Creativity and Collaborative Learning

Creativity and Collaborative Learning

The Practical Guide to Empowering Students, Teachers, and Families

Second Edition

edited by

Jacqueline S. Thousand, Ph.D.
California State University–San Marcos

Richard A. Villa, Ed.D.
Bayridge Consortium
San Marcos, California

and

Ann I. Nevin, Ph.D.
Arizona State University–West
Phoenix

·P·A·U·L·H·
BROOKES
PUBLISHING CO®

Baltimore • London • Sydney

Paul H. Brookes Publishing Co.
Post Office Box 10624
Baltimore, Maryland 21285-0624

www.brookespublishing.com

Typeset by A.W. Bennett, Inc., Hartland, Vermont.
Manufactured in the United States of America by
Victor Graphics, Inc., Baltimore, Maryland.

Quotation from Silverstein, S. (1981). The little boy and the old man. In *A light in the attic* (p. 95). New York: Harper & Row. Copyright © 1981 by Evil Eye Music, Inc. Reprinted by permission of the Harper-Collins Publishers.

"In Which Christopher Robin Leads an Expotition to the North Pole" from WINNIE-THE-POOH by A.A. Milne, illustrated by E.H. Shepard, copyright 1926 by E.P. Dutton, renewed 1954 by A.A. Milne. Used by permission of Dutton Children's Books, an imprint of Penguin Putnam Books for Young Readers, a division of Penguin Putnam Inc. All rights reserved.

Most of the case studies that appear in this book are based on synthesized composites of the authors' experiences in using cooperative group learning techniques. However, a few of the case studies are based on actual cases; fictitious names have been used in these instances.

Library of Congress Cataloging-in-Publication Data

Creativity and collaborative learning: the practical guide to empowering students,
   teachers, and families / [edited by] Jacqueline S. Thousand, Richard A. Villa,
   and Ann I. Nevin. — 2nd ed.
      p.   cm.
   Includes bibliographical references and index.
      ISBN 1-55766-578-8
      1. Group work in education—United States.   2. Peer-group turoring of students—
   United States.   I. Thousand, Jacqueline S., 1950–   II. Villa, Richard A., 1952–
   III. Nevin, Ann I.
      LB10323 .C73 2002
      371.39'5—dc21

                                                            2002022248

British Library Cataloging in Publication data are available from the British Library.

To the Future

To our children

Rebecca
Chang
David
Jonathan
Ruth
Rosemarie

and

grandchildren

Rith
Junior
Nyda
Jme Suanna
Shawn
Jodie
Kelsi
William Nevin "Liam"

and

great-grandchild

Daryn

With love and hope
that your education
has and will be
creative, collaborative,
and empowering

Contents

About the Editors

Jacqueline S. Thousand, Ph.D., Professor, College of Education, California State University–San Marcos, San Marcos, California 92069

Jacqueline S. Thousand is a professor and coordinator of special education teacher preparation and graduate programs in the College of Education at California State University–San Marcos (CSUSM). She joined the CSUSM faculty in 1996 after 15 years at the University of Vermont, where she directed inclusion facilitator and early childhood/special education graduate and postgraduate programs and coordinated several federal grants. These initiatives focused on the inclusion of students with disabilities in local school and community environments. Dr. Thousand is a well-known national and international teacher, author, systems change consultant, and disability rights and inclusive education advocate. She has authored numerous books, research articles, and chapters on issues related to inclusive schooling, organizational change strategies, universal design of curriculum and instruction, student self-determination, collaborative teaming processes, creative problem solving, discipline with dignity, and critical pedagogy. She is actively involved in international teacher education and inclusive education endeavors and serves on the editorial and advisory boards of several national and international journals and professional organizations.

Richard A. Villa, Ed.D., President, Bayridge Consortium, 767 Pebble Beach Drive, San Marcos, California 92069

Richard A. Villa is a renowned educational consultant and motivational speaker who has presented at numerous national and international conferences. He is known for his extensive knowledge in organizational change and his enthusiastic, inspirational, and humorous presentation style. Dr. Villa has worked with hundreds of thousands of teachers, administrators, families, university faculty, and state and national governmental and non-governmental agencies throughout the United States of America and the world to develop and implement organizational and instructional support systems for educating all students within general education. Dr. Villa is an adjunct faculty member at California State University–San Marcos. He has been a middle school and high school teacher, a special educator, a special education coordinator, a pupil personnel services director, and a director of instructional services. Dr. Villa has authored five books and more than 75 chapters and articles regarding inclusive education and has created videos on collaborative teaming and co-teaching.

Ann I. Nevin, Ph.D., Professor, College of Education, Arizona State University–West, Phoenix, Arizona 85069

Ann I. Nevin earned her doctoral degree in educational psychology in 1970 from the University of Minnesota with Maynard C. Reynolds, one of the pioneers of the mainstreaming movement. As a scholar and teacher, Dr. Nevin is passionately committed to discovering what educators, parents, advocates, and students can use to improve academic and social success of students who are difficult to teach. Since 1968, she has been involved in university-level experimental teacher education programs (e.g., in 1969, she collaborated in the development and evaluation of the Vermont Consulting Teacher Program; since 1979, she worked with consulting teachers to replicate the Johnson and Johnson cooperative group learning model for students with special needs). Since 2000, she has collaborated with public school administrators and mentor teachers to empower special education interns to teach self-determination skills and student-led individualized education programs within the K–12 curriculum. Most recently, Dr. Nevin collaborated with technology experts, continuing education programs, and various interdisciplinary faculty to create, implement, evaluate, and redesign graduate-level classes in special education for teachers to learn entirely over the Internet.

About the Authors

Barbara J. Ayres, Ph.D., Associate Professor, College of Education and Human Services, Montana State University–Billings, 1500 University Drive, Billings, Montana 59101

Barbara J. Ayres teaches undergraduate and graduate courses in special education and consults with school districts in the areas of accommodating student diversity, positive behavioral supports, and adult collaboration. Her research interests focus on supporting students with difficult behaviors in general education classrooms. Dr. Ayres has co-authored several book chapters and articles on inclusive education, cooperative learning, and positive behavioral supports.

Barbara E. Buswell, M.A., Executive Director, PEAK Parent Center, 611 North Weber, Suite 200, Colorado Springs, Colorado 80903

Barbara E. Buswell is Executive Director of Colorado's Parent Training and Information Center and is the mother of three children, one of whom received special education supports. Prior to creating PEAK Parent Center, she was a high school English teacher. She has a master's degree in inclusive education reform.

Chigee J. Cloninger, Ph.D., Associate Professor, University of Vermont, Center on Disability and Community Inclusion, 101 Cherry Street, Suite 450, Burlington, Vermont 05401

Chigee J. Cloninger is Executive Director of the Center on Disability and Community Inclusion and the University Center for Excellence in Developmental Disabilities Education, Research, and Service at the University of Vermont. In addition, Dr. Cloninger is Director of the Vermont State I-Team, a statewide technical assistance and training team; Director of the Vermont State Project for Children and Youth with Deafblindness; and an advocate and board member of several advisory councils and task forces.

Neil Davidson, Ph.D., Professor Emeritus and Senior Scholar, Department of Curriculum and Instruction, Benjamin Building, University of Maryland, College Park, Maryland 20742

Neil Davidson serves as senior scholar in the university's Center for Teaching Excellence and in the K–12 university/school partnership development program. He is a pioneer in the development of cooperative learning in mathematics and served for 5 years as president of the International Association for the Study of Cooperation in Education. He publishes extensively on cooperative learning in mathematics and general education, enhancing thinking through cooperative learning, and professional development for cooperative learning. Dr. Davidson is an internationally recognized presenter and consultant in these areas.

Ruth E. Dennis, Ed.D., Research Assistant Professor, College of Education and Social Services, University of Vermont, 101 Cherry Street, Suite 450, Burlington, Vermont 05401

Ruth E. Dennis is Research Assistant Professor at the Center on Disability and Community Inclusion at the University of Vermont. She is a statewide consultant on occupational therapy for the Vermont State I-Team and for the interdisciplinary faculty for the Vermont Interdisciplinary Leadership Education for Health Professionals (ILEHP) program.

Rosario Diaz-Greenberg, Ed.D., Associate Professor, College of Education, California State University–San Marcos, 13754 Pomerado Road, Poway, California 92064

Rosario Diaz-Greenberg was born and raised in El Salvador and came to the United States of America at the age of 17 to learn English. After working for the United Nations, she became a bilingual teacher and worked overseas and in the United States of America for 23 years. Dr. Diaz-Greenberg received her doctorate from the University of San Francisco in 1995.

Janet Duncan, Ph.D., Assistant Professor, State University of New York–Cortland, Education Department, Cornish D-221, Cortland, New York 13145

Janet Duncan teaches inclusive education courses for graduate and undergraduate students and supports students with challenging behaviors in urban settings.

Susan W. Edelman, Ed.D., Research Assistant Professor, Center on Disability and Community Inclusion, University of Vermont, 101 Cherry Street, Suite 450, Burlington, Vermont 05401

Susan W. Edelman is Coordinator of the Vermont State I-Team and Vermont Project for Children and Youth with Deafblindness. She serves as a consultant in the areas of physical therapy and deafblindness and is involved with personnel preparation at the University of Vermont for educators, special educators, speech-language pathologists, and physical and occupational therapists.

Lori Eshilian, M.A., Teacher, California High School, 9800 Mills Avenue, Whittier, California, 90603

Lori Eshilian has been a public school teacher for 25 years and an education consultant specializing in secondary inclusive education and differentiated instruction. She has taught within the field of special education, supporting students and adults with a wide range of learning differences as well as students who are experiencing other significant challenges that place them at risk in school systems and communities.

Mary A. Falvey, Ph.D., Professor, California State University–Los Angeles, 5151 State University Drive, Los Angeles, California 90032

Mary A. Falvey is Professor at California State University–Los Angeles and works within the urban school districts within southern California, including Los Angeles Unified School District. She has authored numerous chapters and books related to inclusive education.

Marsha S. Forest, Ed.D. (1942–2000)

Marsha S. Forest held a master's degree in communication from Teachers College, Columbia University, and a doctorate in education from the University of Massachusetts. Her doctoral work was in the area of leadership and administration. Dr. Forest designed an experimental teacher education program called Explorations! that has been a model of excellence in staff development and education reform. She also served as a visiting scholar at the National Institute on Mental Retardation in Toronto, as Director of Education at Frontier College, and as an adjunct professor at McGill University, where she was the founder and director of the McGill Summer Institute on Integrated Education and Community. Dr. Forest passed away on June 2, 2000, after a 12-year struggle with cancer.

Douglas Fuchs, Ph.D., Professor of Special Education, Peabody College of Vanderbilt University, Magnolia Drive, MRL Building, Nashville, Tennessee 37220

Douglas Fuchs is Professor of Special Education at Peabody College of Vanderbilt University where he conducts research on the assessment and instruction of children at risk for school failure. He is Co-director of two federally funded research centers: The Center for Accelerating Student Learning and The National Center for Research on Learning Disabilities.

Lynn S. Fuchs, Ph.D., Professor of Special Education, Peabody College of Vanderbilt University, Box 328 GPC, Nashville, Tennessee 37203

Lynn S. Fuchs is Professor in the Department of Special Education at Peabody College of Vanderbilt University where she holds the Joseph B. Wyatt Distinguished Professorship. She received her doctoral degree in educational psychology, with emphasis in special education, from the University of Minnesota, where she worked at the Institute for Research on Learning Disabilities. Dr. Fuchs conducts research on classroom-based assessment and instructional methods to enhance outcomes for students with disabilities.

Michael F. Giangreco, Ph.D., Research Associate Professor, Center on Disability and Community Inclusion, University of Vermont, 101 Cherry Street, Suite 450, Burlington, Vermont 05401

Prior to joining the faculty at the University of Vermont in 1988, Michael F. Giangreco spent several years working directly with people with disabilities as a counselor in community residential services, a special education teacher, and a special education coordinator. His research and training efforts have focused primarily on individualized education program services, decision making, and coordination; inclusive education; paraprofessional issues and practices; and curriculum planning and adaptation. Dr. Giangreco is a co-author of several publications, including *Choosing Outcomes and Accommodations for Children: A Guide to Educational Planning for Students with Disabilities, Second Edition* (co-authored with C.J. Cloninger & V.S. Iverson, Paul H. Brookes Publishing Co., 1998).

Antonette W. Hood, Ed.D., Assistant Professor, College of Education, California State University–San Marcos, San Marcos, California 92069

Antonette (Toni) W. Hood was a public school special educator for 19 years and has been teaching at California State University–San Marcos since 1993. Her research interests include creating adaptive and responsive learning environments; inclusion; educational restructuring; the teacher voice; peer support structures; and the self-actualization of students, parents, and teachers.

Golie G. Jansen, Ph.D., Associate Professor, Eastern Washington University School of Social Work, Senior Hall 203, Cheney, Washington 99004

Golie G. Jansen received her doctorate from the University of Illinois at Urbana-Champaign. She teaches courses at Eastern Washington University in leadership and organizational change; prevention, advocacy, and community organization; and policy analysis. Dr. Jansen is active in the areas of violence against women and human rights. She has presented several workshops on conflict resolution and diversity for the Illinois Institute for Dispute Resolution.

David W. Johnson, Ed.D., Professor of Education Psychology, University of Minnesota, 60 Peik Hall, Minneapolis, Minnesota 55455

David W. Johnson received his doctoral degree from Teachers College, Columbia University. His interests include cooperation and competition, conflict resolution, and group dynamics.

Roger T. Johnson, Ed.D., Professor, Curriculum and Instruction, University of Minnesota, 60 Peik Hall, Minneapolis, Minnesota 55455

Roger T. Johnson is Professor of Science Education and Co-director of the Cooperative Learning Center at the University of Minnesota. He has written numerous books and research articles on cooperative learning and conflict resolution in schools with his brother David W. Johnson. Dr. Johnson is currently serving on the Council on Education of the American Veterinary Medical Association and is the chair of the American Educational Research Association (AERA) special interest group on conflict resolution and violence prevention.

Brian Kelly, M.Ed., Student Services Consultant/Psychometrist, School District 12, Woodstock, New Brunswick EOJ 2BO, Canada

Brian Kelly's work has focused on inclusive education for students with challenging behaviors, students at risk of leaving school, crisis intervention, and alternative assessment techniques. As a volunteer, he has been a board member and chairperson for the community's early intervention agency and residential living board, serving individuals with special needs.

Kathleen Kesson, Ed.D., Director of Teacher Education, Goddard College, 123 Pitkin Road, Plainfield, Vermont 05667

Kathleen Kesson directs the teacher education program at Goddard College, a historic progressive school in central Vermont. She is also director of the John Dewey Project on Progressive Education, a research and policy institute at the University of Vermont.

Paula Kluth, Ph.D., Assistant Professor, Syracuse University, 150 Huntington Hall, Syracuse, New York 13244

Paula Kluth is Assistant Professor in the Department of Teaching and Leadership at Syracuse University. She received her master's degree in educational policy from the Harvard Graduate School of Education and her doctoral degree in special education from the University of Wisconsin–Madison. Dr. Kluth is a former special educator who has served as a classroom teacher, consulting teacher, and vocational educator. She has taught in and engages in research in both elementary and secondary schools. Dr. Kluth's professional and research interests center on differentiating instruction and educating students with significant disabilities in inclusive classrooms.

Christopher J. Koliba, Ph.D., Research Assistant Professor, John Dewey Project, University of Vermont, 405 Waterman Building, Burlington, Vermont 05405

Christopher J. Koliba received his doctorate from Syracuse University and is a research assistant professor with the John Dewey Project at the University of Vermont. He is currently pursuing a research agenda that includes the study of school culture, school–community relations, the development of social responsibility in students, and the relationship between democracy and education.

Norman Kunc, M.Sc., 340 Machleary Street, Nanaimo, British Columbia V9R 2G9, Canada

Norman Kunc is a well-known disability rights advocate. Born with cerebral palsy, Mr. Kunc attended a segregated school for children with physical disabilities; then, at age 13, he was integrated into a regular school. From there, he went on to complete a bachelor's degree in humanities and a master of science degree in family therapy. Although Mr.

Kunc's initial advocacy focused on educational rights of students with disabilities, more recently he has directed his attention to how schools and communities can utilize the diversity of people to build a sense of belonging and avoid a climate of allegiance that results from stratification, competition, and group identification.

Laurie LaPlant, M.Ed., Learning Specialist, Essex Town School District, Essex Elementary School, 1 Bixby Hill Road, Essex, Vermont 05452

Laurie LaPlant teaches in an inclusive elementary school in Essex, Vermont. She was the first integration facilitator in Vermont and has spent more than 20 years supporting children with disabilities in general classrooms. Ms. LaPlant has taught several workshops and courses throughout the United States of America, assisting other educators in embracing children with a variety of needs into their school communities. She resides in Colchester, Vermont, with her husband and two children.

Herbert L. Leff, Ph.D., Associate Professor of Psychology, University of Vermont, John Dewey Hall, Burlington, Vermont 05405

Herbert L. Leff is Associate Professor of Psychology at the University of Vermont, where he has served since 1970. His primary research focus has been on metacognitive and educational processes that enhance creativity and the enjoyment of life.

Kristen L. McMaster, M.Ed., Doctoral Student, Peabody College of Vanderbilt University, Box 328, Nashville, Tennessee 37203

Kristen L. McMaster's teaching experience includes working with elementary and high school students in self-contained, resource, and inclusive classrooms. Her interests include accommodating diverse learners in general classrooms and preventing early reading failure.

Mary E. McNeil, Ed.D., Professor of Education, Plymouth State College of the University System of New Hampshire, 17 High Street, Plymouth, New Hampshire 03264

Mary E. McNeil is Professor of Education with the University System of New Hampshire at Plymouth. She is Director of the Center for Professional Educational Partnerships and the Certificate of Advanced Studies in Educational Leadership. Dr. McNeil currently serves as president of New Hampshire Association for Supervision and Curriculum Development. She is past president of the Partners of the Americas Vermont–Honduras Partnership and has published widely in the area of special education and consults in Europe and Latin America. In addition, Dr. McNeil is editor of the *New Hampshire Journal of Education.* Her specialty areas include partner learning, collaborative consultation, and systems change.

Jeff Moyer, M.A., President, Music from the Heart, 670 Radford Drive, Cleveland, Ohio 44143

Jeff Moyer is an internationally known advocate, songwriter, author, and creative thinker whose presentations have touched and inspired audiences throughout the United States of America and internationally. His materials integrate positive and upbeat music that celebrate the diversity of the human family with dynamic and effective group processes that help school communities to deeply incorporate the healing of exclusion, ridicule, and violence against those devalued because of their differences.

Frank B. Murray, Ph.D., H. Rodney Sharp Professor of Education and Psychology, School of Education, University of Delaware, Willard Hall Education Building, Suite 101, Newark, Delaware 19716

Prior to his appointment as H. Rodney Sharp Professor at the University of Delaware, Frank B. Murray served as dean of the College of Education from 1979 to 1995. Currently, Dr. Murray is president of the Teacher Education Accreditation Council in Washington, D.C. For his contributions to the fields of child development and teacher education, Dr. Murray was awarded an honorary doctorate from Heriot-Watt University in Edinburgh, Scotland, in 1994.

Kate Paxton, Graduate Assistant, John Dewey Project, University of Vermont, 411 Waterman Building, Burlington, Vermont 05405

Jack Pearpoint, Founding Director of Inclusion Press and the Marsha Forest Centre: Inclusion.Family.Community, 24 Thome Crescent, Toronto M6H 255, Canada

Jack Pearpoint has more than 35 years of organizational experience that includes spending 7 years in Africa implementing post-war reconstruction, 16 years as full-time president of Canada's oldest national literacy organization—Frontier College, and more than 10 years as a full-time publisher, presenter, and problem solver with individuals, organizations, and governments on five continents. Mr. Pearpoint, along with his wife Marsha S. Forest, created several person-centered planning tools, including Circles, MAPs, and PATH.

J. Michael Peterson, Ph.D., Professor, Wayne State University, 217 Education, Detroit, Michigan 48202

J. Michael Peterson is a professor in teacher education at Wayne State University. He has 25 years experience working with students with special needs in urban, suburban, and rural settings. Dr. Peterson co-founded and coordinates the Whole Schooling Consortium.

Alice M.L. Quiocho, Ed.D., Associate Professor, College of Education, California State University–San Marcos, 872 Orla Street, San Marcos, California 92069

Alice M.L. Quiocho has 28 years of public school experience as a teacher, principal, and coordinator of professional development for teachers and school administrators at the district and county level. Her areas of expertise are literacy for second language learners and bilingual education.

Richard L. Rosenberg, Ph.D., Lead Vocational Coordinator, Whittier Union High School District, 9401 South Painter Avenue, Whittier, California 90605

Richard L. Rosenberg provides support and coordination for the WorkAbility and Transition Partnership Project. He also coordinates and facilitates person-centered planning meetings and orchestrates inclusive services at school and in the community.

Mara Sapon-Shevin, Ed.D., Professor of Inclusive Education, Syracuse University, 150 Huntington Hall, Syracuse, New York 13244

Mara Sapon-Shevin prepares teachers for heterogeneous, inclusive classrooms through Syracuse University's inclusive elementary and special education teacher education program. For more than 25 years, her work has focused on multiple aspects of diversity in schools and communities. Active in the area of cooperative learning, Dr. Sapon-Shevin is a past co-president of the International Association for the Study of Cooperation in Education. She is actively involved in community diversity and anti-racism training as well as being the co-author of a curriculum for anti-racism teaching for high school and college students. Dr. Sapon-Shevin is the author of many articles and book chapters on cooperative learning, inclusion, the politics of gifted education, and teacher for social justice. Her most recent book is *Because We Can Change the World: A Practical Guide to Building Cooperative, Inclusive Classroom Communities* (Allyn & Bacon, 1999).

C. Beth Schaffner, B.A., Director of Curriculum and Technical Assistance Curriculum, PEAK Parent Center, 611 North Weber Street, Suite 200, Colorado Springs, Colorado 80903

C. Beth Schaffner is the Director of Curriculum and Technical Assistance for PEAK Parent Center, which is Colorado's federally funded Parent Training and Information Center. She has been at PEAK Parent Center for 14 years and co-authored several popular PEAK Parent Center publications. Ms. Schaffner worked for 20 years as a special education teacher in a role that evolved from providing direct services in a self-contained classroom to serving as an inclusion facilitator for the school district. She is the mother of a 29-year-old man who has significant disabilities who was fully included in middle and high school and who now lives in his own home and works in the community with necessary supports.

Fred Schrumpf, M.S.W., M.Ed., Coordinator of Student Services, Spokane Public Schools, 200 North Bernard, Spokane, Washington 99201

Fred Schrumpf holds master's degrees in both social work and education from the University of Illinois at Urbana-Champaign. He has practiced and taught school social work for more than 20 years at the University of Illinois, Idaho State University, and Eastern Washington University. He is co-author of *Peer Mediation: Conflict Resolution in the Schools, Revised Edition* (Research Press, 1997) and *Creating the Peaceable School* (Research Press, 1994). He is a former trainer/consultant for the Illinois Institute for Dispute Resolution and the National Center for Conflict Resolution Education. He is supervisor of student services for the Spokane School District #81.

Deborah Tweit-Hull, M.A., Project Director, Interwork Institute, San Diego State University, 4283 El Cajon Boulevard, Suite 100, San Diego, California 92105

Deborah Tweit-Hull has directed and coordinated numerous federal grants focusing on the inclusion of students and adults in their schools, homes, and communities. She has served as adjunct faculty in the Department of Special Education at San Diego State University and is currently the co-director of an agency that provides supported living services to adults with developmental disabilities.

Jonathan Udis, M.Ed., Educational Consultant, Upstream Educational Services, 46 East Hill, Middlesex, Vermont 05602

Prior to starting his own consulting practice in 1991, Jonathan Udis worked as a classroom teacher, public school administrator, and residential treatment educational director. His areas of interest include promoting social and emotional competence and cooperative group learning. He has provided support and training to school districts throughout North America.

Alice Udvari-Solner, Ph.D., Faculty Associate, Department of Curriculum and Instruction, University of Wisconsin–Madison, 225 North Mills Street, Room 204, Madison, Wisconsin 53706

Alice Udvari-Solner holds a joint appointment at the University of Wisconsin–Madison in the Department of Curriculum and Instruction and the Office of Education Outreach. The graduate and undergraduate courses she teaches on accommodating diverse learners in general education settings are integral to the elementary, secondary, and special education teacher certification programs. The design of differentiated curriculum, collaborative teamwork between general and special educators, and systems change toward inclusive education are central to her research.

Emma Van der Klift, 340 Machleary Street, Nanaimo, British Columbia V9R 2G9, Canada

For more than 20 years, Emma Van der Klift has assisted families, agencies, and school districts to support people with varying abilities to live meaningful and enjoyable lives within their communities. Prior to joining forces with Norman Kunc, Ms. Van der Klift worked for a nonprofit organization on Vancouver Island in a variety of capacities, including supported employment, residential options, program director, and labor relations director. In addition, she received training in conflict resolution and mediation at the Justice Institute in Vancouver, British Columbia, Canada.

Pamela J. Villalobos, M.A., Educational Consultant, Interwork Institute, San Diego State University, Post Office Box 922, Pine Valley, California 91962

As an educator, consultant/presenter, and author, Pamela J. Villalobos focuses on student empowerment and teacher and paraeducator training to provide inclusive education for students with disabilities, particularly at the secondary level. She has facilitated student leadership training on human diversity, social justice and inclusion, and peer tutor training to support peers learning together in inclusive classrooms. Ms. Villalobos has provided technical assistance to schools through state and national inclusive education projects, taught as a high school inclusion support teacher and transition instructor, and directed an agency providing supported employment and living services to adults with disabilities.

Gwendolyn C. Webb-Johnson, Ed.D., Assistant Professor, The University of Texas at Austin, Sanchez 408A D5300, Austin, Texas 78712

As Assistant Professor of Special Education, Gwendolyn C. Webb-Johnson teaches classes in behavior management, individual differences, characteristics of learning disabilities and behavior disorders, and multicultural education. Her research focuses on culturally respectful, relevant, and responsive pedagogy and disproportionate representation of learners of color in special education.

Amie Wong, M.A., Special Education Teacher, San Diego Unified School District, 4100 Normal Street, San Diego, California 92103

Amie Wong has been a special education teacher for 11 years in the San Diego Unified School District. She successfully implemented an inclusion program at the junior high school level that was supported with a comprehensive peer tutor program. Currently, Ms. Wong is working as an intern support provider assisting new teachers with their classroom, working in special education.

Nadine Zane, M.A., Special Educator, Malletts Bay School, Post Office Box 28, Colchester, Vermont 05446

Nadine Zane has taught elementary school students to graduate students in general and special education programs. She has participated in presentations and training sessions related to inclusive schooling, collaboration, adaptations, accommodations, behavior management, autism, and peer support systems. Ms. Zane has been functioning as a special educator serving elementary school students in an inclusive school since 1987.

Preface

We, the three editors, have focused our professional and much of our personal lives on working with educators, parents, and students to restructure schools so that all children may be educated together. History is at a point when inclusive education is no longer an idealistic vision but a reality and obligation.

In our collective years of work, we discovered that a critical element for successful academic and social development and inclusion of children with disabilities is for students to support other students. Furthermore, we learned to broaden our discussions to include *all* children, rather than focusing only on a subset of the school population (e.g., "special" education, "general" education).

Our career paths intertwined as we each pursued unique opportunities that demanded collaboration, consultation, and cooperation with people who had differing ideas about educating students with various educational characteristics. Through these interactions, we learned many of the principles and processes that we showcase in this book. We learned from experience that practices such as cooperative learning, partner and peer-mediated learning, and creative thinking increase the likelihood of success for all students.

Our vision in writing the second edition of *Creativity and Collaborative Learning* was to go beyond the rhetoric of explaining *why* students with educational challenges must be educated in general education and have access to the general education curriculum. Instead, we wanted to show how peer support in instruction, advocacy, and decision making could be structured to facilitate the educational success of students with and without identified disabilities and support needs.

As with the first edition of this book, we knew that none of us could write or edit this book on our own. However, with the help of the creative partnerships of the contributing authors, we believe we have created a text that provides educators with detailed "how to" strategies and lesson plans to meaningfully involve a diverse study body in learning. We emphasize practical ways for classroom teachers, students, special educators and other support personnel, curriculum coordinators, administrators, family members, and university professors to invent schools and classrooms in which students with varying abilities can be creatively and actively involved in their own and others' academic and social learning.

Included in this book are research reviews presented in everyday language, sample lesson plans and lesson plan formats, suggestions for peer support and coaching, and forms and materials that teachers may duplicate. Our partnerships involved classroom teachers, teacher credential candidates, graduate students, students and their families, and other school personnel whose experiences are represented throughout the book. We include lessons with examples at a variety of grade levels from preschool through high school; a focus on curriculum areas such as science, mathematics, and language arts; and specific adaptations to meet the needs of students with unique learning characteristics and challenges. Our hope is that this second edition of *Creativity and Collaborative Learning* will join the first edition as one of the most useful and most used books in your professional library. Our dream is that you will use this book to celebrate student diversity, capitalize on students' individual differences, welcome each and every child as an important member of the classroom community, and prepare each child for life in a multicultural and democratic society.

For the Reader

Have you wondered why and how you could make it possible for students to experience collaborative and creative roles in advocacy, instruction, conflict resolution, and decision making? Have you experienced positive collaboration and creativity between parents, students, and school personnel in the design of effective personalized responses? Do you want to increase positive peer support systems such as social support, buddy networks, and opportunities for every child to be a contributing member of an inclusive multicultural school? We co-created this book to make it possible for future students to experience collaborative arrangements and strategies that engage them in instructional and advocacy roles for and with their peers with and without disabilities.

Before you begin your examination of the strategies, we invite you to reflect on your personal experiences as a student and assess the extent to which those experiences incorporated a collaborative and creative approach. Please take a moment and respond to the 14 questions in the Student Collaboration Quiz shown on page xxii. Taking this quiz not only will heighten your awareness of your own experiences as a student but also will prepare you to pick out salient points of the theoretical and practical aspects you will discover in this book.

While you read this book, please imagine yourself as a student enrolled in a school where teachers and administrators use the recommended peer empowerment strategies, collaborative planning and teaching skills, and creative solution-finding techniques. Then, once you've finished the book, retake the quiz. Expect to experience dramatic positive changes in the scores. Our hope is that you will commit to making it possible for future generations of school children to check more ratings of "often" and "very often."

1. Did you as a student observe or experience your teachers modeling collaboration in instruction (e.g., team teaching), planning, or evaluation?

   ☐ Never   ☐ Rarely   ☐ Sometimes   ☐ Often   ☐ Very Often

2. Were you as a student given the opportunity and training to serve as an instructor for a peer?

   ☐ Never   ☐ Rarely   ☐ Sometimes   ☐ Often   ☐ Very Often

3. Were you as a student given the opportunity to receive instruction from a trained peer?

   ☐ Never   ☐ Rarely   ☐ Sometimes   ☐ Often   ☐ Very Often

4. How often was the instruction you received structured to encourage the use of higher level reasoning skills (e.g., analysis, synthesis, evaluation, creative problem solving, meta-cognition)?

   ☐ Never   ☐ Rarely   ☐ Sometimes   ☐ Often   ☐ Very Often

5. How often were you expected to support the academic and social learning of other students as well as be accountable for your own learning?

   ☐ Never   ☐ Rarely   ☐ Sometimes   ☐ Often   ☐ Very Often

6. Were you as a student given the opportunity and training to serve as a mediator of conflict between peers?

   ☐ Never   ☐ Rarely   ☐ Sometimes   ☐ Often   ☐ Very Often

7. How often were you asked to evaluate your own learning?

   ☐ Never   ☐ Rarely   ☐ Sometimes   ☐ Often   ☐ Very Often

8. How often were you given the opportunity to assist in determining the educational outcomes for yourself and your classmates?

   ☐ Never   ☐ Rarely   ☐ Sometimes   ☐ Often   ☐ Very Often

9. How often were you given the opportunity to advocate for the educational interests of a classmate or asked to assist in determining modifications and accommodations to the curriculum?

   ☐ Never   ☐ Rarely   ☐ Sometimes   ☐ Often   ☐ Very Often

10. How often were you as a student encouraged to bring a support person to a difficult meeting to provide you with moral support?

    ☐ Never   ☐ Rarely   ☐ Sometimes   ☐ Often   ☐ Very Often

11. How often were you involved in a discussion about teaching with a teacher?

    ☐ Never   ☐ Rarely   ☐ Sometimes   ☐ Often   ☐ Very Often

12. How often were you asked to provide your teachers with feedback as to the effectiveness and appropriateness of their instruction and classroom management?

    ☐ Never   ☐ Rarely   ☐ Sometimes   ☐ Often   ☐ Very Often

13. How often did you participate as an equal with teachers, administrators, and community members on school committees (e.g., curriculum committee, discipline committee, hiring committee, school board)?

    ☐ Never   ☐ Rarely   ☐ Sometimes   ☐ Often   ☐ Very Often

14. How often did you as a student feel that the school "belonged" to you, that school experiences were structured primarily with student interests in mind?

    ☐ Never   ☐ Rarely   ☐ Sometimes   ☐ Often   ☐ Very Often

Creativity and
Collaborative
Learning

Toward Creativity and Collaborative Learning in the 21st Century

Toward Whole Schools

Building a Movement for Creativity and
Collaborative Learning in the 21st Century

J. Michael Peterson

The editors of this book and the author of this introduction ask an important question—one of the most critical educational questions for the 21st century: "How can we harness the capacity of people to collaborate and to use human creativity to create learning that will lead toward an inclusive, multicultural society?" When talking about education, we have some fundamental questions to address—questions that affect any and everything else we do, questions such as

- Why do people go to school? What is the real purpose?

- Who is school for? Who goes to school together? Who gets separated and why?

- How do we do schooling (a broader term and concept than "teaching")? What does it look like?

It is clear that schools will look different depending on their social purpose. Schools have served many, often conflicting, purposes—acculturating immigrants, preparing the elite for their "proper role" in society, teaching technical skills to the working class, and sorting who belongs in what role. Schools were also supposed to help solve great social problems—poverty, violence, and social unrest. Many had hopes that schools would be tools of a new, strong democratic culture—a view best known in the works of John Dewey (1916).

The purpose of schooling, of course, depends on our image of the type of society for which schools prepare young people. At the beginning of the 21st century, we are in the midst of fundamental social decisions—whether we move toward greater democracy, inclusion, and equality or toward autocracy, segregation, and inequality. Virtually every political conflict can be framed in these terms. Schools are critical conflicted territories in this struggle because children will learn to either be obedient to the existing social order or thoughtful, creative actors who help analyze and shape our world.

Table I.1. Five principles of whole schooling

1. **Empower citizens in a democracy:** The goal of education is to help students learn to function as effective citizens in a democracy.
2. **Include all:** All children learn together across culture, ethnicity, language, ability, gender, and age.
3. **Design authentic, multilevel teaching for learners of diverse abilities:** Teachers design instruction for diverse learners that engages them in active learning in meaningful, real-world activities; and develop accommodations and adaptations for learners with diverse needs, interests, and abilities.
4. **Build community and support learning:** The school uses specialized school and community resources (e.g., special education, Title I, gifted education) to build support for students, parents, and teachers. All people work together to build community and mutual support within the classroom and school and provide pro-active supports for students with behavioral challenges.
5. **Partner with families and the community:** Educators build genuine collaboration within the school and with families and the community; engage the school in strengthening the community; and provide guidance to engage students, parents, teachers, and others in decision making and direction of learning and school activities.

For more information, go to http://www.coe.wayne.edu/CommunityBuilding/WSC.html

We are, however, the makers of our social world. Collaboration, which brings people together under a joined vision of a caring, inclusive, democratic community, has power. Creativity, which will allow us to use our resources and energy, holds great promise. We hold in our hands more than we know. We have choices. This book provides a thoughtful analysis and practical strategies for creating a new, better future.

SCHOOLING FOR AN INCLUSIVE DEMOCRACY

We have challenges and opportunities to take the values and strategies described in this book and make them real in our schools. This work must simultaneously occur in schools, classrooms, and university courses and by building new networks, movements, and organizations that are centered in these values and approaches. The Whole Schooling Consortium was founded in 1997 to build empowering, democratic, inclusive, multicultural schools based on the concepts in this book (see the five principles Table I.1). Since the inception of the Whole Schooling Consortium (Peterson, Beloin, & Gibson, 1997), there has been an amazing response to these ideas. A growing network of individuals have joined the Consortium as collaborating members, and schools in several states have adopted the Whole Schooling principles. We have held several local and national conferences, conducted research to explore the interaction of inclusion with other principles and associated practices, and gathered with a group of people who are crafting and implementing Whole Schooling as a model of school renewal. Our experience leads us to believe that, indeed, we *can* establish caring, inclusive, multicultural communities of learning in schools *if*, with a sense of vision and courage, we creatively harness our resources and collaboratively build a community of change agents. May the ideas and strategies within these pages spur us to thought and action.

REFERENCES

Dewey, J. (1916). *Democracy and education.* New York: Macmillan.
Peterson, M., Beloin, K., & Gibson, R. (1997). *Whole schooling: Education for a democratic society.* Detroit, MI: Wayne State University, Whole Schooling Consortium.

Democratic Education
and the Creation of a
Loving and Just Community

Kathleen Kesson
Christopher J. Koliba
Kate Paxton

HARMONY SCHOOL: FAMILY MEETING
AND THE DEVELOPMENT OF STUDENT VOICE

[handwritten margin note: school designed to develop life skills "being a responsible citizen"]

Harmony School, an independent pre-K through secondary school located in a university town in southern Indiana, was founded in 1974 with the purpose of renewing the civic mission of public schooling. Its handbook states that the school is "designed for the development of the 'whole person,' encouraging the students to achieve academic excellence, feel good about themselves, and see learning as a lifelong activity, . . . [while striving] to give the students a sense of personal control over their lives" (Cosgray & Bonchek, 1996, p. 1). In addition to its innovative curricula and methods, Harmony also provides professional development opportunities for public school teachers and carries out research on democratic education and school change. Harmony has become host to the National School Reform Faculty, an organization of more than 20,000 teachers and principals working in more than 1,000 schools to create more caring and just communities in schools throughout the country.

The commitment to democratic education is described in the handbook as the effort to "provide a real-life environment that would foster the skills necessary for active and constructive participation in our country's democratic process" (Cosgray & Bonchek, 1996, p. 3). Harmony's democratic orientation is interpreted in different ways by each member of the school community. One teacher explains,

We're trying to teach kids to be responsible citizens, and we're trying to do that in a way where we teach them by having them practice what it means to be a responsible citizen. So the democratic education part of Harmony is about practicing being a responsible citizen. It's not necessarily just about the kids getting power over X, Y, or Z; it's really about practicing being a responsible citizen. So I think that's the base philosophy behind the entire school.

In the years since its founding, Harmony has gradually strengthened its democratic ethos through innumerable hours of committee meetings, schoolwide Family Meetings, and the daily workings of the classroom. Like any community, Harmony has struggled with negotiating the boundaries of democracy and power and maintaining the delicate balance between the individual and the community.

The Family Meeting takes place regularly in all of Harmony's programs and is one of the foundations of the school's democratic practice. At the Family Meeting, students learn to solve their own problems, make meaningful decisions, plan future group learning experiences and social activities, and assess the work of the group. The structure of the Family Meeting differs from program to program depending on "age-appropriateness," but all Family Meetings emphasize student leadership, community feedback, and collective decision making. In the middle and high school Family Meetings, students chair meetings, set the agenda, and are responsible for maintaining order during the discussion. Teachers are subject to the same guidelines as students for adding items to the agenda, contributing feedback, and voting. Harmony's faculty members stress the importance of the Family Meetings as learning opportunities. In the high school, students receive one credit per semester in social studies for participating in the Family Meeting, underscoring the emphasis placed on learning. A high school teacher explains,

> *We really seriously do think that Family Meeting is training for engaged citizenship and responsible citizenship. Because that's really how communities . . . work in the first place; they have to have meetings. And for you to be able to deal with the kind of meetings that you're going to be dealing with later on in your life, to be an engaged person, Family Meeting's a [great] model. Because it's hard. It's really hard. And you can observe people making mistakes, and you can observe people doing it right.*

For teachers at Harmony, practicing democratic decision making means a commitment not only to innumerable discussions amongst themselves but also to nurturing this process with their students in classrooms, Family Meetings, and all other school activities. Democratic process goes beyond the limitations of weak democracy, encompassing more than the simple definition of *majority rules;* it means a commitment to instilling a sense of confidence and leadership in students, the responsibility to share one's opinions while knowing that compromise is essential, and the humility and humor to accept that each individual will not always get his or her way. A teacher explains,

> *The big thing is that we expect the kids to be leaders. And to have 60 leaders is really hard; it makes it very difficult to deal with a lot of situations, but we think it's worth the trouble, because that's really what we're asking them to do—to speak up, and to understand that just because you speak up doesn't mean you're gonna get your way all the time, but at least you have a responsibility and an obligation to let people know what you think, and that that's important. And if you can't accept that you may not get your way, then your perspective might be really off, and so your sense of humor will certainly be off.*

A commitment to democratic practice at Harmony School means, first and foremost, acknowledging that children should be active participants in making choices about their learning and their school. Here, democratic education is an ethos—it encompasses the ongoing efforts to help children learn who they want to be, what they want to do, and how they can accomplish these dreams, as well as a respect for Harmony's teachers, their professionalism, and their high quality teaching, independence, and innovation.

Finally, the practice of strong democracy in the school is connected with a vision, not only for the children who attend Harmony but also for the society in which they live; a vision that affirms the rights and responsibilities of all citizens to be who they want to be, to be treated and to treat others with care and respect; to celebrate differences while, in the words of Harmony's director, Steve Bonchek, continuing efforts to "compromise and work out decisions with people unlike yourself."

BARRE TOWN SCHOOL:
PROBLEM SOLVING AND MORAL DEVELOPMENT THROUGH LITERATURE

In the Barre Town School in central Vermont, students in the fifth through eighth grades can take a class called Problem Solving Through Literature (PSTL), an alternative to a traditional English class. Using literary works, students identify with a character in the literature to gain insight into the character's situation; to learn how the character took action and developed strategies to deal with problems in life; and, in many cases, how the character contributed to society. The students then apply what they learn from the character to their own lives. The two teachers who oversee this project, Ravell Allen and Beverly Scofield, introduce students to metacognitive concepts such as Maslow's "hierarchy of needs" and Kohlberg's "stages of moral development," utilizing these concepts in their analyses of literature and in reflecting on their own experiences. Every topic of study has an activity that is based on academic considerations as well as personal exploration and involvement.

Skills learned in each grade level build so by the end of the eighth grade, students have learned how to exercise

- Independent study (e.g., note taking, interviewing, résumé writing, letter writing, research, creative problem solving)

- Self-regulated learning (e.g., time management, planning, decision making, goal setting, cooperative work, self-evaluation)

- Metacognition (e.g., thinking about thinking, articulation through journaling)

- Meta-awareness (e.g., reflection through discussion, reflection through journaling, listening)

Students in the sixth through eighth grade are asked to complete a service-learning project by the end of the year. These projects emerge out of their reflections over the course of the year. Discussions about moral reasoning lay the foundation for students to engage in meaningful service to their community. These service-learning projects emerge from stated community needs, which are discovered through periodic community-needs surveys that the students employ. One of the PSTL teachers comments on how the service-learning component of the curriculum evolved:

> *In a way, when we first started doing this, we didn't even think of it as community service-learning (CSL). It really seemed to be a natural extension of what we were doing with the literature. . . . We talked with the kids about issues of concern for them in the world, things that were going on that they were concerned with but felt powerless to do anything about. So I think it was the second year of the program, it almost seemed that both Bev and I without even talking with each other were thinking along the same lines. Why don't we try to match these kids up with somebody who could be a mentor? We must have heard something about CSL because we thought students would work with a mentor to develop their abilities to try to solve some problem in the community.*

Students carry out various individually designed service-learning projects, often based on inspirational biographies of service-oriented individuals such as Eleanor Roosevelt. One student wrote and published a story, then donated her profits to the local women's center. Some of them engaged in teaching, such as the student who won a national award for teaching children with physical disabilities to ride horseback.

By combining discussions about moral reasoning with the reading of literature and service-learning projects, these students learn the skills and dispositions of active democratic citizenship. They gain the ability to apply concepts to real-life situations. These concepts are derived from the stories they read and are applied to actions that they undertake as a part of their service-learning projects. By developing relationships with adult community mentors, students are afforded the opportunity to expand their intergenerational connections. This provides them with the "social capital" that some researchers are now saying is so important to the cultivation of democratic character. They develop the abilities to deliberate, to negotiate, and to organize their work. As one principal explains,

> I can't say enough about how much these kids learn about how to work with other people and other organizations. They learn how to schedule space; they learn about organizations; they learn about hierarchies, how organizations function, and to respect other parts of the organization needing to be informed of certain activities.

The students develop the capacity to take an active role in the decisions that affect the life of their school. One seventh-grade student found that the skills she learned in PSTL have helped her become more articulate and thoughtful in her work on the student council.

Research on this project is designed to follow students through their school experience to assess the effectiveness of service-learning on their future development as citizens. One senior at the local high school reflects back to his experiences in this program in the sixth grade:

> When the topic of community service-learning was mentioned, since we didn't know much about it, it seemed like just another assignment. . . . So, sure you were doing a lot and investing a lot of time in it and eventually it caught up with you and you realized this is all that I've done, and it wasn't that bad and it's benefiting not only myself, and is a learning experience, but it addresses some of the needs of the community. And then this project (setting up a teen center) that began in seventh grade, I'm still working on. Five years has been a long time. I never would have imagined that I would still be doing it. . . . I think I've learned from the experience of always taking an active leadership role. I've gained great skills from working on this project and interacting with different people. Since almost none of the other classes have any community service-learning component, I carry these traits: . . . more questioning, more critical thinking, definitely not as passive . . . I would be willing to say that this community service-learning back in the sixth grade has shaped who I am today.

We believe that this literature-based curriculum, combined with service-learning projects, is a fine example of how students learn to take action in the world based on moral decision making. Studies of programs that involve students in active engagement in their communities, either through service or, as we will see in the next narrative, through direct political action, "indicate that this involvement may, in fact, be an important stepping stone to later (democratic) participation" (Berman, 1997, p. 145).

TAR CREEK: EDUCATION AND POLITICAL ACTIVISM

In a somewhat isolated rural middle/high school in northeastern Oklahoma, home to a population comprising numerous Native American tribal groups as well as Caucasians, students participate in a service-learning club called the Cherokee Volunteer Society. Since 1995, the group has been facilitated by Rebecca Jim, a local environmental activist and clanmother with the Tribal Efforts Against Lead (an environmental organization based with the Quapaw Tribe), and the school's guidance counselor. Students began their service-learning venture with a community recycling project. The next year, they decided, with financial assistance from the Cherokee Council, to build a traditional council house in the schoolyard. The third year of their existence, they began to tackle the serious environmental problems in their community.

The community in which these young people live is one of the nation's worst hazardous waste sites, a result of extensive lead and zinc mining in the early part of the century. The community is home to acres of toxic lead tailings (that children play on), a water system contaminated with heavy metals, a solid waste incinerator, poisoned creeks, contaminated wells, asbestos waste from an abandoned tire plant, and abandoned mine shafts that periodically cave in (sometimes destroying buildings and roads). The people of this community suffer exceptionally high rates of cancers; kidney disease; miscarriages; immune deficiency disorders; and, most notably in the children, physical and cognitive symptoms associated with high levels of lead. There was little public outcry or activism over these alarming issues until 1995, when students of Ms. Jim's Learn and Serve club got interested enough to tackle the problems.

Students began investigating the environmental problems in their community using the Internet, primary source documents, interviews with community members, and on-site analysis of water and soil. From their research, students began to identify some causal connections between the contamination in their community, chronic (and in some cases terminal) illnesses in their families, and some of their own learning disabilities. These students, many of whom had been disengaged from school and learning, became informed, passionate activists.

One of the first things these students learned was that there was a vast amount of information about the environmental problems in their community, but it was not accessible to the general public. So, one of their first tasks was to research various aspects of the problem—fish contamination, lead poisoning, asbestos pollution, mine water flooding, environmental racism, and jobs versus the environment. Their research papers were collected, along with poetry, songs, and first-person narratives, in an anthology titled *The Legacy*, which was published by the Cherokee Nation.

Every year, students host the Tar Creek Fish Tournament and Toxic Tour (ironic because there are no fish in Tar Creek, except for the occasional neon green or orange creature that has somehow survived the poisons). Started on Earth Day, 1998, these annual events are designed to heighten public awareness about the Tar Creek Superfund Site. The students host speakers from the Environmental Protection Agency, the U.S. Fish and Wildlife Service, the Bureau of Indian Affairs, and the Indian Health Service as well as representatives from local Native American tribes. As part of the events, they guide people on "Toxic Tours" (walking, running, bicycling, rollerblading, and riding) to see the acres of chat piles (mine tailings), neon waters, and devastated ecosystems that pervade this community. They organize local musicians for a "Heavy Metal Blues Fest." (Clearly, they have maintained their sense of humor throughout this work!) These events raise money for their other projects: the purchase of outdoor signs to be posted along the polluted creeks and chat piles, educational programs for elementary school children, the collection and analysis of teeth and hair of affected adults and children, and travel to national conferences to present their findings.

These students have developed many skills and capacities working on these projects. They have mastered the art of identifying significant problems in their community. They have learned to carry out research in the public interest and to share their new knowledge in a useful and appropriate way. In addition to building the science and math concepts necessary for understanding the problems, they have learned a great deal about the structures of civic life—practical skills such as how to write to legislators, contact government officials, organize cultural events, circulate petitions, participate in peaceful protests (they have, on occasion, picketed polluters in the community), and engage in public relations. They have had to hone their public speaking talents for appearances on television; on radio; at community meetings; and at local, state, and national conferences. Their writing skills improve as they write for newspapers, magazines, and their own published book projects. Nancy Scott, the coordinator of Cherokee National Learn and Serve, expressed her admiration for the things these students have accomplished:

> *There was a lot of denial in that community before the students started this Tar Creek Project. I mean [the contamination] was something you just never discussed. It was there in the community, everybody knew, but nobody really talked about it. But you know . . . to me, the students are the key to getting Tar Creek . . . cleaned up or improved or whatever is going to happen.*

The Tar Creek story demonstrates how service-learning, in a context rich with academic content, can be used to teach and practice active citizenship. Last year, the governor of Oklahoma formed the Tar Creek Task Force to investigate the environmental problems. A major statewide newspaper, *The Daily Oklahoman,* gave these students credit for getting the story on its radar screen. The students gave the governor an award for his initiative, and he came to the school to receive it. While there, he listened to the essays and poetry (pro and con) on moving two of the undermined towns, giving voice to affected youth.

All of these group projects build team spirit and a sense of the collective that crosses social and cultural differences and class boundaries. The activities contribute to the students' understanding of their rights and responsibilities as democratic citizens. As noted in Kesson and Oyler, "teaching for moral decision-making and social responsibility, with complex community-based issues at the center, requires moral courage on the part of the teacher" (1999, p. 147). There are many challenges and obstacles to overcome. We were impressed with the moral courage, integrity, passion, and commitment of these students, teachers, and community members working collaboratively on matters of genuine social concern. The Tar Creek story challenges us all to imagine the possibilities of an education committed to the development of democratic citizens.

CRISIS OF DEMOCRACY

It is sometimes easy to forget that the United States of America is the world's first *constitutional democracy.* Barely 200 years old, we are still, in the larger scheme of things, an experiment. In the early days of the republic, America faced a particular historical challenge—educating citizens for the various roles they would need to play in order to sustain a fragile new political system. In 1846, Horace Mann argued that a system of education should be provided for all, at public expense, that would "qualify each citizen for the civil and social duties he [sic] will be called upon to discharge" (as cited in Noddings, 2001, p. 174). Because of these early conceptualizations of the public school, an important educational imperative in America has been the education of students as *citizens.* Educating for democracy in these first two centuries has been fraught with conflicts over the meaning of democracy—what it means to be a citizen and what skills, attitudes, and concepts are necessary in order to educate people for active participation in public life.

The United States of America faces new historical challenges. Many contemporary factors point to a "crisis of democracy" (Trend, 1996). These challenges include the decline of voter participation, the growing gap between rich and poor, the globalization of the economy, and the concentration of the media (McChesney, 1999).

The crisis of democracy is connected to a well-documented sense that our communities are losing their coherence and meaning. Bellah, Madison, Sullivan, Swindler, and Tiptoe (1985) pointed to individualism, isolation, and fragmentation as root causes of the decline in participation in public life. Robert Putnam, noted researcher on civil society and social capital, claims that "there is striking evidence that the vibrancy of American civil society has notably declined over the past several decades" (1995, p. 65). Indicators of the interlocking crises of democracy, community, and civil society are paralleled by troubling studies showing that student knowledge of the responsibilities of citizenship and of political processes is alarmingly low (Hart Research Associates, 1989). Studies have found that students

> *Do not see community participation as necessary for good citizenship, that they speak of their personal rights but not of the common good, that their notions of democracy are vague at best and often border on advertising slogans, that nationalism and authoritarian values are often preferable to democratic values, and that the only way they plan on participating in public decision-making is through voting.* (Berman, 1997, p. 5)

All of the studies conclude that if student apathy and cynicism about the political process continues unabated, our democracy is indeed at risk.

Like most crises, this one presents both dangers and opportunities. Although we do not wish to underestimate the magnitude of this multifaceted problem, we see signs of hope, both in renewed citizen activism and in the efforts many teachers are making to create opportunities for community service, political participation, and the development of skills that are crucial to active democratic citizenship. In the opening pages of this chapter, we highlighted three schools that are, in very different ways, educating for active citizenship. In the remainder of the chapter, we draw insights from these schools to explore the role that schools have to play in responding to the crisis of democracy.

The ideas in this chapter are based on a number of deeply held personal beliefs about the relationship between democracy and education. Because schools are the primary social institutions that have sustained contact with children throughout their formative years, we believe that they have a responsibility to educate students for active citizenship. Furthermore, we believe that this is best accomplished not just through a few isolated lessons in civics but through a comprehensive approach that includes attention to curriculum, instructional practices, governance, school culture and structures, relationships, and opportunities to practice civic learning in real-life situations. We believe that schools need to be *inclusive,* in that they welcome differences as valuable opportunities for practicing the skills of citizenship and community building. We believe that schools should be places where *all students* find their voices and are *empowered* to participate in public life. And we believe that schools should foster the sort of face-to-face interactions, within and without the school walls, which are necessary to building strong communities, vibrant civil societies, and strong democracies.

Characteristics of Democratic Schools

Following John Dewey, progressive educators see the classroom as a microcosm of society, with many possibilities for developing the dispositions and capacities necessary for active citizenship. In contrast to a classroom organized around competitive self-interest, the democratic classroom attempts to emulate the "loving and just community." "Care, trust, and responsibility are important norms . . . members . . . develop common values, goals, and a sense of collective responsibility . . . [and] conflicts become group opportunities for ethical problem-solving" (Berman, 1997, p. 131).

The development of democratic dispositions and capacities cannot take place in a vacuum; thus, the issue of school culture becomes an important consideration. Various studies suggest that "a higher level of institutional justice is a condition for individual development of a higher sense of justice" (Kohlberg, 1996, p. 216). Some of the criteria for assessing the level of institutional justice in a school include (but are not limited to) the following:

- Are the rules and regulations considered fair?

- Do students participate in rule setting?

- How are rewards, punishments, and privileges distributed?

- Do all students have opportunities to participate in governance?

- Are there fair and equitable processes in place for conflict resolution?

- Do students and teachers collaborate on curricular decisions?

- Are students with varied capacities and abilities encouraged to work together on projects of mutual concern?

- Is there a rich curriculum, accessible to all, with modifications and adaptations appropriate to differing student abilities?

The Harmony School, documented more extensively in the book *Elementary Schooling for Critical Democracy* (Goodman, 1992), provides one of the most interesting case studies of an entire school culture organized around democratic principles and institutional justice. Many other models of democratic school culture are unsung, and some are documented in books such as *Democratic Schools* (Apple & Beane, 1995). There are no "formulas" for creating democratic schools and classrooms. Each situation, depending on differences in the students, teachers, and community, will be unique. Sehr (1997) listed some characteristics of school life that are likely to lead to students' engagement with a program of educating for strong democracy:

- An atmosphere in which students feel a sense of belonging or membership in the school community

- A feeling of students' safety, both physical and emotional/psychological

- Schoolwork with intrinsic interest for students

- Schoolwork that is meaningful, not only for school purposes but also in the real world

- A sense of ownership of their school

Sehr (1997) provided a list of school practices that nurture public democratic values and attributes. His list is consistent with the practices that we believe are essential to the creation and maintenance of a democratic school:

- Creating opportunities for students to explore their interdependence with others and with nature

- Encouraging study of issues of equality and social justice

- Encouraging discussion, debate, and action on public issues

- Encouraging students to critically examine and evaluate the social reality in which they live

- Developing students' capacities for public democratic participation

All of the previous characteristics and practices are designed to foster a school culture that supports students' development as active, democratic citizens. In one review of the relationship between schooling and political socialization, a strong, if not conclusive, link was found between decision-making participation in school governance and the development of democratic political values: "The evidence is fairly convincing that there may be relationships between school organization and governance climate and student political attitudes and behavior" (Berman, 1997, p. 125). Given this convincing evidence, we think it is important to maximize the opportunities for students to participate in the decisions that affect their school life: schedules, curriculum, governance, rules and regulations, and assessment. And given that students learn much through the "hidden curriculum," we want to emphasize the importance of creating a school culture in which teachers, staff, and administrators model, in their relationships and practices, the dispositions and capacities that we hope to develop in students. Perhaps most important, we believe that students should be presented with opportunities throughout their school careers to engage in meaningful, problem-focused activities, both within and outside of the school walls.

CONCLUSION

Schools cannot solve the problems of democracy. In many ways, they are microcosms of the wider society and will necessarily reflect the dominant interests, concerns, and moral commitments of the times. Teachers, however, have a historic mission to educate students for active participation in their society. Sometimes, this means having to "teach against the grain" of the existing social order. We hope that we have interested you in the idea of democracy as a moral way of living and illuminated some ways that attention to curriculum, school culture, instructional practices, and opportunities for reaching outside the boundaries of the school walls can foster the capacities and dispositions that students need to become active, compassionate citizens. We hope that you will experiment with some of the ideas in this book for creating caring, collaborative, creative, and democratic classrooms. We believe that students fortunate enough to have such educational experiences are likely to develop an interest in strong democracy and to be creators of the loving and just society that we all hope for.

REFERENCES

Apple, M.W., & Beane, J.A. (1995). *Democratic schools.* Alexandria, VA: Association for Supervision and Curriculum Development.

Bellah, R., Madison, R., Sullivan, W., Swindler, A., & Tiptoe, S. (1985). *Habits of the heart: Individualism and commitment in American life.* New York: Harper and Row.

Berman, S. (1997). *Children's social consciousness and the development of social responsibility.* New York: State University of New York Press.

Cosgray, L., & Bonchek, B. (1996). *Harmony School Handbook.* Unpublished document. Available: Harmony School Education Center, Post Office Box 1787, Bloomington, Indiana 47402.

Goodman, J. (1992). *Elementary schooling for critical democracy.* Albany: State University of New York Press.

Hart Research Associates. (1989). *Democracy's next generation: A study of youth and teachers.* Washington, DC: People for the American Way.

Kesson, K., & Oyler, C. (January, 1999). Integrated curriculum and service-learning. *English Education, 31*(2), 135–149.

Kohlberg, L. (1996). Moral reasoning. In W.C. Parker (Ed.), *Educating the democratic mind* (pp. 201–221). Albany: State University of New York Press.

McChesney, R.W. (1999). Rich media, poor democracy: Communication politics in dubious times. New York: The New Press.

Noddings, N. (2001). Public schooling, democracy, and religious dissent. In R. Soder, J.I. Goodlad, & T.J. McMannon (Eds.), *Developing democratic character in the young* (pp. 152–169). San Francisco: Jossey-Bass.

Putnam, R. (1995). Bowling alone: America's declining social capital. *Journal of Democracy, 6*(1), 65.

Sehr, D.T. (1997). *Education for public democracy.* Albany: State University of New York Press.

Trend, D. (1996). Democracy's crisis of meaning. In D. Trend (Ed.), *Radical democracy: Identity, citizenship, and the state* (pp. 1–18). New York: Routledge.

Families as Creative and Resourceful Collaborators in Inclusive Schooling

Barbara E. Buswell
C. Beth Schaffner

Most advice for creating powerful and resourceful collaboration with families tends to come from professionals. In this chapter, we, parents of two young adults with disabilities who were fully included during their school years, offer advice on initiating partnerships to facilitate inclusive schooling. We speak from our firsthand experiences as advocates for our own children, but we also speak as professional educators working on behalf of all children.

WILSON'S FAMILY'S STORY

Barbara Buswell, Wilson's mother, graduated from college and was excited to teach; she found that watching students learn was fun and interesting. She taught English and French in a variety of schools, geographic locations, and levels from middle school through high school. She remembers the Education for All Handicapped Children Act of 1975, PL 94-142 (now re-authorized as the Individuals with Disabilities Education Act Amendments of 1997, PL 105-17) and the resulting special education teacher preparation programs that emerged. Barb was recruited by several universities to consider their programs but didn't attend because she felt that she lacked the qualities required to teach students with disabilities. All she knew about students with disabilities was that in the small Midwest town in which she was raised, these students were bussed to a special school miles away.

Wilson has one brother and one sister. He is the second-born son in the Buswell family. Wilson was deprived of oxygen at birth and as a result developed a severe physical disability. At the time, this was a shock, as it would be for most families. The entire family felt unprepared and unskilled to meet his physical needs. He was a fun, bright-eyed baby who was not able to talk, move around to explore and play, suck or eat easily, or be positioned comfortably. Intuitively, they knew that in spite of his "problems" (the word professionals used to describe his differences), Wilson needed to be included in every activity so that he could learn to communicate, develop emotionally, grow cognitively, and be an active family participant.

When it was time for Wilson to go to school, the family received a real shock. They had assumed that his teachers would learn from their son, as they had, that there are ways to support him physically so that he can participate actively, that supporting him is very interesting and creative, and that the other children are great resources. In other words, they thought that Wilson would be an asset rather than a burden to the classroom. They also had assumed that because both of Wilson's parents were teachers, his teachers would be receptive to their input as part of the team. However, they discovered that:

- Providing the supports that helped him learn successfully were viewed as a debatable provision; each teacher could decide if he or she was interested or felt capable of accepting.

- Most people in the school system wanted him to be in the physically disabled program where the children who could not move or talk were educated.

- Special education was viewed as a program rather than a system of individually designed supports and services.

- There was a perception that parents whose children are in general education classes aren't supposed to give advice on instructional approaches, so the family's expertise and perspectives about ways to include and support Wilson were dismissed.

Wilson spent his kindergarten year in an inclusive preschool with a lively learning environment, and his mother and father spent that year refining their knowledge and advocacy to ensure that Wilson would begin first grade in general education with the supports that he needed. From this point on in his school years, he was educated in general education classrooms with needed supports and accommodations.

Each year in the spring, as transition planning occurred for the next school year, Wilson and his family encountered various challenges. However, they also discovered some positive "truths." They discovered that good teachers can and do teach all students effectively, that a key to success is involving classmates in designing supports so that everyone can participate, that students without disability labels are not afraid to come forth and be supports and friends, and that no teacher or student is harmed by having Wilson in the class. They also learned that in their culture there are many misperceptions about what special education is and who can successfully teach diverse learners; even Wilson's parents had held those misperceptions before Wilson came along. Finally, they discovered that advocacy and collaboration year after year takes a tremendous amount of energy and work, and it is worth it.

As Wilson went through school, advocates for Wilson came along who helped smooth transitions. Not surprisingly, his fellow classmates and his brother and sister proved to be the most effective advocates in framing how and why it was important that Wilson progress to the next grade and level. Previous teachers and support staff also helped to smooth transitions and identify supports to ensure continuity.

ROB'S FAMILY'S STORY

Rob is a sportsman, a homeowner, a humorist, a former public school student who was fully included in general education in his middle and high school years, a college student, a friend, an occasional gambler, a frequent party man, and a generally wonderful human being. Most important, for his family, Rob is a teacher. He teaches what really matters in life. He teaches the importance of inclusion—a way of life that everyone needs and how important it is for educators. Rob's birth into the family was a pivotal point in their understanding of many things.

Prior to Rob's birth, Rob's mother, Beth Schaffner, experienced the old paradigm of special education, the one that focused on clinical judgments, remediation of impairments, and the old "readiness model" for inclusion (i.e., "You have to be deemed ready before you can be included and have a regular life"). Beth's special education teacher role began as a surrogate mother for 12–20 five- to seven-year-olds with disabilities whose classroom was next to the janitor's closet, down the hall and around the corner from the other classrooms in the building. Over the years, her role evolved so that she became her students' bridge to general education, ensuring that students' needs were met but in ways that would not segregate them from the life and culture of the school.

It was Rob, however, who taught Beth about the importance of holding students' families in high regard, listening and learning from them, and working in tandem with them. Beth had been a special educator who thought she had the expertise to tell families what needed to happen for their children. When Beth became Rob's mother, she realized that families, with their singular focus on their children's well-being, are the keepers of a vision of possibilities of a great life for their children. She understood that it is the general and special educators who need to recognize and acknowledge the expertise of families, help them to create and hold on to their long-term vision for their children, and create the kind of education that will lead to a life of possibilities. Just as families cannot realize quality inclusive education without educators, educators cannot make the changes needed to make inclusive education work without families' knowledge and support.

LEARNING FROM WILSON'S AND ROB'S EDUCATIONAL JOURNEYS

Wilson is now in college studying political science, although he still doesn't speak, is unable to sit or move without his wheelchair, and needs accommodations to demonstrate his knowledge. Rob works in a grocery store. He really would like a career in video production—the focus of his college classes. Yet, no one has been able to see beyond his disability to give him the chance.

It is still difficult for colleges, employers, and new people in Wilson's and Rob's lives to figure out ways to support, communicate with, and include them—at first. Nevertheless, Wilson, Rob, and their friends have become ardent spokespeople for inclusive schooling, and Wilson's and Rob's families are committed to helping people who enter their lives develop the skills and have the information they need to smooth the way for Wilson's and Rob's next experiences.

In 1988, out of a commitment to share their families' journeys and struggles, Wilson's and Rob's mothers, the authors of this chapter, became colleagues and friends as they worked at the PEAK Parent Center in Colorado Springs (Schaffner & Buswell, 1988, 1992, 1997). Here, Barb and Beth realized that inclusive education was really part of a larger overall school reform movement and that their struggles were shared by other families across the nation. Here, they also had the opportunity to learn about other families' creative and resourceful actions to initiate school reform on behalf of their children. Some examples of families' creative activism are

- The mother of a middle school student with a disability meets regularly with her son's support team to brainstorm strategies to ensure his active engagement in classroom activities.

- Families who attend their state's annual inclusion conference bring back information to their children's support teams. The following year, the children's general and special education teachers attend the conference with them to learn more about inclusive schooling strategies.

- The parent of a child with a disability joins his district's accountability committee and initiates efforts to bring a nationally known consultant on inclusion to help the district move forward.

- A family that was provided information about inclusion by the local Parent Training and Information Center share this information with other families at the monthly parent support group meeting at their local school.

Table 2.1. What families offer and need in collaborative relationships

What do families bring to the table?	What do families need in the relationship?
Experience	Equality
Unconditional, unwavering commitment	Access to resources
	Networking at all levels
Perspective	Partnership
Urgency	To be part of discussion
Passion	Continuity for what works
Creativity	Coordination of supports
Dual perspective	Ongoing relationships
Expertise	Respect for their time
A long-term vision	To be valued–NOT A TOKEN
Representation of their children	Information on a regular basis
A bridge to a successful life for their children	A nonadversarial way to do the individualized education program (IEP) process
An avenue for networking and education	
Their own culture and strength	A TEAM process
Activism	A supportive system
A resource to professionals	Acceptance as an asset

As these examples illustrate, families of children with disabilities clearly bring many strengths to the table. To be valuable and valued members at that table, however, they need relationships with others that emphasize equal partnership, continuity, and a nonadversarial way of solving problems. Table 2.1 identifies what families offer and need in their collaboration with others on behalf of their children.

CULTURAL FAULT LINES AND ROLE REDEFINITION

In *The Magic of Dialogue: Transforming Conflict into Cooperation* (1999), social scientist Daniel Yankelovich offers strategies to help individuals master communication skills to successfully dialogue with others and achieve shared objectives. He identified what he calls *cultural fault lines* that lie beneath the surface of daily life in our society and significantly damage relationships.

One cultural fault line involves too much "top-down" talk, resulting in miscommunications and misunderstandings that separate those considered experts in a field from the general public. Families of children with disabilities can feel disrespected when educators (the experts) use educational jargon and, in this way, "talk down" to them. Both educators and family members can create barriers in communication and trust if either fail to attend to this potential fault line and do not take the time to move to a deeper level of dialogue, acceptance, and understanding.

A second cultural fault line is the tendency of our culture to fragment itself into subcultures according to professions, traditional roles, gender, ethnicity, and so forth. People often are locked into their own subculture and the expectations of that subculture and are unable or unwilling to break out. To illustrate, the cultural and life experiences of families of children with disabilities can differ significantly from those of the educators who work with their children. When families have ethnic or socioeconomic backgrounds that are different from their children's teachers, the fragmentation can be even more pronounced.

It is critical to be aware of the value conflict that can be inherent between the subcultures of educators and the families of children with disabilities.

While the issue of value conflict is of concern for teachers working with all families, it becomes most crucial when teachers are working with families whose life circum-

stances or cultural beliefs and practices differ greatly from their own. Most are not aware of how deeply their beliefs are conditioned by their own . . . experiences. (Harry, Torguson, Katkavich, & Guerrero, 1993, p. 48)

As long as educators and parents fail to explore how the other views learning, teaching, belonging, community, and a variety of other dimensions of the schooling experience, cultural fragmentation will remain. We all know that changing long-held views is not easy. However, through talking and listening, family members and educators can discover their common beliefs, ideas, and concerns and step across the subcultural fragmentation fault line and break down subcultural stereotypes of one another.

One way to overcome the human tendency to categorize people and create cultural fragmentation is to encourage and support people to step out of their traditionally perceived roles. For example, a resource room teacher can transform his or her way of delivering services and become an inclusion facilitator who team-teaches with general education classroom teachers. A school cafeteria worker can join a student's planning team and share great strategies for increasing the student's social relationships during lunch. A school principal can call a student's parents to report a budding friendship that he or she has observed in the halls and after school. Collaboration, then, requires a blurring of expected, traditional roles of team members.

Family members who advocate for their child's inclusion often develop a different kind of relationship with their child's teachers, and their own roles change. Specifically, many parents deliberately develop expertise in developing curriculum modifications, positive behavioral supports, and augmentative and alternative communication. Families also deliberately become involved in various school decision-making and policy-setting groups (e.g., local school board, parent advisory committee).

These changes in role and level of involvement can be a different experience for educators who are accustomed to meeting with families only at parent–teacher conferences and communicating in a unidirectional (i.e., from educator to family) manner (e.g., sending permission slips home for signatures, calling home only when a child is struggling academically or behaviorally). In fact, when educators and administrators overcome their own cultural stereotypes to embrace their own role redefinition and the role redefinition of families, they can provide a model of the kind of active family engagement currently promoted by most school reform groups, including the National Parent Teacher Association (1997).

CREATIVE AND RESOURCEFUL ACTIONS FOR FAMILY COLLABORATION

In order to collaborate in new ways, people need to think and act in new ways. Four sets of suggested actions to help family members and educators get started in transforming their relationships so that they are more powerful and mutually beneficial follow. The first set relates to knowledge of the change process and strategic planning and demonstration of effective leadership. The second set targets effective teaching practices that promote a welcoming learning community. The third set suggests ways to stimulate information sharing and support network development. The final set offers suggestions for ensuring accountability in the individualized education program (IEP) process. Each recommendation takes the form of a bulleted action item. The recommendations are derived from the knowledge of the chapter authors and the families with whom they have worked.

Use Change Processes to Create Shared Leadership

- Get to know the members of your school board and key district administrators. Invite them to meet with you and other parents to discuss inclusive education and school reform issues. Provide them with information to help them understand the issues and your perspective.

- Identify your allies in the school and the district. Ask key questions to determine their beliefs, understanding, and expertise about inclusive schooling practices.

- Ask questions to learn about the policies, cultures, operating practices of the school, and school improvement plans to help develop new strategic change plans.

- Develop a plan of action to make inclusive education happen successfully in the school and district.

- Clearly communicate your expectations that your child will be a fully participating member of the school community and receive the supports necessary to be successful there. Be firm and persistent about what you want. Know your bottom line.

- Become knowledgeable about the change process.

- Do not allow the size and complexity of the change process to paralyze you, and do not "buy" rationalizations for changing slowly and incrementally or not at all.

- Let school personnel know that you understand that change is difficult and that you want to help however you can. Offer support to school projects and functions that promote inclusive practices.

- Recognize that new efforts take ongoing monitoring to continue and be effective.

- If things slip back, don't give up; talk with your allies or find new allies, and revise the plan of action.

- Join with other families around school issues of concern in your community. A well-organized group of parents united behind a common cause will command attention and prompt action.

Promote Welcoming Learning Communities Through Effective Teaching Practices

- Be a community resource and materials locator for your child's teachers.

- Volunteer in your child's class and help with creative classroom activities requiring extra adult assistance.

- Advocate for your child to have access, with needed supports, to the richness of the general education curriculum by inclusion in all classroom and other school activities. Students often don't demonstrate what they actually gain in a class until later. It is important that your child's *learning opportunities* not be limited.

- Brainstorm with your child's teacher and team about ways to implement new ideas and teaching approaches and to make accommodations so all students can actively participate in class and other school activities.

- Encourage your child's special education teachers, therapists, and other service providers to be extra resources in the general classroom to encourage the teacher to try innovative inclusive teaching approaches.

- Engage your child's support team to find opportunities for students to be together, emphasize students' strengths and contributions rather than weaknesses or disability label, and infuse goals for belonging and friendship into all aspects of the curriculum.

- Ask your child's support team to identify budding relationships between your child and classmates so that you can encourage opportunities to get together outside of school.

Stimulate Information Sharing and Support Network Development

- Help your child's support team honor the fact that you have critical information and perspectives about your child that no one else has by participating actively and consistently on your child's team.

- Nurture positive relationships as much as possible while recognizing that sometimes parents must speak out and challenge existing attitudes and practices.

- Focus on student and adult strengths. Celebrate even small successes. Usually, problems and challenges are more easily solved when they are framed as opportunities for improvement, rather than as failures.

- Give resource information such as articles, books, and videos on best practices for inclusion and school reform to key people in your child's school and district. Be sure that resource materials you share with others are current, as new information is continually emerging.

- Locate upcoming local, state, and national training opportunities and invite families and educators to participate with you.

- Participate in planning for staff development in your district.

- Actively recruit parents who have been successful advocates for inclusive practices to be presenters and trainers for parents, teachers, youth, and community members.

Promote Accountability in the IEP Process

- Suggest that your child's and other planning teams use a collaborative teaming process that ensures effective communication, creative problem solving, efficiency, and accountability (Castagnera, Fisher, Rodifer, & Sax, 1998; Fisher, Frey, & Sax, 1999; Thousand & Villa, 2000).

- Suggest using chart paper during IEP meetings for recording your child's strengths, needs, support strategy ideas, and so forth.

- Hold team members accountable for what they say they will do and what is written on the IEP by documenting commitments in minutes at each team meeting.

- Document through the IEP process your child's needs for friends, language and behavior role models, and social relationships inside and outside of school by including goals in these areas in the IEP.

- Contact your community or state Parent Training and Information Center for additional information on student planning tools and processes (http://www.taalliance .org).

CONCLUSION

Families of children with disabilities have provoked positive change in how students are educated at all levels. Families can provide the impetus for entire schools to be more responsive to students. It is their vision, knowledge, expertise, and advocacy as they work alongside committed, visionary, and skilled educators that makes the difference.

This work to create inclusive schools and communities requires knowledge, courage, persistence, and true collaboration among everyone involved. Families have a great sense of urgency to move to craft inclusive communities because their children with disabilities have no time to wait. If their children grow through their childhood and school-age years excluded in special classes, pulled out of programs, or denied the supports that they need to learn and interact successfully in general education classrooms, then rich opportunities for learning and priceless experiences of friendship and belonging will pass them by. These particular kinds of opportunities never come again in a person's lifetime.

For educators who wish to join families in making inclusive schooling a reality, we offer four suggestions. First, critically evaluate your own values and attitudes about families, students, and disabilities. Second, focus on the strengths and contributions of all families. Third, regardless of your professional area of expertise, look at a student as a whole person with strengths and interests as well as needs for support. Finally, reach out to and encourage families to participate as equal contributors with important knowledge in the collaborative process.

The inclusive schooling movement has come a long way since our sons were young and we were finding our way as educators and parents who were advocates for inclusion. For us, the journey continues as we support our sons to realize their dreams as adult members of their communities. And we find we *still* must be vigilant in our advocacy. We *still* must develop and nurture collaborative relationships with people who share our values and dreams and will work alongside us. And we must guard our children from those systems and practices that might take them down a different path toward segregation and isolation.

We all must continue to work together vigilantly to build and nurture a society where inclusion is a given and everyone belongs. Acting now will make a powerful, positive difference in our students' lives. Not acting or allowing the status quo to continue can have an equally powerful but negative, damaging impact on many students.

REFERENCES

Castagnera, L., Fisher, D., Rodifer, K., & Sax, C. (1998). *Deciding what to teach and how to teach it: Connecting students through curriculum and instruction.* Colorado Springs: PEAK Parent Center, Inc.

Education for All Handicapped Children Act of 1975, PL 94-142, 20 U.S.C. §§ 1400 *et seq.*

Fisher, D., Frey, N., & Sax, C. (1999). *Inclusive elementary schools: Recipes for success.* Colorado Springs: PEAK Parent Center, Inc.

Harry, B., Torguson, C., Katkavich, J., & Guerrero, M. (1993). Crossing social class and cultural barriers in working with families. *Teaching Exceptional Children, 26*(1), 48–51.

Individuals with Disabilities Education Act Amendments of 1997, PL 105-17, 20 U.S.C. §§ 1400 *et seq.*

National Parent Teacher Association (PTA). (1997). *National standards for parent/family involvement programs.* Chicago: Author.

Schaffner, C.B., & Buswell, B. (1988). *Discover the possibilities: A curriculum for teaching parents about integration.* Colorado Springs: PEAK Parent Center, Inc.

Schaffner, C.B., & Buswell, B. (1992). *Connecting students: A guide to thoughtful friendship facilitation for educators and families.* Colorado Springs: PEAK Parent Center, Inc.

Schaffner, C.B., & Buswell, B.E. (1997). *Inherently equal: An inclusion action guide for families and educators.* Boston: The Federation for Children with Special Needs.

Thousand, J., & Villa, R. (2000). Collaborative teaming: A powerful tool in school restructuring. In R. Villa & J. Thousand (Eds.), *Restructuring for caring and effective education: Piecing the puzzle together* (2nd ed., pp. 254–291). Baltimore: Paul H. Brookes Publishing Co.

Yankelovich, D. (1999). *The magic of dialogue: Transforming conflict into cooperation.* New York: Simon & Schuster.

Beyond Benevolence

Supporting Genuine Friendship in Inclusive Schools

Emma Van der Klift
Norman Kunc

In the 21st century, children with and without disabilities have the opportunity to grow up and be educated together. Therefore, we are optimistic that the generation growing up now will be different from those of the past. We are hopeful that increased contact between children will begin to break down the barriers of misunderstanding and dispel the myths that have shaped society's response to disability.

At first glance, this change might seem to be already taking place. Individuals with disabilities are more visible and increasingly involved in community life. If we believe that greater proximity leads to greater acceptance, then it could be argued that we are successfully participating in the creation of a new social order. Unfortunately, this is only partly true. Instead, we are finding that increased visibility and "presence" do not necessarily ensure that those with disabilities are fully included.

True inclusion is dependent on the development of meaningful and reciprocal relationships between children. As classrooms become increasingly diverse, new strategies are being developed to ensure that students with disabilities are more than simply present. Friendship circles, school clubs, and special buddy systems have been implemented as formalized attempts to foster interaction and develop relationships.

Although increased interaction may result from such efforts, true friendship often remains elusive. Children may have buddies during school hours and still be isolated and friendless after 3:00 P.M. Children without disabilities may be helpful and involved, without developing genuine friendships with children without disabilities. The difficult and often frustrating question is, therefore, "What are the barriers impeding the development of friendship, and how can we move past them?"

FRIENDSHIP AND HELP

At the beginning of the 21st century, the most significant barrier to full school and community participation is attitudinal. Specifically, our society still perceives those with disabilities as constant receivers of help. Descriptors such as "less fortunate" and "needy" and telethons and tearjerker journalism all continue to perpetuate this view. Friendship clubs and buddy systems based on stereotypical beliefs risk perpetuating prejudices and myths and even exacerbating the problem.

It is essential that students be provided with opportunities to interact. Although formalized friendship and support circles may be effective ways to build relationships, an overemphasis on the "helper–helpee" relationship can easily skew the delicate balance of giving and receiving that is the precursor to true friendship. It is critical, therefore, to examine regularly and carefully the nature of the interaction we facilitate and the attitudes that inform it. Consider the following scenario:

Four third-grade children from a local elementary school have been invited, with their teacher, to speak to a room full of adults about friendship. Actually, three of them are there to talk about their friendship with the fourth child. Children in third grade make friends all the time. What is unusual about this group is that while three of the four children in the room can speak and walk, one of them can do neither. The three children are here to talk about their relationship with the boy in the wheelchair.

Adults in the room begin to smile as the first classmate talks. Approving nods accompany the child's words: "He's different on the outside, but inside he's just like me." The conversation whirls around the boy in the wheelchair as he scans the room, looks at his communication board, and sometimes watches his classmates. "We take turns being his buddy," offers one young girl. "Everyone has a turn."

As the children talk and answer questions, it is interesting to watch the interplay between the boy in the wheelchair and the girl to his left. She has one arm around his shoulders and in the other hand she holds a washcloth. She wipes his mouth repeatedly.

At one point, he appears to lose patience and struggles a bit. One hand jerks forward. His friend seizes his hand and holds it still. He makes a noise of clear irritation and attempts to pull his hand free. His classmate smiles fondly at him, continuing to restrain his hand, and wipes his mouth again.

There doesn't appear to be anything wrong with this scene: A 9-year-old, who in other times or other places might have been attending segregated classes, and a group of third graders are learning lessons about differences and similarities. We might even agree with comments made by audience members. We heard the boy's three classmates being called "the hope for tomorrow" and "exceptional kids." All over the room, adults were beaming. After all, this relatively new phenomenon seems to hold some hope for an end to discrimination and distance between those who have disabilities and those who do not.

As the presentation continues, however, it becomes increasingly apparent that although both adults and children think they are talking about friendship, much of the discussion taking place is really about help. Although there is undeniable warmth between the children, most of the comments and nonverbal interactions reflect a helper–helpee relationship, not a reciprocal friendship.

When initially attempting to foster relationships between children with disabilities and their classmates without disabilities, it is common practice to have children "help" the new student. Such help may take the form of providing physical care, "keeping company" during breaks, or assisting with schoolwork. Helping can reduce an initial sense of strangeness or fear and, if carefully done, can lay the groundwork for friendship.

Clearly, there is nothing wrong with help; friends often help each other. It is essential to acknowledge, however, that help is not and can never be the basis of friendship. We must be careful not to overemphasize the helper–helpee aspect of a relationship. Unless help is reciprocal, the inherent inequity between helper and helpee will contaminate the authenticity of a relationship.

Friendship is not the same as help. Attempts to include children with disabilities have sometimes blurred this distinction. Friendship clubs are often really assistance clubs. For example, how much time is spent on the logistics of help? "Who can take Jane to the library on Monday?" "Who can help George eat lunch on Friday?" Still more insidious, how much time is spent bringing George's classmates into a "multidisciplinary team system" to analyze the effectiveness of his current behavior management plan?

Professional caregivers are made, not born. Put a third-grade helper next to a third-grade helpee, add a sizable amount of adult approval, and there you have it. An unfortunate result, however, is that a lot of children and adults with mental and physical disabilities have legions of professional caregivers but no friends in their lives. We must guard against merely creating another generation of "professionals" and "clients," with the former group seen as perpetually competent and the latter as perpetually needy.

But what is a teacher to do? To create a helper is relatively easy; to facilitate a friendship is tough. After all, friendship cannot simply be mandated. At best, it seems to be made up of one third proximity and two thirds alchemy!

Perhaps we must begin by acknowledging what should be but is not always obvious. That is, no one has the power to conjure up friendship at will. Friendship is about choice and chemistry and cannot even be readily defined, much less forced. This is precisely its magic. Realizing this, we can acknowledge without any sense of inadequacy that we are not, nor do we need to be, friendship sorcerers.

Teachers and others, however, do have some influence over the nature of proximity. Thus, to create and foster an environment in which it is possible for friendship to emerge might be a more reasonable goal. To achieve this goal, it is essential that we examine the nature of the interactions we facilitate. In particular, we must look closely at the role of help in our classrooms and not so much at whether children should help each other but how that help takes place.

MOVING TO VALUING

Throughout our lives, we have observed societies and educators experiencing different responses to diversity. As Table 3.1 shows, there are at least four responses to human difference or diversity—*marginalization, reform, tolerance,* and *valuing.* The first response, *marginalization,* is expressed by avoiding; segregating; and, in some cases, putting an end to people who are different. This was a prevalent response in the 1960s and 1970s, a time when many children with disabilities were in segregated schools and in institutions that were more like prisons than classrooms. Society examined such practices and changed or eliminated many of them. Yet, other hurdles arose to replace marginalization.

Remedial, therapeutic, and life-skills programs were developed expressly to help minimize children's disabilities and make them more like children without disabilities. This response among educators was that of *reform.* Educators went from saying "you cannot be with us" to saying "you can be with us, but first you must be like us." In other words, chil-

Table 3.1. Responses to diversity

Response	Expression of response
Marginalization	Avoidance
	Segregation
	Aggression
Reform	Rehabilitation
	Assimilation
Tolerance	Resignation
	Benevolence (false belonging)
Valuing (diversity as typical)	Equal worth
	Mutual benefit
	Belonging

dren with disabilities and other differences were thought to need rehabilitation and assimilation in order to be welcomed into society. The intent was to improve their quality of life through increased functioning and skills development. The promise was future belonging, but the real message was, "You are not valuable as you are." Although the reform response to diversity remains in some places, it has been challenged by the inclusive education movement since the 1980s.

Tolerance, the third response to diversity, may seem more appealing than the first two; many view intolerance of human diversity as morally reprehensible and strive for tolerant schools and societies. Yet, although the intent to create more acceptance of diversity is a worthy goal, it will never lead to true social justice. We have seen this firsthand in our travels to schools around North America. In some schools, when proposals of educating students with disabilities in local classrooms are made, we hear statements of resignation (e.g., "We will, if we have to") or statements of benevolence or false belonging (e.g., "Well, I guess it would be the right thing to do to help those poor, unfortunate children"). These statements represent tolerance, and simply being tolerated is not the same as being valued. Few have as their life's goal to simply be tolerated.

To move beyond mere tolerance to the fourth and ultimate response of genuine *valuing,* human diversity must be viewed as typical. Educators can begin this process by genuinely valuing the natural diversity that students possess and express and by focusing on creating classroom communities that promote belonging and acceptance for all. For example, both cooperative group learning and partner learning strategies can achieve valuing. Teachers can also consciously nurture proximity among students and friendship development. Following are some practical ideas to assist in the process.

Do Not Make Friendship a Big Deal

Friendship between children is wonderful; however, it is not a big deal. If we commend and praise children without disabilities for their interactions with their peers with disabilities (either publicly or in other ways), then we inadvertently make friendship a big deal and imply that all children are not created equal. We reinforce the idea that it is morally and socially admirable to "help the disabled," and, therefore, may remove the opportunity for equality and reciprocity.

Respect Personal Boundaries

Adults are seldom comfortable talking about childhood sexuality. But the truth is that children start noticing each other in kindergarten. People with disabilities, however, often receive messages that tell them they are asexual; these messages begin early. Boundaries of touch that would not be crossed between kids without disabilities should never be crossed with their classmates with disabilities.

An unfortunate side effect of tolerant or benevolent interaction is a tendency to treat the child with disabilities like a life-size doll, pet, or classroom mascot with whom the usual physical boundaries of touch may be violated. We must always ask, "Do the interactions between children in any way compromise the dignity of the individual with the disability?"

Model Valuing Behavior

There is a lot of discussion of how kids model behavior for each other and how a child's peers are effective arbiters of social appropriateness. Although this is most certainly true, we must also remember that teachers remain the most powerful modeling agents in the classroom. If interactions between the teacher and the child with the disability are respectful, then the other students will take their cues accordingly.

Share Information

A child's classmates may provide useful information about the nature of puzzling behaviors. Sometimes, children will see things that remain invisible to adult observers. The risk involved in eliciting input about behavior, however, may be the development of an increased sense of difference and distance. People with disabilities tell us that it is easier to be ignored than to be patronized or seen as a "class project."

We can still get the information we need without compromising the equity of peer relationships by positing the issue as the school's problem, rather than the child's problem. This way, it appears that we do not yet have the insight, experience, or information necessary to support the student. In fact, it may emerge that the real issue has more to do with making schools more responsive to all members.

Acknowledge Reciprocity and Contribution

Although a majority of educators acknowledge that the rights of students with disabilities should be respected, there is an ongoing debate about whether reciprocity is really possible and what kind of contribution is realistic to expect. "What," we are often asked, "can a student with a disability really bring to a relationship?"

This question usually reveals more about our own stereotypical views about the idea of disability than about the limitations of a disability itself. After all, there is nothing universally "true" about any disability. Generalizations about "the disabled" will never generate the information necessary to address serious questions about the nature of reciprocity or contribution.

Dembo, Leviton, and Wright (as cited in Wright, 1983) first identified a societal tendency to generalize and make broad inferences about the nature of disability. They called this common phenomenon *disability spread*. Specifically, disability spread is what happens when we extrapolate the characteristics that we associate with the notion of disability to the particular individuals we meet. These perceptions are often based on stereotypes, are often what we think we know about a particular disability, and are often expressed in predictable ways, such as "All people with Down syndrome are happy," or "People with cerebral palsy usually have a cognitive disability." In fact, these characteristics may or may not actually be true of any individual. Figure 3.1 illustrates this concept.

Many inferences and assumptions are made about disability in our society. For example, we are inclined to see people with disabilities as a collection of needs and deficiencies (McKnight, 1989). We are led to evaluate people based on what is missing rather than what is present. When our perceptions are based on stereotypical myths and misperceptions, we will not see a real person with any clarity.

In fact, every individual is a complex collection of components. Each of us has a variety of interests, skills, and capacities, as well as a unique background. We all have different physical characteristics and our own idiosyncratic personalities. In our interactions with others, we want to be understood and seen for who we are, and we hope that we will not be judged simply at face value. For individuals who have visible disabilities, however, being judged at face value is precisely what happens most often.

When disability is seen as the largest component of a person, much of what is unique and "human" about him or her is obscured. When needs and impairments are all that we see, we focus on what that person cannot do.

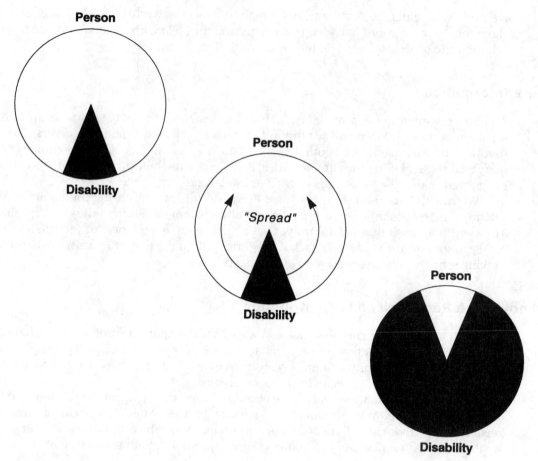

Figure 3.1. Disability spread.

We cannot recognize the diverse contributions of all citizens until we shift our focus from the disability to the complexity and individuality of all people. Only by getting to know a person in all of his or her multifaceted individuality can disability assume its real proportion—as one small facet of a person's identity.

Merge Respect and Help

Too much help can be a disabling force. One of the biggest challenges teachers face in inclusive classrooms is getting other kids to stop doing everything for the child with a disability. Too much help, even when enthusiastically given, is fundamentally disempowering. Help should always be "natural and situation-rooted" (Wright, 1983, p. 311) and should only be what individuals of a fascinating study on help and disability termed *necessary help* (Ladieu, Hanfmann, & Dembo, as cited in Wright, 1983, p. 310).

Help outside the context of choice and self-determination is disrespectful. We all want to feel needed; however, when this desire is at the expense of someone else's sense of competence and autonomy, we commit a lasting act of injustice. People with disabilities literally spend lifetimes struggling to be heard. We must learn to listen. Marsha Saxton wrote:

All of those people trying so hard to help me . . . All of them hoping for me to . . . do well, all wanting to be kind and useful, all feeling how important helping me was. Yet never did anyone of them ask me what it was like for me. They never asked me what I wanted for myself. They never asked me if I wanted their help. I do not feel entirely grateful. I feel, instead, a remote anger stored beneath my coping pattern of compla-cent understanding. People do the best they can to help in meaningful ways, I know. I just wish all the disabled children would say to their helpers: "Before you do anything else, just listen to me." (1985, pp. 133–134)

We must listen to both the verbal and nonverbal messages expressed by someone who may or may not want help. We must use this information to guide our actions and increase our sensitivity. It does not sound like much, but the ramifications are enormous. It is often during times when we are hell-bent on helping that we listen least well. We all know sto-ries of people with visual impairments being forcibly "escorted" over crosswalks by well-meaning pedestrians, of people in nursing homes being fed when they are not hungry, or of what the participants in the Dembo study aptly called "unexpected attacks" of help (Ladieu, Hanfmann, & Dembo, as cited in Wright, 1983, p. 309).

Appeal to Children's Empathy and Social Justice

Most children are acutely aware of what is fair and what is not. Furthermore, powerless-ness and social stigma are not the sole experience of those with disabilities. Children, by virtue of their status in society, generally understand what it feels like to be without influ-ence. They know how it feels to be silenced, to be disregarded, and to have decisions that concern them made arbitrarily and regularly by others.

We have downplayed and underutilized these experiences, thinking that "Caucasian, middle-class, able-bodied children" do not experience oppression and will not understand. In fact, most children experience rejection, isolation, and a sense of powerlessness at some time. Whether these are children of color, children who must learn English as a second language, children who dress differently, children who eat different foods, children who have ethnically different last names, or children who just do not seem to fit in somehow, there is a kernel of commonality in these experiences.

Too often, in discussions of social justice between educators and children, the issues are portrayed as "theirs." We show kids what institutional life looks like, we talk about the negative effects of segregation, and we ask them to think about how it feels to be teased because of a disability. We even subject them to simulated situations or role plays that sup-posedly allow participants to feel, for example, what it is like to be blind.

Unfortunately, the unintentional result is more distance and a greater sense of fun-damental "otherness." At best, this approach fosters sympathy, and at worst, a guilty relief—"thank heaven it's not me."

We must not inadvertently reinforce the notion that those with disabilities are objects of pity. Equitable relationships cannot be built on a foundation of pity. Instead, we must build on the shared experiences, the shared stories between us, to create a sense of empa-thy and a sense of "I know what you mean." This does not disregard our different ex-periences. It is certainly true that having a disability and being an immigrant are not completely comparable experiences. Likewise, being left out of games on the playground and being the victim of racist behavior are not the same. When experiences do intersect, however, we have an opportunity to build connection and understanding that may ex-trapolate to other situations in unexpected ways. Social justice is an important aspect of education. The development of empathy and shared understanding between individuals of diverse background and ability is critical if our world is to survive the next century. We need people to work together to address issues of inequity and injustice.

You may wonder why, in a book primarily devoted to collaborative learning and creativity within heterogeneous schools, this chapter has focused almost exclusively on inclusive education. We believe that individuals with mental and physical disabilities may well prove to be the proverbial canaries in the experimental coal mines of education. These are the people who will teach us most about the nature of help. Through our interactions with those who have disabilities, we stand to learn valuable lessons that will lead us to greater appreciation of diversity in all of its forms. The creation of a better world is dependent on our collective ability to learn these lessons well.

REFERENCES

McKnight, J. (1989). *Do no harm: A policymaker's guide to evaluating human services and their alternatives.* Evanston, IL: Center for Urban Affairs & Policy Research.

Saxton, M. (1985). The something that happened before I was born. In A.J. Brightman (Ed.), *Ordinary moments: The disabled experience* (pp. 127–140). Syracuse, NY: Human Policy Press.

Wright, B.A. (1983). *Physical disability: A psychosocial approach* (2nd ed.). New York: Harper & Row.

4

Building Connections

Mary A. Falvey
Marsha S. Forest
Jack Pearpoint
Richard L. Rosenberg

Schools that include all students also systematically build connections between the school and the participants in the school community. Building such community connections is essential to fostering a sense of belonging to the school community (Falvey, Eshilian, & Rosenberg, 2001; Meyer, Park, Grenot-Scheyer, Schwartz, & Harry, 1998; O'Brien & Mount, 1991; Strully & Strully, 1985). These community connections and friendships are critical for many reasons—to avoid loneliness; to develop social, communicative, and even cognitive skills; to feel like a valued member of the community; and to develop the support needed to co-exist in a community (Gilson & Gilson, 1998; Salisbury & Palombaro, 1998; Stainback, Stainback, & Wilkinson, 1992).

One of the key characteristics to building connections and friendships is being in close proximity to people and having frequent opportunities to interact with each other (Asher, Odem, & Gottman, 1977; Hartup, 1975; Howes, 1983; Lewis & Rosenblum, 1975). Research has demonstrated that in order for children and adults to form the necessary bonds for friendships, they must have frequent access to one another. This access is facilitated when students are in close proximity to one another on a regular basis. So, it follows that students who attend the same school as others who live in their neighborhood are more likely to form bonds that are strong enough to result in friendship (Grenot-Scheyer, Coots, & Falvey, 1989; Grenot-Scheyer, Staub, Peck, & Schwartz, 1998).

Traditionally, special educators have taught students to be independent; however, today more emphasis is being placed on interdependence (Condeluci, 1991; O'Brien & Mount, 1991; Wehmeyer, 2001). *Interdependence* is the ability to connect with individuals within one's own community and develop a network of supports to assist in accomplishing life goals.

There are too many unhappy, unloving, untrusting, mediocre schools. These schools do not teach nor do they emulate such principles as love, passion, openness, and the love of learning. Academic subjects are important only if they are used to teach these principles, as illustrated in Figure 4.1.

Teachers burn out in schools and classrooms that teach basic core academic skills out of the context of teaching values. Schools must teach such skills as creating a just community and society and caring for and helping one another.

For 5 years, a group of teenagers fought a school district in a Western state that refused to allow one of their peers, Louise, to enter or attend the same high school as the rest of them. The school district claimed that because of her diabetes and severe cognitive and physical disabilities, she had to attend a special education class in a different high school. When the school district forced Louise to attend a different high school, her friends were

Dear Teacher,

I am a survivor of a concentration camp.

My eyes saw what no man should witness.

Gas chambers built by learned engineers.

Children poisoned by educated physicians.

Infants killed by trained nurses.

Women and babies shot and burned by high school and college graduates.

So I am suspicious of education.

My request is that teachers help students become human.

Your efforts must never produce learned monsters, skilled psychopaths, educated Eichmanns.

Read, writing, arithmetic are important only if they serve to make our children more human.

Figure 4.1. Letter to teachers. (From Ginott, H. [1972]. *Teacher and child.* New York: Collier Books; reprinted by permission of the author's estate.)

outraged. They had learned about the U.S. Constitution in their eighth-grade civics class and felt that by denying Louise access to her neighborhood high school, her rights and their rights were being violated. They launched a campaign seeking support from advocates and their community. Their plight and their struggle were frequently written about in the newspaper; they appeared on local television news programs; and they presented to local governmental and advocacy groups, including the local city council and the board of education. In addition, they wrote and performed a rap song titled *Friends,* which tells their story—what they wanted and why. Finally, 2 years after they began, their struggle was over—the school district reversed its decision and granted Louise the opportunity to attend the same school and classes as her peers and friends. What is so compelling about this true story is that the students, Louise, and her Circle of Friends initially formed their relationship and subsequent friendships based on their opportunity to go to school and classes together while in junior high school. No adults told the students to care about Louise because she was "special" or to treat her differently because she had diabetes and severe disabilities. Going to school and classes together gave these students the opportunity to know each other and become friends.

This story dramatizes the natural way in which friendships develop. Unfortunately, frequent opportunities and close proximity are not always enough for children and adolescents to feel connected and to build a network of friends. Several tools have been used successfully to facilitate such connections and eventual friendships. These tools are designed to tap into the creative energy of students and educators. Circle of Friends, Making Action Plans (MAPs), and Planning Alternative Tomorrows with Hope (PATH) are three person-centered tools based on hope for the future and assume that all people belong, all people can learn, everyone is better off together, and diversity is one of our most critical strengths. These tools are described in detail in the remainder of this chapter.

CIRCLE OF FRIENDS

A Circle of Friends is something that many of us take for granted. A Circle of Friends provides us with a support network of family and friends who listen, give loving advice, and

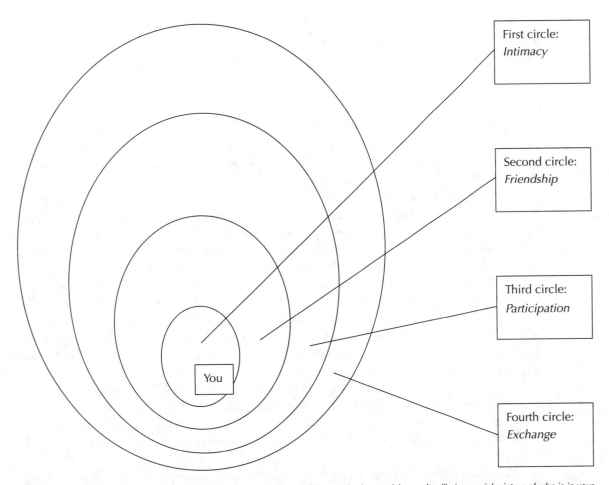

First circle:
Intimacy

Second circle:
Friendship

Third circle:
Participation

You

Fourth circle:
Exchange

Figure 4.2. Steps involved in conducting a Circle of Friends process. This exercise is a social scan. It will give a quick picture of who is in your life. It is very useful to gain clarity about who might be involved in certain activities or circles that need to be filled. We recommend it personally and consider it an essential preventative health check for students and teachers. The key hidden question is, "Who loves this person?" *Instructions:* 1) Draw four concentric circles; and 2) put yourself right in the middle, then take a few minutes to fill in the people in each of your four circles. First circle: the people most intimate in your life—those you cannot imagine living without; second circle: good friends—those who almost made the first circle; third circle: people, organizations, and networks with whom you are involved (e.g., work colleagues, the church choir, the square dance club, the softball team); fourth circle: people you pay to provide services in your life (e.g., medical professionals, tax accountants, mechanics, teachers). *Note:* People can be in more than one circle (e.g., your doctor or teacher could also be a close friend; a deceased parent/friend may be in a circle; an inanimate object may be in a circle).

provide support when it is needed (Perske, 1989). In the absence of a naturally formed Circle of Friends, educators can facilitate a circle process to enlist the involvement and commitment of peers around an individual student. For a student who is not well connected or does not have an extensive network of friends, a Circle of Friends process can be useful.

A Circle of Friends involves gathering a group of students together for the purpose of discovering their own Circle of Friends and then reflecting on each other's circles (Sherwood, 1990). Figure 4.2 provides a list of the steps involved in conducting a Circle of Friends process.

A high school teacher wanted to inject life back into her students, herself, and the school. She knew she could not change everything but wanted to instill some hope and build community connections and friendships for a few of her students who were at risk or had severe disabilities and were on the verge of dropping out of school.

The teacher gathered about 50 students together and told them she wanted to have a frank discussion about friends and how to build more solid relationships in the school. She did not single out any individual but talked in general for half an hour about her own vision and beliefs in relationships and friendship as the core of a good school. She played music softly in the background and drew colorful images as she spoke. She then drew four concentric circles on the chalkboard. She gave each student a sheet of paper that also had four concentric circles and requested that each student put his or her name in the center of his or her inner circle. She modeled this by putting her name in the center of her circle. Then she directed them to write the names of all the people closest to their heart on the first and smallest circle. She gave an example from her own life by putting her husband, her mother, her two children, and, for fun, her computer (she is an avid computer fan) in her first circle. She also added the spirit of a friend of hers who had died 2 years prior.

Then, she explained that the second circle is for people who are friends but who are not as close as those identified in the first circle. Again, she modeled this by using examples from her own life; she has six friends whom she sees all the time and two others whom she sees once a year but whom she speaks to frequently. She also included some family members, a few teachers she works with, and her cat. She then asked the students to fill in their second circle and found that the classroom was very quiet, as the students were taking the activity seriously.

The teacher explained that the third circle was for individuals or groups of people whom the students really liked but to whom they were not very close. She modeled by identifying some of the teachers at the high school, members of the church choir in which she sings, some of her tennis partners, and some members of her exercise class. She also listed individuals she sees occasionally, but who come and go, and three relatives she likes but seldom sees.

After the students completed their third circle, she explained that the fourth circle was for people who are paid to be in their lives, such as teachers and doctors. She identified her doctor, chiropractor, and housekeeper as people who are paid to be in her life. The students followed by identifying those people in their lives who are paid to be there. The circles were then complete.

The teacher told the students that she could tell a lot about people by looking at their completed circles. She asked for a student to volunteer his or her completed circles. She held up the completed circles of the student who volunteered and read the names of the people in each circle (see Figure 4.3). Then she showed the students the completed set of circles for Jane, a student with disabilities, and asked her class to describe how they would feel if those were their circles. Figure 4.4 shows Jane's completed set of circles. The most frequent response was that "the only people who are involved in Jane's life are her family and those people who are paid to be there." In addition, the students also responded with the following descriptors:

- Lonely

- Depressed

- Unwanted

- Rejected

- Isolated

- Confused

- Upset

- Horrible

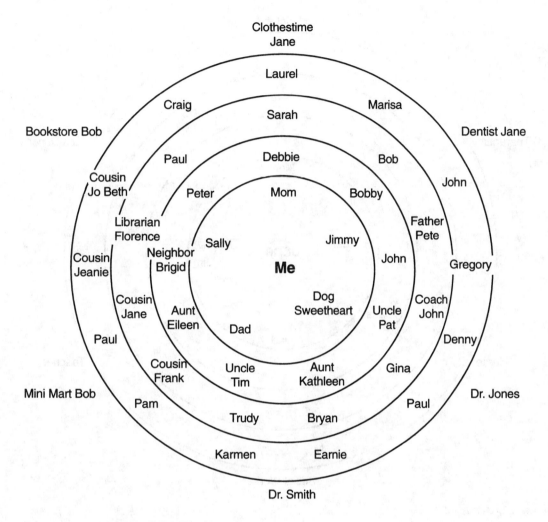

Figure 4.3. A high school student's Circle of Friends.

- Humorless

- Distraught

- Frustrated

- Suicidal

The teacher then asked the students to identify what they would do if this were representative of their life. Their responses included

- Commit suicide

- Try to make friends

- Move to a deserted island

- Do something really drastic

- Kick

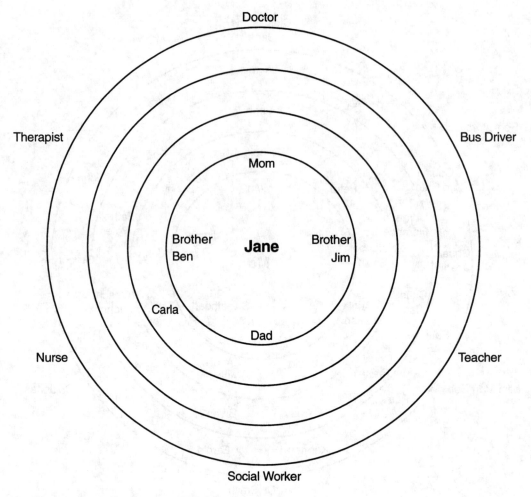

Figure 4.4. A Circle of Friends for Jane.

- Do drugs

- Have a baby

- Stay in bed

- Drink

- Kill someone

- Get a tutor

A passionate discussion ensued. The students began talking about all the pressures they feel from their families, the school, their teachers, and society in general. They identified that they felt "pressure," as they put it, "to look good, to do well, and to achieve a lot." They felt that the general attitude of teachers was that if they could not pass the tests and get good grades to get accepted to a university, then they were total failures. The teacher listened, contributed to the discussion, and explained that she initiated the discussion to see how many students would be interested in helping her figure out how to fill in the circles of those students who were isolated and without friends.

She explained that her strategy would be to fill in circles from the outside circle to the inner circle. For example, if Jane is lonely, they would start by getting Jane involved in groups and organizations to gradually find people who are interested in more personal commitments. She explained that she was not asking, "Who wants to be Jane's friend?" but, "Who knows Jane and is willing to brainstorm ideas with me for getting Jane more involved?" For example, if Jane likes films, maybe the students can identify someone who would invite her to the film club.

The teacher asked the students if there was anyone who wanted to carry on this discussion and help figure out ways to build community and circles in their school. To her delight, all but three students signed up and said they wanted to meet again and often.

Circle of Friends is not a trick or a gimmick; it is a powerful tool. Like a chisel, it can be used to pry open one's heart, soul, and thoughts or create a work of art. A work of art does not happen overnight; neither does building circles or communities. Circle of Friends is a community-building process that requires a commitment. It is as important as math, physics, or history. It is part of a curriculum of caring. It is holistic and powerful and requires dedication and commitment. It is an ongoing strategy for growth, change, and development.

A young man named Tracy learned to read and write at the age of 33 after years of believing he could not. As an adult, he spent time in a high school that was implementing Circle of Friends and including all students in general education. He wondered what would have happened if someone gently and slowly had helped him to build a Circle of Friends and to understand the difference between a drug pusher and a friend or a "gang" and a group of friends. After hearing about and observing Circles of Friends in action, he wrote the powerful poem presented in Figure 4.5, which describes how Circles of Friends are helping teachers and students not to pass each other without stopping, listening, and really seeing.

MAKING ACTION PLANS

MAPs is a tool designed to help individuals, organizations, and families determine how to move into the future effectively and creatively. MAPs is a tool that can be used by "artists"—people dedicated to making others' lives better, richer, and spiritually stronger (Forest & Lusthaus, 1989, 1990; Forest & Pearpoint, 1992; Vandercook, York, & Forest, 1989).

The MAPs process facilitates the collection of information about the person and/or family in question. In his book titled *Reflections on Inclusive Education*, Patrick Mackan wrote,

> *There is a temptation for teachers and other professionals to judge people in terms of their behavior and outward appearance. It is all too seldom that we see through the apparent and visible which makes the person who has been wounded by rejection and segregation. We fail to realize that much behavior and acting out is not inherent but learned as a response to not being truly loved and accepted as a person. Masks are worn only as long as they are needed. Only genuine acceptance and a sense of belonging will lure the rejected supposedly inferior person out from behind the mask. (1991, p. 65)*

In the hands of a creative facilitator who truly listens, MAPs is a very effective tool, focusing on the positive—the person's gifts and strengths. Facilitators must believe in the capacity of all human beings to see the glass as half full, not half empty and must have faith that each person belongs, each person can learn, and that in living we can discover the truth and dignity of each person. Can there be a guarantee? Absolutely not! Does the process at

> ## Don't Pass Me By
> ### By Tracy LeQuyere
>
> I'm a man at thirty-three
>
> Who just learned to read,
>
> I was here all the time
>
> But people passed me by.
>
> One day a woman said I will show you a lie.
>
> I know you can read with
>
> A little time,
>
> But people just passed me by.
>
> So I gave me a little time,
>
> And I gave her a little time.
>
> See this writing,
>
> I will have more time.
>
> Don't pass me by.

Figure 4.5.   Poem reflecting the need to be connected. (From LeQuyere, T. [1991]. *Don't pass me by*. Toronto: Inclusion Press; reprinted by permission.)

least allow the chance of survival? Absolutely! The process promises nothing; however, it gives hope. The opposite of hope is despair, and there is far too much of that, especially in schools.

There are eight key questions to MAPs, as shown in Figure 4.6 (Forest & Pearpoint, 1992). The order of the questions is flexible and can be altered to accommodate the dynamics of the group and the flow of contributions.

MAPs gatherings can be held anywhere—in living rooms, backyards, classrooms, school cafeterias, corporate board rooms, small offices—that a group of volunteers can explore the process and choose others to invite. With MAPs, the key people are the person with disabilities and those people he or she invites. The person will define his or her own problems, dreams, nightmares, and so forth with a little help from his or her friends.

During a MAPs gathering, everyone should be seated comfortably facing a wall. Each person is given several large sheets of paper. A leading facilitator acts as the "host." This person welcomes the group, explains the process, guides the questions, and keeps the session paced and on track. A second facilitator can be the "graphic guide." He or she records, listens, and creates a colorful record of the proceedings. In addition, the session should be audio recorded for those who understand information better with sound than with visuals. The public record is an essential part of the MAPs process. A personal, comfortable, and informal atmosphere is essential. The facilitator urges everyone to trust and be honest with one another and not to use acronyms or too much jargon. The leading facilitator begins by asking everyone to introduce him- or herself and to share his or her relationship to the key person.

This MAPs process may take between 1 and 2 hours. The process is energizing and relevant and leads to a new way to look at the individual. The process has been completed with students who no one believed could sit still for 5 minutes, yet they did. It is understood through MAPs that all people are vitally interested in their own lives. For young children, invite them to be present for as long as they wish, and have people available for child care when they decide to leave.

The process addresses the following questions; however, the questions are not shared for each MAP in the exact same manner. At the end of each question, the facilitator confirms that the emerging picture accurately represents the person's dreams and asks if anyone has something to add. This check constantly reaffirms the ownership of the MAP to the participants.

Question 1: What Is a MAP?

A MAP includes the purpose, the specific questions to be asked, and a general description of what will happen at the gathering. At a MAPs gathering, the participants are asked what a MAP means to them. A MAP can

- Help you get from one place to another

- Act as a guide

- Provide a way to go from here to there

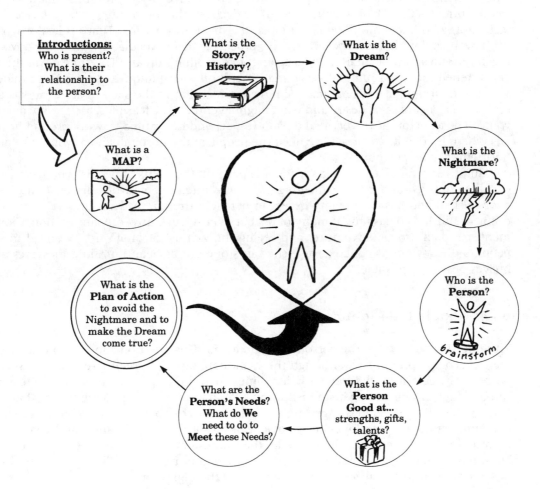

Figure 4.6. Eight key questions involved in MAPs.

The leading facilitator can say, "We are here to help _____ get from where he or she is today to where he or she wants to go. We want this day to be a guide for how to go from here to there—a perfect start."

Question 2: What Is the Person's History or Story?

The individual or family tells the participants the story—the history of the family member's disability and how the family relates to one another. A time limit is set, but it is up to the person talking to say what is essential to him or her. The graphics facilitator draws the story and then summarizes.

Question 3: What Is the Dream?

This question is the heart and soul of the MAPs process and helps the person and the participants know where to go in developing the eventual plan of action. If the individual is nonverbal, then the group, based on history and relationship, can discuss the person's future dreams.

It is essential that the facilitator be nonjudgmental, in both words and body language. One facilitator stymied the MAPs process for a boy named Jason. Jason had hardly even spoken until his first MAPs meeting, when he declared that he wanted to be a doctor. The facilitator, who knew him, literally stopped the process and said, "That's ridiculous! You can't even do your homework." The MAPs process ended immediately. At the next MAPs meeting, with a new facilitator, Jason again spoke about his dream. This time it was drawn and listened to with a full and accepting heart by the facilitator. As the MAP unfolded, Jason himself modified his dream. We have learned that in the seed of all dreams is the essence of a person's real desire and what might eventually be feasible. Jason really did not want to be a doctor; however, he did want respect and he wanted to work around hospitals where his dad had worked. He liked the people at the hospital, and a wonderful doctor friend had helped him.

Judith Snow, one of Canada's leading experts on the rights of people who have been excluded, relayed in her MAPs meeting that she wanted to be a truck driver. Judith uses a wheelchair and has no mobility except in her right thumb. "A truck driver!" many exclaimed. But Judith has taught many of us that to be a truck driver means motion, movement, freedom, travel, adventure, and seeing the world from high up. We need to see people's dreams not as concrete or etched in stone but as beautiful, fluid messages and images of what is possible.

Question 4: What Is the Nightmare?

This question elicits what the person wants to avoid. This question should not cause people to become upset or sad, although the nightmare and the dream are equal in importance. Many parents of children with disabilities answer this question by saying, "I fear my son or daughter will end up in an institution." We have never heard a nightmare that had to do with getting bad grades or getting a less-than-perfect job. It is always about more fundamental issues, such as loneliness, poverty, a life of crime and gangs, and death. The nightmare allows people the dignity to let their monsters and demons out of the closet in an atmosphere in which they are heard, recorded, and respected. The entire aim of the MAPs process is to actualize the dream and avoid the nightmare.

Question 5: Who Is the Person?

Question 5 is a brainstorming question. Everyone is asked to throw out words about the person. A large outline of the person is drawn, and the facilitator gives each participant two sticky notes to write their thoughts on. The graphic facilitator groups words into themes. The person is asked to describe him- or herself and then to choose three favorite words from all the descriptions.

To demonstrate the power of the words identified in this question, the facilitator may ask, "What other words have people used to describe the person?" In Jason's case, for example, the words that others used were *troublemaker, bad, behavior disordered,* and *manic depressive.* None of those were mentioned at the MAP. Instead, words such as *energetic, active, stubborn, tense, intense, terrific,* and *energetic* poured forth.

Thomas Armstrong (1987, p. 128) illustrated how one person's negative perception of a person could actually be a positive characteristic with his suggestions of how to "turn lead into gold" (see Table 4.1).

Question 6: What Are the Person's Strengths, Gifts, and Talents?

Here, the concept of "giftedness" is stressed not as an academic ability but as a part of a well-rounded person. The graphic facilitator can draw a gift box with gifts coming out of it to portray this image. Gifts identified by the participants may be his or her smile, personality, family, and spirit.

Question 7: What Does the Person Need?

To answer this question, the participants must think about what it will take—people and resources—to make the dream come true. This is the time to explore the biological, health, safety, and security needs of the person. This information can help focus on opportunities and identify the formal and informal supports that are needed.

Table 4.1. Turning lead into gold

A child who is judged to be	Can also be considered
Learning disabled	Learning different
Hyperactive	A kinesthetic learner
Dyslexic	A spatial learner
Aggressive	Assertive
Plodding	Thorough
Lazy	Relaxed
Immature	Late blooming
Phobic	Cautious
Scattered	Divergent
Daydreaming	Imaginative
Irritable	Sensitive
Perseverative	Persistent

Question 8: What Is the Plan of Action?

To avoid the nightmare and to facilitate the dream, the participants are asked to identify a plan. Plans should include who will do what and when they will do it.

Carla's MAP

The following story is about a high school student named Carla who decided to have a MAP developed about her life and her future. Her family participated in the development of this summary and perspective.

Carla and her parents made up a "guest list" of the people they wanted to invite to the MAPs session. Carla wrote a short note inviting people to her house on the day they had planned (see Figure 4.7.)

Everyone gathered at Carla's home, which was set up for the meeting and dinner. Carla's friends, Jamie and Shannon, had come home with her on a "minimum day" from school (i.e., a weekly shortened school day for students so that teachers can plan and meet) and helped prepare for the afternoon. When Richard, the facilitator, arrived, he worked on getting everyone comfortable and ready to look at Carla's future. Carla came out from hiding behind the living room sofa and interacted with Richard and the other guests. The team was selected by Carla and her parents based on their friendship with Carla, their loyalty and contributions to her over the years, their values, and their knowledge related to life and education.

White poster boards were taped to the dining room wall awaiting information about Carla's history, dreams, gifts, and fears. As the discussion progressed, themes emerged that fit into one or more of the designated areas, and the team began to put words to feelings and previously unspoken dreams. An overview of Carla's past, present, and future was created.

The process was hard work, but it was successful because the meeting took place in a safe environment with people who were trusted. The family reflected that nothing on the poster boards reflected "weaknesses" or "impairments"; however, there was a lot of discussion about areas that needed to be developed and addressed. Because the meeting was informational, the family didn't feel defensive. Photographs of Carla's dreams, nightmares, and gifts are represented in Figure 4.8.

Dear Family and Friends:

I want you to come for dinner; now that I am 16, I want to look to the future. Can you come for a meeting and dinner to talk about my dreams for the future?

Date: January 31, 2002

Time: 4–8 p.m.

Place: Carla's home

This meeting is being planned to bring my friends and supporters together to examine my life, my dreams, and my hopes for the future and to consider ways to support me in reaching my goals.

Figure 4.7. Carla's letter of invitation to her MAPs participants.

Figure 4.8. Carla's pictures of the MAPs process.

The team began with introductions and an overview of the process—warming up with Carla's date of birth, reviewing her history, and talking about her dreams. Carla was hesitant to say much, and 15 minutes into the discussion, with talk of graduation, she became anxious and close to losing complete control of herself, so she left the group and went to her room. Her mom checked on her, and Carla said that she needed some time alone. The group continued filling in information as follows.

History

- Carla was born March 7, 1984.

- Carla attended physical and speech-language therapy three times a week at age 1; the techniques were taught by the therapist to Alex (Carla's brother), who worked with Carla for best results.

- Carla had kidney problems, and she was treated by a urologist. The family followed the general practitioner's direction for treating the whole person.

- Carla participated in Project Child at the University of California at Los Angeles at age 2. (She was recommended for the project by a speech-language pathologist at Shriners' Hall in Long Beach.)

- Carla had a seizure at age 2.

- Carla's genetic workup was clean.

Schooling

- Carla was tested at age 3.

- Carla went to preschool at the Child Center.

- Carla pioneered inclusion in the local elementary school.

  - Carla went to a self-contained day classroom in presecond grade.

  - Carla did not meet goals in the second grade.

  - Carla was in a restricted program.

- Carla was supported to explore inclusion at elementary school.

- Carla attended a new school in which a sympathetic principal and an interested teacher welcomed Carla.

- Carla was included in the third grade at her neighborhood school.

- Carla entered sixth grade at a new middle school.

- Carla attends high school.

Social

- Carla goes to Disneyland with friends.

Carla came back to the MAPs group, bringing her choir dress and also a long satin skirt that she might wear to the prom one day. Everyone supported her and shared the excitement that these two outfits represented. She also agreed to share her dreams, which she had written in her journal on her own a few months before. Carla's dreams, as well as contributions from the group, are as follows.

- Go to prom
- Participate in the community playhouse; go to movies; be in the choir; try art; bowl; stay on the Queen Mary
- Find a job
- Have a boyfriend, get married, have two daughters
- Call parents by their first names (instead of Mom and Dad)
- Locate a townhouse to share with roommates
- Go on trips to Hawaii, Lakewood, and Las Vegas
- Own a pink recreational vehicle
- When independent, visit dad every day at his office
- Be on her own and have a family
- Be happy
- Enjoy being around costumes and shows
- Stay calm; deal with anger
- Get the job *she* wants
- Attend California State University, Long Beach, for college

Some of Carla's fears started coming out as she talked about her dreams. She was aware of death and mourning because one of her classmates in choir had died the week before, and she also had lost a distant family member. Carla's other fears are as follows.

- Change; new classes
- Fast, dark, scary rides at Disneyland
- Scary movies
- Anger—at her brother and those who call her names
- People looking/staring at her—frustration for not being able to communicate
- Choking on gum
- Being alone
- Sadness

The group was enthusiastic about contributing to Carla's "gifts" poster and wrote her strengths inside a gift box she had drawn. Her talents include

- Artistic
  - Ceramics
  - Painting
  - Drawing
- Social—likes to be around people

- Musical—practices her choir performances (almost daily and with a passion)
- Creative—makes costumes out of curtains
- Good on the Internet
- Imaginative
- Good cook
- Persistent—knows what she wants
- Enjoys the moment

Surrounding the gift box were three important messages:

- Good community support
  - Education
  - Department of Rehabilitation
  - Regional center
- Great support from friends
- Good family support

With that much accomplished, the group proceeded to dinner and continued sharing in an open environment. Richard was setting the stage for the "planning" segment, and before dessert, the group was back "on the posters." The final two posters were labeled *Plan of Action* (see Figure 4.9 for a summary).

The evening concluded with renewed excitement and friendship, and from the family's position, renewed energy, strength, commitment, and most of all thanks for an event that underscored the human experience.

Postscript: The day after this event, Carla examined the posters and took them to her room. Then, she made one poster on her own, borrowing from the original posters, and taped it to her bedroom door. She asked me not to share that one, saying, "it's private." In reference to the Plan of Action, Carla did want to add one more thing: a job at Disneyland.

Mikel's MAP from Elementary to Middle School

The following is a brief example of utilizing the MAPs process to identify issues and steps in the transition from elementary school to middle school for Mikel, who has Down syndrome and has been fully included since preschool. The students and staff with Mikel explored their dreams and goals as well as their nightmares and concerns for the transition from elementary school with one teacher to middle school with seven periods and a larger campus.

The process was considered a person-centered planning meeting for Mikel as well as a transition planning meeting for the whole class of fifth graders. The facilitator started by sharing that the meeting was for all of the students as well as Mikel, who would receive some unique information about being successful in middle school. The facilitator asked the following questions:

- What is great about this elementary school?
- Why are they scared about going to middle school?

Plan of Action for Carla

1. To walk with Certificate of Attendance
2. Transition services, age 18–22
3. School, college classes, clubs, student worker
4. Art, dance, social dance, choir
5. Physical education, aerobics, swimming
6. English
7. Mobility—bus, 911 preparation
8. Dating—social
9. Money—budget, money management
10. Daily living—cooking, cleaning, organization
11. Job(s)—movie usher, downtown Disney, California adventure
12. Community arts

Plan of Action with agencies—School

1. Individualized education program (IEP)—with school district, March 2002
2. Friends—Shannon, Jamie, and Alex—participating with Carla
3. Planning 2002–2003 grad night, prom, choir, vital link
4. Individualized transition plan (ITP)—school and Department of Vocational Rehabilitation collaborating
5. Being a teacher's assistant—math
6. Instruction—with support of Regional Occupational Training Program (ROTP)
7. Community participation—full membership
8. Employment—job shadow
9. Money management

Adult agencies individualized program plan (IPP) with regional center from the Department of Developmental Services

1. Support transition from home to supported living
2. Explore adult support services
3. Explore supported employment agencies
4. Explore social recreation opportunities

Figure 4.9. Carla's Plan of Action summary.

- What questions do they have about middle school?

- What are the next steps they would want to go through to prepare for middle school?

The facilitator had two large sheets of paper documenting responses targeting the whole class and Mikel, specifically. Specific questions regarding Mikel were

- What has been great about this elementary school for Mikel?

- What have the students and adults done at this school for Mikel to be successful?

- What are the concerns they have for Mikel going to middle school?

- What can students do for and with Mikel going to middle school?

- What can adults and staff do for Mikel to be successful at middle school?

- What are the next steps, from their point of view, to help Mikel go to middle school?

Mikel's mother utilized facilitation and shared some of Mikel's responses to the questions regarding going to middle school. Mikel wanted to know if a specific student, Justin, was going to middle school. He also asked who would be with him at middle school and whether they would facilitate. Illustrations and a summary of this meeting are presented in Figure 4.10.

PLANNING ALTERNATIVE TOMORROWS WITH HOPE

PATH evolved from the MAPs process and offers an opportunity to extend the MAPs steps and put a plan of action into place (see Figure 4.11). PATH, as with the Circle of Friends and MAPs, is another strategy to address long- and short-range planning. This is another eight-step process—it is an exercise in thinking backward. Once again, this process is best undertaken with a lead facilitator and a graphic facilitator. It is often better to have a facilitator (or two) who is immersed in the process and who does not know the people involved. The facilitators can then bring out the information without a preconceived scenario.

Where to Begin

To illustrate the PATH process, consider the story of Caleb, an eighth grader who has braces and has some communicative means (pointing and using simple gestures). Caleb is fully included in his neighborhood school, and his family wanted to explore what educational services are available as he moves into high school and later into transition services. Caleb lives at home with his parents, and he is close to his two brothers and his niece. He has told his parents that he is not sure where he will go after high school. The meeting included Caleb, his family, his extended family, his friends, and support staff from school and after school. His brothers provided some of the most insightful comments and thoughts throughout Caleb's meeting. The room was filled with people whom Caleb trusts and with whom he feels comfortable discussing personal issues.

Step 1: The North Star—The Dream

The North Star is the far-reaching dream for an individual. This may or may not be reachable; however, the North Star dream is used as a catalyst for creating a valued and desired future. Time is spent focusing the individual on identifying his or her dreams and ultimately his or her North Star. Some of the questions that can assist a person in identifying his or her North Star include

- What ideals do you most want to realize?

- What values do you want to guide you?

- What gives direction to your life?

- What drives you?

Caleb's North Star is to live in a home with a few people; have friends; have consistent and reliable support; and be able to travel, have a job, and have fun. The facilitator finished this step by summarizing the dream and soliciting from Caleb his perspective on the accuracy of the information that had been depicted graphically.

Step 2: The Goal

The second step is to choose a future time just beyond the scope of a time that can be easily predicted—6 months, 1 year, 2 years—and pretend to go there for a few minutes. It is important to assist the group in this visualization/planning activity. The facilitator may suggest that everyone get in a time capsule. The future is in that time capsule and everyone should share what is happening. The facilitator coaches everyone to discuss positive events that are occurring (remember they really have not occurred). The facilitator may say, "It was Caleb's birthday a couple of months ago, and he received a Game Boy as a gift. Now that it is 3 years later and Caleb is out of school as he transitions from high school to the adult world, what does the transition look and feel like?"

Ask the person and the group to share what is happening. This is the development of the goals for the person. The facilitator will encourage the individual to describe the smells, tastes, touches, and overall feelings in the past. For example, part of Caleb's goal in the past was to go to high school and have more friends. Caleb stated that in the future he goes on a number of field trips. The facilitator will turn the discussion to a point in time that is 3 years later and ask, "What field trips have you gone to? What jobs have you had? What places have you gone as you have traveled with your family and friends?" The group generated a number of activities that "have been completed" as if it was 3 years later, which generated great positive energy.

Step 3: Now

The third step is to bring everyone back to reality. The facilitator asks the participant, "What is it like now? Don't use good words or bad words, just give a description of what life looks like now."

Caleb and the group generated descriptions such as school is good, family is good, support staff changes a lot, traveling is great, and health has been good. The PATH process is now a visual representation of the differences between the present on the left, and the positive possible future (goal) and the North Star dream on the right. The facilitator helps the participants see that these differences are often necessary and good for moving forward. The facilitator now takes more control by simply declaring that for the purposes of the PATH, the objective will be to get from the present to the goal in the time span articulated. The facilitator finishes this step by summarizing the individual's sense of the present and getting confirmation that the summary is accurate.

Step 4: Who Do You Need to Enroll to Support You to Achieve Your Goals?

To accomplish this step, the facilitator points out that there are some preconditions. First, no one can do PATH alone; thus, the facilitator asks, "Who do you need to enroll to support you to achieve your goals?" Again, this supports the notion of striving for everyone to be interdependent, not independent—working as teams and depending on each other.

It is entirely acceptable that people may answer the question with funders, government agencies, or a whole range of generic groups that need to be enrolled. However, the

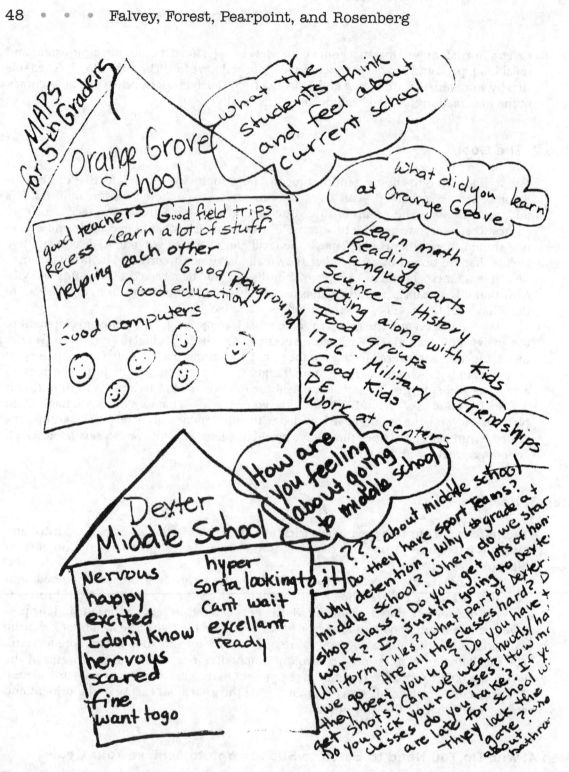

Figure 4.10. Considerations for Mikel from elementary school to middle school.

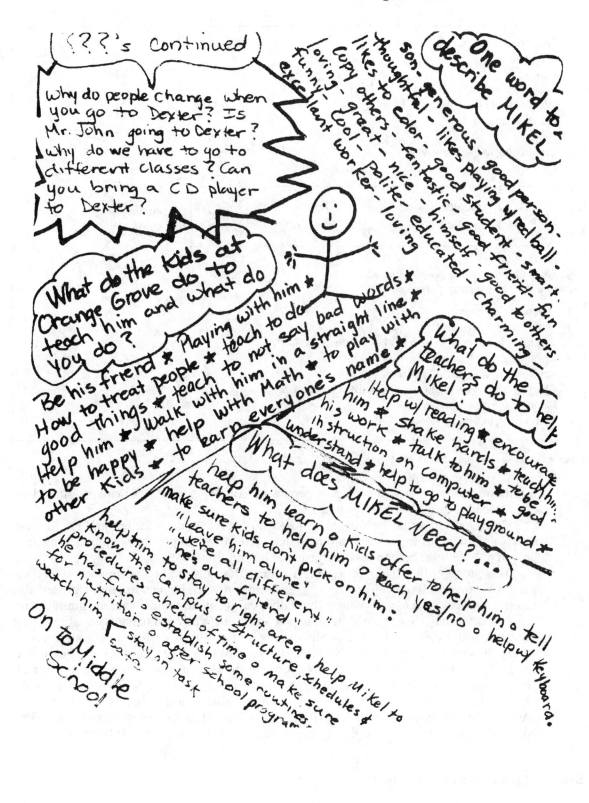

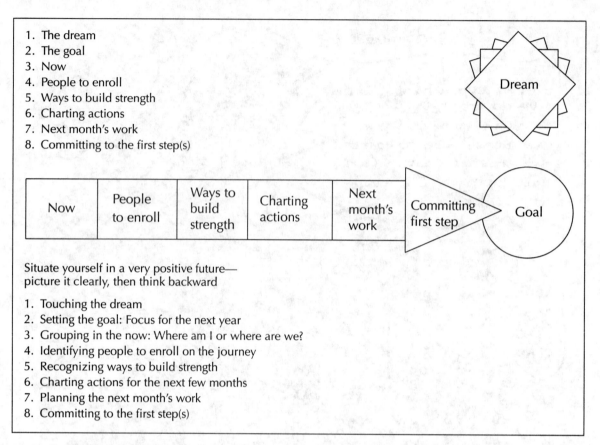

1. The dream
2. The goal
3. Now
4. People to enroll
5. Ways to build strength
6. Charting actions
7. Next month's work
8. Committing to the first step(s)

| Now | People to enroll | Ways to build strength | Charting actions | Next month's work | Committing first step | Goal |

Situate yourself in a very positive future—
picture it clearly, then think backward

1. Touching the dream
2. Setting the goal: Focus for the next year
3. Grouping in the now: Where am I or where are we?
4. Identifying people to enroll on the journey
5. Recognizing ways to build strength
6. Charting actions for the next few months
7. Planning the next month's work
8. Committing to the first step(s)

Figure 4.11.   Graphic representation of a PATH.

facilitator needs to look for specific people or contact people. Participants should be encouraged to enroll themselves to assist.

Caleb indicated that he was going to enroll his teacher, his father, and his mother. Caleb also asked his friends and family to help, too. He asked people by approaching each person and leading them to his graphic paper on the front wall.

This process of enrolling others means more than just getting permission to participate; it means one is sharing and making a commitment in the person's life. This step also recognizes those people with whom the individual wants to build a shared commitment. The facilitator may choose at this time to give everyone a piece of paper with adhesive on the back to allow everyone to place their name on two sheets and give a commitment of where they would like to be involved in Caleb's life. When the facilitator is confident that the list is complete, he or she reminds everyone that this is a process and one can add, change, and delete here as well as any other place along the PATH, as long as the significant participant agrees. At this time, the facilitator also reviews the PATH and adds any names or resources that are needed. Then, the facilitator has the group share some feeling words associated with the list of people enrolled and what they are enrolled to do.

Step 5: Ways to Build Strength

The fifth step is about getting stronger. The facilitator coaches the group through the reality that an enormous amount of work is required in order to enroll people and to move from now to the future. This will be added to everyone's already busy life. So the real question is, "What do we need to do as a group, team, and/or family to be strong enough to reach the goal and keep this team moving forward?" Similarly, "What does each person have to do to be strong enough to be able to make his or her contribution at the personal level?" Caleb's list contained the following:

- Have teachers and teaching assistants with whom to share and communicate
- Communicate effectively with my mother, father, family, and support staff
- Be able to go into the community with various people
- Have time to work on sharing my feelings
- Get involved in social and self-advocacy groups
- Learn from adults with disabilities about what they are able to do and how
- Travel

Step 6: Charting Three Months

In the process of events, the next two steps are similar. Again, the facilitator gives directions and takes the group into the near future, such as 3 months from the present. Everyone should think positively and assume that things have been going really well; that is, the direction of progress is correct and people are feeling some momentum. The easiest way to see this near future is to pick a clear element in the goal and think of what has happened already. If there is time, the facilitator can explore several of the elements to see what steps were (are to be) implemented within the 3 months.

The facilitator must be extremely time conscious at this point, and it is good to indicate to the participants that it is unlikely that every detail of the PATH will be completed at this time. However, once the process is understood, people can fill in their details later.

Step 7: One Month

The seventh step is a repeat of the sixth, except that the time is even closer to the present—1 month. What is important at this step is to push everyone for specific steps.

- Who will do what?
- When will they do it?
- Where will they do it?

Some members of the group may find this difficult as they realize that this exercise is getting out of the dreaming process and moving close to reality. This step is also used to identify specifics for the more immediate future and can be used to measure people's true commitment.

Step 8: Committing to the First Step(s)

The final step is the first step. What *is* the first step? The facilitator should insist that this be some action that can be taken almost immediately (e.g., by tomorrow or next week). It does not need to be a gigantic step, but if the process is going to begin, it is essential that it begin now. If someone has to make a telephone call, a target should be set (e.g., by noon tomorrow). If someone has to contact the funding agency, another target time should be set. Figure 4.12 provides graphic representation of Caleb's PATH.

At this point, as well as throughout the process, it is essential that the goal of interdependence be at the forefront. All of the participants must form a new habit of asking for support and not assume that everything will be done. Many times the first step does not flow; that is okay. It is up to the group and the facilitator to see if there is a block. In many situations, something or someone is standing in the way of progress. The PATH identifies these blocks and then takes the steps to deal with them. A block could have to do with funding or medical, social, or emotional needs. The energy and commitment of the team, at this time, must come together to strategize about any and all blocks that are identified.

Closure is important in any process. The facilitator asks the group to simply give a word or a phrase about what they felt about the process. Caleb offered and noted that he was excited and scared. Others offered and noted that they were confident, energized, and ready to go for it. The excitement and reality of this process is in the implementation and the follow-up.

Each facilitator or co-facilitator has his or her own unique style and character. The goal is that the meeting and the process remain focused on the individual and that the individual and his or her significant others have a say in the development of the process. It is up to the team to allow that North Star dream to become a reality.

CONSIDERATIONS AND CAUTIONS

There are several cautions and considerations to be aware of when using any of the three strategies: Circle of Friends, MAPs, and/or PATH. The facilitator always needs to remember the process is for, by, and with the individual. The facilitator needs to continually

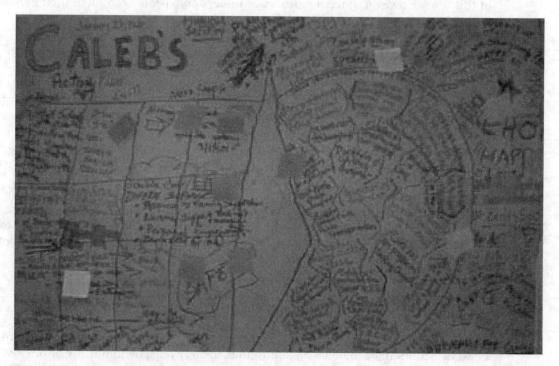

Figure 4.12. Graphic representation of Caleb's PATH.

return to the individual and ensure that what is being written is accurate, relevant, meaningful, and true.

Various communication means may be necessary to ensure that the focus person is involved, understands the process, and is a true participant. One may utilize facilitated or other augmentative communication systems; pictures; or someone else speaking with the individual, verifying with a head nod or eye wink. The process has been successful with individuals who are highly verbal as well as individuals who do not communicate using standard means.

Trust and confidentiality are two issues that must be addressed and reinforced. The process places the focus person in a vulnerable position, and the facilitator must reassure the person and remind the participants that this meeting is personal and confidential.

It is important that the facilitator and the participants discuss when the process will be implemented and when results may be observed. The focus person may become excited by the process and then become frustrated when the dream or North Star does not come true within a week. Timing is sensitive and is an issue that must be addressed during the process. The facilitator should be sure that a support process is in place for all participants to deal with the excitement and any other emotions that may have been brought out as a result of the process.

Remember, this is not a trick, gimmick, or quick fix. The three strategies are all long-range planning processes. The process will bring people together to have a common vision for a person, family, or organization. It will take time, commitment, and knowledge to follow through with what has been generated by the Circle of Friends, MAPs, and/or PATH (Forest & Pearpoint, 1992). Recognizing that the three processes outlined are personal, it may be a good strategy to provide the questions to the person ahead of time to allow him or her time to review them and feel comfortable with the process.

The process does not replace the IEP. It can be a means to generate a functional IEP because the process and write-up may be a strong complement to it. The process is similar to transition planning for the school-to-adult transition process. The outcome can be presented as an individualized transition plan.

The process should not be controlled by experts and is not simply an academic task. The process is a means to develop person-centered planning that leads to people working together for the common goals and dreams of an individual.

The process may be utilized for a class of students or an organization exploring their mission, values, and next steps as well as transition for a student from one class or grade to another or from one school to another. A combination of a MAP and PATH are also options as one becomes comfortable with the process.

CONCLUSION

The value of friends and colleagues cannot be emphasized enough. To embrace all children, schools and educators developing services in schools need to change their views. It is also important for schools to reflect in their educational service delivery model that all children belong and all children want to belong. This chapter provides three ways to change how schools look and how services are developed: Circle of Friends, MAPs, and PATH.

REFERENCES

Armstrong, T. (1987). *In their own way.* Los Angeles: Tarcher.
Asher, S.R., Odem, S.L., & Gottman, J.M. (1977). Children's friendships in school settings. In L.G. Katz (Ed.), *Current topics in early childhood education* (Vol. 1, pp. 33–61). Norwood, NJ: Ablex.

Condeluci, A. (1991). *Interdependence—The route to community.* Orlando, FL: Paul M. Deutsch Press.

Falvey, M.A., Eshilian, L., & Rosenberg, R.L. (2001). Secondary school restructuring. In P. Wehman, *Life beyond the classroom: Transition strategies for young people with disabilities* (3rd ed., pp. 127–144). Baltimore: Paul H. Brookes Publishing Co.

Forest, M., & Lusthaus, E. (1989). Promoting educational equality for all students: Circles and MAPs. In S. Stainback, W. Stainback, & M. Forest (Eds.), *Educating all students in the mainstream of regular education* (pp. 43–58). Baltimore: Paul H. Brookes Publishing Co.

Forest, M.,& Lusthaus, E. (1990). Everyone belongs with the MAPs action planning system. *Teaching Exceptional Children, 22*(2), 32–35.

Forest, M., & Pearpoint, J. (1992). Everyone belongs: Building the vision with MAPs—The McGill Action Planning System. In D. Wetherow (Ed.), *The whole community catalogue: Welcoming people with disabilities into the heart of community life* (pp. 95–99). Manchester, CT: Communitas, Inc.

Gilson, B.B., & Gilson, S.F. (1998). Making friends and building relationships. In P. Wehman & J. Kregel (Eds.), *More than a job: Securing satisfying careers for people with disabilities* (pp. 301–318). Baltimore: Paul H. Brookes Publishing Co.

Ginott, H. (1972). *Teacher and child.* New York: Macmillan.

Grenot-Scheyer, M., Coots, J., & Falvey, M.A. (1989). Developing and fostering friendships. In M.A. Falvey (Ed.), *Community-based curriculum: Instructional strategies for students with severe handicaps* (2nd ed., pp. 345–358). Baltimore: Paul H. Brookes Publishing Co.

Grenot-Scheyer, M., Staub, D., Peck, C.A., & Schwartz, I.S. (1998). Reciprocity and friendships: Listening to the voices of children and youth with and without disabilities. In L.H. Meyer, H.S. Park, M. Grenot-Scheyer, I.S. Schwartz, & B. Harry (Eds.), *Making friends: The influences of culture and development* (pp. 149–168). Baltimore: Paul H. Brookes Publishing Co.

Hartup, W.W. (1975). The origins of friendship. In M. Lewis & L.A. Rosenblum (Eds.), *Friendships and peer relations* (pp. 11–26). New York: John Wiley & Sons.

Howes, C. (1983). Patterns of friendship. *Child Development, 54,* 1041–1053.

LeQuyere, T. (1991). *Don't pass me by.* Toronto: Inclusion Press.

Lewis, M., & Rosenblum, L.A. (Eds.). (1975). *Friendships and peer relations.* New York: John Wiley & Sons.

Mackan, P. (1991). *Reflections on inclusive education.* Toronto: Inclusion Press.

Meyer, L.H., Park, H.S., Grenot-Scheyer, M., Schwartz, I.S., & Harry, B. (Eds.). (1998). *Making friends: The influences of culture and development.* Baltimore: Paul H. Brookes Publishing Co.

O'Brien, J., & Mount, B. (1991). Telling new stories: The search for capacity among people with severe handicaps. In L.H. Meyer, C.A. Peck, & L. Brown (Eds.), *Critical issues in the lives of people with severe disabilities* (pp. 89–92). Baltimore: Paul H. Brookes Publishing Co.

Perske, R. (1989). *Circles of friends.* Nashville: Abingdon Press.

Salisbury, C.L., & Palombro, M.M. (1998). Friends and acquaintances: Evolving relationships in an inclusive elementary school. In L.H. Meyer, H.S. Park, M. Grenot-Scheyer, I.S. Schwartz, B. Harry (Eds.), *Making friends: The influence of culture and development* (pp. 81–104). Baltimore: Paul H. Brookes Publishing Co.

Sherwood, S.K. (1990). A circle of friends in a 1st grade classroom. *Educational Leadership, 48*(3), 41.

Stainback, W., Stainback, S., & Wilkinson, A. (1992). Encouraging peer supports and friendships. *Teaching Exceptional Children, 24*(2), 6–11.

Strully, J., & Strully, C. (1985). Friendship and our children. *Journal of The Association for Persons with Severe Handicaps, 10*(4), 224–227.

Vandercook, T., York, J., & Forest, M. (1989). The McGill Action Planning System (MAPS): A strategy for building the vision. *Journal of The Association for Persons with Severe Handicaps, 14,* 205–215.

Wehmeyer, M.L. (2001). Self-determination and transition. In P. Wehman, *Life beyond the classroom: Transition strategies for young people with disabilities* (3rd ed., pp. 35–60). Baltimore: Paul H. Brookes Publishing Co.

5

Strategies for Creating Multicultural and Pluralistic Societies

A Mind Is a Wonderful Thing to Develop

Gwendolyn C. Webb-Johnson

An Urban Classroom

Ayinde saunters into his fifth-period English class. He is a 13-year-old African American who is deeply steeped in an oral tradition. Ms. Cautious learned these descriptors of African American learners at a multicultural workshop last week. She is very concerned, however. She clearly sees some of the patterns of behavior described in the workshop, but she worries about students like Ayinde. The way he walks is so arrogant. She believes he is just trying to get the attention of his peers. She has been trying to increase the number of times she calls on students like Ayinde. She really wants to give him a chance to demonstrate his way of "knowing," but she is so frustrated. Why should she pay closer attention to differences when she knows learners like Ayinde can behave the way that the majority of learners behave in school?

The bell rings as Ayinde straddles the seat and takes out his novel. Ms. Cautious quickly reminds the entire class, "Remember how we are expected to be seated in this freshman classroom. Young men and young women are expected to seat themselves appropriately. Now, let's take out our books. Ayinde, why don't we begin with you? I won't talk about the way you sat down, but I do hope you have your homework today. Have you read today's assignment?"

"Yeah, Ms. Cautious. Why you always picking on me? I just sat down."

"Ayinde," she said in a frustrated tone.

"I said, yes, I read."

"Good, let's begin. What did you think about the ending to *Of Mice and Men*?"

"It was a real trip how George took Lennie out. I mean why he have to kill him?"

Several students looked up. "He killed Lennie?"

"Yeah man. It was a trip. You know, I guess he thought he was doing the right thing, but man. It was a trip. It made me think about his brain probably spattering all over the place. Did you know that even though the brain only weighs about 3 pounds, it's all spongy and stuff? Can you imagine? It pumps like 198 gallons of blood through it every day. I wonder how much was pumping through when Lennie got shot. I wonder if you could see all of those billion neurons splattered all over the place."

Ms. Cautious interrupts, "Ayinde, are you on the topic? That talk about a splattered brain is clearly not appropriate."

"Excuse me Ms. Cautious, I was on the topic. You always tripping and interrupting. You ask a question and then you can't wait till I finish."

"Are you getting smart young man? You really need to watch your language. Standard English is the mode for this classroom."

Ayinde mutters under his breath, "I'm not getting smart. I am smart. But you know you work my nerves."

"What did you say young man? I believe I have had quite enough. Maybe yet another trip to the office will teach you the importance of good manners and staying on the topic at hand."

She writes Ayinde a pass to the office.

Ayinde leaves the classroom softly singing, "Ya'll go' make me lose my mind, up in here."

MS. CAUTIOUS' RESPONSE

Ayinde is sent to the office for the second time this week. This scene might be commonplace in some classrooms. When teachers like Ms. Cautious attempt to teach meaningful literature and believe that students who demonstrate "inappropriate attitudes" often interrupt them, teachable moments may be lost. Was it necessary for Ms. Cautious to single out Ayinde because of his walk and the way he sat in his chair? Was it appropriate to interrupt his response to her question? Were Ayinde's responses inappropriate? Many in the field of education might find it easy to respond in realms of "best practice." They might conclude that a student's responsibility is to respond appropriately to a teacher's inquiry. Seasoned teachers might say that Ms. Cautious should have waited to see where he was going with his story but also conclude that the attitude demonstrated by Ayinde was not necessary. Still, others might surmise that more information is necessary before any conclusions can be made.

This scenario includes concerns often raised in discussions about effective pedagogy for African Americans or learners of color. Monumental demands are made of educators, families, and students as service providers attempt to provide pedagogy that serves all learners. The sociopolitical context of schooling (Nieto, 1999) highlights the importance of teachers like Ms. Cautious understanding the challenge of teaching in meaningful and responsive ways. They must also teach learners what is expected of them in an inclusive, multicultural, pluralistic, and democratic society (Gay, 2000; Howard, 2000; Ladson-Billings, 2001; Nieto, 1999). This chapter will explore the importance of "becoming multicultural" from a teacher educator's perspective. By first defining multicultural education and using its tenets as a framework, this chapter will explore the development of a multicultural teacher prepared to meet the growing diversity in U.S. schools and then share organizational and curricular strategies to assist teachers like Ms. Cautious in meeting the needs of learners like Ayinde.

MULTICULTURAL EDUCATION

"Multicultural education is a reform movement designed to make some major changes in the education of students" (Banks, 1999, p. 1). As a movement designed to transform the traditional canon of education delivery, it is often misunderstood. Many educators and community members demonstrate misconceptions about multicultural education rather than an understanding of the goals and objectives of this ideology. The field of education is often hesitant to accept change. Because we often operate under the assumption that a "good" education will meet the needs of all learners, "status quo" has become the norm in most elementary and secondary schools in the United States of America. Although the intent of a "common culture" to meet the needs of all U.S. citizens has idealistically been a good one, it is important to note that historically, many schools have implemented practices that are harmful to students who differ racially, ethnically, culturally, by gender, by disability, and by social class (Banks, 2001b). Such practices have served as vehicles to reinforce stereotypes and discriminatory practices not only in schools but also throughout society. As a result, it is important to understand what multicultural education is not and to replace such beliefs with factual information that champions the goals and objectives that highlight what multicultural education is in a 21st century society (see Table 5.1).

Multicultural education does not set as a primary goal the desire for everyone to "get along" and live happily ever after. Although such a goal might be wonderful, it is unrealistic as educators attempt to reconstruct society's notions of what is right or wrong for a pluralistic society. A multicultural framework supports the notion that a community of learners is entitled to a voice when determining what is necessary and best for all learners. As a process and ideology, multicultural education champions a creative and collaborative partnership throughout the community. Proponents of multicultural education believe that the movement provides an opportunity to construct meaningful change in the education of *all* learners. As a systems approach promoting an equitable education, the theory, research, and practice developed in multicultural education since 1980 is successfully assisting institutions in reconstructing education so that all students will develop "the skills, attitudes, and knowledge they need to function within their community culture and the mainstream culture, as well as within and across other ethnic cultures" (Banks, 2001a, p. 46). There are many who resist such a movement. Some of their concern is understandable. The requirements of teachers and a society who are multicultural are multifaceted, multidimensional, and multilayered. The sharing of power is clearly a prerequisite in such a transformative process. The systematic process has not been, nor will it be, an easy one. Yet, it is a necessary process if we are to embrace the growing diversity in the United States of America.

Table 5.1. Perspectives in multicultural education

Multicultural education is not a	Multicultural education is a(n)
Hate agenda: Mode of teaching benefiting only groups of color while promoting the dislike and hate of European Americans	Process, ideology: Way of thinking and viewing reality, inclusive of dimensions supported by theory, research, and practice
Segregation effort: Method of further separating groups from promoting a democratic society	Collaborative partnership: Reform movement that involves all U.S. citizens participating in a meaningful education for all children
Kum Ba Yah: Promotion of an educational system in which a common culture strives to make everyone happy while pretending that historical injustice no longer exists	Opportunity to construct meaningful change: Chance to construct an educational system that serves all learners by embracing the realities of past and present injustice while promoting and creating equity for all
Translucent system: Transparent educational process in which all learners are able to achieve success when provided a standard, "one size fits all" education	Systems approach: Assemblage of content integration, knowledge construction, equity pedagogy, prejudice reduction, school culture and social structure empowerment, inclusion of multiple perspectives

CHANGING DEMOGRAPHICS

Current Demographics in Public Schools and the Nation

Diversity is not new to the United States of America; however, our commitment to respond to increasing diversity with a proactive response must be continuously renewed. Continuing to marginalize those who differ from the norm is not acceptable, especially in public schools. The nation's population is culturally diverse. Although a growing number of European Americans are choosing to educate their children in private schools, they currently represent 63% of the nation's public school students. African Americans make up 17% of the school-age population, whereas Hispanic Americans, Asian Americans, and Native Americans account for 15%, 4%, and 1%, respectively (Newsweek, September 18, 2000). These representations are predicted to change dramatically in the next 50 years. Although European Americans currently comprise 71% of the nation's population; it is predicted that by 2050 their representation will be reduced to 52.7%. African Americans currently represent approximately 12% of the nation's population; however, their predicted growth to 13.5% in 2050 will be greatly surpassed by the Hispanic American population, which is also presently 12%. By 2050, Hispanic Americans will comprise 24.4% of the nation's population (see Table 5.2). This nationally predicted trend would greatly affect the growing diversity in U.S. schools.

School Response to Changing Demographics—Deficit Modes

Although there is a tendency by the public to oversimplify the process of "becoming multicultural" (Geneva Gay, personal communication, April 2001), it is important to note that teacher educators are attempting to reconstruct teacher education to address the ethics, power, and privilege asserted in traditional teacher preparation paradigms (Gay, 1999, 2000; Ladson-Billings, 2001; Townsend & Patton, 2000, 2001; Voltz, Dooley, & Jefferies, 1999; Webb-Johnson, Artiles, Trent, Jackson, & Velox, 1998). Resistance to such change is often met because many teachers have been socialized in traditional teacher preparation programs to seek clear, logical, and concise answers to their classroom challenges. However, multifaceted, multidimensional, and multilayered responses and actions are necessary to counter resistance and promote proactive change.

Teacher Education Response　Teacher educators are realizing that meeting the needs of learners who demonstrate behavioral characteristics such as those observed in students who look and behave like Ayinde requires more than a standard recipe of intervention. Teacher educators are further challenged to ensure that developing teachers see a connection between theory, research, and practice. For example, many new teachers reflect on the fact that a "script" or "recipe" does not often work for students of color or for students of low socioeconomic status, nor do they positively impact students of color who have disabilities. Yet, these teachers often persist in their attitude of "cultural blind-

Table 5.2.　Changing demographics in United States public schools and general population

Ethnic groups	School population 2000	General population 2000	Projected general population 2050
African American	17%	12%	13.5%
Asian American	4%	3.8%	8.2%
European American	63%	71%	52.7%
Hispanic	15%	12%	24.4%
Native American	1%	.7%	.9%

ness." Their socialized patterns of interaction support a belief that treating children the same will produce the most desired school outcomes. They are uncertain about strategies that ensure learning for all learners, and each year their classrooms continue to become more diverse. Do they understand the cultural dimensions that often guide the socialization and development of these students? Did their teacher preparation programs support good teaching as transcendent, thereby asserting that, theoretically, such teaching should work for all students (Gay, 2000)? Such a dilemma often motivates teachers to "blame the victim" or succumb to a deficit mindset in their pedagogical delivery. Teacher educators, therefore, must provide renewed responses to this growing dilemma. Can they teach developing teachers to serve as social change agents who function as cultural brokers, able to build and support cultural bridges designed to improve academic outcomes (Gay, 1999)?

General Education Response   In the attempts to assert transcendent teaching, students of color fall further and further behind in the expected standards set by school accountability systems. Although there has been consistent improvement in the academic skills demonstrated by students of color since the 1970s, the National Assessment of Educational Progress report revealed the impact of deficit modes of intervention in the area of reading.

> *Over the past eight years, we have seen a gradual widening of the gap between the reading skills of the highest and lowest performing students. Asian/Pacific Islanders were the only racial/ethnic group to show an overall improvement in their average scores over the period 1992–2000. As in the past, white and Asian/Pacific Islander fourth graders had higher average reading scores than their Black, Hispanic, and American Indian classmates. (Gary Phillips, Acting Commissioner, National Center for Education Statistics, Press Release, March 6, 2001)*

General educators experience frustration and confusion when best practice, especially in the area of reading, falls short in its ability to affect all learners. Reading instruction is a central focus of school reform, as evidenced in Title I initiatives that support programs such as Success for All, Reading Recovery, and peer tutoring. Although these programs are often successful in assisting struggling readers, students who fail are often blamed for their lack of success, again supporting a deficit model of intervention. Many of these students are students of color or students of low socioeconomic status.

Special Education Response   Deficit models of intervention are also found in the area of special education. The Individuals with Disabilities Education Act (IDEA) Amendments of 1997, PL 105-17, has heralded and guaranteed the right of children with disabilities to a free and appropriate public education. Its intent is to better serve *all* children. However, as in general education, the services often received by children of color in special education fails to meet their "unique" needs. In fact, not only do the specialized services fall short in meeting the educational and disability needs of children of color, masses of these youth are disproportionately represented in special education (Artiles & Trent, 1994; Children's Defense Fund, 1999). Although this is a complex reality impacted by several variables, it appears that race and ethnicity are tied to special education placement (Oswald, Coutinho, & Best, 2000; Oswald, Coutinho, Best, & Singh, 1998). The field's void in the implementation of a cultural context in pedagogical understanding and delivery may contribute to this growing trend. For example, African American learners, who represent 17% of the school-age population, are overrepresented (U.S. Department of Education, 2001) in 5 of the 13 disability categories (e.g., mental retardation—34.3%; emotional disturbance—26.4%; multiple disabilities—19.3%; autism—20.9%; developmental delay—33.7%). African Americans' special education representation should not exceed 10% of their overall representation in the general school population (Chinn & Hughes, 1987).

Although more medically involved areas of disability are assisted by more accurate assessment procedures and practices, more subjective disability categories such as mental retardation and emotional disturbance appear more prone to misidentify African American learners because of the lack of systematic understanding of the impact of race and culture (Larke, Webb-Johnson, & Rochon, 1999). In contrast, African American youth are underrepresented in the gifted and talented area, making up only 8% of the gifted category throughout the country.

Such grossly disproportionate representation leaves educators at a loss in developing reform initiatives that will reverse the trend in school failure in these specialized programs that ideally are designed to meet unique needs. Again, the void in cultural perspective has a devastating impact in school outcomes for many children of color placed in special education. Many of these youth leave school with inadequate reading and math skills. They also have difficulty finding and maintaining gainful employment (The Civil Rights Project, 2000).

Discipline Response   To further complicate the results of "deficit mindsets," the implementation of "zero tolerance" policies has also negatively affected the educational services afforded children of color. For example, there is a clear trend indicating that the "color" of zero tolerance is racially and ethnically biased. This practice has been deemed developmentally inappropriate (The Civil Rights Project, 2000; Gordon, Piana, & Keleher, 2000). Although there was a consistent overrepresentation of students of color in discipline, suspension, and expulsion rates prior to the implementation of zero tolerance policies, those numbers have increased significantly since 1994.

> *Racial disparities in the application of school disciplinary policies have long-been documented. . . . Most recent data from the Department of Education indicates that while African-American children only represent 17% of public school enrollment nationally, they constitute 32% of out-of-school suspensions. White students, 63% of enrollment, represent only 50% of suspensions and 50% of expulsions. A recent study by the Applied Research Center shows that black children, particularly black males, are disciplined more often and more severely than any other minority group. . . . almost 25% of all African-American male students were suspended at least once over a four-year period for disciplinary issues. (The Civil Rights Project, 2000, p. 7)*

What will a pluralistic society demand of schools in reversing these trends toward incomplete school success for children of color? What will it mean to truly construct a democratic society with educational institutions that serve all learners? Teacher educators are exploring strength paradigms to assist teachers on a journey to meet the educational needs of all learners and answer the call for creative and collaborative "community building" in a pluralistic society.

School Response to Changing Demographics—Strength Modes   Proponents of multicultural education are not interested in a sparring contest noting one particular group as the "most" responsible when examining the dismal outcomes experienced academically and behaviorally by students of color. However, they do assert that the nation is greatly challenged and deeply divided in matters of understanding race, gender, disability, sexual orientation, and social class distinctions. As a result, they advocate that the education of all learners move beyond assimilation. Multiculturalists advocate gaining access to a system of acculturation that includes negotiation, discussion, and the restructuring of school systems to reflect the sharing of power, while being inclusive of multiple perspectives.

> *The increasing diversification of the nation's schools requires that the curriculum and the school be reformed in significant ways so that students from diverse racial, ethnic,*

and language groups will learn how to live together in civic, moral and just communities, that respect and value the rights and cultural characteristics of all students. (Banks, 2001a, p. 152)

Consequently, culturally responsive pedagogy (CRP) is emerging as a mode of intervention to increase the likelihood of academic and social skill success among *all* learners (Boykin, 2001; Gay, 2000; Hale, 2001; Howard, 2000; Irvine & Armento, 2001; Ladson-Billings, 2001; Larke et al., 1999; Neal, McCray, & Webb-Johnson, 2001; Nichols, 1976). Although Gay (2000) made it clear that culturally responsive (CR) teaching alone will not solve all the problems inherent in the dismal academic outcomes among children of color and children of low socioeconomic status, she advocated for a position that clearly centers the efforts of teacher educators and teachers. Funding, administration, and policy making are also tenets that must become a part of systemic change in a democratic society. However, the scope of this chapter examines change agency from the perspective of the teacher educator and the K–12 teacher.

Theoretic Frameworks of Knowing　Most educators will agree that academic achievement is a great predictor of success and stability in the United States of America. If a teacher is to affect the lives of all learners, then he or she must teach them the skills and knowledge that will increase their likelihood of successful achievement. As a result, it may be important for educators to develop a more comprehensive understanding of the patterns of knowing and interactions among the diverse groups of people who are "American" (e.g., African American, Asian American, European American, Hispanic American, Native American).

A Comparison of Cultures　What information, then, is necessary in the reconstruction of education to serve such diversity? A cadre of theorists and researchers are calling for the development of CR pedagogy delivered through CR teaching. Such teaching is supported by CR teaching strategies (Boykin, 2001; Delpit, 1988, 1995; Gay, 2000; Hale, 2001; Irvine & Armento, 2001; Ladson-Billings, 1995a, 1995b, 2001; Larke et al., 1999; Neal, McCray, & Webb-Johnson, 2001; Nichols, 1976; Rothstein-Fisch, Greenfield, & Trumbull, 1999; Tatum, 1997; Townsend, 2000). When comparing cultures, educators will find many commonalities. These commonalities are advantageous in our efforts to educate all learners. However, a comparison of cultures may assist developing educators in their ability to also value difference as an opportunity to construct meaningful change.

The theoretical framework of CR teaching stresses culture as "dynamic, complex, interactive, and changing, yet a stabilizing force in human life" (Gay, 2000, p. 10). Culture is a foundational anchor for behavior and learning modes. Traditional pedagogy is based on hegemony that does not serve all children (Gadsen, 2001; Hilliard, 2001; Scheurich & Young, 1997). Educators have the opportunity to construct what is indeed "American" in the development of CR pedagogy designed to meet the needs of a dynamically diverse society. Difference does not mean deficit.

CULTURALLY RESPONSIVE PEDAGOGY (CRP)

Theoretical Framework

CRP empowers teachers to, in turn, empower learners "intellectually, socially, emotionally, and politically by using cultural referents to impart knowledge, skills, and attitudes . . . culturally relevant pedagogy urges collective action grounded in cultural understanding, experiences, and ways of knowing the world" (Ladson-Billings, 1992, pp. 382–383). Irvine and Armento (2001) identified four critical elements that support a CRP theoretical framework:

1. Culture is a powerful variable that influences teaching and learning processes.

2. The effective teaching research is compatible with and supportive of the principles of CRP.

3. Teacher knowledge and reflection are important considerations when designing and implementing a CR lesson.

4. High standards and high expectations are important components of CRP.

Ayinde demonstrated a cultural model of strength that teachers can benefit from if they better understand what might appear as an "attitude." He may be an African American student who has been inundated with Eurocentric perspectives based on individualistic and competitive modes of discourse in the classroom context (Boykin, 2001; Cartledge & Milburn, 1996). Because he may have been systematically devalued as demonstrated in the opening scenario, his "brilliance" could go unnoticed, especially if teachers do not know how to gain access to the critical elements of CRP. Ayinde will benefit from a teaching framework that values multiple perspectives in inclusive settings based also on cooperative and communal modes of discourse in the classroom context. Such classrooms move away from traditional curriculum and instruction to promote a more critical and culturally relevant pedagogy (see Table 5.3).

A CR teaching framework requires teaching demeanors and strategies that support CR pedagogical thinking and action. Such pedagogy embraces multiple perspectives in inclusive, cooperative, and communal ways. Learners and their families become partners in negotiations steeped in critical thinking that champion teachers as cultural brokers who help communities build cultural bridges in pluralistic classrooms. Each partner is supportive of context teaching that promotes reflective practice. Teachers prepare themselves to empower learners to become vibrant and contributing participants in a liberatory society.

Teaching Demeanor and Strategies Supporting CRP

Exploration of "Self" as a Cultural Being   Ms. Cautious provides an example that may assist all teachers in grasping the concepts that lead to conclusions that promote a belief that students like Ayinde have negative attitudes or do not care about an educational context. Many teachers are threatened by what they do not know, especially when what they do not know has potential for challenging what they think they know. As a result, it is extremely important that teachers first explore who they are as cultural beings and instructional leaders. CR teachers have a foundational understanding of 1) self-knowledge,

Table 5.3.   Modes of pedagogy

Traditional pedagogy	Culturally relevant pedagogy
Eurocentric perspective	Multiple perspectives
Exclusive	Inclusive
Dichotomous (either/or)	Diunital (union of opposites)
Compliance oriented	Critical thinking and problem-solving oriented
Teachers as maintenance workers of "status quo"	Teachers as cultural brokers
Common culture context teaching	Cultural context teaching
Classics-based curriculum	Cultural affirmation–based curriculum
Hegemonic classrooms	Pluralistic classrooms
Compliant practitioners	Reflective practitioners

2) self-esteem, and 3) self-ideal (Webb-Johnson, Obiakor, & Algozzine, 1995). They know who they are as individuals, as cultural people, and as teachers. They reflect on how they have come to be the person and teacher they are. They explore issues of privilege in American society and they challenge how privilege has affected their personal journey, especially as it relates to education. CR teachers understand how they feel about their development on personal, cultural, and professional levels. They are able to assess and challenge their self-esteem in each of these areas. Finally, these teachers are able to reflect on and project their self-ideal on each of these levels. They have keen knowledge of the kind of educator and person they strive to become.

This multifaceted identity process prepares teachers to embrace students who may come to their classrooms with different experiences and different ways of knowing. Instead of teachers being motivated to reject and/or fear what they do not know, they use their foundational knowledge to "meet children where they are, and then take them where they need to go." CR teachers teach in such a way that learners are able to participate in a journey to become vibrant and contributing members of society. Ms. Cautious demonstrated disdain for Ayinde. His walk, talk, and attitude appeared inappropriate for the school context. CR teachers, who are journeying to "become multicultural," have decreased opportunities to develop disdain for their students. They see difference as opportunity. This does not mean that they do not set high standards; indeed, it ensures that high standards are initiated and maintained.

Ms. Cautious may have found more success in gaining access to and developing Ayinde's talents (Boykin, 2001) rather than merely assessing her perception of his attitude and academic skills. For example, she would benefit from practicing and implementing ways to take his shared knowledge and incorporate it into the context of the class discussion. He was answering her question, and he was exploring the questions he encountered as he thought about the ending of the novel. He also shared his belief that she did not allow him to complete his answer. She could have asked what motivated this apparent interest in brain activity. If she was knowledgeable of the recent educational brain research (Jensen, 1998), then she could have affirmed his factual accounts of the information he shared. If she was not knowledgeable, then she could have affirmed him for his knowledge and committed herself to learning more about the topic so that she could engage in a conversation with him about the topic and the resulting connections he was making about the end of the novel. She could have zeroed in on what he said about euthanasia by using his statement, "I guess he thought he was doing the right thing," as support for those who indeed believe that George was doing the right thing. Her impatience and assumption of his inadequacy because of behavioral representations interfered with potentially powerful classroom interactions.

Cross-Cultural Progression   CR teachers utilize cross-cultural progressions (REACH, 1997) to assist them in situations such as the one experienced by Ms. Cautious. A CR teacher assumes that most individuals have been culturally encapsulated. One knows what they know as a result of their life experiences. *Encapsulation* typically works for individuals in their respective communities as a result of consistent use and affirmation in that cultural context. Difference often creates fear and/or misunderstanding when encapsulated views are encountered. When individuals enter schools or travel in circles that foster different ways of knowing, *culture shock* might occur. This new experience requires one to take risks in order to better deal with the culture shock. *Risk taking* challenges the CR teacher to ask questions to assist him or her in understanding the differences encountered. Such probing does not mean that agreement with the difference is in order; however, such risk taking assists the CR teacher in gaining more *awareness* of the difference. Increased awareness assists the CR teacher in developing a better foundation in the *understanding* of that difference. Such a stance does not mean that agreement with the difference is to be supported.

A CR teacher might, in fact, disagree with the difference encountered, but listening and exploring the difference will assist in a more appropriate appreciation and respect for the difference. This enhanced knowledge base provides a foundation that assists the CR educator in considering the appropriate *action* important in a community of learners. It is necessary to gain access to the input of families, other service providers, and learners to reach a consensus of meaning that can be employed to support the learning context of the classroom.

Ms. Cautious would benefit from moving beyond her shock to explore and build her awareness and understanding of Ayinde's way of knowing. Dialogue with family members, Ayinde, and other African American learners would assist her in challenging some of her preconceived notions. Although she might still be concerned about his sauntering and "attitude" because she is aware that other uninformed service providers and society might view those behaviors as negative, she will challenge herself to truly "know" Ayinde as a person. Valuing rather than devaluing his contributions will guide her interactions and teaching behaviors. She may be able to develop a relationship in which she discusses with Ayinde the impact of code switching when he encounters resistance to the demeanor he brings to the classroom. Without respect for his identity and his personae, however, such a possibility is unlikely. As a change agent and CR educator, Ms. Cautious would examine and develop curriculum in culturally respectful, relevant, and responsive ways.

Examining and Developing Curricula There is a growing body of research and practice that highlights the impact and efficacy of CR curricula.

- Culturally supported teaching strategies (Gay, 2000; Harry, Rueda, & Kalyanpur, 1999; Irvine & Armento, 2001; Kline, 1995; Ladson-Billings, 1994, 2001; Larke et al.,1999; Neal, McCray, & Webb-Johnson, 2001; Nieto, 1999; Rothstein-Fisch, Greenfield, & Trumbull, 1999; Saravia-Shore & Garcia, 1995; Tatum, 1997; Van Bockern, Brendtro, & Brokenleg, 2000; Webb-Johnson & Albert, 1995; Webb-Johnson & Briscoe, in press)

- Strategies for improving reading and writing achievement (Adams & Welsch, 1999; Carbo & Kapinos, 1995; Hampton, 1995; Maldonado-Colon, 1993)

- Strategies for improving mathematics and science achievement (D'Ambrosio, Johnson, & Hobbs, 1995)

- Strategies for improving oral communication (Chesebro, Berko, Hopson, Cooper, & Hodges, 1995; Perry & Delpit, 1998)

- Strategies for improving academic skills among African American youth (Bondy & Ross, 1998; Boykin, 2001; Cartledge and Milburn, 1996; Delpit, 1995; Gadsen, 2001; Gay, 2000; Harry & Anderson, 1994, 1999; Hilliard, 2000, 2001; Ladson-Billings, 1994, 2001; Larke et al., 1999; Neal et al., 2001; Spencer, 2001; Tatum, 1997; Townsend, 2000; Townsend & Patton, 2001; Webb-Johnson, 1999; Webb-Johnson & Albert, 1995; Webb-Johnson & Anderson, 1999)

Much of this research and practice center on infusing multiple perspectives into existing curriculum. For example, "western expansion" is examined also as "western invasion" as students learn the perceptions of Native, African, Hispanic, Asian, and European Americans. Literature includes works by and about the diverse individuals who compose the United States of America. The classical literature canon is expanded. Math is introduced as a diverse field of study that has its foundations in many cultures. Critical thinking becomes a foundational support system for curriculum development as all students are challenged to assess the sociopolitical context of learning in U.S. public schools (Nieto, 2000).

When students study science and social studies, they learn that diversity has framed the development of the United States of America, especially in this area. As students learn about the significant contributions made by individuals such as Thomas Edison and Alexander Graham Bell, they also learn that Thomas Edison was bicultural (of European and Hispanic American heritage). They study and come to know Lewis Latimer, an African American scientist and inventor who worked for both Thomas Edison and Alexander Graham Bell. They begin to understand that diversity defines the development of this country. It was Latimer's invention of the carbon filament that made it possible for Edison's light bulb to burn for extended periods of time. It was Latimer who drew the plans for Bell's telephone so that the documents could be submitted to the U.S. Patent Office for patent approval (Turner, 1991).

Irvine and Armento (2001) identified three principles in CR curriculum. The first principle, *instructional examples,* is supported by inclusive cultural experiences, alternative perspectives, diversity, commonalities, and the CR learner. *Student engagement,* supported by purposeful and multiple preferences, guides student participation while gaining access to their curiosity and anticipation in learning. Learners are provided with choices that gain access to competitive, cooperative, and individual goals while also supporting their desired choices in educational decision-making processes. Finally, *ongoing assessment* guides the educator's ability to provide feedback that informs the learners of their improvement.

As a CR educator, Ms. Cautious might explore the following as she teaches the novel *Of Mice and Men.* How relevant is the concept of cognitive disabilities to this classroom? Are students prepared to understand why Lennie's cognitive difference motivated the varying perspectives of the other characters in the book? Are they able to make comparisons that are still prevalent in today's society? What experience and examples do they bring to this curriculum material? How does present day society react to those who demonstrate such differences? How does the treatment of the African American character parallel treatment of modern day African Americans? What does euthanasia mean to these learners? Who typically participates in this act? What curriculum is presented to them to assist in their understanding of such concepts in the time period when Lennie and George traveled from ranch to ranch in comparison to what might happen in more recent times? Students in CR settings would be actively involved in exploring notions of disability, difference, racism, sexism, commonalities, and their evolution over time.

Enhancing Instructional Delivery The classroom atmosphere in which curriculum reform is highlighted is also transformed in CR classrooms. Teachers learn "how" to present curriculum in ways that are relevant and responsive to the prior experiences learners bring with them to the classroom. Educators who are "becoming multicultural" use multiple ways of knowing to assist them in designing instructional delivery to address the perspectives of diversity. Multiple ways of knowing is the norm in classrooms in which diversity is valued. Traditional hegemonic themes are challenged by multiple ways of perceiving and knowing. Teachers move beyond merely "training" students and champion efforts to facilitate the "education" of learners who are critical consumers of knowledge. Learners become active participants in their educational process. Multiple voices are accessed, power is shared, and negotiation in all subject areas becomes the norm. For example, when students learn that cowboys were indeed "multicultural," they become excited about the significant contributions of African, Hispanic, and European American "cowboys." Because they are challenged to critically assess what they learn, they become vibrant participants in analyzing why European American cowboys were and are portrayed as the only cowboys. They also begin to question and explore what traditional perceptions of the cowboy have taught society about Native Americans. They begin to discuss and move toward social change and actively challenge how the nation continues to objectify Native Americans as animal like and unworthy of respect. They write letters protesting sports teams that are named after Native Americans, and they want to study and read more about cowboys such as Nat Love and George McJunkin (Folsom, 1992; Miller, 1991).

Teachers who are "becoming multicultural" learn frameworks that support difference. They learn how to infuse and transform curriculum content to embrace communal learners like Ayinde (Boykin, 2001). Activity and community support in learning becomes the norm. It is doubtful that a CR teacher would ask students what happened at the end of the novel. CR initiatives would support pedagogy in which students would generate the questions to be explored from sociopolitical perspectives that move beyond merely providing proof that one has read the end of a book. Critical thinking frameworks guide their exploration of the issues of race, class, gender, and disability presented in *Of Mice and Men*. They study recent brain research and then are able to capitalize on the connections Ayinde was making in his assessment of this novel. Multicultural teachers who engage in CR teaching are not threatened by difference; in fact, they are challenged by the opportunities it provides in stimulating, motivating, and effectively teaching all learners.

EMPOWERMENT PARADIGMS

Culturally Responsive (CR) Goals

The ultimate goal of CR educators is to become and be multicultural (Gay, 2000). Therefore, they are involved in sociopolitical contexts that explore self, while learning to teach in respectful, relevant, and responsive ways. Teacher educators are charged to create programs that empower educators to empower students to become dynamic learners in a race-conscious society. Such pedagogy is truthful, inclusive, democratic, collaborative, and sometimes painful. Effective communication, guided by standards of excellence, is the foundation of effective pedagogical development and delivery. Such efforts are designed to result in improved outcomes among *all* learners. Twenty-first century access to technology and multiple ways of knowing contribute significantly to collaborative visions for a future deeply steeped in liberatory education (Shujaa & Afrik, 1996). Such empowerment brings out the voices of many. Those voices bring a variety of concerns and needs to the table. Educators must make meaningful differences in the educational lives of *all* children in U.S. public schools. CR pedagogy in a multicultural society demonstrates and holds great promise in working toward that goal.

Behavior of Culturally Responsive (CR) Teachers and Learners

Empowered teachers and learners share promising reactions in response to their journey to become "multicultural." For example, when CR lessons were shared with preservice and practicing teachers, as well as their learners in K–12 settings in urban, suburban, and rural school districts throughout a southwestern state, accessed voices consistently shared their excitement and enthusiasm. They requested more sample lessons, and they were eager to develop future lessons. These teachers and students shared critical and reflective insight in response to new or unknown information. Some of their responses follow.

Preservice Teacher Responses   "I have an entirely different mind-set now that I know more about Hispanic culture. My reading unit in my field experience was so much more exciting when we read about Hispanic people. Students really wanted to share their insights. They even volunteered to read favorite passages. This did not happen before."

"So many of the mentor teachers have negative attitudes about African American boys. But when I began to redirect some of the great energy this one little boy had, my supervising teacher wanted to read that article because she could not believe how well

I connected with him. She actually said she had no idea he was that intelligent. Isn't that amazing?"

Practicing Teacher Responses "I have really changed. I teach in a completely different way. I am no longer so threatened by difference. When I admit I do not understand a particular perspective, my students actually try to help me understand. I had one African American student tell me that he knew I didn't like the way he walked, but he at least respected me for admitting that it really had nothing to do with his learning. He is participating more now and his grades have improved. I realize that it is the way that I come and what I bring to the learning environment. He really was willing and able to learn. I had to change."

"This stuff is painful. I never realized I had so much baggage and that it got in the way of my teaching. I learn so much from my students, and to think I used to be afraid."

"I have always considered myself a good teacher, but with the changes that I have made in an effort to be more responsive, I am now becoming my best at teaching."

Student Responses "Why don't we have lessons on the African American cowboy every day?"

"Is there also information on Hispanic American cowboys that I can read about?"

"Why do the books we read in school leave so much of this information out?"

"Yeah, why are they trying to hide the real knowledge about diversity?"

"It is fun to learn that all of the groups have made this country a better place to live."

"Before today, I knew about Thomas Edison and Alexander Graham Bell, but I sure am glad to hear that a brother helped them out. What was his name? Yeah, Lewis Latimer. That's the bomb!"

"I didn't know that people like Frederick Douglass used to trick people into teaching them to read."

"*Of Mice and Men* really deals with issues we face every day. We still treat people who are different like crap. I can really understand why George decided to kill Lennie. Not that I think it is right, but I can see his point. Lots of people make decisions about me based on what they think I know."

Collaborative and Creative Paradigms for the Future

"A mind is a terrible thing to waste." This slogan, made popular by the United Negro Scholarship Fund (Nettles, 1997), has framed for the nation the importance of not wasting the intellectual potential of masses of African American youth. However, new paradigms for equitable change for all learners would offer, "A mind is something wonderful to develop." Ayinde's mind was not being wasted; rather, it was not being accessed and developed in a pluralistic school context. He is a vibrant and dynamic learner. He brought with him the support of a culturally strong community that continues to face sociopolitical challenges. In order to gain access to his brilliance, CR educators need to initiate collaborative paradigms for the future.

All children are worthy of the best education U.S. public schools can offer. The dialogue and action of the entire community must participate in retooling education and its ultimate outcomes. Such an agenda will require gaining access to the voices of difference that compose U.S. public schools (e.g., African American, Asian American, European American, Hispanic American, Native American). An African proverb notes that "It takes an entire village to raise a child." Proponents of multicultural education and CR pedagogy would submit that indeed, it does take an entire community to educate a child, but we must first reconstruct the village.

REFERENCES

Adams, J.Q., & Welsch, J.R. (1999). *Cultural diversity: Curriculum, classroom, & climate*. Macomb: Illinois Staff and Curriculum Developers Association.

America 2000: A Map of the mix. (2000, September 18). *Newsweek, 48*.

Artiles, A., & Trent, S. (1994). Overrepresentation of minority students in special education: A continuing debate. *Journal of Special Education, 27*(4), 410–437.

Banks, J.A. (1999). *An introduction to multicultural education* (2nd ed.). Needham Heights, MA: Allyn & Bacon.

Banks, J.A. (2001a). *Cultural diversity and education: Foundations, curriculum, and teaching* (4th ed.). Needham Heights, MA: Allyn & Bacon.

Banks, J.A. (2001b). Multicultural education. In C.F. Diaz (Ed.), *Multicultural education for the 21st century* (pp. 11–22). New York: Addison-Wesley Educational Publishers.

Bondy, E., & Ross, D.D. (1998). Confronting myths about teaching Black children: A challenge for teacher educators. *Teacher Education and Special Education, 21*(4), 241–254.

Boykin, A.W. (2001). Comment: The challenges of cultural socialization in the schooling of African American elementary school children. Exposing the hidden curriculum. In W.H. Watkins, J.H. Lewis, & V. Chou (Eds.), *Race and education: The roles of history and society in educating African American students* (pp. 190–199). Needham Heights, MA: Allyn & Bacon.

Carbo, M., & Kapinos, B. (1995). Strategies for increasing achievement in reading. In R.W. Cole (Ed.), *Educating everybody's children: Diverse teaching strategies for diverse learners: What research and practice say about improving achievement* (pp. 75–98). Alexandria, VA: Association for Supervision and Curriculum Development.

Cartledge, G., & Milburn, J.F. (1996). *Cultural diversity and social skills curriculum*. Champaign, IL: Research Press.

Chesebro, J., Berko, R., Hopson, C., Cooper, P., & Hodges, H. (1995). Effective strategies for increasing achievement in oral communication. In R.W. Cole (Ed.), *Educating everybody's children: Diverse teaching strategies for diverse learners: What research and practice say about improving achievement* (pp. 139–168). Alexandria, VA: Association for Supervision and Curriculum Development.

Children's Defense Fund. (1999). *The state of America's children yearbook*. Washington, DC: Author.

Chinn, P., & Hughes, S. (1987). Representation of minority students in special education classes. *Remedial and Special Education, 84*, 41–46.

The Civil Rights Project. (2000). *Opportunities suspended: The devastating consequences of zero tolerance and school discipline policies. Report by the Advancement Project and The Civil Rights Project, Harvard University*. Available on-line at http://www.law.harvard.edu/groups/civilrights/conferences/zero/zt_report2 .html.

D'Ambrosio, B., Johnson, H., & Hobbs, L. (1995). Strategies for increasing achievement in mathematics. In R.W. Cole (Ed.), *Educating everybody's children: Diverse teaching strategies for diverse learners, what research and practice say about improving achievement* (pp. 121–138). Alexandria, VA: Association for Supervision and Curriculum Development.

Delpit, L.D. (1988). The silenced dialogue: Power and pedagogy in educating other people's children. *Harvard Educational Review, 58*, 280–298.

Delpit, L.D. (1995). *Other people's children: Cultural conflict in the classroom*. New York: The New Press.

Folsom, F. (1992). *Black cowboy: The life and legend of George McJunkin*. Niwot, CO: Roberts Rinehart Publishers.

Gadsen, V.L. (2001). Comment: Cultural discontinuity, race, gender, and the school experiences of children. In W.H. Watkins, J.H. Lewis, & V. Chou (Eds.), *Race and education: The roles of history and society in educating African American students* (pp. 159–172). Needham Heights, MA: Allyn & Bacon.

Gay, G. (1999). Building cultural bridges: A bold proposal for teacher education. In J.Q. Adams & J.R. Welsch (Eds.), *Cultural diversity: Curriculum, classroom, & climate* (pp. 339–351). Macomb: Illinois Staff and Curriculum Developers Association.

Gay, G. (2000). *Culturally responsive teaching*. New York: Teachers College Press.

Gordon, R., Piana, L.P., & Keleher, T. (2000). *Facing the consequences: An examination of racial discrimination in U.S. public schools*. Oakland, CA: Applied Research Center, Expose Racism & Advance School Excellence. Available on-line at http://www.arc.org.

Hale, J.E. (2001). Culturally appropriate pedagogy. In W.H. Watkins, J.H. Lewis, & V. Chou (Eds.), *Race and education: The roles of history and society in educating African American students* (pp. 173–189). Needham Heights, MA: Allyn & Bacon.

Hampton, S. (1995). Strategies for increased achievement in writing. In R.W. Cole (Ed.), *Educating everybody's children: Diverse teaching strategies for diverse learners: What research and practice say about improving achievement* (pp. 99–120). Alexandria, VA: Association for Supervision and Curriculum Development.

Harry, B., & Anderson, M.G. (1994). The disproportionate placement of African American males in special education programs: A critique of the process. *Journal of Negro Education, 63,* 602–619.

Harry, B., & Anderson, M.G. (1999). The social construction of high-incidence disabilities: The effect on African American males. In V. Polite & J. Davis (Eds.), *African American males in school and society: Practices and policies for effective education* (pp. 34–50). New York: Teachers College Press.

Harry, B., Rueda, R., & Kalyanpur, M. (1999). Cultural reciprocity in sociocultural perspective: Adapting the normalization principle for family collaboration. *Exceptional Children, 66*(1), 123–136.

Hilliard, A.G. (2000). Excellence in education versus high-stakes standardized testing. *Journal of Teacher Education, 51*(4), 293–304.

Hilliard, A.G. (2001). Race, identity, hegemony, and education: What do we need to know now? In W.H. Watkins, J.H. Lewis, & V. Chou (Eds.), *Race and education: The roles of history and society in educating African American students* (pp. 1–36). Needham Heights, MA: Allyn & Bacon.

Howard, G. (2000). *We can't teach what we don't know: White teachers, multiracial schools.* New York: Teachers College Press.

Individuals with Disabilities Education Act Amendments of 1997, PL 105-17, 20 U.S.C. §§ 1400 *et seq.*

Irvine, J.J., & Armento, B.J. (2001). *Culturally responsive teaching: Lesson planning for elementary and middle grades.* Boston: McGraw-Hill.

Jensen, E. (1998). *Teaching with the brain in mind.* Alexandria, VA: Association for Supervision and Curriculum Development.

Kline, L.W. (1995). A baker's dozen: Effective instructional strategies. In R.W. Cole (Ed.), *Educating everybody's children: Diverse teaching strategies for diverse learners: What research and practice say about improving achievement* (pp. 21–43). Alexandria, VA: Association for Supervision and Curriculum Development.

Ladson-Billings, G. (1992). Liberatory consequences of literacy: A case of culturally relevant instructions for African American students. *Journal of Negro Education, 61*(3), 378–391.

Ladson-Billings, G. (1994). What we can learn from multicultural education research. *Educational Leadership, 51*(8), 22–26.

Ladson-Billings, G. (1995a). Multicultural teacher education: Research, practice, and policy. In J.A. Banks & C.A. Banks (Eds.), *Handbook of research on multicultural education* (pp. 747–759). New York: MacMillan Publishing USA.

Ladson-Billings, G. (1995b). Toward a theory of culturally relevant pedagogy. *American Educational Research Journal, 32,* 465–491.

Ladson-Billings, G. (2001). The power of pedagogy: Does teaching matter? In W.H. Watkins, J.H. Lewis, & V. Chou (Eds.), *Race and education: The roles of history and society in educating African American students* (pp. 73–88). Needham Heights, MA: Allyn & Bacon.

Larke, P., Webb-Johnson, G.C., & Rochon, R. (1999). Instructional racism in American schools: A call for culturally responsive pedagogy. In N.L. Quisenberry & D.J. McIntyre (Eds.), *ATE commission on racism from healing prospective* (pp. 49–66). Reston, VA: Association of Teacher Educators.

Maldonado-Colon, E. (1993). Cultural integration of children's literature. In J.V. Tinajero & A.F. Ada (Eds.), *The power of two languages: Literacy and biliteracy for Spanish-speaking students* (pp. 138–147). New York: Macmillan/McGraw-Hill.

Miller, R. (1991). *Reflections of a Black cowboy: Book one.* Englewood Cliffs, NJ: Silver Burdett Press.

Neal, L.I., McCray, A.D., & Webb-Johnson, G.C. (2001). Teachers' reactions to African American students' movement styles. *Intervention in School and Clinic, 36*(3), 168–174.

Nettles, M.T. (1997). *The African American education data book. Volume II: Preschool through high school.* Arlington, VA: Frederick D. Patterson Institute of The College Fund/UNCF.

Nichols, E.J. (1976). Cultural foundations for teaching black children. *Proceedings of the World Psychiatric Association and Association of Psychiatrists in Nigeria Conference,* 1–8.

Nieto, S. (1999). *The light in their eyes.* New York: Teachers College Press.

Nieto, S. (2000). *Affirming diversity: The sociopolitical context of multicultural education* (3rd ed.). New York: Longman.

Oswald, D.P., Coutinho, M.J., & Best, A.M. (2000). *Community and school predictors of over representation of minority children in special education.* Cambridge, MA: The Civil Rights Project.

Oswald, D.P., Coutinho, M.J., Best, A.M., & Singh, N.N. (1998). Ethnic representation in special education: The influence of school-related economic and demographic variables. *The Journal of Special Education, 32*(4), 194–206.

Perry, T., & Delpit, L. (1998). *The real Ebonics debate: Power, language, and the education of African American children.* Boston: Beacon Press.

Phillips, G. (2001). *National assessment of educational progress.* Washington, DC: National Center for Education Statistics.

REACH. (1997). *Respecting ethnic and cultural heritage training manual.* Seattle: REACH Center.

Rothstein-Fisch, C., Greenfield, P., & Trumbull, E. (1999). Bridging cultures with classroom strategies. *Educational Leadership, 56*(7), 64–67.

Saravia-Shore, M., & Garcia, E. (1995). Diverse teaching strategies for diverse learners. In R.W. Cole (Ed.), *Educating everybody's children: Diverse teaching strategies for diverse learners: What research and practice say about improving achievement* (pp. 47–74). Alexandria, VA: Association for Supervision and Curriculum Development.

Scheurich, J., & Young, M. (1997). Coloring epistemologies: Are our research epistemologies racially biased? *Educational Researcher, 26*(4), 4–16.

Shujaa, M. (Ed.). (1996). *Beyond desegregation: The politics of quality in African American schooling.* Thousand Oaks, CA: Corwin Press, Inc.

Shujaa, M.J. & Afrik, H.T. (1996). School desegregation, the politics of culture, and the Council of Independent Black Institutions. In M.J. Shujaa (Ed.), *Beyond segregation: The politics of quality African American schooling* (pp. 253–268). Thousand Oaks, CA: Corwin Press.

Spencer, M.B. (2001). Identity, achievement orientation, and race: Lessons learned about the normative developmental experiences of African American males. In W.H. Watkins, J.H. Lewis, & V. Chou (Eds.), *Race and education: The roles of history and society in educating African American students* (pp. 100–127). Needham Heights, MA: Allyn & Bacon.

Tatum, B. (1997). *Why are all the Black kids sitting together in the cafeteria?* New York: Basic Books.

Townsend, B.L. (2000). The disproportionate discipline of African American learners: Reducing school suspensions, and expulsions. *Exceptional Children, 66*(3), 381–391.

Townsend B.L., & Patton, J.M. (2000). Exploring some missing dimensions: Ethics, power & privilege in the education of African American learners with disabilities and gifts and talents. *Teacher Education and Special Education, 23*(1), 1–2.

Townsend, B.L., & Patton, J.M. (2001). The discourse on ethics, power, and privilege and African American learners: Guest editors' post notes. *Teacher Education and Special Education, 24*(1), 48–49.

Turner, G.T. (1991). *Lewis Howard Latimer.* Englewood Cliffs, NJ: Silver Burdett Press.

U.S. Department of Education. (2001). To assure the free and appropriate public education of all handicapped children. *22nd Annual Report to Congress on the Implementation of the Handicapped Act.* Washington, DC: Author.

Van Bockern, S., Brendtro, S., Brokenleg, M. (2000). Reclaiming our youth. In R. Villa & J. Thousand (Eds.), *Restructuring for caring and effective education: Piecing the puzzle together* (2nd ed., pp. 56–76). Baltimore: Paul H. Brookes Publishing Co.

Voltz, D.L., Dooley, E., & Jefferies, P. (1999). Preparing special educators for cultural diversity: How far have we come? *Teacher Education and Special Education, 22*(1), 66–77.

Webb-Johnson, G.C. (1999). Cultural contexts: Confronting the overrepresentation of African American learners in special education. In L. Meyer & J. Scotti (Eds.), *Behavioral intervention: Principles, models, and practices* (pp. 449–464). Baltimore: Paul H. Brookes Publishing Co.

Webb-Johnson, G.C., & Albert, H. (1995). Integrity/strength models: Empowering African American youth through culturally based curricular, instructional and counseling strategies. *Proceedings of the 4th Biennial International Special Education Conference, Brighton, England,* 75–79.

Webb-Johnson, G.C., & Anderson, M.G. (1999). Review of the McIntrye assessment of culture. *Multiple Voices, 3*(1), 37–47.

Webb-Johnson, G.C., Artiles, A., Trent, S., Jackson, C.W., & Velox, A. (1998). The status of research on multicultural education in teacher education and special education: Problems, pitfalls, and promises. *Remedial and Special Education, 19*(1), 7–15.

Webb-Johnson, G.C., & Briscoe, M.L. (in press). *Affirming all children and youth: The oral tradition as an integral part of classroom interactions.* College Station, TX: Joy Publications.

Webb-Johnson, G.C., Obiakor, F.E., & Algozzine, B. (1995). Self-concept development: An effective tool for behavior management. In F.E. Obiakor & B. Algozzine (Eds.), *Managing problem behaviors: Perspectives for general and special educators* (pp. 155–172). Dubuque, IA: Kendall/Hunt.

6

Teaching for Liberation

Promising Practices from Critical Pedagogy

Paula Kluth
Rosario Diaz-Greenberg
Jacqueline S. Thousand
Ann I. Nevin

Listen to the Voices of Three Students

Clemencia

Clemencia, a 15-year-old sophomore born and raised in Colombia, had been in the United States of America for only 2 years. While in Colombia, she had attended a private school. Upon arriving [in her school in a southeastern metropolitan area], she spent her first year in an English-as-a-second-language class. The school's 1,662 students had only 65 students of Hispanic ethnic origin, although the Hispanic population living in the surrounding community itself had substantially increased. No administrators or guidance counselors at her high school spoke Spanish, although there were a few faculty and staff who did (one male teacher, three female teachers, one female office clerk, one female cafeteria worker, and one Latina parent volunteer who helped in the Media Center). The community happened to include an active Ku Klux Klan organization that influenced the school district to limit the number of Spanish language classes at the high school.

Clemencia was well versed in Latin American literature and culture, and she enjoyed writing poetry in Spanish. She wrote about the uniqueness imprinted on her identity by her family's cultural ties:

> My culture is very important to me because it signifies my identity and my individuality. It makes me feel that I am unique and that my family has different traditions from others. My culture is what makes me feel that we are not made out of the same mold and that we have certain qualities that distinguish us from the rest. If I were to forget this, it would be as if I forget a part of my own identity. I feel that I am important and I am worth something.

Clemencia's classmate, Carolina, stated, "Unfortunately, some teachers are very ignorant and do not appreciate what we have to offer to help others learn about us in our classes." Her classmate, Alexia, stated, "In this school, one can grow intellectually but not personally when it refers to the history, culture, and family of the student. The teachers and administrators don't have the time or the desire and wouldn't even consider...to appreciate the cultural contribution that the students can provide." Clemencia summarized the general feelings of all her classmates by stating,

"It is hard not to feel rejected and marginalized because we speak a different language and belong to a different culture. We try to keep on thinking that we are not inferior, only different, but just as important in one way or another. Some people tell me not to speak Spanish because I am not in my country; but I don't pay attention because my language is a part of me and no one can make me hide it or feel ashamed of it. . . . Well, I wish education would not be so automatizada [automatic]. The teachers have everything they need to teach in a Teacher's Guide Book, even the tests, and they don't go any further than that. I believe the teachers should give of themselves and delve deeper [profundizar] in what is taught." (Diaz-Greenberg, 1997, pp. 30–31)

Gena

Gena (a pseudonym), a 19-year-old Norwegian Irish-American woman, attended a university secondary teacher education program majoring in English. At 15, Gena was diagnosed as having bipolar disorder:

"First I was diagnosed with just basic depression. Then I was diagnosed with bipolar, and then I was diagnosed with alcoholism and drug addiction. They put me on loads of medication–Prozac and Lithium. Looking back, it's the most detrimental thing you can do to a person because you are teaching them that numbness is the solution." She explained, "I value honesty and being true to myself. I am a person who questions, I don't know if authority is the right word, but just questions things. . . . "[In high school,] I made certain cries for help that were quite large. I was not fooling around. I gave my suicide note to my English teacher, and she just said, "Why did you give this to me? I think [my] teachers had a habit of ignoring my voice or voices in general. But I don't think school has shown me who I am. I guess a big thing that school did for me is it showed me that I want to be a teacher, because when I have real bad teachers, I don't want to be like them. I don't want to talk down to kids. The same as when I have excellent teachers, I see qualities [in them] that I want to have." (Diaz-Greenberg et al., 1999, pp. 10–11)

Candy

Candy, a 21-year-old woman, apparently learned academic skills while listening to her sisters as they engaged in nightly homework assignments and developed literacy skills from watching television programs and looking at her sisters' schoolbooks.

Candy's medical diagnosis is microcephaly. She does not speak and cannot reliably point or manipulate a pencil to write; for most of her life, she had been unable to show what she knows. For example, when she was 9, her educators reported that she was "functioning overall in the severely retarded range." . . . When she was 12, a speech and language evaluation reported her language comprehension to be in the "6–12 month range with few skills emerging at the 12–18 month range." By the time she was 16, her individualized education program (IEP) indicated that her "severe cognitive disabilities" prevented her from "adequate learning at a high school curriculum level." However, a few months later, after she learned to use facilitated communication, her diagnosis was changed to mild mental retardation. Candy was placed in a less restrictive classroom in the same school her sisters attended.

With the use of a communication device and a skilled facilitator, Candy initiated conversations, attended to verbal interactions, and used a few verbalizations appropriately (e.g., saying "hi" when walking into a room). She began to laugh during humorous moments. She studied general education content (mathematics, health, home economics, horticulture, and reading), albeit with students with disabilities in special education classes. Candy pushed for an opportunity to participate in general education classes by repeatedly asking her teachers to enroll her in a Spanish language class. When she joined an introductory Spanish class, she seemed to relish the social opportunities to talk in the class. Candy's Spanish teacher welcomed her and used Spanish to greet her during the school lunch period. Even though the behaviors exhibited in Spanish class (she was sometimes seen as too vocal by some educators) resulted in her leaving the class, Candy and others in her life felt she had been successful in the Spanish class.

In response to the huge transition in her life—from silence to written expression—Candy began to receive counseling at the high school where she shared her thoughts with the school psychologist (rather than just being tested for her intelligence). She relished the opportunity to have a more personal and interactive experience with a psychology professional because her previous experiences with psychologists involved assessments of her intelligence and other measurements of her disability. Candy expressed her need to be seen as an intelligent person. She also frequently expressed her need for social opportunities. For example, she wanted to have people talk to her like they "do to each other." She wanted her facilitators to support her physically but to "stay out" of her communication with others. Candy typed over and over again, "Want friends, need friends." (Kluth, 1998, p. 167)

When reflecting on these three scenarios just described, what questions might be posed for educators and advocates of school reform? What made it possible for Clemencia to articulate the differences between those teachers who somehow elicited and listened to her voice and those who only followed a teacher's manual to teach? What can teachers do to become more resourceful so as to help, rather than be embarrassed, when students like Gena need help? What can be done to give students like Candy access to the technology that they need to be heard?

These are just some of the questions that might be posed when teachers apply the principles of critical pedagogy and inclusive education that are summarized in Table 6.1. In this chapter, we create a connection between two heretofore unrelated social justice approaches—critical pedagogy and inclusive schooling. Critical pedagogy is presented as a framework for creating an inclusive, multicultural, and pluralistic schooling experience for all students, including students with disabilities. In this chapter, we explain the potential benefits that result when critical pedagogy and inclusive education principles are combined to increase social justice on behalf of students whose voices are typically silenced. We explore similarities and differences between the two philosophies/approaches in eliciting voice, facilitating collaboration, and advocating empowerment.

Frederick Douglass (an eminent advocate for emancipation of slaves prior to the United States Civil War era) stated, "If there is no struggle, there is no progress" (as cited in Bartlett & Kaplan, 1992, p. 480). As these words indicate, social justice can be better achieved when educators combine their knowledge and skills with educators who apply critical pedagogy principles to their work through a process of dialogue, reflection, and action referred to by Friere (1970) as *conscientization*.

Conscientization refers to the development of an awareness of one's self in the world. Through the process of a dialogical interaction (e.g., using empowering language, providing supports for communication), the individual can create a mental awareness of one point of view and its opposite, thus creating a *dialectic*. This dialectic can lead to the expe-

Table 6.1. Key principles of critical pedagogy contrasted with principles of inclusive education

Critical pedagogy	Inclusive education movement
Dialogue: creating an inner space to know what my view/voice is; knowing my voice requires me to be reflective; being willing to enter another's culture; showing that I listen. The goal is to "make the soul come out naked" (student's statement of how successful dialogue feels in Diaz-Greenberg, 1997).	All means all: based on the zero reject principle first described in the Education for All Handicapped Children Act of 1975, PL 94-142, and reiterated in the Individuals with Disabilities Education Act (IDEA) of 1990, PL 101-476, and its reauthorization in 1997, PL 105-17; no student is refused services in the neighborhood school because of any characteristic (i.e., disability).
Dialectic: creating a space to take an opposite point of view and provide the self and others with tools to go against the establishment.	Empowering language: people first, disability second references (e.g., *student with mental retardation* rather than *mentally retarded student*) and a focus on ability (e.g., *wheelchair mobile* rather than *wheelchair bound*).
	Self-determination: the notion that the student with a disability has the right to participate actively in choosing and evaluating the programs being offered.
Praxis: action, reflection, action cycle that leads to the transformation of one's reality and new perspectives.	Supports in natural environments: a philosophy that appropriate and effective support for learning within the classroom environment, playground, or neighborhood can be created by collaborating with people from multiple disciplines.
Conscientization: becoming aware that "I have a voice," "I matter," and "I can transform myself and others."	Valuing as the preferred response to diversity: in contrast to stereotyping and rejecting people because of their differences, or tolerating people with individual differences, or requiring people with individual differences to become rehabilitated before entering normal society, the preferred response is to value each person for their uniqueness (see Chapter 7).

rience of *praxis,* or a cycle of action–reflection–new action, such as self-determination, that can transform the individual's experience of the world. Critical pedagogy forwards a firm belief that no person can or should be rejected from the opportunity to experience this type of self-awareness.

RESEARCH PROMISE OF CRITICAL PEDAGOGY FOR INCLUSIVE EDUCATION

As the voices of the students at the beginning of this chapter indicate, in the prevailing model of special education in North American schools, most approaches to assessment, instruction, and curriculum ignore or minimize students' culture and personal historical life experiences. Many students' experiences are marginalized due to their ethnic backgrounds or uniqueness of their learning needs. Critical pedagogy and inclusive education offer a different perspective that values the learner's strengths as well as the sociopolitical and cultural context of the learner (Diaz-Greenberg, Thousand, Cardelle-Elawar, & Nevin, 2000; Thousand et al., 1999; Thousand & Kluth, 2000).

Diaz-Greenberg (1997) explained some of the characteristics of critical pedagogy that encourage teachers to affect positive changes in their classrooms. For example, they consciously organize to decrease isolation by using cooperative learning groups, holding high expectations for all, and implementing a child-centered curriculum. Teachers can use the critical pedagogy principles—dialogue, dialectic, voice, praxis, and reflection—that are defined and described in Table 6.1 to enable new actions to come from experience. These principles interface with key principles involved in moving from a separatist perspective to an inclusive perspective for teaching students with disabilities by using a zero-reject philosophy, building in direct teaching of and opportunities to use self-determination skills, empowering students with language that helps them attribute their successes to their actions, and inventing effective assessments and instruction that allows students with disabilities to thrive.

Freire stated, "There is no *teaching* without *learning,* and by that I mean more than that the act of teaching demands the existence of those who teach and those who learn" (1998, p. 17). What Freire emphasized is the professional responsibility of teachers to critically analyze their "well lived and apprehended" teaching experiences (p. 18). Freire's position is that literacy has the potential for empowerment; that is, literacy involves "reading the word" in such a way that one can "read the world" and that by engaging in "reading the wor(l)d" one can emerge with a different, more liberating view of the world. By naming the world (codifying the world), we have the possibility of changing our experience of the world we live in.

In one of the only published special education applications of critical pedagogy, Goldstein (1995) applied critical pedagogy principles in a bilingual special education classroom with first- and second-grade bilingual Latino children with limited English proficiency. Goldstein's analysis of the children's oral language interactions showed that "even young children with the added challenges of learning disabilities and language differences are aware of the economic and social barriers that education often cannot bridge" (p. 472). Using a thematic integrated approach to the curriculum, Goldstein coaxed dialogue from her young students with bilingual Spanish/English books related to themes of illness, family, and immigration, and had the children compare their thoughts with books related to themes of prejudice, poverty, authority, and family. At the heart of a critical pedagogy approach, there is a subtle but important shift of attention to the student and the student's culture. Goldstein's study showed that students began to behave as decision makers in their own learning, as lessons and activities emerged from their dialogue.

Another classroom application of critical pedagogy with culturally and linguistically diverse learners, some with learning disabilities, was documented by Pruyn (1999). As a researcher collaborating with two teachers, Pruyn examined the discursive classroom interactions of students and their teachers in two classroom settings in a predominantly Latina/o inner-city school in Los Angeles with a population of pre-K through fifth grade in which 97% were Latina/o, and Spanish was the predominant language. Pruyn used verbatim discourses between the teachers and the children to show the differences between the roles demonstrated by two different educators: Susana "the pedagogue proper" and Pedro's "situational literacy" role. Pedro's specific techniques included 1) giving explicit praise for all attempts at reading, 2) pointing out the reading strategy being used by the student, 3) asking prediction and story sequence questions interspersed with the reading, 4) using visual representations such as story webs to link story themes to events in the children's lives, and 5) scaffolding difficult English words with Spanish words. Pedro's teaching techniques yielded a qualitatively different outcome: His students were learning to *become* successful readers by *practicing* being successful readers, in comparison with Susanna's students who were learning to be remedial and low readers by practicing being remedial and low readers. Pedro's bilingual students gained competence in a set of skills that served to define and produce them as competent and capable.

Thoma (1999) demonstrated that students whose voices were elicited through participation in their own transition planning and implementation (i.e., exercised choices over some aspect of their high school curriculum) were more likely to have jobs upon graduation from high school. For those whose plans included a goal of community living, students were living outside their parents' homes and were not on waiting lists (p. 4).

Thoma concluded that the voices of young adults with disabilities can be increased through role playing, participating, and talking with transition planners and that the voices of young adults with disabilities regarding their preferences can and must be elicited and regarded.

ACTIONS FOR LIBERATORY EDUCATION

This section of the chapter offers actions for teachers and students who want to use a critical pedagogy approach to inclusive education. Liberatory teaching involves both pedagogy and philosophy; it is a political and social act. Liberatory teachers work to understand their students beyond the boundaries of the classroom and school. They question and help their students to question the teaching and learning relationship, language and paradigms used in curriclum and instruction, and the power dynamics at work in education. Being a liberatory teacher involves action and ideology inside and outside of the classroom and community. Perhaps the easiest way to describe what it means to be a liberatory teacher is to highlight some of the practices commonly associated with liberatory education.

The authors pose that the following eight types of actions may be taken by those interested in a liberatory agenda in the classroom: break the culture of silence, shift power relationships in the classroom, promote a collaborative pedagogy, practice dialogue teaching, listen, engage in critical literacy, create spaces for sharing, and act outside the classroom. Proposed actions in each of these eight areas are derived from the emerging research on the applications of critical pedagogy for the purpose of inclusive education, the authors' own research and professional experiences in this area, and the theory and best practices in both the critical pedagogy and inclusive education worlds.

Action 1: Break the Culture of Silence

Critical pedagogists and inclusive educators are concerned with eliciting the voices of students. Students in North American schools quickly learn to be quiet about their respective cultures as well as their learning differences. To counteract this silence, Diaz-Greenberg (2001) guided her Latina/o teenagers through authentic writing processes in which students interviewed family members, authored a book with their family members, and published the results. The culture of silence was broken when students and family members realized that new curriculum content emerged so that students could then learn more about their respective cultures.

For students with disabilities, they can learn not only about their own particular disabilities but also that people with disabilities do, in fact, have their own history. We can promote students' self-awareness by encouraging them to write brief statements about their strengths and weaknesses and by supporting them to speak with their teachers about instructional and assessment approaches as well as accommodations and modifications

Table 6.2. Teaching for liberation: Teacher actions to break through the culture of silence

Encourage students to interview each other and family members to discover basic information about their countries of origin, their special needs, and their customs.

Guide the students through a brainstorming process to generate questions they most want to have answered.

Use the information from the interviews to orally share and then write with a partner.

Expand information into a "book" form and "publish" either orally or in writing.

that help them learn. Table 6.2 offers additional teacher actions to break the culture of silence.

Action 2: Shift Power Relationships in the Classroom

A liberatory teacher is one who looks to the students as the experts, asks them what they would like to learn, invites students to teach and lead in the classroom, and listens to learners as they speak about the generative themes that grip them as they struggle to live their lives. Liberatory teachers examine their own power and the perceptions that their students have about "teacher's power" in the classroom. They can release their power roles to the students (e.g., determining study topics).

Power shifting can even include the use of new labels and conceptualizations. Roles of the teacher and student become collaborative, not hierarchical. The students and teachers work as a team to educate one another and to co-create understanding of their shared world. Thus, a student with learning disabilities might educate her teachers about her own strengths and needs. She might write a letter to teachers sharing tips on "how to help me in the classroom"; she might construct a portfolio complete with her favorite work samples and reflections on how her disability impacts her education; or she might create her own adaptations for certain lessons. A Jewish student or a Muslim student might educate the classroom community about his or her culture, religion, and beliefs. The students might work with teachers to provide ongoing educational experiences to peers and help school staff become more sensitive to religious differences in the classroom. See Table 6.3 for additional teacher actions to shift power relationships in the classroom.

Action 3: Promote a Collaborative Pedagogy

Teachers interested in adopting more liberatory practices[1] can explore practices centered on collaboration and community; a student-centered and relevant curriculum; a multicultural, democratic, and dynamic pedagogy; and a safe, tolerant, sensitive, and active learning environment. Teachers adopting collaborative practices might support students to challenge institutional knowledge and create their own interpretations of classroom material. Teachers help students see that knowledge is continually created and re-created through reflection and action. Teachers and students in the collaborative classroom see themselves as learners and teachers, and they understand education as a cooperative task. In a collaborative classroom, students often, colloquially speaking, "run the show." Teachers who implement a collaborative pedagogy can be seen doing many of the actions shown in Table 6.4.

---

[1]These liberatory teaching practices are provided as an antidote to the banking practices that Freire (1970, p. 59) posited underlying conventional classroom instruction.

Table 6.3. Teaching for liberation: Teacher actions to shift power relationships

Change where students and teachers sit in the classroom.
Change who evaluates the assignments.
Co-construct classroom rules.
Teach children to question decisions made by the teacher.
Elicit from students what they want to learn in the curriculum.

Action 4: Practice Dialogue Teaching

Liberatory teachers use dialogue teaching because it involves teachers and students as they mutually become engaged in a discussion focused on critical problem solving. Freire (1970, 1998) posited that dialogue allowed students to name the world and thus mediate their experience of the world. Student ideas are the center of the dialogue, with the instructor acting as an active listener and facilitator. Teachers who use dialogue teaching will prompt students to think critically and listen openly.

Part of the challenge of being a skilled dialogue teacher is investigating the verbal style and linguistic habits of the students (Shor, 1987). This may be particularly important for the teacher in the inclusive classroom in which some students may have minimal speech and communicate in alternative ways. In addition, students in diverse, inclusive classrooms will most likely differ in linguistic habits and style. Some students will be native English speakers, whereas others will be learning English as a second or third language. Similar to some of Clemencia's and Candy's teachers, a teacher interested in dialogue teaching will attend to these differences in order to inspire the richest and deepest conversations possible.

Whether students are working to solve a classroom social problem or a more academic task, teachers who use dialogue teaching must be careful not to overshadow their students by directing them or by using language all learners cannot understand. The students, meanwhile, must be attentive to the needs of every participant by carefully watching for initiation of communication and allowing for the full and uninterrupted expression of each speaker. Students might need some instruction in active and compassionate listening. In order to prepare students for dialogue teaching, teachers might provide opportunities to practice active listening, to engage in community-building exercises, and to debrief issues related to teaming and cooperation. Teachers and students might role-play examples of good listening or thoughtful feedback.

Dialogue teaching may be the perfect activity for students who have been the object of study—specifically, students of color, those at risk, second language learners, and students with disabilities—and who have been rewarded for compliance and silence for much of their lives. Students will enter a new and unfamiliar role in dialogue teaching. They will no longer have an authority to follow, nor will they need to attend to commands. Dialogue teaching is an especially important strategy to use with heterogeneous groups of students so as to benefit from diverse perspectives.

Dialogue can be used as a tool for eradicating traditional didactic student–teacher interactions, rejecting the often one-way hierarchical model of knower versus learner and

Table 6.4. Teaching for liberation: Teacher actions to promote a collaborative pedagogy

Work with small groups of students to present different aspects of content to the group.
Interact with the students as a coach, mentor, or advisor to different groups.
Set up students as active learners who construct knowledge.
Speak with students about their work, prompting them to evaluate the experience.

Table 6.5. Teaching for liberation: Teacher actions to practice dialogue teaching

Change pace of the dialogue, giving more time to think before providing responses.
Show that different types of contributions—laughter, gestures, typed words on a communication board, and verbalizations—are valued.
Make sure topics are relevant and important to the group, such as issues related to race, gender, ability, and class.

seeing students as people and as experts in their own lives/experiences. All perspectives and experiences are valuable and necessary in order to build new meanings and knowledge and to inspire change. Dialogue teaching can result in powerful new knowledge of one's strengths, as Clemencia discovered the strengths of her own culture and Candy gained a new community of peers in her Spanish class. Table 6.5 offers examples of teacher actions to practice dialogue teaching.

Action 5: Listen

Teachers have not always been in the business of listening to their students.[2] Liberatory teachers find that students can contribute to an exceptional education about teaching, learning, and dozens of other topics. This may be especially true of students who have been marginalized because students identified as being different are often seen as needing support or help. This view of learners is in stark contrast to an orientation based on seeing students as able to provide insight and education to their educators. Noticing when and where teachers are listening to topics of importance to students is also informative: Students talk during free time, in hallways, and while socializing between class activities. What are students excited about? Worried about? Knowledgeable about? Interested in? Afraid of? Teachers may find keys to teaching and learning by listening broadly during informal but important moments. More examples of teacher actions to listen are found in Table 6.6.

Action 6: Engage in Critical Literacy

Critical literacy is an idea that sprouted from Freire's original work in Brazil. Critical literacy is not technical. It involves much more than decoding, fluency, and phonetic exercises and extends beyond the promotion of reading and the identification of good literature. Critical literacy inspires reading, thinking, and speaking development. It encourages questioning of historical products and knowledge discovered through literacy experiences. In this model of literacy, teaching and learning become forms of research and experimentation in which students and teachers discuss and scrutinize language and the society in which language and meanings are created (Shor, 1987).

Students who can read text are empowered. Students who have opportunities to engage in the world through literacy experiences will have the necessary tools to contemplate and act on their future. They can identify the experiences that have limited them in the past and concentrate on those that may serve to free them. For many students, they will be emancipated by honing their literacy skills—by reading, writing, speaking, and listening in critical and relevant ways. Students can be taught a language of "critique and possibility" (Brady & Dentith, 2000). For example, in their work with pregnant teenagers,

---

[2]Traditional "banking educators" do not value their students' contributions because, with a banking education, "students know nothing" (Freire, 1970, p. 59).

Table 6.6.   Teaching for liberation: Teacher actions to listen

Listen to the communication of students without speech, those without formal communication, those who speak limited English, those with different accents or linguistic styles, and those who struggle to be expressive in whole- or small-group situations.

Encourage students to create some listening adaptations in order to elicit the voices of all.

Make a conscious effort to respond to the verbalizations and gestures of peers who do not speak. If a student laughs or screams, then peers might turn and say, "Jim, you sure seem to have a strong feeling about that. . . . Can you tell us more using your communication device/picture board/signs?"

Teach all students to communicate in a variety of ways. Encourage the whole class to use gesticulations, sign language, or Taiwanese jokes, for instance.

Find generative themes everywhere.

Brady and Dentith found that a critical literacy approach helped young mothers become both more knowledgeable about parenting and more politically aware of issues in their lives. Critical literacy in this curriculum involved the interrogation of discourse and culture. The curriculum helped students to "develop ways of speaking that refute dominant discourses regarding teen pregnancy" (p. 8). As the students became more literate around social issues, they created new ways of regarding their lives and began to see themselves as powerful and capable.

In order to engage students in critical literacy, they will need to be exposed to a variety of materials and experiences. They will need to listen and speak to peers as well as educators. They will need to be provided with experiences that support reading and writing. Students can be invited to learn about self-advocacy, politics, and issues of social justice. For students with disabilities, this new perspective may result in students who question the label of disability they have been handed as the response of others to their diversity and the type of educational life that has been constructed for them. For students who are gay and lesbian, this perspective might involve examining the heterosexism of schools.

Teachers must also value all skills that students bring to the classroom and revise their vision of what it means to be skilled or literate. This revised vision must include valuing sequences of actions, conversations, performances, reading and writing, interpreting context, and listening actively or carefully. Complex literacy expressions were demonstrated by Clemencia in her essays about her culture, Candy in her discussions with the psychologist, and Gena when writing her suicide note.

Adopting a critical literacy approach to teaching and learning is important for many reasons; perhaps the most important being the direct relationship between literacy and being perceived as intelligent. Freire (1970) reported the results of working with a Brazilian peasant who wrote, "Before I could read I was not a man." These parallel statements seem to indicate that literacy is not just about skills, it is also strongly linked to power, to perceptions of being human, and to awareness of selfhood.

The power of literacy expressions can be seen in Candy's typed praise for the student whom she tutored, Gena's note to her English teacher, and Clemencia's essays regarding her newfound respect for her Colombian culture. More examples of teacher actions to promote critical literacy are found in Table 6.7.

Action 7: Create Spaces for Sharing

Teachers can elicit their students' voices. Curriculum and teaching activities can be set up to help students better understand their experiences, actualize their dreams, learn new interests, and have their special needs met. Time must be carved out for communicating and sharing ideas. Students must have mechanisms for initiating communication and, furthermore, must have the power to direct the topics of communication. They must have choices

Table 6.7.   Teaching for liberation: Teacher actions to engage in critical literacy

Help students become more self-aware through literacy activities.

Provide opportunities to learn about and interrogate their own label and the system that serves them.

Give students tools to communicate their ideas and opinions.

Promote critical literacy as a component of students' education as a way to liberate and empower those who have been uninvolved in their own education and life decisions for too long.

Implement both functional and critical literacy curriculum into the lives of students to provide them with skills to know and challenge their world in a new way.

regarding who facilitates them and, furthermore, must be given opportunities to form relationships and make the connections necessary for effective communication. Students' voices must be central to work in the classroom.

They must take part in constructing curriculum—lessons and school events must be culturally and personally relevant. Students must be provided opportunities to construct learning experiences on their own—they must have opportunities to teach peers, to talk, to lead, and to share. Teachers interested in incorporating students' voices might begin by increasing forums for student participation and leadership. Table 6.8 shows teacher actions for creating spaces for sharing.

Action 8: Act Outside the Classroom

Liberatory teachers look for opportunities to create change in their school communities. Teachers need to study the greater school community, the curriculum, the organization of the school, and the politics and culture of the school. Teachers committed to being change agents will also question their own education. They will look for opportunities to create change in their school communities through staff development, partnerships with the greater community, and political participation.

For example, groups of teachers from Detroit to Seattle to New York were actively resisting the standardized testing movement. Many educators believed that the tests favored students who were Caucasian and middle to upper class (Sacks, 2000), and educators and educational advocates across the country worked together to change the ways in which standardized tests were used and interpreted (see the introduction to Section I).

Advocacy groups and individual teachers worked specifically to ensure that evaluations of students and workers were fair and educationally appropriate. Some teachers involved in this anti-testing movement refused to administer the tests because the tests promote rather than ameliorate racial, class, gender, and cultural barriers to equal opportunity and equal access to education. Others attended school board meetings to protest the

Table 6.8.   Teaching for liberation: Teacher actions to create spaces for sharing

Expect students to lead class meetings.

Work with students to develop curriculum.

Listen when students ask to extend a unit of study.

Develop curriculum around students' life experiences (e.g., community celebrations, popular music, family histories).

Put students in charge of certain lessons or work with them to co-teach a lesson.

Ask students to form policies for the classroom (e.g., discipline, tardiness).

Table 6.9. Teaching for liberation: Teacher actions to act outside the classroom

Study the greater school community, the curriculum, the organization of the school, and the politics and culture of the school.

Question educational experiences.

Engage in change making by working collaboratively with families and by working with colleagues to empower students.

Encourage students to become agents of change.

assessments. A group of teachers in Florida traveled 6 hours to Governor Jeb Bush's office to return a stipend they had received for their school's high performance on the state examination ("Florida Teachers Refuse Bonuses," 1999–2000). Table 6.9 lists suggestions for teacher actions to act outside the classroom.

CONCLUSION

In order to truly make a difference, teachers and students must be committed to inspiring change in a way that respects and values all participants equally. Clearly, all students are capable of making contributions to their own education. People without disabilities do not know enough information about experiencing disability to begin to answer to the multiplicity of issues that students face in their educational lives. For some students, being a change agent will involve self-advocacy. Teachers subscribing to liberatory education will teach students to articulate their preferences and needs, manage their IEPs, and challenge their service providers. Educators must shed their desire to be in charge and to make all the decisions. They must team with their students to develop more evolved and respectful educational experiences.

Although there appear to be common goals between critical pedagogy and inclusive education advocates, there may be some areas of silence that neither group can hear at this time. However, it is clear that critical pedagogy advocates want a transformative education in which learners can self-reflect and take action to experience a freer self and a freer life (liberatory education at its best). Similarly, inclusive education advocates have a goal for transformation of schooling itself that will welcome, value, empower, and support the academic and social learning of all students in shared environments and experiences (Villa, 2001).

By adopting the principles of critical pedagogy and inclusive education, all educators are encouraged to adopt the value that, to be successful, education must include liberation. What would a school look like if liberation were a valued outcome? We would look to the students from a multicultural, ethnically, and linguistically diverse population for information and direction in planning their educational experiences. We would look to even the youngest learners for direction on curriculum and instruction. We would collaborate to build democratic schools and classrooms in which multicultural communities are established that allow every student to feel welcome, comfortable, and valued. We would listen to students' critiques of their schools and their schooling experiences. We would then change our instruction, curriculum, and assessments so as to build on their strength, giving every student an engaging and respectful curriculum. We would help students to advocate for themselves and their classmates, to choose from among a variety of options, and to become self-determined and self-actualized humans. When teachers help students name their worlds, the students learn to change their worlds.

REFERENCES

Bartlett, J., & Kaplan, J. (1992). *Bartlett's familiar quotations* (16th ed.). Boston: Little, Brown and Company.

Brady, J.F., & Dentith, A.M. (2000, April). *A critical feminist postmodern pedagogy: Linking theory with practice.* Paper presented at the meeting of the American Educational Research Association, New Orleans, LA.

Diaz-Greenberg, R. (1997). The emergence of voice in Latino students: A critical approach. In J. Fredrickson (Ed.), *Reclaiming our voices: Emancipatory narratives on critical literacy, praxis, and pedagogy. An occasional paper series for entering the 21st century* (pp. 5–38). Los Angeles: California Association for Bilingual Education.

Diaz-Greenberg, R. (2001). Breaking through the culture of silence. In L. Ramierez & O. Gallardo (Eds.), *Portraits of teachers in multicultural settings: A critical literacy approach* (pp. 27–40). Needham Heights, MA: Allyn & Bacon.

Diaz-Greenberg, R., Thousand, J., Beckett, C., Cardelle-Elawar, M., Nevin, A., & Reese, R. (1999, February). *Critical pedagogy and inclusion: Common struggles for change as expressed by voices from the field.* Paper presented at the meeting of the California Association for Bilingual Education, Los Angeles.

Diaz-Greenberg, R., Thousand, J., Cardelle-Elawar, M., & Nevin, A. (2000). What teachers need to know about the struggle for self-determination (conscientization) and self-regulation: Adults with disabilities speak about their education experiences. *Teaching and Teacher Education, 16*(8), 873–887.

Education for All Handicapped Children Act of 1975, PL 94-142, 20 U.S.C. §§ 1400 *et seq.*

Florida teachers refuse bonuses for high test scores. (1999–2000, Winter). *FairTest Examiner, 14*, 5.

Freire, P. (1970). *Pedagogy of the oppressed.* New York: Newbury Park.

Freire, P. (1998). First letter: Reading the world/reading the word. In P. Freire (Ed.), *Teachers as cultural workers: Letters to those who dare to teach* (pp. 17–26). Boulder, CO: Westview Press.

Goldstein, B. (1995). Critical pedagogy in a bilingual special education classroom. *Journal of Learning Disabilities, 28*(8), 463–475.

Individuals with Disabilities Education Act (IDEA) Amendments of 1997, PL 105-17, 20 U.S.C. §§ 1400 *et seq.*

Individuals with Disabilities Education Act of 1990, PL 101-476, U.S.C. §§ 1400 *et seq.*

Kluth, P. (1998). *The impact of facilitated communication on the educational lives of students: Three case studies.* Doctoral dissertation. Madison: University of Wisconsin–Madison, Special Education Department.

Pruyn, M. (1999). The power of classroom hegemony: An examination of the impact of formal and postformal teacher thinking in an inner-city latina/o school. In J. Kincheloe, S. Steinberg, & L. Villaverde (Eds.), *Rethinking intelligence: Confronting psychological assumptions about teaching and learning* (pp. 189–216). New York: Routledge.

Sacks, P. (2000). *Standardized minds: The high price of America's testing culture and what we can do to change it.* Cambridge, MA: Perseus Books.

Shor, I. (1987). *Freire for the classroom: A sourcebook for liberatory teaching.* Westport, CT: Heinemann.

Thoma, C. (1999). Supporting student voices in transition planning. *TEACHING Exceptional Children, 31*(5), 4–9.

Thousand, J., Diaz-Greenberg, R., Nevin, A., Cardelle-Elawar, M., Beckett, E.C., & Reese, R. (1999). Perspectives on a Freirean critical pedagogy approach to inclusion. *Remedial and Special Education, 20*(6), 5–8.

Thousand, J., & Kluth, P. (2000, December). *Paulo Freire & liberatory theory: A pedagogy for inspiring inclusion.* Paper presented at the Annual Conference of The Association for Persons with Severe Handicaps, Miami, FL.

Villa, R. (2001). *The inclusive school: Restructuring for caring and effective education.* Paper presented at the meeting of the British Psychological Society, Century Conference, Glasgow, Scotland.

Access to the General Education Curriculum for All

The Universal Design Process

Alice Udvari-Solner
Richard A. Villa
Jacqueline S. Thousand

Consider the descriptions of the following fourth-grade students:

Jamal

Jamal is a highly motivated learner, especially when he is posed with real-world problems. Jamal loves storytelling and acting out his experiences with animation and exaggeration. He readily offers relevant answers to questions in class but often breaks the social rules of the classroom with excessive talking, interruptions, and too much physical movement. Jamal likes to play practical jokes on his classmates and teachers. Occasionally, he is observed "parallel teaching" (i.e., teaching while the teacher is teaching). He is a particularly talented drummer and excels in mathematics.

Holly

Holly is a quiet, yet social, student who selectively speaks in single words or short phrases. She enjoys the company of other students and will share information more readily with a familiar peer than with an adult. She can be charming and can negotiate her way into a group with her low-key demeanor. She is an emerging reader with a small vocabulary of sight words and relies on pictures, line drawings, or context to gain information from text. Visual media also is helpful for Holly to express her knowledge because she is sometimes unable or unwilling to do so verbally. Holly does not write but can draw pictures. Her favorite pastime is to create designs using colored markers. Her penchant for this activity sometimes interferes with learning as she tries to collect and hoard markers throughout the day.

This chapter is dedicated to my parents, who have influenced me so profoundly by their examples and teaching. Together, they have woven fury and endurance and humanity and conviction into my being. This is for my father who came too close to dying and for my mother whose spirit transcends the limitations of Parkinson's disease. They are my heroes in this life and will be my guides thereafter. —AUS

Rafael

Rafael arrived in the United States of America 2 years ago from Honduras having had no prior English instruction. He is fascinated by "how things work" and has become the resident expert in fixing or creating anything requiring mechanical or electronic know-how. He takes a logical and methodical approach to most academic activities. Advanced organizers and lecture guides assist Rafael in his learning. His teacher noted that he was shy. He enjoys sports, and his coaches describe him as "average" in athletic abilities. When Rafael writes about things, he usually relates them to an insight about himself, his previous home, or cultural heritage. Rafael is sensitive to other people's feelings and listens well to his classmates.

These student profiles represent 3 of the 27 students in Mr. Carbone's fourth-grade classroom. All of his students span the entire range of life experiences, interests, learning styles, talents, and abilities. Mr. Carbone's classroom composition, with its diversity in student characteristics and needs, is not an unusual phenomenon. Rather, it is the norm in today's multicultural and multilingual inclusive schools.

Since the 1990s, a major focus of educational reform has been to develop and implement rigorous state and local learning standards. Although debate continues as to the exact nature and extent of the standards, national consensus has been reached on three guiding principles (McDonnell & McLaughlin, 1997):

1. There will be challenging standards.

2. All students, including students with disabilities, should have the opportunity to achieve these challenging standards.

3. Policy makers and educators should be held publicly accountable for each student's performance.

Historically, the general education curriculum has been viewed as a standard set of requirements or pieces of knowledge and skills that every student must achieve to successfully complete a grade level. This view is based on a presumption that there are predefined bodies of knowledge, information, and skills that, when achieved in sequence, result in postschool success (Poplin & Stone, 1992). This set of sequenced information became the curriculum in many classrooms and was delivered through lecture, single grade-level textbooks, and worksheets as the only means to teach subject matter. As Vaughn and Schuman (1994) discovered through their research, teachers often planned with a whole class mentality and "taught to the middle," rather than taking the unique needs of individual students, including students with disabilities, into consideration.

In this approach, the child who failed to learn "the curriculum" on schedule often was held back, was referred to special education, chose to avoid that subject area, or dropped out of school altogether. Clearly, students who chose to drop out of certain subjects or school no longer had access to the core curriculum. For the students who were held back, instructional strategies likely were not altered, making access to the curriculum just as difficult the second time. For students referred to special education, there was no guarantee that what was being taught reflected or reinforced the general education curriculum. Past special education practice is notorious for having alternative curricula loosely related or unrelated to the general education curriculum and the supplanting of instruction in certain subject areas such as social studies and science for the sake of concentrated reading and math remediation.

Although this "lock step" and standardized view of curriculum and curriculum delivery has fallen into disfavor among general and special educators, it still remains a fundamental challenge to enabling today's diverse student population access to the core general education curriculum. This is particularly disconcerting, given that increasing numbers of students with identified learning differences and challenges are spending all or the majority of their day in general education classrooms. Nationally, the proportion of students with disabilities with primary placements in general education increased from 33% in 1992 to 46.4% in 2000 (U.S. Department of Education, 2000). This percentage will continue to rise, given the national trend toward inclusive educational practices and the curricular emphasis of the 1997 reauthorization of the Individuals with Disabilities Education Act (IDEA) Amendments (PL 105-17). IDEA '97 specifically addresses the need to include students with disabilities as full participants in the rigorous academic and vocational general education core curriculum.

ACCESS TO CURRICULUM THROUGH UNIVERSAL DESIGN VERSUS RETRO-FITTING

The term *general curriculum* has been defined from a special education perspective by the U.S. *Federal Register* (March 12, 1999) as "curriculum that is used with nondisabled children" (p. 1470). The general curriculum, then, is the whole of the educational experiences typically afforded students without disabilities. This whole includes not only what we usually think of as curriculum, that is, the curricular content, but also includes the processes and products associated with curriculum delivery and assessment.

The authors of this chapter have extensive experience working with teachers in inclusive educational environments who are attempting to assist students to gain access to the curriculum. For the most part, we have observed teachers struggling to *retro-fit* the curriculum; in other words, changing or altering pre-existing curriculum and methods of instruction. This approach is similar to the retro-fitting of buildings built prior to federal wheelchair access requirements or the retro-fitting of buildings on or near fault lines for a possible earthquake. In a retro-fit scenario, educators find themselves developing accommodations and modifications for individual students who step into a pre-existing educational situation in which there are particular materials, a typical way of delivering instruction, and a typical way in which students are assessed. Teachers problem solve by asking questions such as, "Given this grade-level textbook and the ways the classroom teacher usually teaches this content and lesson, in what ways might we find alternative materials at the student's reading level or modify the nature or quantity of what we ask the student to do?" Essentially, we are finding a solution after the fact in an attempt to fit a student into what already exists.

An alternative to retro-fitting is an approach known as *universal design*. "Universal design is a concept that refers to the creation and design of products and environments in such a way that they can be used without the need for modifications or specialized designs for particular circumstances" (Fortini & Fitzpatrick, 2000, p. 581). Curb cuts are an example of universal design. They are expensive to add after the fact but cost virtually nothing if designed from the start. Curb cuts not only allow wheelchair access to sidewalks, but they ease stroller access and reduce the probability of joint stress for joggers and faulty footing for all sidewalk users.

So then, what might universal design look like when applied to curriculum? In accordance with the previous definition of universal design, curriculum would be designed so that it could be accessed without the need for specialized modifications and adaptations for particular students. With the broad range of students' learning and language differences in mind, materials, methods, and assessment alternatives would be considered and created in advance. Schools and classrooms would have books on tape and alternate reading materials of high interest at multiple levels of difficulty. Teachers would be versed in and would employ the instructional technologies described in this text that reflect the best educational practices and take advantage of natural peer supports. We would see teachers routinely using partner learning, cooperative group learning, integrated thematic units and lessons, and hands-on learning experiences. We would see teachers bringing the community to the classroom and the classroom to the community and incorporating service learning, the Internet, and other technology into learning opportunities. We would see teachers employing authentic assessment methods such as curriculum-based assessment, artifact collections and portfolios, individual learning contracts, and demonstrations. We would see these elements and more as educators applied the five characteristics of universal design described in Table 7.1 and implemented the three goals of universal design for learning (UDL) identified by the Center for Applied Special Technology (2001). The three goals of UDL are to provide students with multiple means of

1. *Representation*

2. *Engagement*

3. *Expression*

In this chapter, the authors offer ways to move from a retro-fit to a universal design approach for addressing student diversity and curriculum access. This is not to say that curriculum retro-fitting will never be needed. Clearly, there will be times when we will encounter student–curriculum mismatches that have not been thought of or encountered before. At those times, we will need to engage our collaborative and creative problem-solving skills and energies to invent unique accommodations and modifications.

To initiate a universal design approach to universal curriculum access, educators need to think about three distinct curriculum "access points"—content, process, and product. The *content* access point concerns what is taught and what we want students to learn, know, and do. The *process* access point concerns how students go about making sense of what they are learning. The *product* access point concerns how students demonstrate what is learned (Tomlinson, 1995a, 1995b). These three curriculum access points directly reflect the three goals of universal design for learning. Specifically, the *content* access point requires multiple *representation* of the material to be learned, the *process* access point requires multiple means for student *engagement*, and the *product* access point requires multiple

Table 7.1. Five characteristics of universal design

1. Pro-active

   It is assumed that students have different needs. Educators provide students with multiple means of representation, engagement, and expression.

2. More qualitative than quantitative

   It is more than giving some students additional work to do and some students less to do. Differentiated instruction involves changing the nature of the assignment.

3. Provides multiple approaches to content, process, and product/assessment

   By adjusting each of these teaching elements, teachers design different approaches to what students learn, how students learn, how they integrate and apply what they have learned, and how they demonstrate proficiency.

4. Student centered and student led

   Learning experiences are most effective when they are engaging, relevant, and interesting to the learner.

5. Blend of whole-class, small-group, and individualized instruction

   Differentiated instruction utilizes a variety of instructional groupings depending on the desired outcomes.

From Tomlinson, C. (1995b). *How to differentiate instruction in mixed-ability classrooms.* Alexandria, VA: Association for Supervision and Curriculum Development; adapted by permission.

means for student *expression* of learning. The next section offers strategies for facilitating access to the core curriculum at these three access points.

ACCESS TO CONTENT, PROCESS, AND PRODUCT OF LEARNING

Before moving on to more in-depth discussions of content, process, and product access points, it is critical to emphasize that collaboration, creativity, and creative problem solving (the overarching themes of this book) serve as bedrock foundations on which universal curriculum access is crafted. Regardless of whether we find ourselves in a situation of retro-fitting or pro-actively designing curriculum, collaborative and creative dispositions and actions among key stakeholders (e.g., educators, administrators, parents, students) are essential to inventing new ways of doing things more effectively in schools.

Access to the Content of Learning

"Access (cognitive as well as sensorimotor) to the curriculum begins with a student being able to interact with it to learn" (Orkwis & McLane, 1998, p. 6). The starting point in curriculum access for any student involves determining the curricular *content* and ways of *representing* information deemed to be important for students to learn. Content has multiple dimensions, including: 1) what is to be taught; 2) the level of knowledge or proficiency the student is to demonstrate; and 3) the context, materials, and differentiation necessary to offer all students, including those with disabilities, a point of entry and access to learning.

Content is not formulated, selected, or delivered in a vacuum. Public policy and national standards have a huge influence over content. For example, a call for high standards has become a national cry and, with the IDEA '97 mandates, students with disabilities are included in this call. Almost every state has adopted curriculum standards, frameworks, and assessment systems that drive the content decisions that teachers make daily. Yet, interestingly, in the establishment of such standards, there has been virtually no involvement of professionals, parents, or students who are knowledgeable about disabilities (Thurlow, Ysseldyke, Gutman, & Geeman, 1997). This is a significant oversight from a universal design perspective because content and material decisions must take into consideration all students—10% of whom have identified disabilities that require differentiation in content and materials. In addition, there are more students with language and formally unidentified learning challenges that would require similar differentiation and multiple means of representing information.

Access to the Process of Learning

The second curricular access point, *process* access, concerns instructional strategies that afford students multiple means of *engaging* with the curriculum. Since 1980, research has been conducted to determine effective instructional strategies for assisting students with disabilities to gain access to curriculum. Among the demonstrated organizational and instructional approaches for assisting students to engage with the curriculum are the use of assistive technology, positive approaches to supporting challenging behavior, collaborative planning and co-teaching among general and special educators, teaching students "learning-to-learn" strategies, use of constructivist principles to have students discover and construct their own knowledge, as well as strategies previously mentioned in this chapter (i.e., peer-mediated instructional arrangements such as partner and cooperative group learning, integrated cross-curricular thematic units, hands-on methods that utilize realia, accessing the Internet, connecting school and community through service learning and community-based projects; Kronberg & York-Barr, 1997; Udvari-Solner & Thousand, 1995).

In a comprehensive review of inclusive schooling practices derived from both general and special education research, McGregor and Vogelsberg (1998) identified themes that seem to run through the discourse about making the process of learning more responsive. They concluded the following:

- There currently exist an array of strategies to enable students to learn the general education curriculum.

- Some students require explicit instruction in how to learn in general education environments.

- The inclusion of students with severe disabilities as valued members of the classroom has broadened the curricular accommodations and modifications available to all students.

- Learning is promoted through integrated, child-centered processes.

- Instruction must be delivered in ways that acknowledge and capitalize on students' different ways of learning because thinking, learning, and intelligence are not singular constructs.

- Teaching for understanding and problem solving increases student achievement.

- Teaching, learning, and assessment need to be integrally connected.

- Heterogeneous student grouping practices promote student performance and avoid the pedagogical, moral, and ethical problems associated with tracking.

- Time for team planning and reflection is critical to enable collaborative approaches to instruction to develop and be successful.

- Collaborative planning for the full range of students at the "design point" of instruction minimizes the amount of retro-fitting that must be provided by special education personnel working to support students in general education classrooms.

Access to the Product of Learning

Product access or assessment of learning outcomes requires developing and using multiple means for students to *express* their understanding of the curriculum. Here, the notion of multiple intelligences (MI) becomes important as a guide to thinking about the assessment—the products of learning—in new ways. Howard Gardner (1983), through his research, concluded that the notion of intelligence previously had been defined too narrowly. Instead, intelligence is multifaceted and includes abilities in at least eight domains, including visual-spatial, musical, bodily/kinesthetic, interpersonal, intrapersonal, and naturalistic, as well as the verbal/linguistic and logical/mathematical areas traditionally valued and assessed in schools. As Falvey and colleagues pointed out,

> The question that educators and psychologists often struggle with is, How smart is this student? Gardner suggested that this is the wrong question to ask. The question that needs to be addressed is, How is the student smart? This question presumes that all students are smart; they are just smart in different ways. (Falvey, Blair, Dingle, & Franklin, 2000, p. 194)

So, then, what are ways (the products of learning, the assessment methods) for students to demonstrate their knowledge in the best and most accurate ways? Authentic performance assessment methods such as curriculum-based assessment, artifact collections and portfolios, individual learning contracts, and demonstrations are a starting point. Performance assessments are built around tasks that are open ended, allow for a variety of methods or approaches for a student to achieve a "correct" response, and can reflect a student's unique experiences and interests. For example, instead of students filling out a true/false test on the scientific method, they are expected to demonstrate the scientific method while performing an experiment about the principles of flotation. Performance tasks are authentic because they provide for "real world" application of skills and knowledge.

Hock (2000) noted that authentic performance assessments such as classroom-based portfolios and even statewide portfolio systems can easily be adapted to replace the test-based assessments historically used to measure the progress of students eligible for special education in their individualized education programs (IEPs). The value of portfolios becomes obvious as IEP team members see the real work collected over the year rather than the artificial snapshots yielded from traditional testing. Videotapes may even replace paper and pencil task samples. Such a shift in the curriculum product eliminates the jargon and technical language that can be an insurmountable obstacle to really seeing a student's progress and, instead, enables teachers, parents, and the students themselves to understand progress in the curriculum in the most meaningful of ways (Harry, 1992).

A PROCESS FOR UNIVERSAL DESIGN OF CONTENT, PROCESS, AND PRODUCT

Given state and district curriculum standards and the demands of an increasingly diverse learner population, how can a teacher design meaningful learning activities that address the standards and the educational needs of all of the students in the class? How can a teacher minimize the need to retro-fit lessons and units for students with disabilities and other learning, language, and motivational differences? Is there some step-by-step process for thinking through lesson plans so access to curriculum and learning is maximized? In this section, the authors propose a decision-making process for differentiating instruction at the instructional "design points"—when a teacher is deliberately thinking about the content, processes, and products that will comprise an upcoming lesson or unit. The following vignette illustrates the outcome of deliberate universal design.

> Mr. Carbone enters the room dressed as a pioneer girl! In high top boots, bonnet, and pinafore he begins describing his day on the winter prairie where he struggles to stay warm, grinds wheat, and prepares a meager meal. He is met with a few giggles and the wide, attentive eyes of his entire fourth-grade class. He continues to enact the details of an early settler's daily responsibilities, utilizing a few historical artifacts and props. Mr. Carbone ends the scene as his character shivers and struggles to sleep under a threadbare quilt. He explains that he has just acted out one page of a young girl's diary written in 1860 and gives the class a simple assignment: "Consider what I've shown you about life in Wisconsin in the 1800s, and make a comment or develop a question. You may write your thoughts in your journal or exchange ideas with a classmate. I'll check in with some of you to talk through your ideas."
>
> A low buzz of conversation begins as some students choose partners and some write quietly in journals. Mr. Carbone stops at several tables invit-

ing a small group to join him at the front of the class to examine the historical artifacts he used in the role play. Included in this small group is Holly, the student with significant disabilities who was described at the beginning of this chapter. This introductory "kick-off" activity provided the teacher with a sense of his students' knowledge and misconceptions about the subject matter based directly on their comments and questions.

As a fourth-grade teacher, Mr. Carbone is responsible for designing instruction that meets the state's social studies standards in Wisconsin history and the learning needs of students such as Jamal, Holly, and Rafael. Among the many skills and abilities expected of fourth graders, this teacher is trying to arrange experiences for his students to

- Identify and examine various sources of information that are used for constructing an understanding of the past, such as artifacts, documents, letters, diaries, maps, textbooks, photos, paintings, architecture, oral presentations, graphs, and charts.

- Use a time line to select, organize, and sequence information describing eras in history.

- Examine biographies, stories, narratives, and folk tales to understand the lives of ordinary and extraordinary people, place them in time and context, and explain their relationship to important historical events.

- Compare and contrast changes in contemporary life with life in the past by looking at social, economic, political, and cultural roles played by individuals and groups (see Madison Metropolitan School District Curriculum Standards at http://www.madison .k12.wi.us/tnl/social00.htm).

Mr. Carbone addresses these standards in part by designing five learning stations that are integral to the study of pioneer life in the state of Wisconsin. Students participate in learning stations in flexible groups throughout the week. Activities can be completed individually, in partnerships, or in small groups that allow the teacher to determine and influence student groupings throughout this unit. At each station, the students can select from a menu of products or activities to demonstrate their learning. Figure 7.1 summarizes guidelines for completion of each learning station.

In Station 1, students examine historical documents and media that include photos, letters, diaries, maps, textbooks, stories, narratives, folk tales, and music recordings representing details of the late 19th century in the Wisconsin area. Using this media, students are asked to identify elements of pioneer life that differ from current-day experiences. The analysis may be as simple as examining a photograph or as lengthy as reading an excerpt from a historical biography. Students initially are allowed to self-select materials and then are guided by the teacher to analyze increasingly more challenging material at each subsequent station visit. A product from this station is a collective wall chart to which each student contributes his or her findings. While engaged in this activity, students have a variety of options to show their understanding, including telling a friend one finding, describing the finding in writing, drawing a picture of the finding, pointing to the finding or answering questions about the finding when requested by a teacher or peer, or acting out the finding for others to observe.

A variety of present-day products, along with their historical counterparts, are available for exploration in Station 2 (e.g., an early Thomas Edison recording and a compact disc, a stereoscope slide and a digital camera). These materials assist students not only to hypothesize uses for objects unfamiliar to their generation but also to compare real, contemporary objects with historical artifacts to uncover similarities, differences, and evolving technology. Products from this station may include a research report tracing the

Station #1

Look at the photographs, journals, textbooks, and other items at this station.

What do they tell us about life in Wisconsin in the 1800s?

Find one thing that is different from living in Wisconsin today.

You can . . .

1. Tell a friend one thing you have found.
2. Write down one thing you have found.
3. Draw a picture of one thing you have found.
4. Point to one thing you see that is different and speak with a teacher or friend.
5. Act out what you have found.

Station #2

Explore the objects at your table. Some are used today (contemporary). Some were used in the late 1800s or early 1900s. Compare these things.

What is the same? What is different? What do the old objects tell us about life in the 1800s?

1. Sort the items into groups of old and new.
2. Pair the old item with its new (contemporary) version.
3. Ask a question about one object and research the answer through interviews.
4. Use an item to tell a story or act out a scene from daily life in the past.
5. Trace the evolution of one item through history in a written or pictorial report using the Internet as one source.

Station #3

Use the materials and try the activities that were common in the 1800s. What did you discover about life in these times?

Experience Options

Weaving on a loom
Spinning on a spinning wheel

Station #3 (continued)

Cooking food from scratch
Making soap
Making candles
Churning butter
Writing or dictating an entry in your journal from the perspective of a pioneer child

Station #4–Creating a time line

Explore the photos, drawings, record of historical events, and actual items.

Organize them by topics and display them in a time line.

For example: Use the pictures or actual items to construct a time line of the clothes worn by your parents, grandparents, great-grandparents, etc.

Other Activity Options:

Bring in pictures of your own family history—organize and display them in a time line.

You may develop your own time line based on other common objects (household utensils, games, tools, etc.) or key events in this state's history.

Station #5

Creating a Museum Exhibit For Our Local Children's Museum

Participate with a team to design a pioneer cabin and replicate the household items in each room.

Create exhibit descriptions that compare/contrast current and past details of daily life.

Figure 7.1. Guidelines for the completion of Wisconsin history learning stations.

technological changes in an object from the 1800s to present day or using an item to tell a story about daily life in the past, as Mr. Carbone demonstrated at the beginning of the unit.

Station 3 offers students hands-on experiences in daily activities of the 1800s. Among the real activities in which students can choose to participate are weaving on a loom, spinning yarn from wool, cooking food from scratch using a pioneer recipe, making soap, fashioning candles, or churning butter. Among the purposes of this station are speculating how these activities are accomplished now and conjecturing what changes in technology, culture, and social roles have taken place to contribute to that change.

Constructing time lines is the focus of Station 4. Here, students examine and organize photos, drawings, descriptions of historical events, or actual items by placing them in chronological order by their use, evolution, or occurrence. Students may begin with a time line of their own history to place past and present events into a personal context.

A cooperative agreement between Mr. Carbone and the local children's museum creates a service learning initiative for Station 5. In cooperative learning teams, students use the knowledge gained from resources and activities in the previous stations to design and construct an interactive exhibit of a pioneer cabin that will be displayed in the children's museum. The students develop blueprints of each room, study replicas of artifacts, and write exhibit descriptions that contrast current and past details of daily life. This station provides opportunities for community-referenced instruction as groups of students take turns working on-site with the museum curator. Photographs from one such collaborative school–community museum exhibit are shown in Figure 7.2.

The learning stations in this unit of instruction promoted active and meaningful participation for the range of students in Mr. Carbone's class, including Holly, Jamal, and Rafael. The universal design process by which this set of learning experiences was developed is outlined in Figure 7.3. The process that results in differentiated lessons is presented as a series of considerations or decision points related specifically to the content, process, and products of learning.

UNIVERSAL LESSON DESIGN: DECISION POINTS IN THE PROCESS

Design Point 1: Facts About Students

For every educator, the process to differentiate curriculum and instruction begins by *knowing your students*. A positive profile of the student that identifies social and academic abilities, strengths, and learning concerns is an essential first step. These facts about a student help establish for the team a shared vision of that student's active involvement and can reveal pertinent strategies for effective teaching.

Some teams begin this exchange informally, simply by talking about the student's preferences and learning style; looking at past instructional methods; and, if the student has an identified disability, reviewing the most current IEP. Other more formal communication tools such as the Creative Problem-Solving Process and Making Action Plans (MAPs; see Chapter 4) can be employed to promote team members' deeper understanding of the individual. The learner, his or her family, current and previous teachers, peers, and others close to the student must be solicited and involved in information sharing. In addition, the team should consider how the student performs in multiple contexts (e.g., How does the student function at home, in school, and in the presence of peers?). Only when these multiple perspectives are considered can team members have a clear and comprehensive understanding of the student's capabilities, needs, and educational priorities.

As noted previously, a helpful framework for understanding and finding strengths in all students is the theory of multiple intelligences (MI) proposed by Howard Gardner (1983). MI theory assumes that all students possess an array of human intelligences that can be cultivated and emerge in unique configurations for each individual. The descriptions of each of the three focus students—Jamal, Holly, and Rafael—that were presented at the beginning of this chapter can be interpreted using an MI framework, as illustrated in Table 7.2. Examining students' characteristics through an MI lens helps to highlight their learning strengths or needs.

Acknowledging Jamal's, Holly's, and Rafael's MI profiles, Mr. Carbone designed elements of content, process, and product in the pioneer unit that matched students' strength areas or cultivated the intelligences that were "nonstrengths" or less evident for given stu-

Figure 7.2. Children's museum exhibit of a pioneer household in the 1800s.

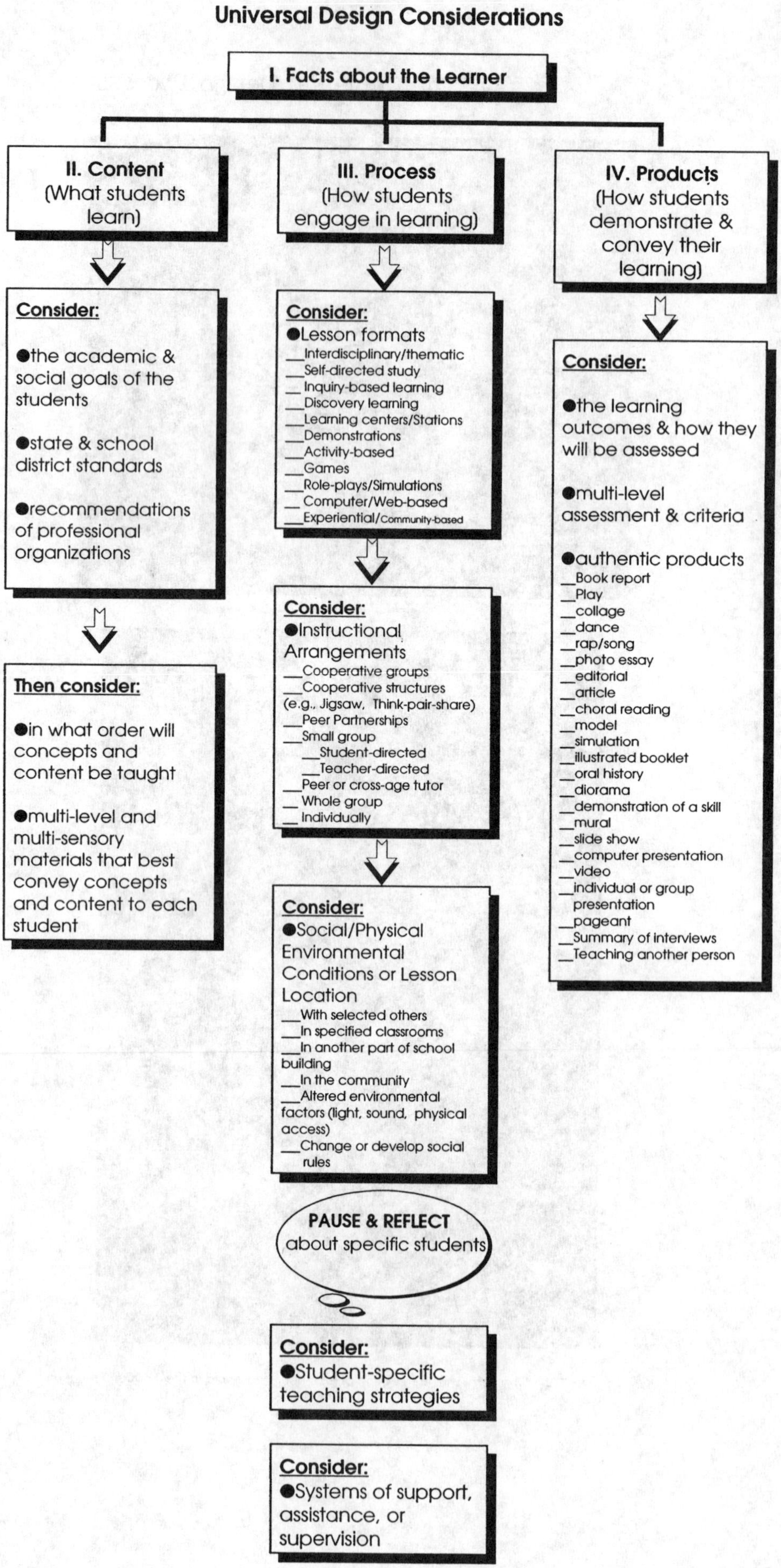

Universal Design Considerations

I. Facts about the Learner

II. Content
(What students learn)

III. Process
(How students engage in learning)

IV. Products
(How students demonstrate & convey their learning)

Consider:

● the academic & social goals of the students

● state & school district standards

● recommendations of professional organizations

Consider:
● Lesson formats
___ Interdisciplinary/thematic
___ Self-directed study
___ Inquiry-based learning
___ Discovery learning
___ Learning centers/Stations
___ Demonstrations
___ Activity-based
___ Games
___ Role-plays/Simulations
___ Computer/Web-based
___ Experiential/Community-based

Consider:

● the learning outcomes & how they will be assessed

● multi-level assessment & criteria

● authentic products
___ Book report
___ Play
___ collage
___ dance
___ rap/song
___ photo essay
___ editorial
___ article
___ choral reading
___ model
___ simulation
___ illustrated booklet
___ oral history
___ diorama
___ demonstration of a skill
___ mural
___ slide show
___ computer presentation
___ video
___ individual or group presentation
___ pageant
___ Summary of interviews
___ Teaching another person

Then consider:

● in what order will concepts and content be taught

● multi-level and multi-sensory materials that best convey concepts and content to each student

Consider:
● Instructional Arrangements
___ Cooperative groups
___ Cooperative structures (e.g., Jigsaw, Think-pair-share)
___ Peer Partnerships
___ Small group
___ ___ Student-directed
___ ___ Teacher-directed
___ Peer or cross-age tutor
___ Whole group
___ Individually

Consider:
● Social/Physical Environmental Conditions or Lesson Location
___ With selected others
___ In specified classrooms
___ In another part of school building
___ In the community
___ Altered environmental factors (light, sound, physical access)
___ Change or develop social rules

PAUSE & REFLECT
about specific students

Consider:
● Student-specific teaching strategies

Consider:
● Systems of support, assistance, or supervision

Figure 7.3. Universal design considerations.

Table 7.2. A multiple intelligences framework for viewing student abilities

Student	Areas of intelligence	Description
Jamal	Verbal/linguistic	Loves storytelling, talks excessively, plays practical jokes, offers relevant answers
	Musical	Talented drummer
	Logical/mathematical	Excels in mathematics, motivated by real-world problems
	Bodily/kinesthetic	Always moving, drummer, acts our stories with animation and exaggeration
	Interpersonal	Tries to parallel teach, interacts readily with others
Holly	Interpersonal	Quiet yet social, enjoys company of other students, shares readily with peers, charming, has nonverbal skills of negotiation
	Verbal/linguistic	Emerging reader, speaks selectively
	Visual/spatial	Relies on pictures, line drawings, or context for text meaning; visual media facilitates expression; draws designs with markers
Rafael	Verbal/linguistic	Non-English speaker learning a second language
	Logical/mathematical	Fascinated by how things work, expert in mechanical and electronic know-how, logical and methodical approach to academics
	Intrapersonal	Shy, writing is introspective
	Interpersonal	Sensitive, a good listener

dents. Consequently, the lesson became responsive to the needs of students representing a wide spectrum of abilities.

Design Point 2: Content

The state and school district standards in social studies, as well as curriculum guides for this subject at the fourth-grade level, gave Mr. Carbone broad parameters for the *content* of this unit. To create meaningful learning experiences from these broad guidelines, however, the academic and social needs of the students had to be considered. Facts about the students' MI profiles, past learning experiences, prior knowledge, and current interests and abilities are invaluable in designing *multilevel goals and objectives* for members of the class.

Acquiring, extending, refining, and using knowledge meaningfully are all elements of what we want all students to know and be able to do. The scope and degree of the mastery we expect of these elements, however, will vary across students. Examples of selected goals for each of the three students in Mr. Carbone's class illustrate this notion.

For Jamal, a relevant goal that capitalizes on his verbal/linguistic and bodily/kinesthetic abilities is to analyze three different documents or media (e.g., a photograph, a diary excerpt, the lyrics to a 19th-century song) to develop an original story that could be told to or performed for the class. Rafael, who is fascinated by how things work, will compare and contrast the 19th century and current technology of a selected object. He will diagram the differences and write a brief explanation that includes at least three grammatically correct English sentences. This goal bolsters his verbal/linguistic skills and engages his logical/mathematical inclinations with the exploration of technology. For Holly, improving her verbal communication and understanding of the basic concepts of past and present are high priority IEP goals. In the context of this unit, Mr. Carbone expects her to use two- or three-word phrases to respond to a question posed by a classmate at the learning stations. By the end of the unit, Holly is expected to differentiate symbols, objects, and activities that belong to the 19th century from those of today. Holly's performance goals capitalize on her interpersonal capacities while promoting declarative knowledge.

Within a lesson, unit, or class, multilevel goals can take a variety of forms. For example, students may engage in the same curricular content, but the focus may be more or less complex for individual students. Students may address the same content but be required to use different response modes to demonstrate their knowledge (e.g., to speak rather than write, to point rather than speak). The teacher may require increased or decreased rate of completion, varied pacing of the content, or differentiated expectations in the level of mastery, degree of quality, or quantity of the curricular requirements. Finally, students may focus on similar content, but some students may have more functional applications (Udvari-Solner, 1995, 1998).

An important content decision is the selection of appropriate instructional *materials*. Materials are the means by which students gain access to information and demonstrate their comprehension of content. Consequently, materials must be multilevel and multisensory in order to reach and teach the range of students. The more varied and rich the materials, the more likely the teacher is to capture evidence of a student's knowledge. In constructing each station, Mr. Carbone offered materials that could be examined visually and tactually (e.g., pictures, text, real objects) or accessed auditorally (e.g., audio and video tapes). Some materials were concrete; some were complex. Furthermore, a range of reading levels were represented. For example, at a single station, one student could analyze an 1850 McGuffy first-grade reader while another could read a chronicle about the African American ex-slave settlements in the Wisconsin region.

Because such an array of materials was available, students could show their knowledge in alternative ways that departed from traditional paper and pencil tasks. Students could arrange or order real items in time lines or produce products for the museum exhibit. In combination with multilevel goals, these varied materials ensured reasonable and meaningful expectations and challenges within a given unit of instruction.

Design Point 3: Process

Process—how students engage in learning—requires decisions about lesson formats, instructional groupings, the nature of the learning environment, and, for some students, specific decisions about optimal teaching strategies and systems of support or supervision (Udvari-Solner, 1996).

The organizational design of a learning experience or the *lesson format* dictates how information is imparted to students and how they will interact with that content. Teachers have a wide range of lesson formats from which to choose, including interdisciplinary/ thematic approaches, self-directed study, inquiry-based learning, learning by discovery, centers or station learning, computer-based learning, student conferencing, Socratic dialogue, games, simulations, role plays, activity-based or experiential learning, or community-referenced learning. Because these formats allow for multisensory experiences and are more active and interactive, more avenues for participation are available for students who don't respond well to a traditional lecture/demonstration/practice orientation.

Mr. Carbone chose a combination of formats that included station learning, learning by discovery, experiential and community-referenced learning, and options for self-study. He provided diversified materials and artifacts and asked students to discover differences and similarities to current-day contexts. Given the make-up of his class, he could not assume that all students had sufficient or accurate prior knowledge of this era in history, so he planned to solidify concepts through real experiences. He also knew that learners such as Rafael and Holly would be particularly motivated by the service learning museum project because it made the purpose of their learning more evident. Station learning was particularly helpful for Jamal, who could move through activities at his own pace, sometimes sitting, sometimes standing, with the freedom to interact with others informally.

A related consideration at this decision point concerns methods of grouping students and the learning configurations for structuring a lesson. *Instructional arrangements* dictate whether a student will be working alone, functioning as part of a large group, or operating in coordination with a small number of classmates. There is a calculated balance when using a variety of instructional arrangements throughout the day or week, including: 1) large-group or whole-class instruction; 2) teacher-directed small-group instruction; 3) small-group learning; 4) one-to-one teacher–student instruction; 5) independent or individual work; 6) partner learning, peer tutors, or cross-age tutors; and 7) cooperative learning groups (Tomlinson, 1999; Udvari-Solner, 1996).

Given the nature of his learners, Mr. Carbone used whole-class instruction selectively and for only 15–20 minutes at a time. He introduced the lesson to the whole class using the format of a role play (i.e., describing a winter day dressed as a pioneer girl). Before beginning station work each day, he delivered a 5- to 10-minute mini-lecture about historical events of this era that were not summarized or represented in the available materials. During the remaining instructional time, students could work alone, in pairs, or loosely organized groups to engage in the station activities. Cooperative groups in which specific student roles were assigned kept the museum exhibition station highly structured. To manage these multiple groupings, Mr. Carbone and a parent volunteer rotated through the stations to answer questions, prompt inquiries, and keep students appropriately challenged.

Holly functions well with a partner, Rafael prefers solitary work, and Jamal is at his best with a small group of peers. The flexible groupings inherent in the learning stations allowed time in each of these arrangements for these three students and the other class members. The teacher also had the freedom to engineer deliberate associations between specific students or bring the class together as a whole group at appropriate times.

Environmental conditions are yet another consideration in the process of how students engage in learning. The location of the lesson; the physical arrangement of the room space parameters for individual students; and factors such as lighting, noise level, seating, physical location, and accessibility to learning materials are all important environmental design decisions. The social rules (e.g., hand raising is required to answer a question) observed in the classroom also are an integral part of the environmental conditions that set the climate and activity level and guide acceptable interactions. Using the hallway as additional instructional space for two of the experiential learning stations and employing music to cue students to switch locations are examples of simple, yet important, environmental decisions made by Mr. Carbone.

Due to Jamal's active physical nature, he often interferes with other students' "personal space" and has difficulty sitting for long periods of time. As a consequence, to maximize Jamal's learning, his teacher made explicit decisions about his seating and altered a common social rule for classroom behavior. Staying seated while working is a typical social rule in most classrooms. Mr. Carbone relaxed these guidelines for the entire class by allowing the choice of sitting on chairs, sitting on the floor, or standing while engaged in station activities as long as students were not interfering with the work of others. Jamal's need for frequent movement, which under different social rules could be considered a behavior management problem, was easily accommodated by this simple alteration in a classroom prescript.

At this juncture, after clearly considering the optimal lesson format, instructional arrangement, and environmental conditions, it is important to *pause and reflect* about the lesson and consider whether specific students may need *unique* teaching or support strategies. *Teaching strategies* are the explicit and implicit ways an educator 1) gives directions, cues, prompts, and corrective feedback; 2) checks for understanding; 3) questions; 4) manages behavior; or 5) provides physical assistance. Student-specific teaching strategies are techniques that go beyond the structured technical aspects of delivering instruction and may include strategies to connect the content of a lesson to a particular student's culture, home, and community life (Udvari-Solner, 1996).

As noted in her profile, Holly has the tendency to hoard or collect markers. At times, this interferes with her learning. Without access to the markers, her anxiety and distraction increase. Using a student-specific teaching strategy to reduce her anxiety and increase her ability to stay engaged, the teacher has provided Holly with a small shoulder bag to carry a few markers. As a calming technique, Holly is allowed short periodic breaks to draw a picture of an artifact from her station using the markers. Whenever possible, the use of the markers is incorporated into the task at hand.

For Rafael, a student-specific teaching strategy is employed during a large-group question and answer session. First, adequate "think time" is given to all students that allows a full 20–30 seconds to formulate and write down an answer. Rafael is allowed to write his answer and share it aloud in Spanish so that his participation is not slowed by his less fluent use of English. After sharing his answer in Spanish, the class is challenged to translate his answer into English. The expectation is that Rafael also will use this time to rephrase his answer in English.

In a truly heterogeneous classroom, some students may need higher levels of assistance, intervention, or supervision than are typically provided to other students. Support needs may vary daily or be required at predictable times but rarely does a student need continuous, one-to-one supervision. Clearly, the amount and type of support needed for an individual student to meaningfully participate is a necessary design consideration. When additional support is warranted, *natural supports*—assistance that can be provided by the general education teacher and classmates—is preferable. Additional instructional staff (e.g., a paraprofessional) may be needed at times but only with clear goals to fade assistance, teach students self-management, or model strategies to transfer the support back to the natural support system of the classroom. For Holly, periodic breaks to draw pictures were employed as an instructional strategy to reduce anxiety. The support to do this came from a peer who simply asked her every half hour, "How are you feeling? Do you need a break?" In most cases, once the strategy, frequency, and type of support is known by class members and becomes part of the routine, special planning is rarely needed.

Design Point 4: Product

The fourth decision point in the universal design process is to determine how students will demonstrate and convey their learning. Here, the teacher must consider the learning outcomes and arrange for multilevel assessments that promote the development of authentic products. Authentic assessment occurs when students are expected to perform, produce, or otherwise demonstrate skills that represent realistic learning demands (Choate & Evans, 1992; Diez & Moon, 1992). To ensure that assessments represent the integration and application of what students have learned, teachers should 1) encourage student choice in product selection, 2) incorporate key concepts and relevant skills into final products, and 3) use multiple criteria to assess the project. Multiple criteria to assess one type of project could include accuracy in historical representation, use of multiple sources for research, creativity, and integration of writing and speaking skills. Mr. Carbone's unit promoted varied demonstrations of knowledge in the forms of tangible time lines, journal entries, written or pictorial reports, storytelling and role plays, collective charts of findings, oral responses to directed questions, and a culminating classwide project of a museum exhibition that allowed this fourth grade class to share their knowledge with a wider community. This diversity of product options created ample venues for Holly, Jamal, and Rafael to show their knowledge. A number of additional ideas for authentic products are offered in the right hand column of Figure 7.3.

CONCLUSION

Access to the general curriculum is most readily available by providing services in the regular education classroom. We need collaborative opportunities to define and develop a vision in public education where all students, including students with disabilities, actively engage in learning and progress in the general curriculum. Access to the general curriculum must not be viewed as exclusively a special education concern; it is dependent on factors associated with regular education and the general curriculum. Therefore, all students benefit when the general education curriculum becomes more accessible. (Office of Special Education and Rehabilitative Services, 1999)

This quote summarizes the rationale for universal access to curriculum—it has the potential to benefit all students, each with their unique learning styles and histories. To successfully engage in universal design, however, requires particular dispositions of teachers about teaching and their learners. Among the many necessary dispositions that we have observed, teachers acknowledge that

- Teaching is a complex act because of the unique learning characteristics of each student who enters the classroom every day and every year.

- Differentiation is a natural part of curriculum development, delivery, and refinement and should not be perceived as an extra step or a process reserved for a select group of students.

- Teachers already differentiate curriculum offerings and instructional design; universal design simply shifts the priority given to the learning needs and active participation of specific students (i.e., up-front rather than after-the-fact consideration).

- The initial effort and time spent to jointly design curriculum and instruction among general and special educators is both equitable and more efficient.

- Effective teaching for students with disabilities is substantively the same as effective teaching for all students, and it enriches and expands learning options (Castangnera, Fisher, Rodifer, & Sax, 1998).

The universal design process offered in this chapter complements and uses concepts and processes of creative problem solving and participation options, person-centered assessment and planning processes, research findings regarding best practices in inclusive education, dimensions of differentiation described by Tomlinson (1999), instruction and evaluation based on MI theory, and methods of authentic assessment. The proposed process is intended to demystify the task of differentiation as well as provide a collaborative tool for facilitating ongoing dialogue among those concerned with the educational outcomes of all of our children and youth.

Crafting quality education is an evolutionary process. With our collective attempts at differentiation, the technology of teaching and the understanding of the learning process will be advanced. Engaging in curricular and instructional differentiation is an act of change. In the words of Leo Buscaglia (as cited at Utah's Project for Inclusion web site, http://www.usoe.k12.ut.us/sars/Upi/index.htm), "Change. It has the power to uplift, to heal, to stimulate, surprise, open new doors, bring fresh experience and create excitement in life. Certainly it is worth the risk." Standing beside and among educators who have responded to this call, we recognize that changing or refining our practices does feel risky and, at times, uncomfortable. Allowing all students access to the general education curriculum by engaging in the universal design process may be new and different for educators. It is in this state of temporary imbalance, however, when the most creative solutions are generated.

REFERENCES

Castangnera, E., Fisher, D., Rodifer, K., & Sax, C. (1998). *Deciding what to teach and how to teach it: Connecting students through curriculum and instruction.* Colorado Springs, CO: PEAK Parent Center, Inc.

Center for Applied Special Technology. (2001). *Universal design for learning.* Retrieved from http://www.cast.org/udl.

Choate, J.S., & Evans, S. (1992). Authentic assessment of special learners: Problem or promise? *Preventing School Failure, 37*(1), 6–9.

Diez, M., & Moon, J. (1992). What do we want students to know?...and other important questions. *Educational Leadership, 49*(8), 38–41.

Falvey, M.A., Blair, M., Dingle, M.P., & Franklin, N. (2000). Creating a community of learners with varied needs. In R. Villa & J. Thousand (Eds.), *Restructuring for caring and effective education: Piecing the puzzle together* (2nd ed., pp. 186–207). Baltimore: Paul H. Brookes Publishing Co.

Federal Register. (March 12, 1999). *Rules and Regulations, 64*(48).

Fortini, M., & Fitzpatrick, M. (2000). The universal design for promoting self-determination. In R. Villa & J. Thousand (Eds.), *Restructuring for caring and effective education: Piecing the puzzle together* (2nd ed., pp. 575–589). Baltimore: Paul H. Brookes Publishing Co.

Gardner, H. (1983). *Frames of mind: The theory of multiple intelligences.* New York: Basic Books.

Harry, B. (1992). An ethnographic study of cross-cultural communication with Puerto Rican-American families in the special education system. *American Educational Research Journal, 29,* 471–494.

Hock, M.L. (2000). Standards, assessments, and individualized education programs: Planning for success in the general education curriculum. In R. Villa & J. Thousand (Eds.), *Restructuring for caring and effective education: Piecing the puzzle together* (2nd ed., pp. 208–241). Baltimore: Paul H. Brookes Publishing Co.

Individuals with Disabilities Education Act (IDEA) Amendments of 1997, PL 105-17, 20 U.S.C. §§ 1400 *et seq.*

Kronberg, R., & York-Barr, J. (1997). *Differentiated teaching and learning in heterogeneous classrooms: Strategies for meeting the needs of all students.* Minneapolis: Institute on Community Integration (UAP), College of Education and Human Development, University of Minnesota.

Madison Metropolitan School District Curriculum Standards. (2001). *Social studies fourth grade performance standards: History, time, continuity, and change.* Available on-line at http://www.madison.k12.wi.us/tnl/social00.html.

McDonnell, L., & McLaughlin, M. (Eds.). (1997). *Educating one and all: Students with disabilities and standards-based reform.* Washington, DC: National Academy Press.

McGregor, G., & Vogelsberg, T. (1998). *Inclusive schooling practices: Pedagogical and research foundations.* Baltimore: Paul H. Brookes Publishing Co.

Office of Special Education and Rehabilitative Services. (1999). *Request for proposals 84-324H, C-1 & 2.* Washington DC: U.S. Department of Education.

Orkwis, R., & McLane, K. (1998). *A curriculum every student can use: Design principles for student access* (Report No. RR93002005). (ERIC Document Reproduction Service No. ED423654)

Poplin, M., & Stone, S. (1992). Paradigm shifts in instructional strategies: From reductionism to holistic/constructivism. In S. Stainback & S. Stainback, (Eds.), *Controversial issues confronting special education* (pp. 153–180). Needham Heights, MA: Allyn & Bacon.

Thurlow, M.L., Ysseldyke, J.E., Gutman, S., & Geeman, K. (1997). *State level policies and practices: Where are students with disabilities?* College Park: University of Maryland, Center for Policy Research on the Impact of General and Special Education Reform.

Tomlinson, C. (1995a). Deciding to differentiate instruction in middle school: One school's journey. *Gifted Child Quarterly, 39*(2), 77–87.

Tomlinson, C. (1995b). *How to differentiate instruction in mixed-ability classrooms.* Alexandria, VA: Association for Supervision and Curriculum Development.

Tomlinson, C. (1999). *The differential classroom: Responding to the needs of all learners.* Alexandria, VA: Association for Supervision and Curriculum Development.

Udvari-Solner, A. (1995). A process for adapting curriculum in inclusive classrooms. In R. Villa and J. Thousand (Eds.), *Creating an inclusive school* (pp. 110–124). Alexandria, VA: Association for Supervision and Curriculum Development.

Udvari-Solner, A. (1996). Examining teacher thinking: Constructing a process to design curricular adaptations. *Remedial and Special Education, 17*(4), 245–254.

Udvari-Solner, A.(1998). Adapting curriculum. In M. Giangreco (Ed.), *Quick-guides to inclusion 2: Ideas for educating students with disabilities* (pp. 1–27). Baltimore: Paul H. Brookes Publishing Co.

Udvari-Solner, A., & Thousand, J. (l995). Promising practices that foster inclusive education. In R. Villa & J. Thousand (Eds.), *Creating an inclusive school* (pp. 87–109). Alexandria, VA: Association for Supervision and Curriculum Development.

U.S. Department of Education. (2000). *Twenty-second annual report to Congress on the implementation of the Individuals with Disabilities Education Act.* Washington, DC: Author.

Utah's Project for Inclusion. (2002). Retrieved from http://www.usoe.k12.ut.us/sars.

Vaughn, S., & Schuman, J. (1994). Middle school teachers planning for students with disabilities. *Remedial and Special Education, 15,* 152–161.

Perspectives on Creativity and Collaborative Learning

Cooperative Group Learning as a Form of Creativity

Alice M.L. Quiocho

Picture it—a classroom full of adolescents and a teacher who wants them all to be their very best. Included in this classroom is Anthony. Anthony won't cooperate with anyone. It doesn't matter in which group he is placed. He has decided that working with others is not something he wants to do.

I was that teacher, and Anthony was my student. He had the brightest eyes of anyone I had ever met. He had a pocketful of smiles that he used skillfully in a variety of contexts. And, Anthony was a challenge—my personal challenge. I felt frustrated because he would not engage with other students. So, I did what I thought would work. I decided to hold a conference with Anthony and talk about what I saw happening. I told him that I would like to see him perform his assigned role. I told him that I wanted him to be the best and that working together can make all of us better. In return, I got a blank stare.

Still, I forged ahead. I gave Anthony more reasons to consider cooperation as a positive way to learn. I told him about the real work world where groups of people solve problems together. I even gave him an example. I told him about the tour I took through the Sony Corporation plant, where they operate in teams. Anyone on the team—a man on the floor, an administrator, or a mid-management person—can come up with the best solution to any problem. This company understood that working together to solve problems was the most important thing they could do to include everyone in the process of teamwork.

"Good for them," he said with as much sarcasm as an adolescent can summon. "I don't plan to work for them anyway. I have other plans."

I took another stab at it. I told him that other companies used team problem solving as well. They used what they called *Quality Circles* for the purpose of group problem solving. And after all, I reminded him, "We are really preparing you for the work world." Silence. He gave me that "you've got to be kidding" look and just shook his head.

"When we work together, we build community," I reminded him. He pulled out his "oh please, spare me" smile. I was beginning to get agitated, but I had worked with adolescents for at least 14 years. I could do this. "Think about it, Anthony. When we work together on something, we can do more than if we worked alone. Do you ever help your older brother at home get something done?" He looked beyond me at the trees swaying in the cool spring breeze.

He informed me that if I wanted him to, he would do everything by himself. He didn't need anyone. He topped this response off with a smile that makes a teacher think twice about the possibility of throttling a child for the first time ever in his or her career! He tossed his head of shiny black curls, slouched back down in his chair, crossed his arms, sighed, and took everything in. Although I was pleased with what I saw happening, I could hear him say in his head, "What losers! Look at them. Giving it up to her." What had gone wrong? No, I didn't throttle Anthony, although I thought about it. I did what I had been taught to do when things don't go right. I reflected on what I had done.

I wanted my class to learn how to work together. I wanted to create a learning community where we all realized that we needed each other to be our best. I wanted us to feel that none of us could fail at anything because there were too many of us in the classroom that could help each other learn. I believed that cooperative learning was the best way to achieve the goals I had set for my class. I had read Johnson and Johnson's (1984) *Circles of Learning: Cooperation in the Classroom.* I wanted a democratic classroom. I realized how important it was that everyone in my room have a voice in learning. I knew I had to teach social skills and have an academic or cognitive goal for the group to achieve. I had heard Spencer Kagan (1985) speak and decided that I would ease into cooperative learning with pairing activities first. I had listened to William Glasser and realized that tasks had to be designed so that each person needed everyone else in the group in order to complete them. I re-read *Circles of Learning: Cooperation in the Classroom,* studied up on the importance of teaching social skills, and used the role descriptions to support the social skills. I learned how to assign roles and to train students to perform their respective roles. We even practiced how to talk to one another using positive language such as, "Good job! I like what you said." I knew students were supposed to learn interdependence through cooperative learning. I knew I had to structure the cooperative learning process. And, here was the caveat—I had read an article on *Quality Circles* and decided that because the work world had discovered the importance of collaboration, cooperative learning was perfect to prepare my students for their futures. The Secretary's Commission on Achieving Necessary Skills (SCANS) report that had just been released from the U.S. Department of the Interior (1991) laid out the skills students need to learn to be productive in the work world where technology is integral to organizational function. It focused on the collaboration necessary for problem solving as well as the language and thinking students should learn and practice in reading, writing, listening, speaking, and using technology. Surely, eighth graders could profit from these goals and from cooperative learning. I was ready.

Except I had forgotten about Anthony. After studying up on what I was going to do, I started to teach my students about cooperative learning with a determination and commitment of which I was proud. I was even metacognitive about my own teaching. I constantly questioned myself about my lessons. Did I consider the prerequisite skills? Did I have clear academic objectives for the lesson? Was I being clear about the purpose for teaching social skills? Was I monitoring thoroughly enough? Did students understand how the roles were related to the social skills and all were related to working cooperatively to achieve the assigned task? Did students understand the criteria for success? Were the self- and group evaluation processes working? Were the evaluations informative for me as well as for my students? Had I set clear standards that students and I could use to evaluate the process? I was really working hard at making cooperative learning a success. I began to feel a surge of confidence. I proudly looked out on a sea of students, all engaged in learning. It was working. It was a success. Then, I saw Anthony.

There he was—Mr. Independent. He would decide what he wanted to do. He would decide whether this was the day to work with the group, or he would use his "winning" smile on some girl in the group and *she* would do the work he was supposed to do. He could just sit back in his seat basking in the attention and smile while she did his work. In all of the preparation and studying I had done, I had not planned for Anthony. I had forgotten about group rewards. I had started with pairs, but it didn't dawn on me that I could plan a fishbowl activity in which a group of students volunteer to practice the necessary skills while other students watch, followed by a group evaluation process. I had not counted on opposition that could and would become a disruption in the classroom. I had not considered peer mediation or thought about "students who do not do the work." And, more important, I had forgotten about the cultural capital that Anthony brought to school. My assessment of the situation was a surface one.

Anthony was a bi-racial child of Native American and African American descent with strong ties to the Native American culture. To date, his schooling had been focused on making him like everyone else—making him conform. As an adolescent, Anthony realized that he was a nonconformist. He was different. He was his own man. I don't think he knew why.

Anthony was not like Ayinde. He did not share all he knew. He was quiet most of the time. He always observed the activity in the classroom from the fringe. Sometimes, when he felt like it, he would begin the assigned work after everyone else was almost finished. He spent a lot of time watching, sharpening pencils, circling the activities, and smiling. Anthony only engaged when he wanted to. It was always on his terms, I thought. I assessed his reading and writing and got inconsistent results. He would achieve independence in reading on one eighth-grade passage and plummet to frustration on another. He struggled to get his thoughts on paper. When asked to write, he did a lot of sitting and staring. "I'm thinking," he would respond when asked if he was going to get started with his work. I was positive Anthony was just avoiding work. I didn't understand what was going on. I was frustrated and challenged by Anthony. I decided to step back, far back, and take another look. I had some work to do.

First, I spoke with Anthony's older brother, the chair of his tribe. At first he told me that he wanted Anthony to conform, to be like the other students. I said that I didn't think that was going to happen soon, and I wanted the best learning situation for Anthony. His brother wanted to help, and I needed it. During our talk, Anthony's brother shared that he knew Anthony was not the typical adolescent. Anthony had been referred to by his teachers as quietly defiant, and his brother had been asked to come to school many times. He shared that Anthony always had to watch what was going on around him for a long time before he did anything.

"I thought," his brother shared, "that he was slow, but now I don't think that. I think maybe that's the way Anthony learns. When we learn the tribal dances, we are taught to watch the older dancers and imitate what they are doing. That's the way we learn. We listen to the overall tones of the chants, the pitch, the volume and cadence of the drums, and the chanter. We watch, and we learn. Maybe that's what's going on with Anthony."

Maybe it was. I modeled cooperative learning structures and roles. I allowed time for students to practice. I thought that I had provided sufficient modeling, but maybe it was not enough for Anthony. Perhaps he needed more scaffolding (Crawford, as cited in Leyba, 1991). I hadn't taken Anthony's culture into consideration. I had to look at what Anthony brought and work those cultural factors into the cooperative learning process.

I decided to think about inclusive cooperative learning using the information Anthony's brother had shared with me. Observation was a piece of the cultural capital Anthony brought with him to school. I was going to take a risk—I was going to let Anthony use observation and reflection to learn. I revisited the concept of a learning community with my students. We talked about what was easy in the cooperative learning work that we had been doing and what was hard. We used a think-pair-share structure to do this. We talked about when to help others and when not to help. We talked about how each of us learned differently—that some of us need more time to learn about concepts as well as about the way the learning might be structured when it looks and feels different from more traditional contexts of learning. I learned that the quiet students felt intimidated in groups of four. I learned that I had to see roles as being flexible and individualized to address student needs. It was then that I decided to add time for observation of how cooperative learning worked—just like learning the tribal dances. I set up a fishbowl using volunteers. We all evaluated what we saw, and the group evaluated what they did. Anthony was allowed to continue to observe. He could engage when he was ready, but he had to engage at some time. We had an agreement. I wondered how long it would take. I was nervous. We had talked, and he agreed that he needed more time to watch and learn than the other students did and that he would become involved when he understood how things worked. We modeled several examples of tasks using the fishbowl. When we broke into groups of four, I asked Anthony to share with me how the observations were going. He was allowed to sit in on groups and listen. The waiting was killing me. I was sure I had made the wrong decision and Anthony was taking advantage of me. I was asked why Anthony got to "walk around looking." I reminded the students who asked that we had talked about how some of us needed more time than others to learn. After all, if we were a learning community, we all had an obligation to be the best models for Anthony so he could learn how things worked through the process of observation. I saw doubt in their eyes, and I understood. I felt the same way. I would talk with Anthony during and after each cooperative learning activity. I asked him to tell me how he felt he would work in the group structure and if he understood how it worked—that everyone needed each other to get the work done. "Not sure," he would reply sometimes, or "I don't know." As I observed him, though, I found that he was beginning to engage with the groups that he was observing. He was actually listening, sharing information, and laughing with the group. One day, about a week and a half later, Anthony asked to be assigned to a group. I used positive rewards in the form of positive, verbal feedback. I would quietly tell him how his presence and his work made the group better. He'd smile.

We continued using cooperative learning in my classroom. We started in the fall, and by the end of spring we all understood how it worked for us. We became a learning community. We did learn that we were all better because we were together. We all learned that we were better because each of us was unique and that was okay—that's the way the world is. My students became "tight." They stuck up for and supported each other in and out of the classroom. I did have to continue to be attentive to the way I structured the tasks for cooperative learning. I continued to involve students in the evaluation process, and I learned to adjust or design roles to ensure active involvement of all students. I learned that I needed to look at cooperative learning as a form of creativity. Once I became creative with the way I implemented cooperative learning, paying close attention to the needs of each of my students, my students became more creative in their thinking and their work. They took risks. I had taken a risk. Anthony stopped cruising and became engaged in the classroom's activities. By June, I breathed a sigh of relief, and I was pleased about our progress as a learning and creative community that academic school year. I felt a twinge in my heart when Anthony gave me a hug the last day of school and said he would miss me and everyone in the class. They were all going on to different high schools.

I saw Anthony 10 years later. He came to interview me, now the principal of the middle school. "You're not the same teacher I had in eighth grade?" he asked. "Yes, I am" I replied, "just older." He beamed and shook his head. Anthony interviewed me as the editor of his tribal newspaper. He sat there with his laptop and pecked away as we talked. We talked about learning in middle school, about the need for cooperative learning in schools to support and increase student achievement, and about desktop publishing programs as a way to support and share student learning. We walked around the school, and he was able to see cooperative learning in the classrooms. "We used to do that," he said with a broad smile. "Yes, we did, didn't we?" I replied. "It's a good thing," he replied. I shared my school newsletter with him, and he shared his newspaper with me. Later on in our conversation, he shared how he was working collaboratively as a tribal representative with the surrounding schools to improve the achievement of Native American children attending public schools. He still had that beautiful shiny hair and that winning smile. I just smiled and shook my head. Anthony. Imagine that.

REFERENCES

Crawford, A. (1991). Communicative approaches to second language acquisition: From oral language development into the core curriculum and L2 literacy. In C.F. Leyba (Ed.), *Schooling for minority students: A theoretical framework* (pp. 79–132). Los Angeles: California State University.

Johnson, D.W. (1984). *Circles of learning: Cooperation in the classroom.* Alexandria, VA: Association for Supervision and Curriculum Development.

Kagan, S. (1985). *Cooperative learning.* San Clemente, CA: Resources for Teachers.

U.S. Department of the Interior. (1991, June). *What work requires of schools: Secretary's Commission on Achieving Necessary Skills (SCANS).* Washington, DC: Author.

8

Problem-Solving Methods to Facilitate Inclusive Education

Michael F. Giangreco
Chigee J. Cloninger
Ruth E. Dennis
Susan W. Edelman

Inclusive educational practices require people to work together to maximize learning experiences for all children. This chapter presents ways of planning, adapting, and implementing inclusive educational experiences for students of varying abilities. It is a how-to chapter based on the assumption that inclusive educational experiences benefit all children. As Giangreco and Putnam (1991) pointed out, when people use terms such as *inclusion*, they may mean different things. To assist the reader in understanding what the authors mean, a five-point definition of inclusive education is presented in Table 8.1. Education is inclusive only when all five features occur on an ongoing, daily basis.

An inclusive school is "a place where everyone belongs, is accepted, supports, and is supported by his or her peers and other members of the school community in the course of having his or her educational needs met" (Stainback & Stainback, 1990, p. 3). It is designed to benefit everyone—students of varying characteristics (including those with disabilities) as well as teachers and other school personnel (e.g., Bauer & Shea, 1999; Hunt & Goetz, 1997; Lipsky & Gartner, 1997; McGregor & Vogelsberg, 1998; Stainback & Stainback, 1996; Thousand & Villa, 2000; Villa & Thousand, 1995).

The remainder of this chapter is divided into four sections. The first section presents contextual information regarding the challenges associated with educating a diverse group of students in general education environments and activities. The second section describes characteristics of effective problem solvers as well as the complete Osborn-Parnes Creative Problem-Solving (CPS) process. The third section delineates three variations of the CPS process that use the creative powers of children and adults to generate options for the inclusion of classmates with diverse needs. The final section discusses implications of using CPS in education.

CHALLENGE OF EDUCATING DIVERSE GROUPS IN HETEROGENEOUS GENERAL EDUCATION ENVIRONMENTS AND ACTIVITIES

We can, whenever and wherever we choose, successfully teach all children whose schooling is of interest to us. We already know more than we need in order to do this. Whether we do it must finally depend on how we feel about the fact that we haven't done it so far. (Edmonds, 1979, p. 29)

Table 8.1. Basic components of inclusive education

Inclusive education is in place when each of these five features occur on an ongoing, daily basis:

1. Heterogeneous grouping: All students are educated together in groups in which the number of those with and without disabilities approximates the natural proportion. The premise is that "students develop most when in the physical, social, emotional, and intellectual presence of nonhandicapped persons in reasonable approximations to the natural proportions" (Brown et al., 1983, p. 17). Thus, in a class of 25 students, perhaps there is one student with severe disabilities, a couple of others with less significant disabilities, and many students without identified disabilities working at various levels.

2. A sense of belonging to a group: All students are considered members of the class rather than visitors, guests, or outsiders. Within these groups, students who have disabilities are welcomed, as are students without disabilities.

3. Shared activities with individualized outcomes: Students share educational experiences (e.g., lessons, labs, field studies, group learning) at the same time (Schnorr, 1990). Even though students are involved in the same activities, their learning objectives are individualized and, therefore, may be different. Students may have different objectives in the same curriculum area (e.g., language arts) during a shared activity. This is referred to as *multilevel instruction* (Campbell, Campbell, Collicott, Perner, & Stone, 1988; Collicott, 1991; Giangreco & Meyer, 1988; Giangreco & Putnam, 1991). Within a shared activity, a student also may have individualized objectives from a curriculum area (e.g., social skills) other than that on which other students are focused (e.g., science). This practice is referred to as *curriculum overlapping* (Giangreco & Meyer, 1988; Giangreco & Putnam, 1991).

4. Use of environments frequented by persons without disabilities: Shared educational experiences take place in environments predominantly frequented by people without disabilities (e.g., general education classroom, community worksites).

5. A balanced educational experience: Inclusive education seeks an individualized balance between the academic/functional and social/personal aspects of schooling (Giangreco, 1992). For example, teachers in inclusion-oriented schools would be as concerned about students' self-image and social network as they would be about developing literacy competencies or learning vocational skills.

Edmonds's (1979) vision of American education remains unfulfilled but acknowledges the challenges faced by schools in realizing this vision. Table 8.2 contrasts major distinctions between "traditional" approaches of dealing with student diversity and more contemporary, inclusion-oriented approaches. These distinctions are presented in order to set a context—to highlight the assumptions and approaches that enable educators to meet the challenge of educating diverse groups of students in heterogeneous general education environments and activities more effectively.

It should be noted that even if educators embrace the inclusion-oriented educational tenets presented in Table 8.2, they still should and do have legitimate questions about how educational alternatives work and what the impact of these practices will be. Their questions include

- How can I, as a teacher, accommodate a wide array of student needs without sacrificing quality?

- Is it not a lot of pressure on one person—the teacher—to generate all the accommodations that need to be made?

- How will the inclusion of students with diverse needs affect the social and academic outcomes of the other students?

- How will the inclusion of students with diverse needs affect my capacity to provide quality education to all of my students?

Research in North American schools has yielded sufficient evidence to convince us that the answers to these questions are positive, although much remains to be done. Specifically, we have concluded that

- Diverse student needs can be accommodated within general class activities while maintaining high quality for all students.

- The responsibility for developing accommodations can and should be shared among many members of the classroom community that include not only the adults of the school but also the students.

- Well-planned inclusion can have positive social and academic outcomes for students with and without disabilities.

Teachers who choose to meet the challenge of educating diverse groups of students improve their teaching for the entire class (Hunt & Goetz, 1997; McGregor & Vogelsberg, 1998).

OSBORN-PARNES CREATIVE PROBLEM-SOLVING (CPS) AS A METHOD FOR INCLUDING STUDENTS WITH DIVERSE NEEDS IN THE CLASSROOM

The CPS process (Parnes, 1985, 1988, 1992, 1997) is one method for empowering teams of teachers and students to work together to meet the challenges of educating a heterogeneous school population. CPS is a generic strategy designed for addressing a variety of challenges and opportunities. The process was articulated first by Osborn (1953/1993) and was further developed by Osborn's protégé and colleague, Parnes, who promoted the use of CPS in many fields—advertising, product development, business, and education. Clearly, creativity is recognized as a valuable process and outcome in education and a necessary

Table 8.2. Approaches to educating students with diverse characteristics

Traditional approaches	Inclusion-oriented alternatives
The teacher is the instructional leader.	Collaborative teams share leadership.
Students learn from teachers, and teachers solve the problems.	Students and teachers learn from each other and solve problems together.
Students are purposely grouped by similar ability.	Students are purposely grouped by differing abilities.
Instruction is geared toward middle-achieving students.	Instruction is geared to match students at all levels of achievement.
Grade-level placement is considered synonymous with curricular content.	Grade-level placement and individual curricular content are independent of each other.
Instruction is often passive, competitive, didactic, and/or teacher directed.	Instruction is active, creative, and collaborative among members of the classroom community.
People who provide instructional supports are located, or come primarily from, sources external to the classroom.	People who provide instructional supports are located, or come primarily from, sources internal to the classroom.
Some students do not "fit" in general education classes.	All students "fit" in general education classes.
Students who do not "fit in" are excluded from general classes and/or activities.	All students are included in general class activities.
The classroom teacher and general education team assume ownership for the education of general education students, and special education staff assume ownership for the education of students with special needs.	The classroom teacher and general education team (including special educators, related service staff, and families) assume ownership for educating all students attending the school.
Students are evaluated by common standards.	Students are evaluated by individually appropriate standards.
Students' success is achieved by meeting common standards.	The system of education is considered successful when it strives to meet each student's needs.

skill for professionals faced with restructuring schools to meet the changing needs of modern society. Within education, CPS historically was associated with the education of children labeled *gifted*. Only since the late 1980s has CPS been applied to inclusion-oriented education issues. As a consequence, people increasingly recognize that approaches to teaching students at "opposite ends" of the academic achievement continuum hold benefits for the multitude of children in between. Following are some basic tenets of the CPS process represented as characteristics of effective problem solvers.

CHARACTERISTICS OF PROBLEM SOLVERS

To be optimally successful in using the CPS process, participants must exhibit certain behaviors and dispositions identified as characteristics of effective problem solvers. Six of these characteristics are described in this section:

1. Problem solvers are optimistic.

2. Problem solvers believe everyone is creative and has the capacity to solve problems.

3. Problem solvers alternate between divergent and convergent thinking.

4. Problem solvers actively defer and engage their judgment.

5. Problem solvers encourage "free-wheeling" and fun.

6. Problem solvers take action.

Problem Solvers Are Optimistic

CPS, or any other problem-solving method, is based on optimism. Problem solvers enter the process with the knowledge that every challenge they face can be solved, usually in more than one way.

Problem Solvers Believe Everyone
Is Creative and Has the Capacity to Solve Problems

Everyone has heard statements such as "I'm not creative," or "I could never come up with those kinds of ideas." Many people limit the ideas they can generate by minimizing their personal creative potential. The fact is that people use their creative problem-solving abilities constantly in daily life without even noticing it. Creative abilities are being used every time a person rearranges furniture in a room, makes a substitution in a recipe, improvises by using an object in place of an absent tool, adapts a game to play with a child, or plans a schedule.

In education, as in many other fields, people have been encouraged to believe that certain experts hold the key to special knowledge or creative solutions. As a result, there is a tendency to become unnecessarily dependent on outside consultants to solve problems while becoming increasingly less confident in one's own abilities. In contrast, we believe any group of people has the ability to solve the challenges of inclusion-oriented schooling through the use of CPS. By working together, teams of people can identify solutions and take actions that no individual could accomplish alone. The practice of using creative problem-solving strategies within teams also can enhance individual team members' personal growth and creative capacity in a broader range of situations.

The steps of CPS take advantage of the abilities people already have and encourage people to deliberately use their existing abilities to solve problems. Learning the basics of CPS is easy. People already know how to do most or all of what is needed, and they have been doing it naturally all of their lives. The new learning comes in practicing the use of these existing skills in new and deliberate ways.

Problem Solvers Alternate Between Divergent and Convergent Thinking

A central concept embedded in the CPS process is actively alternating between divergent and convergent thinking. This means that at each stage of the CPS process, there is a time to consider the challenge in broad, divergent ways—to open up to many possibilities. Then, within the same stage, the problem solver is encouraged to think convergently—to narrow the focus and make a choice from among many possibilities, allowing the process to continue.

Problem Solvers Actively Defer and Engage Their Judgment

People frequently inhibit their creative abilities by prematurely engaging their judgment; in essence, they are generating ideas and attempting to evaluate them at the same time. Firestien (1989) likened this to driving a car with your feet on the brake and the gas pedal at the same time. Firestien's analogy pointed out that such an approach is unlikely to get anyone very far. Effective problem solvers refrain from this practice and identify times to actively defer judgment and times to engage judgment purposefully. These times correspond with divergent and convergent thinking. In a divergent phase, judgment is actively deferred. In a convergent phase, judgment is purposefully engaged.

Problem Solvers Encourage "Free-Wheeling" and Fun

Having fun and being playful with ideas is crucial to effective problem solving. We might think of humor and playfulness as the oil that keeps the creativity engine lubricated and running smooth. Creative insights, as well as humor, can be facilitated by bringing together things that seem incongruent.

Sometimes it may be difficult for people to be playful when the challenges they are facing are serious; yet, playfulness is essential. During training workshops, we have observed teachers practicing the use of CPS on noneducational examples and doing an excellent job of being playful and having fun with their ideas. However, when the same teachers were asked to apply CPS skills to educational challenges, many reverted to old "school meeting behaviors" that were anything but fun and that seriously interfered with their capacity to creatively problem solve. It is easy for people to fall back into familiar patterns and traditional group interactions. Therefore, when using CPS, it is critical to be mindful of this hazard and guard against it with collective playfulness.

Problem Solvers Take Action

Problem solvers extend the power of their optimism by acting on their ideas. Ideas that are generated do not have to be earth shattering or world changing. Some people do not use the ideas they generate because they judge the ideas as "not good enough." Yet, as Osborn observed, "A fair idea put to use is better than a good idea kept on the polishing wheel" (as cited in Parnes, 1988, p. 37). As people start to use CPS and get into new habits that accentuate their creative problem-solving abilities, they find themselves generating more and better ideas. The key is to act, not to wait for the perfect solution before taking action.

STAGES OF THE OSBORN-PARNES CREATIVE PROBLEM-SOLVING (CPS) PROCESS

The information regarding the six stages of the CPS process presented in Table 8.3 and described on the following pages is based on descriptions of the process outlined by Osborn (1953/1993) and Parnes (1985, 1988, 1992, 1997) and insights gained from the authors' use of the process (Giangreco, 1993).

Developing creativity capabilities is a lifelong undertaking (Parnes, 1985, 1988) that should be thought of more as the development of a creative attitude than the learning and application of specific steps and procedures. Thus, the CPS process should be used as a springboard for inventing or personalizing CPS models and techniques. Some of the variations developed by these authors to help with the challenges of school and community inclusion are highlighted later in this section. Cycling and recycling through the CPS process and its variations internalize the creative attitude and make CPS a part of one's daily routine rather than an isolated tool used only in certain contexts (e.g., school versus home or family) or with certain problems (e.g., student versus systems change issues in educational reform).

Table 8.3. Stages of the Osborn-Parnes creative problem-solving (CPS) process

Stage 1: Envisioning or objective finding

At this initial stage, the problem solvers heighten their awareness through imagining potential challenges. First, they are divergent, considering a variety of possible challenges. Then, they converge by selecting one challenge to begin solving.

Stage 2: Fact finding

Problem solvers gather as much information as possible about the selected challenge by using all of their perceptions and senses. By asking "who," "what," "where," "when," "why," and "how" questions, problem solvers are divergent in considering multiple perspectives regarding the challenge. They finish this stage by identifying facts they believe to be most relevant to the challenge.

Stage 3: Problem finding

The purpose of this stage is to clarify the challenge or problem by redefining it in new and different ways; by rephrasing the challenge as a question, "In what ways might I/we . . . ?"; and by asking the question "Why?" or "What do I/we really want to accomplish?" This process is repeated until the problem solvers restate the problem in a way that makes the most sense and is most appealing to them.

Stage 4: Idea finding

At this stage, the objective is to defer judgment while generating as many ideas as possible to potentially solve the challenge. Playfulness and wild ideas are encouraged. To come up with ideas beyond the obvious, problem solvers attempt to make new connections between ideas through analogies, manipulation of ideas (e.g., magnifying, minifying, reversing, eliminating), and hitchhiking (i.e., making new associations by building on someone else's idea).

Stage 5: Solution finding

At this stage of the process, a variety of criteria are considered and ultimately selected for evaluating the merit of ideas. Problem solvers use the criteria to assist in selecting the best solution.

Stage 6: Acceptance finding

The problem solvers refine the solutions to make them more workable. The objective is to turn ideas into action through the development and implementation of an action plan. Regular evaluation of the solution helps problem solvers discover new challenges and ways of addressing them as the action plan is carried out.

Sources: Osborn (1953/1993) and Parnes (1985, 1988, 1992, 1997).

Stage 1: Envisioning or Objective Finding

Have you driven down the same road many times and later realized that there was something on that road you had not noticed before? The first stage of CPS helps us become increasingly aware of challenges and opportunities around us by sharpening our powers of observation. It prepares us to use all of our senses and perceptions to explore new possibilities and search for opportunities. The following rules or dispositions will help a problem solver at this stage:

- Think of objective finding as a starting point or a general challenge.

- Think divergently by considering a variety of potential problems to solve; remember to defer judgment and have fun.

- Expand the possibilities and free yourself from real or perceived boundaries by imagining, wishing, dreaming, and fantasizing.

- Think convergently by focusing in on one challenge you really want to solve.

- Remember that challenges come in all different sizes. Pick one that is small enough to be solved in the time available. By starting with manageable challenges, teams and individuals are more likely to experience success, develop a creative attitude, and practice and improve creativity skills.

Stage 2: Fact Finding

The purpose of fact finding is to identify and list as many facts about the challenge as team members can think of. There is an important relationship between facts and potential solutions. From obvious facts come obvious ideas; from less obvious facts come less obvious and possibly more inventive solutions. To start fact finding, set a short time limit, such as 5–8 minutes. Fact finding is a quick-paced, rapid-fire listing of what people believe to be true about the challenging situation. The facts should be presented briefly without explanation, judgment, or discussion. In other words, use the approach of the fictional Joe Friday (the character from the famed television series, *Dragnet* [Webb, 1952–1959/1967–1971]) and solicit "just the facts, ma'am; just the facts." Always record and save the list of facts for use later during the CPS process (e.g., during idea finding). The following are tips for increasing the likelihood that all of the relevant facts emerge:

- Use all of your senses and perceptions to describe what you know about the challenge. Remember that facts can be feelings.

- Ask "who," "what," "where," "when," "why," and "how" questions about what is and is not true of the challenge situation.

- Be divergent and defer judgment to generate a large quantity and variety of facts. If someone states an opinion with which you do not agree, then do not dispute it; rather, accept the fact as that person's opinion (e.g., "Larry believes that students act out because they simply are bored during class").

- Stretch beyond the obvious facts.

- Ask yourself, "What does the challenge or facts about the challenge remind me of?"

- Be convergent by selecting a subset of relevant facts to assist problem finding in the next stage.

- Record and save the list of facts. These will be used again later in the process, especially during idea finding.

Stage 3: Problem Finding

Sometimes the initial selection of a challenge is right on target; at other times, the initial selection is just a starting point. The purpose of problem finding is to clarify the challenge or problem by considering different ways of viewing it. When rephrasing the challenge at this stage, it is helpful to state the challenge in positive words by using the starter phrase, "In what ways might we . . . ?" and repeating the question until the team feels comfortable that it has teased out the real issues.

Next, be convergent and select one of the new challenge statements that the team agrees it wants to solve. Problem finding is an important stage of CPS because, as John Dewey observed, "A problem well defined is half solved" (as cited in Parnes, 1988, p. 72).

Stage 4: Idea Finding

Ideas are potential solutions to the challenge statement selected at Stage 3. Where do these ideas come from? Ideas may emerge through the deliberate use of approaches such as the awareness plans described in Chapter 10 of this volume. Central to idea finding is the awareness plan of brainstorming (Osborn, 1953/1993). *Brainstorming* is a divergent, idea-generating process in which judgment or even praise is deferred in order to help problem solvers stretch beyond the obvious. Quantity is the key, as it is likely that the first ideas generated will be the "same old" ideas. It is important to keep the ideas flowing quickly and to limit sessions to 5–10 minutes. Good brainstorming sessions do not look anything like a typical group meeting; in brainstorming sessions, there is little quiet time and people speak in single words or short phrases rather than sentences. Other important techniques are forced relationships (Parnes, 1988), incubation, and making the familiar strange.

Forced relationships are achieved when two objects, ideas, or concepts that appear to have little or no relationship to each other are combined or rearranged in some way to generate a new idea to solve a problem. These new connections are made by looking for similarities, analogies, metaphors, or other comparisons between characteristics of the two objects or ideas. *Incubation* involves moving away from the challenge for a time to engage in different activities and returning to the challenge later. Creativity and invention also are facilitated when people *make the familiar strange*. One way to make the familiar strange is to search for new ways of seeing the challenge and facts by identifying new relationships through paradox, analogies, metaphors, associations, and connections (e.g., Gordon, 1987; Gordon & Poze, 1979).

As mentioned previously, ideas also may emanate from facts. Thus, it is important to use facts from Stage 2 in conjunction with idea-joggers, by combining or manipulating facts or their dimensions. Idea-joggers include questions such as, "What would the situation look like if something (e.g., a fact about the situation) were: 1) minimized/made smaller, 2) magnified/made bigger, 3) rearranged, 4) eliminated, 5) reversed, or 6) turned upside down or inside out?"

Idea-joggers may involve manipulating dimensions of a fact—for example, if part of a problem situation is visual (e.g., "In what ways might the school building or classroom be improved in appearance?"). Applying idea-joggers to visual dimensions such as color, shade, brightness, design, or contrast can generate ideas. Although facts can lead directly to ideas, theoretically, the more idea-joggers applied and combined, the more ideas are likely to be generated.

Some ideas that are generated may be wild and unusable. These ideas have tremendous potential, however, as other ideas may be spurred by them in a hitchhiking effect. For example, a class of first graders was presented with the forced relationship of a magazine photo of a tropical beach scene and the challenge, "In what ways might we help our new classmate, Amy, feel welcome?" One student enthusiastically blurted out, "Let's take her to Bermuda!" The next student said, "I could play with her in the sandbox during recess." This student apparently hitchhiked or piggybacked on the previous idea by identifying similarities between the beach in Bermuda and facts she knew about the schoolyard (e.g., both use sand for play; Giangreco, 1993). Idea finding concludes by focusing in on promising ideas.

Stage 5: Solution Finding

Solution finding involves evaluating and selecting ideas generated in Stage 4. It begins divergently by considering a wide variety of potential criteria that might be used to evaluate the ideas. For example, ideas about potential accommodations for an individual student might be judged by the following criteria framed in question form:

- Is the accommodation feasible?

- Is the accommodation time efficient for the teacher?

- Does the student like the idea?

- Will the accommodation likely enhance the image of the student among his or her peers?

- Is it consistent with the team's philosophical orientation or shared values?

- Will the accommodation promote independence and responsibility rather than dependence and helplessness?

Next, the individual or team converges on a subset of criteria and uses them to evaluate the ideas. Select solutions by using a matrix in which ideas are listed along the side and criteria are listed across the top. The matrix offers space to rate each idea based on each criterion. Rating may be as simple as a plus versus minus scoring system or as complex as a scale that weighs criteria differently. Remember, whatever scoring method is used, it is not intended to be a formula that removes decision-making power. Rather, the criteria and rating method are intended to provide a rational framework for considering the merits of each idea. Fundamentally, solution finding is a convergent stage of CPS in which judgment is engaged to select or combine ideas for which a plan of action is then formulated and carried out.

Stage 6: Acceptance Finding

In acceptance finding, the problem-solving task is to first think divergently by asking and answering "who," "what," "where," "when," "why," and "how" questions in order to explore a variety of ways to make the selected solution(s) workable and effective. The team then acts convergently developing a step-by-step plan of action. The entire process ends with the problem solvers taking action and regularly evaluating the effectiveness of the selected solution(s). New challenges that arise during implementation may be viewed as opportunities—opportunities to cycle through the CPS process again, to invent yet more new solutions, to continue to develop a creative attitude and disposition, and to hone creativity skills.

VARIATIONS OF THE OSBORN-PARNES CREATIVE PROBLEM-SOLVING (CPS) PROCESS THAT TAP STUDENTS' NATURAL CREATIVITY

This section describes three variations of the CPS process that have been field-tested in some Vermont classrooms. The variations are dedicated specifically to developing ways of enhancing meaningful participation for class members when the group includes students with a wide range of abilities and characteristics. The variations focus on the challenge of including an individual student. Although this approach was successful as a starting point, users of the variations are encouraged to consider the challenge as the meaningful inclusion of all class members in the classroom community.

The variations described in this section tap the innate creative abilities of students. Although it may be preferable to teach children a complete problem-solving process (e.g., Eberle & Stanish, 1985), less complete variations have proven to be effective for on-the-fly classroom use. CPS variations work so well because people are, by their nature, creative; the variations simply "fill in the blank" for steps missing from the creative processes each of us develops on our own. It should be emphasized that CPS and its variations are generic tools for students to use to address—individually or in groups—a range of academic, social, or personal challenges other than those described in this chapter.

Heterogeneous Grouping and Inclusion-Oriented Education: A Prime Opportunity To Engage Creative Processes

Before detailing each of the three CPS variations, we would like to return to an examination of the context in which the variations are useful. We all know educators who look at students who have differing educational needs and use that observation to justify ability-grouping within a classroom or the exclusion of some students from typical classes rather than to determine in what ways students' uniqueness can be appreciated and supported. For problem solvers with an inclusive educational orientation, placement in the classroom of students with widely differing educational needs is a naturally occurring incongruity or forced relationship. Therefore, heterogeneous, inclusive classrooms offer a prime opportunity for many creative ideas and solutions to be developed and tried. Inclusive education and creative problem solving are positively interdependent characteristics of effective schooling.

CPS and its variations work best if a creative attitude, atmosphere, and culture exist within the classroom and school community. An additional issue, therefore, in using CPS with and for children in schools, is how to promote a culture of creativity so that students eventually identify and engage creative problem-solving strategies, even when they are not asked to. The following are some strategies classroom teachers and administrators have used to establish more creative school cultures.

- Establish and use a collaborative team approach in which members of the classroom and school community work together toward common goals (Thousand & Villa, 2000).

- Be sure adults model collaborative, open, creative, and problem-solving behaviors (e.g., deferring judgment) for students.

- Involve students in making important instructional decisions.

- Give students ongoing opportunities to solve important problems in an atmosphere in which their ideas are welcomed and acted on.

- Create opportunities for students to see that there can be more than one "right answer" to any problem or question.

- Create ongoing opportunities for learning to be active and fun.

- As adults, be ready, willing, and able to learn from your students as well as from each other.

Issues in Peer-Supported Problem Solving

Because the problem-solving strategies described here engage children in problem solving for a peer, concerns arise as to whether having classmates focus on a particular student unnecessarily draws negative attention to the student or otherwise infringes on the privacy and rights of the individual. Such concerns should always be considered seriously. Peer-supported problem solving can be a powerful and effective strategy if precautions designed to protect student rights and dignity are observed. Specifically, educators should be sure to

- Obtain parental consent and permission.

- Obtain student consent. Discuss in private the possibility of peer-supported problem solving with the student who will be the focus of discussion, and seek feedback and approval before proceeding. For students with communication challenges, explore various observational strategies and augmentative approaches to determine their interest in involving peers in planning processes.

- Respect student privacy and confidentiality needs. (For some students, the type of personal information that may be revealed and used in problem solving with classmates may be nonthreatening; for others, the same information may be considered extremely sensitive and private.)

- Use CPS variations respectfully with other class members, regardless of ability. This establishes the process as a general classroom tool for addressing daily challenges and building class community.

CPS Variation 1: "One-Minute Idea Finding" or "Ask the Kids"

The simplest and quickest variation used in inclusive classrooms is to have the teacher ask the students for their ideas, using the steps presented in Table 8.4. It is remarkable how many excellent ideas students will generate when they simply are presented with information, a challenge, and a request for their ideas. To illustrate the "Ask the Kids" variation, consider the experience of a class of third graders who are preparing a mural as a culminating activity of their social studies unit on cities (Giangreco, 1993).

The teacher divided the class into four heterogeneous groups of five students each. One group included Betty, a girl with intensive educational needs. The teacher assigned each group a part of the city to paint or draw (e.g., downtown business area, residential

Table 8.4. Steps in the "One-Minute Idea Finding" or "Ask the Kids" strategy

Step 1. The teacher presents introductory lesson content or activity directions to the class. This provides the students with some information about the challenge (i.e., fact finding). They already know other general information about themselves and the classroom.

Step 2. The teacher presents a selected challenge to the class. For example, a teacher might say, "We are going to be conducting a science experiment in small groups. In what ways can we make sure Molly (a student with educational challenges) is included in the activity?" This step combines objective finding (Stage 1 of creative problem-solving [CPS] process) and problem finding (Stage 3 of CPS). An alternative phrasing that might be more inclusive and respectful would be to ask, "We are going to be conducting a science experiment in small groups. In what ways can we make sure that everyone in each group is included in the activity?"

Step 3. The teacher asks the students to offer their suggestions for 1 minute in an atmosphere of deferred judgment. This is the idea-finding stage of the CPS process. The ideas may be recorded on the chalkboard or elsewhere.

Step 4. The class selects the ideas they wish to use. This is the solution-finding stage of CPS.

Step 5. The students participate in the class activity and use their ideas. This last step represents the acceptance-finding stage of CPS.

neighborhoods, waterfront, industrial sites). Using cooperative group skills (Johnson, Johnson, & Holubec, 1993) the class had practiced throughout the year, each group was asked to reach consensus about what would be included in their part and decide who would be responsible for each part. Each group also had to coordinate with every other group so that the four pieces could be joined to make a single large mural of a city to be displayed in the hallway. The teacher told the students that they should be prepared to explain what they did within and between groups and why.

> The teacher then asked the class, "How can we make sure that Betty has ways to participate in this activity?" Mark said, "She's up there in her wheelchair and we're here on the floor with this big paper; we could get her out of her chair and bring her down here with us." Karen suggested, "It's good for Betty to have her arms moved, and I know blue is her favorite color; I could help her hold and move the paintbrush to paint the sky and water." Janet thought, "Betty could help carry our group's list of ideas to the other group so we can see how our parts will fit together." "Hey! That makes me think, maybe we could have Betty run the tape recorder so we can tape our list rather than writing it!" said Joe. (Giangreco, 1993, p. 122)

The key is to ask students for their ideas. This CPS variation is quick, easy, and effective but is limited for two reasons. First, students may come up short on ideas or, after using this strategy repeatedly, give "standard" answers rather than developing new, creative alternatives. Second, although student ideas may lead to meaningful inclusion of the classmate with disabilities, their suggestions may or may not address the individualized learning needs of the student. This represents a common problem in inclusion-oriented classrooms. A student may be welcomed and included, but individual learning objectives may not be adequately or deliberately addressed through participation in class activities. Despite its limitations, this simple variation is consistent with the notion of developing natural supports internal to a classroom and simultaneously facilitating inclusion and a culture of creativity.

CPS Variation 2: "One-Minute Idea Finding with a Fact-Finding Back-Up"

The "One-Minute Idea Finding with a Fact-Finding Back-Up" variation addresses the problem of students' getting stuck for ideas or giving standard solutions. This variation takes advantage of the relationship between facts and ideas. As previously noted, ideas can come directly from facts or idea-joggers used to consider facts from new perspectives.

The steps of this variation parallel those of the first "One-Minute Idea Finding" variation (see Table 8.4). The back-up procedure occurs at Step 3, as outlined in Table 8.5. Using the previous example about Betty's participation in the social studies mural activity, Giangreco offered the following example of how a teacher might assist students to break through to new ideas.

> The teacher could say, "Okay, what do we know about this activity?" As the students use their powers of observation to fact find, ideas might be spurred. The teacher could continue to facilitate idea finding by asking probing, idea-jogging questions, such as "What would happen if we took that fact and reversed it, cut it in half, or made it bigger?" Perhaps the teacher then would present an object as a forced relationship to stimulate the students to look for similarities, connections, analogies, or metaphors between the object and the challenge that might help solve the problem. Using these procedures, Andrea realized, "We need to get paper and paints from the supply room (fact finding); Betty could go to the supply room with us and help carry back the stuff we need and give it to the other kids" (idea finding). Marc added, "We'll be painting with a lot of different colors (fact finding). Hey, maybe Betty could use her switch to turn on a fan. Then the paint would dry faster and we could do more painting" (idea finding). (1993, p. 123)

This variation is quick and addresses the issue of what to do if students get stuck for ideas. However, it does not address the problem of inclusion-oriented classrooms mentioned previously; that is, a student being welcomed and included but individual learning objectives not being adequately or deliberately addressed.

CPS Variation 3: "Get Some Help from SAM—A Good Friend"

The third variation was once called the "Short-Focused Option" (Giangreco, 1993) because the variation, being less extensive than the full CPS process, can be completed in a short period of time (i.e., less than 10 minutes) while deliberately focusing on the individualized learning objectives of a student. The deliberate attention on learning objectives distinguishes this third variation from the two previously described. Because the Short-Focused Option is not a friendly name, one colleague jokingly suggested renaming the variation "John." Another hitchhiked, saying, "Why not just a name?" Using the forced relationship technique in combination with metaphors and connections between a person's name and the Short-Focused Option were explored. The name Sam came to mind because of a good friend named Sam. The Short-Focused Option also could be considered a good friend in helping us pursue quality, inclusive education. Thus, this variation was fondly renamed SAM, which is not an acronym for anything.

When To Call on SAM for Assistance   SAM may be called on prior to a lesson as a preplanning activity by the teacher or a team (e.g., teacher and paraprofessional, teacher

Table 8.5.   Fact finding back-up procedure for Step 3 of "One-Minute Idea Finding"

Step 3:   The teacher asks the students to offer their suggestions for 1 minute in an atmosphere of deferred judgment (idea finding). The ideas may be recorded on the chalkboard or elsewhere.

Fact finding back-up procedures

3a.   If students do not answer, then offer a limited number of ideas or offer standard ideas—the teacher stops and has the students list facts about the activity and class.

3b.   The teacher encourages the students to search for ideas that may be spurred by looking at the facts.

3c.   If an insufficient number of ideas is generated by looking at direct relationships between the facts and ideas, then idea-joggers can be applied to the facts to generate additional ideas.

and special educator). When done in advance, the classroom teacher must have an idea of how the lesson or activity will be presented, as SAM can assist in adapting the original plans to address a mismatch between the planned lesson and the needs of one or more students.

Certain types of activities (e.g., large-group discussions, small-group tasks, independent work, quizzes, labs) may be a consistent part of a classroom scene. If the activities are reoccurring formats, with variations in content, then facts generated by observations of these activities may be useful in generating adaptation ideas for a series of similar situations. This avoids continually having to reinvent the same wheel. For example, a series of options may be developed for giving a quiz, planning a lab experiment, or implementing a large-group lesson.

Examples: Double-Edged Sword   Although examples are desirable because they can illustrate a process, they are included here with some hesitation. Any time an example is used, there always is the danger that it will become a standard response. The caution, therefore, is to remember that the examples offered here are not the only solutions. They may prompt piggybacking or hitchhiking of ideas onto them, but they clearly are not the only usable ideas.

The examples embedded within the following steps are based on the student description presented next. As discussed previously, approaches that focus on the inclusive challenges of an entire class rather than an individual student may be beneficial. In such instances, knowing the learning objectives for other students is needed to use the SAM variation effectively.

Molly is 11 years old and attends fifth grade at Mountainview Middle School. Molly lives at home with her mom, dad, and younger brother. She is known for her smile and personality and is sought after for friendship by her classmates and the children who live in her neighborhood. Molly is considered stubborn and noncompliant by some people, but those who know her best view her simply as strong-willed. Molly enjoys using headphones to listen to music. She likes to go on outings with family or friends, especially shopping trips with her parents. Her favorite activities include playing on playground equipment, going swimming, playing with her dog, and sledding in the winter.

Molly seems to enjoy being around other people but does not always react as if she knows others are present. This may be due, in part, to the fact that Molly has some hearing and vision loss. Molly has some physical disabilities as well and no formal mode of communication. Thus, it is difficult to determine her sensory abilities precisely. Although Molly has been labeled "intellectually delayed," those who know her have been unwilling to accept any label that limits expectations of her abilities. As her dad pointed out, "We just can't be sure how much she understands or what her potential is, so let's proceed as if she understands everything!"

Currently, Molly communicates primarily through facial expressions (e.g., smiling, frowning). She makes some sounds to represent pleasure or discomfort that family members understand. Her parents expect few other people to understand the meaning of these vocalizations unless their meaning had been previously explained. People communicate with Molly by speaking (to take advantage of her residual hearing), using gestures, and showing her objects and pictures (to accommodate for her impairments).

Molly gets from place to place by having others push her wheelchair. Molly has limited use of her arms and needs at least partial assistance with most daily activities. Her favorite foods are tacos, fruit, and pizza; she needs to have these and other foods cut into small pieces and fed to her. Molly, her teacher, the paraprofessional who supports her, classmates, and family members receive the support of an inclusion facilitator (special educator), occupational therapist, physical therapist, speech-language pathologist, and a dual sensory impairment specialist.

Steps in Using SAM   Before getting assistance from SAM, it is important to become familiar enough with the basic principles of CPS (e.g., alternating between divergent and convergent thinking, deferring judgment, using idea-joggers) and the characteristics of problem solvers to apply them throughout the SAM process. The steps of SAM presented here parallel the six stages of the generic CPS process.

Step 1: Identify the Challenge and Develop a Challenge Statement   SAM starts by identifying a class, activity, or situation in which the needs of a particular student differ significantly from the range of educational needs of other students. For example, Molly, described previously, attends a fifth-grade science class in which much of the curricular content appears not to match her individual educational needs. Yet, there are many opportunities for Molly's educational needs to be met through existing class activities if the activities are adapted slightly or if new science activities are invented.

Next, a challenge statement is developed. Figure 8.1 offers a worksheet format for getting assistance from SAM. As Figure 8.1 illustrates, with the SAM variation of CPS, objective finding and problem finding have been combined into a single challenge statement. The challenge statement, "In what ways might we address the educational needs of (insert student name) in (insert name of class or activity) class/activity?" is applied to the student and the situation to become, for example, "In what ways might we address the educational needs of Molly in science class?"

Step 2: Identify the Facts About the Student's Educational Needs and the Class/Activity   The left-hand column of Figure 8.1 is used to list facts about the student's program and educational needs. Student facts include a brief description of priority individualized education program (IEP) goals, desired learning outcomes beyond current IEP priorities, and the general supports necessary to successfully participate in the educational program. As the left-hand column of Figure 8.2 shows, the following are Molly's priority learning outcomes identified by her support team, which includes her parents.

- Make choices when presented with options.
- Greet others.
- Follow instructions.
- React to people by displaying an observable change in behavior.
- Offer assistance to others.
- Engage in active leisure with others (e.g., play group games).
- Use adapted microswitch to activate battery-operated devices.
- Perform a classroom job with peer(s).

This is only a partial listing of all of the learning outcomes generated by Molly's support team.

In the second column of the SAM worksheet (Figures 8.1 and 8.2), observations about the class or activity may be listed. These facts should include the things the teacher and students actually do (e.g., teacher shows a videotape, class plays an educational game, students draw diagrams, groups of students build a model). To gain accurate information

OBJECTIVE-FINDING AND PROBLEM-FINDING:

In what ways might we address the educational needs of _____ (student's name) **in** _____ (class/activity) **?**

FACT-FINDING		IDEA-FINDING	
Facts about student's needs 1	Facts about class/activity 2	Direct Ideas 3	Indirect Ideas 4

continued

Figure 8.1. SAM creative problem-solving worksheet. (_Sources:_ Osborn-Parnes Creative Problem-Solving Process [Parnes, 1985, 1988, 1992, 1997]).

Figure 8.1. *(continued)*

SOLUTION-FINDING

Potential Ideas	Criteria				
	Addresses student need	Neutral or positive for students without disabilities	Likely to support valued life outcomes	Perceived as usable by users (e.g., teacher)	Other: _____ _____ _____
1.					
2.					
3.					
4.					
5.					
6.					
7.					
8.					
9.					
10.					
11.					
12.					

ACCEPTANCE-FINDING

What needs to be done?

Who is going to do it?

When is it going to be done?

How can the ideas be improved?

Where will it be done?

**OBJECTIVE-FINDING
AND PROBLEM-FINDING:**

In what ways might we address the educational needs
of ___Molly___ in ___Science___ ?
  (student's name)   (class/activity)

FACT-FINDING

Facts about student's needs[1]	Facts about class/activity (partial[2] listing)
1. Makes choices	1. Students greet each other and teacher before class bell rings.
2. Greets others	
3. Follows instructions	2. Students hand in homework to box on teacher's desk.
4. Reacts to people	
5. Offers assistance	3. Teacher tells students agenda for class.
6. Engages in active leisure	4. Teacher turns off lights and shows short video.
7. Uses "switch"	5. Teacher assigns small groups to play educational games to reinforce video.
8. Does classroom job with peer(s)	6. Teacher passes out quiz.
	7. Some students who finish early feed class fish and gerbils.

IDEA-FINDING

Direct Ideas (partial[3] listing)	Indirect Ideas (partial[4] listing)
Teach/practice greeting before bell rings.	Student chooses which game to play.
Work on active leisure (game skills) during educational games and instruction following.	Student gets opportunity to react to classmates by having "homework box" on her desk.
Caring for class pets with a peer may be a classroom job.	Student offers assistance to others and gets opportunities to react by handing out quizzes.
	Student uses switch to activate TV/VCR and listen to music when adapted quiz is completed.

continued

Figure 8.2. SAM creative problem-solving worksheets completed for Molly.

Figure 8.2. (*continued*)

SOLUTION-FINDING *(partial listing)* Potential Ideas	Criteria				
	Addresses student need	Neutral or positive for students without disabilities	Likely to support valued life outcomes	Perceived as usable by users (e.g., teacher)	Other: ___ ___ ___
① Student chooses game	+	+	+	+	
② Homework box on desk	+	+	+	+	
③ Handout quizzes	+	+	+	+	
4. Switch for lights	+	+	+	—	
5. Switch for TV/VCR	+	+	+	—	
⑥ Switch for tape player	+	+	+	+	
⑦ Greeting before class	+	+	+	+	
⑧ Cares for class pets	+	+	+	+	
⑨ Plays educational games	+	+	+	+	
10. Grades quizzes with key	+	—	—	—	
11. Record and play tape of class agenda	+	+	+	—	
12.					

ACCEPTANCE-FINDING

What needs to be done?

Who is going to do it?

When is it going to be done?

How can the ideas be improved?

Where will it be done?

about a class may require one or more members of a student's support team to observe in the classroom. Here, it is more crucial to identify what the teacher and students do than to identify the curricular content of the general education lesson. Thus, no observed event is insignificant, as any activity may prove to be useful in either prompting or being an idea for adapting a lesson. For example, what adaptations or accommodations for Molly do the following facts about science class (see Figure 8.2) bring to mind?[1]

- Before the bell rings, the teacher and students greet each other and talk informally.

- Students hand in homework to a box on the teacher's desk.

- A student turns off the lights before a film is shown.

- The teacher passes out the quiz.

Remember, when facing the challenges of curriculum overlap, the nature of activity in a classroom is critical. When classroom approaches are primarily passive and teacher directed, opportunities for meaningful participation for curriculum overlapping are more limited. When classroom approaches are active and participatory, opportunities for meaningful participation expand. A goal of creative problem solving, therefore, is to increase teachers' use of more active and participatory instructional approaches.[2]

Step 3: Generate Direct and Indirect Ideas   A "first level" of idea finding involves a systematic comparison of each fact about the student (see the first column in Figure 8.2) with each fact about the class/activity (see the second column in Figure 8.2) to look for direct, obvious relationships. Any direct ideas that arise through this comparison are recorded in the third column of Figure 8.2, labeled *Direct Ideas*. Given eight to ten facts in each of the two fact columns, the comparison process should take no more than a few minutes.

Let us compare the facts about Molly and her class listed in Figure 8.2. It is immediately apparent that there is a direct relationship between the second fact in Column 1 (i.e., greets others) and first fact in Column 2 (i.e., students greet each other and teacher before the bell rings). This class appears to offer a natural time to teach and practice greetings. Notice also that Molly's goal of participating in active leisure with peers relates directly with the teacher's planned activity for students to play educational games. Their activity is a natural opportunity for Molly to follow instructions related to game playing (e.g., rolling dice, picking up cards, moving a marker). Another direct relationship exists between Molly's need for doing a classroom job and the activity of feeding and caring for the classroom fish and gerbils. Clearly, caring for the classroom animals could be a class job done with a classmate.

Systematically comparing facts about a student's needs and classroom routines may reveal that naturally occurring opportunities for meaningful inclusion already exist, with-

---

[1]The SAM worksheet presented in Figure 8.1 is meant to offer a format to facilitate systematic exploration of possibilities at each step of the SAM process. The authors acknowledge that the SAM form has limited space and likely will be insufficient for all of the ideas that will be generated. It may be easier, therefore, to simply have the form available as a reminder of the SAM process and to write ideas as lists on blank sheets of paper. SAM users also are encouraged to modify or develop their own SAM worksheet formats and share them with the authors.

[2]Information about the student may come from any of several sources. If using the COACH assessment (Giangreco, Cloninger, & Iverson, 1998), this information may come from one of three sources: 1) the Program-at-a-Glance, 2) the Scheduling Matrix, or 3) the student's schedule. A Program-at-a-Glance lists a full set of facts regarding the content of the student's educational program. A Scheduling Matrix provides a set of facts as they relate to particular classes or major class activities. Both identify priority objectives for a student, other anticipated learning outcomes, and general supports the child's team has decided are needed for student participation in classes. SAM has been pilot-tested in environments where COACH was used to generate information about the focus student. Of course, information about a student may be generated or collected in many other ways, directly (e.g., direct observation) and indirectly (e.g., record review, interviews with the student, family members, friends, school personnel).

out the need for significant changes in routine. The number of such opportunities, however, may be insufficient for an educational experience of adequate quality; therefore, it may be necessary to invent adaptations to existing routines or invent completely new experiences.[3]

After identifying direct ideas, it may be necessary to look for indirect ideas by applying idea-joggers to facts. Following the same pattern used to find direct ideas, facts about the student and facts about the class/activity are compared while applying an idea-jogger (e.g., ask, "What would happen if we eliminated this fact or made it bigger or smaller?"). At this point, it is critical to defer judgment about the quality, usefulness, or feasibility of the ideas that result. For example, suppose the idea-jogger of reversing were applied to the facts in Figure 8.2. The teacher intends to assign small groups to play educational games to reinforce content presented in the videotape. By reversing who chooses the game from teacher to student, an idea is generated for Molly to work on choice making—a priority goal for her (see Column 4 of Figure 8.2).

Suppose the idea-jogger of rearranging were applied to Molly's goal of reacting to the presence of other people and the fact that, in this science class, students hand in homework by placing it in a box on the teacher's desk. Rearranging the place where homework is turned in so that the homework box is on Molly's desk would create as many opportunities for interaction as there are students in the class.

Combining rearranging with the idea-jogger of minimizing/making smaller and applying them to the fact that the science teacher passes out quizzes and Molly needs practice reacting to and offering assistance to others could lead to the indirect idea of having Molly and a classmate, rather than the teacher, pass out quizzes. To keep the pace of classroom activities typical, the task could be made smaller so that Molly hands out five quizzes in the same time that her partner hands out 20. Although all of the ideas just described may seem small, they do match the student's identified needs.

Step 4: Evaluate Ideas and Choose Solutions

Step 4 involves solution finding and convergent thinking. Here, direct and indirect ideas are evaluated based on a set of criteria. The four criteria on the SAM worksheet (see Figures 8.1 and 8.2) are offered as starting points for evaluating ideas. Ideas are listed in abbreviated form in the left-hand column of the worksheet. Then, each idea is judged according to the selected criteria. Using the four criteria included on the worksheet, one may ask

- Does this idea address an identified student need?

- Is the idea positive or at least neutral in terms of likely impact on students without disabilities?

- Is the idea likely to yield valued life outcomes (e.g., friendships and affiliations; access to meaningful places and activities; choice and control that matches a person's age, health, and safety)?

- Is the idea perceived as feasible and meaningful by the user (e.g., the teacher)?

As already noted, the process of applying criteria to potential ideas is intended to assist decision making. Criteria, therefore, must match the situation and be adjusted, replaced, eliminated, or otherwise changed to match the unique characteristics of a situation. Items may be rated using whatever method is preferred and makes sense, as long as preferred solutions have been selected by the end of this step.

---

[3]Although the two fact-finding and idea-finding steps are presented here in a linear, sequential fashion, these authors have found shifting attention back and forth between the two sets of facts to be a powerful technique for prompting ideas for adaptations. For example, once educational needs are listed, each new class/activity fact can be compared with the needs to see if an idea is immediately spurred. These ideas should be recorded as they are generated.

Table 8.6. Implications of using the Osborn-Parnes Creative Problem-Solving (CPS) process for students with and without disabilities

CPS engages students in the solution of real-life problems and challenges, which are an essential characteristic of effective education (Dewey, 1998).

CPS encourages students to believe they can solve problems, either independently or with the support of others in the class.

CPS offers students of low academic achievement levels the opportunity to assist in solving relevant challenges faced by them or their classmates and establishes all students as valued contributors.

CPS offers opportunities for students to be included in general class activities in ways that meet their individualized educational needs.

CPS offers opportunities for students to participate in the design of their own instruction.

CPS offers opportunities for students to learn and practice problem-solving skills on an ongoing basis to address relevant challenges.

The collaborative, nonjudgmental, and action-oriented aspects of CPS encourage community building among classmates when the process is used to address challenges of concern to the group.

CPS encourages and reinforces many desirable academic and affective skills (e.g., observation, analysis, evaluation, perspective taking, building on another's ideas, synthesizing ideas).

Step 5: Refine Ideas To Develop and Carry Out an Action Plan Once solutions have been selected, they must be refined. Idea-joggers continue to be helpful in accomplishing this end. For example, suppose that a direct idea was generated about playing an educational game as an accommodation for Molly. When looking carefully at the nature of the game, Molly's physical characteristics likely would prompt the question, "What if the game parts were bigger?" This type of simple adaptation might allow Molly to participate, at least partially, with game materials. The "who," "what," "where," "when," "why," and "how" questions facilitate the development and delivery of a CPS action plan. As ideas are implemented, CPS users must remember to be alert to new facts and new ways to make the familiar strange. Also, it should be noted how repeatedly cycling through the SAM and other CPS variations develops a creative attitude and competence.

EDUCATIONAL IMPLICATIONS OF USING THE OSBORN-PARNES CREATIVE PROBLEM-SOLVING (CPS) PROCESS

This chapter opened with the proposition that inclusive educational arrangements are desired alternatives to more exclusionary traditional approaches. The CPS process and its variations are offered as a set of procedures for empowering teams to meet the challenge of instructing heterogeneous groups of learners.

There are many implications of mastering and using CPS and its variations, particularly in the education of students who otherwise might be excluded from the general education opportunities. Table 8.6 offers anticipated benefits for students with disabilities and

Table 8.7. Implications for professionals working with students in heterogeneous groups

The Osborn-Parnes Creative Problem-Solving (CPS) process encourages teachers to be open to the possibility that there is more than one "right" answer.

CPS encourages teachers to provide active, problem-solving learning experiences that educational leaders have advised are essential as we begin the 21st century.

CPS encourages teachers to be ongoing learners and to open themselves to learn from the children in their classes.

CPS provides a method for distributing the pressures of instructional accommodations in inclusive classrooms across a wider group of problem solvers.

CPS used by teachers can enhance their capacity to teach all children by recognizing existing options for teaching heterogeneous groups, adapting other existing options, and inventing new options.

CPS encourages teachers to design interesting, active approaches to education that account for student input and result in motivating learning experiences.

their peers without disabilities. Table 8.7 suggests positive outcomes educators should expect when they use the problem-solving methods described in this chapter.

Taking action is the first, middle, and culminating step for any problem solver, including those of us who are interested in excellence, excitement, and equity in education. We would do well, therefore, to follow the advice of Charles Kettering to "keep on going and chances are you will stumble on something, perhaps when you least expect it. I have never heard of anyone stumbling on something sitting down" (as cited in Parnes, 1988, p. 89). The creative problem-solving strategies offered in this chapter should help us to keep on going, for as Cheyette noted, "creativity is converting wishful thinking into willful doing" (as cited in Parnes, 1988, p. 105).

REFERENCES

Bauer, A.M., & Shea, T.M. (1999). *Inclusion 101: How to teach all learners.* Baltimore: Paul H. Brookes Publishing Co.

Brown, L., Ford, A., Nisbet, J., Sweet, M., Donnellan, A., & Gruenewald, L. (1983). Opportunities available when severely handicapped students attend chronological age appropriate regular schools. *Journal of The Association for Persons with Severe Handicaps, 8,* 16–24.

Campbell, C., Campbell, S., Collicott, J., Perner, D., & Stone, J. (1988). Individualized instruction. *Education New Brunswick—Journal Education, 3,* 17–20.

Collicott, J. (1991). Implementing multi-level instruction: Strategies for classroom teachers. In G. Porter & D. Richler (Eds.), *Changing Canadian schools: Perspectives on disability and inclusion* (pp. 191–218). Ottawa, Ontario, Canada: The Roeher Institute.

Eberle, B., & Stanish, B. (1985). *CPS for kids: A resource book for teaching creative problem-solving to children.* East Aurora, NY: D.O.K. Publishing.

Edmonds, R. (1979). Some schools work and more can. *Social Policy, 9*(5), 25–29.

Firestien, R. (1989). *Why didn't I think of that? A personal and professional guide to better ideas and decision making.* East Aurora, NY: D.O.K. Publishing.

Giangreco, M.F. (1992). Curriculum in inclusion-oriented schools: Trends, issues, challenges, and potential solutions. In S. Stainback & W. Stainback (Eds.), *Curriculum considerations in inclusive classrooms: Facilitating learning for all students* (pp. 239–263). Baltimore: Paul H. Brookes Publishing Co.

Giangreco, M.F. (1993). Using creative problem solving methods to include students with severe disabilities in general education classroom activities. *Journal of Educational and Psychological Consultation, 4,* 113–135.

Giangreco, M.F., Cloninger, C.J., & Iverson, V.S. (1998). *Choosing outcomes and accommodations for children (COACH): A guide for educational planning for students with disabilities* (2nd ed.). Baltimore: Paul H. Brookes Publishing Co.

Giangreco, M.F., & Meyer, L.H. (1988). Expanding service delivery options in regular schools and classrooms for students with severe disabilities. In J.L. Graden, J.E. Zins, & M.J. Curtis (Eds.), *Alternative educational delivery systems: Enhancing instructional options for all students* (pp. 241–267). Washington, DC: National Association of School Psychologists.

Giangreco, M.F., & Putnam, J.W. (1991). Supporting the education of students with severe disabilities in regular education environments. In L.H. Meyer, C.A. Peck, & L. Brown (Eds.), *Critical issues in the lives of people with severe disabilities* (pp. 245–270). Baltimore: Paul H. Brookes Publishing Co.

Gordon, W.J.J. (1987). *The new art of the possible: The basic course in synectics.* Cambridge, MA: Porpoise.

Gordon, W.J.J., & Poze, T. (1979). *The metaphorical way of learning and knowing.* Cambridge, MA: SES Associates.

Hunt, P., & Goetz, L. (1997). Research on inclusive educational programs, practices, and outcomes for students with severe disabilities. *Journal of Special Education, 31*(1), 3–29.

Johnson, D.W., Johnson, R.T., & Holubec, E.J. (1993). *Circles of learning: Cooperation in the classroom* (4th ed.). Edina, MN: Interaction Book Company.

Lipsky, D.K., & Gartner, A. (Eds.). (1997). *Inclusion and school reform: Transforming America's schools.* Baltimore: Paul H. Brookes Publishing Co.

McGregor, G., & Vogelsberg, R.T. (1998). *Inclusive schooling practices: Pedagogical and research foundations: A synthesis of the literature that informs best practices about inclusive schooling.* Baltimore: Paul H. Brookes Publishing Co.

Osborn, A.F. (1993). *Applied imagination: Principles and procedures of creative problem-solving* (3rd ed.). Buffalo, NY: Creative Education Foundation Press. (Original work published 1953)

Parnes, S.J. (1985). *A facilitating style of leadership*. Buffalo, NY: Bearly Limited.

Parnes, S.J. (1988). *Visionizing: State-of-the-art processes for encouraging innovative excellence*. East Aurora, NY: D.O.K. Publishing.

Parnes, S.J. (1992). *Source book for creative problem-solving: A fifty year digest of proven innovation processes*. Buffalo, NY: Creative Education Foundation Press.

Parnes, S.J. (1997). *Optimize the magic of your mind*. Buffalo, NY: Creative Education Foundation Press.

Schnorr, R. (1990). "Peter? He comes and he goes . . .": First-graders' perspectives on a part-time mainstream student. *Journal of The Association for Persons with Severe Handicaps, 15*, 231–240.

Stainback, S., & Stainback, W. (1990). Inclusive schooling. In W. Stainback & S. Stainback (Eds.), *Support networks for inclusive schooling: Interdependent integrated education* (pp. 3–23). Baltimore: Paul H. Brookes Publishing Co.

Stainback, S., & Stainback, W. (Eds.). (1996). *Inclusion: A guide for educators*. Baltimore: Paul H. Brookes Publishing Co.

Thousand, J.S., & Villa, R.A. (2000). Collaborative teams: A powerful tool in school restructuring. In R.A. Villa & J.S. Thousand (Eds.), *Restructuring for caring and effective education: Piecing the puzzle together* (2nd ed., pp. 254–291). Baltimore: Paul H. Brookes Publishing Co.

Villa, R.A., & Thousand, J.S. (1995). *Creating an inclusive school*. Alexandria, VA: Association for Supervision and Curriculum Development.

Webb, J. [Producer and Director]. (1952–1959/1967–1971). *Dragnet* [Television series]. Los Angeles: Mark VII.m.

Supporting Students with Troubling Behavior

Richard A. Villa
Jonathan Udis
Jacqueline S. Thousand

In America they have begun to talk of troubled children as "throw-away" children. Who can be less fortunate than those who are thrown away (Thom Garfat, as cited in Brendtro, Brokenleg, & Van Bockern, 1990, p. 12)?

Mariah

Mariah has spent the past 3 weeks in the psychiatric ward of her local community hospital. She is 16 years old and lives with her father and 14-year-old sister. Prior to her hospitalization, Mariah had begun "experimenting" with drugs and alcohol. Her father is concerned that Mariah's substance use may have turned to substance abuse and may have been a catalyst for her hospitalization. There is a history of alcoholism in their family. Last year, Mariah's mother died of injuries sustained when driving a car while intoxicated. Teachers describe Mariah as a "good, solid B student"; they were shocked to learn of her hospitalization. While in the psychiatric ward, she revealed that her father had sexually abused her. Mariah was hospitalized for a nearly successful suicide attempt.

Billy

"F— you! You can't make me do it," Billy yelled at his eighth-grade social studies teacher for the fourth time this week as he threw a chair toward the corner of the room and stormed out of the room. Billy lives with his parents and two sisters. He usually comes to school dressed in dirty clothes and occasionally smells of urine. Although he often comes to school late, he rarely misses a day. Billy reads at a third-grade level; math is his area of strength. Billy's guidance counselor states that he has no "real friends." A review of discipline records reveals that Billy spends more than 50% of his time in the in-school suspension room or with the guidance counselor or the assistant principal.

Ricardo

Ricardo enrolled as a new student on the second day of the school year. Because his family has moved seven times in the past year, no records of his past schooling have been located.

For the first 6 weeks of school, Ricardo would walk into his fourth-grade classroom, put his head on his desk, and sleep. Whenever the teacher was able to get Ricardo to communicate, he would speak in a whisper and turn his eyes to the floor. Despite repeated efforts by school personnel to contact Ricardo's parents by telephone, letters, and home visits, contact has yet to be made with an adult in his home. In mid-October Ricardo stopped coming to school.

CHILDREN WHO ARE TROUBLED OR TROUBLING—WHO ARE THEY?

Mariah, Billy, and Ricardo—we all know children like them. For a variety of administrative, fiscal, legal, educational, and theoretical reasons, many different labels (and accompanying definitions) have been developed and attached to students who appear troubled or troubling in school. Labels include emotionally disturbed, disruptive, delinquent, acting out, unmanageable, conduct disordered, socially maladjusted, antisocial, noncompliant, and serious behavior problem (Hobbs, 1982). Regardless of the origins of these labels and definitions, they all have an extraordinary impact on the children to whom they are applied.

> Once a particular verbal commitment has been made in describing a child or an adolescent, there follows inexorably a chain of actions bent to institutional forms. . . . Thus, it makes a big difference how one talks about a child or an adolescent and what encompassing rubrics one uses to define his [or her] status. (Hobbs, 1982, p. 23)

At the local school level, what gets labeled as a serious behavior problem or a significant emotional disturbance varies from one school to the next and from class to class. Such variability is contingent on a number of factors, including

- Federal, state, and local policies such as "zero tolerance" with respect to weapons, drugs, tobacco, alcohol, and school disruptions

- Tendencies to respond to children's behavioral, social, or emotional coping patterns with medicalization (e.g., assigning psychologically or biologically based labels such as attention-deficit/hyperactivity disorder [ADHD], oppositional defiant disorder [ODD], attachment disorder, or Asperger syndrome) and the use of drugs rather than relationship-inspired teaching and the creation of loving, disciplined, and engaging relationships (Breggin, 2000)

- Local perceptions of what is "deviant"

- Past successes (or failures) with students whose needs go beyond what is viewed as a school's standard discipline, guidance, or instructional responsibility or capacity

Members of a school community with little experience individualizing for any particular student might view and label Mariah, Billy, and Ricardo as candidates for exclusion, expulsion, or restrictive placement outside of general education. Another school, with extensive experience educating students with a broad range of needs, might view them as three of many students with unique needs that must be met. This phenomenon of "relativity," combined with the chain of often negative, institutionalized reactions that result when a label is attached to a child, has led us to be very deliberate about the terms we use. Therefore, throughout this chapter, we use terms such as *children who are troubled or troubling, students who are challenged or challenging, children who demonstrate high rates of rule-violating behavior, students who are easily frustrated,* or *students who have acquired nonadaptive ways of relating* to represent Mariah, Billy, and Ricardo and other students who, for whatever reason, are perceived as the "most challenging" to the current school organizational structure or culture.

HOW MANY CHILDREN ARE TROUBLED OR TROUBLING?

How many of our children are troubled or troubling to their teachers, community, or family? This question is difficult to answer, but consider the following:

- Kauffman (2001) noted that the prevalence data vary widely—from 0.5% to 20% of school-age students—depending on the method of counting or "guesstimation."

- Knitzer, Steinberg, and Bleisch (1990) speculated that the national rate of less than 1% of the school population represents only one third to one half of the anticipated prevalence of children identified as emotionally/behaviorally disordered.

- Fink and Janssen (1992) noted that in 1989 almost 2 million reports of child abuse and neglect officially were filed and that conservative estimates suggest two or three times this number of youth actually are systematically abused. Their review of the literature demonstrated that systematic abuse leads to significant dysfunction in emotional, developmental, and intellectual capacities and at-risk psychological, medical, motivational, academic, and legal conditions. The difficulties experienced by maltreated youth resemble those usually associated with youth that are labeled behaviorally or emotionally disabled.

- Curwin and Mendler (1997) noted the following trends:

  1. There are more disruptive students than ever before and the rate is increasing.

  2. Children are becoming more disruptive at earlier ages.

  3. Children are more violent.

  4. Many children lack any sense of caring or remorse.

  5. Students are increasingly described by those who teach them as aggressive and hostile.

- Kunc observed that "teen-age suicide is increasing at an exponential rate and has now become the second leading cause of adolescent death. Extreme violence, drug dependency, gangs, anorexia nervosa, and depression among students have risen to the point that these problems now are perceived almost as an expected part of high school culture" (1992, p. 37).

- Students identified as having a behavior or emotional disability have one of the lowest rates of promotion as well as one of the highest rates of dropout and exit prior to graduation (Leone, McLaughlin, & Meisel, 1992).

- It has become one of the realities of life that adults who work in schools will be called on to deal with children's anger. In our modern age, a growing number of students come to school from homes that fail to foster positive values. The effects of abuse, neglect, homelessness, poverty, and ignorance exert a powerful effect on the emotional health and well being of a growing number of students. For those more materially fortunate youngsters, our hurried society all too often short-changes them of the family-based nurturing and guidance that was available to previous generations (Romaneck, 2000).

What does the previous information suggest about the emotional turmoil, stress, and pre-occupations our children bring with them when they walk through a school's doors? What does it suggest about how their life circumstances affect their behavior, their interactions with others, and their capacity to learn?

WHERE ARE THE CHILDREN WHO ARE TROUBLED OR TROUBLING BEING EDUCATED?

In the 21st century, American public schools primarily educate children identified as "behaviorally disordered" in self-contained, separate classrooms (Leone et al., 1992). In descending order of frequency, resource rooms, special schools, itinerant support, out-of-district placements, and homebound instruction are also used (Morgan, 1990). With the exception of itinerant support in general classrooms, the common characteristics of these service options is that they immerse children in a community and culture of disturbance and dysfunction in which students have limited access to pro-social models and in which they are given the message that they do not belong with their peers (Kunc, 2000). Yet, as Kunc emphasized, "belonging—having a social context—is requisite for the development of self-esteem and self-confidence" (p. 83). The predicted consequences of not belonging combined with lackluster efficacy data regarding segregated special education programs (Lipsky & Gartner, 1997; Villa & Thousand, 2000) have convinced us that educators have a professional and social responsibility to discover, invent, and share with others successful strategies for addressing the needs of troubled or troubling children in integrated general education and community environments. In our view, what is needed in schools is not *zero tolerance* but rather *zero indifference* to the wide range of behaviors that make schools uncomfortable and sometimes unsafe environments for students and staff (Skiba & Peterson, 1999; Stein, 2000). Furthermore, it is considerably more cost effective to individualize services for a child with severely maladjusted behavior in the community than to place the child in a segregated residential program, and the services provided are considered to be "better" (Burchard & Clarke, 1990).

RATIONALE AND OBJECTIVES

This chapter presents an alternative to a continuum of placement conceptualization and approach to providing support and services for children who are troubled or troubling. The alternative has been described as a "constellation of services" (Nevin, Villa, & Thousand, 1992, p. 44) approach in which supports and services are brought to the child rather than the child's being taken to the services. The constellation is an assemblage of approaches and strategies that represent current research and writing concerning discipline, social skills, and the promotion of responsibility and that which has been discovered when tra-

Table 9.1. Assumptions and beliefs underlying the constellation of resources, supports, and services

Each child is an individual, and no matter what we do, our foremost responsibilities are to cause no harm to the child and to help the child meet his or her need to belong in a valued community (Donnellan, 2000; Knitzer et al., 1990; Van Bockern, Brendtro, & Brokenleg, 2000).

All behavior is an attempt to communicate and satisfy basic human needs (Glasser, 1986; Maslow, 1970).

Students and their families are central to solution-finding processes; the responsibility of educators is to work with and for students and their families rather than blame them for their troubles.

Interagency collaboration promotes a unified community response that is more likely to meet the individual needs of children, their families, and the school personnel who work with and for them.

Creative outcomes result from collaborative teaming and creative problem solving among people committed to establishing caring and effective communities of learners.

Table 9.2. Student Bill of Rights

Students have the right to experience, and schools have a responsibility to ensure

- Effective instruction
- Personalized accommodations
- A motivating school climate in which basic human needs are met and students are provided supports for dealing with the societal stresses of early 21st-century life

ditional strategies have failed. The constellation further reflects the assumptions and beliefs presented in Table 9.1. Before describing the constellation, however, we offer a "Student Bill of Rights" that reminds us of the purpose of schooling and our responsibility as educators.

Student Bill of Rights

The characteristics of schooling described in this section are intended to create, promote, and/or sustain a caring, responsive, and quality learning environment. Collectively, they serve as a keystone to effectively supporting and serving troubled or troubling learners and making school a desirable and motivating place for all students. We conceptualize this collection of school characteristics as the Student Bill of Rights, which is represented in Table 9.2. A brief explanation of these rights follows.

Effective Instruction and Personalized Accommodations Ron Edmonds (1979) noted that the field of education has the knowledge and tools to enable any school to be effective. Specifically, he wrote, "We can, whenever and wherever we choose, successfully teach all children whose schooling is of interest to us; . . . we already know more than we need to do that" (p. 22). Edmonds' statement is even truer today as more is learned about quality instruction and meaningful accommodations. When children are active participants in developmentally appropriate activities, they are less likely to present troubling behaviors. They may still be troubled but not troubling. With the presence of effective instruction and meaningful accommodations for individual differences, it is less likely that teachers will need to resort to emotional responses and interventions that are based on punishment, control, conformity, and obedience (e.g., humiliation, public sarcasm, detention, demerits, suspension, expulsion).

What are the characteristics of effective instruction? At a minimum, effective instruction involves high rates of active student involvement, student use of higher level reasoning skills, and discovery and constructivist learning approaches. The literature is rich with descriptions of practices that promote effective instruction. Among the highly promoted and researched practices are 1) cooperative group learning (see Section I); 2) differentiated instruction (Tomlinson, 1995, 1999); 3) authentic assessment (Perrone, 1991); 4) multiple intelligences theory (Armstrong, 2000); and 5) social and emotional learning (Elias et al., 1997). For a more in-depth description of research-based strategies that promote student achievement, the reader is referred to Marzano, Pickering, and Pollock (2001). Of course, the foundations of all effective instruction are positive teacher–student relationships and teacher reflection and decision making for the purpose of matching task demands and learner characteristics.

A Motivating School Climate Children who are troubled or troubling often do not seem motivated or are unable to change their interpersonal behaviors or their relationship with school or learning. Different theorists (e.g., Bandura, 1977; Brendtro et al., 1990; Glasser, 1975, 1986, 1998; Johnson & Johnson, 1991; Maslow, 1970; Skinner, 1974) offer different conceptualizations of motivation—how to enhance learner interest in engaging in learning versus troubling behaviors. Educators are more likely to succeed in motivating students if they take an eclectic, divergent approach to understanding and enhancing student motivation. What this requires is that all educators study as much as they can about theory and practice regarding human motivation and use that knowledge to 1) increase students' capacity to sustain problem-solving efforts in the face of frustration and 2) entice students to engage in the acquisition of knowledge and skills.

Adversity at home and in the community always has affected some or many of the children attending school; there always have been troubled and troubling youth. However, the number and intensity of stressors of early 21st-century life (e.g., poverty, neglect, abuse, divorce, lack of adequate health care, lack of family or informal community support networks) have increased so that more and more students come to school with their ability and motivation to learn negatively affected. To create a motivating school climate for these students, educators must acknowledge and attempt to address stressors by offering a variety of supports (e.g., a breakfast program, free lunch, mental health and other human services available as on-campus school support services), including the constellation of resources, responses, and services described in the remainder of this chapter. This, of course, makes the job of educator more complex, broadening it to include the issues of safety, health, and the psychological well-being of children.

A CONSTELLATION OF RESOURCES, RESPONSES, AND SERVICES

Suppose a school community made a commitment to actualize the Student Bill of Rights presented in Table 9.2 and to meet the needs of all students, including those who are troubled or troubling. To fulfill this commitment, members of the school community must be able to answer "yes" to at least the following three questions:

1. Are the adults of the school equipped and empowered to deliver effective instruction, personalize accommodations for learners, and create a motivating school climate?

2. Do students of the school community know and understand their Student Bill of Rights?

3. Are students empowered to exercise their rights and the responsibilities that accompany these rights?

What are your responses to these three questions? In our experience, in even the most committed schools, many educators and students answer "no" to at least one of these questions. The remainder of this chapter offers a constellation of resources, responses, and services for equipping and empowering educators and students to change their answers from "no" to "yes." The constellation includes strategies for 1) promoting student responsibility, 2) supporting and empowering students, 3) involving and supporting families, 4) redefining the role of adults in the school, and 5) reconceptualizing "schooling" and the student's day. Table 9.3 outlines the strategies of the constellation that are detailed in the text that follows.

Teaching Students Responsibility

Educators recognize that student mastery of content areas (e.g., language arts, mathematics, science) specified in most schools' scope and sequence frameworks requires continuous and complex instruction during a period of 10–12 years. When students fail to learn new skills or concepts, we respond by reteaching the material, providing additional or dif-

Table 9.3.   A constellation of resources and strategies for serving troubled or troubling learners

Strategies for promoting student responsibility
   Schoolwide discipline system
   Social skills training to promote social and emotional responsibility, competence, and self-determination
   Teaching students anger management and impulse control techniques
   Setting limits to ensure safety

Strategies for involving, empowering, and promoting self-determination
   Students as instructors
   Students as advocates
   Students as decision makers

Strategies for involving, supporting, and empowering family members
   Home–school partnerships
   The individualized education program (IEP) planning process
   Core teams for individual students
   Intensive family-based wraparound services
   Local and state-level interagency collaboration

Redefining the role of the adults
   Collaborative planning for the development of accommodations
   Teaching teams of educators, community members, and students
   Awareness training for all staff
   Mentors and advisors to students
   Adult advocates for students
   Individual support personnel for students

Rethinking the traditional paradigm of schooling and the student's day
   "Jumping the tracks"
   Creative placements
   Shortened days
   Altered school weeks and years

ferent types of supports, and making accommodations. We respond with a "teaching response" to a student's inability to learn material. Yet, for the content area known as "responsibility," the teaching of patterns of behavior and habits of mind representative of "responsible" behavior often is relegated to "add on" or "quick fix" instructional methods (e.g., seeing the guidance counselor, attending a 6-week social skills group, making an oral or a written plan, talking about it after school). Furthermore, when a student demonstrates a lack of responsibility (frequently in the form of rule-violating behavior such as tardiness, verbal aggression, rudeness, or failure to follow instructions), we (the adults of the school) often "take the behavior personally" and respond with an emotional, punishing response rather than an emotionally neutral teaching response. The teaching of responsibility is no less demanding a task than the teaching of any other curriculum area; it requires careful thought and reflection, complex instruction starting at the earliest ages and continuing throughout the school years, and patience.

It is within the context of a caring relationship that the concept of responsibility acquires meaning. Thus, a condition for promoting the learning of responsibility is that students perceive that someone in the school community cares about them. In order to facilitate students' acquisition of responsible values, attitudes, and behaviors, educators must engage in positive, systematic approaches for developing relationships with students. Relationships may be promoted by teachers acknowledging and validating students' achievement, progress, or goal attainment. With students who are troubled or troubling, it is particularly important to demonstrate caring, concern, and support by teaching responsibility through 1) the establishment of a schoolwide discipline system that promotes the learning of responsibility, 2) direct instruction of pro-social communication skills, 3) nurturance of social and emotional competency and self-determination, 4) direct instruction of anger management and impulse control techniques, and 5) the setting of limits to ensure safety.

A Schoolwide Disciplinary System that Promotes Responsibility Many disciplinary systems often fail for some of the reasons cited in Table 9.4. We conceptualize an effective disciplinary system as a pyramid (see Figure 9.1). The strength of the pyramid is its base, in which the focus is on developing a classroom climate of caring and interdependence through class meetings, use of cooperative learning as a primary instructional approach, establishment of predictable routines and rituals, and the use of a range of quick and nonintrusive recovery responses to classroom distractions and disruptions. The next level of the pyramid represents the "somewhere else"—a planning room, a time away thinking space, problem solving with a counselor or teacher advisor—where students can go when they and/or their teachers are unable or unwilling to resolve a conflict or issue at the classroom level. Here, the student is given the opportunity to calm down and immediately engage in social problem solving (under adult guidance), with the goal being a quick return to the classroom. The pinnacle of the pyramid involves assembling a group of caring individuals who collaborate and engage in creative problem solving to develop an effective support plan that will result in a long-term behavioral change for a student.

Proactive discipline systems are those that promote positive behavior and respond to troubling (rule-violating) behavior in ways that teach the relationship between a behavior and its consequence as well as alternative ways of getting needs met (Curwin & Mendler, 1999; Glasser, 1986). Such systems are based on a solid understanding of the differences between discipline and punishment. They recognize that responsibility is learned over a period of time and only with opportunities for students to make meaningful choices and to make mistakes without retribution. Although safety and orderliness are desired outcomes of a disciplinary system, obedience and compliance are not, as they fail to instill or teach ownership for one's own behavior (i.e., responsibility). Proactive disciplinary models acknowledge that the adults of the school have a responsibility to control the learning environment but not to control the students. Instead, students are expected and supported to acquire the coping strategies to control themselves.

Table 9.4. Why do many disciplinary policies and systems often fail?

1. There is an expectation that *rules* change behavior, when they do not. *Action* changes behavior.
2. There is a belief that somewhere there is a commonly agreed on view of unacceptable behavior as well as a common set of consequences that, if only universally and equally applied, would always be effective.
3. Roles and responsibilities are not clearly defined or shared.
4. People believe the myth that consequences by themselves change behavior rather than appreciating that chronic misbehavior almost always is an attempt to communicate a need for mastery, belonging, generosity, power and control, independence, attention, and so forth. Without an understanding of the communicative intent of a behavior, it is unlikely that consequences alone will be effective in promoting long-term behavior change.
5. Many disciplinary systems and procedures are based on one or more of the following (often incorrect) assumptions:
   - Students continually misbehave because they want to or think they can get away with it.
   - Students continually misbehave because the system is not tough enough.
   - Students continually misbehave because of poor parenting, poverty, and other life circumstances.
   - Students continually misbehave because they do not want to learn.
   - Students continually misbehave in order to drive adults crazy.

From Bennett, B., & Smilanich, P. (1994). *Classroom management: A thinking and caring approach.* Toronto: Bookation Inc.; and Udis, J. (April, 2001). *Exchanging dissonance for harmony: Promoting the social and emotional competence of youth at risk.* Bedford, New Hampshire: ASCD 2000–2001 Conference Series; adapted by permission.

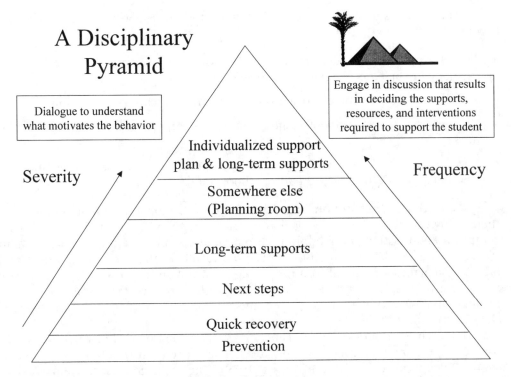

Figure 9.1.　A conceptualization for effective disciplinary systems.

     With responsibility-based models of discipline, responses to rule-violating behavior are congruent with the goals of the system and strive to ensure that each student is treated "fairly" but not necessarily "equally" (Curwin & Mendler, 1988, p. 68). Although classroom and schoolwide rules may be the same for everyone, responses to rule violations are individualized. They are based on the unique characteristics of the student and the situation and not on predetermined, arbitrarily established, and rigidly enforced "if–then" consequences (e.g., 10 absences equals a grade of *F* in the missed classes, three tardies equals a detention). Arbitrary consequences are few. Instead, creative disciplinary interventions and the establishment of consequences are guided by the questions, "What will the student learn?" and "How will responsibility be promoted?"

     Responsibility-based models of discipline acknowledge that conflict is a natural and ongoing part of human existence. Such models take teachers and administrators out of the traditional role of police officer and place them in the role of facilitator. Behavior is treated as contextual. Therefore, responses to either rule-following or rule-violating behavior are dependent on a variety of factors, such as the time of day, the activity during which the behavior occurred, the frequency and severity of the behavior, and the number of people demonstrating the behavior. Reminders, warnings, cues and self-monitoring techniques, positive practice, restitution, oral or written plans, behavioral contracts, redirection, prompts, direct teaching of interpersonal behaviors, "sit and watch" (being asked to briefly sit and watch classmates who model acceptable behavior), and "time out" from positive reinforcement are all potential responses to rule-violating behavior that, when delivered in a thoughtful, calm, and predictable manner, teach students instead of punishing them (Curwin & Mendler, 1988; Glasser, 1986; Jackson, Jackson, & Monroe, 1983). A caution here is that removal of reinforcement may be a traumatic experience, especially for youth who have been victimized by being locked up or whose pattern of response to abuse is to escape from reality through fantasy (Fink & Janssen, 1992).

Perhaps most important to the promotion of student responsibility is an acknowledgment that

- The development of student responsibility should be primarily concerned with teaching young people how to have their needs met

- The development of student responsibility is part of a school's curriculum

- The development of student responsibility is as important as any other curriculum area

- The development of student responsibility requires modeling, coaching, and ongoing thought and reflection on the part of school staff

Social Skills Instruction   Students who are troubled or troubling often express their thoughts and feelings in ways that violate either explicit or implicit rules governing communication within the school environment (e.g., no swearing, no name calling of teachers). Rule-violating communication often results in the student "getting into trouble"; it also makes it more difficult for people to "hear" and understand what the student needs or is requesting. Teaching children and youth how to communicate their thoughts, feelings, and needs in ways that allow adults and peers to hear them is the goal of social skills instruction (Kahler, 1988).

The teaching of pro-social skills encompasses a wide range of instructional strategies that include behavioral, cognitive, and affective approaches (e.g., Elias et al., 1997; Goldstein, 1998a; Jackson et al., 1983; Vernon, 1989). One of the greatest challenges associated with social skill instruction is student generalization of learned skills to real-life situations—particularly stressful situations. Some strategies for promoting generalization include

- Teaching social skills in heterogeneous "general classrooms" versus "pull-out" situations

- Direct teaching of social skills in association with intentional cooperative group learning structures (Johnson & Johnson, 1991)

- Frequent, thoughtful teacher feedback and group processing of students' social skills performance

- Frequent recognition, within classrooms and schoolwide, of student effort and skill mastery

- Opportunities for practice of social skills in real-life community situations

- Social skills newsletters for parents and community members

- Use of social skills in cross-age and same-age partner learning/peer tutoring structures

- Bulletin boards and assemblies that remind students of the importance of social skills to school climate

Teaching Students Anger Management and Impulse Control Strategies   Many students labeled troubled or troubling are characterized as impulsive or having difficulty managing their anger. It is not adequate or satisfactory to simply request, tell, or remind students to "stop and think" prior to acting. Instead, to promote students' control over anger and impulsiveness, schools must offer direct, quality instruction in anger management and impulse control strategies. Anger management strategies often include

- Teaching students to recognize and monitor the dimensions and cycle of anger—the external triggers (e.g., someone says or does something you do not like), the internal triggers (e.g., internal dialogue about the external trigger such as, "That's not fair. I'll get her!"), and physiological signals of anger (e.g., sweaty palms, increased heartbeat)

- Teaching students a series of anger-reducing techniques, such as pleasant images, deep breathing, counting strategies, relaxation strategies, and new internal dialogue scripts

- Strategies for self-assessment, self-monitoring, and self-reinforcement through hassle logs and journals (Goldstein, 1998b)

Classroom teachers may promote tentativeness and impulse control by offering choices on how to approach tasks, teaching and encouraging self-correcting procedures, instituting a 3- to 5-second "wait time" between a teacher asking a question and calling on a student to provide an answer, using informal cooperative structures (e.g., think-pair-share, round robin format), teaching the difference between open- and closed-ended tasks and offering opportunities to do both, implementing long-term projects, identifying and rewarding different levels of performance, and asking students to think and teach out loud.

Behavioral, cognitive, and affective instructional strategies have been employed, often in combination, to assist students to develop impulse and anger control. For instance, Goldstein (1998a) also took a cognitive-behavioral approach in *The Prepare Curriculum* and offers problem-solving training, social skills training, aggression replacement training, stress management, empathy training, moral reasoning, recruitment of supportive models, and cooperation training as elements of a comprehensive program. Of course, critical to any self-control training program are activities for promoting the generalization of acquired skills such as role playing, coaching, and ongoing practice and reinforcement of learned self-control strategies in a broad range of contexts.

Setting Limits to Ensure Safety   It is the responsibility of the school to ensure that students are free from physical danger. It must be recognized that, at times, youth who are troubled or troubling present safety concerns to the school community and themselves. Therefore, part of a school's commitment to ensure safety for all must be a well-articulated and well-understood crisis management system that promotes student responsibility and choice at each stage of a crisis. Allowing students opportunities to "calm down" and problem-solve in a less stressful environment such as a planning room (see Table 9.5); allowing students the choice to leave the school grounds or to go home for a certain amount of time; and in-school suspension and parent, social services, mental health, and even police removal are all possible options within a crisis response system. Although an unpleasant and a last-resort intervention, passive physical restraint is something a number of school personnel need to know how to perform. People most likely to restrain a student must receive training in this procedure. Finally, out-of-school suspension is an option that may need to be considered for short periods of time until a team (which includes the student) can convene to consider the next steps. It is critical that, if a student is asked to leave the school, he or she has a safe and supervised place to go.

Involving, Supporting, and Promoting Self-Determination

We offer three reasons for giving students voice by placing them in collaborative roles as instructors, decision makers, self-advocates, and advocates for others. First, given the diverse needs of an increasingly heterogeneous student population, school personnel need to take advantage of any and all available human resources; students offer a rich source of expertise, enthusiasm, and refreshing creativity at no extra cost to the school district. Second, educational reform leaders have called for more opportunities for students to develop and use higher level thinking skills through "a new collaborative role . . . in which students accept an active senior partnership role in the learning enterprise" (Benjamin, 1989, p. 9). Having students plan, teach, problem-solve, and evaluate educational activities responds to these calls for active involvement. Third, reform leaders have

Table 9.5. Critical elements and questions to consider when establishing a planning room

The planning room should exist as part of a schoolwide discipline system. (Where and how does the planning room fit into the system? How does the planning room promote the goals of the disciplinary system?)

Students and faculty need to be taught the purposes and procedures of the planning room. (How and when will this teaching happen? How will ongoing review, reteaching, and practice be built into the system?)

The focus of the planning process is on present and future behavior and the teaching of strategies that promote rule-following behavior. Although counseling and academic support may be part of a student's plan, such support should occur outside of the planning room. (How does the planning room offer support and instruction for the student? How will the system ensure that the planning process remains the focus of the interaction between the student and the planning room staff person?)

A space is needed for a planning room. This room should be used only for planning and no other purposes. Ideally, it should be removed from the traffic of the school and have enough room to accommodate three to four students at one time.

The planning room should be staffed throughout the school day. Whether one person or several people work in the room, what is provided to students is ongoing training and support in developing effective plans, social skills training, anger management, problem solving, and so forth.

There must be clearly defined entry and exit procedures for students requiring the planning room. This requires that classroom teachers understand the need for and goals of a planning room and the planning process. (What are the expectations of teachers prior to sending a student to the planning room? How does the student get from the classroom to the planning room? How does the student leave the planning room and re-enter the classroom?)

There must be clearly defined procedures in the planning room and procedures for when students do not follow the planning room rules. These procedures should be simple. (What happens when students engage in significant, chronic rule-violating behavior in the planning room?)

Use of a planning room does not preclude the use of other strategies that promote rule-following behavior and reduce rule-violating behavior. (How does the system provide additional problem solving and planning for students?)

It is critical to establish a communication system between the planning room and classroom teachers to ensure follow-up to a student's written plans.

The development of a data-keeping system to help evaluate the effectiveness of the planning room for individual students and the program as a whole will facilitate program improvement over time. (How will you keep track of who uses the planning room, for what behaviors, for how long, and to what end?)

advised schools to expand opportunities for students to develop empathy for others and practice being contributing and caring members of society (Van Bockern et al., 2000). By encouraging students to advocate for their own and fellow classmates' educational interests, schools create such opportunities.

Enfranchising students as responsible citizens of a school is the goal of collaborative student–student and student–adult arrangements. Table 9.6 presents collaborative strategies intended to

- Empower students to better advocate for and support one another

- Increase the likelihood that any student (including one who is troubled or troubling) will experience a sense of belonging and community

- Motivate and support students to engage as positive members of a school community

A caution in giving one student responsibility over another is that students who have been identified as sexual offenders should not be given responsibility or power over other children unless an adult supervises the interaction.

Involving, Supporting, and Empowering Families

The Education for All Handicapped Children Act of 1975, PL 94-142, and its subsequent reauthorizations promise the design and delivery of a free appropriate public education for every child with a disability. They also provide for strong parent involvement. The architects of these documents were astute in their recognition of the critical role that families play in determining and evaluating the appropriateness of academic and behavioral interventions for their children. One of the most powerful interventions for meeting the needs of children who are troubled or troubling is the development of a strong, meaningful home–school partnership, one characterized by equity and parity in decision making.

For a variety of reasons, the establishment of a meaningful partnership is not always easy. Many parents may have had negative experiences themselves in school. Previous patterns of interaction with the school may have consisted primarily of frequent telephone calls home to report how poorly their child was doing, academically and behaviorally. School personnel may not be available when parents are able to meet (e.g., in the evenings, on weekends). At times, parents may be overwhelmed with life's circumstances and unable to participate more meaningfully in their child's education. Finally, school personnel may, intentionally or unintentionally, communicate to parents that they are failing as parents and that their child does not belong in school. Clearly, school personnel committed to meeting the needs of children who are troubled or troubling must confront and attempt to overcome these obstacles.

The annual individualized education program (IEP) meeting required by law for children eligible for special education provides one avenue for developing a trusting home–school partnership. To be meaningful, these meetings must afford parents opportunities to express their feelings as well as share their expertise and knowledge regarding their child's unique needs and the successful strategies they have used to meet these needs. School personnel must be open to and invite parent input. Otherwise, as parents report happening far too often, educators end up talking at parents and presenting them with documents and plans that are already completed.

School-Based Supports and Services for Families In a number of school districts, core teams have been assembled to support children who are troubled or troubling and their families. Ideally, a student's core team includes the parent(s); a support person for the parent; the student; a peer, selected by the student, who provides support to the student; a classroom teacher; a special educator; a paraeducator (if one is assigned to work with the student); and, perhaps, an administrator. Initially, core teams meet weekly or biweekly for 30 minutes to 1 hour to plan and problem-solve with regard to the target student. Sometimes, the student and/or family members are reluctant to participate fully in the collaborative decision-making process. In some cases, it has taken a year or two for a student or parent to actively and regularly participate as a core team member because it took that long for a meaningful and trusting relationship to develop. Yet, waiting is worth the effort. For many families, the ongoing trust and communication that result from the

Table 9.6. Collaborative roles for students as instructors, decision makers, and advocates for themselves and others

Students as instructors in partner learning, cooperative group learning, and adult–student teaching team arrangements

Students as members of collaborative planning teams that determine accommodations for themselves and other classmates experiencing academic or behavioral challenges

Students supporting a challenged classmate through a "peer buddy" system or a Circle of Friends (see Chapter 24)

Students as coaches for their teachers, offering feedback regarding the effectiveness and consistency of their instructional and discipline procedures

Students who are troubled or troubling serving on a student council to make recommendations on how to improve the school climate (Curwin & Mendler, 1988)

Students trained to serve as peacemakers in conflict situations on the playground, in the school building, and in life outside of school (see Chapter 20)

Students establishing a violence- or crime-prevention club in which they identify crime problems and develop strategies to reduce them (Pitcher & Poland, 1992)

Students as members of curriculum, in-service, and other school governance committees, such as the school board or a student-operated "Jury of Peers" for dealing with student behavioral infractions core team's frequent face-to-face interaction has transformed their relationship with the school and the lives of their troubled children.

Schools may show respect for and support families in a number of other ways. First, personnel should avoid talking in jargon—in their respective discipline-specific expert language. Second, schools can respond to parents' requests for training related to their rights, collaboration and conflict resolution, meaningful accommodations, appropriate academic and behavioral interventions, and transition services. This information is intended to empower parents to participate more fully in the design of their child's program as equal partners on collaborative teams. Third, it is recommended that information for parents be delivered through a team-teaching arrangement of a parent and a professional so that parents observe in the instructor role another parent with whom they can identify and who has credibility because of similar experiences. The parent–teacher teaching arrangement also models equity and parity between school personnel and families.

Finally, parents may choose to influence decisions that affect them and their child by serving the greater school community as members and leaders of school organizations such as the parent–teacher organization and the school board. Parents in these roles can provide a powerful perspective as well as strong advocacy for their own and others' children as they volunteer time and energy in service to the school.

Community-Based Supports and Services for Families   Given the current organizational structure of public schools, school personnel often are not able to provide all of the supports a family may need in order to deal with the family dynamics and the behavior of a child who is troubled or troubling. Families of many children who are troubled or troubling require the services of multiple agencies (e.g., social services, mental health, and interagency cooperation among education, corrections, and human health services).

Family counseling often is a proactive intervention for addressing the needs of a family that, for whatever reason, is in distress. School personnel can facilitate a family's participation in counseling by serving as a "linking pin," helping the family to gain access to appropriate, affordable counseling services.

A promising intensive community-based intervention for families of children who are troubled or troubling is known as wraparound services (Burchard & Clarke 1990). In a Wrap Around approach, a broad range of supports are individually crafted to support the family of a student identified as troubled and troubling. Such supports might include 1) support to parents to set and attain goals for themselves and their child; 2) the modeling of effective parenting practices; 3) training to help family members to learn new ways of responding to their children's challenging behavior; 4) individual or group counseling for the child and/or family members; 5) connecting families to employment, welfare, child care, and other community resources; 6) coordination with other agencies; and 7) joint interagency funding and training of individual support personnel to shadow and enable students to be successful in and outside of school.

Respite, foster care, and emergency mental health placements are other community-based supports that have proven to be effective in assisting families with a child who is troubled or troubling. School personnel can facilitate the family's access to these important resources through interagency coordination. A benefit of available respite and emergency care is that the family gets a break and has the opportunity to come together to work out problems in a less stressed state. Occasionally, short-term foster care is deemed in the best interest of the child and the family. It must be emphasized that the goals of respite or foster care are family reconciliation and, when necessary, positive change in traditional family behavior patterns.

Regrettably, in many communities, school- and community-based supports and services for families such as those described are the exception rather than the rule. School personnel are encouraged to advocate for more creative and collaborative interagency responses for gaining access to, designing, and delivering family-centered supports for children who are troubled or troubling.

Redefining the Role of the Adult in the School

In our view, we cannot expect children to support and respect others (children and adults) as equals if we are not willing to do the same. This proposition suggests a shift in the role of the adults of the school from authority figure—a type of policing official, responsible for ensuring that students conform to standardized rules, norms, and standards, to support person—an active listener and partner in the construction of meaningful educational experiences for each individual learner. Skrtic, in an interview with Thousand (1990), further proposed viewing the educator as a collaborative inventor, who through adhocracies—ad hoc collaborative teams that pool skills and knowledge to invent unique, personalized programs for each student—exercises an implicit understanding that educational programs must be "continuously invented and reinvented by teachers in actual practice with students who have unique and changing needs" (p. 32). What follows are strategies for supporting students identified as troubled or troubling that assume that the appropriate role of the educator is that of collaborative supporter and inventor.

Adults as Members of Planning and Teaching Teams   Personnel in schools that have been most successful in responding to the needs of students who are troubled or troubling consistently identify as the cornerstone to their success the establishment of individual student core teams that meet regularly to address the challenges experienced and presented by a student. Any adult or student interested in supporting the education of a student is a potential member of that student's core planning and support team. The strongest, most effective core teams are skilled in the use of problem-solving and decision-making processes referred to as *collaborative teaming* (Thousand & Villa, 2000).

In some schools, long-term team teaching arrangements, described as teaching teams, have been established. A *teaching team* is "an organizational and instructional arrangement of two or more members of the school and greater community who distribute among themselves planning, instructional, and evaluation responsibilities for the same students on a regular basis for an extended period of time" (Thousand & Villa, 1990, p. 152). As with individual student core teams, members of teaching teams engage in an ongoing exchange of knowledge and skills and the generation of creative responses to children, including those identified as troubled or troubling. In teaching teams, members release professional labels and distribute job functions across formerly separate school personnel (e.g., special versus general educators), community volunteers, and students.

In summary, it is important to remember that each member of the school community who comes in contact with a student with challenging behaviors needs to have an adequate understanding of the student's needs and strategies for responding to the student's behavior. Thus, central to a student's success in a school is ongoing communication and awareness training with all of the people who work in and for the school, including custodial staff, secretaries, cafeteria workers, and volunteers, regarding principles of behavior management, effective communication, active listening, and conflict resolution.

Adults as Mentors and Advocates for Students   Adults, consciously and unconsciously, serve as models for children. Children who are troubled or troubling may have had limited or no access to adult models that demonstrate effective communication, anger management, and creative problem-solving skills. Thus, it is critical for teachers and other adults who work with and for children who are troubled or troubling to remain aware of their potential power as positive role models. Through their consistent actions they can teach students new patterns for communicating, managing anger, and dealing with adversity in socially acceptable ways.

Adult members of the school community can also support students who are troubled or troubling by serving as mentors or teacher advisors. Typical adult mentoring or teacher advisor programs pair each adult member of the school (e.g., teachers, custodians, administrators, secretaries) with a small group of fewer than nine students. Mentors or teacher advisors meet daily with their advisee groups and attend pro-active or reactive meetings in which academic or behavioral issues are addressed. In some schools, advisor–advisee relationships are long term, extending throughout all of the secondary school years. For children who are troubled or troubling, advisors frequently begin and end each day with a brief meeting in which the day is previewed or reviewed. In some instances, more frequent contact is scheduled throughout the day. A natural extension of the mentor/advisor role that is emerging in some schools is the adult advocate role. An adult advocate functions not as a school representative but as a support person for a student. It is recommended, therefore, that a student participate in the selection of his or her advocate. The advocate accompanies and represents a student at planning, discipline, and other school-related meetings. An adult advocate may prepare a student for a meeting and discuss the results with the student following the meeting. The advocate represents the student's "voice" in dealings with authority figures (e.g., other school personnel, parents) and helps a student plan how to successfully carry out and monitor any oral or written plan developed to affect positive changes in the student's behavior.

Individual Support Personnel   Valuable supports for some students who are troubled or troubling have been individual support personnel. Serious consideration must be given as to whether an individual assistant is needed to help a student monitor his or her behavior. Many students view the assignment of a support person as stigmatizing. However, support personnel are essential if a student's behavior is disruptive and places him- or herself or others in physical danger.

We offer the following advice to educators considering assigning a support person to a student. First, be sure to spend adequate time discussing and clarifying with the school community that the purpose of support is to enable the student to gain independence and form natural relationships with peers. Second, clearly delineate the job as a support to the teacher and the classroom, as well as the challenged student. Third, use the collaborative teaming processes to plan, deliver, and evaluate the student's program, and expect support personnel to join the team as equally valued, vocal members. Fourth, do not presume that all students who are troubled or troubling require full- or part-time personal support. Instead, require and establish procedures for the documentation of need for support personnel that include a description of the other types of accommodations and supports that already have been attempted. Finally, develop and regularly re-examine a plan to fade out direct instructional and personal support provided by support personnel. Many students who are troubled or troubling have expressed dissatisfaction with being assigned support personnel. Through involvement on their collaborative core teams, these students have participated in designing plans for fading and, eventually, eliminating support (e.g., contracting to systematically reduce the support contingent on appropriate behavior for a set period of time).

Rethinking School and the Student's Day

It is no secret that there is a widespread belief that schools are failing to meet the needs of a significant number of children, among whom are children who become identified as troubled or troubling. The term *school* conjures up various images. The Oxford American Dictionary defines *school* as

1. An institution for educating children or for giving instruction; 2. its buildings; 3. its pupils; 4. the time during which teaching is done there, school ends at 4:30 p.m.; *5. the process of being educated in a school,* always hated school. *(1980, p. 810)*

In other words, a school consists of many components—the organizational structure, the building, time usage, the students and adults, and the processes of learning. Furthermore, a school does not operate in a vacuum but in the context of a larger local and global community. Therefore, when thinking about how to respond to the needs of students who are troubled or troubling, all of these variables must be considered.

In rethinking schools, one of the first places to look for assistance is motivational theory. Choice, self-determination, independence, competence, and belonging are central concepts to most contemporary motivational theories. Therefore, enhancing student choice in the learning enterprise—the "what," "where," "when," and "how" of learning—is a key to restructuring schools so as to entice students to be actively engaged in learning versus disrupting the process. Choice is particularly important for troubled or troubling youth who feel that life and school have been imposed on them, that freedom and choice have been denied, or that they are the victims of adult authority. Choice can help to break a student's cycle of apathy, resistance, or defiance. Students are more likely to make a commitment to participate in schooling when the components of schooling are, at least in part, of their own design. The following are examples of nontraditional designs of the school day that afford students more choice.

"Jumping the Tracks" In 1985, Jeannie Oakes estimated that 80% of American secondary schools and 60% of elementary schools employed some form of ability grouping or tracking. The practice of tracking and ability grouping remains prevalent in schools today. Encouraging students to "jump the tracks" and enroll in any class or course usually limited to a subset of students (e.g., jumping the college preparatory track to take a vocational child care half-day internship; jumping the "slow learner" track to participate in a "gifted program," such as the Odyssey of the Mind competition) has proven to be a successful strategy for reducing the level and frequency of some students' rule-violating behavior. The increased choice, self-determination, and empowerment from this practice has resulted in increased student interest, motivation, and engagement in learning activities and a corresponding reduction in students' need to gain attention through means that are unacceptable to teachers.

Creative Placement Creative placement involves children being allowed to sample experiences and course offerings that traditionally have been unavailable to them because of their chronological age, grade level, or location within the building walls. It expands on the "jumping the track" notion by opening up all of the school and community as potential learning environments and experiences. For example, a sixth grader identified as "gifted," who was not motivated by the middle school social studies curriculum, was allowed to enroll in the twelfth-grade government class. Another middle school student, who refused to come to school, was motivated to return by enrollment in a high school automotive course. Employment, apprenticeships, and community service also represent creative placement options that not only expand the traditional curriculum but also increase the relevance of learning to future life as a worker and community member.

Shortened Days and Altered School Weeks and Years Consider a student perceived as troubling because he routinely arrived at school at 10:00 A.M. versus the usual 7:45 A.M. start time. When questioned, he revealed that both of his parents worked the late shift and that he stayed up until 3:00 A.M. so that he could spend some time with them. This was the only time they all were at home. Rather than continue to demand that the student attend first- and second-period classes, which he had failed to attend for 3 years, the decision was made to shift the starting and ending time of his school day so that he began school with the third-period class and ended the day with his employment program, which extended his school day until 5:00 P.M. For some students, 12 years of 190 7-hour school days does not constitute the "magic formula" for learning. Some students may be most responsive to shortened or extended school days or school years. For example, some students may need support and continued education in the summer months in order to "stay out of trouble" in the community. Students who are engaged in the determination of the time, locations, and duration of their educational careers may be more motivated and committed to the learning process and less inclined to engage in behaviors that are incompatible with learning.

In summary, we advocate replacing the current categorical, multitracked educational system with a "one-track system" (Nuzzi, 1992, p. 7) in which all students' differing abilities, interests, learning styles, and psychological needs are recognized, valued, and addressed. As the Reverend Ronald Nuzzi suggested:

> If we truly wish to respond to different student interests within a one-track system, we have to rethink the notion that learning happens only within the confines of the school building. Opportunities for distance learning must be created at every level; and the neighborhood, the community, and the world must become the classroom. Would this still be a one-track system? Maybe it would be one track per student, one student per track. (1992, p. 7)

DISCUSSION

Successfully addressing the diverse psychological and educational needs of children and youth who have been identified as troubled and troubling can be a complex, frustrating, and continual challenge. In this chapter, we present a constellation of resources, supports, and services that have been employed by school personnel committed to successfully meeting this challenge. Clearly, matching intervention strategies to the life circumstances, stresses, and context from which a child operates requires careful and thoughtful consideration; in other words, the suggested strategies should not be used in a simple, "cookbook" manner.

To illustrate the power of the resources, supports, and services recommended in this chapter, we offer strategies selected by teams supporting Mariah, Billy, and Ricardo—the students introduced at the start of this chapter.

Mariah

While Mariah was still hospitalized for her suicide attempt, an interagency team that comprised Mariah, her maternal aunt, and representatives from the school and mental health and social services agencies was formed and met to design a plan to coordinate services and supports for Mariah after her hospital release. The primary goal of the team was to reduce the likelihood of future suicide attempts. The service plan that was developed for Mariah included 1) temporary residence for Mariah and her sister with her maternal aunt; 2) a suicide prevention contract with Mariah; 3) individual counseling for Mariah that focused on her drug and alcohol abuse; 4) Mariah's participation in a peer support group for survivors of sexual abuse; and 5) family counseling for Mariah, her father, and her sister. Criminal charges were brought against Mariah's father. While the charges were pending, the father voluntarily agreed to participate in an outpatient sex offender program. All contact between Mariah and her sister with their father was supervised. Upon return to school, Mariah was taught creative problem-solving strategies to identify alternatives other than self-destructive behavior to manage her thoughts and feelings. She also selected an adult mentor/advisor in the school with whom she "checked in" daily, before and after school. Mariah's support team made a commitment to continue meeting to assist Mariah in planning for her transition from school to college, independent living, and work.

Billy

Billy's social studies teacher, concerned by the increase in his swearing and chair throwing, requested that a core team be established to support Billy and his teachers by developing interventions for dealing with his rule-violating behaviors. The core team members included Billy, a classmate selected by him, Billy's mother, the social studies teacher, the assistant principal, and a special educator. This team met weekly on Friday afternoons from 2:30 P.M. to 3:00 P.M.

One of the team's first considerations was whether an individual support person should be assigned to Billy's classes. It was agreed that this would be a premature, excessively intrusive, and costly response at this point in time. It was decided that the special educator would team teach with the social studies teacher 4 days a week. The role of the special educator was to implement accommodations and modifications to the curriculum and instruction to enable Billy and other students to be more successful and to be available to intervene with Billy, if necessary. The social studies teacher agreed to increase the use of partner and cooperative group learning structures in order to give students more of an opportunity to work with one another and to increase Billy's opportunity to develop friendships. In addition, because Billy expressed an interest in participating in a reciprocal tutoring program, he was trained as a tutor in mathematics and delivered instruction three times a week to a small group of students in a fifth-grade classroom. He also received tutoring in reading from an eighth-grade classmate during their assigned study hall.

A multidimensional approach was used to address Billy's aggressive outbursts. First, he joined an anger management and impulse control social skills group facilitated by his guidance counselor. The social studies teacher also agreed to team teach with the guidance counselor so that he would be able to incorporate social skill instruction and practice into his regular social studies curriculum. Second, Billy was given the option to remove himself from class when he felt he might engage in swearing or aggressive behavior. Third, in response to the social studies teacher's request to learn appropriate passive physical restraint procedures, the teacher was given 9 hours of training from certified personnel from a recognized training organization. The training emphasized strategies for avoiding and de-escalating aggressive behavior. Finally, in an effort to promote responsibility and enhance self-esteem, Billy was given a school job in the cafeteria. It also was arranged for Billy to shower and change into clean clothes whenever he came to school smelling of urine.

Ricardo

After repeated visits to their home at various times during the day and night, the school social worker finally made contact with Ricardo's family. Although the social worker's Spanish vocabulary was limited, she was able to communicate with Ricardo's parents and learned that they both were migrant farm workers who worked 14–16 hours a day. She also discovered that Ricardo routinely got up in the middle of the night to welcome his parents home and to spend time with them. Ricardo's parents did not know that Ricardo had stopped going to school.

A core team was established for Ricardo that included a professional from the Migrant Worker Education Center, Ricardo's classroom teacher, the school social worker, and a classmate selected by Ricardo. Supports developed for Ricardo included a flexible school schedule so that he could come to school late. When the social worker visited his home, she observed that Ricardo was very good at playing with and taking care of his younger cousins. This prompted school personnel to offer Ricardo a job in the after-school child care program on Mondays, Wednesdays, and Fridays. Ricardo eagerly accepted the job, and it decreased the amount of time that he was alone and unsupervised. It also provided him with a healthy after-school snack. On Tuesdays and Thursdays, Ricardo was enrolled in the YMCA after-school recreation and homework support program where he made a number of new friends from his neighborhood. Summer program options, including volunteer community service, are being explored.

JUST THE BEGINNING

Clearly, much remains to be discovered about providing appropriate support and education for children and youth who are troubled or troubling. Nevertheless, we are confident that teams of educators, students, and family and community members using collaborative and creative planning processes will invent solutions to the challenges faced and presented by these youth (see Chapters 8 and 10). Successful inventors are passionate. They are willing to challenge the status quo, deal with the cognitive dissonance and emotional turmoil that frequently accompany change, remain focused on their vision, and learn from their experiences. In our experience, the school personnel most successful in dealing with youth who have been identified as troubled or troubling have this passion. Given this passion, they choose to perceive problems, barriers, and challenges as opportunities. They also maintain and display a sense of humor.

As previously stated, many North American schools are failing an ever increasing number of children. To turn this around, it is imperative to recognize that far too often the disability is not in the child who gets labeled and, often, ejected from the educational system, but rather the disability is in the structure, policies, and traditions of school and social services systems. It also is imperative to recognize that it sometimes is easier to blame the victim than to struggle to change the system.

In our view, children and youth labeled as troubled or troubling offer schools a gift. Their behavior forces us to see the inadequacies of many of the organizational, curricular, instructional, cultural, and interactive patterns that have become tradition in North American schools. If we have the courage to confront the inadequacies of the current schooling paradigm to creatively respond to the challenges posed by Mariah, Billy, and Ricardo, the gift will be new and renewed school communities with a greater capacity to be caring, respectful, effective, and inviting for children and adults alike. The gift has been offered. Will we accept it and commit?

> *Until one is committed there is hesitancy, the chance to draw back, always ineffectiveness. Concerning all acts of initiative . . . there is one elementary truth, the ignorance of which kills countless ideas and splendid plans: That the moment one definitely commits oneself, then providence moves too. (W.H. Murray as quoted in Gore, 1992, p. 16)*

REFERENCES

Armstrong, T. (2000). *Multiple intelligences in the classroom* (2nd ed.). Alexandria, VA: Association for Supervision and Curriculum Development.

Bandura, A. (1977). *Social learning theory.* Upper Saddle River, NJ: Prentice Hall.

Benjamin, S. (1989). An ideascape for education: What futurists recommend. *Educational Leadership, 47*(1), 8–14.

Bennett, B., & Smilanich, P. (1994). *Classroom management: A thinking and caring approach.* Toronto: Bookation, Inc.

Breggin, P.R. (2000). *Reclaiming our children: A healing plan for a nation in crisis.* Cambridge, MA: Perseus Books.

Brendtro, L.K., Brokenleg, M., & Van Bockern, S. (1990). *Reclaiming youth at risk: Our hope for the future.* Bloomington, IN: National Educational Service.

Burchard, J.D., & Clarke, R.T. (1990). The role of individualized care in a service delivery system for children and adolescents with severely maladjusted behavior. *The Journal of Mental Health Administration, 17*(1), 48–60.

Curwin, R.L., & Mendler, A.N. (1988). *Discipline with dignity.* Alexandria, VA: Association for Supervision and Curriculum Development.

Curwin, R.L., & Mendler, A.N. (1997). *As tough as necessary: Countering violence, aggression, and hostility in our schools.* Alexandria, VA: Association for Supervision and Curriculum Development.

Curwin, R.L. & Mendler, A.N. (1999). *Discipline with dignity for challenging youth.* Bloomington, IN: National Educational Service.

Donnellan, A. (2000). Absence of evidence: Myths about autism and autism and mental retardation. In D. Fisher, K. Craig, & B. Buzwell (Eds.), *1999 TASH conference yearbook— "TASH 2000: Our turn now"* (pp. 15–22). Baltimore: The Association for Persons with Severe Handicaps.

Edmonds, R. (1979). Effective schools for the urban poor. *Educational Leadership, 37*(1), 15–24.

Education for All Handicapped Children Act of 1975, PL 94-142, 20 U.S.C. §§ 1400 *et seq.*

Elias, M.J., Zins, J.E., Weissberg, R., Frey, K.S., Greenberg, M.T., Heynes, N.M., Kessler, R., Schwab-Stone, M.E., & Shriver, T.P. (1997). *Promoting social and emotional learning: Guidelines for educators.* Alexandria, VA: Association for Supervision and Curriculum Development.

Fink, A.H., & Janssen, K.N. (1992). The management of the maltreated adolescent in school settings. *Preventing School Failure, 36*(3), 33–36.

Glasser, W. (1975). *Schools without failure.* New York: Harper & Row.

Glasser, W. (1986). *Control theory in the classroom.* New York: Harper & Row.

Glasser, W. (1998). *The quality school: Managing students without coercion* (3rd ed.). New York: Harper & Row.

Goldstein, A. (1998a). *The prepare curriculum* (2nd ed.). Champaign, IL: Research Press.

Goldstein, A. (1998b). *Aggression replacement training.* Champaign, IL: Research Press.

Gore, A. (1992). *Earth in the balance: Ecology and the human spirit.* Boston: Houghton Mifflin.

Hobbs, N. (1982). *The troubled and troubling child.* San Francisco: Jossey-Bass.

Jackson, N.E., Jackson, D.A., & Monroe, C. (1983). *Getting along with others: Teaching social effectiveness to children.* Champaign, IL: Research Press.

Johnson, D.W., & Johnson, R.T. (1991). *Teaching children to be peacemakers.* Edina, MN: Interaction Book Company.

Kahler, T. (1988). *Quality relations: Using the Process Communication Model.* Little Rock, AR: Kahler Communications, Inc.

Kauffman, J.M. (2001). *Characteristics of emotional and behavioral disorders of children and youth* (7th ed.). Upper Saddle River, NJ: Prentice Hall.

Knitzer, J., Steinberg, Z., & Bleisch, B. (1990). *At the schoolhouse door: An examination of programs and policies for children with behavioral and emotional problems.* New York: Bank Street College of Education.

Kunc, N. (1992). The need to belong: Rediscovering Maslow's hierarchy of needs. In R.A. Villa, J.S. Thousand, W. Stainback, & S. Stainback (Eds.), *Restructuring for caring and effective education: An administrative guide to creating heterogeneous schools* (pp. 25–39). Baltimore: Paul H. Brookes Publishing.

Kunc, N. (2000). The need to belong: Rediscovering the right to belong. In R.A. Villa & J.S. Thousand (Eds.), *Restructuring for caring and effective education: Piecing the puzzle together* (2nd ed., pp. 77–92). Baltimore: Paul H. Brookes Publishing Co.

Leone, P., McLaughlin, M., & Meisel, S. (1992). School reform and adolescents with behavioral disorders. *Focus on Exceptional Children, 25*(1), 1–24.

Lipsky, D.K., & Gartner, A. (1997). *Inclusion and school reform: Transforming America's classrooms.* Baltimore: Paul H. Brookes Publishing Co.

Marzano, R.J., Pickering, D.J., Pollock, J.E. (2001). *Classroom instruction that works: Research-based strategies for increasing student achievement.* Alexandria, VA: Association for Supervision and Curriculum Development.

Maslow, A. (1970). *Motivation and personality.* New York: Harper & Row.

Morgan, D.P. (1990). *Teaching behaviorally disordered students: Preferred practices.* Upper Saddle River, NJ: Prentice Hall.

Nevin, A., Villa, R., & Thousand, J. (1992). An invitation to invent the extraordinary: A response to Morsink. *Remedial and Special Education, 13*(6), 44–46.

Nuzzi, R. (1992). Issue: The practice of "tracking" students is under heavy attack. How can schools offer only one track and still address students' different abilities and interests? *ASCD Update, 34*(9), 7.

Oakes, J. (1985). *Keeping track: How schools structure inequity.* New Haven, CT: Yale University Press.

Oxford American dictionary. (1980). New York: Oxford University Press, Inc.

Perrone, V. (1991). *Expanding student assessment.* Alexandria, VA: Association for Supervision and Curriculum Development.

Pitcher, G.D., & Poland, S. (1992). *Crisis intervention in the schools.* New York: The Guilford Press.

Romaneck, G. (2001, February). Proactive approaches to help students control their anger. *Today, 7*(6), 1, 9, 13.

Skiba, R., & Peterson, R. (1999). *The dark side of zero tolerance: Can punishment lead to safe schools?* Available on-line at http://pdkintl.org/kappan/kski9901.htm.

Skinner, B. (1974). *About behaviorism.* New York: Alfred A. Knopf.

Stein, N. (2000). Sexual harassment in an era of zero tolerance. *The Wellesley Centers for Women Research Report, 22*(1), 18–20.

Thousand, J. (1990). Organizational perspectives on teacher education and school renewal: A conversation with Tom Skrtic. *Teacher Education and Special Education, 13*(1), 30–35.

Thousand, J., & Villa, R. (1990). Sharing expertise and responsibilities through teaching teams. In W. Stainback and S. Stainback (Eds.), *Support networks for inclusive schooling: Integrated interdependent education* (pp. 151–156). Baltimore: Paul H. Brookes Publishing Co.

Thousand, J.S., & Villa, R.A. (2000). Collaborative teaming: A powerful tool in school restructuring. In R.A. Villa & J.S. Thousand (Eds.), *Restructuring for caring and effective education: Piecing the puzzle together* (2nd ed., pp. 254–291). Baltimore: Paul H. Brookes Publishing Co.

Tomlinson, C. (1995). *How to differentiate instruction in mixed-ability classrooms.* Alexandria, VA: Association for Supervision and Curriculum Development.

Tomlinson, C. (1999). *The differential classroom: Responding to the needs of all learners.* Alexandria, VA: Association for Supervision and Curriculum Development.

Udis, J. (April, 2001). *Exchanging dissonance for harmony: Promoting the social and emotional competence of youth at risk.* Bedford: New Hampshire ASCD 2000–2001 Conference Series.

Vernon, A. (1989). *Thinking, feeling, behaving.* Champaign, IL: Research Press.

Van Bockern, S.L., Brendtro, L.K., & Brokenleg, M. (2000). Reclaiming our youth. In R.A. Villa & J.S. Thousand (Eds.), *Restructuring for caring and effective education: Piecing the puzzle together* (2nd ed., pp. 56–76). Baltimore: Paul H. Brookes Publishing Co.

Villa, R.A., & Thousand, J.S. (2000). Setting the context: History and rationale for inclusive schooling. In R.A. Villa & J.S. Thousand (Eds.), *Restructuring for caring and effective education: Piecing the puzzle together* (2nd ed., pp. 7–37). Baltimore: Paul H. Brookes Publishing Co.

10

Awareness Plans for Facilitating Creative Thinking

Herbert L. Leff
Jacqueline S. Thousand
Ann I. Nevin
Alice M.L. Quiocho

Our school has made a commitment to serving all children regardless of their needs and gifts through teaching teams of educators who used to work apart from one another (e.g., classroom teachers, special educators, guidance personnel). Our challenge is that there is no scheduled time for us to meet to plan and evaluate our students' and our own performance.

Johnnie doesn't seem to be motivated by anything I am doing in my classroom. I am concerned that he will start acting out or simply choose to stop coming to school. In what ways might I adapt the curriculum, change my instructional approach, or engage Johnnie's classmates in idea finding so that Johnnie becomes more involved in class? It is critical that whatever we do, Johnnie not stand out from the rest of the kids.

Our new teaching team has been meeting regularly every other day for 6 weeks now, but we are having problems. One member dominates the discussions and fails to listen carefully to the needs and concerns of the other teachers. Another member is chronically late for meetings. And most of the members seem to shoot down every suggestion before we can figure out how to make it feasible. What can we do to deal with these small-group interpersonal issues and make our team more effective?

These are only three of the challenges encountered by teams and individuals attempting to create caring and effective educational experiences for children and adults. Left unsolved, any of these situations could lead those involved to throw in the towel—to give up on a student or a promising innovation. The good news is that there are numerous strategies for enhancing the creative spirit, thinking, and developing actions of an individual or a team so that effective solutions to challenges such as these can be more readily found. This chapter is about how to promote creativity in human imagination and actions, with *creativity* defined simply as the process of being "productive, . . . imaginative" (*Webster's New Collegiate Dictionary,* 1973, p. 276), and inventive.

Throughout this chapter, we rely on a conceptual tool called an *awareness plan* (Leff, 1984) to discuss creative thinking strategies. An *awareness plan* is simply one's mental procedure for selecting and processing information. Clearly, any thinking activity uses some awareness plan. However, people usually do not consciously think about or deliberately select the way in which to process information, examine issues, or explore possible actions in response to a problem (see also Leff, 1978).

Leff and Nevin (1990; Nevin & Leff, 1991) emphasized that children and adults can increase their creative thinking capacity by learning and practicing a variety of new awareness plans. To illustrate this point, several different awareness plans from the book *Playful Perception: Choosing How to Experience Your World* (Leff, 1984) can be applied to Johnnie's challenging situation described at the beginning of this chapter. In response to the motivational concerns expressed by Johnnie's teacher, the awareness plan of viewing everything in school and the classroom as alive could be tried. Thinking of school in this way certainly would add fun and flexibility to the search for ideas. Another awareness plan—searching for the most boring things in the classroom and then identifying what is interesting about them—might help Johnnie's teacher tune into what is happening in her educational environment and discover untapped possibilities. As for the third scenario described previously about team difficulties (members quickly judging and discarding suggestions), it might be enlightening for them to exaggerate even further their tendency to judge by engaging in an orgy of evaluation (using many different criteria for judging), and, afterward, discussing the potential negative effects of judgment on team productivity.

Barriers to creative thinking and action abound, particularly in group situations. Thoughts and actions identified by Adams (1986) as common barriers to the creativity of teams are summarized in Table 10.1. Clearly, learning new ways of thinking takes commitment and energy. In fact, a subtle, but pervasive, barrier to creativity is the amount of mental effort and intellectual commitment it takes to learn and practice anything new or unfamiliar.

A TOOLBOX FOR CREATIVE THINKING AND ACTION

What follows is a toolbox for breaking down the barriers to creativity. All of the awareness plans are drawn from *Playful Perception: Choosing How to Experience Your World* (Leff, 1984) and the discussion builds directly on the presentation in that book. The first dozen tools presented are awareness plans for imagining an improvement and formulating actions to accomplish the improvement. Following these are awareness plans that capitalize on the "two heads are better than one" phenomenon known as *synergy*, in which contributions reinforce each other to create a "total effect [that] is greater than the sum of the effects taken independently" (*Webster's New Collegiate Dictionary*, 1973, p. 1183). This second set of

Table 10.1. Actions and thoughts that discourage creativity

Insisting on early precision or being correct	Setting up win–lose conflicts
Cross examining	Supporting confusion, ambiguity, or uncertainty
Misinterpreting, arguing, or challenging	Pointing out only the flaws
Reacting negatively, discounting, or putting down	Not listening
Being cynical, skeptical, or non-committal	Being dominant and in command
Disapproving, preaching, or moralizing	Ordering, directing, threatening, or warning
Being critical, judgmental, or pessimistic	Taking the "ball away from" another
Blaming, name calling	Correcting
Being competitive, making fun of others	Getting angry, scaring others
	Demanding
Acting distant, not joining in, or using silence to work against others	Assuming it cannot be done
	Putting the burden of proof on "others"

Source: Adams (1986).

tools is intended for use by teams of people. The third and last set of tools includes basic enlightenment awareness plans that may be employed by teams or individuals. *Basic enlightenment*, as defined by Leff (1984, p. 103), refers to a way of experiencing events (including problems) so as to maximize personal fulfillment and joy, which, in turn, should enhance outcomes of the experience (including the solutions to problems).

A Dozen Awareness Plans for Imagining Improvements and Planning for Change

Throughout every day, each one of us imagines improvements in our lives and surroundings. We imagine improving our personal relationships, making our homes more comfortable and attractive places to live, and creating a more harmonious country and world. Educators and others concerned with education and student learning are asked and expected to imagine beneficial changes in curriculum, instruction, classroom management, school governance, individual student programs, teacher collaboration, and many other organizational and instructional issues. It is common to imagine improvements. What is not common is to deliberately use awareness plans to stimulate new ideas that lead to action.

The power of the dozen awareness plans for imagining improvement, represented in Figure 10.1 and in the numbered questions and statements below, is that they address some common barriers to creative thinking by helping to

- Break traditional and usual assumptions about what is and is not possible (e.g., 2: Ask, "What if . . . ?" questions; 4: Think of unusual, nutty things; 6: Use magic wand wishes as guides to feasible ideas).

- Take on new and different perspectives (e.g., 7: Take on different roles of people, animals, things; 8: Use all senses and emotions).

- Think of unusual and new combinations (e.g., 3: Reverse goals; 11: Form new mental connections; 12: Invent games that inspire your thinking).

- Generate a lot of ideas (e.g., 5: Force yourself to think of many alternative ideas; 10: Break the problem into smaller problems).

- Go beyond merely correcting a problem to thinking of potential positive possibilities (e.g., 9: Define the goal in different ways).

Remember, the more quickly these aids are incorporated into your automatic thinking and problem-solving repertoire, the sooner and more often you can try them out. Although a dozen awareness plans are offered, even one can be enough to help with a problem. Experimentation will inform you as to which works best for you and which works best with the adults and students with whom you collaborate.

A difficult barrier to overcome has to do with stepping out of one's cultural comfort zone. A question to ask to determine the fit between the awareness plans and one's culture is, "How do I culturally respond when I am asked to perform one of the awareness plans?" The assumption of the model is that when asked to actively participate in one of the awareness plans, the participants know how to engage in the behavior. As with students, there is as much diversity among team members as there is in the classroom. You may have, for example, people who do not understand "playing a game" or "inventing a game" for Awareness Plan 12. You may have people who do not know what *invent* means. Do I know or even have an idea that a game could inspire my thinking? To think of unusual, nutty things (Awareness Plan 4) assumes that *nutty* means unusual but humor-

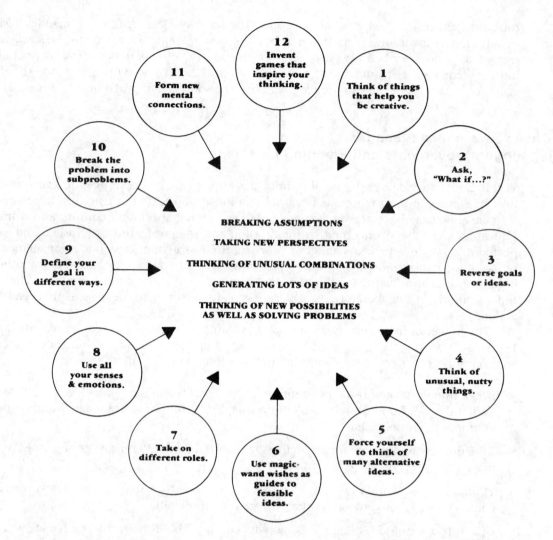

Figure 10.1. A dozen awareness plans for imagining improvements. (From Leff, H.L. [1984]. *Playful perception: Choosing how to experience your world* [pp. 89]. Burlington, VT: Waterfront Books. For copies of this book, please call 1-800-639-6063. Copyright © by Herbert L. Leff; reprinted by permission.)

ous and, therefore, potentially inspiring, relaxing, and allowing your creativity to blossom. What if you have people who think of *nutty* as something to do with food or who cannot think about it as appropriate to the process of problem solving or an academic task? So, instead of becoming more relaxed and open, it could create stress and actually have the opposite effect on their thinking. Somebody, therefore, has to model the behavior involved in the awareness plan and show participants how the plan actually accomplishes the goal of inspiring thinking in different ways.

If I am on a team and am asked to look at these 12 awareness plans, no one has asked me how I personally solve a problem that I encounter. To ask participants to share how they personally solve problems can activate their background knowledge. With the collective background knowledge that has been activated, people then could see the diversity in problem-solving approaches and then make a transition or application to the diversity of solving problems within their own classrooms with their students. This also could help them to see and appreciate the potential value of the 12 awareness plans and the new awareness that can emerge from their personal sharing of the problem-solving strategies. This, in turn, might motivate the reluctant members of the group and inspire group members to invent even more "culturally appropriate" awareness plans to help their students.

Awareness Plan 1: Think of Everything that Helps You to Be Creative   When is your creativity boosted? During which activities are you most inventive in your thinking? What feelings, which people, and what states of mind help you to be creative? After you have made a list, your awareness plan is to put yourself into a creative frame of mind for imagining improvements by either 1) vividly imagining experiencing each of these things or 2) actually doing the things that prompt your creative spirit. Things that may enhance creativity include

- Exercising
- Falling asleep
- Sitting by the ocean
- Feeling independent
- Thinking out loud
- Sailing
- Waking up
- Reading poetry
- Feeling confident
- Not straining
- Running
- Meditating
- Listening to music from a different culture
- Being playful
- Playing an instrument such as the bongo or chimes
- Not fearing criticism
- Becoming immersed in the problem
- Acting and talking crazy with a best friend or colleague

Awareness Plan 2: Use "What if . . . ?" Questions to Challenge Usual Assumptions and Expectations   One purpose of the "What if . . . ?" awareness plan is to remove limitations and expectations that we consciously or unconsciously assume must be in operation in situations we are trying to change. This strategy is particularly effective and energizing when used with a group of people. Suppose, for example, that you are a member of a team charged with imagining improvements in the community's school building and playground. Questions that might help the team to abandon the usual assumptions of what a school "looks like" are

- What if nothing could touch the floor?
- What if rooms had three or four levels?
- What if the building and rooms allowed for dancing, leaping, jumping, and running to occur at a moment's notice?

- What if only people with no sight (or no hearing) were to use the building and the playground?

- What if infants and toddlers attended school daily?

- What if senior citizens, some of whom use wheelchairs, were part of the school staff or student body?

- What if everyone spoke a different language?

Each of the questions should trigger ideas for new "What if . . . ?" questions as well as novel and nontraditional changes—hanging ornamentation and furnishings from the ceiling, having furniture fold out of the walls, having all furniture on wheels, having walls that recede into the ceiling, relying primarily on soft furniture, having wide doors that automatically recede into the walls when people and objects approach, or having the playground indoors as an integral part of the school.

"What if . . . ?" questions can be particularly useful in coming up with alternative actions for carrying out a change. For example, consider the different possible actions regarding school design suggested by these questions:

- What if this change were the most important thing in our lives?

- What if we did not need to spend money to accomplish this change?

- What if we could wait twice (or half) as long for the change?

- What if everything we did to get this done had to be fun?

Another "What if . . . ?" question you might ask is, "What if I am a member of the group and am asked to try this 'What if . . . ?' strategy and I don't see how 'What if . . . ?' questions encourage thinking? I might disconnect and not engage, become confused, or even get angry at being asked to do something that does not have meaning to me. This can happen. What do I do? Maybe the best thing to do is accept this current reality and move on to another awareness plan. Or, if I am daring, I might work with a few other group members to see how they build new ideas from 'What if . . . ?' questions."

Awareness Plan 3: Reverse Goals or Ideas Interpreting things as the reverse of what we normally think they are is an awareness plan intended to stretch mental flexibility as well as stimulate constructive alternatives. Let's use the school redesign challenge discussed previously to illustrate how reversing works. Suppose, for example, your team thought of replacing the old window blinds with new colored blinds. Reverse the idea by taking away all window coverings and thinking of ways to decorate windows that would never block light. Imagine the ceiling used as the floor, the walls as the ceiling, and the floor as the walls. Reverse your view of what is inside and what is outside, so that bushes, flowers, and trees become interior furniture and blackboards, and computers and televisions become play equipment. Or, try mentally reversing the relative values of things—things in trash cans and left on shelves unused for years are priceless, and the school building, property, and money are worthless junk.

Thinking of possible actions for improving education, we might reverse cause and effect relationships and think of children's learning as causing teachers' instructional behaviors. We also might imagine working against our goals. For example, imagine a school as the most physically and psychologically uninviting environment in which to spend time (e.g., as a prison camp, as a place where physical and emotional garbage is dumped on children). Does such imagining offer deeper insight into current problems with schooling and how to deal with them constructively? Suppose that the goal of a sixth-grade teaching team is to have a more harmonious relationship with a new principal with whom team members have numerous conflicts. Reversing the goal, think of ways the team could decrease harmonious relationships (e.g., as a group, storm into the principal's office to present written documentation of his or her failings and call him or her names in front of the superintendent and school board chairperson). Now, imagine reversing these actions to achieve your goal (e.g., send flowers to the office, drop in one by one to develop more personal relationships, deliver public praise for positive actions concerning students, write a note to the superintendent and school board praising the principal for actions that represent more effective communication with the team).

There is no limit to the reversals we can perform in our minds. At the very least, reversal awareness plans can provide users with endless possibilities for free entertainment while contemplating the usually "unthought of" or the "unthinkable."

Awareness Plan 4: Deliberately Think of Unusual, Nutty Things How ridiculous, strange, and crazy can we be in our thinking? The awareness plan of deliberately thinking in unusual and nutty ways is a starting place for genuinely useful ideas that nonetheless depart from old assumptions of what is possible or appropriate. For example, in imagining improvements to classrooms, in how many ridiculous ways can we cover the floors, the walls, and the ceilings? What are the most bizarre furnishings (e.g., from history, other cultures, the future) imaginable? What unexpected activities (e.g., wrestling, shopping, ballet, opera, art show, space travel, moon walking) can be envisioned for classrooms?

Off-the-wall notions can be called on to suggest feasible actions as well. Let's focus on making the school's playground more interesting. What are some wild ideas for action? Teachers could quit teaching and work full time on the playground; so could the students. The school could be sold to pay for the playground, or the faculty could apply for a federal grant. Finally, the children could be brainwashed to think the playground already has been made more interesting. Assuming none of these ideas are feasible, how could they be massaged to become feasible? Perhaps teachers, parents, community members, and students could work after school, on weekends, or on a special community project day to renovate the playground. This has been done in many communities. Maybe parts of the school building could be rented out for meetings or classes at night or over the summer, thus raising money for improvements. Perhaps a special physical fitness project that would merit a federal grant could be proposed and written with the help of community college faculty. Perhaps the children could be encouraged to play more imaginative games and make more imaginative use of existing equipment and facilities.

Awareness Plan 5: Force Yourself to Think of Many Alternative Ideas *Brainstorming* is now a commonly used term describing the awareness plan of forcing yourself or a group to generate a large number of alternative ideas. The procedure initially was described by Alex Osborn (1953) in *Applied Imagination: Principles and Procedures of Creative Thinking*. Application of the brainstorming awareness plan, illustrated in more depth in Chapter 22, requires adherence to at least five essential rules.

1. No negative reactions to comments are allowed. A judgment may interrupt the flow of ideas or stop the next idea from being expressed.

2. Free-wheeling is welcomed. Wild ideas are desired. Ideas will be critically examined later.

3. Quantity is the desired outcome; the more the better. Skip talking about details, as it slows down the process. Details come later.

4. The time limit must be short. Several minutes is about as long as the mind can stay intensely creative in a group.

5. Assign a recorder, but do not let the recording slow down the idea generating. The job of the recorder is to quickly jot down a key word or phrase to represent each idea and to move on.

The importance of quantity is that the first run of ideas that usually represent the "same old ideas" clear out the cobwebs, so to speak, and pave the way for more novel, imagined improvements. One aid for envisioning actions is to make each new action as different as possible from the previous one. Thus, if your team already imagined five ways to make money to improve the school's playground, try for a sixth and seventh way that have nothing to do with money. For example, work to change community members' attitudes so they will volunteer time or materials to construct the playground; or perhaps recycle materials—tires, railroad ties, old barn board—already on hand.

A caution for the brainstorming procedure has to do with "essential rules 3 and 4" regarding quantity, lack of details, and time limit. What if you have representatives of cultural groups that view talking, telling stories, and elaborating as critical to thinking and problem solving. For example, this is true with the "talk story" practice of the Hawaiian culture that involves unstructured conversation peppered with personal experiences about a variety of topics to which everyone contributes simultaneously (Au, 1993). Given this context, the western brainstorming practice of quick idea generating might communicate the message that "my contributions are not heard or valued because there is no space in the conversation for me or my friends/colleagues to elaborate." What would happen to the process if the rules of brainstorming were changed to include a "talk story" model to encourage participants to elaborate on ideas rather than just stating them briefly and moving on. For "essential rule 5" regarding recording, why not substitute it with multiple recorders in order to capture the rich details of the simultaneous conversations.

Awareness Plan 6: Imagine Having a Magic Wand If you had a magic wand that could allow all things to be possible and remove all barriers, how fanciful could you be in dreaming up changes or actions? The magic wand awareness plan is intended to help an individual or team to temporarily forget about the genuine barriers to change and defer judgment so that the imagination can run wild.

After thinking of magical wishes, the next step is to identify the specific features of the wishes that are particularly appealing and to figure out feasible ways to embody them. Suppose the goal is to come up with actions for getting the school's administrators to be more open to teachers' suggestions. You might imagine spiking their morning coffee with a magical potion that prevents people from being closed minded for up to 8 hours. Appealing features of this magic wand inspire ideas that are simple, fast, effortless, and nonthreatening to everyone concerned. What are some real actions that share some of these features? As a faculty, you might send each administrator a holiday gift of an audio tape or a book that conveys the advantages and skills of open mindedness, such as David Johnson's (1997) *Reaching Out: Interpersonal Effectiveness and Self-Actualization.* Anonymously distribute to all administrators and teachers a current article that deals with the same topic. Gift wrap suggestions and slip them in with the morning coffee as presents. What other actions resemble a "magic pill" in effect? Given the magic wand, what more can you think of?

There are some potential problems to the magic wand awareness plan. What if people in the group object to the term *magic* because the term and concept is considered dark, satanic, negative and destructive, or reminiscent of witchcraft? For example, parents and school boards have objected to or banned from school libraries children's books that have references to witchcraft or paranormal activity. Perhaps, when members of a group tell their personal stories, it will become evident if some members may be offended by reference to magic or the use of magic. In these cases, do not use this strategy, or change the language that refers to the strategy to remove the negative connotations of magic.

Awareness Plan 7: Take on Different Roles While Imagining Improvements
Taking on the role of other people, creatures, or things has the power of expanding our capacity for viewing a situation and imagining actions from others' points of view. The basic idea is to switch among different roles. As you switch among different roles and values, notice how your thoughts change. This sort of self-observation while taking on new mental roles is a powerful technique for helping people to develop empathy with others.

To illustrate this awareness plan, suppose several educators are meeting to plan instructional accommodations for a student with intensive educational needs. The team's creativity might be boosted by a role-reversal awareness plan. The classroom teacher might take the student's perspective, the special educator might take the perspective of the student's classmates and friends, the teaching assistant might take the role of a parent, and the parent might take the role of the classroom teacher. Team members could switch roles several times as they explore alternative actions for accommodating instruction, materials, and classroom arrangements. When we tried this technique with teaching teams in inclusion-oriented schools, accommodations tended to be more fun, less disruptive to daily routines, and more reliant on classmate support than when the adults stayed in their usual roles.

Academic roles also can be used to broaden thinking. Leff and Nevin (1994) encouraged teachers to instruct students to take on the thinking patterns associated with specialists in various academic subject areas and fields of work. How would you think and act if you had the role and values of the following people?

- Historian

- Mathematician

- Daredevil race car driver

- Teacher who is blind

- Environmental activist

- Bomb defuser

- Hang glider

As you try out each role, intensify the values associated with it. As a mathematician, nothing is more important than logic combined with tentativeness and tenacity. A mathematician values sticking with a problem until it is solved, even if it takes years. Therefore, time is of little importance. As a daredevil racer, however, time and speed, as well as excitement and competition, are very important.

To maximize flexibility in perspective taking, try using the role-reversal awareness plan to switch between the values, ideas, and actions of a particular role and its opposite. For instance, first think like the race car driver who values competition as the spice of life, then shift to regarding cooperation as the most crucial value. In what ways might you act differently in a team meeting when in either of these opposing roles? Next, adopt the values of a historian (e.g., preservation of the past), then switch to the values of a futurist (e.g., accurate prediction of the future). What ideas and actions for restructuring a school's physical plant or reorganizing the people who work within it are suggested by the opposing values of these two roles?

Finally, viewing the world as an animal or even a thing cannot only shift thinking away from the usual, but be entertaining and emotionally enriching as well. For example, what kinds of things in school would be important if you, the teachers, and the learners were dogs? What would dogs need or want to learn? How would dogs teach? What would be important to know about a dog's home environment? Now, imagine that you are an object or thing. For example, you are a school building and all of the school's contents, material and human, are part of you. The parts of the school and the school community are cells in your body. Imagine the emotions, sensations, and thoughts you would experience and how you would react to what's going on "inside of you." Now, use this information to think of ways in which to restructure a school organization to be maximally responsive to the emotions, sensations, and thoughts that you experienced.

One of the co-authors describes how, as a school principal, she used this awareness plan to help teachers time travel and recapture their personal histories to empower themselves to restructure schooling to support students at risk of academic failure, social maladjustment, and low quality of life. At the time, the teachers felt as if they did not have the skills to address the needs of their at-risk students; they felt they needed help from an outside expert. Faced with this situation, the principal gathered the teachers together and asked them each to write on a sticky page about a time in their lives when they felt at risk. The sticky pages were handed to the vice principal who compiled the list outside of the room while the teachers generated a list of the factors they felt contributed to their students being at risk (e.g., coming from a single parent home, living in poverty, living with one parent who was an active alcoholic, having been physically or sexually abused, having low expectations of attending college).

When the vice principal brought the teacher's list back in and posted it next to the list generated by the group, there was silence as they compared the lists and realized that they were virtually identical. Each teacher had been in danger of being at risk for school failure as a child.

The principal then had the teachers identify resilience factors that had "saved" them. This list included a compassionate teacher, an elder who took the time to listen, a mother or grandmother who advocated for them, and other individuals who in some way showed that they cared and were willing to act on their behalf. The teachers realized that collectively they had the power to be the resilient factors for the students they were teaching; they needed to share what they had learned from their own lives; they needed to look to the past to see what had been helpful to students who were at risk or who succeeded in school. The teachers had forgotten what it was like to be at risk; they had shoved it out of their consciousness. The experience that the principal guided the teachers through allowed them to take on the perspective of students. The overall outcome was that the teachers decided to transform the school from a strictly departmentalized model to a family model where teachers were committed to advocating for students and time was structured into the school day to collaborate and get to know each student personally. They changed the culture and structure of the school to allow resiliency factors to be activated. This likely would not have happened if they had not been prompted to take on the "different role" of student while imagining improvements.

Awareness Plan 8: Use Different Senses and Emotions to Suggest New Possibilities   In Western culture, we are schooled to process information using our sight and hearing. In redesigning a school building, what if you focused on the sense of touch to guide your design. Touch might suggest the use of new textures or it might suggest creating a closer atmosphere where children and adults could more easily connect with one another. Taste sensations (e.g., hot, spicy, sweet, cool) might suggest a more exciting, ethnic-oriented lunch menu or lunch room design, or different tastes might suggest different color schemes throughout the building—hot and spicy reds and oranges in one section, cool blues in another. As for emotions, anger might suggest more flamboyant, vibrant colors and arrangements, whereas joy might suggest a more open, flowing Eastern decor with movable partitions.

Turning to the domain of actions, suppose your school has a goal of increasing harmony and excitement among staff. The sense of smell might suggest the scent of roses or the aroma of fresh-brewed coffee and fresh-baked cookies, which, in turn, might suggest having floral arrangements and homemade snacks at meetings, in the teachers' room, or throughout the school.

Again, the full range of human emotions—from humor and joy to anger and sadness—can be used in awareness plans. What if everyone in the school were engaged in thinking of the funniest ways to increase harmony, infuse excitement, or achieve any other change? How might the "positive qualities" of anger (e.g., intensity, focus) be constructively channeled into an attack on a problem rather than on a person?

Even the active expression of sadness might be used to forward a beneficial goal, as was the sorrow of the classmates of a young man with disabilities after his sudden and unexpected death. These students learned of a girl with disabilities similar to those of their friend who was being denied access to her local school, which was in another city. Amazed that any community would do this to a child, they wrote newspaper articles and letters to the school board and the superintendent advocating for her admission into general classes. Three students even traveled to her community and, in front of several hundred people, presented the benefits of educating all children together. These actions helped to speed the healing process for the young man's classmates and heightened the public's awareness of the contributions that a student with disabilities can make to the lives of others.

Awareness Plan 9: Define Your Problem or Goal in Many Ways Define your problem or goal in many ways. For example, with regard to the problem of teachers not having enough time to meet, the starter phrase, "In what ways might we . . . ," could be used to brainstorm positive restatements of the problem. Actual alternative problem statements generated by teachers include the following: In what ways might we . . .

- Define the problem in terms of the student's culture?

- Use community volunteers to free up teachers so they can meet?

- Rearrange the master schedule so teachers who need to meet have common preparation periods?

- Use some in-service training days as planning days?

- Have a "floating" permanent substitute to cover for teachers who need to meet?

- Build up a store of student contact hours by lengthening the school day by 20 minutes and, through a biweekly early release of students, exchanging the earned hours for a half-day time block for collaboration?

Whether the objective is to restate a goal or envision alternative means to achieve a goal, each new definition points thinking toward different possibilities.

Awareness Plan 10: Break the Problem into Subproblems If it is hard to think of where to begin with a seemingly massive or complex problem or goal (e.g., school restructuring), try to focus on just one part of the problem at a time (e.g., student empowerment), and list the various actions you personally could take that conceivably could contribute to solving the problem (e.g., involving students as instructors, advocates, and decision makers). Once you have thought of potential actions or improvements, mentally follow through by imagining the consequences each action or improvement might have. Select the most promising approaches and break them down into subparts (e.g., implementing cooperative learning and partner learning in daily lessons). Then, try them. The key to creating change is to search until you find a way that you can enter the process of working toward a final goal.

Awareness Plan 11: Form New Mental Connections Awareness plans in this category link thoughts about a thing, event, idea, or feeling together with another, with the goal of jogging novel ideas. The simplest of the awareness plans is to think of things or situations that are similar to what you want to change or do, and use them to jog thinking. In improving a school building, you might think of a famous hotel and hotel lobby or an architectural gem, such as a home designed by Frank Lloyd Wright, and use it as a model. Going farther afield, try deriving ideas from museums, parks, or the "homes" of animals and birds. Try picking decidedly unattractive or repulsive things (e.g., a bus terminal, a prison) and, using the reversal awareness plan, reverse their features as your source of inspiration.

One way to form new mental connections is to tell a personal story. For example, Quiocho (2000) involved 50 teachers in telling stories about their students in the positive narrative style modeled by a variety of authors, such as Kuzmekus (1996) in *We Teach Them All: Teachers Writing About Diversity.* The outcome was that teachers learned that storytelling is a way to construct meaning and make positive connections with students from diverse cultures. New mental connections also can be used to think of new actions. If you are trying to come up with ways to increase the amount of laughter and play among the adults in your school, then try thinking of the people with whom you have had the most fun and laughs and recall how that fun and laughter was created. Or, think of analogies from the animal kingdom—how do various animals play and "have fun"?

To push thinking further, connect things to your goal that have no logical reason to be connected. Connect the first thing that you sense or think of to your goal. What, for instance, does a deck of cards suggest for the goal of making the school grounds safer at night? Perhaps a bridge tournament or a casino night could be organized to raise money for improving lighting of the grounds, or safety tips might be printed onto cards and made into an educational game.

Awareness Plan 12: Invent Imaginative Games to Inspire Thinking　Inventing games is an awareness plan that can be employed to help groups reach a goal more easily, learn a task or concept, or solve a problem. Leff and Nevin (1994), for instance, proposed that teachers use the inventing games awareness plan to liven up academic content previously considered mundane. Games can increase students' motivation, achievement, and appreciation of subject matter. As an example, Susan Underhill (personal communication, April, 1991), a fifth-grade teacher in an inner-city elementary school, developed a "Preposition Game" for grammar exercises. In an overnight game assignment, she challenged the students to notice and list every preposition they heard or used as they talked with family members, neighbors, friends, and so forth. All 32 students—including those with chaotic home lives or special education needs—brought in a list of three or more examples. Working in groups, students checked to be sure the examples actually did represent prepositions. They wrote each example on an index card and posted the cards around the room. Within 15 minutes, hundreds of accurate examples lined the walls. The students' competence in using and labeling the examples of prepositions was publicly displayed for all to see and celebrate. Over time, other grammar exercises turned into games, and students began to state that grammar was fun and easy.

Games also can be used to make it fun to apply several awareness plans (e.g., the ones presented thus far) to the same problem or goal. Here, for instance is a possible game for imagining improvements in a school library.

Step 1.　Gather a few members of the school community into the library and briefly explain the procedure.

Step 2.　Ask one another "What if . . . ?" questions for 5 minutes to loosen up assumptions about what can be done in and with a library.

Step 3.　Spend some time taking on various animal roles. From each animal's perspective, discuss how each animal would most like the library to change.

Step 4.   Translate the animal suggestions into feasible ideas for improving the library for children and adults.

Step 5.   Ask the group to invent yet another new game, and use it to come up with creative actions to achieve the improvements identified in Step 4. For instance, a new game might use the "magic wand" and the "form new mental connections" awareness plans to come up with creative actions.

Thus far, we have presented techniques for teams and individuals to be more creative in envisioning improvements and inventing strategies for accomplishing the improvements. The next two sections offer awareness plans for harnessing the synergistic potential of human interaction and making any situation in life more fulfilling.

THINKING FOR SYNERGISTIC (TEAM) OUTCOMES

Synergy refers to combined action in which individual contributions reinforce one another. It is an exciting phenomenon of human interaction that relies on the ongoing interchange of thoughts and actions of members of a group. Synergy connotes creativity, inventiveness, and excitement in human exchange and requires (as well as develops) honest communication, inviting rather than manipulating others to consider ideas, and mutual problem solving rather than competitive approaches to conflicts. In our view, synergistic thinking is highly related to valuing the well-being of all people.

The awareness plans presented in this section are particularly useful for teams. They are intended to illustrate ways of thinking and perceiving to enhance the "two heads are better than one" phenomenon of synergy. Four synergistic awareness plans are explored in depth; five additional plans are presented in Table 10.2.

Look for Points in Other People's Ideas on Which to Build

The next time you are in the middle of a disagreement, stop and deliberately focus on as many good points as you can find in the other person's ideas, and build on them to generate even better ideas. Let's say you are in a discussion about discipline and someone says that punishment through suspension or expulsion is the best way to handle a student's violation of school rules. If you disagree, rather than immediately trying to shoot down the other person's position, see if you can find something in the idea that you can genuinely agree with or use as a place to start generating better ideas. For instance, you might think suspension is a mistake but agree with the idea of letting students know when their behavior violates rules. You could then build on this positive aspect of suspension and start suggesting alternative, nonpunitive ways of achieving the same effect (e.g., developing an oral plan or written contract for improved behavior with the student).

Table 10.2.   Additional synergistic awareness plans

1. Carefully consider how the feelings or emotional states of others (e.g., teammates) affect your feelings and vice versa.
2. Consciously take the points of view of others; imagine you are the other people.
3. Think of advantages of sharing power and decision making with others.
4. Identify and question the underlying assumptions about your goal or situation.
5. Imagine being openly cooperative, creative, and synergistic; then tackle a troubling situation while in that state of mind.

Source: Leff (1984).

This awareness plan is based on the spectrum policy described by George Prince (1970) in his book *The Practice of Creativity*. The policy is to always pick out the best part of the total spectrum of a person's ideas and think of the weaker parts as challenges to address, rather than as points to reject or attack. The net effect of this constructive orientation is that it both stimulates one's own creativity and promotes a productive and more friendly social atmosphere.

A different way to use the spectrum policy is to adapt the round robin method of discussion (Kagan, 1995) with a ground rule that no person's idea is rejected as invalid. What if we talked about a problem in terms of our own personal experiences to similar problems. We would each tell a story in the following manner. In a triad, the first person shares one personal or cultural response to a similar problem. The second person paraphrases the first person's personal story and adds his or her own story. The third person paraphrases both stories and adds his or her personal story. The group now has more ideas to bring back to the larger group to propose as potential solutions.

Think of People's Ideas as Gifts or Invitations

What if disagreements were considered celebrations or parties of diverse ideas rather than a kind of war or competition? What if members of a group thought of themselves as living in a shared pool of thoughts rather than each person being the "owner" or originator of unique ideas? What if, rather than judging a thought or idea as "wrong," we viewed it as an opportunity to teach or learn something new? What if we thought of our own proposals as invitations to others to propose and explore even better ideas? What if we thought of our past experiences, positive or negative, as resources (gifts) for solving current problems? If awareness plans such as these were routinely used within groups, then it would not be much of a struggle at all to find exciting, shared goals and the means to achieving them.

Define Conflicts in Terms of Underlying Needs Rather than Incompatible Solutions

This awareness plan involves thinking of a conflict with others and imagining how it might be handled if everyone determined ways to satisfy one another's underlying needs or desires. For example, imagine two teachers attempting to team teach, embroiled in an argument over the noise level in the room. One teacher likes to hear the "hum" of children talking and making noise; the other wants quiet. If the two teachers define the problem strictly in terms of preconceived solutions—having it either noisy or quiet in the room—then the conflict likely will be difficult to resolve to both teachers' satisfaction.

What if, instead, the teachers began their discussion by determining what basic needs or desires underlie their preferences and then framed the problem as finding a way to meet both of their needs or desires? They might discover that one teacher's need is to structure cooperative learning groups where students' dialogue is a part of the classroom routine; the other teacher's need is to have relative silence in order to run focused reading comprehension groups with selected students. If both were committed to finding a resolution that satisfied each of these needs, then they might come up with possibilities such as finding mutually agreeable times of the days for quiet work versus more noisy group work or searching out alternative places in the school building to do reading or cooperative groups. The net result should be satisfied needs and a strengthened partnership.

Focusing first on needs rather than preconceived solutions can do wonders for resolving many educational issues. Just think of the possibilities for issues such as inclusive educational practices, student empowerment, teacher empowerment, school busing, and school choice. The key to success in using an awareness plan that focuses on underlying needs is for all parties to enter the process with a firm commitment to divulging real needs and taking the time to find solutions that work for everyone.

Think of Superordinate Goals that Could Resolve Conflicts and Foster Excitement

A superordinate goal is one that is so big, important, or exciting that people who previously were either apathetic or in conflict enthusiastically unite to pursue it. Survival often provides the basis for superordinate goals. For example, a polarized community pulls together to rebuild after a hurricane or tornado or unites to save a small rural school from being closed in a school-consolidation drive. Superordinate goals also may be based on seeking creative improvements. For example, a group of students energize and mobilize themselves to raise money for new athletic facilities and equipment. In numerous communities, formerly unconnected families have united in the highly cooperative, superordinate effort of designing and building a community recreation area. As with the awareness plan that focuses on underlying needs, discovering goals that are truly superordinate requires people to communicate honestly about what they really value and want.

EMPLOYING BASIC ENLIGHTENMENT TO ENHANCE INDIVIDUAL AND TEAM EXPERIENCES

The purpose of this final section is to present a few awareness plans that help make any situation in life more fulfilling, including working with students and colleagues in school. The underlying disposition to develop is referred to as *basic enlightenment* (Leff, 1984). *Enlightenment* has many meanings, most of which involve a spiritual connotation. (Therefore, be considerate of people on your team who might be reluctant to engage with the concept of enlightenment as spirituality.) *Basic enlightenment,* however, refers to a way of experiencing events (including problems) so as to maximize personal fulfillment or joy, which, in turn, should enhance any outcomes of the experience (including the solutions to problems). What follows is advice on how to immediately experience each moment in richer ways. The four awareness plans for basic enlightenment presented are useful for both individuals and teams.

Think of Every Moment as an Opportunity

A powerful way to bring choice to life is to view each moment as an opportunity for choosing how to experience or act. Regardless of the situation, try thinking or saying out loud, "Well, here I am. This is all I have to work with. I commit myself to treating this situation as an opportunity for a constructive and fulfilling experience." It is important to recognize that feelings and thoughts are as much a part of a situation as external circumstances. So, suppose you are facing a stressful event. The "opportunity" involves not only how you treat the event itself, but also how you treat the feelings of stress. For example, one of these authors, faced with the stress of several impending writing deadlines and intensive job and family responsibilities, used the feeling of stress as an opportunity to identify stress-reducing activities. This, in turn, led to the re-introduction into the author's life of two favorite calming and fulfilling activities—piano playing and weight lifting—activities that had been lost in the rush of a busy life.

Although this awareness plan may be applied to any situation, it is especially useful for "reframing" problematic or disturbing circumstances. What positive opportunities are provided by an otherwise disappointing cold and rainy weekend, an automobile break-down, or having to stay home because of illness? How could an argument with a supervisor be turned into an opportunity for personal growth? As an exercise in the use of this awareness plan, take a single problem that particularly bothers you and spend 30 minutes exploring opportunities it might offer for enriching your life.

Regard Everything as If It Were Your Hobby

Imagine that you are doing some required paperwork for school that you really hate do-ing. Now, see if you can change your feeling about paperwork by regarding it as a long-standing favorite hobby. To do this, however, first you need to think about how it feels to engage in a hobby you genuinely like. Picture the activities and feelings associated with hobbies. You may experience aesthetic pleasure, intense attention to detail, feelings of having chosen to do what you are doing, loving the activity involved, enjoying the people who also have the same hobby, and so forth. Now, transfer these thoughts and feelings to the activity of doing paperwork.

Is it possible to think of paperwork as a hobby, something to look forward to and savor, take pride in, and do for recreation? Do "hobby feelings" change your experience when you actually do paperwork? If it is hard for you to imagine paperwork as an enjoy-able pastime because you dislike it so much, perhaps you could regard hating paperwork as a hobby and think: "Yeah! Another opportunity to hate paperwork. Let's think up all of the reasons why and ways in which to hate it today." The value of the awareness plan of treating a feeling of dislike as a genuine hobby is that it reminds us that we can always choose to welcome our feelings.

Focus on What You Can Do

For any problematic situation, focus on what you are doing and especially on what you can do rather than focusing on what you might see as being done to you. In your most cre-ative frame of mind, imagine possible actions to change the situation or even to get out of it. Or, if the situation cannot be changed or you cannot get out of it, think of new ways to experience it so that it feels better. For example, instead of struggling or resisting, treat the whole thing as an educational experience, a game, or as unimportant and silly.

The trick to effectively using this awareness plan in a situation that you truly want to change is to start by committing yourself to finding something—anything—that you actu-ally can do to make a difference. In some cases, it simply may be to choose to experience the situation differently, perhaps with a playful awareness plan.

Learn from Whatever You Encounter

Regarding all things and experiences as having something important to teach is the last and possibly the most powerful awareness plan offered in this chapter. This awareness plan works best if you actively seek ways to identify possible lessons rather than waiting for the lessons to appear. In the search, be sure to use any of the other awareness plans presented in this chapter to 1) help you suspend your assumptions about what is impor-tant, 2) look for new connections, and 3) learn from unexpected or overlooked sources (e.g., discarded materials, outdated texts, the most troubled or troubling children in the school, senior citizens). Finally, be sure to attend to your own feelings, emotions, thoughts, and actions as well as those of others as sources of information. In summary, just about everything in life offers a lesson, even though it may take some mental digging to find it.

AN INVITATION TO INVENT THE EXTRAORDINARY

A main message of this chapter is that there are many strategies for individuals and teams to employ to overcome traditional barriers to creativity. In our experience, when collaborative teams have used the awareness plans presented in this chapter, they have successfully created time for collaboration, developed meaningful accommodations and modifications to curriculum and instruction, and redefined the roles of educator and student so that all children, regardless of their needs and gifts, experience quality education in schools that are both caring and effective (Thousand & Villa, 2000).

A second message of this chapter is that each person can choose how to experience the world at each moment by trying out new and different awareness plans. Although the awareness plans in this chapter should prove useful and enjoyable, coming up with your own will allow you to personalize new plans to the specifics of your life—your work; your relationships; and your interests, goals, and pleasures. And so, we end this chapter with an invitation to invent the extraordinary—to devise your own awareness plans, try them out, and share them with others through your actions. Finally, we invite you to directly teach them to children. After all, the imagination and creativity of our children represent the future of our planet.

REFERENCES

Adams, J. (1986). *Conceptual blockbusting: A guide to better ideas* (3rd ed.). Reading, MA: Addison-Wesley.

Au, K.H. (1993). *Literacy instruction in multicultural settings.* San Diego, CA: Harcourt Brace College Publishers.

Johnson, D. (1997). *Reaching out: Interpersonal effectiveness and self-actualization* (6th ed.). Needham Heights, MA: Allyn & Bacon.

Kagan, S. (1995). *Cooperative learning* (Rev. ed.). San Clemente, CA: Kagan Publishing.

Kuzmekus, J. (1996). *We teach them all: Teachers writing about diversity.* York, ME: Stenhouse Publishers.

Leff, H. (1978). *Experience, environment, and human potentials.* New York: Oxford University Press.

Leff, H.L. (1984). *Playful perception: Choosing how to experience your world.* Burlington, VT: Waterfront Books.

Leff, H., & Nevin, A. (1990). Dissolving barriers to teaching creative thinking (and meta-thinking). *Teacher Education and Special Education, 13*(1), 36–39.

Leff, H., & Nevin, A. (1994). *Turning learning inside out.* Tucson, AZ: Zephyr Press.

Nevin, A., & Leff, H. (1991). Is there room for playfulness? *Teaching Exceptional Children, 22*(2), 71–73.

Osborn, A. (1953). *Applied imagination: Principles and procedures of creative thinking.* New York: Charles Scribner & Sons.

Prince, G. (1970). *The practice of creativity.* New York: Macmillan.

Quiocho, A. (2000). Narrative as transformation. *The New England Journal of Education, 3,* 30–36.

Thousand, J.S., & Villa, R.A. (2000). Collaborative teams: A powerful tool in school restructuring. In R.A. Villa & J.S. Thousand (Eds.), *Restructuring for caring and effective education: Piecing the puzzle together* (2nd ed., pp. 73–108). Baltimore: Paul H. Brookes Publishing Co.

Webster's new collegiate dictionary. (1973). Springfield, MA: G & C Merriman Company.

11

Why Understanding the Theoretical Basis of Cooperative Learning Enhances Teaching Success

Frank B. Murray

The term *cooperative learning* refers to a family of instructional practices in which the teacher gives various directions to groups of pupils about how to work together. It is a teaching practice rarely employed by novices; yet, it is a powerful, if somewhat counterintuitive, teaching technique.

In a cooperative learning exercise, the class is divided into groups of four to six children, usually of similar age but differing in perceived ability, ethnicity, and gender. The teacher's directions are designed, one way or another, to have the children work together as a team on some academic task. The children, of course, must learn to cooperate to follow the teacher's instructions, but cooperation itself, although a worthy curriculum objective, is not the principal objective in cooperative learning instruction. The claim of cooperative learning advocates, usually supported by field research, is that ordinary school learning is enhanced considerably when children, following cooperative learning procedures, learn in groups rather than on their own or in competition with other pupils.

Schooling, largely for reasons of economy and efficiency, invariably takes place in class groups. We know that overall academic achievement is usually, but not always, superior when the groups are small—optimally seven or fewer—and when the members of the group are of different or mixed academic levels. We know also that a disproportionate share of the academic benefits in mixed classrooms of 30 or so pupils tend to go to those of lower academic accomplishment. Although traditional classroom instruction has always entailed a degree of cooperation and competition among pupils, cooperative learning practices *require* pupils to cooperate as a team as a *necessary* condition of acquiring academic information. This usually means that 1) the instructional outcome results from the pupils' common effort, 2) the instructional goal is shared, and 3) each pupil's success depends on and is linked with every other pupil's success and never their failure. Cooperative learning practices typically have pupils share materials, divide up the labor required to complete the assignment, assist the other members of the group, and receive rewards based on the group's performance.

SUCCESS AND UNDERSTANDING

The link between successful teaching practice and the teacher's understanding of the reasons for the success of the practice is subtle (Floden & Klinzing, 1990). Sound practices can be derived from sound theories, but, surprisingly, they can also be validly derived from unsound theories. Thus, the fact that practice works does not guarantee that the theory from which it was derived is sound. Technically, unsound practices cannot be derived from sound theories, but theories in education or the behavioral sciences are rarely stated with the precision that one would need to make a proper deduction from them in any case. Nevertheless, the way in which the teacher thinks about the practice is important in determining which aspects of the pupil's accomplishment will be stressed and cultivated.

Basically, the various kinds of cooperative learning structures teachers may set up for their pupils are based on four theoretical perspectives: social learning theory, Piagetian theory, Vygotskian theory, and the newer cognitive science theories on experts and novices. Each of these perspectives is focused on one of the following basic characteristics of cooperative learning: tutoring (cognitive science), conflict resolution (Piagetian theory), community collaboration (Vygotsky), and teamwork (social learning theory).

Cognitive Science: Tutoring

The characteristics of ideal learning environments derived from the cognitive science perspective (Bransford, Brown, & Cocking, 1999; Collins, Brown, & Newman, 1986) closely parallel many features embedded in the common cooperative learning formats, all of which make provisions, for example, for modeling, coaching, and scaffolding. However, some novel cooperative learning procedures, such as reciprocal teaching, have been developed by cognitive scientists for classroom instruction.

Reciprocal teaching, developed by Palincsar and Brown (1984), is a method of teaching reading in which the teacher and students take turns as teacher. Specifically, they both read a passage to themselves, and then the teacher demonstrates the process of formulating a question based on the passage—summarizing the passage, clarifying it, and making predictions based on the information contained in it. When the pupil takes a turn as teacher, the teacher carefully coaches the pupil in the skills of comprehension and offers prompts and criticism until the pupil achieves the skill, at which time the teacher's role becomes more passive. Both laboratory and classroom studies have demonstrated that the reciprocal teaching method is effective in significantly raising and maintaining the reading comprehension scores of poor readers (Collins et al., 1986; Symons, Snyder, Cariglia-Bull, & Pressley, 1989).

Basically, the method is thought to be successful because the pupil gradually, but solidly, develops a new conceptual model for the skill and couples it with specific strategies that are used by expert readers. The cooperative learning features of these expert–novice teaching procedures lead the pupil to integrate the multiple roles that the successful problem solver inevitably masters. Thus, student writers are helped as writers when they read and critique other pupil's work and when they have their own work read by others, and so on. By taking turns writing and reading, they acquire a larger view of the writing task, a new conceptual model for it, and a model closer to that possessed by the expert writer.

Cooperative learning also occurs when tutors receive benefits from their work, although it is difficult to know to what to attribute the benefits—the tutoring act itself, the preparation for tutoring, or the kind of study the tutor engages in (Hufnagel, 1984).

Piagetian Theory: Conflict Resolution

Teachers working within the Piagetian tradition use cooperative learning lessons to accelerate the pupil's intellectual development by forcing the child to systematically confront another child who holds an opposing point of view about the answer to some school task. Basically, the teacher places two pupils who disagree about the answer to a problem in a group called a *dyad* and tells them to work together until they can agree or come to a common answer, at which time the lesson will conclude. Once the pupils agree, the teacher who tests the children alone usually finds that the pupils who initially do poorly on the problem now, on their own, solve the problem in a way that is indistinguishable from the way a correct problem solver solved it in the first place (see Murray, 1986, for a review of this literature).

In some instances, teachers may also instruct the pupils in the dyad to simply imitate a correct problem solver, and on other occasions, the teacher may instruct one child, in the presence of the other, to pretend to reason in a mature way. In other words, the teacher places the pupil in some social situation in which he or she is forced to take a viewpoint that conflicts with his or her own point of view.

The practice of using dyads works best if the teacher ensures that one pupil understands the task. Some cognitive growth occurs, however, when neither child knows the correct answer to the problem and only when each initially offers an incorrect answer that contradicts the other's answer.

Overall, these social interaction or cooperative learning effects, documented consistently in some 30 studies, are limited to mental tasks that have strong relationships with age, but they do occur across a wide variety of tasks and with groups of various sizes (two to five students), grades (K–5), and ethnic and social diversity. These developmental tasks, nevertheless, are important parts of the school curriculum because they are about information that is necessarily true (e.g., if A is older than B and B is older than C, then A is also older than C). These social interaction versions of cooperative learning, apart from being effective ways to promote cognitive growth, are also more effective for developmental tasks in the school curriculum than traditional instructional practices that are based on direct teaching or conditioning.

The techniques are rooted in the Genevan notion of egocentrism, or the tendency of school children to center on one aspect of a situation, usually their own perspective. The technique is designed to address this pivotal factor in the child's reasoning by encouraging the child to attend to other dimensions and perspectives and to integrate these and his or her prior views into a new, more inclusive, view of the problem.

Throughout the 1960s and early 1970s, it was widely held that one implication of Piagetian theory was that the young child (younger than 7 years) was structurally incapable of taking a cognitive point of view different from his or her own (Cox, 1980). Researchers all over the world confirmed the young child's stubborn egocentrism in scores of laboratory studies, and the extensions of the fact of egocentrism were found in curriculum and instructional designs that accepted the immutability of the young child's limited competence. However, when teachers and mothers researched these issues based on their own unique familiarity with children and as part of their own graduate research training in the 1970s, they quickly devised experiments that showed that young children were able to take the point of view of others in many situations. These experiments led to substantial modifications in the prevailing interpretations of the child's cognitive competence that, in turn, supported the invention of pedagogical techniques, such as cooperative learning, that now presuppose the young pupil's competence to take the point of view of another pupil.

Vygotskian Theory: Community Collaboration

The most compelling theoretical rationale for cooperative learning comes from the Russian psychologist, L.S. Vygotsky. Vygotsky claimed that our distinctively human mental functions and accomplishments have their origins in our social relationships and in particular the slot or role into which we are socialized in the cultural group of which we are a part. In this view, mental functioning is the internalized and transformed version of the accomplishments of the group to which one belongs. It is always more than what an individual could have accomplished on his or her own. The theory gives great weight to a group's common perspectives and solutions to problems through debate, argument, negotiation, discussion, compromise, and dialectic. This collaboration by a community of learners is seen as indispensable for cognitive growth. Its role is more than a mere facilitator of events. It is the means by which such growth occurs, and a provision for it must be made in schooling.

Researchers and teachers often find that the dyad can solve a problem that individuals working on their own cannot solve. There is a distance, called a *zone of proximal development* (ZPD), by Vygotsky, between what the pupil can do on his or her own and what the child could achieve were he or she to work under the guidance of teachers or in collaboration with more capable peers. Thus, teachers who wish to maximize what the child can accomplish will minimize the time the child works alone on school tasks.

Research in this tradition (see Forman & Cazden, 1985) has not resulted in novel practices in the schools, but it has provided a demonstration of the growth in individual children's problem solving when the problems are approached collaboratively and when the teacher sees the other children in the class as an indispensable part of the lesson and not as a barrier to each pupil's accomplishments. The other pupils are an instructional resource in this approach and an asset in assimilating the child into the role of pupil or student.

Social Learning Theory: Teamwork

Practices derived from the social learning tradition are the most widely used in schools. They are based on the common principle that pupils will work hard on those tasks for which they secure a reward of some sort and will fail to work on tasks that yield no reward or yield punishment. In cooperative learning instruction, the teacher employs the approval of other pupils and the expectations of the group and relies heavily on the ability of the pupil to imitate the academic behavior of others. These are the tools of the cooperative learning teacher in the social learning tradition.

When individuals work together toward a common goal, their mutual dependency often motivates them to work harder to help the group, and thereby themselves, to succeed. In addition, they often must help specific members of the group do well, and they often come to like and value the members of the group.

The cooperative learning practices in the social learning tradition are designed to provide incentives for the members of the group to participate in a group effort because children will not spontaneously help their colleagues or work toward a common goal. Thus, it is critical that the teacher deliver incentives to a pupil only when all members of the group succeed in learning the assignment or, in the case in which the teacher assigned the pupils different parts of a complicated task, only on the basis of the group's overall achievement and not according to the merit of any individual pupil's contribution to the group's effort.

Also, the teacher must ensure that the contributions of the "weaker" members of the group are genuinely important so that the group's success cannot be attributed merely to the work of one or two pupils. If the teacher merely instructs the pupils to work together and to help each other, then the academic gains are generally no greater than if the pupils worked alone on the task.

The most thoroughly researched cooperative learning practices are Johnson and Johnson's Learning Together; Sharan and Sharan's Student Teams Achievement Divisions (STAD) or STAD Group Investigation; Slavin, Leavey, and Madden's Team Assisted Individualization; DeVries and Slavin's Teams-Games-Tournaments (TGT); and Aronson's Jigsaw. All of these models are described and referenced by Slavin (1986, 1998) and Stallings and Stipek (1985).

In a typical cooperative learning exercise, the teacher might divide academic material into parts, and ask each member of the team to read and study one of the parts. Then, the members of the different teams who have studied the same parts might meet to discuss and clarify their sections, after which they would return to their original group to teach and quiz their teammates about their section; or, they might enter into an academic game contest with their counterparts on the other teams to determine who performed best. Often, each student is assessed individually, with no help from the others, on the entire subject matter and a "team score" is derived from individual performance outcomes by a scheme that allows each member to contribute to the team's score in a significant way (e.g., the team score might be based on the amount of improvement in each member's grasp of the subject matter). The team with the highest group score also can be rewarded with a certificate or some other attractive form of recognition. In some schemes, the grade a student receives is the team score or a combination of both the individual and team performances; in other schemes, the grade follows the conventional practice and is based solely on the pupil's own work.

The positive outcomes of cooperative learning structures have been widely documented over the last several decades. For example, Johnson and his colleagues (Johnson, Maruyama, Johnson, Nelson, & Skon, 1981), in an examination of 156 research studies, found 108 studies in which cooperation promoted higher academic achievement than independent work, six studies in which the reverse was true, and 42 in which no difference was found. In Slavin's (1986) review of research studies that had equivalent control groups and took place in real schools over a period of at least 2 weeks, cooperative groups achieved at higher levels than the control groups in 22 of the 33 studies, with no difference being found in 10 studies.

Some cooperative schemes have been very carefully researched. For example, TGT (Stallings & Stipek, 1985) has been evaluated in sample sizes ranging from 53 to 1,742 at both elementary and secondary levels and in several subject matter domains. In these studies, TGT was administered by classroom teachers with random assignment of teachers and pupils to the cooperative and control groups and with both groups having the same curriculum materials and objectives. On four of the seven standardized achievement tests and eight of the nine classroom tests, the TGT group outscored the control group as well as showed positive effects for race relations, friendship, attitudes toward school, and self-esteem.

CONCLUSION

The research literature supports the conclusion that teachers can increase their pupil's performance on academic tasks if they have their pupils work on the tasks in groups of two to six under rules by which the pupils teach each other, coach each other, and succeed as a group. These gains occur only if teachers show their pupils how to do and think about these things and if they are rewarded individually and as a group for doing them. The various theories explain how the cooperative learning innovations produce their impressive results and guide the teacher in ways of dealing with novel problems presented in the lesson. Over and above accomplishment on school tasks, cooperative learning among pupils and between pupils and teachers may be the essential means, as both Vygotsky and Piaget claimed, by which the mind constructs knowledge and invents meaning. Teaching techniques that fail to make a provision for this kind of cooperation run the risk that although pupils may learn their lessons and may imitate their teachers, they will not understand their lessons. In other words, the meaning derived from the instructional experience will fall short of what would have been possible. The teacher who grasps the reasons behind a successful, even if counter-intuitive, teaching strategy such as cooperative learning will be guided to the core of education, the development of the child's mind, and the child's ability to use it well. Such a teacher also will understand why simple administrative devices such as retention never have been and never could be the solution to the problem of a child failing to understand key aspects of the curriculum.

REFERENCES

Bransford, J., Brown, A., & Cocking, R. (Eds.). (1999). *How people learn: Brain, mind, experience, and school.* Washington DC: National Academy Press.

Collins, A., Brown, J., & Newman, S. (1986). Cognitive apprenticeship: Teaching the craft of reading, writing, and mathematics. In L. Resnick (Ed.), *Cognition and instruction: Issues and agendas* (pp. 1–41). Mahwah, NJ: Lawrence Erlbaum Associates.

Cox, M.V. (Ed.). (1980). *Are young children egocentric?* New York: St. Martin's Press.

Floden, R., & Klinzing, H. (1990). What can research on teacher thinking contribute to teacher preparation? A second opinion. *Educational Researcher, 19*(5), 15–20.

Forman, E., & Cazden, C. (1985). Exploring Vygotskian perspectives in education: The cognitive value of peer interaction. In J.V. Wertsch (Ed.), *Culture, communication and cognition: Vygotskian perspectives* (pp. 323–347). New York: Academic Press.

Hufnagel, P. (1984). *Effects of tutoring on tutors.* Unpublished doctoral dissertation, University of Delaware.

Johnson, D., Maruyama, G., Johnson, R., Nelson, D., & Skon, L. (1981). Effects of cooperative, competitive, and individualistic goal structures on achievement: A meta-analysis. *Psychological Bulletin, 89,* 47–62.

Murray, F. (1986). Micro-mainstreaming. In J. Meisel (Ed.), *The consequences of mainstreaming handicapped children* (pp. 43–54). Mahwah, NJ: Lawrence Erlbaum Associates.

Palincsar, A., & Brown, A. (1984). Reciprocal teaching of comprehension—fostering and monitoring activities. *Cognition and Instruction, 1,* 117–175.

Slavin, R. (1986). Small group methods. In M. Dunkin (Ed.), *The international encyclopedia of teaching and teacher education* (pp. 327–245). New York: Pergamon Press.

Slavin, R. (1998). Success for all: Policy consequences of replicable schoolwide reform. In G. Cizek (Ed.), *Handbook of educational policy* (pp. 326–347). New York: Academic Press.

Stallings, J., & Stipek, D. (1985). Research on early childhood and elementary school teaching programs. In M. Wittrock (Ed.), *Handbook of research on teaching* (3rd ed., pp. 727–753). New York: Macmillan.

Symons, S., Snyder, B., Cariglia-Bull, T., & Pressley, M. (1989). Why be so optimistic about cognitive strategy instruction? In C. McCormick, G. Miller, & M. Pressley (Eds.), *Cognitive strategy research: From basic research to educational applications* (pp. 1–32). New York: Springer-Verlag.

12

Cooperative and Collaborative Learning

An Integrative Perspective

Neil Davidson

This chapter explores some of the diversity in the field of cooperative and collaborative learning. In contrast to some other innovations, there is no single guru on cooperative learning who is accepted on all points. The field has a number of diverse viewpoints, which can result in arguments over which approach is better or more "right." However, diversity can be viewed as a source of strength in terms of flexibility and mutually enriching perspectives, with all approaches having more similarities than differences. This chapter outlines six major approaches to cooperative and collaborative learning and examines commonalties and variations among the approaches. The approaches are Student Team Learning (STL) (Slavin, 1983a, 1983b, 1990, 1994); Learning Together (Johnson & Johnson, 1975/1991/1999, 1987, 1989a, 1989b); Group Investigation (Sharan & Hertz-Lazarowitz, 1980, 1982; Sharan, 1993/1999); the Structural Approach (Kagan, 1992/1994); Complex Instruction (Cohen, 1986, 1994); and the Collaborative Approach (Barnes, Britton, & Torbe, 1986; Britton, 1970; Reid, Forrestal, & Cook, 1989).

Table 12.1 shows five attributes that are common to all of the cooperative/collaborative approaches; nine attributes vary. In this chapter, each cooperative/collaborative learning approach is explained and analyzed in terms of the common and varying attributes.

STUDENT TEAM LEARNING

Student Team Learning (STL) approaches were developed by Robert Slavin (1983a/1994, 1983b, 1986, 1990) and his associates at The Johns Hopkins University. Student Teams Achievement Divisions (STAD), Teams-Games-Tournaments (TGT), and Jigsaw II are examples of STL methods. Some STL techniques, notably Team Assisted Individualization (TAI) in math and Cooperative Integrated Reading and Composition (CIRC), have specific curricular materials to go with them. In STAD, worksheets and quizzes are provided to help teachers, but these are not intended to be complete or prescriptive.

A central feature of STL is the combination of individual accountability and either group rewards or group goals. This combination is cited by Slavin (1983b, 1990) as a cen-

---

Drafts of this chapter were sent for review to at least one of the authors of each of the approaches. This chapter reflects their comments and suggestions.

Neil Davidson has served as President of the International Association for the Study of Cooperation in Education (IASCE). This chapter is based on a portion of his keynote address for the IASCE Convention in Baltimore in July 1990.

Table 12.1. Common and varying attributes among cooperative and collaborative learning approaches

Attributes common to all approaches

1. Common task or learning activity suitable for group work
2. Small-group learning
3. Cooperative behavior
4. Interdependence (often referred to as *positive interdependence*)
5. Individual accountability and responsibility

Attributes that vary among approaches

6. Grouping procedure (e.g., heterogeneous, random, student selected, common interest)
7. Structuring positive interdependence (e.g., goals, tasks, resources, roles, division of labor, rewards)
8. Explicit teaching of interpersonal, relationship, cooperative, or collaborative skills
9. Reflection (or processing) on social skills, academic skills, or group dynamics
10. Climate setting through class building, team building, trust building, or cooperative norms
11. Group structure
12. Attention to student status by the teacher (identifying competencies of low-status students and focusing peers' attention on those competencies when demonstrated).
13. Group leadership
14. Teacher's role

tral finding in the research for increasing student achievement. Space allows for an analysis of only one STL method, namely STAD. A different analysis would be required for TAI or CIRC. In STAD, students are grouped heterogeneously based on past achievement, race/ethnicity, and gender. This is also true of the other STL methods. Groups are called *teams* in order to transfer some of the motivational dynamics of team sports into the classroom arena. Typically, the teacher follows a cycle of teacher presentation/direct instruction, team study and practice, individual quizzes, and team recognition. Individual students receive grades based on their own quiz scores. Teams also receive points based on individual members' improvement over past performance (i.e., individuals earn improvement points that are used solely for team recognition). Recognition often takes place through class newsletters, bulletin boards, and posters; team names are prominently featured.

In terms of the five common and nine varying attributes of cooperative/collaborative approaches, STAD is structured as follows.

Common attributes:

1. The task for group work is for all members to practice and master facts and skills, as well as solve problems in math and identify main ideas in literature.

2. Student interaction occurs in small teams of four or, occasionally, five members. Students often practice in pairs within their teams.

3. Cooperative behaviors include students discussing the problems or questions together, comparing their answers, explaining, and correcting any misconceptions or mistakes. Peer norms support academic effort and achievement.

4. Positive interdependence occurs when teammates encourage each other to do their best; individual learning is important for team success. The only way for the team to succeed is to concentrate on enhancing the learning of every team member.

5. Individual accountability occurs when all team members take individual quizzes and receive individual grades. Individual improvement points contribute to team recognition, not grades.

Varying attributes:

6. Team formation is heterogeneous, based on past academic performance (e.g., a high performer, two medium performers, a low performer), gender, and race/ethnicity.

7. Positive interdependence is structured in a variety of ways. Goals are for all team members to master the material or improve their own past performances and for the team to receive recognition or a reward. Tasks require discussion and mutual help for all team members to succeed. Resources are limited; there are two worksheets for a team of four. Roles typically are not assigned, but team members sometimes take turns quizzing each other. Team rewards are based on the team's average improvement points. Rewards include certificates or other team recognition via a newsletter or bulletin board, special privileges, or small prizes.

8. Explicit teaching of social skills does not occur unless there is a specific need for it.

9. Reflection (or processing) on team functioning is not highly emphasized.

10. Climate setting occurs via team building through the use of and emphasis on team names.

11. Group structure is not specified, except that practice often occurs in pairs within teams.

12. Attention to student status treatments is not emphasized.

13. Group leadership is not specified; no single leader is selected for a team.

14. The teacher's role varies in different phases of the instructional cycle. The teacher presents information; circulates among and praises the teams; computes base scores, improvement points, and team improvement scores; and presents certificates or rewards to high-performing teams.

LEARNING TOGETHER

David and Roger Johnson (1975/1991/1999, 1987, 1989a, 1989b) from the University of Minnesota designed a conceptual approach to cooperative learning, sometimes known as Learning Together, taken from the title of their book, *Learning Together and Alone: Cooperative, Competitive, and Individualistic Learning* (1975/1991/1999). The Johnsons emphasized the distinction among cooperative, competitive, and individualistic learning situations. In the cooperative learning situation, students perceive that their goal achievements are positively related—"We sink or swim together." In competition, students work against each other. In individualistic learning situations, students work individually to accomplish goals unrelated to those of their peers.

The Johnsons emphasized certain basic elements of cooperative learning, including positive interdependence, face-to-face interaction, direct teaching of interpersonal and small-group skills, processing of those skills, and individual accountability. They use a group discussion procedure, often with assigned roles (e.g., facilitator, encourager, praiser). Interdependence is structured in various ways. The Learning Together method of cooperative learning is used for both higher cognitive processes as well as mastery of basic facts and skills and has been extensively researched over many years (Johnson & Johnson, 1989a).

The Johnsons' conceptual approach to cooperative learning does not involve direct application curriculum packages or specific strategies applied in detailed or structured ways. Following is the Learning Together approach analyzed in terms of the common and varying attributes of cooperative learning models.

Common attributes:

1. Common tasks or learning activities suitable for group work can occur at all cognitive levels; however, more conceptual learning requires more discussion, explanation, and elaboration.

2. Small-group learning occurs in groups of two, three, or four members, with groups of three preferred.

3. Cooperative behaviors are emphasized. Students work together, discuss, listen, question, explain, elaborate, share ideas and materials, encourage, and so forth.

4. Positive interdependence is interpreted as the perception that one is linked with others so that one cannot succeed unless the other team members also succeed. Groups are structured so students seek outcomes that are beneficial to their group mates.

5. Individual accountability or responsibility is attained by checking responses on individual worksheets, randomly selecting one group member to explain, or giving individual quizzes or tests. Group members are to hold one another accountable for their learning.

Varying attributes:

6. Grouping typically is done heterogeneously by mixing gender, race/ethnicity, social class, and achievement levels (e.g., high, medium, low). However, a teacher may sometimes form homogeneous groups of students who need to work on a specific skill, procedure, or set of facts.

7. Positive interdependence is structured in multiple ways. Goal achievements by students are positively correlated; that is, students perceive that they can reach their learning goals if and only if group mates also reach their goals. The mutual learning goals are to learn the assigned material and to make sure that all group members do the same. Tasks require students not only to agree on answers but also to be able to explain their group's reasoning or strategies. Resource materials can be limited to one copy per group or jigsawed with each member having different materials. Division of labor sometimes occurs for suitable tasks. Roles are assigned and rotated frequently. Each member is assigned a role that is essential to the group's functioning (e.g., reader, checker, relater/elaborator, accuracy coach, summarizer, encourager, confidence builder). Rewards may be given in the form of bonus points if all members of a group achieve a preset criteria of excellence.

8. Interpersonal and small-group skills of leadership, decision making, trust building, communication, and conflict management are purposefully and explicitly taught. Skills often are practiced while performing assigned roles.

9. Reflection (processing) on social skills, academic skills, and group dynamics occurs regularly after group work is completed. Students discuss how well group members are learning and maintaining effective working relationships. They also identify helpful or unhelpful behaviors of members and behaviors to continue or to change.

10. Climate setting occurs within teams and across the whole class through a variety of trust-building activities (see Johnson & Johnson, 1991).

11. Group structure is not prescribed in detail; teachers apply the basic elements in planning their own lessons.

12. Attention to status treatments for individual students sometimes occurs but is not emphasized.

13. Shared leadership occurs through assigning and rotating roles essential to a group's work.

14. The teacher's role is complex and varies in different phases of the lesson. The teacher specifies academic and social objectives, makes a number of decisions prior to instruction, explains the academic task and cooperative goal structure, monitors and intervenes during group work, and evaluates learning and facilitates processing. All of these teacher actions are described in detail in the varied works by the Johnsons (see also Chapters 11 and 14).

The Johnsons employ a combination of ad-hoc informal cooperative learning groups that last up to one class period, formal cooperative learning groups that last up to several weeks, and base groups with stable membership for long-term mutual support. Note that the previous analysis applies to the basic conceptual model of cooperative learning. For more advanced information, see the Johnsons' works on leading the cooperative school (1989b), creative conflict (1987), and cooperation in the college classroom (Johnson, Johnson, & Smith, 1991/1998).

GROUP INVESTIGATION

The Group Investigation model, based on the ideas of Thelen (1967, 1981), has been applied and investigated extensively in Israel in the works of Sharan (1993/1999), Sharan and Hertz-Lazarowitz (1980, 1982), and Sharan and Sharan (1992). In the Group Investigation model, a complex topic is divided into multiple subtopics to be studied by different research groups. The model has six components or stages:

1. The class determines subtopics and organizes into research groups.

2. Groups plan their investigations—what they will study, how they will go about it, and how they will divide the work among the group members.

3. Groups carry out their investigations. Members of each group gather, organize, and analyze information on their subtopic.

4. Groups plan their presentations. Members share and discuss their data with their group and plan the group report together.

5. Groups make their presentations. Reports are delivered to the entire class in a variety of forms and with the participation of all group members.

6. Teachers and students evaluate the group investigations individually, in groups, and as a class. There are varied means for assessing contributions of individual members as well as the group presentation as a whole.

The six stages of the model, including the teacher's role and the students' role at each stage, have been described in detail by Sharan (1993/1999) and Sharan and Sharan (1992). Additional stages may be added if needed with a particular project. Critical components of the model are investigation, interaction, interpretation, and intrinsic motivation. Positive effects of the group investigation model have been found on student achievement, intrinsic motivation, and social interaction.

The Group Investigation model is analyzed in terms of the common and varying attributes of cooperative learning.

Common attributes:

1. The common task or learning activity is to investigate a complex topic divided into subtopics for groups to research. The task should allow all group members to readily

participate and have an opportunity to talk, and should require members to make choices and group decisions.

2. Small-group learning takes place in research groups with no more than four or five members.

3. Cooperative behavior includes jointly planning the investigation using detailed suggestions given for cooperative planning. Students work together and sometimes individually; assign roles and divide the tasks among themselves; exchange materials, ideas, and information; plan their presentation together; and give feedback to their classmates.

4. Positive interdependence begins with the identification of a broad problem of common concern to the class, which then leads to jointly planning, coordinating, and conducting the investigation. Interdependence takes different forms at different phases of the complex undertaking.

5. Individual accountability or responsibility occurs when students divide up and take responsibility for a part of the task, carry out their investigations, present their findings with all members taking part, receive feedback and perhaps written evaluations of their work, and take individual tests.

Varying attributes:

6. Grouping procedures include random assignment, common interest in a topic, and student or teacher selection. Factors to consider in grouping include individual student characteristics, task characteristics, and duration of the group investigation.

7. Structuring positive interdependence is promoted when 1) common goals are set by the class through cooperative planning, and tasks are jointly determined by each research group; 2) resources for the investigation are exchanged and divided among and within groups; 3) roles are determined and assigned by each research group; and 4) division of labor occurs as the class and each group divide the research topics and tasks associated with each subtopic. Rewards are not used to promote interdependence; instead, intrinsic motivation is strongly emphasized.

8. Explicit teaching of cooperative skills often occurs prior to the investigation. In addition to establishing a climate for interactive talk, the teacher may conduct skill-building exercises to develop students' skills in discussion and reaching consensus. Cooperative skills are taught during the investigation only if a need arises.

9. Reflection by the group members may occur in the final stage of the investigation by students identifying and analyzing what happened, generalizing their learning outcomes to different situations, and setting goals for the improvement of group behavior. Students may be asked to reflect on their own academic and social learnings, as well as on the presentations of others.

10. The climate is set for interactive talk through cooperative norms, such as mutual help and sharing ideas and information, teacher modeling of listening with respect, teacher encouragement of student talk, and establishing cooperative planning.

11. Group structure is not made explicit by the teacher but is determined by the student groups at different stages of the investigation.

12. Attention to student status may occur but is not a prominent part of this method.

13. Shared leadership occurs when students plan together and select their tasks and roles in the investigation. There are no assigned leaders and no pre-assigned roles.

14. The teacher's role changes at different stages in the investigation. The teacher leads exploratory discussions to determine subtopics; helps groups formulate their plans; helps maintain cooperative norms; helps students find information and use study skills; coordinates planning, presentations, and feedback; and evaluates learning of information, higher level thinking, and cooperative behavior.

STRUCTURAL APPROACH

The Structural Approach (Kagan, 1992/1994) represents and derives its name from an array of simple group structures (e.g., Think-Pair-Share, Roundtable, Numbered Heads Together, Three-Step Interview, Jigsaw, Pairs Check) that teachers can readily add to their repertoire and use immediately. The goal is for teachers to become skilled with the individual simple structures and then begin to combine and sequence them in a meaningful and artistic way to form more complex lessons. Kagan recommends trying one new structure at a time, working it solidly into the repertoire of both the teacher and students. In the Structural Approach, there are structures for practice and mastery, structures that foster thinking, structures for information sharing, and so forth. The job of the teacher is to choose and use the structure(s) most appropriate for the task at hand.

The Structural Approach incorporates some procedures from other models of cooperative and collaborative learning. For example, STAD is considered a lesson design for developing mastery, and Jigsaw II is a "division of labor" design. One design, Co-op Co-op, is the Sharans' (1992, 1993/1997) Group Investigation model expanded from 6 to 11 steps.

Kagan has developed six key concepts for his model of cooperative learning: teams, management, skills to cooperate, will to cooperate, structure, and principle. Kagan's four principles are described by the acronym PIES—positive interdependence, individual accountability, equal participation, and simultaneous interaction. With the fourth principle, a goal of group learning is to maximize the number of students who can speak at any given time in order to maximize simultaneous interaction (e.g., pairs allow for more simultaneous interaction than groups of four).

There is research support for the Structural Approach in that it incorporates procedures from other models that have an established research base. However, there is a need to investigate specific structures as well as their effectiveness in a multistructural lesson. The Structural Approach may be described in terms of the attributes of cooperative and collaborative learning as follows.

Common attributes:

1. Common tasks or learning activities for group work can be designed at all cognitive levels, ranging from mastery of basic facts and skills to the development of higher-level thinking skills. Different structures are matched to different types of tasks.

2. Small-group learning occurs in teams of four, which sometimes divide into pairs.

3. Cooperative behaviors include listening, paying attention, giving ideas, praising, encouraging, and a host of other behaviors that are taught through a variety of methods.

4. Interdependence is a key concept in the Structural Approach. Kagan distinguishes among weak, intermediate, and strong forms of positive interdependence. The strength of the interdependence depends on the degree to which success of each team member is linked to the success of other team members.

5. Individual accountability or responsibility is structured for 1) student achievement (e.g., the team recognition score is based on individual scores); 2) participation (e.g.,

using "talking chips"); and 3) listening (e.g., using a three-step peer interview process). Grades are based on individual performance, not on any form of team scoring.

Varying attributes:

6. Grouping may be heterogeneous, random, common interest, or homogeneous by language. Each grouping procedure is used for a different purpose and has distinct advantages and disadvantages.

7. Structuring of positive interdependence varies depending on the academic and social goals of the lesson and the specific structure employed. In some lessons, group members have the same goal, such as producing an essay, model, or mural. Tasks may be structured so that no individual is able to do them alone. Resources are shared among group members. Roles are chosen so they are complementary and necessary (e.g., materials monitor, coach, encourager, reflector, quiet captain, praiser, checker). Division of labor (e.g., Jigsaw II) occurs in some lesson designs. Rewards are used differently in various reward structures. Team scores and rewards are used to promote cooperative relations within a team; team scores contributing to a total class score fosters cooperation among teams.

8. Explicit teaching of social skills occurs through a "structured natural approach." Teachers set up a "social skills center," where important information about each social skill may be found. They select and introduce a skill-of-the-week, develop roles that use the skill, and identify the verbal and nonverbal behaviors needed to fulfill the role. Next, they choose a cooperative structure that requires or fosters that skill (e.g., listening is required for the "interview" and "round-robin" structures). Finally, they model and reinforce the skill and guide students to reflect on their use of the skill.

9. Teachers encourage reflection on academic and group performance through varied means such as reflection questions, linking with the social skills center, using a particular cooperative structure for reflection, student self-monitoring, observers, and formal reflection forms.

10. Class and team climate-building efforts attempt to help students get acquainted, develop class and team identity, provide mutual support, value differences, and experience synergy through interactions. Numerous techniques are used to accomplish these purposes.

11. Group structure is highly explicit in the Structural Approach. Numerous specific, simple structures are offered for organizing the interaction of individuals in a classroom or small group.

12. Attention to students' status may occur, but is not a principal feature of this approach.

13. Leadership is shared through the use of varied structures and rotating roles that develop social skills.

14. The teacher's role is complex. It involves selecting academic and social goals, choosing the appropriate cooperative structure(s) to accomplish the goals, observing and consulting during group work, and so forth. The teacher also employs a cooperative classroom management system that includes the use of a quiet signal, the setting of class norms or rules, positive attention for following norms, and public recognition systems.

COMPLEX INSTRUCTION

Complex Instruction, a model developed by Elizabeth Cohen and associates (1986, 1994), is complex both in terms of the tasks given to the students and the way in which student groups are organized. Complex Instruction originally was designed for investigations in math and science, using the Finding Out/Descubrimiento curriculum of DeAvila, Duncan, and Navarette (1986). Now, the method is being applied in other subject areas as well.

In Complex Instruction, the class is divided into groups of four or five. Each group has a different learning station, and roles are assigned to group members. Different groups often investigate related phenomenon (e.g., issues related to the melting point of ice) and then report their results to the entire class. Complex Instruction is similar to Group Investigation approaches, except that it is organized and orchestrated by the teacher, and members of groups work together rather than separating into individual investigations. Multiple-ability tasks are designed to incorporate all levels of performance—not only cognitive but also psychomotor, visual, organizational, and so forth. Tasks are designed so that all members of the group are needed; each individual brings unique talents or knowledge to the task. The Complex Instruction model also employs a cooperative management system involving delegation of authority to students, cooperative norms, assigned roles, and group decision making.

A unique and prominent feature of Cohen's (1986, 1994) approach is attention to individual students' status within the classroom. The multiple abilities orientation sets the stage for the assignment of competence. This occurs when the teacher first identifies students of low status and looks for their areas of competence. The teacher then specifically identifies that competence when it is displayed and calls it to the attention of teammates and other classmates. Students who are publicly recognized as competent in one area may perceive themselves more positively and become motivated to develop competence in other areas.

The Complex Instruction model may be characterized in terms of the 14 common and varying attributes of cooperative learning as follows.

Common attributes:

1. Common tasks and learning activities are multiple-ability tasks that require skills in manipulating materials, observing, reasoning, organizing, recording, and communicating. Tasks are designed to be intrinsically motivating and highly challenging.

2. Learning takes place in groups of five or, sometimes, four members.

3. Cooperative behavior is established through a system of cooperative norms (e.g., asking for help when necessary, providing assistance, taking turns, giving everyone an opportunity to contribute).

4. Interdependence is stimulated, in part, by the delegation of authority; that is, students must act as resources for one another to be able to complete a task successfully. Children cannot move on to the next learning center unless all group members have completed the task and their individual worksheets. Although Cohen (1986, 1994) did not emphasize the concept of positive interdependence, it is provided in many ways.

5. Individual accountability and responsibility are promoted when students perform their assigned roles and complete their individual worksheets. Students are responsible for their own learning and task engagement.

Varying attributes:

6. Grouping is random in the context of a heterogeneous classroom (e.g., academic, social, and linguistic heterogeneity). Groupings also are heterogeneous with respect to gender, ethnic background, and linguistic proficiency.

7. Positive interdependence is promoted incidentally and directly with the Complex Instruction method. Students have a common goal—to explore and learn about a challenging, intrinsically interesting phenomenon. Conceptual learning, including the development of thinking skills and problem-solving strategies, is the main objective; however, this requires interpersonal interactions—opportunities to talk and work together on the task. Tasks are designed so that multiple abilities are required for their completion; thus, children must work together to successfully complete these tasks. Resources, such as manipulative materials and activity cards (available in English and Spanish), are limited and must be shared at each learning center. Depending on the task, various roles are assigned and rotated (e.g., facilitator, checker, reporter, safety officer, clean-up supervisor, equipment manager, harmonizer). Division of labor occurs between groups; different groups work with different materials and perform different tasks. Rewards are not used in Complex Instruction, as tasks are designed to be intrinsically motivating.

8. Cooperative behaviors are taught using procedures from social learning theory; that is, new behaviors are labeled and discussed, recognized when they occur, practiced, and reinforced. Cooperative behaviors are learned through structured games and exercises and practiced during group work.

9. Reflection on the quality of group work is accomplished in several ways. For teachers, there is an observation guide and a participation scoring instrument for use by an "outside observer." During the wrap-up phase of the lesson, the teacher gives specific feedback to groups and individuals, comments on groups' collaborative processes, discusses with the class how group functioning could be improved in the future, and emphasizes connections among activities.

10. The climate is set for cooperation by training students to use specific cooperative behaviors, setting norms for equal participation and cooperation, and discussing the importance of being responsive to the needs of members within a group.

11. Group structure is affected by the system of assigned roles and task directions but otherwise is not specified.

12. Student status issues are attended to through the multiple abilities orientation and by highlighting the competence of students with low-status characteristics. The teacher publicly and specifically identifies and acknowledges quality performances of a child of (potential) low status.

13. Shared leadership develops as students perform their assigned roles.

14. The teacher's role may be described as "letting go and teaming up." The teacher's cooperative management system involves setting cooperative norms; assigning groups and roles; describing specific cooperative behaviors; and giving clear, specific orientation and instructions for the task. During group work, the teacher plays a supportive role but does not directly supervise groups. The teacher asks questions to stimulate and extend children's thinking, provides specific feedback to groups and individuals during group work or the wrap-up, and addresses "status" issues as needed.

COLLABORATIVE APPROACH

The Collaborative Approach is most often associated with theories about language and learning developed by James Britton (1970) and Douglas Barnes (1976). Used initially in language arts and literature, the Collaborative Approach is practiced extensively in the United Kingdom, Australia, Canada, and the United States of America. Its intention is to focus on the creation of personal meaning and internally persuasive understandings through dialogue and discussion. The methodology of Collaborative Learning is described by Barnes et al. (1986); Barnes and Todd (1977); Brubacher, Payne, and Rickett (1990); and Reid et al. (1989).

In the Collaborative Learning model described by Reid et al. (1989), instruction is organized into five phases labeled *engagement, exploration, transformation, presentation,* and *reflection.* In the engagement phase, the teacher provides a perspective to the whole class, producing the basis for the ensuing group activities. In the exploration phase, students engage in initial exploration of ideas or information; this is done in small groups called *home groups.* In the transformation phase, students in home groups engage in an activity to "reshape" the information—organize, clarify, elaborate, or practice the information. In the presentation phase, students present their findings to an interested and critical peer audience called a *sharing group.* Sharing groups are larger than home groups and are formed by combining together or reconstituting home groups. In the final phase—reflection—students "look back" at what they have learned and the process they experienced. Reflection may be done by individuals, pairs, small groups, or the whole class.

This particular collaborative approach is like a Jigsaw procedure with a more leisurely pace and less structure. There is no attempt to directly teach social skills, even though social skills may be discussed during processing. Students are given plenty of time to do their work. In addition, they are given discretion in how they organize themselves as long as they get the task done. The intent is to foster meaning and understanding of the world and one's place in it and for people to come to know and articulate their own values and beliefs.

Historically, there has been some tension between "collaborative" and "cooperative" learning approaches, with some (but not all) cooperative learning approaches tending to be more structured and focused on specific behaviors and rewards. Those of the collaborative learning tradition tend not to "micro-manage," not to break tasks into small component parts, and not to provide rewards. Although interdependence and individual accountability are clearly present in collaborative models, they are emphasized less than in cooperative approaches.

In analyzing Collaborative Learning in terms of the 14 common and varying attributes of small-group approaches, it should be noted that the analysis presented next for items 2, 5, 6, 9, 10, and 14 is based mainly on the one model of collaborative learning described by Reid et al. (1989). These items are marked with an asterisk below.

Common attributes:

1. The common task or learning activity is clarified so group members know the purpose of the group discussion, and its desired outcomes are clear to them.

2. Small-group learning takes place in home groups with four members and in larger sharing groups.*

3. Cooperative behavior involves a lot of discussion in which everyone takes part in clarifying the task, listening, disagreeing, and honestly stating ideas.

4. Interdependence is present in collaborative learning more as an underlying assumption than a technique. The assumption is that learning which takes place in daily life

is predominantly social, with language as a primary means of communication. Thus, social and collaborative interaction are fundamental in human learning and the classroom is a place where language should flow readily and freely among the learners.

5. Individual accountability and responsibility occur as students take notes and keep their own records. Students also must make their findings public and receive feedback in their sharing groups. During the presentation stage, students are accountable for clear and precise communication about their findings (Reid et al., 1989).*

Varying attributes:

6. Grouping is done by "friendship selection" in home groups. The teacher helps compose the sharing groups.*

7. Interdependence is loosely structured. It is assumed that an innate need to make sense and meaning of the world and curiosity about the learning situation will motivate group members to work jointly toward a goal. An explicit goal for the home group is to prepare a public presentation of its findings. Tasks require dialogue in exploration, discussion, elaboration, and critique and typically are structured so students must be interdependent in order for the task to be completed. Tasks also culminate with a presentation of the group's findings. Resources are shared within groups, but different materials may be used for different home groups. Roles are not explicitly assigned. Division of labor may occur when different groups perform different tasks or activities. Rewards are not used; instead, emphasis is placed on engaging intrinsic motivation to inquire and make sense of our world.

8. Explicit teaching of social skills does not occur in a structured way.

9. Reflection on group dynamics and learning takes place during the reflection stage, both individually and collaboratively. Reflective use of a group checklist helps students understand the group process.*

10. Climate setting includes providing introductory lessons to help students understand how groups work. These experiential lessons deal with students as learners, working in small groups, and characteristics of effective and ineffective groups.*

11. Group structure is not made explicit.

12. Attention to student status issues may occur, but is not emphasized.

13. Shared leadership occurs through the different leadership functions (e.g., recording, reporting) assumed by different group members at different times. A group of four does not need a designated leader to "chair" its discussions.

14. The teacher's role includes carefully structuring the learning experiences, assisting students with their learning, listening carefully to small-group discussions, and making personal contact with students. The teacher's role in planning each phase of the lesson, monitoring small groups, and facilitating whole-class discussion is described in detail by Reid et al. (1989).*

OTHER MODELS AND RESOURCES

There are many more approaches to cooperative and collaborative learning than the ones described in this chapter. For example, McCabe and Rhoades (1990; Rhoades & McCabe, 1992) have developed a Simple Cooperation model that features 1) direct instruction of social skills in a somewhat sequential manner based on a social skills continuum, 2) use of

Table 12.2. Analysis of attributes that vary among approaches

	STAD	Learning Together	Group Investigation	Structural Approach	Complex Instruction	Collaborative Approach
6. Grouping procedure	Heterogeneous	Usually heterogeneous	Varied	Varied	Random heterogeneous	Friendship
7. Structuring positive interdependence						
Goals	Everyone masters material; improves over own past performance	Mutual learning goals; make sure everyone learns	Set by cooperative planning	Sometimes produce a group product	Conceptual learning goals	Arise from need to make sense and meaning of the word
Tasks	Require mutual help	Require ability to explain reasoning or strategies	Set by cooperative planning	Designed so they cannot be done alone	Require multiple abilities	Include use of language and presentation of findings
Resources	Limited	Limited or jigsawed	Shared; divided among groups	Shared	Limited; shared	Shared
Roles	No	Yes	Set by group	In some structures	Yes	Not explicitly assigned
Division of labor	No	Sometimes	Within and between groups	In some designs between groups	Between groups	Sometimes between groups
Rewards	Yes, team recognition	Sometimes, bonus points	No	Team recognition scores	No	No
8. Explicit teaching of social skills	Only as needed	Major emphasis	As needed, sometimes prior to Group Investigation	Structured natural approach	Using Social Learning Theory	No
9. Reflection on social and academic skills or group process	Not emphasized	Yes	May occur in final stage	Yes	Yes	Yes
10. Climate setting	Team building via team names	Trust-building activities	Cooperative norms	Class building; team building	Cooperative norms and training for cooperation	Sometimes through introductory lessons
11. Group structure	Not specified; sometimes paired	Not prescribed; affected by practice roles	Determined by students	High degree of explicit nature	Not specified; affected by roles	Not specified
12. Attention to student status	Not emphasized	Not emphasized	Not emphasized	Not emphasized	Highly emphasized	Not emphasized
13. Group leadership	Not designated	Shared via roles	Not designated; develops in joint planning	Shared via structures and roles	Shared via roles	Shared via assuming different functions
14. Teacher's role	Complex and varied	Complex and varied	Complex and varied	Complex and varied	Complex and varied	Complex and varied

The numbering of the attributes (6–14) in the table above corresponds to the numerical order of the varying attributes that follow the analysis of each of the six collaborative approaches presented in this chapter.

group rewards and bonus points instead of group grades, 3) three authentic assessment techniques, 4) processes for effective meeting management, 5) distributed leadership, 6) a direct link between cooperative learning and varied thinking behaviors and thinking processes, and 7) an outcomes-based learning model.

The reference list and bibliography at the end of this chapter include selected additional references for cooperative and collaborative learning. A more comprehensive listing of resources may be found in *Resource Guide* (Graves, 1993), which is a special issue of the *Cooperative Learning Magazine* published by the International Association for the Study of Cooperation in Education (IASCE), and the organization's web site at http://www.iasce.net.

CONCLUSION

Six major approaches to cooperative and collaborative learning are described and compared in this chapter. Five attributes considered "critical attributes" of cooperative and collaborative learning are identified as common to all six approaches. These attributes are 1) a common task or learning activity suitable for group work, 2) small-group learning, 3) cooperative behavior, 4) interdependence, and 5) individual accountability and responsibility.

Beyond these five critical attributes, nine attributes are identified that are employed to varying degrees in the different models of cooperative/collaborative learning. Table 12.2 provides a summary analysis of the approaches presented in this chapter, using the nine attributes that vary among approaches.

I have had considerable experience in supporting the professional development of teachers who use cooperative learning (see, for example, Brody & Davidson, 1998). In my opinion, it is useful for teachers to emphasize the five attributes common to all cooperative and collaborative approaches. Teachers can then make careful selections among approaches and additional attributes that fit their own personal philosophies, instructional goals, and classroom settings. The five common attributes establish a coherent unity underlying all of the diverse approaches to cooperative and collaborative learning. The diversity of approaches within this underlying unity provides flexibility based on a strong conceptual foundation.

REFERENCES

Baloche, L. (1998). *The cooperative classroom: Empowering learning.* Upper Saddle River, NJ: Prentice Hall.
Barnes, D. (1976). *From communication to curriculum.* Portsmouth, NH: Boynton/Cook.
Barnes, D., Britton, J., & Torbe, M. (1986). *Language, the learner and the school* (2nd ed.). Portsmouth, NH: Boynton/Cook.
Barnes, D., & Todd, F. (1977). *Communicating and learning in small groups.* London: Routledge, Kegan Paul.
Britton, J. (1970). *Language and learning.* Portsmouth, NH: Boynton/Cook.
Brody, C., & Davidson, N. (Eds.). (1998). *Professional development for cooperative development: Issues and approaches.* Albany: State University of New York.
Brubacher, M., Payne, R., & Rickett, K. (1990). *Perspectives on small group learning: Theory and practice.* Oakvale, Ontario, Canada: Rubicon Publishing, Inc.
Cohen, E. (1986). *Designing groupwork: Strategies for the heterogeneous classroom.* New York: Teachers College Press.
Cohen, E. (1994). *Designing groupwork: Strategies for the heterogeneous classroom* (2nd ed.). New York: Teachers College Press.
DeAvila, E., Duncan, S., & Navarette, C. (1986). *Finding out/Descubrimiento.* Northvale, NJ: Santilla Publishing Company.

Forest, L. (2001). *Crafting creative community: Combining cooperative learning, multiple intelligences, and nature's wisdom.* San Clemente, CA: Kagan Publishing Co.

Groves, T. (1993). Resource Guide. *Cooperative Learning Magazine, 12*(4).

Jensen, E., & Davidson, N. (1997). 12-step recovery program for lectureholics. *College Teaching, 45*(3), 102–103.

Johnson, D.W., & Johnson, F. (1991). *Joining together: Group theory and group skills.* Upper Saddle River, NJ: Prentice Hall.

Johnson, D.W., & Johnson, R. (1975/1991/1999). *Learning together and alone: Cooperative, competitive, and individualistic learning.* Needham Heights, MA: Allyn & Bacon.

Johnson, D.W., & Johnson, R. (1987). *Creative conflict.* Edina, MN: Interaction Book Company.

Johnson, D.W., & Johnson, R. (1989a). *Cooperation and competition: Theory and research.* Edina, MN: Interaction Book Company.

Johnson, D.W., & Johnson, R. (1989b). *Leading the cooperative school.* Edina, MN: Interaction Book Company.

Johnson, D.W., Johnson, R., & Holubec, E. (1986/1998). *Circles of learning: Cooperation in the classroom* (6th ed.). Edina, MN: Interaction Book Company.

Johnson, D.W., Johnson, R., & Smith, K. (1991/1998). *Active learning: Cooperation in the college classroom* (2nd ed.). Edina, MN: Interaction Book Company.

Kagan, S. (1992/1994). *Cooperative learning: Resources for teachers.* San Clemente, CA: Kagan Publishing.

Lotan, R.A. & Cohen, E.G. (1997). *Working for equity in heterogeneous classrooms: Sociological theory in practice.* New York: Teachers College Press.

Lyman, F. (1992). Think-pair-share, thinktrix, thinklinks, and weird facts: An interactive system for cooperative thinking. In N. Davidson & T. Worsham (Eds.), *Enhancing thinking through cooperative learning.* New York: Teachers College Press.

McCabe, M., & Rhoades, J. (1990). *The nurturing classroom.* Sacramento, CA: ITA Publications.

Millis, B., & Cottell, P. (1998). *Cooperative learning in higher education.* Phoenix, AZ: Oryx Press.

Reid, J., Forrestal, P., & Cook, J. (1989). *Small group learning in the classroom.* Scarborough, Australia: Chalkface Press.

Rhoades, J., & McCabe, M. (1992). *Outcome-based learning: A teacher's guide to restructuring the classroom.* Sacramento, CA: ITA Publications.

Rogers, E., Reynolds, B., Davidson, N., & Thomas, A. (2001). *Cooperative learning in undergraduate mathematics: Issues that matter and strategies that work.* Washington, DC: Mathematical Association of America.

Sharan, S. (1990). *Cooperative learning: Theory and research.* New York: Praeger.

Sharan, S. (Ed.). (1993/1999). *Handbook of cooperative learning methods* (2nd ed.). Westport, CT: Greenwood.

Sharan, S., & Hertz-Lazarowitz, R. (1980). A group investigation method of cooperative learning in the classroom. In S. Sharan, P. Hare, C. Webb, & R. Hertz-Lazarowitz (Eds.), *Cooperation in education* (pp. 14–46). Provo, UT: Brigham Young University Press.

Sharan, S., & Hertz-Lazarowitz, R. (1982). Effects of an instructional change program on teachers' behavior, attitudes and perceptions. *Journal of Applied Behavioral Science, 18*, 185–201.

Slavin, R. (1983a/1994). *Cooperative learning: Theory, research and practice* (2nd ed.). Needham Heights, MA: Allyn & Bacon.

Slavin, R. (1983b). When does cooperative learning increase student achievement? *Psychological Bulletin, 94*, 429–445.

Slavin, R.E. (1986). *Using student team learning* (3rd ed.). Baltimore: Johns Hopkins University, Center for Research on Elementary and Middle Schools.

Slavin, R. (1990). *Cooperative learning: Theory, research and practice.* Upper Saddle River, NJ: Prentice Hall.

Thelen, H. (1967). Group interactional factors in learning. In E. Bower & W. Hollister (Eds.), *Behavioral science frontiers in education* (pp. 257–287). New York: John Wiley & Sons.

Thelen, H. (1981). *The classroom society.* London: Croom Helm.

13

Ensuring Diversity Is Positive

Cooperative Community, Constructive Conflict, and Civic Values

David W. Johnson
Roger T. Johnson

In order for the promise of diversity to be realized, diverse students must be brought together in the same classroom and school, united under a common superordinate identity. Cooperative efforts, constructive conflict, and civic values are required among students, faculty, and administrators to educate diverse students to understand and take pride in their heritage, understand and appreciate the heritage of others, develop a superordinate identity, and internalize the democratic values expressed in the U.S. Constitution and Bill of Rights.

THREE Cs PROGRAM

The promise of diversity is built on the three Cs: cooperative community, constructive conflict resolution, and civic values. The school is a cooperative system in which faculty/staff, students, and parents work together to achieve mutual goals concerning quality education. Sometimes, conflicts arise over how best to achieve goals and coordinate actions. These conflicts have to be resolved constructively if the community is to survive. Both cooperative community and constructive conflict resolution are based on civic values that recognize and support the long-term benefits of working together and contributing to the welfare of others and the common good (as well as working for one's own well-being).

The Three Cs Program, described next, has been implemented in a wide variety of schools throughout North America and many other parts of the world including Europe, the Middle East, Africa, Asia, the South Pacific, and Central and South America. It has been used with inner-city, lower-class students and with upper-class private school students and with everyone in between. In short, the program has been field tested throughout the world in widely diverse situations (Johnson, D.W. & Johnson, R., 2000).

First C: Cooperative Community

Nature of Community and Social Interdependence Realizing the promise of diversity begins with establishing a learning community based on cooperation (i.e., working together to achieve mutual goals). Scholarship, learning, and positive relationships among students do not exist in isolation; they are products of a community and a culture characterized by mutual respect and trust. *Community* may be defined as a group of people who live in the same locality and share common goals and a common culture. Broadly, the school community includes all stakeholders, including central administrators, college admission officers, and future employers; but in practice, the school community is made up of the faculty and staff, the students, their parents, and members of the neighborhood.

The heart of community and culture is social interdependence. Social interdependence exists when each individual's outcomes are affected by the actions of others (Deutsch, 1949; Johnson & Johnson, 1989). Social interdependence may be positive or negative. Positive interdependence (cooperation) exists when individuals work together to achieve mutual goals, and negative interdependence (competition) exists when individuals work against each other to achieve a goal that only one or a few may attain. Social independence—in which the outcomes of each person are unaffected by others' actions—is characterized by individualistic actions. The effectiveness of a school increases the positive interdependence (i.e., cooperation) that is structured at all levels of the school: learning groups, classrooms, interclass, schools, school–parent and school–neighborhood relationships.

Power of Cooperation The type of interdependence structured among individuals determines how they interact with each other, which, in turn, determines outcomes. Structuring situations cooperatively results in individuals promoting each other's success (individuals help, assist, support, and encourage each other's efforts). Structuring situations competitively results in individuals opposing each other's success (individuals obstruct and block each other's efforts). Structuring situations individualistically results in ignoring each other's success or failure (individuals work alone). These interaction patterns affect numerous variables, which may be subsumed within the three broad and interrelated outcomes of (Johnson & Johnson, 1989)

1. Effort exerted to achieve (higher achievement and greater productivity, more frequent use of higher level reasoning, more frequent generation of new ideas and solutions, greater intrinsic and achievement motivation, greater long-term retention, more on-task behavior, and greater transfer of what is learned within one situation to another situation)

2. Quality of relationships among participants (greater interpersonal attraction, liking, cohesion and esprit de corps, valuing of heterogeneity, and greater task-oriented and personal support)

3. Psychological adjustment (greater psychological health, greater social competencies, higher self-esteem, a shared identity, and greater ability to cope with stress and adversity)

Much of the research on social interdependence and interpersonal relationships has been conducted on relationships between students of various racial identities, students from various ethnic groups, and students with and without disabilities (Johnson & Johnson, 1989). The results are consistent. Working cooperatively creates far more positive relationships among diverse and heterogeneous students than does learning competitively or individualistically. Within cooperative situations there tends to be a process of acceptance, and within competitive and individualistic situations there tends to be a process of rejection (see Table 13.1). The *process of acceptance* is based on the individuals' promoting mutual goal accomplishment as a result of their perceived positive interdependence. The promotive interaction tends to result in frequent, accurate, and open communication; accurate understanding of each other's perspectives; openness to being influenced by collaborators; differentiated, dynamic, and realistic views of each other; high self-esteem; success and productivity; and expectations for positive and productive future interaction. The *process of rejection* results from oppositional or no interaction based on perceptions of negative or no interdependence. Both lead to inaccurate or no communication; egocentrism; resistance

Table 13.1. Processes of acceptance and rejection

Process of acceptance	Process of rejection
Positive interdependence	Negative interdependence
Promotive interaction	Oppositional or no interaction
Frequent and open communication	Inaccurate or no communication
Understanding of other perspectives	Egocentrism
Inducibility	Resistance to influence
Differentiated views of each other	Monopolistic views of each other
High self-esteem	Low self-esteem
Successful achievement, productivity	Failure, lack of productivity
Expectations of positive and productive	Expectations of negative and unproductive
Future interaction with others	Future interaction with others

to influence; monopolistic, stereotyped, and static views of others; low self-esteem; failure; and expectations of distasteful and unpleasant interaction with others. The processes of acceptance and rejection are self-perpetuating. Any part of the process tends to elicit all the other parts of the process.

Benefits of Cooperative Learning for Diversity A focus on cooperative learning and persistence in implementing it in every classroom is instrumental in laying the foundation for capitalizing on the benefits of diversity (Johnson & Johnson, 1989). First, cooperative learning ensures that all students are meaningfully and actively involved in learning. Active, involved students do not tend to engage in rejecting, bullying, or prejudiced behavior. Second, cooperative learning ensures that students are achieving up to their potential and are experiencing psychological success so they are motivated to continue to invest energy and effort in learning. Those who experience academic failure are at risk for tuning out and acting up, which often leads to physical or verbal aggression against stereotyped classmates. Third, systematic use of cooperative learning promotes the development of caring and committed relationships among students, including between majority and minority students. Students who are isolated or alienated from their peers and who do not have friends are at risk for physical or verbal aggression against stereotyped classmates. The negative impact of isolation may be even more severe on minority students in a wider variety of areas.

Fourth, cooperative groups provide an arena in which students develop the interpersonal and small-group skills needed to work effectively with diverse schoolmates. Students learn how to communicate effectively, provide leadership, engage in effective decision making, build trust, and understand others' perspectives. Fifth, cooperative learning groups provide an arena for discussions in which personal problems are shared and solved. As a result, students' resilience and ability to cope with adversity and stress tend to increase. Children who do not share their problems and who do not have caring, supportive help in solving them are at greater risk to commit physical or verbal aggression against stereotyped classmates.

Sixth, cooperative groups promote a sense of meaning, pride, and esteem by academically helping and assisting classmates and contributing to their well-being and quality of life. This increases the social acceptance of diverse classmates. Seventh, all the benefits of cooperation for students can result from the cooperation among faculty and staff. Finally, the systematic use of cooperative learning provides the context for resolving conflicts in constructive ways; this is essential for positive relationships among diverse individuals. To constructively resolve conflicts, students, faculty, and staff need a common set of procedures, which is why academic controversy needs to be used and a schoolwide conflict resolution and peer mediation program is implemented.

Classroom Interdependence   Consider the following classroom scenario.

One class that was studying geography turned the ceiling of their classroom into a large grid giving latitude and longitude. The class was divided into eight cooperative groups. Each group was assigned a geographical location on which to do a report. The groups summarized the essential information about their location on a placard, located where on the ceiling it should be placed, and placed it there. The class then planned an itinerary for a trip to visit all eight places. Yarn was used to mark their journey. As they arrived at each spot, the appropriate group presented its report on the location, including its latitude and longitude.

The positive interdependence in learning groups may be extended to the class as a whole through class goals (a criterion for each student or a total class score as a specified criterion), class rewards or celebrations (academic and nonacademic rewards or a class party), class roles (establishing a classroom government, placing teams in charge of daily class cleanup, running a class bank or business), or dividing resources (having the class publish a newsletter in which each cooperative group contributes one article). Class meetings can be held as a forum for discussing how well the class is functioning and how the quality of classroom life may be improved. Finally, a common identity may be created by such things as a class name, slogan, flag, or song.

Interclass Interdependence   There are many ways to structure cross-class cooperation. An interdisciplinary team of three to six teachers may organize their classes into a "neighborhood" or a "school within a school" where classes work together and engage in joint projects for a number of years. Science and math or English literature and social studies may be integrated and the classes combined. Students of different ages can be involved in cross-class "reading buddies" who meet weekly throughout the year so they can jointly share and explore literature. Several classes can do periodic projects on learning specific social skills and values so students from different classes can demonstrate the skills and values to each other and use them in the hallways, on the playground, and in the lunchroom. In these and many other ways, cross-class interdependence may be created.

School Interdependence   Consider this scenario at a local public school.

One challenge we face each year is bringing new faculty on board. We want them to become part of our school community as quickly as possible and that means training them in the components of our program. Study groups help accomplish this. We have one study group, for example, on the *Nuts and Bolts of Cooperative Learning* for new faculty who have not been trained in cooperative learning and another study group on *Teaching Students to be Peacemakers* for new faculty who have not been trained in conflict resolution. A trained, experienced teacher leads each study group. In each meeting, we take a chapter in the book and go over it in detail. Then, we plan how to implement it in our classrooms. We make sure we have those programs in every classroom in the school. This is how we keep the climate the way it is.

There are at least four ways positive interdependence may be established at the school level (Johnson & Johnson, 1994b). First, the school mission statement may articulate the mutual goals shared by all members of the school and may be displayed on the school's walls and printed at the top of the agenda of every meeting involving faculty and staff. This "keeps the dream" in front of the faculty and staff and is a constant reminder of their commitment.

Second, just as students work in cooperative learning groups, ideally, teachers will work in a variety of cooperative teams (Johnson & Johnson, 1994b). All faculty and staff can meet weekly in teaching teams and/or study groups. *Collegial teaching teams* consist of two to five teachers who plan lessons together, orchestrate their use of integrated curriculum units, schedule the times they will teach together and apart, and explore how best to promote each other's instructional success for the following week. *Collegial study groups* are formed to discuss a book about an instructional method (e.g., cooperative learning, block scheduling, creating an integrated curriculum).

Third, in addition to the collegial teaching teams and study groups, teachers may be assigned to *task forces* to plan and implement solutions to schoolwide issues and problems such as curriculum adoptions and lunchroom behavior and *ad-hoc decision-making groups* during faculty meetings to involve all staff members in important school decisions.

Finally, school interdependence may be highlighted in a variety of schoolwide activities, such as the weekly student-produced school news broadcasts, special activities organized by the student council, all-school projects, and regular school assemblies.

School–Parent Interdependence   Parents and other family members can be involved in establishing the school's goals and the "strategic plan" to achieve the goals. Family members, with the help of students, can produce a weekly newsletter or publish the school yearbook. Parents and family members can volunteer in their children's classes and help conduct special projects. Family members may serve on all school committees and the site council. The ideal goal is to have 100% of the parents and family members participating in the school.

School–Neighborhood Interdependence   There are many creative ways that the school community may be extended into the neighborhood. Local merchants can support the school mission by giving a discount to students who achieve a *B* average or above. Members of the neighborhood could play in the school band. Classes could do neighborhood service projects, such as cleaning up a park or mowing the yards of older residents.

Second C: Constructive Conflict Resolution

Conflict is the moment of truth among diverse individuals. It is almost paradoxical that conflicts are more frequent and intense the more caring and committed the relationships among participants and the more committed participants are to the community's goals. When they are managed constructively, conflicts can result in such positive outcomes as 1) increased energy, excitement, and emotion; 2) increased achievement, retention, insight, creativity, problem solving, and synthesis; 3) increased healthy cognitive and social development; 4) clarified identity, commitments, and values; and 5) strengthened relationships (Johnson & Johnson, 1995a, 1995c, 1995d, 1996a). If the conflicts are managed destructively, then they destroy relationships and tear the cooperative system apart.

Whether conflicts result in positive or negative outcomes depends largely on 1) participants having clear procedures for managing conflicts; 2) participants being skilled in the use of the procedures; and 3) whether the norms, values, and climate of the school encourage and support the use of the procedures. If one or more of these conditions are not met, then conflicts will tend to be managed destructively. Faculty and staff need to teach students (and learn themselves) three procedures for managing conflicts: academic controversy, problem-solving negotiation, and peer mediation (see Table 13.2; Johnson & Johnson, 1995a, 1995c). Each of these procedures is essential for constructive relationships among diverse individuals (see Chapter 19).

Table 13.2. Types of conflict

Academic controversy	Conflicts of interest
One person's ideas, information, theories, conclusions, and opinions are incompatible with those of another and the two seek to reach an agreement.	The actions of one person attempting to maximize benefits prevents, blocks, or interferes with another person maximizing his or her benefits.
Controversy procedure	Integrative (problem-solving) negotiations
Research and prepare positions	Describe wants
Present and advocate positions	Describe feelings
Refute opposing position and refute attacks on own position	Describe reasons for wants and feelings
Reverse perspectives	Take other's perspective
Synthesize and integrate best evidence and reasoning from all sides	Invent three optional agreements that maximize joint outcomes
	Choose one and formalize agreement

Academic Controversies A *controversy* exists when one person's ideas, opinions, information, theories, or conclusions are incompatible with those of another and the two seek to reach an agreement (Johnson & Johnson, 1995c). Controversies are resolved by engaging in what Aristotle called *deliberate discourse* (i.e., the discussion of the advantages and disadvantages of proposed actions) aimed at synthesizing novel solutions (i.e., *creative problem solving*). Teaching students how to engage in the controversy process begins with randomly assigning students to heterogeneous cooperative learning groups of four members (Johnson & Johnson, 1979, 1989, 1995c). The groups are given an issue on which to write a report and pass a test. Each cooperative group is divided into two pairs. One pair is given the con position on the issue and the other pair is given the pro position. Each pair is given the instructional materials needed to define their position and point them toward supporting information. The cooperative goal of reaching a consensus on the issue (by synthesizing the best reasoning from both sides) and writing a quality group report is highlighted. Students then

1. *Research, learn, and prepare a position:* Students prepare the best case possible for their assigned position by researching the assigned position, organizing the information into a persuasive argument, and planning how to advocate the assigned position effectively to ensure it receives a fair and complete hearing.

2. *Present and advocate the position:* Students present the best case for their assigned position to ensure it gets a fair and complete hearing.

3. *Engage in an open discussion in which there is spirited disagreement:* Students freely exchange information and ideas while 1) arguing forcefully and persuasively for their position, 2) critically analyzing and refuting the opposing position, and 3) rebutting attacks on their position and presenting counter arguments.

4. *Reverse perspectives:* Students reverse perspectives and present the best case for the opposing position.

5. *Synthesize:* Students drop all advocacy and find a synthesis on which all members can agree. Students summarize the best evidence and reasoning from both sides and integrate it into a joint position that is a new and unique. Students are to write a group report on the group's synthesis with the supporting evidence and rationale and take a test on both positions. Groups then process how well the group functioned and celebrate the group's success and hard work.

Validating Research Evidence   Since 1970, the authors have published 15 research studies on the impact of academic controversy, and numerous other researchers have conducted studies directly on controversy and in related areas (Johnson & Johnson, 1989, 1995c). The considerable research available indicates that intellectual "disputed passages" create higher achievement (characterized by higher achievement, longer retention, more frequent use of higher level reasoning and metacognitive thought, more critical thinking, greater creativity, and continuing motivation to learn), more positive interpersonal relationships, and greater psychological health when they 1) occur within cooperative learning groups and 2) are carefully structured to ensure that students manage them constructively (Johnson & Johnson, 1989, 1995c). Engaging in a controversy can also be fun, enjoyable, and exciting. Two of the most important aspects for managing conflicts among diverse individuals, however, are 1) the emphasis on viewing issues from all perspectives and 2) learning that conflicts can have positive outcomes when people listen to each other and work cooperatively to reach solutions.

Conflict Resolution Training   The "Teaching Students to be Peacemakers Program" began in the 1960s (Johnson & Johnson, 1995b, 1995c) to teach all students in a school how to resolve conflicts of interest constructively. All students are taught how to engage in problem-solving (integrative) negotiations and mediate their schoolmates' conflicts. The program is then implemented and all students take turns mediating.

Problem-Solving Negotiations   In addition to intellectual conflicts, conflicts based on individuals' differing interests within a situation must be resolved constructively. *Conflicts of interest* exist when the actions of one person attempting to maximize his or her wants and benefits prevents, blocks, or interferes with another person maximizing his or her wants and benefits. Such conflicts are resolved through negotiation (when negotiation does not work, then mediation is required). There are two types of negotiations: *distributive* or "win–lose" (in which one person benefits only if the opponent agrees to make a concession) and *integrative* or problem solving (in which disputants work together to create an agreement that benefits everyone involved). In ongoing relationships, distributive negotiations tend to result in destructive outcomes and problem solving tends to lead to constructive outcomes. The steps in using problem-solving negotiations are (Johnson & Johnson, 1995b, 1995c)

1. *Describing what you want:* "I want to use the book now." This includes using good communication skills and defining the conflict as a small and specific mutual problem.

2. *Describing how you feel:* "I'm frustrated." Disputants must understand how they feel and communicate it openly and clearly.

3. *Describing the reasons for your wants and feelings:* "You have been using the book for the past hour. If I don't get to use the book soon, then my report will not be done on time. It's frustrating to have to wait so long." This includes expressing cooperative intentions, listening carefully, separating interests from positions, and differentiating before trying to integrate the two sets of interests.

4. *Taking the other's perspective and summarizing your understanding of what the other person wants, how the other person feels, and the reasons underlying both:* "My understanding of you is . . . " This includes understanding the perspective of the opposing disputant and being able to see the problem from both perspectives simultaneously.

5. *Inventing three optional plans to resolve the conflict that maximize joint benefits:* "Plan A is . . . , Plan B is . . . , Plan C is . . ." This includes inventing creative options to solve the problem.

6. *Choosing one and formalizing the agreement with a hand shake:* "Let's agree on Plan B!" A wise agreement is fair to all disputants and is based on principles. It maximizes joint benefits and strengthens disputants' ability to work together cooperatively and resolve conflicts constructively in the future. It specifies how each disputant should act in the future and how the agreement will be reviewed and renegotiated if it does not work.

Peer Mediation   A *mediator* is a neutral person who helps two or more people resolve their conflict, usually by negotiating an integrative agreement. In contrast, *arbitration* is the submission of a dispute to a disinterested third party (such as a teacher or principal) who makes a final and binding judgment as to how the conflict will be resolved. Mediation consists of four steps (Johnson & Johnson, 1995b, 1995c):

1. *Ending hostilities:* Break up hostile encounters and cool off students.

2. *Ensuring disputants are committed to the mediation process:* To ensure that disputants are committed to the mediation process and are ready to negotiate in good faith, the mediator introduces the process of mediation and sets the ground rules that 1) mediation is voluntary, 2) the mediator is neutral, 3) each person will have the chance to state his or her view of the conflict without interruption, and 4) each person agrees to solve the problem with no name calling or interrupting, being as honest as he or she can, abiding by any agreement made, and keeping anything said in mediation confidential.

3. *Helping disputants successfully negotiate with each other:* The disputants are carefully taken through the problem-solving negotiation steps.

4. *Formalizing the agreement:* The agreement is solidified into a contract.

Continuing Lessons To Refine and Upgrade Students' Skills   Gaining real expertise in resolving conflicts constructively takes years of training and practice. A few hours of training are clearly insufficient. Negotiation and mediation training need to be integrated into academic lessons. Almost any lesson in literature and history, for example, can be modified to include role-playing situations in which the negotiation and/or mediation procedures are used. In addition, the "Teaching Students to be Peacemakers Program" was conceived to be a 12-year spiral program that is retaught each year in an increasingly sophisticated and complex way. Twelve years of training and practice will result in a person with considerable expertise in resolving conflicts constructively.

Benefits of Conflict Resolution and Peer Mediation Programs   We have conducted 17 studies on implementing the "Teaching Students to be Peacemakers Program" in schools involving students from kindergarten through the tenth grade, and several other researchers have conducted relevant studies (Johnson & Johnson, 1995c, 1995d, 1996a). There are many benefits of teaching diverse students the problem-solving negotiation and the peer mediation procedures.

First, students and faculty tended to develop a shared understanding of how conflicts should be managed and a common vocabulary to discuss conflicts. Second, students tended to learn the negotiation and mediation procedures, retain their knowledge throughout the school year and into the following year, apply the procedures to their and other people's conflicts, transfer the procedures to nonclassroom settings such as the playground and lunchroom, transfer the procedures to nonschool settings such as the home, use the procedures similarly in family and school settings, and (when given the option) engage in problem-solving rather than win–lose negotiations. Third, students' attitudes toward conflict tended to became more positive. Students learned to view conflicts as potentially positive, and faculty and parents viewed the conflict training as constructive and helpful.

Fourth, students tended to resolve their conflicts without the involvement of faculty and administrators. A teacher noted:

> It's so great to be able to say, "These people are having a conflict; is there someone who can help them resolve it?" Twenty hands go up and everybody wants to help them. And I choose someone and say, "All right, take these people back to the mediation table and solve the conflict and let me know how it goes." Sometimes it will take 2 minutes and sometimes it will take 15 minutes. As a teacher, I respect so much and appreciate immensely that students can do that for themselves. It enables everybody in the class, including me, to focus on what we're learning.

Classroom management problems, in other words, tended to be significantly reduced. The number of discipline problems teachers have to deal with decreased by about 60% and referrals to administrators dropped about 90%. Faculty and administrators no longer have to arbitrate conflicts among students; instead, they spend their time maintaining and supporting the peer mediation process. A teacher commented, "Classroom management problems are nil as far as I'm concerned. We don't do a lot of disciplining per se. A lot of times, when a conflict occurs on the playground, they resolve it there and do not bring it back to the classroom. So there is a lot less I have to deal with in the classroom."

Fifth, the conflict resolution procedures tended to enhance the basic values of the classroom and school. A teacher who emphasizes the value of "respect" states, "The procedures are a very respectful way to resolve conflicts. There's a calmness in the classroom because the students know the negotiation and mediation procedures." Sixth, students generally liked to engage in the procedures. A teacher states, "They never refuse to negotiate or mediate. When there's a conflict and you say it's time for conflict resolution, you never have either one say I won't do it. There are no refusals."

Finally, when integrated into academic units, the conflict resolution training tended to increase academic achievement and long-term retention of the academic material. Academic units, especially in subject areas such as literature and history, provide a setting to understand conflicts, practice how to resolve them, and use them to gain insight into the material being studied.

Third C: Civic Values

For a community to sustain itself, members must share common goals and values aimed at increasing the quality of life within the community (Johnson & Johnson, 1996b, 1999). To create positive relationships among diverse individuals, common goals and shared values must help define appropriate behavior. The constructive outcomes resulting from diversity tend not to result in schools dominated by 1) competition in which students are taught to value striving for their personal success at the expense of others or 2) individualistic efforts in which students value only their own self-interests. Rather, students need to internalize values underlying cooperation and constructive conflict.

Civic values may be taught through direct instruction, modeling and identification, the enactment of assigned and voluntary roles, group influences, and the hidden curriculum existing in the pattern and flow of daily school life (Johnson, D.W. & Johnson, F., 2000). First, the core values can be directly taught by placing them in the school's mission statement, role playing how to put them into action, pointing out instances in which a student demonstrated the values, and integrating them into the curriculum (children's literature may be used to teach values). Second, faculty and administrators can teach students values through identification by 1) building positive, caring, supportive relationships with the students and 2) consistently modeling the values in interactions with the students.

Third, values may be taught by assigning students social roles. In school, students learn the roles of "student" as well as other roles such as "American," "citizen," "collaborator," and "mediator." Fourth, individuals adopt the values of their reference groups. By adopting the school community as a reference group, students will adopt its civic values.

Perhaps the most effective way to teach values is through the ebb and flow of everyday life within the school. The value systems underlying competitive, individualistic, and cooperative situations, for example, are a hidden curriculum beneath the surface of school life. Whenever students engage in *competitive efforts,* for example, they learn the following values: 1) commitment to getting more than others (there is a built-in concern that one is smarter, faster, stronger, more competent, and more successful than others so that one will win and others will lose); 2) success depends on beating, defeating, and getting more than other people (triumphing over others and being "number one" are valued); 3) what is important is winning, not mastery or excellence; 4) opposing, obstructing, and sabotaging the success of others is a natural way of life (winning depends on a good offense—doing better than others—and a good defense—not letting anyone do better than you); 5) feeling joy and pride in one's wins and others' losses (the pleasure of winning is associated with others' disappointment with losing); 6) others are a threat to one's success; 7) a person's worth (own and others) is conditional and contingent on his or her "wins," (a person's worth is never fixed, it depends on the latest victory); 8) winning, not learning, is the goal of academic work; and 9) people who are different are to be either feared (if they have an advantage) or held in contempt (if they have a disability).

The values inherently taught by *individualistic experiences* are 1) commitment to one's own self-interest (only personal success is viewed as important, others' success is irrelevant); 2) success depends on one's own efforts; 3) the pleasure of succeeding is personal and relevant to only oneself; 4) other people are irrelevant; 5) self-worth is based on a unidimensional view that the characteristics that help the person succeed are valued (in school that is primarily reading and math ability); 6) extrinsic motivation to gain rewards for achieving up to criteria is valued; and 7) similar people are liked and dissimilar people are disliked.

The values inherently taught by *cooperative efforts* are that 1) commitment to own and others' success and well-being as well as to the common good; 2) success depends on joint efforts to achieve mutual goals; 3) facilitating, promoting, and encouraging the success of others is a natural way of life (a smart cooperator will always find ways to promote, facilitate, and encourage the efforts of others); 4) the pleasure of succeeding is associated with others' happiness in their success; 5) other people are potential contributors to one's success; 6) own and other people's worth is unconditional (because there are so many diverse ways that a person may contribute to a joint effort, everyone has value all the time); 7) intrinsic motivation based on striving to learn, grow, develop, and succeed is valued (learning is the goal, not winning); 8) people who are different from oneself are to be valued as they can make unique contributions to the joint effort.

Constructive controversy inherently teaches the values of respecting the diverse nature and efforts of others, strongly stating one's views, subjecting one's conclusions to intellectual challenge, viewing issues from all perspectives, ensuring all sides receive a fair hearing and a critical analysis, and seeking a synthesis or integration of the best information and reasoning from all sides. *Problem-solving negotiations and mediation* inherently teaches the values of behaving with integrity, honestly sharing one's wants and feelings, viewing issues from all perspectives, seeking agreements that maximize joint outcomes, and maintaining effective long-term relationships.

Benefits of Civic Values Program　　There are too many developmental and personal benefits from learning civic values to detail all of them here. Relationships among diverse individuals are based on the civil values of respect, equality, freedom, and justice.

At the personal level, civic values provide the internal gyroscope each child and youth needs to guide his or her behavior. It ensures that each individual becomes inner directed (as opposed to other directed) and has the inner principles needed to regulate his or her behavior. At the school management level, teaching civic values takes the guesswork out of knowing what the school stands for. The values guide decision making about the curriculum, instruction, and resources. They provide a standard for making selections of curriculum materials. The values provide a structure for faculty and staff to talk to parents, students, visitors, and each other about what is important and why.

FUTURE OF THE THREE Cs APPROACH TO DIVERSITY

Educational practices come and go, but cooperative learning, constructive conflict, and civic values will always be with us for many reasons. First, the amount and consistency of research demonstrating the effectiveness of cooperative efforts and constructive conflict resolution is staggering. Any teacher who does *not* use cooperative learning and constructive conflict procedures may not be considered fully competent. In schools where practice follows what we know about effective teaching, the three Cs are foundational.

Second, as the diversity of students in American schools increases, the three Cs are required to ensure that creative energy results rather than prejudice and ethnocentrism. By 2020, demographers predict people from ethnic and racial groups other than European Americans will compose nearly half of school-age students. Such diversity provides opportunities and problems. Students need to learn about and take pride in their cultural and ethnic heritage, understand and appreciate the cultural and ethnic heritage of others, develop a superordinate identity as Americans, and internalize the democratic values expressed in our U.S. Constitution and Bill of Rights. In order to ensure that our heterogeneity is a source of creativity, energy, entrepreneurism, and sophistication, cooperative community, constructive conflict, and civic values are required.

Third, changes in family and community structure have reduced the social support and quality of relationships experienced by many children. Caring, committed, supportive relationships are an absolute necessity for healthy social, cognitive, and physical development and psychological health. For many children, school has become the primary place where they are involved with peers and adults. The three Cs are essential for developing the caring relationships, social competencies, and coping skills required to grow and develop in healthy ways and deal with adversity. To manage stress and deal with adversity, the coping skills and social competencies resulting from working cooperatively with others, resolving conflicts constructively, and internalizing civic values gives students a developmental advantage.

Fourth, understanding interdependence, constructive conflict, and civic values are requirements for citizenship in the world community. Because of technological, economic, ecological, and political interdependence, the solution to most problems cannot be achieved by one individual or country alone. The major problems faced by individuals (e.g., contamination of the environment, warming of the atmosphere, world hunger, international terrorism, nuclear war) are increasingly ones that cannot be solved by actions taken only at the national level. The internationalization of problems has increased so that there are no clear lines between domestic and international problems. The international affairs of one country are the internal affairs of other nations and vice versa. Cooperation and constructive conflict, therefore, must be established among disparate peoples and nations. The three Cs simultaneously model interdependence and provide students with the experiences they need to understand the nature of cooperation. Students who have had 12–20 years of the three Cs will be better able to understand and manage interdependent systems than will students who have had 12–20 years of competitive and individualistic learning.

In order for diversity to enrich students' learning and school experiences, schooling must be based on a cooperative community, constructive conflict resolution, and civic values. To establish a learning community, cooperation must be carefully structured at all levels in the school. To maintain the learning community, constructive conflict resolution procedures must be taught to all members of the school. To guide and direct the cooperation and constructive conflict resolution, civic values must be inculcated in all school members. Together, the three Cs are a complete program for creating effective and nurturing schools where diversity is a resource and children and youth learn and develop in positive and healthy ways.

REFERENCES

Deutsch, M. (1949). A theory of cooperation and competition. *Human Relations, 2,* 129–152.

Johnson, D.W., & Johnson, F. (2000). *Joining together: Group theory and group skills* (7th ed.). Needham Heights, MA: Allyn & Bacon.

Johnson, D.W., & Johnson, R. (1979). Conflict in the classroom: Controversy and learning. *Review of Educational Research, 49,* 51–61.

Johnson, D.W., & Johnson, R. (1989). *Cooperation and competition: Theory and research.* Edina, MN: Interaction Book Company.

Johnson, D.W., & Johnson, R. (1994a). Cooperative learning and American values. *The Cooperative Link, 9*(3), 3–4.

Johnson, D.W., & Johnson, R. (1994b). *Leading the cooperative school* (2nd ed.). Edina, MN: Interaction Book Company.

Johnson, D.W., & Johnson, R. (1995a). *Creative controversy: Intellectual challenge in the classroom* (3rd ed.). Edina, MN: Interaction Book Company.

Johnson, D.W., & Johnson, R. (1995b). *My mediation notebook* (3rd ed.). Edina, MN: Interaction Book Company.

Johnson, D.W., & Johnson, R. (1995c). *Teaching students to be peacemakers* (3rd ed.). Edina, MN: Interaction Book Company.

Johnson, D.W., & Johnson, R. (1995d). Teaching students to be peacemakers: Results of five years of research. *Peace and Conflict: Journal of Peace Psychology, 1*(4), 417–438.

Johnson, D.W., & Johnson, R. (1996a). Conflict resolution and peer mediation programs in elementary and secondary schools: A review of the research. *Review of Educational Research, 66*(4), 459–506.

Johnson, D.W., & Johnson, R. (1996b). Cooperative learning and traditional American values. *NASSP Bulletin, 80*(579), 11–18.

Johnson, D.W., & Johnson, R. (2000). Cooperative learning, values, and culturally plural classrooms. In M. Leicester, S. Modgill, & C. Modgill (Eds.), *Classroom issues: Practice, pedagogy, and curriculum* (Vol. 3, pp. 15–29). London: Falmer Press, Limited.

14

Cooperative Learning and Inclusion

Mara Sapon-Shevin
Barbara J. Ayres
Janet Duncan

In writing this chapter, we were guided by our beliefs about the importance of cooperative learning to inclusive schooling. First, cooperative learning benefits all students. Second, cooperative learning is an integral part of current school reform efforts. Finally, cooperative learning promotes collaboration between educators who have traditionally worked in isolation.

COOPERATIVE LEARNING IS GOOD FOR ALL STUDENTS

Cooperative learning makes sense in inclusive classrooms because it builds on heterogeneity and formalizes and encourages peer support and connection. However, cooperative learning is not of value only to children with disabilities. Cooperative learning is of value for all students including those who have been identified as "at risk," "bilingual," "gifted," and "normal." Cooperative learning encourages mutual respect and learning among students with varying talents and abilities, languages, and racial and ethnic backgrounds (Marr, 1997). Sudzina (1993) reported that cooperative learning is effective in reducing prejudice among students and in meeting the academic and social needs of students who are at risk. All students need to learn and work in environments where their individual strengths are recognized and their individual needs are addressed. Many educators strive to ensure that multiple intelligences theory is incorporated into their curricula (Armstrong, 2000; Gardner, 1993) and that emotional intelligence is also an important facet of classroom community (Goleman, 1997). All students need to learn within a supportive community in order to feel safe enough to take risks. Cooperative learning arrangements have been found to be effective for increasing achievement, encouraging student involvement, and enhancing motivation for learning (Polloway, Patton, & Serna, 2001). There is increasing recognition that all students, even those currently educated in what appear to be relatively less diverse settings, will need to live and work successfully in diverse, multicultural environments. Cooperative learning can provide students with the skills demanded by our increasingly diverse society.

Some educators have challenged the use of cooperative learning in classrooms with students who are identified as "gifted," claiming that gifted students become permanent tutors and are resentful of having to work with students of differing abilities (Matthews, 1992). Such arguments must be examined critically; we must ask ourselves what we want students to learn in school. Beyond academic subjects, don't we want all students to be comfortable with and accepting of individual differences (their own and others)? Don't we want all students to have sophisticated social skills that will allow them to work with people they perceive as "different" or even "difficult"? Furthermore, don't we want to model inclusion and community and demonstrate in the microcosm of the classroom what a society in which all people are valued would look like? Surely, learning to work with others is a vital part of becoming a productive citizen within a diverse world.

One student we know who was initially resistant to group work commented, "What I like best about this class is that everyone cooperates and shares" (Ayres, O'Brien, & Rogers, 1992, p. 26). This is an important lesson for all students to learn, not just students with disabilities. Another student said, "Sometimes I can't understand Jingyu—it's kind of hard to understand him, but he can read pretty good. Like on math problems, people say, 'Why don't you help Jingyu?' but sometimes he helps us. He is good at math." Thoughtfully implemented cooperative learning disrupts typical hierarchies of who is "smart" and who is not and allows all students to work together, each student experiencing the role of teacher and of learner. The acknowledgement that there are many ways of being "smart," often described as "multiple intelligences" (Armstrong, 2000; Gardner, 1993), is supported by designing cooperative activities that demand a wide variety of skills and abilities (Cohen, 1994).

If teachers or students are uncomfortable with cooperative learning, it is often because they have adopted a technique without a firm understanding of the underlying principles and without sufficient support to implement creative, multilevel cooperative learning activities. Teachers must be encouraged to be thoughtful about all aspects of cooperative learning (Sapon-Shevin & Schniedewind, 1989/1990) and to garner enough support for themselves so that they are not isolated and overwhelmed by the truly complex task of meeting the needs of many different children within the same environment.

COOPERATIVE LEARNING IS PART OF COMPREHENSIVE SCHOOL REFORM

Teachers are confronted on a regular basis with educational innovations that must be incorporated into their teaching: whole language, critical thinking, authentic assessment, and so forth. Some teachers (and administrators) hope they can ignore these "fads" in education, and, by waiting for them to pass and be replaced by "the next thing," save themselves the time and energy needed to learn about and implement new practices. Yet, not only is cooperative learning supported by a compelling research base, it is also fully compatible with other best practices currently being promoted (Gambrell, 1996).

Balanced literacy instruction that involves having students read literature and write stories has been implemented successfully in cooperative groups. Many of the current best practices promoted by reading experts are inherently cooperative (e.g., peer editing, partner reading, literature circles, readers' theater). One teacher, for example, had each student in the class write an "I like" book; some of the students wrote long narratives—"I like walking in the rain in my new boots"—whereas others cut out pictures of things they liked and pasted them in the book. Every child completed a book, thus engaging in the literacy activity. Every child shared his or her book by "reading" it to an attentive listener. In contrast to grouping children into homogeneous reading groups by skill, this activity was structured in heterogeneous cooperative groups, and all children could succeed at their own level.

Important skills such as critical thinking, creative problem solving, and the synthesis of knowledge can easily be accomplished through cooperative group activities in inclusive classrooms. Many of the principles of differentiated instruction (Tomlinson, 1999), which structures a variety of learning and assessment tasks for individual students, are consistent with the principles of inclusive cooperative learning. In addition, authentic assessment (anecdotal reporting, portfolio assessment, and observational recording) is fully compatible with cooperative learning in inclusive contexts.

Teachers need not envision cooperative learning as "one more thing" they need to do but rather as an organizing value and principle for all the instruction in their classroom. Building a cooperative, inclusive classroom community can be the framework within which other teaching strategies and practices are woven.

COOPERATIVE LEARNING MEANS TEACHERS COOPERATING

In order for cooperative learning to be successful in inclusive classrooms, teachers who have traditionally worked in isolation will need to find new ways of collaborating and sharing their expertise (Watson, 1995). This kind of collaboration can be challenging because it involves sharing responsibilities and communicating with others, but it can also be exciting and rewarding. One teacher commented that planning cooperative learning lessons was stimulating: "For us, it really gets the creative juices flowing." Another teacher said, "It's fun, there are no two ways about it, it's fun. How can it not be fun? Plus [the students] get to know each other's abilities and they can get excited about each other's growth, even though it's not the same as theirs" (Ayres et al., 1992, pp. 25–26).

Not only can students get to know each other's abilities within a cooperative process but teachers can as well. A general education teacher and a special education teacher planning together often find that they have unique skills and ideas to contribute to the process (Friend & Cook, 1998). The general education teacher may have a broader perspective on the curriculum and on curriculum integration, whereas the special education teacher may have special skills in modifying instruction and developing adaptations that benefit many children. General education teachers who are used to working with larger groups of children often can contribute important classroom management and organizational strategies to balance some of the individualized approaches proposed by the special education teacher.

It is often acknowledged that when students are learning to work in groups, they need support and encouragement to get them over the rough spots. "I don't want to work with Pam," or "Danny's taking over the whole project" are indications that time and attention must be devoted to developing appropriate social skills for negotiating conflict and moving toward consensus. Similarly, teachers learning to work together may encounter struggles over turf, expertise, ownership, and responsibility—these also need to be negotiated. Teachers must find ways to support one another as they learn to be cooperative, inclusive educators at the same time they support their students in this goal. Learning how to use the expertise of the speech-language therapist or physical therapist, for example, or how to balance a child's individualized education program (IEP) objectives with broader classroom objectives requires time for teachers to meet, talk, listen, plan, and develop a trusting working relationship. Implementing cooperative learning in inclusive classrooms benefits not only the students but also provides an important opportunity for educators to develop their own teaching skills. Supportive administrators have found creative ways of providing teachers with adequate planning and preparation time so that inclusion becomes an opportunity for better teaching rather than an imposed burden.

PRINCIPLES OF INCLUSIVE COOPERATIVE LEARNING

Once teachers have decided that they will begin to implement formal cooperative group lessons in their classrooms, many decisions must be made. Teachers must decide how they will incorporate cooperative learning lessons within their classroom structure, how they will decide the content to be taught using cooperative learning, how they will form groups, how they will ensure active participation for all students, and how they will evaluate students' learning. On the following pages, we explore some principles of inclusive cooperative learning that must be taken into consideration for successful implementation.

Cooperative Learning Means Establishing a Cooperative Classroom Ethic

For cooperative learning to be maximally effective, it must take place within an overall context of cooperation and peer support (Sapon-Shevin, 1999; Sapon-Shevin, Dobblelaere, Corrigan, Goodman, & Mastin, 1998). Attempts to implement cooperative learning activities when the classroom norms are those of isolation, competition, or interpersonal indifference are apt to result in contradictory messages to students and have limited positive impact on the goal of creating a safe, inclusive community. Creating a safe, caring community for all students within which cooperative learning is simply the formalized expression of classroom values and orientations involves attention to overall community and connections, open communication about differences and classroom practices, and helping.

Overall Community Connections Cooperative learning should not be something that is done on Tuesdays and Thursdays from 9 A.M. to 10 A.M., nor should it be something we do only when we have children with disabilities included. An example of what not to do is when one school posted a sign on a wall announcing "Cooperative Learning, May 14th." When a visitor inquired about the sign, she was told, "That's the day the students with mental retardation go into the third-grade classroom to work."

A feeling of cooperation, community, and connection should be part of everything that happens in the classroom. For example, hanging up for display only those papers graded with As communicates to students that not everyone's work is valued. Teachers might instead want to hang up a "proud paper" from every student or let students decide what they would like to display. Having students line up for music and gym in a girls' line and a boys' line communicates that gender divisions are important ones (and pity the boy who accidentally gets in the girls' line). There are an infinite number of other ways to line students up that encourage them to interact with a variety of their classmates across boundaries of race, gender, and ability. Behavior management strategies that single students out for praise or punishment (e.g., names on the board; statements such as, "I like the way Nicole is sitting") must be challenged with reference to how such practices affect the way students look at one another and their differences. Classroom holiday celebrations, posters on the wall, and the racial and ethnic representation of the books in the classroom library all affect the school community and the extent to which students feel that they are (or are not) a valued part of the classroom. Teachers must be encouraged to think about all aspects of their classroom practice in reference to questions such as the following: Will this practice contribute to or detract from a sense of classroom community? Will what I say or do in this situation encourage students to see each other positively or negatively?

Open Communication About Differences and Classroom Practices Creating a classroom community in which all students feel comfortable and supported in their learning requires that teachers deal directly with issues that affect the classroom (Sapon-Shevin, 1999). When a child in the classroom is displaying some challenging behavior, for example, other students are generally aware of this. Not talking about the situation and exploring various solutions with students may leave them frightened or disenfranchised, wondering why something so obvious is not being discussed and what their role in the classroom should be. Teachers certainly need to be thoughtful about how and when they talk to students about Mark's biting or the fact that LeAnn is being teased on the playground because she smells. However, ignoring such issues in the hope that they will "work themselves out" often results not only in escalation of the problem but also a classroom atmosphere in which students do not feel empowered to talk about what is happening or to explore their role in generating and implementing solutions (Sapon-Shevin, 2001).

In Johnson City, New York (Salisbury, Palombaro, & Hollowood, 1993), students and teachers use a collaborative problem-solving process in which they identify issues, generate possible solutions, screen solutions for feasibility, choose a solution to implement, and then evaluate it. Teachers have used this system to address barriers to inclusion at multiple levels: physical (e.g., "How can Marie be involved in the puppet show her group has written when she cannot stand up and hold her puppet at the same time?"), social (e.g., "What might Taylor be trying to communicate when he pulls hair?"), and instructional (e.g., "What are some ways we can help Luis, who has a hearing impairment, learn to count?"). Including children in identifying problems and generating and implementing solutions sends the clear message that we can talk about what is happening in our classroom, and, as a group, we can figure out ways to do things so that everyone is included.

Similarly, teachers who implement cooperative learning strategies should also talk to students about why they are doing so, what they hope to accomplish, and what some of the barriers might be. Students who are involved in the process of cooperative learning, as opposed to those who are simply doing what the teacher told them to do, are far more likely to take ownership of cooperative activities and generalize them to other areas of classroom and home life.

Helping   Establishing norms about when, how, and why we help others is critical to the full implementation of cooperative learning. Because many teachers and students have received cultural messages that say that "needing help is bad or shameful" and "offering help to others will embarrass them," it is important to establish new classroom norms. Two of the most critical values are 1) everyone is good at something and can help others, and 2) everyone is entitled to and can benefit from help and support from others. Teachers may want to help students structure a "Classroom Classifieds," in which students identify their own strengths and skills and name these as "Help Offered" (can help with multiplication, good at jumping rope, can teach sign language, know a lot about frogs). Concurrently, they can identify their needs and learning goals and identify these as "Help Wanted" (want to learn to make friendship bracelets, need help with spelling, want to learn how to play ball games at recess). It is important that such activities be structured so that every child is both a teacher and a learner as a way of challenging rigid notions that there are some people who give help and some people who need help. It is important to create a classroom space for people to proudly claim what they are good at and safely ask for the help and support they need without fear or embarrassment, humiliation, or isolation. When a fourth-grade teacher implemented this activity in her inclusive classroom, she found that many of the students had difficulty identifying something they were good at. She observed that when students announced that "they weren't good at anything," other students jumped in to remind them about their strengths (e.g., "You're really good at the computer," "You're a good artist").

Cooperative Learning Facilitates Teaching Meaningful Content

Unfortunately, neither deciding to have an inclusive classroom nor implementing cooperative learning guarantees that the curriculum will be creative or meaningful. Teachers who feel constrained by or limited to a fixed curriculum or set of materials often try to "bend" the child to fit the curriculum, and we have seen cooperative learning used to encourage children to complete unimaginative worksheets and dittos.

Including a child with a significant disability in an activity and structuring that activity cooperatively gives us an opportunity (and sometimes forces us) to examine the curriculum critically and unleash our creative pedagogical and curricular inventiveness. Combining a commitment to inclusion with an orientation toward cooperative learning can be a catalyst for thinking carefully about the following questions: "What is really important for students to learn? How can I make learning meaningful and functional for all students?"

One of the often unexpected but welcome benefits of including children with specific behavioral and educational challenges in the classroom is that teachers are encouraged to rethink previous beliefs and practices related to the curriculum and pedagogy. The teacher who decides to use manipulatives for math (instead of worksheets) because one child quite clearly requires that approach often finds that many other students also benefit from this hands-on, participatory approach. Teachers who move away from text-based question-and-answer approaches to teaching in order to accommodate students who require more active involvement in the curriculum are generally pleased to find that such an orientation is of benefit to all students.

Cooperative learning in inclusive classrooms will be more effective when it is multilevel, multimodal, and integrated across subject areas (Schniedewind & Davidson, 2000; Tomlinson, 1999). Multilevel teaching involves students working on similar objectives or with the same material but at different levels. All students may be using the telephone book, for example, but some students might be learning to dial 911 in case of an emergency while others learn to compute and compare long-distance charges and optimum calling times. Or, all students may be working on map skills but at different levels. Perhaps Maria is learning about lines of latitude and longitude while Robin is learning the directions "up," "down," "left," and "right."

Multimodality teaching involves moving away from pencil and paper tasks to other forms of active involvement. Writing and performing a puppet show, for example, might involve writing, reading, building a set, singing, cutting, talking, dancing, and so forth. An activity such as a puppet show or a unit on space can also be used to integrate curriculum across subject matter. When one class studied the moon, for example, they incorporated science (facts about the moon and astronomy), creative writing (poems and stories about the moon), social studies (cross-cultural beliefs and traditions around the moon), math (computing distance, density, air pressure), and much more. Broadening the curriculum in these ways provides many opportunities to include students who work at significantly different levels and to design cooperative learning activities in which students can help and support one another in their learning while still maintaining a common theme and a sense of community.

Cooperative Learning Depends on Supportive Heterogeneous Groups

In classrooms where teachers are working to communicate norms of cooperation, students can work together in a number of different ways. In many cooperative classrooms, students sit in heterogeneous base groups so teachers can structure both informal and formal opportunities for cooperation between students throughout the day. For example, students can start their day with an informal group activity at their desk clusters; complete class jobs with a partner from their group; and engage in formal, structured cooperative learning activities with group members. In most classrooms, teachers schedule cooperative learning groups to work together for 1 month or 6 weeks so that students have an opportunity to get to know and work together with group members but also have an opportunity to learn to work with other classmates throughout the year. The goal is for students to have worked in cooperative groups with *all* of their classmates by the end of the year.

One important aspect of creating cooperative learning groups is maximizing the heterogeneity of the students within the small groups. Students should be assigned to groups that are mixed by academic skills, social skills, personality, race, class, and gender. It is often helpful for teachers to work with others who are familiar with their students when groups are being formed. With all of the different aspects of student diversity that need to be taken into consideration, forming groups can seem like an onerous task that will be too difficult for any one person.

Many teachers structure cooperative groups very deliberately. In classrooms where students are functioning at different levels in regard to academic and social abilities, it is important that the teachers structure the groups to ensure heterogeneity, particularly in the beginning of the year or when new students enter. Two first-grade teachers who team teach in a classroom that includes the full range of learners work together to plan cooperative learning groups. They begin the process by identifying one aspect of student diversity and placing one student with this quality in each group. For example, they start with academic diversity and place one student in each group who is able to read. Next, they look at the students who are nonreaders and assign them to the groups. As they place this second student, they always consider how this student and the first student match up in regard to supporting one another socially. For the third student in each group they also consider social aspects—they look for a student who can complement the other two students and help pull the group together. One day their discussion when forming groups went as follows:

> *This is a nice combination, but Katie and Andrew are both quiet. I was thinking about Rachel and Katie because of Rachel's style—she may be more assertive with Katie to help stimulate her involvement.*
>
> *What about Doug and Brent? I'm thinking of this because of Doug's abilities. In many ways Brent is similar but it may build some self-esteem for Brent in that setting. He can really do things but he doesn't think he can do as much as he can.*
>
> *Maybe Madeline should be with Brad because she is so strong in everything—and in that group it is going to take a little more work from two people instead of three. Plus, she is comfortable with Brad and I think she will come up with strategies to involve him—she is real bright and she is good at modifying things. This group is going to have to be able to change and not have to be doing exactly what every other group is doing and not get upset about it. (Ayres et al., 1992, p. 6)*

These comments illustrate the level of complexity of thought that goes into structuring supportive heterogeneous groups. Through careful planning, students have a greater opportunity to receive the social support that is important for establishing a sense of belonging and group membership in the classroom.

In forming groups, some teachers focus on student choice, asking students who they would like to work with. Although it makes sense for teachers to provide students with multiple opportunities to choose within the school day, student choice may not be the best way to form groups. When students choose their own groups and work only with others they already know, the groups often tend to be homogenous terms of gender, race, and ability, which works against the broader goals of cooperative learning. Teachers should strive to help students learn to value the diversity that exists in the classroom and in society.

There are ways for teachers to incorporate some aspects of student choice into group formation. For example, a fourth-grade teacher forms new groups periodically throughout the year and asks each student to respond (privately) to a number of questions including, "Who are two people you think you could work well with?" "Who are two people you don't know well and would like to know?" By asking students these questions, she is allowing them to participate in group formation but also emphasizing that although it is important to work with students they already know, it is also important to learn to accept, value, and work with others they do not know well yet. Once students have learned to work with many others, allowing more choice in group formation may be appropriate.

Cooperative Learning Requires Structures that Ensure the Active Participation of All Students

Equally important to establishing supportive heterogeneous groups is ensuring the active participation of all students within inclusive cooperative learning lessons. All too often, students are placed into groups and given a task to complete without the provision of structures that will promote the active, equitable participation of all members. Key components of participation include the division of labor and materials, flexible interpretation of roles, and individualized student responsibilities.

Division of Labor and Materials The participation of all group members is more likely when teachers carefully structure the cooperative group task. Through the division of labor and materials, the students are given a clear message that each student has an important contribution to make toward the completion of the group's task. In the beginning, or when new groups have formed, it is important that teachers structure this interdependence among the group members. Planning for equitable participation is especially important in inclusive classrooms where the participation of some students may be dependent on the structure that is provided. For example, with a student who is reserved and responds more slowly than her classmates due to a physical disability, if labor and materials are not divided, it is possible that group members will do the task for her. As was mentioned previously, it is also important for teachers to talk with students about the goals of working together and the importance of everyone contributing. In one classroom, the teacher talked to individual groups and asked the students how they were going to make sure that all group members were given a turn.

Flexible Interpretation of Roles To promote active, equitable participation within groups, roles must be interpreted flexibly. Instead of creating static roles for students, flexible roles allow for the individualization that will ensure that all group members are able to assume each role at some point in time. For example, in one classroom, the roles remained the same across time (e.g., writer, reader/questioner, checker), but the *responsibilities* of the roles changed depending on the task and the students who would be given the role on that particular day (Ayres et al., 1992). Through these flexible roles, a student who is unable to write the letters of the alphabet could be the writer when the task is designed so that the writers are gluing something instead of writing words. Another aspect of individualizing roles occurs when teachers think of creative ways for students to fulfill the role responsibilities. Teachers might ask themselves, "What are the different ways that students could encourage group members for this lesson?" or "How could Rachel, who doesn't speak, encourage others?" When teachers work to broaden their thinking about the equitable participation of students, they can come up with many different ways for students to be active contributors (e.g., encourage others by giving a "high five," passing a card with a positive statement or a smiley face written on it to a group member).

Individualized Student Responsibilities Adaptations can be made within groups to promote the active, equitable participation of all members. Sometimes adaptations are necessary to promote the participation of an individual student. For example, in an elementary classroom, heterogeneous cooperative learning groups worked together on math story problems. One student, whose goals for math included writing numbers from 1 to 50 and using a calculator to compute problems, was given the role of writer/checker within her group. The other students in the group determined what mathematical function to use for the problem, helped her write down the problem on the worksheet by dictating the numbers, solved the problem, and dictated to her the numbers to write down for the answer. She was then responsible for checking the group's response on her calculator. In another classroom, a first-grade boy's educational objectives included grasping and holding objects and indicating his preference by choosing between two objects. During a lesson on community helpers, his group was given the role of a doctor to study so that he could use a play doctor's kit to learn about medical instruments. The addition of the hands-on materials provided an opportunity to address his educational objectives of grasping objects and indicating preference (Ayres et al., 1992).

When students are placed in supportive heterogeneous groups and issues of active, equitable participation are addressed by teachers, all students can benefit from the use of cooperative learning in the classroom (Schniedewind & Davidson, 2000). Through these considerations and individualized adaptations, all students are seen as important group members in the eyes of their peers. Although these components initially require more thought and time on the part of teachers, teachers will reap the rewards as students begin to support and expect the maximum involvement of all group members.

Cooperative Learning Provides Opportunities for Ongoing Evaluation

One important and often complex aspect of instruction with cooperative learning is evaluation. How can educators be certain that students are attaining their educational goals within cooperative groups? How should students be evaluated and how should that evaluation be communicated? How can an evaluation system help modify and refine cooperative learning instructional programs? These questions can guide educators as they work to design appropriate evaluation methods for cooperative learning activities. Effective evaluation of cooperative learning in inclusive classrooms must focus on both the content and the process of the group experience.

The issue of grading in inclusive cooperative classrooms is difficult. Educators who are concerned about the self-esteem of all learners reject the use of practices that promote competition between students. Group grades or group rankings work against encouraging cooperation among students and may make group members less willing to support a classmate with a disability. Evaluation should not be structured so that one student's difficulty becomes a group's liability or the cause (real or perceived) of group failure. It is imperative to avoid situations in which students can accurately report that "Tyrone brought our grade down." Teachers must be careful that the structure of group evaluation accounts for different abilities. Schniedewind and Davidson (2000) offered excellent examples of how teachers can differentiate both instruction and evaluation, making both individualized and meaningful.

In inclusive cooperative classrooms, teacher-made tests of subject matter or standardized tests with norm-referenced criteria may not be sufficient or appropriate for assessing achievement. The students who have IEPs may be working at different levels than their peers, a modification we wish to encourage rather than discourage through excessive standardization. Separating students into fixed ability groups that are evaluated through a variety of criterion-referenced tests is not the solution either, particularly as such a process tends to isolate and stigmatize individuals (e.g., "You're *only* on the red book").

Teachers must find ways to assess students who are engaging in significantly different activities within a common structure and begin to describe and evaluate what students have learned and how they are working with their peers. Cooperative learning provides an opportunity for students to complete an activity with an emphasis on group dynamics and interpersonal skills as well as the academic goals of the lesson. Cooperative learning also allows for ongoing evaluation on the part of students and teachers, both during and after group activities.

If we intend to evaluate students on their group process and product, it is crucial that cooperative learning lessons are designed to be just that—cooperative. This can be accomplished through the creation of activities that incorporate many of the principles presented in this chapter, including teaching meaningful content, creating supportive heterogeneous groups, and using structures that ensure the active participation of all students. Many different types of activities are appropriate for the evaluation of students who are working in cooperative groups. Dippong (1992) advocated for evaluation through activities such as group reports, problem solving, seminars and debates, and simulations and role plays. Armstrong (2000) provided examples of ways to assess students using a multiple intelligences framework.

In inclusive cooperative classrooms, teachers may want to assess individual as well as group effort and, perhaps, grade students on individual goals and/or on the basis of improvement. Individual goals can be both academically oriented and social-skill related. For example, one of Martin's objectives might be to say encouraging things to his classmates during the group lesson; Kara's objectives might relate to her writing skills or organizational leadership.

During cooperative learning activities both teachers and students can assume responsibility for evaluating the skills and contributions of group members. While students are engaging in group activities, educators often collect and share information on how groups are functioning in regard to the academic and social aspects of the lesson. This information is shared with groups both during and after the lesson. Direct observation is a valuable tool for teachers who are concerned about a student's performance in a specific area. For example, do all group members have a chance to talk, including the child who uses an alternative communication device? If not, equitable participation can be addressed with this group at the time they most need the feedback—when they are working together to complete a task. In addition, as part of cooperative learning lessons, students are often asked to discuss how they worked together to accomplish the task. This information is shared within small groups and then with the entire class. An important part of cooperative learning includes the instruction of students in how to observe, evaluate, and provide feedback to group members in positive ways. Peer evaluation affords students a chance to appreciate and critique the efforts of their peers with the group project in mind. Self-evaluation can also be a part of cooperative learning activities in which students set their own goals and share them with group members.

Several strategies can be used to provide a more comprehensive examination of progress within cooperative learning activities (see Cullen & Pratt, 1992). The following methods are more qualitative in nature and provide rich information about students that could not be ascertained as readily through traditional testing. For example, some teachers use a cumulative record file review system that outlines teachers' comments in subject areas, patterns of strengths as well as areas that need improvement, and affective observations. This information includes observations of students in cooperative learning groups and comments about their growth in academic and social skills. Other teachers collect both individual and group work in portfolios that can be reviewed by teachers, parents, and students on a periodic basis. The student–teacher interview is another option. Through interviews, the teacher can glean much information about students' interests, motivation, knowledge, and perspectives on their contribution to the group. All of these approaches are compatible with cooperative learning and the use of authentic assessment, which is gaining attention as an important approach to determining whether students have acquired skills to select and use important concepts in authentic open-ended situations (Hibbard, 1992).

Cooperative learning activities provide a unique opportunity to evaluate important collaborative outcomes, such as interactive communication, active listening, taking the perspective of others, acceptance and accommodation of individual differences, and the evaluation of a final product developed through group effort.

APPLYING COOPERATIVE LEARNING BELIEFS AND PRINCIPLES

Knowing where to begin the process of developing cooperative learning lessons for heterogeneous groups may seem daunting. There is not one "right way" to do it; one simply must jump in—with the help of some colleagues (see Chapter 20).

Some teachers begin by designing lessons for their whole class and then later create individualized adaptations for specific students. Others prefer to begin with one student's interests and needs and then expand the teaching concept for the whole group. A more comprehensive model involves looking carefully at *all* the learners in the class and at the intended curriculum and designing cooperative learning lessons that work for the entire group (Sapon-Shevin, 1999). Regardless of the process, the goal is to meet learning goals for individual students within a heterogeneous, cooperative learning lesson (Duncan et al., 1991; Schniedewind & Davidson, 2000).

Educators attending a university course in language arts curricula development designed several cooperative learning units for their classes so that students with specific disabilities could be equal members of groups and meet their IEP goals. To guide their planning, the teachers reflected on the five elements of cooperative learning by Johnson, Johnson, and Holubec (1998): 1) face-to-face interactions, 2) positive interdependence, 3) individual accountability, 4) interpersonal and small-group skills, and 5) group processing. These elements formed the cornerstones of the lessons.

In a university course on teaching language arts, teachers worked cooperatively to design units for their classes that included students with IEP objectives. First, the teachers selected a grade level and a topic of interest. Working in small groups of three and four, they generated ideas for the topic that could be developed into a unit of study. The five most frequently named concepts were chosen as the focal point for the unit. Next, the teachers discussed the makeup of the classroom that had a range of students, including those with disabilities. As the teachers sketched out the lessons that would be a part of the unit, they considered the active participation of all students. They were provided with specific information on the students with disabilities including learning style, interests, talents, and areas in need of support. Teaching strategies for the student were written in terms that teachers found useful; IEP goals were articulated in familiar, everyday phrases. The teachers then answered the following questions: What would be the best student composition of the groups? How would the student be best supported in a group? How would the student offer his or her talents to the group? Finally, effective evaluation strategies for the class were determined (see Chapter 7).

One lesson developed for second-grade students focused on "similarities and differences that exist among people." All aspects of the curriculum (i.e., mathematics, reading, science, social studies) were included in the unit. Students brainstormed questions about similarities and differences, researched their questions, and depicted their findings on a poster with illustrations. For a student with difficulty printing and recording information, coloring the illustrations with jumbo crayons was an appropriate adaptation. Another student who had difficulty processing information worked with a partner to gather information and was responsible for recording their findings as dictated by the partner.

Another lesson developed for fifth graders concerned accessibility for individuals with physical disabilities. The students, working in groups of three, were provided with information on requirements and codes and measuring devices and were asked to survey a number of buildings in their community, including their school. The findings were recorded, and each group submitted a report describing the accessibility of specific locations in the community. They also wrote a letter to the company, store, or restaurant summarizing their findings. For a student with difficulty reading and staying on task, instructions were provided to his or her group in a pictorial format accompanied by words. To record the results of the group's findings, the student dictated his or her responses to a partner. Another student, who was unable to read words and determine measurements, was responsible for indicating what needed to be measured and then holding the measuring devices in place while other group members recorded the results.

These two examples, as well as those detailed in "Creative Cooperative Group Lesson Plans" (see Chapter 21) illustrate how students with disabilities may be meaningfully and effectively included in cooperative learning lessons. Through the consideration of the beliefs and principles articulated in this chapter, teachers can structure cooperative learning lessons that ensure active participation in learning for all students.

CONCLUSION

In summary, we suggest that cooperative learning is good for all students and that it is part of comprehensive school reform efforts. To achieve this reform, teachers must work together to build networks within their school community. Teachers must also establish a cooperative classroom ethic that emphasizes overall community building, open communication about differences and classroom practices, and reciprocal helping relationships. Meaningful content in cooperative lessons is critical for the success of all students. For students to succeed within their groups, careful consideration regarding group heterogeneity must be given in conjunction with roles that ensure active, equal participation by all students. Creative assessment practices must be developed to document achievement of meaningful outcomes for students. All of these considerations require planning and structure in order for the teaching to be successful.

The early literature on mainstreaming assumed that children with special education needs could be considered eligible for participation in the general education classroom when they were able to compete successfully with other children. This orientation implied that the burden of change was on the child and that the general education classroom was a fixed, immutable environment in which some practices, such as competition, were inevitable. A more exciting and far-reaching way of thinking about inclusion and cooperation is based on the beliefs that all children belong in the general education classroom and that it is possible to design curriculum and pedagogy that includes and benefits all students. Through the creation of a community that is cooperative and inclusive, children's acceptance and success in the general education environment will be greatly enhanced. All students and all teachers have much to gain by structuring the classroom and school environment so that it provides generous support for learning, connecting, and caring.

REFERENCES

Armstrong, T. (2000). *Multiple intelligences in the classroom* (3rd ed.). Alexandria, VA: Association for Supervision and Curriculum Development.
Ayres, B., O'Brien, L., & Rogers, T. (1992). *Working together, sharing, and helping each other: Cooperative learning in a first grade classroom that includes students with disabilities.* Syracuse, NY: Inclusive Education Project, Syracuse University.
Cohen, E.G. (1994). *Designing groupwork: Strategies for the heterogeneous classroom* (2nd ed.). New York: Teachers College Press.

Cullen, B., & Pratt, T. (1992). Measuring and reporting student progress. In S. Stainback & W. Stainback (Eds.), *Curriculum considerations in inclusive classrooms: Facilitating learning for all students* (pp. 175–196). Baltimore: Paul H. Brookes Publishing Co.

Dippong, J. (1992). Two large questions in assessing and evaluating CL: Teacher challenges and appropriate student tasks. *Cooperative Learning, 13*(1), 6–8.

Duncan, J., Hedeen, D., Henneberry, M.B., Kraus, J., Weber, C., Jackson, L., Trubisky, M., & Seymour, A. (1991). *Cooperative learning lessons which promote full inclusion of students with disabilities.* Syracuse, NY: Teacher Leadership Inservice Project, Syracuse University.

Friend, M., & Cook, L. (1998). *Interactions: Collaboration skills for school professionals* (3rd ed.). White Plains, NY: Longman Publishers.

Gambrell, L.B. (1996). Creating classroom cultures that foster reading motivation. *The Reading Teacher, 50*(1), 14–25.

Gardner, H. (1993). *Multiple intelligences: The theory in practice.* New York: Basic Books.

Goleman, D. (1997). *Emotional intelligence.* New York: Bantam Books.

Hibbard, K.M. (1992). Bringing authentic performance assessment to life with cooperative learning. *Cooperative Learning, 13*(1), 30–32.

Johnson, D.W., Johnson, R.T., & Holubec, E.J., (1998). *Circles of learning* (2nd ed.). Alexandria, VA: Association for Supervision and Curriculum Development.

Marr, M.B. (1997). Cooperative learning: A brief review. *Reading and Writing Quarterly: Overcoming Learning Difficulties, 13*(1), 7–20.

Matthews, M. (1992). Gifted students talk about cooperative learning. *Educational Leadership, 50*(2), 48–50.

Polloway, E.A., Patton, J.R., & Serna, S. (2001). *Strategies for teaching learners with special needs* (7th ed.). Upper Saddle River, NJ: Prentice Hall.

Salisbury, C., Palombaro, M.M., & Hollowood, T.M. (1993). On the nature and change of an inclusive elementary school. *Journal of The Association for Persons with Severe Handicaps, 18*(2), 75–84.

Sapon-Shevin, M. (1999). *Because we can change the world: A practical guide to building cooperative, inclusive classrooms communities.* Needham Heights, MA: Allyn & Bacon.

Sapon-Shevin, M. (2001). Making inclusion visible: Honoring the process and the struggle. *Democracy in Education, 14*(1), 24–27.

Sapon-Shevin, M., Dobblelaere, A., Corrigan, C.R., Goodman, K., & Mastin, M.C. (1998). Promoting inclusive behavior in inclusive classrooms: "You can't say you can't play." In L.H. Meyer, H.W. Park, M. Grenot-Scheyer, I.S. Schawartz, & B. Harry (Eds.), *Making friends: the influences of culture and development* (pp. 105–132). Baltimore: Paul H. Brookes Publishing Co.

Sapon-Shevin, M., & Schniedewind, N. (1989/1990). Selling cooperative learning without selling it short. *Educational Leadership, 47*(4), 63–65.

Schniedewind, D., & Davidson, E. (2000). Differentiating cooperative learning. *Educational Leadership, 58*(1), 24–27.

Sudzina, M. (1993, February). *Dealing with diversity in the classroom: A case study approach.* Paper presented at the annual meeting of the Association of Teacher Educators, Los Angeles. (ERIC Document Reproduction Service No. ED 354 233).

Tomlinson, C.A. (1999). *The differentiated classroom: Responding to the needs of all learners.* Alexandria, VA: Association for Supervision and Curriculum Development.

Watson, B. (1995). Relinquishing the lecture: Cooperative learning in teacher education. *Journal of Teacher Education, 46*(3), 209–215.

15

Student Disruptions
in the Cooperative Classroom

Experiences in a New Brunswick, Canada, School District

Brian Kelly

This chapter examines teachers' perceptions about the instructional strategies that enable them to accommodate a wider range of student behavior in the classroom. Teachers at the elementary and high school level who use cooperative learning were interviewed to gain their insights on how cooperative learning influenced their teaching and how peer-mediated strategies, such as student problem solving and class meetings, assist students with problematic behavior. Peer-influence strategies, including cooperative learning, were identified as procedures that can be used to address, pro-actively and reactively, students who demonstrate disruptive behavior during academic learning.

In the late 1980s, at one school's forum on school discipline, teachers noted the need for collaboration among school personnel, parents, and students to resolve discipline issues by empowering students to help one another. Subsequently, teachers met to discuss students at risk of school failure and the obstacles, strategies, and solutions for keeping these students in school through grade 12. Discussions regarding discipline issues were lengthy. The number one obstacle was dealing with students who did not want help because of what their peers would think. School personnel, therefore, sought intervention techniques that addressed this issue of peer pressure and receiving help.

TEACHER PERCEPTIONS OF INSTRUCTIONAL STRATEGIES

In examining classroom strategies, teachers stated that classroom management could not be separated from student learning. They recognized that students actively engaging in academic behaviors are less likely to engage in disruptive behavior in the classroom. More effective teaching strategies were seen, therefore, as key to teaching all students and appealing to their various learning styles and abilities. Gilstrap and Martin (1976) identified a range of instructional strategies teachers might use to instruct students (see Table 15.1).

Teachers who were interviewed considered few of these strategies to be purposefully designed to address diverse student needs during a lesson. Only one strategy—cooperative group learning—was identified as an instructional strategy to deal with peer pressure concerns, behavior management, and effective instruction in an integrated fashion. Four additional themes, described next, emerged from the teacher interviews.

Table 15.1. Types of instructional strategies

Lecture
Independent study
Discovery learning
Cooperative group learning
Behavior modification
Discussion
Group investigation
Learning centers
Multilevel instruction
Performance-based learning activities
Drill and practice
Laboratory approach
Simulation
Do-look-learn

Source: Gilstrap and Martin (1976).

Most Instructional Strategies Do Not Provide Enough Evidence That They Work

Teachers thought that some of the instructional strategies represented in Table 15.1 carried assumptions about the type of students they taught. For example, either the classroom was full of students who were well behaved, or, if the teacher was having classroom management difficulties, then they could simply be addressed by using the right type of motivational technique. Other strategies made only superficial attempts to address classroom management issues. These strategies viewed the classroom in very generic terms and, thus, showed limited success in specific classroom situations and problems.

Many Classroom Procedures Fail to Be Comprehensive Enough to Solve a Student's Difficulties

Teachers stated that they believe that instructional strategies and behavior management procedures fail because they do not complement one another. For example, some schedules of reinforcement, if adhered to specifically, disrupt the flow of teaching. As a result, one type of disruption is replaced by another. Furthermore, some behavior management strategies fail because they require so much time and are too complex for the teaching to progress.

Many Classroom Procedures are Simply Too Ambiguous

Sometimes, behavior management advice is unclear; it lacks sufficient detail for complete understanding by the teacher. Procedures often are deployed quickly as immediate responses to crisis situations, rather than planned to fit the overall classroom instructional design. As a result, errors occur and what was intended is often implemented incorrectly. In summary, the procedures are too ambiguous for a teacher to carry out with a high degree of accuracy.

Many Classroom Procedures Fail
Because They Exceed Available Resources

Some procedures are not sustained because of the level of effort they require from a teacher; they become just one more thing to be added to a teacher's responsibilities. The extra time required to implement procedures also may exceed a teacher's expectations and the time available in a school day.

In summary, the previous themes suggest that teachers want and need integrated strategies that enable them to concentrate on academic instruction and, at the same time, maintain high levels of appropriate behavior in the classroom. Teachers are more likely to implement and maintain an instructional strategy that simultaneously addresses instruction and behavior.

PEER INTERVENTIONS

The problems shown by our children reflect their search for alternative outlets, for places to release the pressure, for contexts in which they feel efficacious. If children are not "good enough" in academics and if schools provide few outlets and pathways to a feeling of effectiveness and accomplishment, then students will show that they can be the best at disrupting learning, showing disrespect, and resisting entreaties of teachers and parents to do schoolwork (Elias, 1989, p. 401).

Elias (1989) suggested that students need to feel they have control or a say in what happens. He further suggested that, academics aside, "school is primarily a social experience" (p. 397). Thus, students need opportunities to interact. Kohler and Strain (1990) coined the term *collaborative interventions* to describe a range of strategies that involve teachers and peers working together to help a particular student by implementing an intervention to increase or decrease certain behaviors. Generally, collaborative intervention strategies have the dual purpose of teaching academic skills and managing certain social skills and behaviors of a specific student. Whereas collaborative interventions are a distinct type of intervention, it is perhaps easier to think of them as falling into one of two categories: peer mediation strategies or peer influence strategies. In peer mediation, peers systematically implement behavior change programs to serve in peer mediation roles. Students are trained and monitored by a teacher or guidance counselor. Within one school, peer mediation strategies have been incorporated into peer mediation, peer tutoring and peer support group programs, conflict resolution instruction, and classwide meetings. Peer influence strategies, however, take advantage of natural social interactions and consequences that children in groups provide one another when working toward a mutual goal. Peer influence strategies are typified in cooperative learning lessons.

Peer Mediated Strategies

In this section, two strategies that rely on peer mediation are described: problem solving and class meetings.

Problem Solving Some students are so consistently challenging or unresponsive that they outlast the usual repertoire of interventions. In these situations, it is good to take a team approach in which a group of people bring their particular perspectives to the meeting. The way to approach problem solving in schools can be on a one-to-one basis or in large groups, such as a classroom of students (Kelly & den Otter, 1991). Meetings that involve students in structured problem solving take 20–30 minutes and should follow six steps (Porter, 1994; Porter, Wilson, Kelly, & den Otter, 1991):

1. Define the problem in specific terms.

2. Brainstorm solutions; write whatever comes to mind.

3. For each possible solution, list what might happen that could help the situation.

4. Select or combine the desired solutions.

5. Plan how to carry out the solution.

6. After a week or two, evaluate how the plan is working.

Problem solving should be viewed as something that is used by students and by teachers.

Class Meetings   Class meetings provide a teacher and students with a forum to discuss how a student's behavior is affecting them and what they can do about it. The intensity of a certain behavior or the fear for the personal safety of members of the classroom may necessitate an adult intervening to defuse a potentially explosive situation and initiating a class meeting. Students and teachers discuss how they feel about the situation and the possible precipitating factors or antecedents that may produce the behavior. They also discuss possible solutions. Consider David, whose life situation and low achievement precipitated a high level of disruption in a sixth-grade classroom. This disruptive behavior was being inadvertently reinforced by classmates' responses to his behavior.

Until recently, there had been a lot of violence in David's home. In class, he sought attention and approval from his peers by swearing, making loud vocalizations, and throwing objects. In the beginning, classmates reacted with laughter, which caused David's misbehavior to escalate. One morning, when David was away from class, the teacher initiated a class meeting to discuss David's behavior and how the class reacted to it. The teacher explained that their laughing was a problem when David was disruptive in learning groups. The teacher drew some parallels to similar situations that might occur at home, such as when a sibling is being silly at the dinner table. The children in the class easily related to the issue and offered appropriate alternatives to solve the dilemma. They decided that ignoring and not laughing at David's behavior was the best solution. They also identified and made a list of the cooperative social skills they would encourage.

Clearly, such talks with students should avoid focusing on only negative behaviors and attributes of a student. Rather, the student must be described in a balanced light—as someone who belongs to the class and who has strengths and gifts to contribute to the class but who at times acts in an unacceptable way. For class meetings to work, the teachers must do at least the following:

• Demonstrate true concern and empathy for the student during the meeting. If not, students will quickly perceive the discussion as an opportunity to merely slander the student.

• Model appropriate responses when the child is being disruptive, and cue students in the group or class to do likewise.

• Coach and reinforce appropriate responses to unwanted behavior so that it becomes second nature.

Teachers who have used class meetings identified six advantages of this intervention approach:

1. Immediacy: Teachers as well as students have the opportunity to come up with strategies to help the student with problematic behavior.

2. Ownership: Students who share the same space with a student who has difficulties have a vested interest in seeing that the situation gets resolved.

3. Relevance: Solutions produced through the problem-solving process are tailored to the resources available in the school.

4. Empowerment: Students involved can feel that they are contributing to a solution for ongoing difficulties.

5. Collaboration: None of us is as smart as all of us.

6. Positive orientation: Use positive attributes of the student as the cornerstone for change.

Collaborating with students to generate solutions under nonthreatening conditions is a way to encourage students to own a class problem and demonstrate that they can affect positive change. Class meeting problem solving is premised on the notion that a solution does not necessarily make a problem "go away." Instead, a solution is a temporary accommodation and adjustment in how the school system can meet the needs of the individual child. It requires a positive outlook and confidence that there are ways to resolve a problem.

A PEER INFLUENCE STRATEGY: COOPERATIVE LEARNING AS PRO-ACTIVE MANAGEMENT

The general consensus of teachers in this school was that being pro-active or preventative with regard to disruptive behavior was better than being reactive. For them, pro-active meant to act in advance and to have a plan of action that offered maximum control of a situation. Another aspect of being pro-active was combining appropriate student discipline with effective instruction. One teacher noted that most in-service training "examined either effective teaching or classroom management but seldom were examples presented of how the two work together." Also, recommended classroom management strategies tend to focus on individual student behavior without looking at the whole classroom situation, despite agreement that appropriate behavior demonstrated by a student perceived as disruptive often is the by-product of well-managed groups. Cooperative learning structures, when regularly used in a classroom, embody the characteristics of pro-active management strategies and clearly demonstrate how good teaching and good classroom management can go hand in hand. Specific pro-active strategies of well-designed cooperative group learning classrooms and in-service training opportunities are discussed in the next sections. Experiences of this school's teachers are used to illustrate each aspect.

In-Service and Follow-Up Training

Most of the school's teachers felt that they learned little in their preservice training programs about a variety of the instructional strategies, including cooperative learning models. When they completed their practice teaching, they had little opportunity to practice and receive coaching on the instructional strategies of which they were aware. Teachers noted that the district's in-service instruction and follow-up coaching on cooperative learning taught them how to 1) plan lessons more effectively, 2) implement lessons within a cooperative format, and 3) evaluate what they had taught. Teachers reported that more than any other training, this training enabled them to both provide students with academic instruction and prevent off-task, disruptive behavior. Classroom order depends on a teacher's ability to monitor on-task behavior and model high commitment to work—quality instruction maximizes learning and student accountability for doing assigned work. Cooperative learning seems to increase the teacher's capacity to maximize order and quality in teaching.

Teaching Students Appropriate Behaviors

Another type of information conveyed to students was appropriate behavior. As most cooperative group learning models emphasize, direct instruction of social skills is crucial to effective group work among students. Teachers at this school recognize the power of teaching social skills to curtail the occurrence of disruptive behavior, as well as the importance of beginning the school year by spending time to develop expectations for classroom behavior with students. As one elementary teacher noted,

> We sometimes make real assumptions that students come to school ready to learn and interact with peers. Most of the time when a child gets in trouble it can be attributed to the fact that [he has] not learned an appropriate way of communicating [his] needs. For example, Peter's response to being refused something was to hit other students. I spent a lot of time teaching him simply to say, "That's not fair," or "I'm angry," rather than simply striking out. (S. Langdon, personal communication, November 1993)

In many elementary classrooms, teachers actively teach social skills. Being able to listen, communicate, and work harmoniously are seen as just as important as learning to read, write, and compute. Teachers noted that their students made noticeable and significant gains when social skills were directly taught. Students in cooperative classrooms were reported to "get along better" than they did in years prior to cooperative learning being introduced into the schools. Teachers also noted that unlike individual social skills programs for students with "poor" social skills, social skills taught to the whole class in the context of classroom activities permitted the socially skilled students to readily serve as strong role models for their less skilled peers. When students were taught away from the classroom, the skills taught in isolation often did not generalize to the classroom or other school environments. Taking the time to teach social skills in the classroom context increases the likelihood that the skills can and will be used in the classroom now and in the future.

When instruction addresses social skills, both the teacher and the students learn and experience a common body of information and a common language with which to talk about social skills and expectations. Thus, when a student does something deemed inappropriate, feedback and interventions may be offered in the form of corrective feedback rather than criticism or a threat of punishment. In the words of one teacher,

> Usually students who don't have a lot of self-esteem tend to use put-downs with others in their group. Sometimes other students in the group will have to tell the student to ease up. But there are times when I have felt the need to intervene. Instead of getting on his case, I remind him of why we don't use put-downs and how it makes others feel. (K. Anderson, personal communication, November 1992)

Some of the teachers began to directly teach classroom routines and requisite skills to successfully engage in each activity just as academic content was taught. For example, teachers performed a task analysis for each classroom activity. For each task, they identified the social skills (see Table 15.2) and procedures that were necessary for students to perform as

Table 15.2. Summary of social skills

Self-disclosure
  Being aware of thoughts, feelings, and needs
  Expressing thoughts, feelings, reactions, and needs to others
  Seeking and giving feedback
Trust
  Responding with acceptance and support when others self-disclose
Communication
  Speaking by using "I" messages when expressing thoughts, feelings, reactions, and
    needs
  Describing others' actions without making judgments
  Empathy
Responses
  Using appropriately evaluative, interpretive, supportive, and probing responses
Acceptance and support
  Describing strengths when it is appropriate to do so
  Expressing acceptance of other people when it is appropriate to do so
Influence
  Reinforcing others' actions in order to increase, decrease, or maintain the frequency
    of their behavior, depending on what is in their best interests
  Modeling interpersonal skills for others who wish to acquire them
Conflicts
  Knowing how to define conflict
  Viewing conflict as an opportunity for change
  Taking perspective
  Managing feelings
  Reaching agreement
Stress and anger
  Following rules for the constructive management of anger
  Asserting anger through descriptions of behavior, nonverbal messages, and active
    listening

Source: Johnson & Johnson (1998).

desired. They presented the tasks to students in small steps and with the appropriate level of vocabulary. Finally, students practiced the needed social skills and received feedback on their performance.

By communicating expectations and social skills before each lesson, teachers cued students as to the task demand and, in this way, reduced the likelihood of misbehavior. Consistent expectations added stability to daily routines, leaving less room for unwelcome disruptions.

Monitoring and Processing Classroom Activity

The ongoing student monitoring that is built into cooperative learning serves as another important means of communicating behavioral expectations to students and allows the teacher to take a more active role in facilitating learning. Once task and social demands of a lesson have been set up, students can begin to work. The teacher's role is to monitor how students work together. Rather than focusing on a specific student, teachers carefully observe what is happening within groups. One teacher stated,

It's easy sometimes to blame a student if [he is] not working. If the student isn't work-ing, it's [his] problem. But sometimes these students are just the tip of the iceberg. They are the flag wavers who may represent the others who don't understand what is going on. When I ask a group, "How are you doing?" I get a feeling of how each student is doing in the context of the others in the group. (L. Purvis, personal communication, November 1992)

By asking various questions of the group to ensure social skills and academic accountability, the teacher may pinpoint skills in need of more practice or discover problems in groups as they are first emerging. To develop students' behavioral competence, teachers must stimulate students' self-reflection regarding their social skill and task performance when working with others. The teacher's role of guide or facilitator of this self-reflection (known as *group processing*) is essential for students' interpersonal and self-control development. Processing does not only occur while the teacher observes how students are working in groups but also at the midway point and sometimes at the end of an activity. Self-reflection occurs as members of the groups evaluate how they did and focus on what they need to change to improve their work in the future. To progress to the point where group processing comes naturally and has an effect on individual behavior requires time and encouragement on the part of the teacher. One teacher commented,

> *When groups start processing how they work together, their first attempts seem half-hearted or are token gestures to comply by filling in the sheet. But as time goes on, they get into it. Their comments are more earnest and natural as they talk about their work. (R. Kelly, personal communication, November 1992)*

By asking various questions of the group (e.g., social skills accountability), the teacher can pinpoint skills that need more practice or problems in a group that may just be starting and that affect group interdependence and functioning.

Dealing with Special Challenges

A goal of peer influence strategies, such as cooperative learning, is to create opportunities for students to work and interact in meaningful and positive ways. However, with every opportunity there are potential drawbacks. Some students, because of their previous learning experiences or particular life situations, will resist working with peers. Johnson and Johnson (1998) identified four types of students who may disrupt group processes: students who do not do their work, students who are withdrawn, students who are low achievers, and students who are disruptive in a group. They then recommended some strategies to deal with these students' behaviors.

Students Who Do Not Do Their Work Thinking of the student who will not do his or her assigned work brings to mind group projects that I was required to complete during my studies. A professor would group together people who were mostly unknown to one another and tell them to prepare a paper, a presentation, or a display. As the deadline date would near, it become apparent that some people were working more than others. Some students would skate along doing little; others would work slavishly and pull up the slack in order to meet the deadline. After such projects, students expressed many negative judgments such as, "I never want to do a group project again" or, "I never want to speak to that person." It was not and is not enough to assign students to group projects. If students are put in groups without explicit roles and responsibilities, then there may be someone who tries to do as little as possible in order to get by. When this appears to be taking place in a group, possible interventions include the following:

- Ask the group to discuss the issue with the student and see why he or she is not contributing to the group's work.

- Take the student aside and ask about the situation to determine his or her perception of it. Problem-solve alternative ways in which more commitment or involvement can be obtained.

- Present a skills lesson on problem-solving a situation to be sure that all the students have the skills they need to deal with such a situation.

- Trust the group to resolve the issue.

Another way to change student behavior is to change the way students in the group are evaluated. For example, have part of each student's grade comprise a rating given by each of the other group members. Or, grade the group on the basis of their average performance. If group members are penalized for another student's lack of effort, then they are likely to derive strategies for increasing that student's involvement. Another strategy is for teachers to randomly pick one student in the group to represent the group's overall learning for a particular task. This sense of not knowing whose paper will be chosen may motivate most students to help each other be prepared.

Students Who Are Withdrawn   Some children come to school shy and withdrawn. They may have limited opportunities to socialize, have no siblings, or live in a rural environment. Other students may become isolated over time; they may lack friendships because of poor interpersonal skills, or they may give up on school because of repeated failure, as is the case with many at-risk students. Strategies to help and include these students are discussed next.

Ensure Constructive Teammates   The teacher's decision regarding face-to-face interaction may be to assign students who are likely to be nurturing and supportive to the student's group. Often the key to success is creating opportunities for students to click. One elementary teacher describes such a situation.

> *Tom was very withdrawn. He was happy to just sit and watch what was going on in class. At the beginning of the year, his parents told me about this and asked me to keep an eye on things. So I matched him up with Stephanie. She's very outgoing and is good at including others. For instance, I saw Tom sitting and asked Stephanie to go and play with him. Stephanie went and took his hand, brought him to the group, and announced that they were playing house and he was the father. She gave him a helmet and told him what to do. The same thing happens when they are sitting and doing schoolwork. She becomes what I would call an "enabler." (J. Dunnett, personal communication, November 1992)*

Structure Resource Interdependence   Peer interaction may be promoted by having limited materials (e.g., one pair of scissors per group, one set of crayons) available to necessitate sharing and interaction. Assigning different parts of the academic task to each person in the group, similar to a jigsaw puzzle, also may prompt supportive interactions to help the withdrawn student locate and/or prepare his or her unique contribution.

Structure Role Interdependence   Each student has a role with specific responsibilities such as recorder, observer, or speaker. A specific role can be assigned or invented that is low risk to the withdrawn student but likely to ensure that the student is included (e.g., observer).

Students Who Are Low Achievers   Including students who are low achievers in cooperative learning creates the opportunities for more growth than would be associated with other instructional strategies (e.g., competitive, individualistic). Inclusion of low achievers requires the teacher to adapt lesson requirements so that the student may participate in a way that is valued by the student and the other members of the group. The same suggestions for a withdrawn student may promote active involvement and performance for a low achiever. Coaching the student in advance to make him or her an expert in a specific aspect of the assignment allows the student to be called on to teach other group members.

Students Who Are Disruptive in a Group   If we consider all behavior to be some form of communication, then we may assume that students who disrupt or students who are actively uninvolved in a lesson are attempting to communicate some underlying message, the source of which may be academic or behavioral. In the academic domain, students may be experiencing difficulty with schoolwork. In the social domain, their social or interpersonal skills may be ineffective. Students who disrupt likely are seeking to avoid school work or be noticed through whatever means possible to them. Some strategies for helping these students are discussed next.

Include Constructive Teammates and Avoid Destructive Teammates   Many children with disruptive behaviors have ineffective interpersonal skills and have had negative experiences (e.g., arguments, fights) with other students. When assigning students to groups, try to avoid "deadly combinations" that will exacerbate the situation.

Pretrain Teammates in Procedures for Controlling the Disruption   Create opportunities for classmates to intervene with relevant management strategies that deal with special challenges. It is critical that classmates practice any procedure they are to use consistently (e.g., ignoring, engaging the student in oral planning) with the student when a disruption occurs or is about to occur.

Intervene to Teach Collaborative Skills   When a student disrupts, the teacher may intervene to help group members or the class find ways to influence the disruption. The teacher's role is to guide classmates through problem-solving or brainstorming strategies to come up with some ideas that are acceptable and workable in the classroom.

Teach the Disruptive Student Collaborative Skills   Although most cooperative learning models have a significant social skills component, there may be students who require additional time to practice and master social skills. Students may need someone (e.g., the school counselor, a special educator, a trained paraprofessional, a peer mediator) to coach them before a group activity takes place and to meet with them again after the lesson to discuss progress.

Reduce the Group Size   Some children who disrupt in groups perform much better in one-to-one situations (e.g., partners, peer tutoring) or in triads. In these situations, they receive a more constant flow of directed attention and feedback that keeps them academically engaged.

CONCLUSION

Student behavior is currently one of the most discussed topics in schools. Increasing numbers of educators are turning to instructional strategies that rely on peer mediation and peer influence as they search for ways to effectively deal with behavioral challenges. Cooperative learning has emerged as a preferred, pro-active peer influence strategy that both actively supports the variety of learning styles and abilities that exist within a single classroom and prevents or minimizes disruptive behavior in the classroom.

Teacher interviews revealed a continuum of interventions that address the needs of students with disruptive behavior. One end of the continuum involves reactive measures that respond to misbehavior. The other end involves being pro-active and designing the classroom to inhibit the occurrence of disruptions by communicating appropriate behavior through modeling and teaching social skills. The cooperative learning method, for example, increases student interdependence and learning, reduces disruptive behavior, and demonstrates that disruptive behavior is not a random act beyond the teacher's control. Rather, student behavior is a by-product of the way teachers teach and structure their classrooms.

A direct relationship exists between classroom management and the need for outside school supports. Teachers who use verbal suppression as a means to stop unwanted behavior typically view continued student misbehavior as a problem innate to the child. They see formal assessments and a trip to a psychologist as the route to purge students of their problems. The teacher sees the student as having to meet the teacher's needs in the classroom, and they see no need to change. Thus, they reject the procedures described in this chapter—collaboration, problem solving, restructuring the classroom environment, teaching social skills, and empowering peers. In such a situation, are behavior problems so much a student problem as one of "blaming the victim"? Are discipline problems in some schools as much a reflection of educators' inflexibility as students' behavior characteristics?

As stated previously, students are an untapped resource. When trained and given the opportunity, they can be very effective in mediating their own and their peers' learning and social interactions. When given a voice, even young elementary age students demonstrate a level of maturity and analysis. Cooperative learning is an example of an increasing array of strategies that rely on peers helping peers. When educators and the community support students to run their classrooms, schools become a very different place—a kinder and more meaningful and effective place for everyone.

REFERENCES

Elias, M. (1989). School as a source of stress. *Journal of School Psychology, 27,* 393–407.

Gilstrap, R.L., & Martin, W.R. (1976). *Current strategies for teachers: A resource for personalizing materials.* Santa Monica, CA: Goodyear Publishing.

Johnson, D., & Johnson, R. (1998). *Learning together and alone: Cooperative, competitive, and individualistic learning* (5th ed.). Upper Saddle River, NJ: Prentice Hall.

Kelly, B., & den Otter, J. (1991). Beyond behaviour: A case of social intervention strategies for a student with challenging behaviours. In G.L. Porter & D. Richler (Eds.), *Changing Canadian schools: Perspectives on disability and inclusion* (pp. 257–280). Toronto: The Roeher Institute.

Kohler, F.W., & Strain, P.S. (1990). Peer-assisted interventions: Early promises, notable achievements, and future aspirations. *Clinical Psychology Review, 10,* 411–452.

Porter, G. (Executive Producer). (1994). *Teachers helping teachers: Problem-solving that works* [Video]. Toronto: The Roeher Institute.

Porter, G.L., Wilson, M., Kelly, B., & den Otter, J. (1991). Problem-solving teams: A thirty minute peer-helping model. In G.L. Porter & D. Richler (Eds.), *Changing Canadian schools: Perspectives on disability and inclusion* (pp. 219–238). Toronto: The Roeher Institute.

16

Using Peer Tutoring to Prevent Early Reading Failure

Kristen L. McMaster
Douglas Fuchs
Lynn S. Fuchs

Many students experience significant difficulty in learning to read. By fourth grade, an estimated 38% of American school children are performing below basic proficiency levels in reading (National Center for Education Statistics, 1998). The consequences for these students are serious: They lag behind their peers in other academic areas, have low self-esteem, pose disciplinary problems, and are less likely to graduate from high school (Juel, 1996). Moreover, these students are often referred for special education services; about 73% of students with learning disabilities primarily have difficulties with reading (Riley, 1996).

Detecting and remediating reading problems early is critical for preventing long-term failure (Lyon et al., 2000). Children who are poor readers in first grade are likely to continue to be poor readers in later grades unless they receive early, effective intervention (Juel, 1988). Educators are challenged to find and implement methods that will give poor readers the boost they need to develop reading skills essential for success in school. At the same time, teachers must meet the instructional needs of increasingly diverse groups of students. In addition to the growing presence of students who speak English as a second language, minority children, and children living in poverty (see Fuchs, Fuchs, Mathes, & Simmons, 1997), students with learning disabilities frequently receive their reading instruction in general education classrooms (Vaughn, Gersten, & Chard, 2000). Teachers are finding that conventional instructional methods are not sufficient for addressing the needs of all students in such heterogeneous classrooms (Vaughn et al., 2000).

Peer tutoring, an alternative instructional strategy in which students support each other's learning (Maheady, Harper, & Sacca, 1988), shows promise for enhancing children's early literacy development. Peer tutoring allows teachers to individualize learning materials to address a broader range of instructional needs (Fuchs et al., 2001; Scruggs & Richter, 1985) and provides students with more opportunities to respond to and practice academic content than conventional teaching formats do, which is essential for student success (Delquadri, Greenwood, Whorton, Carta, & Hall, 1986). Moreover, peer tutoring has the potential to facilitate positive changes in students' social behaviors and school adjustment (Fuchs, Fuchs, Martinez, & Mathes, in press; Scruggs & Richter, 1985).

PEER-ASSISTED LEARNING STRATEGIES (PALS): AN EMPIRICALLY VALIDATED PEER TUTORING PROGRAM FOR CLASSWIDE USE

Although empirical evidence supports the use of peer tutoring to improve student achievement, research is still needed to determine the conditions under which peer tutoring is most effective and to compare peer tutoring to other empirically validated interventions (Greenwood, Carta, & Maheady, 1991; Mathes & Fuchs, 1994). What researchers have found thus far is that *specific* tutoring treatments, such as reciprocal classwide programs (e.g., Delquadri et al., 1986; Fuchs et al., 1997), have yielded more powerful results than others. Thus, to maximize students' achievements from peer tutoring, teachers are encouraged to implement empirically validated programs; one such program is Peer-Assisted Learning Strategies (PALS).

The PALS program for reading was developed as a strategy to 1) accommodate diverse groups of learners, including those with disabilities, in regular classrooms (e.g., Fuchs et al., 1997); 2) be feasible for general educators to implement as part of their reading instruction; and 3) provide students with a rich set of strategic, challenging, and motivating activities geared toward enhancing reading achievement (Fuchs et al., 2001). The PALS activities were originally developed for students in second through sixth grade. Since 2000, PALS was extended downward to kindergarten and first grade and upward to meet the needs of high school students with reading difficulties. More than 10 years of pilot studies, component analyses, and large-scale experiments conducted in classrooms have demonstrated that PALS improves the reading achievement of students who are low and average achievers, as well as of students with learning disabilities (e.g., Fuchs et al., 1997; Fuchs et al., 2001; Simmons, Fuchs, Fuchs, Hodge, & Mathes, 1994).

All of the PALS programs share several important features. First, all PALS activities are highly structured. Students are trained to use specific prompts, corrections, and feedback during PALS. Second, PALS incorporates frequent verbal interactions between tutors and tutees, increasing students' opportunities to respond (Delquadri et al., 1986; Greenwood et al., 1991). Third, PALS roles are reciprocal so that both students in a pair serve as tutor and tutee during each PALS session. What follows are detailed descriptions of the PALS program at the kindergarten and first-grade, second- through sixth-grade, and high school levels.

Kindergarten and First-Grade Peer-Assisted Learning Strategies (PALS)

In light of the serious consequences of reading failure and because deficits in reading begin early and are difficult to remediate beyond the early grades (e.g., Juel, 1988), the most recently developed PALS activities have focused on beginning reading skills critical for early literacy acquisition (Fuchs et al., 2001). Specifically, kindergarten and first-grade PALS activities address phonological awareness, beginning decoding, and word recognition—all skills that researchers have demonstrated to be important for successful beginning reading programs. Numerous studies conducted with preschool, kindergarten, and first-grade children (e.g., Ball & Blachman, 1991; Blachman, Ball, Black, & Tangel, 1994; Byrne & Fielding-Barnsley, 1991; O'Connor, Notari-Syverson, & Vadasy, 1996) have shown that early intervention that emphasizes *phonological awareness*—an awareness of the sounds that make up words—facilitates early reading acquisition. In addition, systematic instruction in decoding (i.e., mapping sounds onto letters and blending them into words) and word recognition skills is critical to early reading success (e.g., Adams, 1990; Adams & Bruck, 1995). Intervention programs that emphasize both phonological awareness and word recognition and decoding have had positive effects on the achievement of children at risk for reading failure (e.g., Blachman, Tangel, Ball, Black, & McGraw, 1999; Hatcher, Hulme, & Ellis, 1994; Torgesen, Wagner, & Rashotte, 1997).

Results of several large-scale experimental studies indicate that the kindergarten and first-grade versions of PALS show great promise for developing beginning reading skills in students who are low, average, and high achievers, as well as for those with disabilities (e.g., Fuchs et al., in press; Fuchs et al., 2000). PALS has also proven to be effective in schools with large percentages of minority children and children living in poverty, as well as in schools with predominantly Caucasian, middle-class student populations.

Kindergarten Peer-Assisted Learning Strategies (K-PALS)　As in all PALS programs, K-PALS students work in pairs. Teachers use a rapid letter naming test, a good predictor of future reading performance (e.g., Torgesen et al., 1997), to rank students in the class. The highest scoring student is paired with the lowest scoring student, then the second highest scoring student is paired with the second lowest student, and so on. The pairs change every 4 weeks.

Teachers prepare their children for PALS by modeling the activities in a whole-class format. The teacher acts as the "Coach" and the students are the "Readers" during eight introductory lessons. Gradually, individual students take turns assuming the role of Coach for the whole class. Then, the students tutor each other, alternating as Coach and Reader. The higher performing student is always the Coach first. The teacher circulates among the student pairs, monitoring their progress and providing corrective feedback. K-PALS is conducted three times per week for 20 minutes per session.

Two types of activities are incorporated into PALS: Sound Play and Sounds and Words. Sound Play includes five phonological awareness "games" that address rhyming, isolating first sounds, isolating ending sounds, blending sounds into words, and segmenting words into sounds. Each lesson sheet shows pictures of common animals and objects. Children are trained to use a standard coaching format for each type of lesson. For example, as illustrated in Figure 16.1, the First Sound game shows rows of four pictures (seal, turtle, kite, and saw). Two of the pictures begin with the same sound. In the lesson shown in Figure 16.1, the Coach would point to the first picture and say, "Seal, /sss/." Then he or she would point to the other three pictures and say, "Which one starts with /sss/—turtle, kite, or saw?" The Reader should reply, "Saw, /sss/."

Sounds and Words is made up of four activities. All activities are printed on one side of a lesson sheet (see Figure 16.2). After the Reader has completed an activity one time, the Coach marks one of four happy faces printed at the end of the activity. The students then switch jobs and do the activity again. The first activity, called What Sound?, displays rows of letters that the students read from left to right. A new letter sound is introduced in every other lesson. This letter is in a box along with a picture of an animal or object that starts with that sound. The new letter sound is introduced by the teacher. Then, the Coach points to each letter and asks, "What sound?" The Reader says each sound. Stars are interspersed with the letters to prompt the Coach to praise the Reader. When the Reader makes an error, the Coach says, "Stop, that sound is _____. What sound?" The Reader says the sound, and the Coach says, "Start the line again."

The second activity, What Word?, displays common sight words in rows on the lesson sheet. A new sight word is introduced in every other lesson, and the words build cumulatively across lessons. The teacher introduces the new sight word to the class at the beginning of the lesson. The Coach points to each sight word and asks, "What word?" The reader reads the words, and the Coach corrects errors, just as in the What Sound? activity.

The third activity is called Sound Boxes. Students read decodable words comprised of letter sounds practiced in earlier lessons. The words in each lesson are presented in word families, such as *at, mat,* and *sat.* Again, words build cumulatively across the lessons. Each letter of a word is in a "sound box." The Coach says, "Read it slowly," and the Reader sounds out the word, pointing to each box. Then, the Coach says, "Sing it and read it." This prompts the Reader to blend the sounds together and then read the word. The Coach corrects errors and praises the Reader for appropriate responses.

Finally, the students read sentences comprised of sight words and decodable words practiced in earlier lessons. The Coach says, "Read the sentences" and provides corrective feedback for any errors as the Reader reads. At the end of the lesson, the students count up the happy faces they have marked and record this number on point sheets.

Lesson 6

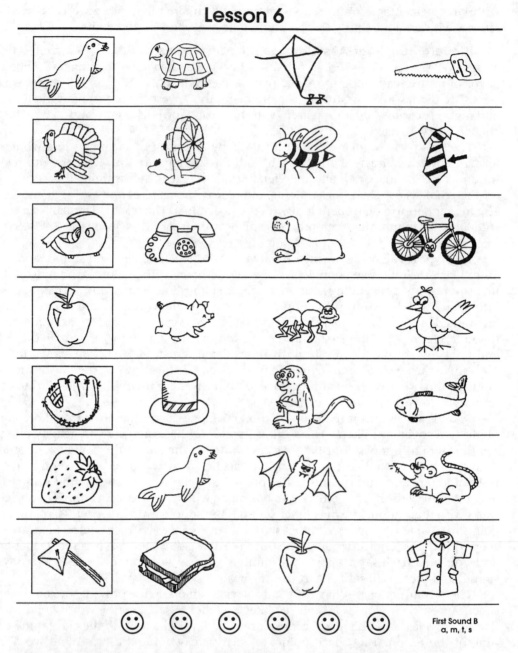

Figure 16.1. Sample Sound Play lesson sheet for kindergarten Peer-Assisted Learning Strategies (K-PALS).

First-Grade Peer-Assisted Learning Strategies (PALS) The first-grade PALS program was developed based on the work of Mathes, Howard, Allen, and Fuchs (1998). As in K-PALS, the first-grade activities emphasize beginning decoding skills and word recognition. In addition, one experimental version of first-grade PALS includes a fluency component designed to include the speed and accuracy with which students read. For the first 2 weeks of PALS, teachers train students to follow PALS rules and work cooperatively to complete the PALS activities. Following training, PALS is conducted three times per week for 35–40 minutes per session.

Teachers use the rapid letter naming test to rank-order their students. The rank-ordered list is then split in half, and the strongest reader from the top half of the list is

Lesson 34

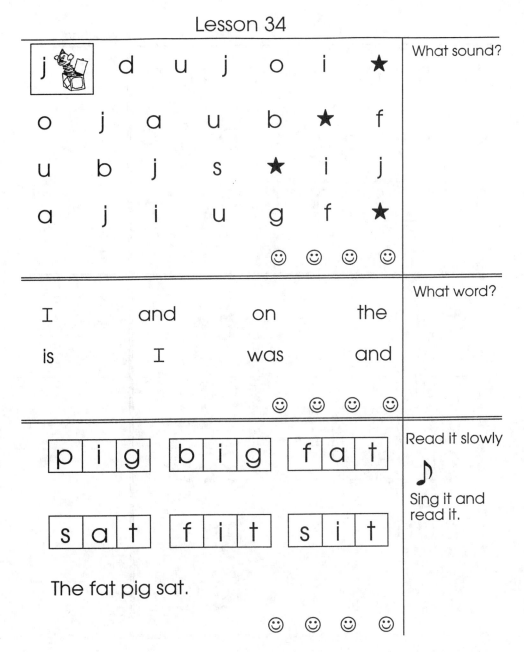

Figure 16.2.   Sample Sounds and Words lesson sheet for kindergarten Peer-Assisted Learning Strategies (K-PALS).

paired with the strongest reader from the bottom half of the list and so on until all students are paired. The higher performing student in each pair is the Coach first, and the lower performing student is the Reader first. New partners are assigned every 4 weeks.

Each PALS lesson begins with a brief teacher-led introduction. The teacher introduces new letter sounds and sight words and then leads the students in segmenting and blending words that they will later decode in the lesson. The teacher says a word, and the students say the sounds in the word, holding up a finger for each sound. The teacher then shows them the word, and they blend the sounds together and read the word.

First-grade PALS activities are comprised of two parts: Sounds and Words and Partner Reading. Sounds and Words is made up of four main activities (see Figure 16.3). The first activity, Saying Sounds, is similar to the What Sound? activity in K-PALS. The Coach

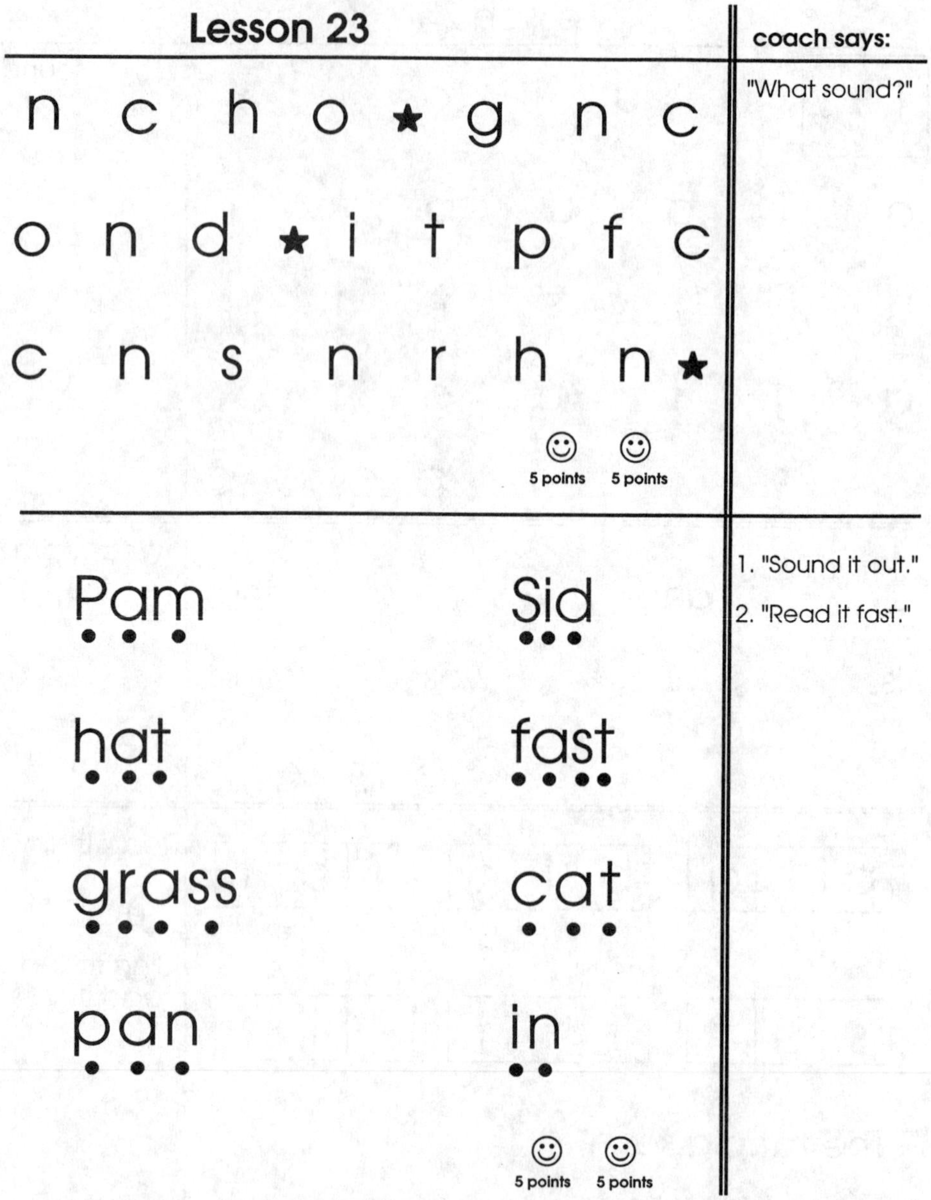

Lesson 23

	coach says:
n c h o ★ g n c	"What sound?"
o n d ★ i t p f c	
c n s n r h n ★	

☺ 5 points ☺ 5 points

Pam	Sid	1. "Sound it out."
hat	fast	2. "Read it fast."
grass	cat	
pan	in	

☺ 5 points ☺ 5 points

Figure 16.3. Sample Sounds and Words lesson sheet for first-grade Peer-Assisted Learning Strategies (PALS).

points to each letter on the lesson sheet and says, "What sound?," and the Reader says each sound. The Coach praises the Reader and provides corrective feedback. When the Reader has said all of the sounds, the Coach marks a happy face and five points on a point sheet. The students then switch roles.

The second activity is a blending task using the words the teacher presented at the beginning of the lesson. An arrow and small dots are printed under each phoneme. The Coach points to the first word and says, "Sound it out." The Reader points to each dot and says the sounds. Then, the Coach says, "Read it fast." The Reader slides his or her finger along the arrow and reads the word fast. If the Reader makes an error, then the Coach models sounding out the word and reading it fast; the Reader repeats the word and starts the line over. Again, the Coach marks a happy face and points, and the students switch roles.

	coach says:
	"Read the words."

are	has to come	have blue	was
he said	are away with	he has no	see no
are blue	are for	have a	are
and he	come find	he has	are for
find	was away		

☺ ☺
5 points 5 points

"Read the story."

Pam and **James**

Pam has a **brother James**.

Pam has a baseball.

Pam throws the baseball to **James**.

Pam and **James** are in the grass

at the park.

☺ ☺ ☺ ☺ ☺ ☺
5 points 5 points 5 points 5 points 5 points 5 points

☆<James>

☆<brother>

Go back to "Read the words."

The third activity is called Read the Words. Common sight words are presented in rows on the lesson sheet. The Coach says, "Read the words," and the Reader points to each word and reads them. In the fluency version of PALS, many of the sight words are grouped into phrases. This prompts the Reader to read words as chunks, rather than in isolation. Also, for the first half of the fluency version, students read the sight words in a Speed Game format. During the Speed Game, the teacher times the Readers for 1 minute as they read the sight words. The Readers then have two chances to try to read more words in 1 minute than they did the first time. Then, the Coaches play the Speed Game. When students beat their times, they mark a star on a Star Chart which, when completed, can be exchanged for small prizes, such as bookmarks or pencils.

Next, students read short stories composed of the sight words and decodable words they've already practiced. Before the students read the story, the teacher introduces "rocket words" that have been added to make the stories more interesting. Then, the teacher reads the story, providing a fluent model. The Readers then read the story. If the Reader makes a mistake or hesitates on a word for 3 seconds, then the Coach says the correct word, and the Reader repeats it and continues reading. Happy faces and points are marked, and the students switch roles. In the fluency version, the Speed Game format is used with the story for the second half of the program. In the regular version, students mark stars on Star Charts when they have earned at least four happy faces for reading the story. The Star Charts are exchanged for prizes when completed.

After first-grade PALS has been conducted for 4–6 weeks, Partner Reading is introduced. This activity is conducted for 10 minutes, immediately following the Sounds and Words activities during each PALS session. During Partner Reading, students use the decoding and word recognition skills that they've practiced during PALS to read books. Teachers select books that are appropriate to the reading level of the lower performing student in each pair. The Coach reads the title of the book, pointing to the words, then the Reader reads the title. Then, the Coach reads a page, pointing to the words, and the Reader repeats the same page. When the partners finish the book, they mark five points, switch roles, and read the book again. Each book is read four times before the pair receives a new book to read.

Peer-Assisted Learning Strategies (PALS) for Second Through Sixth Grades

PALS has been documented to be effective among students in second through sixth grades for improving reading fluency and comprehension for students who are low and average achievers, as well as for students with learning disabilities who are included in PALS classrooms (e.g., Fuchs et al., 1997; Simmons et al., 1994). For this, PALS has been awarded "best practice" status by the U.S. Department of Education's Program Effectiveness Panel (Fuchs et al., 2001). PALS involves pairing high performing readers with low performing readers to conduct a series of activities to promote reading fluency and comprehension. These activities—Partner Reading, Paragraph Shrinking, and Prediction Relay—are described in detail in this section.

Teachers use a set of brief, scripted lessons to train all students in their classrooms to conduct PALS. The six to ten training lessons last 30–60 minutes per session and include direct teacher presentations, student practice, and teacher feedback. Following training, students participate in PALS three times each week for 35 minutes per session.

Every student in the class is paired with another student, and each pair consists of a student who is a high performer and a student who is a low performer. The teacher determines the pairs by first ranking all of the students in the class from the strongest to the weakest reader. The teacher then splits the rank-ordered list of students in half, pairs the strongest reader from the top half with the strongest reader from the bottom half of the list, and so on until all students are paired. Although the tutoring roles are reciprocal during each tutoring session, the student who is a high performer always reads first to serve as a model for the student who is a low performer.

Each pair is assigned to one of two teams for which they earn points during PALS. These points are awarded for correct responses during the PALS activities. Each pair marks their points by slashing through numbers on a score card. Teachers also circulate among the pairs during PALS to monitor their performance and award bonus points for cooperative behavior and for following the PALS procedures. At the end of each week, the pairs report the number of points they earned for their teams, and the teacher adds them up to determine the winning team. The teacher creates new pairs and teams every 4 weeks.

Partner Reading During each PALS session, the first activity is Partner Reading and retelling. Each student reads aloud from connected text for 5 minutes each. This text comes from narrative literature selected by the teacher, and it should be at an appropriate level for the student who is the low performer in each pair. The higher performer reads first, then the lower performer reads the same material. Whenever the reader makes an error, the tutor says, "Stop, you missed that word. Can you figure it out?" If the reader does not figure out the word in 4 seconds, then the tutor says, "That word is _____. What word?" The reader says the word and continues reading. After both students have read, the student who is the lower performer retells the sequence of events just read for 2 minutes. Students earn 1 point for each sentence read correctly and 10 points for the retell.

Paragraph Shrinking   The second PALS activity is Paragraph Shrinking. This activity is designed to develop comprehension through summarization and main idea identification. During Paragraph Shrinking, the students continue reading orally, but they stop at the end of each paragraph to identify the main idea. The tutor asks the reader to identify 1) who or what the paragraph is mainly about and 2) the most important thing about the who or what. The reader must combine or "shrink" this information into 10 words or less. If the tutor determines that the reader's answer is incorrect, then he or she says, "That's not quite right. Skim the paragraph and try again." After the reader provides a new answer, the tutor decides whether the answer is correct. If so, he or she gives 1 point each for correctly identifying the who or what, for stating the most important thing, and for using 10 words or less. If the tutor determines that the answer is incorrect, then he or she provides a correct answer, and the pair continues reading. After 5 minutes, the partners switch roles.

Prediction Relay   The last activity, Prediction Relay, requires students to formulate predictions and then confirm or disconfirm them. This activity is included in PALS because making predictions is a strategy associated with improvements in reading comprehension (Palincsar & Brown, 1984). Four steps make up Prediction Relay. The reader 1) makes a prediction about what will happen on the next half-page to be read, 2) reads the half-page aloud, 3) confirms or disconfirms the prediction, and 4) summarizes the main idea. If the tutor disagrees with the prediction, then he or she says, "I don't agree. Think of a better prediction." Students earn points for each reasonable prediction, for reading each half-page, for accurately confirming or disconfirming the prediction, and for identifying the main idea in 10 words or less. Again, the students switch roles after 5 minutes.

High School Peer-Assisted Learning Strategies (PALS)   High school PALS has been demonstrated to be a promising strategy to promote literacy among adolescents who are seriously reading delayed (Fuchs, Fuchs, & Kazdan, 1999). High school students who have participated in PALS have significantly improved their reading comprehension scores in comparison to similar students in non-PALS programs. In addition, PALS students have reported working harder with their peers and working harder to improve their reading. High school PALS is similar to PALS for second through sixth grades in that students work reciprocally in pairs, earn points for their teams, and work on the same three activities (Partner Reading, Paragraph Shrinking, and Prediction Relay). However, high school PALS differs from second- through sixth-grade PALS in three ways.

First, students switch partners every day instead of every 4 weeks. This accommodates the frequent absences of high school students, which makes partner consistency difficult. Also, high school students seem to prefer interacting with different classmates. Second, the motivational system is based on a "work" theme. Pairs earn PALS dollars, which they deposit into checking accounts. They maintain these accounts and write checks to order items from a PALS catalog, such as CDs, fast-food coupons, and sports apparel that have been donated by local businesses. Third, students involved in high school PALS typically read from expository, rather than narrative, text that is selected to address issues pertinent to their lives, such as work and social relationships.

CONCLUSION

Peer-Assisted Learning Strategies (PALS) Benefits: Teacher Testimonials

Teachers find that PALS provides a unique opportunity for children to intensely practice the basic skills they need to become good readers and to be successful in later grades. In the words of one kindergarten teacher,

> *This is my fourth year teaching kindergarten. I have never had so many students reading at this time. . . . This program is very easy to implement and extremely beneficial to the students. All students will go to first grade knowing letters, sounds and decoding skills and reading many words. Students who participated in this program will have a head start over other children in regard to reading as they enter first grade.*

This sentiment is echoed by first-grade teachers as well. As one teacher pointed out, the "repetition of saying sounds, sounding out, and sight words gave my students the 'nuts and bolts' of reading practice that they needed but seldom get." Another credited PALS with allowing her to promote students at risk for being held back in first grade: "I had three students that I thought would be retained. The PALS approach to reading has really made a difference. I'm not retaining any children this year."

Teachers also find that the reciprocal roles in PALS provides social as well as academic benefits to students of all ability levels. As one teacher explained, "The program really helps my lower performing students and average performing students to read. It also helps to improve students' social skills. They learn to communicate with others. It also helps the high achievers to expand/develop their leadership skills."

Another important benefit of PALS is its capacity to include students with disabilities in the general classroom. Children with learning disabilities, behavior disorders, and mild mental retardation have successfully learned to use the procedures in PALS and to assume the role of both Coach and Reader to complete the PALS activities. Teachers who have students with disabilities included in their classrooms find the structured, predictable routine helpful for developing their reading skills as well as improving overall classroom behavior.

Brandon, a student with learning and behavior disabilities, was included full time in a PALS classroom. As his teacher explains, PALS served as a means of truly including Brandon in classroom activities:

> *Before we started PALS, it was so hard to keep him focused; it was so hard to keep him on task. . . . With him being full-time inclusion in my room, without the PALS program, I don't know what I would have done with [Brandon] during that time. I may have wound up finding other avenues for him—working on the computer and things like that which wouldn't have been tying him in to the classroom, which is what inclusion is supposed to be about. I have seen him grow so much with the PALS program, just in being able to listen to sounds and recognize words that he probably wouldn't have known before.*

Teachers who use PALS also cite the feasibility of PALS and how well it fits within the kindergarten and first grade reading curricula. As one first-grade teacher stated after implementing PALS for a year in her classroom, "The PALS activities were very easy to implement. They provided intensive times of actual reading by every student, as well as interaction with other students. It provided a valuable addition to my regular reading instruction." Similarly, a K-PALS teacher noted that the "program is so organized. I only had to open a manual to find the next lesson or to plan the pacing of my other reading instruction."

Peer-Assisted Learning Strategies (PALS) Nonresponders

As beneficial as PALS appears to be for many students, including those with disabilities, there are still some children who do not make the desired achievement gains after participating in PALS. An estimated 7% of PALS participants do not respond to the instruction (Al Otaiba, Fuchs, & Fuchs, 2000), as measured by tests of phonological awareness, decoding, and word recognition. Those students who have not responded to the program have been characterized as having difficulties in such areas as phonological awareness, attention and behavioral control, and cognitive development or as having received education in economically disadvantaged areas (Al Otaiba, Fuchs, & Fuchs, 2000). When implementing PALS in the classroom, teachers should closely monitor the progress of students most at risk for reading failure. More intensive, individualized interventions will likely be necessary for a small number of these children.

Summary and Ways To Gain Access to
Peer-Assisted Learning Strategies (PALS) Materials

Peer tutoring has shown great promise as an effective supplement to conventional teaching methods to 1) promote critical reading skills and 2) accommodate the increasingly diverse student population and academic diversity in today's classrooms. Peer tutoring makes use of one of the greatest resources in our schools—the students themselves. When empirically validated tutoring programs are implemented carefully and accurately, teachers can help most of their students make great strides toward literacy and success in school.

For more information and access to materials for PALS at all grade levels described in this chapter, visit the PALS web site at http://www.peerassistedlearningstrategies.org or e-mail pals@vanderbilt.edu.

REFERENCES

Adams, M.J. (1990). *Beginning to read: Thinking and learning about print.* Cambridge, MA: MIT Press.

Adams, M.J., & Bruck, M. (1995). Resolving the 'Great Debate.' *American Educator, 19,* 7, 10–20.

Al Otaiba, S., Fuchs, D., & Fuchs, L.S. (April, 2000). *Children who do not respond to early literacy instruction: A longitudinal study.* Paper presented at the annual conference of the Council for Exceptional Children, Vancouver, Canada.

Ball, E.W., & Blachman, B.A. (1991). Does phoneme awareness training in kindergarten make a difference in early word recognition and developmental spelling? *Reading Research Quarterly, 26,* 49–66.

Blachman, B.A., Ball, E., Black, R., & Tangel, D. (1994). Kindergarten teachers develop phoneme awareness in low-income, inner-city classrooms: Does it make a difference? *Reading and Writing: An Interdisciplinary Journal, 6,* 1–17.

Blachman, B.A., Tangel, D.M., Ball, E.W., Black, R., & McGraw, C.K. (1999). Developing phonological awareness and word recognition skills: A two-year intervention with low-income, inner-city children. *Reading and Writing: A Interdisciplinary Journal, 11,* 239–273.

Byrne, B., & Fielding-Barnsley, R. (1991). Evaluation of a program to teach phonemic awareness to young children. *Journal of Educational Psychology, 85,* 104–111.

Delquadri, J., Greenwood, C.R., Whorton, D., Carta, J.J., & Hall, R.V. (1986). Classwide peer tutoring. *Exceptional Children, 52,* 535–542.

Fuchs, D., Fuchs, L.S., Martinez, E., & Mathes, P.G. (in press). *Effects of peer-assisted learning strategies on the social acceptance of students with learning disabilities in mainstream classrooms.* Learning Disabilities Research and Practice.

Fuchs, D., Fuchs, L.S., Mathes, P.G., & Simmons, D.C. (1997). Peer-assisted learning strategies: Making classrooms more responsive to diversity. *American Educational Research Journal, 34,* 174–206.

Fuchs, D., Fuchs, L., Thompson, A., Al Otaiba, S., Nyman, K., Yang, N., & Svenson, E. (2000). *Strengthening kindergartners' reading readiness in Title I and non-Title I schools.* Paper presented at the Pacific Coast Research Conference, La Jolla, CA.

Fuchs, D., Fuchs, L., Thompson, A., Al Otaiba, S., Yen, L., Yang, N., Braun, M., & O'Connor, R. (2001). Is reading important in reading-readiness programs? A randomized field trial with teachers as program implementers. *Journal of Educational Psychology, 93*(2), 251–267.

Fuchs, D., Fuchs, L.S., Thompson, A., Svenson, E., Yen, L., Al Otaiba, S., Yang, N., McMaster, K.N., Prentice, K., Kazdan, S., & Saenz, L. (2001). Peer-assisted learning strategies in reading: Extensions for kindergarten, first grade, and high school. *Remedial and Special Education, 22,* 15–21.

Fuchs, L.S., Fuchs, D., & Kazdan, S. (1999). Effects of peer-assisted learning strategies on high school students with serious reading problems. *Remedial and Special Education, 20,* 309–318.

Greenwood, C.R., Carta, J.J., & Maheady, L. (1991). Peer tutoring programs in the regular education classroom. In G. Storer, M.R. Shinn, & H.M. Walker. (Eds.), *Interventions for achievement and behavior problems* (pp. 179–200). Silver Spring, MD: National Association of School Psychologists.

Hatcher, P.J., Hulme, C., & Ellis, A.W. (1994). Ameliorating early reading failure by integrating the teaching of reading and phonological skills: The phonological linkage hypothesis. *Child Development, 65,* 41–57.

Juel, C. (1988). Learning to read and write: A longitudinal study of fifty-four children from first through fourth grade. *Journal of Educational Psychology, 80,* 437–447.

Juel, C. (1996). What makes literacy tutoring effective? *Reading Research Quarterly, 31,* 268–289.

Levin, H., & Meister, G. (1986). Is CAI cost-effective? *Phi Delta Kappan, 67,* 745–749.

Lyon, R., Fletcher, J., Shaywitz, S., Shaywitz, B., Torgesen, J., Schulte, A., & Olson, R. (2000). *Rethinking learning disabilities.* Unpublished manuscript.

Maheady, L., Harper, G.F., & Sacca, M.K. (1988). Peer-mediated instruction: A promising approach to meeting the diverse needs of LD adolescents. *Learning Disability Quarterly, 11,* 108–113.

Mathes, P.G., & Fuchs, L.S. (1994). The efficacy of peer tutoring in reading for students with mild disabilities: A best-evidence synthesis. *School Psychology Review, 23,* 59–80.

Mathes, P.G., Howard, J.K., Allen, S.H., & Fuchs, D. (1998). Peer-assisted learning strategies for first-grade readers: Responding to the needs of diversity. *Reading Research Quarterly, 31,* 268–289.

National Center for Education Statistics. (1998). *NAEP 1998 reading report card for the nation and states.* Washington, DC: U.S. Department of Education.

O'Connor, R.E., Notari-Syverson, A., & Vadasy, P.F. (1996). Ladders to literacy: The effects of teacher-led phonological activities for kindergarten children with and without disabilities. *Exceptional Children, 63,* 117–130.

Palincsar, A.M., & Brown, A.L. (1984). Reciprocal teaching of comprehension-fostering and comprehension-monitoring activities. *Cognition and Instruction, 2,* 117–175.

Riley, R. (1996). Improving the reading and writing skills of America's students. *Learning Disability Quarterly, 19,* 67–69.

Scruggs, T.E., & Richter, L. (1985). Tutoring learning disabled students: A critical review. *Learning Disability Quarterly, 8,* 286–298.

Simmons, D.C., Fuchs, D., Fuchs, L.S., Hodge, J.P., & Mathes, P.G. (1994). Importance of instructional complexity and role reciprocity to classwide peer tutoring. *Learning Disabilities Research and Practice, 9,* 203–212.

Torgesen, J.K., Wagner, R.K., & Rashotte, C.A. (1997). Prevention and remediation of severe reading disabilities: Keeping the end in mind. *Scientific Studies of Reading, 1,* 217–234.

Vaughn, S., Gersten, R., & Chard, D.J. (2000). The underlying message in LD intervention research: Findings from research syntheses. *Exceptional Children, 67,* 99–114.

17
Partner Learning

The Power Source for Students, Schools, and Communities

Mary E. McNeil
Antonette W. Hood

If we take seriously the challenge to promote creative, collaborative learning models that empower students and teachers, continual refinement of partner learning approaches is essential. Since 1980, an impressive database that recognizes partner learning programs as effective approaches to enhancing student learning in the classroom has been compiled. "Partner learning is an eminent example of individualized instruction in which students work together to achieve educational objectives" (McNeil, 1994, p. 244).

PARTNERING FOR SUCCESS

Structured partnerships may take a variety of forms including peer and cross-age tutoring as well as cooperative learning approaches. Several studies have provided solid evidence that peer tutoring is an effective way to promote the individualization of instruction by increasing students' time on task and their opportunities to respond and receive coaching and feedback (McNeil, 1994; Villa & Thousand, 1996). When teachers incorporate these techniques into their classrooms, extra assistance for students struggling with their learning becomes an integral part of the classroom.

Transformational Effects

Partner learning systems have the power to transform the teaching process. As LaPlant and Zane point out (see Chapter 18), teachers who engage in such programs understand that instruction may come from people other than the adults labeled as "teachers." Teachers who incorporate partner learning programs into their classrooms have reported that, in addition to receiving more individualized instruction, students tend to learn at accelerated rates, enjoy the exciting opportunity to work cooperatively with classmates, demonstrate

We acknowledge the contributions of Ellen Klein and Jane Johnson of the Washington Elementary School for sharing the results of their Cross-Age Tutoring Project and Dr. Leo Corriveau, Superintendent of Schools Hillsboro-Deering School District in New Hampshire, for his enthusiastic support of this project. Special thanks go to Advancement Via Individual Determination (AVID™) Coordinator Mary Duggan, teacher Blaze Newman, and AVID student Marisa. We are also indebted to Betty Mohlenbrock, President, and Madhu Narayan, Program Manager, of the Family Literacy Foundation. Many thanks go to Katelynn Miller, Community Coordinator, Youth Reading Role Models at Escondido High School. Our thanks also go to Natalie Maniace, Project SUCCESS Site Director, and Robert Vater, Project SUCCESS teacher at Sierra High School. In addition, we thank the many students who shared their personal stories with us. They are true partners in every way.

heightened responsibility for their learning and that of their partners, relish the association with the teacher as a member of the instructional team, and be more actively involved in creating a positive classroom learning environment (McNeil, 1994).

Partner learning relationships have been found to offer a great deal to educators and students alike. Data collected by McNeil (1994) indicated that both tutors and tutees demonstrated increases in achievement, communication skills, and self-esteem. LaPlant and Zane report (see Chapter 18) that partner learning may be a source of positive relationships for students who have few outside connections.

There is much to be learned from the outcomes of recent research and the many activities involving the refinement of peer support structures and partner learning systems. Since the 1980s, several of these support structures and systems, including cross-age/cross-grade peer tutoring, same-age/same-grade peer tutoring, peer mediation, social supports, and buddy networks, have established a remarkable foothold in our public schools. Research in this area has yielded substantial benefits to those involved and is described in detail in Sections II and III of this book (see also Cowie & Sharp, 1996; Fuchs, Fuchs, & Kazden, 1999; Lipsky & Gartner, 1997; Mortweet et al., 1999; Thousand & Villa, 1990; Villa & Thousand, 1996).

Academic and Social Growth

Structured partnerships continue to positively influence the academic and social growth of each partner—tutor or tutee. Thousand, Nevin, and McNeil related, "Students who teach concepts and procedures understand them at a deeper level" (2000, p. 148). This phenomenon persists as a focus of studies looking at the effect of partner learning systems and peer support structures on people in education who represent a wide range of ages and positions, from preschoolers to teacher educators (e.g., Cushing & Kennedy, 1997; Thousand, Nevin, & McNeil, 2000; Vaughn, Gersten, & Chard, 2000). Their common findings support the advancement of partner learning as a best practice in education in general and in inclusive education in particular.

Several studies of the effects of peer-assisted learning by school-age children have documented growth in academic skills. For example, Fuchs, Fuchs, and Kazden (1999) and McMaster, Fuchs, and Fuchs (see Chapter 16) found that Peer-Assisted Learning Strategies (PALS) showed potential to increase literacy among some high school students who had serious reading delays. Previous examination of the effectiveness of the use of PALS at the elementary level by Fuchs, Fuchs, Mathes, and Simmons (1997) discovered a significant improvement in reading fluency among students involved in the program. Vaughn et al., (2000) found that "the interactive dialogue between . . . students and proficient peers is critical for effective interventions in reading and writing" (p. 110). Peer-mediated instruction for children with mild disabilities has consistently been found to be an effective instructional strategy to improve spelling skills (e.g., Harper, Maheady, & Mallette, 1994; Harper, Mallette, Maheady, Parkes, & Moore, 1993).

POWER SOURCES: LESSONS FROM MODELS IN THE FIELD

A variety of partnership models exist in our nation's public schools for children to support one another. From Head Start to high school, these programs generally share common characteristics. They build on a cooperative relationship between students; they create structures that facilitate the students' social or academic potential; and they empower children who have been isolated, are at risk of failing in school, or who may otherwise choose to leave school. In this section, four different partnership models are described that support Vygotsky's notion, "What children can do together today, they can do alone tomorrow" (as cited in Johnson & Johnson, 1994, p. 86).

Youth Reading Role Models

Youth Reading Role Models (YRRM) is a program of the Family Literacy Foundation, a community-based organization that was founded in San Diego in 1989. Its mission stems from the notion that "the single most important activity for building the knowledge required for eventual success in reading is reading aloud to children" (Family Literacy Foundation, 2000, p. 23). YRRM was developed to facilitate supportive relationships between children in Head Start programs and the high school students who read aloud to them. The emphasis is on developing communication between the youth (as "extended family") and the preschoolers. It further emphasizes the development of an empowering attitude in both groups. For the high school students, empowering attitudes include an improved sense of self-worth, competence, confidence, and value for service to community. For the children, the focus is on developing a positive attitude toward literacy and an "I can read!" way of thinking.

Part of the success of YRRM is the "intergenerational" involvement in which hundreds of San Diego's high school students have the opportunity to practice valuable citizenship and transform their local communities by giving their time to read with preschool children. They become positive role models in their schools and communities, and they experience and realize the fun and importance of reading aloud to children.

During their two training sessions, the YRRMs are given a workbook that includes a service-learning agreement form (see Figure 17.1) and a detailed job description (see Figure 17.2). The YRRMs commit to reading at a child care center, such as Head Start, in their community for 1 hour per week for an entire school semester. At the end of the semester, the YRRMs are expected to write a reflective essay about their experience. They receive community service credit hours, which satisfy district community service required for graduation. They are awarded a Family Learning Foundation certificate, and they receive a Letter of Commendation from the mayor's office. Their work often enhances college scholarship and placement applications, and they are able to add an important work experience to their résumés.

The YRRMs become a part of the solution to the significant numbers of children in their communities who might otherwise enter school ill-prepared for learning. A high percentage of the preschool children who have participated in the YRRM program have been from homes in which the primary language is not English, and for many of those children, hearing stories in English has been a new experience. As one YRRM reflected in his essay,

> Most of the children who go to the Head Start Center are between the ages of 3 and 5, and the majority have been born of a Hispanic origin and are therefore raised in a Spanish-speaking environment. As a reading role model, I was able to give the children what was for many of them their first experience with books in the English language. But there are practical benefits to participation, as well.

Advancement Via Individual Determination (AVID™)

Established in more than 1,000 schools in 16 states and 13 countries and servicing more than 50,000 students, Advancement Via Individual Determination (AVID™) is a 20-year-old program that began in San Diego in response to the increasing number of minority students of low socioeconomic status at a high school that had previously been mostly

YOUTH READING ROLE MODELSSM

SERVICE LEARNING AGREEMENT

➢ **STUDENT:**

I,_____(print your name) plan to give between 30 and 40 hours of service to the children of San Diego County through the YOUTH READING ROLE MODELS SM program. In doing so, I will fulfill my commitment to this program and receive a certificate of completion from them.

Signature:_____

(NOTE: This agreement is due at Training session #2. If it is not turned in by this date, you could be ineligible to participate in the program.)

➢ **TEACHER/ADVISOR:**

Your student will be participating in the YOUTH READING ROLE MODELS SM program. Your signature is required for your student to participate and receive the appropriate acknowledgements.

Print Name:_____

Signature:_____

Thank you for supporting your student's participation in this important community service program.

©Family Literacy Foundation, 1999

Figure 17.1.   Youth Reading Role Models (YRRM): Service Learning Agreement; reprinted by permission.

FAMILY LITERACY FOUNDATION
A Not-For-Profit Organization

YOUTH READING ROLE MODELS[SM]

Job Description

> Thank you for volunteering to be a YOUTH READING ROLE MODEL this semester. We take your commitment to the young children of your community very seriously. The following are some of the important details and expectations for your participation.

1) You will be expected to read approximately **one hour a week**, with a team of your peers, at a designated Child Care Center location and on a consistent basis. **Attendance is vital to make the experience a beneficial one**. The children will be counting on you to be there with books you have chosen from the Library and looking forward to your visit each week. You are allowed up to **3 excused absences**. If you are unable to attend a session, **you must call your Student Coordinator to let them know you will not be there that day.** If you miss more than 3 sessions, you will be expected to make them up. Ideas for make-up activities should be discussed with a Community Coordinator.

2) You must be available for one hour on the same day each week throughout the semester in order to participate in the program. Center assignments will be given at Training #2. You will be giving approximately **30-40 hours** of your time over the course of the semester, and through doing so, will receive recognition through Family Literacy Foundation, your school, and the Mayor of your municipality. These hours include time spent at the Library finding books to read with the children, time spent preparing for your reading session (practicing reading the books), and 1 hour at the Center actually reading with the children.

3) Prior to beginning your weekly reading sessions at the Child Care Center, you must attend 2 **Training sessions**. There will be paperwork distributed at the 1st session which will need to be returned at the 2nd session, signed by a parent and teacher. Please remember to bring some form of ID to Training #2 to fill out a Library Card application, if you do not already have a Library Card (a driver's license, learner's permit, or school ID are all appropriate forms of identification).

4) You need to be able to travel to the Child Care Center and library on your own or with your Team. You will be provided with bus tokens, route information, and maps, if needed. A parent or guardian must sign a **travel/photo release form**, which will be handed out at Training #1 and returned to us by Training #2.

5) You will be expected to keep track of your hours on a **time card** provided inside your workbook.

6). At the close of the semester, you will be asked to write a one-page **reflective essay** on your experience as a YOUTH READING ROLE MODEL.

©Family Literacy Foundation, 1999

Figure 17.2. Youth Reading Role Models (YRRM): Job Description; reprinted by permission.

middle class and Caucasian. This reform program, initiated by an English teacher, Mary Catherine Swanson, seeks to provide academic attention and support for those under-achieving, underrepresented students who have the potential to succeed at a 4-year university. The participants are generally students who come from low-income backgrounds, whose grades are low or average, and who would potentially be the first in their families to attend college. The mission of AVID™ is to ensure that all students, especially those with academic potential, will

- Succeed in a rigorous curriculum

- Enter mainstream activities of the school

- Increase their enrollment in 4-year colleges

- Become educated and responsible participants and leaders in a democratic society (Swanson, 1998)

All AVID™ candidates and their parents sign a contract (see Figure 17.3) describing the goals and responsibilities of AVID™ participation. Swanson believed the key to success in AVID™ is the combination of rigor and support. "Rigor without support is a prescription for failure," she says. "Support without rigor is a tragic waste of potential" (Wilkens, 2001).

The AVID™ program has three components: academic instruction, tutorial support, and motivational activities. The key to the program's success is that it is not a pull-out program—it is an in-class program. The AVID™ class is a regular, elective class scheduled into the school day for each year of high school. The class focuses on developing student learning patterns by using writing, inquiry, and collaborative grouping as tools for learning. The curriculum covers a variety of study skills and time-management strategies; reading, writing, and presentation skills; and long-range planning and goal setting. Within the classroom, students experience a built-in support system in which expectations are high, and success is common. As one student reported, "They said if we worked a little bit harder, we could get into a 4-year college. No one ever told me I was smart before" (Morita, 2001, paragraph 19).

The tutorial support comes from peers and college-age tutors who engage in inquiry-based, collaborative sessions of group problem solving, group projects, work groups, study groups, and other interactive activities. Strong communication between students is encouraged, and students are constantly nurtured and challenged in a forum of collaboration and independent learning. On a poster in an AVID™ classroom, one of the four maxims of the philosophy declares: "It is better for a student to be an apprentice at a tutor's or teacher's side for five minutes than a disciple at his or her feet for five months."

Perhaps Marisa's story captures best the power of AVID™ in the life of a young immigrant. Marisa was 11 years old when she came to the United States of America from Mexico. She was a bright child who spoke only Spanish. No one in her family had ever graduated from high school. When she entered seventh grade as a struggling reader and writer, a teacher recommended her for the AVID™ program. She observed a spark of self-determination in Marisa. Since 1996, Marisa has thrived in AVID™ and credits her progress in school to the tutors, in particular. Their constant encouragement and support led her to reach higher and dream larger. Marisa is now a senior in high school who excels in the advanced placement English class. She is enthusiastically involved in school activities, is the student representative to her school district's school board, facilitates parent meetings for the high school's Hispanic families, is the school's translator, and has been awarded early acceptance at several universities. Marisa aspires to be an AVID™ English teacher, and her bilingual skills and self-confidence ensure her of many job opportunities. She has chosen to attend a local state university and continue to live at home. Her parents will have

AVID™ Contract
Advancement Via Individual Determination

As an AVID™ student with college goals, I understand and agree to the following:

1. I will complete **all** homework assignments for **all** classes equal to an average of at least two hours per night and weekends.

2. I will be prepared for **all** classes with **all** assigned work completed and ready to submit at the beginning of the class period.

3. I will be an active learner by paying attention in my classes, taking thorough notes using the Cornell method, and being an active participant.

4. I will come prepared to study groups and tutorials: I will have in my possession all of my class notes, texts, handouts, tutorial focus sheet, and any other necessary materials.

5. I am aware that study groups and tutorials **are not** replacements for homework time. I understand that they are study sessions with aid from college tutors. The tutorial goals include the clarification of ideas, concepts, and problems which are difficult to reach working alone. I, as a member of the group, will help others and, in turn, will receive help from members of my group. I do not expect the tutors to "give me the answers" but instead to lead me and the other members to discover our own answers.

6. I will "keep on top" of my grades in each class by taking responsibility for my own learning. If I don't understand something or find myself falling behind, I will request help from my teacher and/or my tutors and study group members.

7. I am aware that AVID™ is also a class. I will complete all AVID™ assignments including binders, writing assignments, and college tests. Remember that AVID™ students write because of the AVID™ maxim, "How do I know what I think until I see what I write?"

8. I realize that I must be enrolled in college preparatory academic classes. I realize that these courses are challenging and that I may be required to repeat a class if significant progress is not made. This will require attendance at summer school and/or doubling up on courses to meet all graduation and A-F requirements.

9. In order to meet all requirements for graduation and the A-F requirements for admission to the universities, I may need to attend summer school.

10. Being in AVID™ is a privilege. I take my enrollment in the program as an honor and I will behave accordingly in all classes and in all activities.

I understand that by not working toward these goals I am jeopardizing my chances of being qualified for college upon graduation. I also understand that if I do not work toward meeting these goals I will be placed on probation in the AVID™ Program or asked to leave the program.

_____   _____
Student Signature   **Date**

Parent or Guardian:

I have discussed the requirements of the AVID™ program and understand what my daughter or son needs to do to succeed. I agree to support my daughter or son in the pursuit of her or his college goals.

_____   _____
Parent/Guardian Signature   **Date**   9/95

Figure 17.3. Advancement Via Individual Determination (AVID™) contract. (From Swanson, M.C. [1997]. *Implementing and managing the AVID program.* San Diego: AVID Press; reprinted by permission.)

time to adjust to the notion that their daughter is breaking the family tradition by choosing to earn a college degree and pursue a career in teaching.

According to Francie Tidey, co-director of the Capital Region AVID™ Center at the Sacramento County Office of Education in Sacramento, California, approximately 92% of AVID™ graduates attend college, and of those students, 60% attend 4-year universities. Many of the students return to their high schools to become tutors during their college years. Swanson's legacy appears to be assured.

Project SUCCESS (Students Understanding Communities and Cherishing Each Student's Service)

An integrated, inclusive, national service-learning program, Project SUCCESS brings together students with and without disabilities who perform community service while applying academic lessons to the community beyond the classroom. The program was designed for middle and high school-age youth and is implemented in both school- and community-based settings. It is founded on a principle of partnering diverse youth who work as teams in service-learning projects. Project SUCCESS helps to counter youth isolation by pairing young people as partners in service to become active and empowered members of their communities. It encourages them to forge lasting friendships with their classmates by providing opportunities for them to work side by side to create social change through community service. A curriculum of preparation, action, reflection, and celebration has been developed that accommodates youth with multiple abilities, interest levels, and learning styles.

In San Diego County, Project SUCCESS has two community-based sites and six school-based sites. Participants are in grades 6 through 12, and their numbers have increased more than 150% in the past 3 years. More than 300 students have performed more than 3,000 hours of community service with their partners. During a typical year in one Project SUCCESS program, partners continued their annual holiday traditions of making holiday cookie baskets for the local police and fire departments, including handwritten thank-you notes for each member of those departments. At Mama's Kitchen, a grass roots, community-based volunteer program for the needy, Project SUCCESS partners have also prepared and served more than 400 hot meals to AIDS patients who live at home; and at Thanksgiving, the partners have made cards and placemats for Mama's Kitchen. Other service-learning activities have included beach clean-ups, storm drain stenciling, graffiti "paint-outs," collections for children's hospital, arts and crafts projects at local convalescent homes, visits to the elderly, and holiday gift collections for struggling families.

The effects of Project SUCCESS have been far reaching (see Figure 17.4). The community's relationship with the high school is certainly strengthened, and parents of the participants notice positive changes in their children. But, perhaps the most important effect has been the active relationships that have developed between the partners as they join forces for the benefit of their community. As one student reported, "Finishing those projects really makes you feel like you've done the right thing, And now when I see (my partner who has a disability) at school, I really see *her* first. We've even been to the mall together after school."

A NEW SPIN ON THE CIRCLE OF COURAGE

The Circle of Courage is a "strength-based model of youth empowerment" (Van Bockern, Brendtro, & Brokenleg, 2000) that proposes an integration of "the practice wisdom of great European pioneers . . . with a Native American child-rearing system that create(s) courageous, respectful children" (Brendtro & Van Bockern, 1994, p. 4). These intuitive understandings of the Native American cultures, which have been validated by contemporary research (Villa & Thousand, 2000), charge the caring adults of every society with an important responsibility: to support the core needs—belonging, mastery, independence, and generosity—of all children. As Van Bockern et al. (2000) asserted,

> *Children in every culture need to belong. Depriving a child of care is universally evil. Children by their nature are created to strive for mastery; thus, schools that sabotage this motivation for competence are maltreating children. Children from any back-*

ground have the need for self-determination; to block this development of indepen-
dence is to commit an injustice. Finally, from the dawn of cooperative civilization, chil-
dren have sought to give back to others the concern they have been shown by others. If
educators fail to provide children with opportunities for caring and generosity, they
extinguish their students' human spirit.

Zone of Empowerment

Maslow (1954) contended that humans seek satisfaction through fulfillment of a hierarchy of needs. This hierarchy of needs can explain what motivates individuals. Maslow pro-

---

What People Are Saying About Project SUCCESS

"With Project SUCCESS, I can visualize terms such as opportunity, growth, development, social skills, awareness, maturity, happiness, and, most importantly, 'success!'"
— E. G., Youth Club Proprietor

"The Project is doing something that my husband and I have had to do individually with our daughter...help her realize that she can positively contribute to improving the lives of others." — P. D., Parent

"The ability of a teen (with a disability) to give back to a community that often gives to them is a rewarding experience, which will promote growth and self assurance for all teens."
— N. G., Family Jewish Community Center

" Now that Project SUCCESS has started, I finally feel like I fit in somewhere. It's about making a difference in my life and others. I don't look any different externally, but I am a new person inside."
— Participant, Project SUCCESS

I believe the self-esteem of the individual involved and the peer acceptance by general education students is greatly raised when our kids are involved in service..."
— J. K., Middle School Teacher

"Project SUCCESS' emphasis on having students pair up and learn about diversity in a number of areas is innovative and will add a new dimension to the service-learning in (our) school district."
— P. C., Community Service Program

Figure 17.4.   What people are saying about Project SUCCESS; reprinted by permission from Molly C. Brannon.

posed that once the lower level needs (physiological, security, and safety) are satisfied, they no longer motivate an individual. In accordance with the Circle of Courage (Brendtro & Van Bockern, 1994; Van Bockern et al., 2000), we can assume that before students have a sense of belonging, mastery, independence, and generosity, they are isolated novices who are dependent and needy. What, then, transports individuals from that place of lower-level need to a place where their social needs (to belong, to be accepted, and to be loved) and their ego needs (to be respected; to gain prestige, recognition, and status) are met?

Partner learning and peer relationships may play an important role in this passage. They represent a power source in a *zone of empowerment*, in which individuals become (through positive interactions, teamwork, growth, and support) welcome members of groups, masters of skills, independent in their academic and social accomplishments, and generous of spirit (see Figure 17.5). This transportation from a place of considerable need to a place of empowerment is compatible with Vygotsky's notion (1978) of the *zone of proximal development* (ZPD). He suggested that there exists a ZPD between *actual development* (in which the learner is able to learn independently, building on previously developed experiences or *schemata*) and *potential development* (in which the learner functions or achieves with support from peers, teachers, or parents). The ZPD is a "construction site" where learners are able to build on their prior knowledge through active engagement in collaborative learning opportunities (Jensen & Kiley, 2000, p. 251).

Villa and Thousand's description of the potential benefits of peer support structures (see Chapter 20) highlights how enhancement of self-esteem, opportunities for practice with higher-level thinking skills, and progression toward content mastery occurs through empowerment strategies that involve students as 1) members of the instructional team,

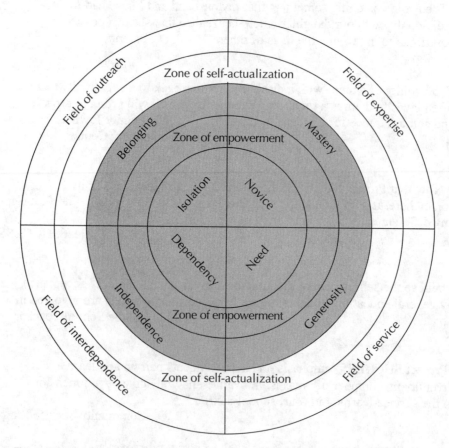

Figure 17.5. Extending the Circle of Courage.

2) advocates for themselves and their peers, and 3) decision makers. Partner learning and peer support processes yield benefits for and from students, schools, and communities. The reciprocal gifts harvested from the zone of empowerment can be observed in the looks of happiness, calm, and pride on children's faces; in the secure and dynamic atmosphere of successful schools; and in the surrounding peaceful, vibrant, and inclusive communities.

EXTENDING THE GOALS OF THE CIRCLE OF COURAGE

Zone of Self-Actualization

Based on our research, we propose a "new spin" on the Circle of Courage (see Figure 17.5) that extends the outcomes of attainment of the goals of education. We contend that peer support structures, a power source for the zone of empowerment, lead to goal attainment. Through the process, or *zone of self-actualization,* an outer field is created—a higher level of possibility—from which a new sense of worth emerges.

In a democratic society, transference to the fields of outreach, expertise, interdependence, and service (aspired to by individuals who have developed a true sense of belonging, mastery, independence, and generosity) are made possible because the zone of self-actualization fosters reflective practices. Each of the partner learning programs includes in its structure many opportunities for participants to engage in written and oral reflection. This process enables students to recognize their value to society as a whole. For many of them, this empowering realization is the very impetus for making decisions about which path their lives will take next. Students spoke of continuing in a field where they would help others, be role models, and encourage others to participate in service activity.

Belonging and Outreach: The Socially Healthy Side of Schooling

Although schools are certainly institutions of academic learning, they are also important social systems in our society. Through their research efforts over the years, we have found that students in socially healthy schools are likely to experience a sense of belonging. They demonstrate this by maintaining healthy friendships with classmates and interacting in positive and productive ways with their teachers. Educators who take seriously the social side of schooling can do much to promote the positive social behaviors that enhance school climate and foster healthy and caring environments for *all* learners.

We have discussed several models of partner learning in this chapter and have noted that

> *Teachers who availed themselves of these partner learning arrangements in their classrooms have discovered that their students receive more individualized instruction, tend to learn at an accelerated rate, enjoy the exciting opportunity of working cooperatively with classmates, demonstrate heightened responsibility for their learning and that of their partners . . . and are found to be more actively involved in creating a positive classroom learning environment. (McNeil, 1994, p. 224)*

These are the very elements that lead to happy memories of school and often to lifelong friendships. The students we have observed and interviewed through our research have shared their sense of personal growth and belonging resulting from the partner learning opportunities they have experienced. For many, this sense of belonging has brought them to a point of wanting to reach out to others, inviting them to belong as well. One student wrote,

My experience as a youth reading role model has allowed me to recognize the importance of being dependable, enhanced my ability to communicate with other individuals, and has increased my own interest in reading for schoolwork and pleasure. My service as a volunteer has been especially beneficial to my younger brother. As a reading role model it was necessary that I visit the public library on a regular basis to choose and check out books appropriate to the age level of the children at the Head Start Center and also that I take the time to prepare reading the books I chose for the children. My little brother helped me choose the books that would interest the young children, and then I was able to take those books I chose and read them to my own brother, who is at the age where it is extremely crucial that he hear the English language and be able to enjoy the experience of reading.

Tutors have recruited new volunteers, gone on to design new partner learning programs, taken on leadership roles in their programs, and selected careers in education and other related fields. In his reflective essay, one YRRM student reported, "My goal in life is to become a teacher, and this program has made me realize that this is what I really want to do."

This desire and commitment to outreach is evident in another student's comment. "I cannot think of a better way to spend my time than volunteering my services for kids. I gain experiences for my future and get the chance to help kids have fun and learn new things." Comments such as these lead us to believe that human relationships can have a very powerful impact on learning. Children who feel they belong are free to enjoy friendships as they learn and grow without the fear of being isolated. This social component of schooling has the potential to afford children some of the best gifts available—wonderful friendships and fond memories of their educational experiences.

The lessons learned from the programs we reviewed and the words of the students have led us to an understanding of the importance of new partnership roles for schools and communities. The YRRM program has provided an excellent example of school–community partnerships at work.

Mastery and Expertise: From Knowledge to Wisdom

The celebration of students' success and effort are common occurrences in today's classrooms. The intrinsic and extrinsic rewards can be readily observed at any level of public school. Applause, recognition, verbal praise, token economies, and class parties have secured their place in the daily and weekly plans of teachers. Students' comments and facial expressions give teachers insights into the satisfaction level that students feel for a job well done.

The value of mastery has become very high as students compete for class rank, grades, scholarships, and college acceptance. It is no surprise, then, that the external support structures, such as individualized instruction, tutoring, and partner learning, have become entrenched in the classroom environment. This has been particularly advantageous to the struggling learners who are, for a variety of reasons, challenged by the pace or scope of the curriculum. Their positive response to partnership relationships has increased the opportunity for mastery and led many to realize their actual expertise.

Generosity and Service: Partners in Learning

For students and educators, service is the natural outcome of generosity. Once empowered with gifts that have been nurtured, developed, honed, and practiced, passing them on is the logical next step. Perhaps this is most clearly illustrated in this anecdote from one of us:

Ann (Nevin) and I were taking a morning walk through the charming city of Limerick, Ireland. We had come there with Mary McNeil to the Association of Teacher Educators Europe (ATEE) Conference to present our work on alternative instructional delivery systems. As we were walking, Ann was convincing me that I should pursue a doctoral program and outlined for me a potential agenda of steps to follow to facilitate that journey. So much of what I was doing was a direct result of Ann's constant generosity. She had invited my participation in the development and delivery of an on-line teacher education course (Nevin, Thousand, & Hood, 1998), in writing a proposal—and then a presentation (Nevin, Hood, & McNeil, 1998)—for ATEE, and in writing a chapter about our work for an international text about changing contexts and challenges in teacher education (Nevin, Hood, & McNeil, 2002). Now, she was giving me just the nudge I needed to begin my doctoral work. Her words and wisdom were so constantly timely and effective, and I was filled with gratitude. "How can I ever thank you . . . " I began. She hastily replied, "Don't you realize that is my responsibility—and yours, too—to pass it on? That is how you will repay me! Pass it on." Ann's generosity pushed me through my own zone of self-actualization, and from that moment I knew that doing service in the field of education was the only possible course to follow. (Hood, personal communication, August 1998)

Feeling empowered, a child who has acquired the ability to read can often be observed spontaneously coaching others whose reading skills are still developing. Based on our experiences, for many students, along with the satisfaction that comes from sharing one's knowledge, skills, and talents comes an exponential desire to continue to share, prompt potential, and perform duty and service.

Jennings (2001) implemented service-learning activities for his middle school students and discovered that his students were "anxious to participate in something of genuine value" (p. 475). In response to his students' desire to help others, Jennings developed the "We C.A.R.E." (Weekly Cross-Age Reading Experiences) program, in which his students were trained to read to younger students. In his G.R.O.W. (Great Reading, Oral language, and Writing) with Grandfriends service-learning project, Jennings' students were paired with senior citizens. The purpose of the program was for the high school students to discover, through an interview process, the similarities that exist between the senior citizens and themselves. They wrote biographical essays about their partners and presented their work at a special gathering. Again, Jennings' students were able to "discover their talents and interests, develop their skills, and experience the rewards of participating in activities that benefit others" (p. 475). In these partnerships, they gained confidence in their skills, a sense of pride and belonging in their community, and "the knowledge that they are valued and can indeed make a difference" (p. 474).

In many secondary schools, students are required to do service-learning projects as a requirement for graduation. The accelerated responsibility for learning that many experience during their earlier grades often leads students into making decisions about service-learning projects in which they will work with other students in partnership or peer support formats. The YRRM program and Project SUCCESS are exemplary illustrations of such service-learning projects. In these programs, students have the opportunity to encounter authentic circumstances and become involved in the problem-solving process required to address the social, economic, environmental, and multicultural needs within their own communities. Student reflections about their involvement reveal that once their zone of self-actualization is reached, their projects proceed with ease, and they willingly and joyfully engage in these service activities.

Independence and Interdependence: The Freedom to Depend

Most schools have developed mission statements that reflect the larger community's vision of the outcomes of education, typically, graduation from high school. One example comes from Merced, California, a multicultural community with one of the largest concentrations of Southeast Asian refugees in the United States of America and a Hispanic presence representing about 40% of the population. Many families faced significant economic challenges, and high school drop-out rates were high. Educators and community members alike were concerned for the education and welfare of all of the students who would be attending the community's new high school. They came together to create the following mission statement and hopes for its graduates:

> *Through a collaborative effort of students, staff, and the community, the mission of Golden Valley High School is to provide academic and real life learning experiences so that its graduates will be creative and innovative; self-aware and self-directed; adaptable problem solvers; respectful, friendly and cooperative; technologically adept; successful in career and life skills; effective communicators; and active contributing members of society. (Thousand, Nevin, & McNeil, 2000, p. 154)*

The mission statement reflects the community committee's eagerness to produce graduates who demonstrated independence. They were mindful of the diversity and the economic, social, and cultural challenges facing the community. Not only did they value success in career and life skills, but they also wanted graduates who were respectful, friendly and cooperative, and active contributing members of society.

We view this as a desire for individuals who are not only independent but also interdependent. Once a person has become sufficiently self-reliant, he or she is then able to experience the freedom to enter relationships in which each member is able to depend on the other. This could be a marriage arrangement; a business partnership; a team-teaching situation; or a collaborative, contributing member of a community. One of the YRRM Tutors put it this way:

> *My consistent visits to the library and hours of reading made my creativity visible. I learned to lose my shyness and let the story come to life through me. I enjoyed making voices and facial expressions, but most of all, I enjoyed the acceptance of the children. I became a more patient person, which helped a lot the first few days of reading. The children taught me to be outgoing and always try new things. Once I actually danced in the middle of a group as we were playing a game. I would have never guessed I would be brave enough to do that in front of a group of people. Yet, it was all because I spend time with the children of my community.*

When educators and community members come together to address the education goals of their community, children and youth are afforded opportunities to experience a carefully planned and supportive move from dependence to independence and then to interdependence. Listening to the voices of our students is key to ascertaining the success of our efforts.

TIPS FOR SUCCESS IN IMPLEMENTING PARTNER LEARNING PROGRAMS

Practical Suggestions for Educators

We are often asked, "How does one get started in designing partnership programs that academically, socially, and personally benefit children and youth?" In addition to the programs highlighted in this chapter, and based on our years of experience and research, we offer the following suggestions:

- *Remember that sometimes the best models are in you own backyard.* Educators often try to locate models of best practices in journals, texts, or on the Internet. Although these are certainly valued (and included in this list), a good place to begin one's research is in one's own community or in nearby school districts. Making inquiries locally frequently yields results.

- *Look for teachers' stories in your local newspaper.* There may be a regular local newspaper column devoted to education, or there may be randomly published articles that showcase exemplary school programs.

- *Talk with local school officials.* Learn the names of the administrators of local schools, and seek their input. Principals of schools usually enjoy the interest of the community in their schools' programs, and this may be your opportunity to be invited to observe their schools' operations.

- *Arrange to visit local partner learning programs.* Perhaps you are already aware of a school's exemplary program. Call the principal's office and ask to arrange an escorted visit. If you are not aware of local partner learning programs, then ask the principal for information about local programs.

- *Interview project leaders, students, teachers, and parents.* This specific arrangement might be an outcome of your visit to the local programs. Whenever you find a program that you feel will complement or exemplify your own school's programmatic vision or plans, it is advisable to make direct contact with those involved in the development and implementation of the established program. A group or individual interview may result in a successful design and implementation at your school.

- *Read professional and popular journals and magazines for ideas.* Many teachers (and many public schools) subscribe to education magazines and journals, which may be good resources of information about exemplary partner learning programs and best practices in education.

- *Contact your local university.* Contact the College of Education at a local university for referrals to faculty who may have information about research, development, and locations of partner learning programs in your area. There are generally several teaching credential programs at universities, such as elementary education (multiple subjects), special education, middle school, and secondary (single subject) programs. In many cases, you may be able to speak with faculty whose disciplines are a good match to your own needs. For example, if you are teaching in a middle school and your student population is primarily Hispanic, then you might consider contacting a member of the faculty in the College of Education whose expertise is in the area of multicultural education in middle schools.

- *Look for announcements of community volunteer opportunities.* These might appear in local newspapers, on local television or radio broadcasts, or on the Internet.

- *Search the Internet* (e.g., key words: peer tutoring, mentorships, partner learning). You can search broadly or within your own geographic region for research articles, for specific information, for web sites of model programs, and for people who share your common vision, questions, and concerns.

- *Look for features on your local news stations.* Scan your local radio and television listings regularly for programming information. After the broadcast, send an e-mail or make a

Partnership Planning Guide A

Type of Program	Possible Resources
School-Based • Peer tutoring • Cross age tutoring • Buddy networks • Peer-assisted learning • Cooperative learning • PALS • Class-Wide Peer Tutoring • Circle of Friends • AVID™	**Professional Books, Journals, & Organizations** ✓ Association for Supervision and Curriculum & Development (1-800-933-ASCD) http://www.ascd.org ✓ Council for Exceptional Children (1-888-232-7733) http://www.cec.sped.org ✓ Phi Delta Kappa (1-800-766-1156) http://www.pdkintl.org ✓ AVID™ Student Handbook http://rims.k12.ca.us/avid ✓ Restructuring for caring and effective education: Piecing the puzzle together (2000) (Villa & Thousand, Eds.) ✓ Inclusion: A guide for educators (1996) (Stainback & Stainback, Eds.)

Figure 17.6.   Partnership Planning Guide A: School-based programs.

telephone call to the administrator of the school or other site of the program, and schedule a visit or a telephone interview or make some other arrangement to gather the information you need.

- *Attend lectures, conferences, and workshops to obtain knowledge and materials.* If you take advantage of checking the resources already mentioned, you will, no doubt, become aware of relevant lectures, conferences, and workshops to attend. Take advantage of learning from those who have successfully implemented partner learning programs.

- *Contact community-based service organizations supporting youth activities* (e.g., YMCA, Boys and Girls Clubs, scouting organizations, preschool and after-school programs). Frequently, these organizations have ongoing projects that involve partner learning and peer mentoring. For local contacts, use the Yellow Pages.

- *Begin today!*

Partnership Planning Guides

We have also included Partnership Planning Guides to assist you in making decisions about your own partnership project. Partnership Planning Guide A (see Figure 17.6) focuses on

Partnership Planning Guide B

Type of Program	Possible Resources
School-Community Based	**Possible Resources**
▪ Project SUCCESS	✓ United Cerebral Palsy of San Diego
▪ Youth Reading Role Models	(1-858-571-7803)
▪ Service learning	http://www.ucpsd.org
▪ GROW	✓ Family Literacy Foundation
	(1-858-482-7323)
Community-Based	http://www.read2kids.org
▪ Scouting Organizations	✓ National Service Learning
▪ YMCA	Clearinghouse
▪ Boys and Girls Clubs	http://nicsl.jaws.umn.edu
▪ Local Libraries	✓ Scouting Resources Online
	http://www.macscouter.com
	✓ World Alliance of YMCAs
	http://www.ymca.int
	✓ Boys and Girls Clubs of America
	http://www.bgca.org/
	✓ organization newsletters
	✓ local media announcements

Figure 17.7. Partnership Planning Guide B: School–community and community-based programs.

developing partnership programs that are school-based and offers suggestions for specific program structures, such as peer tutoring, buddy networks, and cooperative learning. A list of potential resources accompanies the list of programs and includes (but is not limited to) professional books, journals, and organizations that support school-based partnership programs.

Partnership Planning Guide B (see Figure 17.7) lists several partnership programs that reflect partnerships between schools and community-based organizations. For example, YRRM links high school students with preschool programs in local communities. The list of possible resources will continue to grow as schools and communities realize the extraordinary benefits of these programs.

FINAL THOUGHTS: THE FIELD OF HOPES AND DREAMS

In our diverse society, the interrelationships among our youth, our communities, and our schools are quite complex. Yet, the daunting challenges to create safe and productive communities, live generous and confident lives, and continually improve the social landscape of our nation must remain at the forefront of our efforts. Partner learning and youth service programs weave a strong and significant thread through our country's social fabric. The empowering opportunities they afford students, schools, and communities make us hopeful that life can and will be better. The dream of an intentional, wide-scale implementation of these and similar programs in our schools and communities makes the future look very promising.

REFERENCES

Brendtro, L.K., & Van Bockern, S. (1994). Courage for the discouraged: A psychoeductional approach to troubled and troubling children. *Focus on Exceptional Children, 26*(8), 1–15.

Cowie, H., & Sharp, S. (1996). *Peer support forum: Principles of good practice in peer support projects.* Retrieved January 15, 2001, from http://www.mhf.org.uk/peersupport.

Cushing, L.S., & Kennedy, C.H. (1997). Academic effects of providing peer support in general education classrooms on students without disabilities. *Journal of Applied Behavior Analysis, 30*(1), 139–151.

Family Literacy Foundation. (2000). *Youth Reading Role Models: Community Coordinator Manual.* Solana Beach, CA: Author.

Fuchs, D., Fuchs, L.S., Mathes, P.H., & Simmons, D.C. (1997). Peer-assisted strategies: Making classrooms more responsive to diversity. *American Educational Research Journal, 34*(1), 174–206.

Fuchs, L.S., Fuchs, D., & Kazden, S. (1999). Effects of peer-assisted learning strategies on high school students with serious reading problems. *Remedial and Special Education, 20,* 309–318.

Harper, G.F., Maheady, L., & Mallette, B. (1994). The power of peer-mediated instructions: How and why it promotes academic success for all students. In J.S. Thousand, R.A. Villa, & A.I. Nevin (Eds.), *Creativity and collaborative learning: A practical guide to empowering students and teachers* (pp. 228–241). Baltimore: Paul H. Brookes Publishing Co.

Harper, G.F., Mallette, B., Maheady, L., Parkes, V., & Moore, J. (1993). Retention and generalization of spelling words acquired using a peer-mediated instructional procedure by children with mild handicapping conditions. *Journal of Behavioral Education, 3,* 25–38.

Jennings, M. (2001). Two very special service-learning projects. *Kappan, 82,* 474–475.

Jensen, R.A., & Kiley, T.J. (2000). *Teaching, leading, and learning: Becoming caring professionals.* Boston: Houghton Mifflin.

Johnson, D.A., & Johnson, R.T. (1994). *Learning together and alone* (4th ed.) Needham Heights, MA: Allyn & Bacon.

Kamps, D.M., Barbetta, P.M., Leonard, B.R., & Delquadri, J. (1994). Classwide peer tutoring: An integration strategy to improve reading skills and promote peer interaction among students with autism and general education peers. *Journal of Applied Behavior Analysis, 27,* 49–61.

Kohler, F.W., & Greenwood, C.R. (1990). Effects of collateral peer supportive behaviors with the classwide peer tutoring program. *Journal of Applied Behavior Analysis, 23,* 307–322.

Lipsky, D.K., & Gartner, A. (Eds.). (1997). *Inclusion and school reform: Transforming America's classrooms.* Baltimore: Paul H. Brookes Publishing Co.

Maheady, L., Harper, G.F., & Sacca, K. (1988). A classwide peer tutoring system in a secondary, resource room program for the mildly handicapped. *Journal of Research and Development in Education, 21,* 76–83.

Maslow, A.H., (1954). *Motivation and personality.* New York: Harper & Row.

McNeil, M. (1994). Creating powerful partnerships through partner learning. In J.S. Thousand, R.A. Villa, & A.I. Nevin (Eds.), *Creativity and collaborative learning: A practical guide to empowering students and teachers* (pp. 243–259). Baltimore: Paul H. Brookes Publishing Co.

Morita, J.K. (2001). AVID pursuits of educational excellence: Students surpass perceived limits in achievement program. Retrieved January 17, 2001, from http://www.sacbee.com/news/news/local05_20010116.html.

Mortweet, S.L., Utley, C.A., Walker, D., Dawson, H.I., Delquadi, J.C., Reddy, S.S., Greenwood, C.R., Hamilton, S., & Ledford, D. (1999). Classwide peer tutoring: Teaching students with mild mental retardation in inclusive classrooms. *Exceptional Children, 65,* 524–536.

Nevin, A., Hood, A., & McNeil, M. (1998, August). *New directions in university professional education preparation programs: Using the Internet as an instructional delivery model.* Working Group Papers Workshop #2, Conference Papers for the 23rd Annual Conference of the Association for Teacher Education Europe, Limerick, Ireland: Mary Immaculate College, August 24–30. Also available on-line at http://www.west.asu.edu/icaxn/ateecover.html.

Nevin, A., Hood, A., & McNeil, M. (2002). Creating community in on-line (electronic) environments. In H.E. Christiansen & S. Ramadevi (Eds.), *Re-educating the educator: Global perspectives on community building* (pp. 127–149). Albany: State University of New York Press.

Nevin, A., Thousand, J., & Hood, A. (1998). EDUC501: *Mainstream instruction for children with special learning needs.* Available on-line at http://webct.csusm.edu/educ501th.

Sideridis, G.D., Utley, C., Greenwood, C.R., Delquadri, J., Dawson, H., Palmer, P., & Reddy, S. (1997). Classwide peer tutoring: Effects on spelling performance and social interactions of students with mild disabilities and their typical peers in an integrated instructional setting. *Journal of Behavioral Education, 7,* 435–462.

Stainback, S., & Stainback, W. (1996). *Inclusion: A guide for educators.* Baltimore: Paul H. Brookes Publishing Co.

Stevenson, N. (2000). *The Stevenson Learning Skills Program.* Attleboro Falls, MA: Stevenson Learning Skills.

Swanson, M.C. (1998). *AVID™.* Retrieved March 5, 2001, from http://rims.kia.ca.us/avid.

Thousand, J.S., Nevin, A.I., & McNeil, M.E. (2000). Social justice through responsibility education. In R.A. Villa & J.S. Thousand (Eds.), *Restructuring for caring and effective education: Piecing the puzzle together* (2nd ed., pp. 137–165). Baltimore: Paul H. Brookes Publishing Co.

Thousand, J.S., & Villa, R.A. (1990). Sharing expertise and responsibilities through teaching teams. In W. Stainback & S. Stainback (Eds.), *Support networks for inclusive schooling: Interdependent integrated education* (pp.151–166). Baltimore: Paul H. Brookes Publishing Co.

Van Bockern, S., Brendtro, L.K., & Brokenleg, M. (2000). Reclaiming our youth. In R.A. Villa & J.S. Thousand (Eds.), *Restructuring for caring and effective education: Piecing the puzzle together* (2nd ed., pp. 56–76). Baltimore: Paul H. Brookes Publishing Co.

Vaughn, S., Gersten, R., & Chard, D.J. (2000). The underlying message in LD intervention research: Findings from research synthesis. *Exceptional Children, 67,* 99–114.

Villa, R.A., & Thousand, J.S. (1996). Student collaborations: An essential for curriculum delivery in the 21st century. In S. Stainback & W. Stainback (Eds.), *Inclusion: A guide for educators* (pp. 171–191). Baltimore: Paul H. Brookes Publishing Co.

Villa, R.A., & Thousand, J.S. (Eds.). (2000). *Restructuring for caring and effective education: Piecing the puzzle together (2nd ed.).* Baltimore: Paul H. Brookes Publishing Co.

Vygotsky, L. (1978). *Mind and society: The development of higher psychological processes.* Cambridge, MA: Harvard University Press.

Wilkens, J. (2001, January 9). AVID educator. *The San Diego Union Tribune,* pp. E1, E4.

Putting Creativity and Collaborative Learning into Practice

Strategies and Lesson Plans

Creativity

Ann I. Nevin, Jacqueline S. Thousand, and Richard A. Villa

Before you begin reading this introduction or the chapters in this section, we invite you to use the rubric shown in Table III.1 to evaluate your own creativity. Then, as you read the introduction and subsequent chapters, refer to this scale to notice how your perceptions of your creativity may have changed.

We can expect improved outcomes in quality of life in school, home, and community when creativity and creative processes are infused into the work of teaching, advocating for, and raising students with disabilities. However, there are many challenges to creativity. Some of the most pervasive challenges are the range of definitions of creativity, common conceptual blocks to creativity, and self- or society-imposed limits to an individual's creative responses. We hope you will agree that the chapters in this section, in concert with all of the other chapters in this book, can support and stimulate you to release your creative genius.

RANGE OF DEFINITIONS OF CREATIVITY

Cre-a-tive (kre-a-tiv), adj. 1. creating or able to create. 2. productive (of); inventive (Webster, 1966, p. 346).

Cre-a-tive, adj. 1. having the ability or power to create. 2. creating; productive. 3. characterized by originality and expressiveness; imaginative (*The American Heritage Dictionary,* 1985, p. 338).

Cre-a-tiv-ity (measures of): assessing the aptitudes and personality traits that contribute to creative achievement, not direct measures of creative achievement itself (see Torrance Tests of Creative Thinking [Torrance, 1962] or Guilford's Tests of Divergent Thinking [Guilford, 1967]).

Cre-a-tive courage: "Whereas moral courage is the righting of wrongs, creative courage, in contrast, is the discovering of new forms, new symbols, new patterns on which a soci-

Table III.1. Rubric for evaluating creativity

Rating of 1	Rating of 2	Rating of 3	Rating of 4	Rating of 5
I am not creative. I don't have the creativity gene. I think only 1 person in 100,000 can be considered "truly creative." A chair is more creative than I am.	I am not creative, but I do enjoy the arts. I appreciate the creativity of others. I believe that creativity is a rare trait. I can see creativity in others but not in myself.	I do not think of myself as creative, but I do use problem-solving strategies to help others come up with new ideas and solutions to problems.	I am creative in certain situations, although I wasn't born creative. I have developed my creative thinking skills.	I was born creative. I am creative. I will always be creative. I practice my creativity skills every day. I help others become creative. Creativity is a common trait shared by all of us.

Circle the statements that are true for you right now.

ety can be built. Every professional can and does require some creative courage" (May, 1980, p. 14).

Creativity: "First, we define *creativity* as the production of new—and in some way useful or "good"—things or ideas. Second, everybody is creative. Third, creativity skills can be learned" (Leff & Nevin, 1994, p. 29).

These definitions represent the wide range of perspectives about creativity that influence our beliefs and actions with respect to being creative ourselves, recognizing creativity in others, and expecting creative responses (especially from students with disabilities). Another definition that speaks to the necessity for both divergent and convergent thinking in the creative process is, "Creativity is the bringing together of the uninhibited energy of a child with its opposite (and sometimes enemy)—a sense of order imposed by a disciplined adult intelligence" (source unknown).

CONCEPTUAL BLOCKS TO CREATIVITY

A conceptual block to creativity is any mental wall that blocks you from correctly *seeing* the problem or *conceiving* a solution. Adams (1986) described four major blocks to creativity:

1. *Perceptual* blocks include limitations (rules, unnecessary limits), stereotypes (can't picture doing it a different way), and not isolating the real problem (incomplete or incorrect facts, information).

2. *Cultural* blocks to creativity include taboos (ideas that are just not "acceptable"), serious problem solving (no room for fun, humor, play), valuing logic over intuition, and favoring tradition over change.

3. *Emotional* blocks to creativity include fear (of risks, chaos), judging ("yes, but"), not incubating (must solve immediately), and not enough challenge.

4. *Language* barriers are those that underlie one's culture, as represented by the language (culture bound—no common language; and not having the "correct" language [e.g., visual, auditory, mathematical]) to conceive a solution.

No doubt you can point to examples in your own life that show how conceptual barriers blocked your own creative responses. In our experience, we have witnessed individuals and teams of people who prefer to engage in *problem admiration* rather than *creative solution finding*. It is often easier to admire a problem rather than engage the intellectual work involved in thinking. This phenomenon could be referred to as *conceptual laziness*.

STIFLING CREATIVE RESPONSES

In addition to the conceptual barriers identified previously, there are additional barriers that can be described as "attitudes" or "attributions." There is "self-talk" or "internal dialogue" that we inadvertently bring to the challenges that we face. In our experience, the following three internal dialogues are the most pervasive.

1. I doubt my ability to be creative.

2. I accept the culturally created context for believing I am not creative. In other words, only the notable writers, musicians, scientists, artisans, artists, composers, and inventors merit recognition as creative beings.

3. I believe people who are invested in my being are not creative because it makes them uncomfortable when I am creative, or my creativity causes them to question why they don't take action or get results similar to mine.

PURPOSE OF SECTION III

The authors of the chapters in this section present strategies to 1) be creative, 2) overcome barriers and blocks to creativity, and 3) tackle educators' perceived "most challenging" students—students who have been labeled as troubled or troubling. The success stories included within the chapters are intended to motivate you to avoid stifling your own creativity.

LaPlant and Zane (Chapter 18) offer mental tools to overcome the barriers to creativity discussed previously with respect to planning and managing partner learning systems. Schrumpf and Jansen (Chapter 19) provide structured processes for activating both the divergent and convergent dimensions essential to creative thought and action involved in conflict resolution. Villa and Thousand (Chapter 20) describe the creative and collaborative processes in cooperative teaching arrangements. Chapter 21 is a treasure chest of creative cooperative group lesson plans developed and field tested by classroom teachers. To connect students with meaningful relationships and quality life experiences now and in their future, Villalobos, Tweit-Hull, and Wong (Chapters 22 and 23) detail the processes for establishing peer partnerships in secondary schools. Villalobos, Eshilan, and Moyer (Chapter 24) show the creativity involved in developing teaching activities that result in secondary students becoming advocates for inclusion and social justice. The strategies and processes described in these chapters have been shown to increase novel solutions, inventive outcomes, and effective changes on behalf of students with disabilities and their families.

BARRIER BUSTER CHALLENGE

After you have read and reflected on the information in the chapters in this section and employed some of the strategies described, we invite you to revisit the rubric for evaluating your own creativity (see Table III.1). We predict that your perception of your own creativity will have changed in a positive direction. You will have realized that creativity is an inherent part of being human. To be human is to be creative.

REFERENCES

Adams, J.L. (1986). *Conceptual blockbusting: A guide to better ideas.* Reading, MA: Addison-Wesley.

The American heritage dictionary, 2nd college edition. (1985). Boston: Houghton-Mifflin.

Guilford, J. (1967). *The nature of human intelligence.* New York: McGraw-Hill.

Leff, H., & Nevin, A. (1994). *Turning learning inside out.* Tucson, AZ: Zephyr Press.

May, R. (1980). *The courage to create.* New York: Bantam Books.

Torrance, E. (1962). *Guiding creative talent.* Upper Saddle River, NJ: Prentice Hall.

Webster, N. (1966). *New world dictionary of the American language: College edition.* New York: The World Publishing Company.

18

Partner Learning Systems

Laurie LaPlant
Nadine Zane

Partner learning systems are not new. One-room schoolhouses often utilized the knowledge and skills of all the students attending school. Children and adolescents are continually teaching each other informally when playing games and sports. Students' instructional influence not only occurs in school but also at home through interactions in the community among friends, siblings, and neighbors. Schools today need to capitalize on students as resources. This can be accomplished, at least in part, by developing and implementing partner learning systems.

Partner learning systems build relationships between students. They involve students who are of the same or different ages. They can occur within a class, between classes, or across a school or district. The design of partner learning systems can be for academic or nonacademic purposes and can be one-to-one, in small groups, or as whole classes.

COMPONENTS OF EFFECTIVE PARTNER LEARNING SYSTEMS

We have developed a six-component model for creating an effective partner learning system. The components include identification, recruitment, training, supervision, evaluation, and reinforcement. This chapter explains each component in detail and provides examples of systems that have been successfully established.

Identification

The first consideration in developing a partner learning system is to identify who will participate. A student may need a partner to tutor him or her to acquire a skill or more actively participate in a classroom activity. Conversely, a student may be identified to be in a tutor role because of a need to develop skills and to be in a leadership role. For example, Kevin, a fifth grader who has a moderate mental disability, needs frequent adaptations, accommodations, and specific resources to participate successfully in general education activities. His program called for support from a paraprofessional and teacher, as well as peers. His team established a peer tutor program in which Kevin assumed the role of tutor with a second grader who needed to learn sight words similar to the words Kevin was learning in his own program. Serving as a peer tutor helped to reinforce sight word skills for Kevin while providing him with a leadership role and enabling him to be a contributor in his school community.

A parent, teacher, or other staff member may initiate the request for a partner learning system. In many schools, collaborative teams (Thousand & Villa, 2000) work together to support a student or team teach to support a classroom of students. Teams may be particularly effective in identifying who would benefit from being an instructor or learner in a partner learning program.

Recruitment

Recruitment involves considering 1) the various sources of potential student participants, 2) methods for informing participants, and 3) the skills (both technical and interpersonal) students need or will acquire by participating in a partner learning program.

Sources of Tutors and Tutees   Sources for recruiting tutors and tutees are as varied as the children in a school. Sources may include in-school or after-school clubs, classes, or other community organizations. In one of our former schools, classes of older students teamed with kindergarten-age students to assist them in their reading development. On the opposite end of the age spectrum, classroom teachers of a multi-age second/third-grade class recruited residents of a nursing home to listen to their students practice oral reading once a week. In this relationship, students benefited in many ways, including receiving encouragement and nurturing from caring and appreciative older adults.

Methods for Informing Potential Participants   Methods to inform potential participants include flyers; class presentations; direct contact; or referral from a teacher, guidance personnel, or family member. An illustration of class presentations to provide information involved a fifth-grade student named Melissa, who has severe mental and physical disabilities. To facilitate Melissa's transition to a new school, teachers and students discussed her strengths and needs with her future classmates. As a result of these sessions, students were asked to volunteer for tutoring or "buddy" systems that oriented Melissa to her new school prior to her transition. These initial partner learning relationships helped classmates to make informed decisions about whether they wanted to participate in other partner learning programs with Melissa when she began to attend her new school on a full-time basis.

Who Has or Needs To Acquire Teaching Skills?   Students who serve as tutors need to acquire certain effective technical instructional skills, such as direct questioning, checking for understanding, giving feedback, and evaluating another person's performance. Equally important are the affective interpersonal partner skills, such as giving praise, making eye contact, assessing another student's willingness to participate, and problem solving. Furthermore, it is important that students develop the skills to make adjustments during the sessions, just as classroom teachers do whenever they teach a lesson. Thus, in recruiting potential tutors, a teacher wishing to maximize initial success may choose to seek out students who possess or are more likely to grasp some of these skills quickly. Another teacher may wish to do just the opposite—recruit students in the greatest need of learning interpersonal skills.

The deliberate recruitment of a particular student for a partner learning program is illustrated by Alex, a fourth grader. Alex received support because he was identified as gifted and talented. He had advanced understanding and application of a broad range of academic concepts. However, Alex had a difficult time relating to peers in social situations, often resulting in arguing and physically fighting with schoolmates. His support team designed a partner learning program to specifically address his interpersonal needs. A major objective of the program was to intentionally teach Alex how to adjust his language when talking about a content area to a level appropriate for the student he was tutoring. A second objective was to teach Alex to use praise, correction language, and other social skills in accord with the age and experience of his tutee.

Training Partners

Training is the heart of partner learning programs. Decisions must be made regarding 1) who will conduct the training of partners, 2) where training will occur, and 3) the number and length of training sessions. For example, a member of a teaching team might have the skills to conduct the training but have limited time in his or her schedule. Another team member might provide coverage to allow for release time for the training to occur. Trainers can include classroom teachers, special educators, paraprofessionals, secretaries, custodians, administrators, and, most important, other students who have participated in prior partner learning programs.

Another issue to address in training partners is what and how to teach—the actual content and methods needed to teach a lesson effectively (see Chapter 24). The trainer needs to work with the tutors to set the objective, use the materials, and evaluate the effectiveness of their procedures. To illustrate a training procedure, one of us designed a partner learning program for a third-grade classroom teacher to give her students practice in math facts. The objective of the program was for each tutee to practice facts for the operation they were learning (e.g., addition, subtraction). The materials included sets of flash cards with a problem written on one side and the problem and the correct answer written on the other side and recording sheets with a space for tutors to record the problem and for students to respond. The evaluation procedure involved tutors summarizing the lesson by writing the total number of correct responses over the number of facts presented.

The trainer guides tutors to learn and develop their own teaching methods that match their skill and age levels. Instructional methods include procedures as basic as establishing eye contact with the tutee, stating instructions clearly, and using age-appropriate verbal and nonverbal praise. Methods also include procedures as complex as giving corrective feedback in a respectful way and monitoring and then adjusting a lesson's sequence or content. In one third-grade classroom, the instructional methods taught to all tutors were how to present flash cards in a neutral manner, praise correct responding, and neutrally state a correct response when an incorrect response was given.

Supervision of Partner Learning Systems

Planning for ongoing supervision of partners requires teachers to discuss and answer at least the following questions: Who is responsible for supervision? How frequently does supervision need to occur? What should be the intensity of the interaction between the supervisor and the partners? This, of course, requires direct observation of partner learning experiences. Supervisors should examine both the technical (effective) and interpersonal (affective) aspects of a partner learning program. As with trainers, anyone in the school community may supervise. Supervision may occur as infrequently as once a month or as often as daily, depending on the goals of the program (e.g., daily social skills practiced in the context of a classroom in which cooperative learning is the norm) and the intervention needed to validate program success or make changes in the program. Ultimately, supervision should result in validating what partners are doing well and initiate changes to improve the partner learning program as needed.

An example of collaborative supervision involved sixth graders who regularly tutored younger students. Initially, the special educator took on the training and supervisory role. She then gradually reduced the amount of time she spent with the tutors as the classroom teacher assumed a more active supervisory role, monitoring the program and initiating needed changes when necessary. The special educator and teacher continued to check with each other on a regular basis to communicate any issues that arose related to the partner learning program.

Evaluation

Every day, Kaitlyn, a fifth-grade student, worked with Tyler, a second-grade student, in the area of reading. Kaitlyn read story books to Tyler, questioning him about story elements such as characters, plot, and setting. She kept a daily record of the stories she read to Tyler and logged his responses to questions. Kaitlyn and the special educator met periodically to analyze Kaitlyn's records and logs to determine if changes were needed in the objectives or methods of instruction. The special educator met with both Kaitlyn and Tyler to assess their overall working relationship and ongoing interest in continuing as partners in the program.

As the example of Tyler and Kaitlyn illustrates, evaluation involves assessing 1) the content relevance, 2) the effectiveness of methodology, 3) the frequency of teacher evaluation sessions, and 4) the need for changes in any aspect of a partner relationship. Evaluation of content involves assessing whether the learner's objectives are being met and determining the next steps of the instructional program. Evaluation of methodology involves the assessment of the interpersonal relationship between the partners. Frequency of teacher evaluations concerns formative (i.e., daily, weekly, monthly) and summative (i.e., semester, annual) evaluation. Finally, changes should be based on the information gathered during the evaluation process. Change may relate to the content of the lesson, the delivery of instruction, the partners' relationship, the location of the tutoring sessions, the time of the sessions, or any other variables related to a program. The change should revitalize a program by providing it with a booster shot of something new that, in turn, will need to be reflected on in future evaluations.

Reinforcement for Participating in Partner Learning

Designing and implementing ways of reinforcing children for participating in a partner learning relationship is the last component of a comprehensive partner learning program. Reinforcement systems may be formal or informal. Formal systems may take the form of ceremonies and awards, parties (e.g., tutors and tutees having a pizza party together during lunch hour at the end of a program), and recognition in print (e.g., classroom or school newsletters).

Informal reinforcement systems arise in tutoring programs and sometimes arise unpredictably. For example, two students from a fifth/sixth grade multi-age classroom were after-school peer tutors for Nick, a kindergarten student who was labeled as having autism. Nick stayed after school while his mother attended weekly collaborative meetings. The tutors engaged Nick in playful learning activities at a sand table or block area. At the end of the year, Nick's mother wrote unsolicited letters of gratitude to each student's parents expressing thanks for the assistance her son received and the opportunity provided for Nick to develop a peer network. The tutors continued their relationships with Nick throughout the summer. Nick's friendship with the tutors was particularly important to his parents because they had only recently moved into the community and had not yet established many friendship links for Nick.

Another example of informal reinforcement occurred in a partner learning program with Murphy. Murphy had participated in a variety of partner learning programs throughout his elementary school years as both a tutor and a tutee. One day, his class was working through a very difficult math concept. At one point in the lesson, students were required to independently work on the application of the concept. Murphy raised his hand and, when called on, stated that he would be happy to do his work if he could have a peer tutor. Murphy's request was rewarding for everyone. Murphy received help and was successful; it spoke to the success in his past experiences as tutor and tutee. His classmates were validated because it acknowledged the effectiveness and importance of their partner learning relationships with Murphy. For the teacher, Murphy's request validated the use of partner learning programs in the class and demonstrated the ultimate goal of students taking a pro-active role in their own learning. His parents were pleased to know that Murphy was becoming more interdependent. Finally, visitors who happened to be observing the class that day had the opportunity to witness a student spontaneously initiate a request for a technique they had come to observe.

EXAMPLES OF PARTNER LEARNING PROGRAMS

The six components of partner learning (identification, recruitment, training, supervision, evaluation, and reinforcement) are illustrated in the following case studies. Variations include within-class, between-class, schoolwide, and districtwide arrangements, as well as same-age and cross-age relationships.

Cross-Age Partner Learning for a Tutor with Unique Needs

An initial and crucial first step when considering a partner learning relationship is to identify how each student participant is expected to benefit. A team (at times including the student) can activate its creative powers to design unique, powerful partner learning programs. For instance, a team concerned with a second-grade student, Stephen, followed steps similar to the creative problem-solving model of Sidney Parnes (1988; see Chapter 8). In brief, the process involves fact-finding, problem-finding, idea-finding, and solution-finding steps to arrive at an acceptable idea that is subsequently put into action.

Through fact finding (i.e., observing and analyzing Stephen's behavior patterns throughout the day), the team identified that transitions from activity to activity were particularly difficult for Stephen. The team speculated that at the end of the day, Stephen was fatigued, irritable, and anxious about the transition from school to home. Stephen also hesitated to engage in activities at which he perceived himself to be less than competent. Ignoring undesirable behaviors was not effective in engaging Stephen to participate appropriately in class activities. The team agreed that companions were needed throughout the day and adaptations were needed for end-of-the-day activities. Without exception, Stephen demonstrated his most challenging behaviors (e.g., resistance to and defiance toward adults) during the last half hour of each school day, prior to boarding the school bus to go home. However, he displayed a range of challenging behaviors throughout the day that were chronic in nature. His challenging behaviors included resistance to authority figures, difficulty with perceiving another person's perspective appropriate to his age level, a strong tendency to dominate and control the outcomes of student-centered activities, extreme difficulty relating to and interacting with other children, poor social skills in team and group activities, and an unusually competitive spirit for his age level. During fact finding, the team examined resources and identified that it was difficult to provide additional support for Stephen in the classroom on a consistent basis at the end of the day due to scheduling conflicts.

Stephen had not yet been identified under any special education labels during the second grade (he has subsequently been labeled with Tourette syndrome and attention-deficit/hyperactivity disorder). The school he attended provided a noncategorical service delivery model in which all children received supported services and planning as needed, regardless of whether they were identified as eligible for special education (Schattman, 1992). Stephen's needs were intensive enough to receive the ongoing support of a collaborative team and special education support in the classroom.

The team framed the challenge as, "In what ways might we restructure the last 30 minutes of the school day prior to Stephen's boarding the school bus home to reduce or eliminate his power struggles with adults?" When the team moved to an idea-finding stage, many ideas regarding accommodations of current activities and environment were generated, one of which was to explore bringing an older peer into the last activity of each school day. During solution finding, the team refined the idea of having older peers tutor Stephen (with the sustained presence of an adult due to the unpredictability and the potential for unsafe behaviors from Stephen).

Putting a Program in Place for Stephen

In acceptance finding, the team cycled back to facts critical to the consideration of a partner learning relationship and established the following:

- The tutor would need to have an air of confidence when interacting with Stephen.

- Given training, the tutor would need to be able to demonstrate skills of ignoring, staying focused on the task, and engaging in a high rate of praise in his or her interactions with Stephen.

- The tutor would need to be able to initiate "judgment calls" during interactions with Stephen that required negotiating and a "give and take."

Avoiding "burn-out" also was considered in designing the tutor program. Because of Stephen's challenging behaviors, it was speculated that one tutor might quickly become overwhelmed and lose interest in continuing a partner learning relationship. A team member suggested a "tag team" approach in which two tutors would be trained in the program. The two tutors also shared the responsibility of tutoring other students in the classroom as well. While one tutor worked with Stephen, the other worked with another student the teacher identified as needing help for that day. The tutors were given responsibility for how they would share the two jobs. If one tutor was absent, the session was not interrupted because the other tutor would "substitute" teach with Stephen.

The remaining job of the team was to identify two tutors and establish the partner learning program. Team members shared responsibilities for this. The collaborating special educator recruited and trained two tutors. The classroom teacher selected educational activities that Stephen enjoyed. She took responsibility for organizing lesson plans for the tutors, gathering materials, and ensuring space for each session. The principal contacted the parents of the tutors for explanation and permission, Stephen's parents explained and encouraged Stephen to participate in the program, and a special education paraprofessional who supported the classroom on an occasional basis shared with the special educator the adult "supervisor" role in the tutoring sessions.

Evaluation Leading to Change

Shared responsibility among team members for the establishment and implementation of this partner learning program was critical to its success. The program was "doable" because each team member contributed to some aspect of the program. Also critical was the teacher's willingness to individualize for Stephen during this activity time each day. Furthermore, she chose to have primary responsibility for monitoring Stephen's accomplishments during tutoring sessions. When the other team members "picked up" other responsibilities, the teacher was able to focus on ensuring academic outcomes for Stephen's tutorial sessions.

After several sessions in this partner learning relationship, Stephen began to request "to be the tutor." The team recognized that the communicative intent of Stephen's requests was a need to serve in a leadership role as teacher. Not only did Stephen enjoy being helped, but he wanted to experience being a helper as well.

Throughout the teaming process, a second partner learning program was initiated for Stephen. On alternate days from his tutoring sessions with older tutors, Stephen began tutoring a first-grade student who needed to practice oral reading. This partner learning program required more vigorous supervision; anticipating this, the team planned pro-actively. The team took the time to plan for the second program carefully because of their strong belief that Stephen, being in a caring type leadership role, would have short- and long-term positive outcomes in terms of behavioral self-management, self-esteem, a sense of belonging, mastery, and independence (Brendtro, Brokenleg, & Van Bockern, 1990; Van Bockern, Brendtro, & Brokenleg, 2000).

A Schoolwide, Cross-Age Tutoring Program

In a fourth-grade classroom, two students presented significant challenges. As part of the students' educational programs, a variety of same-age support programs of both an academic (peer tutoring) and nonacademic (peer buddy) nature were developed for the classroom. The classroom tutors performed their responsibilities so magnificently that the classroom teacher wanted the skills of the tutors to extend beyond their classroom. The class of tutors eventually became cross-age math tutors in a first-grade classroom for the remainder of the school year. This was the beginning of a schoolwide, cross-age tutor program that involved 75% of the elementary school's student population. Students in five upper elementary classrooms tutor students in five lower elementary classrooms in the areas of math and language. Initially, a collaborating teacher (special educator) matched classrooms and facilitated the scheduling, planning, delivery, evaluation, and reinforcement components of the program. Over time, each cross-age tutoring match developed its own unique approach to implementing the cross-age tutoring program.

Identification

Initially, only a few involved students were identified as likely to benefit from a tutoring situation for either academic or nonacademic reasons. Over time, it became obvious that each individual student could benefit in a partner learning relationship. Any student in the upper and lower elementary classrooms was a potential tutor or tutee.

Recruitment

At the start of each school year, upper elementary students are introduced to the cross-age tutoring program through a class discussion about past student experiences as tutors and tutees, including students' perceptions of the art and science of teaching. Following the discussion, students receive a letter to be shared with their parents that explains the program.

Included with the letter is a sample contract stipulating the student's responsibilities should he or she choose to participate as a tutor in the program. All students who return their contracts with appropriate signatures are allowed to participate in the cross-age tutoring program. In general, 95% or more of the students in each class elect to become tutors. The few students who do not choose to do so often change their minds during the school year.

Training

Generally, training sessions of 30–45 minutes occur either once or twice a month, alternating with bimonthly or biweekly tutorial sessions. Students are required to identify the critical elements of the concept they will teach in their next tutoring session. Then, students either develop their own lesson plan for their tutees or learn how to deliver a previously developed plan. Necessary materials for the tutoring session are prepared, and the lesson is rehearsed. Students usually ask many questions related to lesson development, material preparation, lesson delivery, or behavior management at the training sessions. Students' questions and issues are addressed as they bring them up.

Supervision

Each upper or lower elementary classroom determines its own supervision arrangement. Usually the upper elementary classroom teacher participates in planning sessions with a collaborating teacher (special educator). The lower elementary teacher usually supervises the delivery of the tutoring in the classrooms with the support of a collaborating teacher. All teachers share in monitoring tutors to make sure their contractual responsibilities are being met. This is necessary because tutoring is a privilege contingent on adequate work completion and social responsibility.

Evaluation

At the end of each tutoring session, tutors and tutees alike are asked to evaluate the session. In 3–5 minutes of discussion, students identify "what went well with the lesson" and "what could be done better" for the upcoming sessions. The upper elementary students use this information to develop lessons in their next planning session. Periodically, evaluation occurs to determine if major changes need to occur across the entire elementary school partner learning program. Surveys with open-ended questions, checklists, or class meetings are used to gather information for this summative evaluation. As a result of program evaluations, the cross-age tutor program was changed from a small group of students as tutors to whole classes of tutors and from twice a month tutoring sessions to once a month tutoring sessions in a couple of classrooms.

Reinforcement

Reinforcement can and should be structured for everyone. Tutors may reinforce the tutees at the end of each tutor session with tangible reinforcers or fun activities. Classroom teachers are reinforced through observations of their students in responsible teaching and active learning. They gain information from observations to improve their own work with their students. The school community is reinforced by stories told by students about experiences and the emerging interest of a number of students in becoming teachers. At the end of each school year, all tutors are publicly applauded for their service to their school through a tutor recognition ceremony.

In summary, a cross-age tutoring program is one way a school community can structure opportunities for students to become active participants in their own education and the education of others, help tutors better learn content through learning about the metacognitive aspects of teaching information to another, and give students the opportunity to contribute to a community to which they belong (Van Bockern et al., 2000).

Partner Learning as a Community Service

A tradition of the Swanton (Vermont) Central School fifth- and sixth-grade multi-age program has been to develop a classroom culture and ethos by identifying themselves as the "Songadeewin Family" (meaning "strong heart" in one Native American language), through which children demonstrate how they may be "keepers of the earth through mind and spirit." The class is structured to provide services to others in the belief that one way to help students define who they are is to have them decide how they will contribute to others.

To achieve the goal of generosity for the Songadeewin family, the approximately 50 students in the class are subdivided into groups of six to eight children and one adult advisor. The adults include teachers, teaching assistants, the principal, special educators, parent volunteers, and student teachers. Each group, called a Council Circle, meets twice weekly for approximately 30 minutes to develop and implement service projects in the four areas of Songadeewin—family, school, community, and the earth.

One year, Council Circles developed a service project called "Songadeewin Family Tutees." The advisor of this particular group, Linda, trained students in essential technical and interpersonal tutoring skills. Linda utilized many of the suggestions and followed tutor training strategies such as those described in Chapter 16. Students role-played partner learning situations to develop and practice the tutoring skills, as well as behavior management strategies.

Each student created a folder that included materials they would need for a partner learning program. They had an index card that "introduced" them to their potential tutees. For example, Kalib's card stated, "My name is Kalib. I am in grade 6. My teachers are Ms. LaPlant and Ms. Zane. I am good at spelling and English. The subject I am not good in is math." On the opposite side of the card, Kalib listed "conversation starter" questions to ask his tutee to help them become acquainted, such as, "What are you good at?" and "How old are you?" The folder included a list of teaching skills the tutor had learned that served as a prompt to use the skills in an actual partner learning session. Each tutor also generated a list of positive words and statements that could be used to encourage tutees to respond. A personalized "praise list" was developed. For example, Kalib listed 17 statements, such as, "good," "nice job," "fantastic work," and "You're doing fine." Stickers and awards selected or made by tutors were in the folders, along with a Tutor Log Book. The log was used to record tutee's answers and any information from a tutorial session that could help a tutor reflect on the session. The information was intended to help tutors improve as teachers through self-reflection.

When Council Circle members completed their training and tutoring folders were assembled, each prospective tutor created a brochure advertising the program and the services he or she could provide. Brochures were distributed and the Council Circle advisor promoted the program to other adults in the school community. Teachers "employed" the students and reported that they made excellent teachers in partner learning programs; they needed minimal teacher time in orientation or supervision because of the prior training they received in their Council Circle groups.

The tutoring program subsequently expanded to a "Songadeewin Day Care" program. The same group of students learned child care skills through a process similar to the partner learning training. They developed materials and activities for younger children and performed child care duties during and after school for parents and teachers who needed to attend a variety of school meetings. The Songadeewin Day Care providers were a valuable asset to the school, keeping younger children meaningfully engaged and supervised during adult meeting times. In keeping with the Songadeewin community service ethic, the child care providers volunteered their services.

A Partner Learning Program To Acquire Math Facts

This example of a partner learning program for two students of the same age in a third-grade classroom illustrates how supervision may need to intensify at points during a partner learning relationship. A third-grade teacher was concerned with two students who were not mastering addition and subtraction math facts at a satisfactory rate. The teacher described both students as having difficulty attending and working independently. They both were frustrated in math, voicing a lack of confidence about their abilities.

This teacher's special education support teacher developed a reciprocal peer tutoring program for math fact acquisition that had sequential steps that incorporated auditory, verbal, and writing components in a repeated rehearsal format. The teacher ensured that the students had at least one opportunity a day for reciprocal tutoring. Each tutorial took approximately 10 minutes each day and allowed each partner to play the role of tutor and tutee. The students concentrated on six math facts per session (four "known" and two "unknown" or yet unmastered), practicing them until mastery using an auditory, kinesthetic, and visual program.

It was hoped that once the two students were trained in the procedure and in tutoring, only intermittent supervision would be needed to monitor the program and provide students with reinforcement and feedback. The students did, in fact, master the program steps quickly and demonstrated mastery of the teaching–learning procedure. Once the students demonstrated consistent behaviors during tutoring, the special education support teacher who supervised the program arranged to visit weekly to monitor the program.

Before the first supervisory visitation, the third-grade teacher approached her support teacher with concerns over the way in which the two students were treating each other during tutoring sessions. She observed the students frequently using "put-down" statements and abandoning reinforcement, feedback, and other skills in which they had been trained. They also fought over materials. Nevertheless, the feedback sheets the students filled out after each session indicated they perceived the sessions to be going well. When the support teacher queried the students, they did not take responsibility for what was happening and made strong accusations toward each other.

There was a clear need for more training, modeling, and supervision of the tutoring sessions. Both teachers hoped that the students eventually would not require constant supervision to carry out the program. The support teacher arranged to increase her supervision time daily on a flexible schedule when her presence would not interrupt direct instruction or another critical activity. This resulted in a "win-win" situation for everyone. The third-grade teacher was pleased the students were able to continue the tutoring, the special educator was able to meet her training and supervision obligations, and the students received intensified intervention.

The students did need reinforcement and reminders of the steps of the program, but the emphasis of supervision was to develop the students' skills in making positive statements and sustaining positive interactions with one another while adult supervision was gradually removed. The supervising special education support teacher developed a data sheet that included each step of the teaching sequence, adding the steps of "saying nice things" and "saying thank you." As she supervised, she checked off each step as the tutor performed it, particularly noting examples of partners saying "nice things" and "thank you."

Prior to introducing the data collection system to the partners, she observed them, collecting baseline data on their performance. She then shared the data and her observations with the students and set goals with them to improve their performance. The students could collect "points" based on the number of checkmarks they jointly accrued that could be traded for activity-based reinforcers (e.g., lunch with the supervisor, games, free time).

With this intervention, the students quickly improved in all areas of the partner learning program. Yet, the goal of reducing supervision was slow to be achieved. Supervision was reduced but only to every other day. Nevertheless, the teacher and support teacher agreed to continue the program because the students did show consistent gains in learning math facts and acquiring interpersonal skills. Although supervision in this case remained somewhat intensive, it was seen as a necessary support to the partner learning program. Adult intervention was needed to prompt, guide, and reinforce cooperative behavior rather than to teach actual math skills.

Adam's Positive Experiences as a Classroom Tutor

Several years ago, Michelle, a second-grade teacher, was working in her school's resource center while her student teacher did her "solo week." She met Adam, a fifth grader with severe emotional challenges, who was in the resource center working while he "cooled down" following a disruption in his regular classroom. On this day, Michelle observed Adam as he patiently helped another student who was struggling with a particular concept. She was amazed with his teaching skills and impressed with how well he related to the younger child. This was the beginning of Adam's experience as a classroom tutor in Michelle's second-grade classroom that would continue for almost 3 years. Michelle quickly identified Adam as a student who had developed and was able to apply good tutoring skills. Adam's educational support team had identified Adam's needs for opportunities to practice identified social skills in a normalized environment and to improve his perceptions of himself and his school experiences in general. Collaborating teachers (special educators) in the school brought Michelle and Adam's team together and encouraged them to develop a tutoring program for Adam.

At the time, Adam had a behavior contract to support him in maintaining appropriate school behavior. Recruiting Adam to become a tutor was easy because he grew to like Michelle and wanted to work in her classroom. The educational team ultimately decided to use Adam's strong desire to tutor as a reinforcement when he met his obligations on his behavior contract.

Training and supervision of Adam as a tutor was Michelle's responsibility. Because Adam could tutor any student in the class, he had the chance to deliver many types of lessons in different content areas. Initially, someone needed to spend time explaining and modeling lessons to Adam; Adam's collaborating teacher helped Michelle with this. Over time, as Adam became familiar with the various programs and content areas in Michelle's classroom, the amount of training and supervision decreased dramatically.

Michelle's and Adam's collaborating teacher (special educator) met regularly to evaluate Adam's performance as a tutor; sometimes Adam participated in these meetings. Adam's collaborating teacher also observed to determine the degree to which he generalized to other children the positive social interactions he showed with students in Michelle's second-grade classroom.

Participating as a classroom tutor was very reinforcing to Adam. He rarely failed to meet the requirements of his behavioral contract, thus earning his time to serve as a tutor. One school year at Christmastime, Adam came to a tutoring session with a bag filled with small stuffed animals that he had won at various fairs and carnivals. He gave each student in the class a stuffed animal, surprising everyone including the teacher. Becoming a classroom tutor empowered Adam to expand his social interactions in an atmosphere of acceptance.

CONCLUSION

Partner learning systems can be uniquely tailored to meet the existing needs of an individual student, a classroom, or a school community to achieve both social and academic goals. Intentional planning of the partner learning programs increases the likelihood that the student partnerships will be successful. We have seen, first hand, the benefits of partner learning and have learned that instruction may come from people other than adults with a "teacher" label. For students who have few positive outside connections, partner learning may be a source of positive relationships. By instilling a sense of responsibility for others in a student community, it is our hope that an ethic of generosity will develop, transcend the walls of the school, and follow children into adulthood.

Partner learning relationships offer educators much, including a fresh look at learning, as they observe their students teaching and learning from each other. However, to initiate a partner learning system requires a change in the attitudes of educators, students, and communities about the roles of teachers and learners and how adults and children interact in school. Change is always difficult, but attitudes can affect outcomes, as Winnie the Pooh pointed out.

"We're all going on an Expotition with Christopher Robin!"
"What is it when we're on it?"
"A sort of boat, I think," said Pooh.
"Oh! that sort."
"Yes. And we're going to discover a Pole or something. Or was it a Mole?
Anyhow we're going to discover it." (Milne, 1957, pp. 106–107)

REFERENCES

Brendtro, L., Brokenleg, M., & Van Bockern, S. (1990). *Reclaiming youth at risk.* Bloomington, IN: National Educational Service.

Milne, A.A. (1957). *The world of Pooh.* New York: E.P. Dutton.

Parnes, S. (1988). *Visionizing: State-of-the-art processes for encouraging innovative excellence.* East Aurora, NY: D.O.K. Publishing.

Schattman, R. (1992). The Franklin Northwest Supervisory Union: A case study of an inclusive school system. In R.A. Villa, J.S. Thousand, W. Stainback, & S. Stainback (Eds.), *Restructuring for caring and effective education: An administrative guide to creating heterogeneous schools* (pp. 143–159). Baltimore: Paul H. Brookes Publishing Co.

Thousand, J.S., & Villa, R.A. (2000). Collaborative teaming: A powerful tool in school restructuring. In R.A. Villa & J.S. Thousand (Eds.), *Restructuring for caring and effective education: Piecing the puzzle together* (2nd ed., pp. 254–291). Baltimore: Paul H. Brookes Publishing Co.

Van Bockern, S.L., Brendtro, L.K., & Brokenleg, M. (2000). Reclaiming our youth. In R.A. Villa & J.S. Thousand (Eds.), *Restructuring for caring and effective education: Piecing the puzzle together* (2nd ed., pp. 56–76). Baltimore: Paul H. Brookes Publishing Co.

19

The Role of Students in Resolving Conflict

Fred Schrumpf
Golie G. Jansen

The picture of school violence dramatically changed in February, 1996, when a ninth-grade male student returned to school to gun down a teacher and two students in math class in Moses Lake, Washington. Two years later in Jonesboro, Arkansas, an 11-year-old male and a 13-year-old male opened fire on their classmates as they were leaving the school, and one teacher and four students were killed. A year later, in Littleton, Colorado, two armed male students entered their school, killing 12 students, 1 teacher, and then themselves. The headlines in the last couple of years of the 20th century noted more than 44 deaths in 13 different schools. All perpetrators were Caucasian males. Finding reasons and gaining understanding for these actions has become a major topic and concern for school personnel and researchers alike.

Students are involved daily in conflicts. The question for students is not, "Will I have a conflict today?" but, "How will I handle the conflict?" Statements such as, "You're cheating," "I'm going to get you after school," "Did you hear what she said about you?" "Your momma . . ," "Gay," "Fag," and "Slut" turn anger into aggression and violence. Unresolved conflicts hurt the school climate and can result in increased absenteeism or vandalism. Too often, when students bring conflicts to teachers, adult advice may be to "ignore it" or "walk away." When friends or parents are asked for advice, their response often is to "get 'em back." When students' conflicts reach the principal's desk, the consequences often are detention or suspension. With all of these responses, conflicts fail to get resolved and often escalate.

Curious about what students think about violence in schools, the National Association of Attorneys General (Gregoire, 2000) conducted conferences throughout the country asking students, "What causes violence?" and, "What can we do about it?" Overwhelmingly—and surprisingly—students from across the country stated that the primary cause of youth violence lies in the home and is related to how children are raised, nurtured, listened to, and taught to solve problems. However, the second major cause was the way students treat each other. They cited bullying, "dissing," harassing, and outcasting as major contributors to school violence. Asked about solutions, students welcomed newly installed physical security measures but stated that youth violence would not be solved until root causes were addressed. Recognizing the need for multiple solutions, the people who came to the listening conferences spoke highly of peer mediation, after-school programs, and training to prevent bullying (Gregoire, 2000).

Another concern of schools and parents is the rising incidence of what is referred to as *hate crimes*. "When bias motivates an unlawful act, it is considered a hate crime" (Carrier, 1999, p. 1). Targets of hate crimes are not only individuals of a particular race or religion but also gay and lesbian people and people with disabilities. According to the Federal Bureau of Investigation, 10,700 hate crimes were reported in the United States of America in 1996—approximately 29 incidents per day (U.S. Department of Education, 1998). Schools are not immune to hate crimes. Teenage boys and young adults account for a substantial number of these crimes both as victims and as perpetrators. Teachers and principals struggle with issues and conflicts related to behavior that is hate motivated, such as ethnic conflicts, harassment, intimidation, or graffiti.

Knowledge of how to handle conflicts in an appropriate way is a life skill that can be learned cooperatively with peers; its application will benefit students beyond the school environment and their school years. As a response to the increased awareness of conflicts, North American schools have adopted conflict resolution programs as one way of addressing student conflicts in a pro-active and positive way. Many of these programs employ students as peer mediators. Students who serve as mediators sometimes are called *peacemakers* or *conflict managers*. Peer mediation assumes that 1) conflicts are a normal part of growing up, 2) conflicts can be treated as learning opportunities, and 3) conflict resolution skills are positive forces for personal growth and social change.

A peer mediation approach may be initiated on a schoolwide basis or within a classroom, from the elementary through the high school level. When a peer mediation program is adopted, a small number of students may be selected and trained in the mediation process. The students then are available during the school day to conduct mediations as requested by teachers, principals, or peers. Requests for mediations frequently come from students themselves. In elementary schools, mediators also may frequently be assigned to playground areas to settle disputes on the spot. At some schools, *all* students are trained in the conflict resolution skills of negotiation and mediation (Johnson, Johnson, Dudley, & Burnett, 1992). Teaching these skills may be part of an elementary curriculum or, when taught at the secondary level, may be integrated in subjects such as social studies, language arts, or health classes. Students receive instructions in the nature of conflict, communication skills, problem solving, and the steps of negotiation and mediation. Whenever a peer conflict arises, students are asked to negotiate their differences. If the disputants cannot reach an agreement on their own, then the teacher selects a peer mediator to assist. The teacher becomes the mediator only if the peer mediator cannot help resolve the conflict. Such an approach in an elementary school in Minnesota resulted in an 80% decrease in the frequency of student conflicts that teachers had to manage and a reduction in principal referrals to zero (Johnson et al., 1992).

Research during the late 1990s supports effectiveness of peer mediation (Jones, 1998). The Comprehensive Peer Mediation Evaluation Project (CPMEP) studied the efficacy of peer mediation programs in a 2-year study. The field experiment study compared program models and involved 27 elementary, middle, and high schools in three sites across the nation, with a total sample of 430 peer mediators, 5,400 control students, and 1,225 teachers/administrative staff. Research questions focused on the impact of peer mediation on students' attitudes and behavior and on school climate and whether peer mediation programs effectively handle disputes. The data "reveals that peer mediation programs provide a significant benefit in developing constructive social and conflict behavior in children at all educational levels" and "clearly demonstrates that exposure to peer mediation reduces personal conflict and increases pro-social values, decreases aggressiveness, and increases perspective taking and conflict competence" (Jones, 1998, p. 18). These CPMEP results prove that peer mediation programs can significantly improve school climate (Jones, 1998).

Common to all peer mediation programs are trained peer mediators who respond to student conflict by facilitating a process of communication and problem solving. The mediation process is voluntary and enables two disputants to talk face-to-face and come to some common understanding. Solutions are generated and evaluated, and agreed-upon solutions become a written agreement on the part of the disputants. The remainder of the chapter offers a rationale for peer mediation, discusses the nature of conflict, describes in detail the mediation process and strategies for training students and establishing mediation within a school, and concludes with an example of peer mediation in action.

WHY PEER MEDIATION?

Schools today reflect the problems and conflicts with which students live in their larger environments. Many educators include the teaching of life skills as an essential curriculum domain so that daily conflicts experienced by students become teachable moments and opportunities for cooperative learning. Mediation is a life skill that empowers students to solve their own problems through clear communication, applied decision making, and critical thinking. Peer mediation can reduce the time that teachers, principals, or counselors spend dealing with discipline problems. It can help reduce absenteeism, vandalism, and violence, and it can be more effective than suspensions to teach responsible behaviors. Resolving conflict promotes peace and understanding of individual differences in a multicultural world and creates a safe learning environment.

UNDERSTANDING CONFLICT

It is easy to come up with examples of conflicts in school. At most every grade level, when students are asked to give examples of conflicts, their responses include teasing, put-downs, bullying, being left out, rumors, problems with sharing, lost or damaged property, threats, and aggression. Some schools have more conflicts than others; this often has to do with how school staff handles conflict and the atmosphere of each classroom. Kreidler (1984) identified some common causes for classroom conflicts:

- Competitive atmosphere: Students work against each other and are compelled to win.
- Intolerant atmosphere: Learners mistrust and are intolerant of different ideas or lifestyles, including racial prejudice.
- Poor communication: Students lack understanding or listening skills or cannot express their feelings and needs.
- Misuse of power: Teachers are rigid and have inflexible rules; they use fear or threats.

William Glasser (1986, 1990), examining basic needs, used the Choice Theory to explain the origin of conflict. Glasser stated that people are not controlled by external events, but, instead, are motivated by the desire to satisfy internal basic psychological needs.

- The need to *belong*: loving, sharing, and cooperating
- The need for *power*: being recognized, achieving, and being respected
- The need for *freedom*: making choices in life
- The need for *fun*: laughing and playing

Students want and try to satisfy these needs in the classroom. When students feel excluded or discriminated against, go unrecognized, have no freedom to make classroom decisions, or stop having fun, there will be conflicts in the classroom.

Limited resources can also be a source of school conflict. For example, when students need to share materials, equipment, or teacher time, conflict can arise. It is harder for students to have their basic needs met when school resources are in short supply.

Finally, conflicts may arise because of *different values*. People have different convictions, and when they interact, their values are represented in their words and actions. When students say, "It's not fair," "I'm right and you're wrong," or, "He's not telling the truth," it is often because the concepts of honesty, equality, and fairness are viewed differently by different people.

Conflicts due to cultural or value differences may be bias-based and expressed as racism, classism, sexism, and homophobia (Woolner, 1990). Because people bring learned biases and ethnocentric views of the world to school, prejudice reduction and cross-cultural sensitivity must be part of conflict resolution training. In summary, it takes communication and understanding to discover differing values; it takes communication skills to create shared sets of values.

An important first step in conflict resolution involves awareness of one's response to conflict. The conflict diagram presented in Figure 19.1 illustrates sources and responses to conflict. The *hard* response to conflict is defined as confrontation, threats, aggression, and anger. A second response to conflict is avoidance because sometimes it seems easier to withdraw, ignore, or deny a conflict. This is called the *soft* response. Although resentment is internalized, anger or depression can result in avoidance. The preferred way to handle conflict is the *principled* response that leads toward resolution, which includes understanding, respect, and resolution (Fisher, Ury, & Patton, 1991). Outcomes to these responses are indicated as either win-lose, lose-lose, or the preferred win-win.

Origins of conflict		
Limited resources	*Unmet basic needs*	*Different values*
Time	Belonging	Beliefs
Money	Power	Priorities
Property	Freedom	Principles
	Fun	
Conflict		
Responses to conflict		
Soft	*Hard*	*Principled*
Withdrawing	Threatening	Listening
Ignoring	Pushing	Understanding
Denying	Hitting	Respecting
Giving in	Yelling	Resolving
Outcomes to conflict		
Soft	*Hard*	*Principled*
Lose-lose	Lose-lose	Win-win
Lose-win	Win-lose	

Figure 19.1. Understanding conflict. (From *Creating the peaceable school: A comprehensive program for teaching conflict resolution* [p. 92] by Bodine, R., Crawford, D., & Schrumpf, F. [1994]. Champaign, IL: Research Press. Copyright © 1994 by Bodine, R., Crawford, D., & Schrumpf, F. Reprinted by permission.)

PHASES OF PROGRAM ORGANIZATION AND IMPLEMENTATION

An effective peer mediation program requires schoolwide interest. Teachers, administrators, and students all need information and training on peaceful conflict resolution. The four organizational phases to establishing a successful program are generally followed.

Phase 1: Develop Awareness and Interest

The first phase is to interest a group of staff and parents to form a committee that familiarizes itself with resource materials that teach conflict resolution education and with any available materials on peer mediation programs. The group may also learn from other schools in the area with peer mediation programs. The committee should research and report the frequency of conflict situations in the school. After such a study, a proposal is developed that describes how peer mediation could be initiated and how it would benefit the school.

Phase 2: Establish Schoolwide Support

Phase 2 involves educating staff and students about what peer mediation is and how it operates. Staff may by informed via orientations at regular staff meetings, or, better yet, through in-service training on conflict resolution strategies. Students may be informed through classroom presentations, grade-level assemblies, daily announcements, and informational brochures. All orientations should answer questions such as, What is mediation? Who are student mediators? What are the rules? How do I get a conflict mediated? Why should I try mediation? Figure 19.2 offers further suggestions for questions and responses to include in a brochure.

Next, those who have developed an interest will need to develop the program, adapt materials for the program, arrange for more in-depth training for teachers who want to implement a classroom curriculum, and select students to become mediators. Student mediators should be representative of the diverse student body with regard to race, gender, grade-point average, extracurricular interests, and clique membership. They also should be judged as good listeners, respectful of others, trusted by peers, and motivated to help people work together.

Phase 3: Provide Mediation Training

Mediation is like any other skill, it can be learned and improved with practice. Between 9 and 12 hours of training is needed for students and teachers to learn and practice the basic skills of negotiation and mediation. To implement this phase, several staff members from the school need to complete additional training in conflict resolution in order to train others. Alternatively, an outside trainer may be used to provide the instruction. Details of a model 2-day workshop that would prepare a trainer are presented later in this chapter.

Phase 4: Implement and Evaluate the Program

Peer mediation should have high visibility among teachers and students and be promoted through schoolwide announcements and materials that inform everyone of the program and how it can help. Posters that encourage peace and talking out problems may be de-

Having a conflict?

Has someone made fun of you or teased you?

Did someone say, "Just wait, and I'll get you after school?"

Did "he say" that "she said" that "you said," and a rumor is going around the school?

What is mediation?

Mediation is a chance for you to sit face-to-face and talk, uninterrupted, so each side of the dispute is heard. After the problem is defined, solutions are created and then evaluated. When an agreement is reached, it is written and signed.

What is a student mediator?

A student mediator is one of your peers who has been trained to conduct the mediation meeting. The student mediator makes sure the mediation session is helpful and fair. Your fellow students were selected to help you resolve differences because they might better understand your point of view.

Are there any rules to peer mediation?

To make the process work, there are a few simple rules.

• Mediation is a process that both students choose.

• Everything said during the mediation is kept confidential; what is said stays in the room.

• In mediation, students take turns talking and no one can interrupt.

• The student mediator does not take sides.

If I have a conflict, how do I go about getting it mediated?

It is very easy to request a mediation. Just pick up a mediation request form from a counselor or social worker. Take 2 minutes to fill it out and return it to any counselor or social worker. Within a day, you will receive notification of the time and place of mediation. Mediations will be scheduled when the least amount of class time is missed.

Why should I try mediation?

There are many reasons why mediation will be helpful to you. Here are a few.

• Conflicts that do not get resolved often end in fights, which could result in suspension.

• Conflicts that do not get resolved often hurt feelings, which could cause you to lose friends.

• You will learn to choose a peaceful, responsible way to solve your own problems without an adult doing it for you.

• Mediation will help develop mutual respect and clear communication.

• Mediation will make school a more positive place to learn and grow.

If you answered *yes* to any of the questions at the top of this brochure, check out the Common Ground Student Mediation Center.

Figure 19.2.   Sample brochure. (From *Peer mediation: Conflict resolution in schools* [p. 277] by Schrumpf, F., Crawford, D., & Bodine, R. [1997]. Champaign, IL: Research Press. Copyright © 1997 by Schrumpf, F., Crawford, D., & Bodine, R. Reprinted by permission.)

signed and placed throughout the school. T-shirts, hats, or buttons worn by mediators can help build a positive image of mediation. The goals of promotion should be to encourage student participation and increase the likelihood of requests for mediation from teachers, principals, and students.

It is critical that student mediators receive ongoing training and support for their efforts. Monthly meetings allow peer mediators an opportunity to discuss any problems they have had as mediators, receive more advanced training, and learn that skills improve over time with practice.

Finally, data collection is a critical part of any peer mediation program. Information on the Peer Agreement Form, shown in Figure 19.3, includes type of conflict, place of conflict, if agreement is reached, and length of mediation. This information can be compiled and reported each month. The committee can also compile overall data regarding student conflicts such as overall detentions, suspensions, fights, or absenteeism.

TRAINING MEDIATORS

Conflict resolution can be taught at all grade levels. Classroom curricula have been developed for the elementary grades by Kreidler (1984, 1990) and Johnson and Johnson (1996). Training materials for mediators in grades 4–12 were developed by Schrumpf, Crawford, and Bodine (1997) and Sadalla, Holmberg, and Halligan (1990). These materials build on natural leadership and communication skills that students bring with them. The materials include problem-solving techniques to assist others to resolve their conflicts.

A workshop to train elementary-age student mediators generally involves two half-day sessions that total 6–8 hours of instruction. At the secondary level, a 2-day workshop totaling 10–12 hours is recommended. At both levels, students learn the definition of conflict, the goal of mediation, the role of the mediator, and communication skills. Students also learn each step of the mediation process through role plays of conflict situations. The following is a brief overview of how training is conducted.

Section 1: Understanding Conflict

Students are introduced to the nature of conflict by being asked to brainstorm a list of words that come to mind when the word *conflict* is stated. The list usually includes many words with negative meaning such as *fight, disagreement, argument, yelling, problem, threat,* and *war.* Students are then challenged to think of conflict as positive, with the introduction of words such as *opportunity, change, talk, challenge, risk,* and *problem solving.*

The desired outcome of such an exercise is for students to acquire a new and positive understanding of conflict. Students learn that conflict is to be seen as a natural part of everyday life that can be handled in positive or negative ways, having either creative or destructive results; when handled creatively, conflict can be a positive force for personal growth and social change.

They also learn that in order to resolve a conflict, the conflict's source must be identified, as shown in Figure 19.1. Students must learn that almost every dispute between people involves attempts to meet basic human needs for belonging, power, freedom, and fun (Glasser, 1986, 1990). Needs are discussed by asking students to give personal examples of how they have each of their needs met and clarifying those conflicts that arise because of limited resources or differing values or cultures. Finally, students are asked how they respond to conflict and they examine how chosen responses either escalate or de-escalate a conflict situation.

Students involved in conflict

Name: _____ Grade: _____

Name: _____ Grade: _____

Name: _____ Grade: _____

Name: _____ Grade: _____

Type of conflict

____ Rumor   ____ Harassment   ____ Relationship   ____ Fight

____ Property   ____ Threats   ____ Other: _____

Place of conflict

____ Classroom   ____ Hall   ____ Gym   ____ Cafeteria   ____ Other: _____

What is the conflict about? (What are the major issues?)

Brainstorm possible solutions. (List at least three options.)

1. _____   4. _____

2. _____   5. _____

3. _____   6. _____

Evaluate options and make an agreement.

I, _____ , agree to _____

_____

I, _____ , agree to _____

_____

I, _____ , agree to _____

_____

I, _____ , agree to _____

Mediator's signature: _____

Disputants' signatures: _____

_____

Date: _____ Length of mediation: _____

Figure 19.3. Sample Peer Agreement Form.

Section 2: Goal of Mediation and Role of Mediators

The goals of peer mediation are discussed next. Mediators learn that disputants need to 1) learn to understand and respect different views, 2) open and improve communications, 3) develop cooperation in solving a common problem, and 4) reach agreements that address the interests of both sides.

Students become familiar with peer mediation as a noncompetitive approach to solving differences. They learn how trained peer mediators facilitate cooperative (versus competitive) processes by helping disputants to state honestly what they want and how they feel. The approach is to focus on the problem without blaming the other person.

Roles and qualities of mediators are also taught. Students learn that in all cases, peer mediators remain neutral and do not take sides. Peer mediators are emphatic listeners; they listen for understanding of thoughts and feelings. The mediator is respectful and does not judge or show prejudice. The mediator helps people work together and cooperate in order to find their own solutions. Finally, the peer mediator keeps information confidential in order to build trust and confidence in the process. The mediation is not discussed with other students in the school.

Section 3: Communication Skills

The basic communication skill used in mediation is *active listening* (see Table 19.1). The first step, listening, emphasizes the use of nonverbal behaviors (e.g., eye contact, nodding, facial expressions, not interrupting) to show understanding. The second step is summarizing—the mediator restates the main facts and feelings described by the disputants. Summarizing information ensures facts and feelings are heard correctly; it also shows that the mediator listens. The third step is clarifying, which includes asking open-ended questions to gain more information. Because an open-ended question cannot be answered with a "yes" or "no" response, it serves to help all parties better define the problem and develop understanding. Mediators are instructed to avoid giving advice, interrupting, judging, criticizing, or sharing their own conflicts.

Section 4: The Mediation Process

There are six steps to the mediation process, each of which is practiced using role-play situations. Students may generate conflict situations to role play, and/or the trainers may prepare scenarios in advance. Students work in groups of four: two students to play the disputants and the other two to act as co-mediators. Figure 19.4 summarizes each of the six steps to mediation (Schrumpf et al., 1997). The next section explains each step in more detail.

THE MEDIATION PROCESS

The six-step mediation process employs the problem-solving and communication skills that have already been demonstrated to the peer mediators.

Step 1: Open the Session

The mediator sits between the two disputants at a table, makes introductions, and states the ground rules:

Table 19.1. Three steps in active listening

Listen (eye contact, posture, facial expression, gestures)
Summarize (restating facts and reflecting feelings)
Clarify (using open-ended questions or statements)

"As mediator I remain neutral and do not take sides."

"Each person takes a turn talking and listening with no interruptions."

"Everything said is kept confidential; meaning, what's said in this room stays in this room."

Each person is then asked to agree to the ground rules and commit to try to solve the problem. Once they agree, the mediation begins. If they do not agree, then the dispute is referred to an adult.

Step 2: Gather Information

The purpose of this step is to get "the story" from each disputant's point of view. The mediator asks each party to tell what happened. The mediator first listens to one person and summarizes what was stated. Next, the other party is asked to tell his or her story. Again, the mediator listens and summarizes the relevant information stated. Active listening is important so that each disputant believes he or she is heard and understood. The mediator gives each disputant another chance to clarify and share additional information until the problem is clearly understood and well defined. Many times the mediator will ask clarifying questions such as,

"Is this a long-lasting conflict?"

"Is it a recent problem?"

"Was there a difference in beliefs?"

"Were you friends before?"

The mediator finishes this step by restating the problem.

Step 3: Focus on Interests

The mediator invites the disputants to identify what they want to happen so that the conflict will be resolved. The mediator tries to find common ground by asking questions to each participant, such as,

"What do you really want to happen?"

"Why?"

"What might happen if you don't reach an agreement?"

"Is fighting getting you what you really want?"

The mediator listens and summarizes the shared interests, states what the disputants have in common, and reflects on basic needs.

Step 4: Create Options

This step involves brainstorming possible solutions. The mediator asks disputants to work together to list as many ideas as possible to solve the conflict. The mediator explains that ideas are not to be evaluated at this step. The process is to generate a list of new possibilities. It is helpful for the mediator to list the ideas as they are generated. Each party is encouraged to make at least three suggestions. The mediator refrains from making suggestions so the disputants will "own" the solution as well as the problem.

Step 1 Open the session
Make introductions.
State the ground rules:
- Mediators remain neutral
- Everything said is confidential
- No interruptions
- Agree to solve the conflict

Get commitment to the ground rules.

Step 2 Gather information
Ask each person, "Please tell me what happened."
  (Listen and summarize.)
Ask each person, "Do you want to add anything?"
  (Listen, summarize, and clarify with questions.)
Repeat until the problem is understood. Summarize.

Step 3 Focus on interests
Determine interests; ask each person,
  "What do you really want?" "Why?"
  "What might happen if you don't reach an agreement?"
  "What do each of you have in common?"
  (Listen, summarize, and question.)
Summarize shared interests.
State what disputants have in common.

Step 4 Create options
Brainstorm solutions; ask disputants,
  "What could be done to resolve the problem?"

Step 5 Evaluate options and decide on a solution
Choose a solution; ask each person,
  "Which of these options are you willing to do?"
Restate: "You both agree to . . . "

Step 6 Write an agreement and close
Write an agreement and sign it.
Shake hands.

Figure 19.4. Sample Mediation Process Summary.

Step 5: Evaluate Options and Decide on a Solution

Solutions are evaluated in this step. The mediator asks each disputant which of the listed solutions are acceptable. Often, a disputant will say what he or she wants the *other* person to do. When this occurs, the mediator points out that the agreement states what each person is willing to do—not what the other person should do.

Agreed-on options should be mutually satisfactory to both parties because a balanced agreement is important for a lasting resolution. The solutions should be specific and realistic and include a time frame. Questions that the mediator may ask at this step are,

"Which option is most fair for both of you?"

"Does this help the interests of everyone involved?"

"Can it be done?"

"What will be the results?"

Step 6: Write an Agreement and Close

A mutual agreement is written using a Peer Agreement Form as shown in Figure 19.3. A written and signed agreement increases the disputants' commitment. In some cases, a written agreement might not be used if mediations are taking place on a playground. The agreement is signed by both disputants and the mediator. The mediator shakes hands with everyone and congratulates them for their efforts. Both parties are then asked to shake hands.

Of course, there are times when an agreement will not be reached. In such cases, an effort is made to get the parties to meet again the next day to continue. In the meantime, a truce to the conflict is called. If an impasse is reached, then it may be helpful to talk to each disputant separately. This is called *caucusing*, and the same ground rules apply as for the mediation. A caucus is confidential, so the disputant must agree whether what is discussed may be shared outside of the private session.

CONFLICT RESOLUTION IN ACTION

The following example shows how a peer mediator used the six-step process to cooperatively help two seventh-grade students reach an agreement. In this situation, James and Victor were engaged in a loud, threatening argument in the hallway. When a teacher referred them to Jack, a peer mediator, they both agreed to go.

Step 1: Open the Session

Mediator: Hello, my name is Jack, and I am the mediator assigned to hold this session. James and Victor, welcome to mediation. We are here to cooperate and find a solution to your conflict. We will talk and try to come up with something that works for both of you. Let me explain the ground rules. First, I remain neutral—I do not take sides. Everything said in the mediation is kept confidential. That means what is said in mediation is not discussed outside this room. Each person takes turns talking without interruption. You are expected to do your best to reach an agreement that satisfies both of you. James, do you agree to the rules?

James:	Yes.
Mediator:	Victor, do you agree to the rules?
Victor:	Yeah.

Step 2: Gather Information

Mediator:	James, can you tell me what happened?
James:	Victor and I were arguing in the hallway. I am mad at him because he borrowed my basketball during lunch yesterday. When he brought it into school, he was dribbling it in the hallway, and a teacher took it from him. Now, it's lost, and he says he can't get it back.
Mediator:	You're mad at Victor because he lost your basketball, and you want it back.
James:	That's right. He was responsible for the ball.
Mediator:	Victor, can you tell me what happened?
Victor:	It's true that I borrowed his basketball yesterday during lunch. We all like to shoot baskets after we eat. I was bringing the ball back to his locker after lunch when somebody hit the ball out of my hands and it bounced on the floor until Mr. Thomas picked it up. It wasn't my fault it was lost.
Mediator:	You borrowed the ball and when returning it, someone hit it from your hands. That's when Mr. Thomas took it.
Victor:	Yeah, and Mr. Thomas is very strict, and he says we won't get it until the end of the year.
Mediator:	James, do you have anything to add?
James:	That was a new ball, and I thought we were friends, but now he is just ignoring me.
Mediator:	So, you and Victor are friends, and you don't want to be ignored when there's a problem.
James:	Right.
Mediator:	Victor, do you have anything to add?
Victor:	I don't mean to ignore James, but I don't like to be yelled at in the hallways.
Mediator:	So, you are willing to talk to James to work this out?
Victor:	Sure.

Step 3: Focus on the Interests

Mediator:	James, what do you really want to happen here?
James:	I want my ball back.
Mediator:	Beyond your ball, is there anything else?
James:	Yeah, I want to be friends with Victor.

The conversation continues until it is clear that both boys want to be friends and that they both have a common interest (e.g., they want the ball back so they can use it at lunch). At first, the source of the conflict seems to be over a limited resource (the basketball); however, at closer look, it really is over trying to meet the basic psychological needs of "belonging" and "fun." When the mediator identifies this common ground, Step 3 is complete.

Step 4: Create Options

Mediator:	What are possible ways to solve the problem with the ball and keep your friendship?

Victor and James brainstormed a list that includes

- Both boys going to Mr. Thomas to explain what happened
- Both boys going to the principal to explain what happened
- Victor giving James his ball until school is out
- Victor giving Mr. Thomas his ball to hold until the end of the year
- James accepting an apology and forgetting the ball for *now*

Step 5: Evaluate Options and Decide on a Solution

Mediator: Which of these ideas will probably work best for you?
Victor and James both respond with ideas they believe are the best solutions to the conflict. The boys agree to talk first to Mr. Thomas. After their explanation, if he does not return the ball, Victor agrees to offer his ball to James.

Step 6: Write an Agreement and Close

The mediator writes an agreement to be as specific, realistic, and balanced as possible. The mediator signs it and shakes hands with both Victor and James. Finally, the mediator asks both boys to sign and to shake hands.

This process took about 20 minutes. The boys have made a plan and have not lost their friendship. The mediator has assisted with the plan, but it has really been generated by the two disputants, and the process has been cooperative and structured.

CULTURE AND CONFLICT

The American Heritage Dictionary defined culture as "the behavior patterns, arts, beliefs, and . . . thought characteristic of a community or population" (1985, p. 348). Thus, culture is the way of life of a given society or group. The most important aspects of a culture are its language, norms for behavior, and communication styles. Hall (1959) even considered culture and communication synonymous.

Myers and Filner (1997) identified the following cultural issues as significantly affecting conflict resolution: language use that can lead to misinterpretation, incorrect assumptions about diverse cultures, expectations that others will conform to our values, bias against the unfamiliar, and value conflicts. In terms of values, a number of differences can be identified that distinguish mainstream cultural values and behaviors from those of other cultures (see Table 19.2). The way in which conflicts are resolved is also different in different cultures—some use confrontation, whereas others solve their conflicts with the help of a (often more powerful) third party. Thus, when we do not understand these differences of language, rules, norms, and values when communicating with people from other cultures, it is normal that conflicts occur. When dealing with student conflicts, Woolner remarked,

> *The incident that brought the students into mediation may have been name-calling, pushing, stealing, or any of the usual precipitating events. But the underlying issues were bias, or prejudice, expressed as racism, classism, sexism, homophobia and ethnocentrism. (1990, p. 1)*

Table 19.2.   Cultural values and behaviors that may affect mediation

Mainstream America	Other cultures
The individual is valued; independence and decision making are important. Recognition for personal achievement is expected and honored.	The group's collective and cooperative interests are considered more important than the effort or recognition of the individual. Harmony influences communication.
Informality is the norm; almost everyone uses first names.	Permission is needed to use first names; some never use first names.
Mobility has become important. One must often leave family and friends for a new job and so must make new friends quickly.	A great number of the world's people have never left home; their friends are those they have known all their lives.
Each person is expected to have an opinion and express it freely.	Deference is given to people in power or authority.
Direct communication is expected; saying what's on your mind is important.	Directness and open criticism are considered offensive; intermediaries are often used.
Use of clear ground rules and written agreements is valued.	Oral traditions are valued as well as symbolic gestures.
Individuals have the right to challenge authority.	Great respect is given to authority, which is rarely challenged.
Emphasis is less on the past and more on the present and future.	There is reverence for the past, and the memory and examples of ancestors and heroes drive much of people's behavior.
There is forgiveness and admission of error.	Conflicts can be solved by restitution and payback.
People are measured by what they do to meet individual needs.	People are measured by family and origin and value family and group approval.
Materialism is paramount and power, money, and possessions are highly valued.	Greater emphasis is placed on spiritual issues.

Source: Myers and Filner (1997).

Training Mediators

Training mediators to help resolve conflicts across cultures involves more than teaching the steps of the mediation process. It means helping students actively engage in becoming aware of one's own cultural beliefs and values and recognizing that disputants may bring a different set of values to their conflict. Thus, training includes exercises and discussions about the students' self-knowledge; knowledge of the beliefs, lifestyles, and practices of others; and the development of a commitment to creating a peaceful and just school and community. The old saying, "If you want peace, work for justice," is a good reminder that peace requires relationships that are free of domination and oppression and a situation in which resources are distributed equitably.

Dealing with issues of bias, prejudice, and different values is a challenge and an opportunity for mediators. The challenge is to contribute to a world in which students learn to live together. The opportunity is to learn from each other and to appreciate each others' values, which can be enriching for everyone. The goal of mediation is not to change values but to explore them and encourage understanding and respect.

Differences in Communication Styles

Each mediation is affected by differences in verbal and nonverbal communications. Gender, class, and ethnic background affects initiative and fluency in verbal communication.

Students that speak English as a second language have a disadvantage over native English speakers and are often assumed to be less intelligent or may be seen as being unable to contribute ideas.

Differences in nonverbal communications are plenty and should be understood by mediators but not used to stereotype disputants because this could lead to inaccurate judgments. Aspects of nonverbal communication are eye contact, use of silence, shaking hands, emotional expression, personal space, and voice level. Eye contact for mainstream Americans is seen as paying attention and showing respect to the speaker. Avoiding eye contact is seen as disrespectful, uninterested, or defensive. However, in other cultures, eye contact is considered disrespectful, and avoiding eye contact honors the persons' right to privacy. The same is true with the use of silence, which in mainstream American understanding connotes passivity and unfriendliness. Yet, in many non-Caucasian cultures, the use of silence maintains privacy, gives people time to think, and is not uncomfortable. In the Caucasian culture, shaking hands connotes the closing of a deal or reaching a resolution in conflict. In other cultures, there may be taboos about shaking hands (e.g., women shaking hands with men). Firm handshakes are expected in Caucasian culture, whereas in other cultures a handshake is more gentle—just a touch, rather than a strong shake. Thus, a limp handshake may be interpreted as weak by people from a Caucasian culture, whereas a strong handshake may be interpreted as domineering by people from non-Caucasian cultures. In terms of emotional expression, some cultures value outward expression of feelings, whereas others teach people to be reserved and self-contained. In mainstream American culture, people feel comfortable with others at an arms' length for conversations, whereas in other cultures a much closer proximity, including touching, is comfortable.

In addition, raising one's voice is some cultures is seen as disrespectful and a sign of anger, whereas in other cultures, raising one's voice indicates animation and involvement in the conversation. It takes practice, sensitivity, and sometimes a request for clarification to unravel the meaning of nonverbal communications.

Special Concerns for Mediators

Student disputes in a multicultural school may involve not only conflicts about values but also conflicts about imbalances of status and privilege. The imbalances can be within groups (e.g., classism, sexism) and across groups (e.g., racism). The mediator must pay particular attention to helping the less advantaged person to get his or her needs met. This does not change the neutral stance of the mediator or the equal respect given to each disputant. It means flexibility on the part of the mediator and wisdom about how to influence the process.

Another issue is guilt versus shame. Caucasian students may feel personally guilty when they understand that they engaged in unacceptable or inappropriate behavior. They violated their conscience. Discussing the incident and taking responsibility for it relieves the individual from guilt and restores the relationship. In other cultures, inappropriate or unacceptable behavior reflects on the honor of their family and brings shame to all. Mediation, therefore, as a process of bringing the conflict to a third person, may solve the problem for the disputant but not satisfy the family. Other solutions that satisfy the family may be appropriate.

Finally, trust building, flexible interventions, and other methods that may help solve the conflict are special concerns for mediators. Trust building takes time and may take more time in a cross-cultural mediation because trust is promoted through positive interpersonal experiences and information. Mediating with a disputant with an "underdog" status, a person that has been bullied or ridiculed, a student with disabilities, a student who is gay or a lesbian, or a student who is an extreme loner may take more time for one or both disputants to open up, feel listened to, or trust that the process will be successful. Mediators may need to reinterpret resistance as a coping skill and as part of the process of trust building. Flexibility refers to understanding differences and being open, but it can also refer to using the mediation process and the steps flexibly. This may mean a more active involvement of the mediator. Some examples may be reminding parties that attacks or put-downs are counterproductive, clarifying misconceptions by giving information about cultural differences, interrupting intimidating behavior, reframing statements to prevent disputants from losing face, helping disputants to confront statements and behaviors and not the other person, and cultivating patience. Other methods to help solve the conflicts are caucusing and inviting others to the mediation process. *Caucusing* means that the mediator meets separately with each disputant, which may reduce anxiety when inequality may be a barrier for resolution. This method may be used to explain the process, ask questions, and discuss concerns in a nonthreatening environment. Caucusing may be repeated and may increase respect for the process and give disputants assurance that they are heard. Involvement of others may be an option for mediators when it is clear that personal or cultural barriers exist to a solution. Mediators can check with disputants if having another person present is desirable. If all agree, possible candidates include a friend, a school or nonschool support person, or a family member.

In conclusion, understanding how cultural differences—expressed as bias and prejudice against others "who are not like us"—affect mediation helps mediators to address these differences. Sensitivity to differences, including cultural differences, requires patience and enhances trust and understanding necessary for a successful mediation (Jansen, 1997).

PROGRAM EVALUATION AND EFFECTIVENESS

Peer mediation programs in schools have proliferated. Johnson and Johnson (1996) estimated that in 1994 there were 5,000–8,000 mediation programs, an increase from about 2,000 in 1992. Questions about effectiveness are critical not only because of sustained support for these programs but also to affirm the value of peacemaking for students and staff involved.

One early comprehensive study about conflict resolution in metropolitan schools deserves mentioning. Eight hundred students and 500 faculty members were interviewed in more than 60 junior high and high schools. The study concluded that both students and staff perceived that more than 90% of reported conflicts by students remained unresolved or were resolved destructively. Negotiation of conflicts hardly existed (DeCecco & Richards, 1974).

Schools that implement peer mediation programs show different figures. Early on, Schrumpf, Crawford, and Usadel (1991) described a peer mediation program in a middle school in Illinois with about 1,000 students (25% African American, 70% Caucasian, and 5% Asian) that collected data on conflicts to be mediated. During the 1989–1990 school year, 245 conflicts were resolved through peer mediation; approximately 51% were requested by students, 27% of referrals came from teachers, and 22% came from administrators. Caucasian student disputes were 47% of the total, disputes by African Americans accounted for 26%, and 27% of the disputes were between students of different races. The cause of conflict and their resolutions can be seen in Table 19.3.

Johnson and Johnson (1996) reviewed the available research on conflict resolution and peer mediation and from a variety of studies (Gottman, 1979; Johnson, Johnson, & Dudley, 1992; Laursen & Hartup, 1989) identified that untrained students and trained students differ significantly in how they resolve problems. Untrained students use withdrawal, suppression, force/coercion, intimidation, and win–lose negotiations. Yet, trained students face conflict; learn; retain and apply procedures; transfer the skills learned to nonschool,

Table 19.3. Annual evaluation summary

Cause of conflict	Percentage	Resolution
Name calling	26%	Resolved at a 98% success rate
Rumors	23%	Resolved at a 100% success rate
Hitting/fighting	16%	Resolved at a 100% success rate
Other (lost or damaged property, relationship problems, etc.)	35%	Resolved at a 93% success rate

The number of requests for mediation increased approximately 25% from the previous semester. Referrals from administrators almost doubled from the previous year. But, these figures suggest increased support for and perception of the effectiveness of the program.

From *Peer mediation: Conflict resolution in schools* (p. 98) by Schrumpf, F., Crawford, D., & Usadel, C. (1991). Champaign, IL: Research Press. Copyright © 1991 by Schrumpf, F. Crawford, D., & Usadel, C. Reprinted by permission.

nonclassroom conflicts; engage in problem solving; and use integrative (win-win) negotiations (Johnson & Johnson, 1996, p. 473). For instance, in one study, students reported on 209 school conflicts and 574 conflicts at home. Negotiation only was used once in the experimental group and never in the control group before training. After training, however, nearly 40% of conflicts in the experimental group were resolved in negotiations by seeking a win-win solution through a mutually acceptable agreement (Johnson & Johnson, 1996). Johnson and Johnson concluded that "there is evidence therefore that conflict resolution and peer mediation training results in students knowing the negotiation and mediation procedures, being able to use the procedures in actual conflicts"(p. 479). Peer mediation programs were reviewed by Johnson and Johnson and Crawford and Bodine (1996). Johnson and Johnson reported that success rates of mediated conflicts range from 80% (Burrell & Vogl, 1990) to 96% in an Ohio study (Ohio Commission on Dispute Resolution and Conflict Management, 1994) to 98% in the Schrumpf et al. (1991) study. Crawford and Bodine highlighted a number of evaluation studies, all showing positive outcomes. For instance, they reported a New York City study that saw a 45%–70% reduction in suspensions for fighting during the program's first year. A Palm Beach, Florida, example reported a reduction in the number of referrals and suspensions. The number of referrals at the school dropped from 124 between September and December 1992 to 5 during the same period in 1994. In yet another project, office referrals were reduced from 384 to 67, and suspensions for disruptive behavior were reduced from 52 to 9.

Results indicated a high success rate of peer mediation programs despite a needed caution. Johnson and Johnson (1996) noted that studies about conflict resolution/peer mediation in schools suffer from methodological problems. They stated that most studies do not use randomized samples, do not measure the same interventions, and often rely on self-reported data. Yet, with these problems in mind, they do confirm that there is little doubt that research indicates that peer mediation programs are effective in teaching students how to solve conflicts constructively, reducing the number of student–student conflicts that are taken to teachers and administrators, and thus, reducing suspensions.

REFERENCES

The American heritage dictionary, 2nd college edition. (1985). Boston: Houghton-Mifflin.

Bodine, R., Crawford, D., & Schrumpf, F. (1994). *Creating the peaceable school: A comprehensive program for teaching conflict resolution.* Champaign, IL: Research Press.

Burrell, N., & Vogl, S. (1990). Turf-side conflict mediation for students. *Mediation Quarterly,* 7, 237–250.

Carrier, J. (1999). *Ten ways to fight hate: A community response guide.* Montgomery, AL: The Southern Poverty Law Center.

Crawford, D., & Bodine, D. (1996). *Conflict resolution education: A guide to implementing programs in schools, youth-serving organizations, and community and juvenile justice settings.* Washington, DC: U.S. Department of Education & U.S. Department of Justice.

DeCecco, J., & Richards, A. (1974). *Growing pains: Uses of school conflict.* New York: Aberdeen Press.

Fisher, R., Ury, W., & Patton, B. (1991). *Getting to yes: Negotiating agreements without giving in.* New York: Penguin.

Glasser, W. (1986). *Control theory in the classroom.* New York: Harper and Row.

Glasser, W. (1990). *The quality school.* New York: Harper and Row.

Gottman, J. (1979). *Marital interactions: Experimental investigations.* San Diego: Academic Press.

Gregoire, C. (2000). *Bruised inside: What our children say about youth violence, what causes it, and what we need to do about it.* Washington, DC: National Association of Attorneys General.

Hall, E.T. (1959). *The silent language.* New York: Doubleday.

Jansen, G. (1997). Diversity and conflict resolution. In F. Schrumpf, D.K. Crawford, & R.J. Bodine (Eds.), *Peer mediation: Conflict resolution in schools* (Rev. ed.). Champaign, IL: Research Press.

Johnson, D.W., & Johnson, R. (1996, Winter). Conflict resolution and peer mediation programs in elementary and secondary schools: A review of the research. *Review of Educational Research, 66*(4) 459–506.

Johnson, D.W., Johnson, R., & Dudley, B. (1992). Effects of peer mediation training on elementary school students. *Mediation Quarterly, 10,* 89–99.

Johnson, D.W., Johnson, R., Dudley, B., & Burnett, R. (1992). Teaching students to be peer mediators. *Educational Leadership, 50*(1),10–13.

Jones, T.S. (1998, March/April). Research supports effectiveness of peer mediation. *The Fourth R, 82* 1, 10–12, 18, 21, 25, 27.

Kreidler, W. (1984). *Creative conflict resolution.* Glenview, IL: Scott, Foresman.

Kreidler, W. (1990). *Teaching concepts of peace and conflict.* Cambridge, MA: Educators for Social Responsibility.

Laursen, V., & Hartup, W. (1989). The dynamics of preschool children's conflicts. *Merrill-Palmer Quarterly, 35,* 281–297.

Myers, S., & Filner, B. (1997). *Conflict resolution across cultures: From talking it out to third party mediation.* Amherst, MA: Amherst Educational Publishing.

Ohio Commission on Dispute Resolution and Conflict Management. (1994). *Conflict management in schools: Sowing seeds for a safer society.* Columbus: Author.

Sadalla, G., Holmberg, M., & Halligan, J. (1990). *Conflict resolution: An elementary school curriculum.* San Francisco: Community Boards, Inc.

Schrumpf, F., Crawford, D., & Bodine, R.J. (1997). *Peer mediation: Conflict resolution in schools* (Rev. ed.). Champaign, IL: Research Press.

Schrumpf, F., Crawford, D., & Usadel, C. (1991). *Peer mediation: Conflict resolution in schools.* Champaign, IL: Research Press.

U.S. Department of Education. (1998). *Preventing youth hate crime: A manual for schools and communities.* Washington, DC: Author.

Woolner, C. (1990). *Rethinking mediation: Living peacefully in a multicultural world.* Amherst, MA: National Association of Mediation in Education.

20

One Divided By Two or More

Redefining the Role of a Cooperative Education Team

Richard A. Villa
Jacqueline S. Thousand

Cooperative group learning models are the most researched educational approach to promote heterogeneous student grouping (Johnson & Johnson, 1989; Slavin, 1989; see also Chapters 12 and 13 for research reviews). They are gaining increased popularity and acceptance as school personnel simultaneously recognize the need to 1) address students' social and interpersonal skill development, and 2) create heterogeneous school communities that reflect and prepare students for the "real world" of the 21st century—an ever-changing global community in which diversity (e.g., cultural, racial, ability, ethnic, language, economic) is the norm.

We devote a great deal of time to training administrators, classroom teachers, and support personnel (e.g., special educators, guidance personnel, speech-language specialists, compensatory education personnel) in cooperative learning methods. We have discovered that many school personnel who have a history of working in isolation (e.g., in "self-contained" general education or special class environments) are mystified by the idea of collaborating to educate a more diverse group of learners through interactive processes such as cooperative learning. They, as well as their students, are full of questions regarding the new role of partners in teaching and learning through cooperative structures.

The questions most frequently posed by special educators, who are accustomed to delivering student support primarily through "pull-out" services outside of the general education classroom, include the following:

- "What is my role versus the classroom teacher's role during cooperative learning experiences?"

- "Do I go into the general education classroom with the students I serve in order to support them in their cooperative learning groups?"

- "How do I ensure that the students I serve are successful members of cooperative learning groups in the general education environment?"

- "Do I sit with the students I support as a member of a student-learning group?"

- "Am I to interact with other students in the classroom?"

This chapter was simultaneously prepared for publication in this book and in Putnam, J.W. (Ed.). (1993). *Cooperative Learning and Strategies for Inclusion: Celebrating Diversity in the Classroom* (pp. 57–91). Baltimore: Paul H. Brookes Publishing Co., in which it appeared as "Redefining the role of the special educator and other support personnel." It appears here in slightly edited and revised format, by permission of the authors and publisher.

The questions often asked by classroom teachers are

- "How do I most effectively utilize a special education or other support person during cooperative group learning activities?"

- "What are the benefits of having another educator in the classroom?"

- "Who plans for and evaluates which students?"

- "How do the students I support fit into cooperative learning groups?"

Students most often inquire

- "Which one is my teacher?"

- "Whom do I ask for help?"

- "Whose rules and discipline procedures apply to me?"

- "If the special education teacher helps me, will people think that I'm a 'special education' student?"

- "Will both teachers want to talk so much that we won't have the time we need to work in our groups?"

All of the previous questions reflect the confusion of both educators and students regarding their roles when collaborative and cooperative teaching and learning arrangements are introduced to maximize student success.

A primary purpose of this chapter is to illustrate how classroom teachers and support personnel effectively share expertise and responsibility to promote not only the learning and collaborative skill development of their students but also their own professional and interpersonal growth. We first offer the rationale for professional partnership in the design and delivery of cooperative learning instruction and define a cooperative education team. Then, we offer strategies to reduce role confusion among classroom teachers and support personnel through teachers' systematic analyses and distributions of instructional responsibilities (i.e., planning, teaching, evaluating student performance). The chapter closes with examples of cooperative education teams in action and offers tips for optimizing team effectiveness.

WHY CREATE COOPERATIVE EDUCATION TEAMS?

Modeling What We Preach

Conventional wisdom suggests that a primary learning method for both children and adults is the observation of behaviors displayed by "role models." A critical teacher behavior, therefore, in preparing students for the cooperative workplace and society of the 21st century is to model cooperative teaching. With cooperative teaching, students learn through observation how two or more people coordinate instructional, behavior management, and student-evaluation activities. Although students who experience cooperative learning structures acquire the learnings through active participation in the cooperative learning experience, the adult modeling of the same behavior reinforces the message that cooperative behavior is a norm that extends beyond student life to adult life and lifelong success. Adult modeling increases the likelihood that students will value and cooperate with teachers to create a collaborative classroom culture.

Two Heads Are Better than One

Having worked extensively in public schools with classroom teachers and specialists who regularly partner with each other in instruction and who employ cooperative learning methods in their instructional routines, we have found that these educators experience creative thinking and problem-solving outcomes (Thousand & Villa, 2000) similar to those experienced by students who learn in heterogeneous cooperative groups (Johnson & Johnson, 1989). In particular, collaborating teachers are able to generate new conceptualizations and novel solutions to the daily challenges presented by a diverse student population through the synergistic processes of collective induction (i.e., inducing general principles together that no one could induce individually) and process gain (i.e., generating new ideas through group interaction that are not generated when people work alone).

A primary purpose of assembling a cooperative education team is to increase the potential for individualizing instruction while enabling all students to be educated with their peers. With multiple instructors, the teacher-to-student ratio is higher, which allows for more immediate and accurate diagnosis of and intervention in response to individual student's social and academic needs. Instructors also have a greater opportunity to capitalize on the diverse, unique, and specialized knowledge, skills, and instructional approaches of team members who have different training and experience backgrounds.

Professional Growth and Peer Support

What stereotypic responses are possible to the question, "What do general educators have to offer special educators and vice versa?" One response might be that general education teachers possess content mastery in any number of topical areas from reading and writing to the sciences, whereas special educators have knowledge of specific techniques for remediating or accelerating learning in basic skill areas, such as mathematics or reading. Another response might be that general educators have the experience and skill to manage large numbers of learners, whereas special educators have the skill to design individual behavior management plans and to teach social skills that enhance self-management and social acceptability within the classroom. Whatever the response, it is likely that educators will acknowledge that each person in the school community possesses unique talents and perspectives that, when pooled, create a richer learning environment for adults as well as for children. In other words, in cooperative education team arrangements, teachers may experience professional growth that cannot be attained in formal coursework.

Research on staff development highlights the importance of educators having frequent opportunities 1) to observe models of new instructional methods and 2) to receive coaching and feedback during their efforts to replicate and personalize the new technique (Showers, Joyce, & Bennett, 1987). Cooperative education teams are natural arrangements for modeling and processing to occur. Of course, "peer coaching" requires and promotes a high level of trust and mutual interdependence among cooperating teachers (Cummings, 1985, p. 1). Such an interdependent support system for obtaining feedback is necessary to ensure the integrity and continued improvement of teachers' use of cooperative learning and to sustain one another's interest in doing so (Johnson, Johnson, & Holubec, 1998). Johnson and Johnson (1998) supported the networking of cooperative education teams through a schoolwide professional support group to ensure long-term practice of cooperative methods. In this larger support group, teams may share ideas, lessons, and successes and may solve individual and mutual problems in using cooperative learning methods. They also can structure reciprocal observation and coaching opportunities to improve one another's competence in using cooperative learning procedures.

Support personnel such as special educators who provide technical assistance to several teachers are a very important resource for spreading cooperative learning throughout a school. By offering to teach other teachers' classes, they can model cooperative learning methods for both teachers and students. Support personnel also may "free up" other members of their cooperative education teams so they, too, may model in other classrooms.

WHAT IS A COOPERATIVE EDUCATION TEAM?

A cooperative education team is an instructional arrangement of two or more people in the school and greater community who share cooperative learning, planning, instructional, and evaluation responsibilities for the same students on a regular basis during an extended period of time. Teams may vary in size from two to six people. They should vary in composition as well, using any possible combination of support personnel (e.g., special educator, speech-language pathologist, guidance counselor, health professional); instructional assistant; student teacher; community volunteer (e.g., parent, member of a local "foster grandparent" program); teacher; and students themselves (Thousand & Villa, 1990).

Members of an effective cooperative education team practice the same critical elements that they structure for their student cooperative learning groups. Specifically, members 1) have frequent face-to-face interactions, 2) structure a positive "we are all in this together" sense of interdependence, 3) hold one another individually accountable for agreed-on responsibilities, 4) periodically assess and process their instructional and interpersonal effectiveness, and 5) practice small-group interpersonal skills.

Face-to-Face Interaction

Among the most often posed questions by newly formed cooperative education teams are those that have to do with time for face-to-face interactions. When and how often does the team meet? How much time, during or outside of school hours, will team meetings take? Of the support personnel (e.g., special educators, speech-language pathologists, Title 1 instructors, teaching assistants), who will be regular members of the team? When should other people who support students in the classroom (e.g., guidance counselors, health professionals, "outside" consultants, therapists) attend meetings? What means will members of the team use to communicate information quickly among themselves when a formal planning meeting is not scheduled (e.g., a communication log on the classroom teacher's desk, a bulletin board on the classroom computer, sticky notes stuck to the inside of a storage door in the classroom)?

Questions of face-to-face interaction involve team members discussing and collaboratively agreeing on answers. Time must be arranged for team members not only to plan cooperative lessons but also to evaluate the effectiveness of the lessons. The need for face-to-face interactions also affects team size. The literature on student cooperative learning arrangements suggests a maximum of five or six group members (Johnson et al., 1998). The same size limitations hold for adult teams to allow each team member adequate "air time" during meetings.

Positive Interdependence

In most North American schools, teachers, whether labeled general educators or special support personnel, generally are still expected to work alone, independent of one another. This expectation determines not only how teachers behave but also how they think about the students for whom they have assigned responsibilities. "These students ('general,' 'special') are mine and, therefore, my primary or sole responsibility." "Those students ('special,' not 'general') are not mine, and, therefore, of little instructional concern to me."

For cooperative education teams, positive interdependence changes this. Positive interdependence involves the recognition among team members that no one person can effectively address the diverse educational, social, and psychological needs of a heterogeneous group of students (i.e., "your students and mine"). It encourages members of the team to feel that they all are responsible for arranging for the learning of all their students through the pooling of their diverse skills and knowledge and material resources. The strategies teams may employ to create feelings of positive interdependence include 1) distributing and rotating "classroom leadership" and decision-making powers (i.e., the "who," "what," "where," "when," "why," and "how" of designing and delivering cooperative lessons) among all members of the team and 2) regularly celebrating team success in designing and conducting lessons (e.g., including "positive statements" as the first agenda item for all planning and evaluation meetings and sharing lesson outcomes with other teachers, parents, administrators, or the general community).

A cooperative education team does everything that a "normal" teacher would do except that now there are two or more people doing it. Or, as the title of this chapter suggests, one job is shared by two or more people. What is key here is the implicit recognition that numerous decisions about how the formerly separate "classroom leadership" responsibilities and powers of team members are redistributed and readjusted over time. Some of the questions team members must jointly answer are presented in Table 20.1. Tough decisions have to be made at times; yet, the professional and personal growth that may result from making such decisions is an invaluable outcome not easily achieved in public schools today.

Individual Accountability

Collaboration, as represented by a cooperative teaching team, has the potential to increase teachers' accountability. In a collaborative school, teachers monitor one another's perfor-

Table 20.1. Questions members of a cooperative learning teaching team must answer to distribute leadership responsibilities among team members

1. Who plans for the academic content of the lesson?
2. How will the lesson be presented and explained? Will one person teach the social skills; another the academic material; and other(s) assist in observing, intervening, and processing with student learning groups? Or, will all members share in the instruction, monitoring, and processing?
3. Who adapts the materials, instructional procedures, and performance expectations for individual students?
4. Who evaluates which students? Do team members collaborate in evaluating all students' performances, or is each team member primarily responsible for evaluating a group of students?
5. How is the paperwork for students eligible for special education managed?
6. Who decides on the intervention procedures for disruptive student behavior? Who carries out the procedures? How is consistency ensured?
7. How do team members arrange to share and enhance their skills? Do they observe one another and practice "peer coaching"?
8. Do team members rotate teaching and student monitoring and processing responsibilities? How often do these responsibilities rotate? How is the decision made to shift these responsibilities?
9. Who will have the authority to make on-the-spot adjustments in the lesson? How and when during the lesson will decision makers confer to agree upon needed adjustments?
10. Who communicates with parents and administrators?
11. How is the decision made to expand or contract the team membership?
12. How will an equitable balance of work and decision-making power be maintained among team members?

mance, set limits on one another's behavior, and take responsibility for helping their colleagues to improve. The natural consequence of structuring cooperative education teams is the introduction of additional "eyes" to the learning environment and opportunities for team members to observe and assess one another relative to their agreed-upon planning, teaching, monitoring, and evaluation activities.

There is no question that working as a team reduces the autonomy and freedom enjoyed by teachers when they function independently of one another, as in freestanding one-room schools housed under a single roof (Skrtic, 1991). However, a primary purpose of teaming structures is to maximize the instructional performance of each individual through the modeling, coaching, and feedback that teammates provide (Johnson & Johnson, 1998). The possible loss of freedom that teaming implies is balanced by the freedom of not being solely responsible for students' learning; the potential for power and survival in dealing with an increasingly diverse student population; and the sense of belonging as well as fun that accompanies successful, creative, shared problem solving (Glasser, 1998; Parnes, 1988, 1997).

Small-Group Social Skills

Just because two or more people call themselves a team is no guarantee that they will interact cooperatively. For an adult or student team to collaborate effectively, members must have knowledge of and use small-group interpersonal skills. Unfortunately, few teachers and support personnel who comprise cooperative education teams have had the same opportunity as their students to receive instruction and practice in small-group skills. As a consequence, newly formed teams will include people who were never before required to demonstrate collaborative skills.

The most effective teams are those that are able to maintain equity and parity in decision-making power among their members by arriving at decisions through a consensual (i.e., all members agree) rather than a democratic (i.e., the majority of votes wins) process. To behave in a consensual fashion, however, requires the acquisition and mastery of many small-group social skills; the mastery of these skills does not occur overnight. The four levels of skills that team members need to demonstrate for group growth to occur are 1) initial trust-building skills (forming skills); 2) communication and leadership skills that help to manage and organize team activities so that tasks are completed and relationships are maintained (i.e., functioning skills); 3) skills needed to stimulate creative problem solving and decision making and to create deeper comprehension of unfamiliar or confusing information (i.e., formulating skills); and 4) skills needed to manage controversy and conflict of opinions and interest, search for more information (e.g., obtain technical assistance outside the team), and stimulate revision and refinement of ideas (i.e., fermenting skills; Johnson & Johnson, 1998; Thousand & Villa, 2000).

Of course, small-group interpersonal skills can be learned by adults as well as children. Learning these skills is no different from learning any other skill. It requires opportunities for team members to 1) see the need for the skill, 2) learn how and when to use it, 3) practice using it, and 4) receive feedback on how well they used it (Johnson & Johnson, 1998). A major challenge for beginning cooperative education teams is how to acquire these small-group collaborative skills. One direct method is to arrange for training and guided practice as part of an ongoing in-service agenda. An indirect and natural method, one recommended by David and Roger Johnson (see Chapter 13), is for teachers simply to begin teaching social skills to students as part of cooperative learning lessons. In this way, teachers acquire the same skills as the students through the process of teaching, and they develop an understanding of the importance of these skills to any team's functioning. A third method is to structure, as a regular component of planning meetings, time for team members to process their instructional and interpersonal effectiveness.

Processing Team Effectiveness

As already noted, research on staff development highlights the importance of structuring frequent opportunities for teachers to process and receive feedback regarding the innovative practices they are attempting (Showers et al., 1987). This is particularly true for cooperative education teams in which members are likely to have had little previous experience in co-planning, co-teaching, or exercising small-group interpersonal skills. The final critical element for team success involves the regular structuring of time for team processing of instructional and interpersonal effectiveness and the setting of personal and group social growth goals. Outside observers (e.g., a colleague from another cooperative education team, a supervisor with knowledge and experience in cooperative learning, guidance personnel with knowledge of social skill and group development) may be invited to observe planning meetings or cooperative lessons and to share their observations as part of the team's professional development activities or as an intervention when the team is having trouble functioning.

HOW DO MEMBERS OF THE TEACHING TEAM PLAN, CONDUCT, AND EVALUATE COOPERATIVE LEARNING EXPERIENCES?

Cooperative learning may be incorporated into the culture of the classroom in three ways: 1) formal lessons and learning groups that are more structured and stay together until a task is done (e.g., a group of four completes a week-long science unit and ensures that all members master the assigned information); 2) informal learning groups that are transient and less structured (e.g., "Turn to your neighbor and share with one another your three learnings"); and 3) base groups in which students have long-term (e.g., semester- or year-long) responsibility for providing one another with peer support and long-term accountability (Johnson & Johnson, 1998).

Once a cooperative education team understands how to structure formal lessons cooperatively, the other two types of cooperative learning experiences can (and should) be added to the classroom. Clearly, formal cooperative lessons require the greatest degree of coordination and mutual decision making among members of the cooperative education team. Hence, this section addresses the roles and decisions required of members of a cooperative education team as they develop, teach, and evaluate formal cooperative learning experiences. Of course, what team members learn through these experiences will influence and better enable them to use informal learning groups and base groups.

The roles that members of a cooperative education team distribute among themselves involve strategies and decisions during the planning, conducting, and evaluating stages of a cooperative learning experience (Johnson & Johnson, 1998). In planning a lesson, the first team task is to agree upon and to specify clearly the academic and social skill objectives. The second is to make certain decisions regarding face-to-face interaction (which students will be in which groups, the size of each group, the arrangement of the room); how students will be made interdependent; how academic and social skills will be taught and monitored; and how feedback will be provided to individual students regarding task and social skill performance.

When conducting a formal lesson, one critical role of the cooperative education team is to clearly explain to students the task, the social skills, and the goal structure(s); that is, whether it is a cooperative, individualistic, and/or a competitive learning structure. Another is to monitor the effectiveness of the cooperative learning groups and to intervene to provide assistance in the task (e.g., answer questions, clarify or teach parts of the task) or to improve students' interpersonal and group skills. Two final roles of team members are to evaluate students' achievements and to process with students how well they collaborated with each other.

Evaluation continues following the lesson, with the team's further evaluation of students' performances and the team's self-evaluation of the integrity of the lesson's delivery, the effectiveness of the team's instruction, the team's ability to coordinate their actions and to work together, and the team's acquisition or refinement of skills through the teaming process. Evaluation results inform the team on how they may better design and carry out lessons.

Planning a Cooperative Lesson

Like all effective instruction, planning is the key to the successful delivery of a cooperative group lesson. Figure 20.1 details the diverse factors a cooperative education team must consider when constructing a formal lesson. The team must clearly specify the academic and social skill objectives and make a series of decisions regarding face-to-face interaction, the structuring of positive interdependence among students, social skill instruction and monitoring, and processing with students their task and social skill performance. A great number of these decisions further require the team to agree upon who will do what; for example, how the role of the teacher will be distributed among team members. The questions the team should consider when deciding how the role of teacher should be distributed among team members are presented in Table 20.1. The following additional questions relate to the individualization of instruction for students:

- Will there be different academic objectives, materials, or performance criteria for some learners? Who will select the objectives, measure student performance, and process with the students their performance?

- Will there be different social skill objectives or performance criteria for some learners? Who will select the objectives, measure student performance, and process with the students their performance?

- Will some students receive preteaching in academic or social skill areas? When will this preteaching occur? Who will conduct the instruction?

- Will differences in academic or social objectives be communicated to the class or the group to which the student belongs? When will this communication occur? Who will communicate the information? What is the rationale for communicating or not communicating this information? Is there an issue of confidentiality that should be addressed with families of students eligible for special education?

Creating Positive Interdependence Through a Structured Team Meeting Process　Like student cooperative learning experiences, planning meetings of a cooperative education team must be structured to promote a feeling of positive interdependence among team members (Thousand & Villa, 2000). Positive interdependence may be created through a division of labor during team meetings as well as during the delivery of a lesson. It is a "best practice" for team members to rotate, from one meeting to the next, different leadership roles that promote either the completion of work or the maintenance of relationships among members. With this structure, the team has as many leaders as members

Cooperative Group Lesson Plan

Lesson name:

Authors:

What is the content area?

What are the appropriate age levels for this lesson?

Academic objectives

1. What are the prerequisite skills for taking part in the lesson?

2. What are the academic objectives of this lesson? (Remember also to identify the social skills objective in the Establishing Social Skill Performance section.)

3. What, if any, are the modifications of objectives for learner(s) with special needs?

Face-to-face interaction decisions

1. What is the group size (2–6)?

2. Which students will be in which groups? (Assignments should ensure that groups are heterogeneous.)

3. How is the room arranged? (Draw a diagram.)

Structuring positive interdependence

Members get the messages: "We sink or swim together," "Do your work—we're counting on you," and "How can I help you to do better?"

1. How will you structure one group goal, a single product, or a shared outcome?

2. Will you structure a group reward (e.g., one group grade, dual grades for individual and group products, dual grades for academic and social skill performance, bonus points if preset criterion is exceeded, free time or privileges for meeting criterion)?

3. What student roles will be used to promote positive interdependence? (Define each role using the words you will use with the students.)

4. Will there be division of labor other than roles? Describe.

5. How will materials be arranged to promote positive interdependence (e.g., one set of materials, "jigsawing" of information or materials)?

(continued)

Figure 20.1. Elements of formal cooperative learning groups that team members need to consider when designing a lesson. (It may be helpful for readers to consult the model lesson plan section of this book, Chapters 21 and 23.)

Figure 20.1. *(continued)*

6. How else will positive interdependence be structured? (Optional)

   a. Will you structure intergroup (between group) cooperation? How?

   b. Will you structure intergroup (between group) competition in order to develop within group cohesion? How?

   c. Will you structure positive fantasy or identity interdependence (e.g., a fantasy mission, selecting a group name)? How?

Establishing social skill performance

1. What are the social skills for this lesson?

2. How will the need for each skill be communicated? Who will do this (e.g., after groups have worked for session(s), ask them to brainstorm the behaviors needed to help the group learn and work together well; tell students why the skill(s) is/are important; ask the students why the skill(s) is/are important)?

3. How will each social skill be explained? Who will do this (e.g., someone demonstrates the skill, explains each step of skill performance, and redemonstrates the skill; someone structures a role play of the skill for the whole class, explains each step of skill performance, and structures a second role play of the skill; a videotape is used to demonstrate and explain the skill)?

4. How will the social skill(s) be assigned to group members (e.g., assign the skill(s) generally to the groups so all group members are responsible for engaging in the social skill(s); assign the skill(s) to randomly selected students and rotate the skills around the group until all members have performed each skill several times; select target students who need coaching and special training and pretrain them in the skills)?

Social skill performance: Teacher monitoring and intervention

1. How will the groups be observed? Who will observe which groups (e.g., anecdotal observations and notes are made regarding specific examples of students demonstrating cooperative behaviors; a structured observation form is used and each group is observed for an equal amount of time; a structured observation form is used and only selected groups having trouble are observed)?

2. How will teachers give students feedback if the target social skills are being used (e.g., interrupt the group and compliment the group on the use of the skill; during processing time, compliment the group on the use of the skill; say nothing)?

3. How will teachers give students feedback if the target social skills are not being used (e.g., ask the members of the group what they have done so far to increase the use of the skills; ask the group what it will try next to increase skill use; suggest an action)?

4. What are likely problems in collaboration? What are interventions to avoid/remedy them? (Rules: When you feel like intervening, don't. If you must intervene, do it with a question, not an answer. Move away as soon as you can, even if it is only 3 feet.)

Social skill performance: Student monitoring

1. Will there be student observers?

2. What social skills will the student observers monitor?

3. Will the students observe one or more groups?

4. Will the students observe for the whole lesson?

5. How will student observers be selected?

6. How and when will student observers be trained? Who will train them?

7. How and when will student observers share their observations with group members?

Structuring individual accountability

How do teachers determine whether each student learned the material and contributed to the group effort and product (e.g., roam among groups and randomly question individuals; individually quiz all students; select one paper to represent the group)?

Setting the task

1. How will the academic task and criterion for success be explained? Who will do it?

2. How will the social skill(s) and criterion for success be explained? Who will do it?

(Always tell the students what the objectives are, give or solicit from the students reasons why it is important to learn this content or perform this task, be specific in your directions, and check for individual student's understanding.)

After the lesson: Closure and processing

1. Closure: How will students summarize what they have learned following the lesson (e.g., teachers randomly "beam" questions to individual students; the entire class gives a choral response or signal; students do a quick "5-minute write" in response to questions)?

2. How and when will students receive feedback on their academic performance? Who will assess which students and who will provide the feedback?

3. How will teachers' observations be shared? (As a general rule, share negative comments in private and positive comments in public and private.)

4. In addition to hearing observation reports from teacher and peer observers, how will students assess their individual and their group's success in using social skills?

and the message is communicated that no one person has the expertise, authority, or the material or information resources needed to accomplish the team's goals.

Numerous task (e.g., timekeeper, recorder) and relationship (e.g., observer, encourager) roles have been prescribed and defined by various authors (Glickman, Gordon, & Ross-Gordon, 1997; Johnson & Johnson 1998; Thousand & Villa, 2000). Exactly which roles a team decides to use during a meeting depends on the nature of the lesson being planned and the level of interpersonal skill development among team members. For example, when conflict and controversy are expected, there may be a need for a "conflict recognizer" to identify emerging conflicts and to signal the team to stop and assess whether the steps of conflict resolution should be initiated. A "harmonizer" role also may be needed to help to conciliate differences by looking for ways to reduce tension through humor and nonjudgmental explanations. A "praiser" role is important when a team has become negligent in regularly affirming the contributions of members. When team discussions become dominated by particular participants, the "equalizer" role can be activated. The equalizer encourages quiet members to participate and regulates the flow of communication by ensuring that all members have equal access to "air time."

Any social skill may be transformed into a role to be practiced by and rotated among team members. Two roles recently invented by school-based collaborative teams are the "but watcher" and "jargon buster" roles. The job of the "but watcher" is to help team members to defer judgment during creative idea-generating or problem-solving periods by monitoring and signaling a member's use of blocking, oppositional, or judgmental language, such as, "Yes, but that won't work because. . . ." A "jargon buster" has the job of signaling whenever a specialized term may not be understood. The jargon user then must define the term or use an analogous term that everyone knows. This role is very important for cooperative education teams that include special educators or other support personnel professionals who may use jargon to describe their work and ideas. The jargon-buster role prevents team members who are unfamiliar with particular terms from feeling intimidated or less than equal. It also establishes the norm that it is perfectly all right not to know something. Once team members are familiar with the meaning of jargon, the terms may be used by the group to enhance its efficiency and to promote a feeling of interdependence. A common language tends to increase communication and to build a team's sense of identity and spirit.

The team meeting worksheet, presented in Figure 20.2, has proven to be an effective outline for promoting accountability among team members with regard to meeting attendance and the equitable distribution of work during and after planning meetings (Thousand & Villa, 2000). The worksheet also ensures attention to the other elements of the collaborative teaming process (i.e., face-to-face interaction, positive interdependence, collaborative skill performance, processing).

The worksheet is a valuable guide at team meetings. In order to emphasize individual accountability for meeting attendance and face-to-face interaction, names of present, late, and absent members are recorded on the worksheet. Names of others who are not at the meeting but who need to be informed of team outcomes (e.g., extended team members who may be involved in subsequent lessons, administrators or other teachers in the school interested in cooperative groupings) also are noted; this alerts the team of who may need information regarding the outcomes of planning. Accountability for distributing leadership is prompted by the list of possible roles included on the worksheet and the indication that roles be assigned in advance of the next meeting. This ensures that the people in such roles (e.g., timekeeper, recorder) will bring with them the materials they need to carry out their roles. Advance role assignment also prompts team members to rotate roles from one meeting to the next.

Notice that the team is prompted to create the agenda for the next meeting before it disbands. If all members are alerted (at the meeting and through the minutes) to the date,

Team Meeting Worksheet

Persons Present	Absentees	Others Who Need to Know
(Note late arrivals)		

_____

_____

_____

_____

_____

_____

Roles:	This Meeting	Next Meeting

Timekeeper
Recorder
Equalizer
Other: _____
Other: _____

AGENDA

Items	Time Limit
1. Positive Comments	5 minutes
2.	
3.	
4.	
5. Processing (task and relationship)	5 minutes
6.	
7.	
8.	
9. Processing (task and relationship)	5 minutes

MINUTES OF OUTCOMES

Action Items:	Person(s) Responsible
1. Communicate outcomes to absent member and others who need to know by _____	
2.	
3.	
4.	
5.	

AGENDA BUILDING FOR NEXT MEETING

Date: _____   Time: _____   Location: _____

Expected Agenda Items:

1.
2.
3.
4.
5.

Figure 20.2. Worksheet for promoting effective team meetings. (From Thousand, J.S., & Villa, R.A. [2000]. Collaborative teams: A powerful tool in school restructuring. In R.A. Villa & J.S. Thousand [Eds.], *Restructuring for caring and effective education: Piecing the puzzle together* [2nd e p. 284]. Baltimore: Paul H. Brookes Publishing Co.; reprinted by permission.)

location, purpose, and time of the next meeting, then accountability is ensured. Also, people are motivated to participate in the next meeting; they take an interest in events and objectives that they have helped to formulate.

Examination of the agenda section of the worksheet in Figure 20.2 reveals that incorporated into all meetings are 1) time limits for each agenda item; 2) a time to celebrate the things that went well in the cooperative lessons just taught and other positive educationally related events experienced since the last meeting; and 3) a time, midway and at the end of the meeting, to process members' use of collaborative skills and their progress toward completion of the lesson. The empty numbered spaces listed on the agenda worksheet represent the actual content of each meeting—the subtasks that contribute to the team's achievement of its overall goals, including successful lesson design. Although the agenda proposed at the end of a meeting guides the construction of the actual agenda of the team's next planning meeting, it must be remembered that many events can occur between meetings. Consequently, the actual agenda items should be modified at the beginning of each meeting to reflect the intervening events.

Promoting Equity Through the Planning Process   The ultimate outcome of a planning meeting of a cooperative education team is the actual production of a cooperative lesson, which should be represented in some type of lesson plan format such as that already suggested in Figure 20.1. The minutes of outcomes section of the team meeting worksheet shown in Figure 20.2 is intended to prompt equitable distribution of other tasks that should be accomplished in preparation for teaching the lesson. Periodic review of minutes and lesson plans may help to monitor equity in work distribution. If such monitoring reveals that one or two team members regularly assume the majority of tasks, then it is a signal of problems with positive interdependence. Team members may be "free loading"—taking advantage of the group's size to avoid work. Some members' interest may be waning. Those doing most of the work may not trust others to carry out assignments. Inequity in the division of labor is an enemy of a team's sense of cohesion and requires the team to explore the causes and possible actions to re-establish balance (e.g., limiting the number of responsibilities for which a single person may volunteer).

We offer two final bits of advice regarding the planning of a cooperative lesson. First, plan together, face-to-face; do not attempt to "jigsaw" and separately design lesson components. Jigsaw planning inevitably results in duplications, omissions, and a less efficient, effective, enjoyable cooperative experience for students and teachers alike. Face-to-face interaction is as important for collaborating adults as it is for collaborating students. Second, take the time to identify problem situations that may arise (e.g., absent students, behavior challenges of individual students, confusion regarding complex directions, attempts to compete rather than cooperate) and, more important, detail approaches on which all team members can agree to prevent the situation from occurring or intervene so as to minimize teacher disruption of group work.

Conducting Cooperative Learning Lessons

Conducting a formal cooperative learning lesson involves the cooperative education team's joint adherence to its lesson plan. Conducting a lesson is not simply the delivery of instruction; it is a time to collect data on several levels and to make adjustments that improve the present and future lessons. During the lesson, designated members of the team provide students with a clear explanation of the academic content, the social skills, and the cooperative activities in which students are to engage. Team members monitor not only the effectiveness of the student learning groups but also their own effectiveness in coordinating actions to deliver the lesson as designed or to adjust the objectives, activities, or performance criteria during the lesson if student responses signal this need. Of course, making on-the-spot changes in the lesson requires the team to have a plan for making adjustments. At a minimum, this plan should identify who makes which adjustment decisions as well as how and when the decision makers will confer during the lesson and communicate the changes to the other team members participating in the delivery of the lesson.

During a cooperative group lesson, members of the cooperative education team are responsible for intervening to assist students with task or interpersonal issues and to evaluate and process with students their academic and social skill performance. They are also responsible for intervening to assist one another in performing their agreed-on roles in the lesson (e.g., providing prompts to a team member who forgets or makes an error with an important direction, action, or piece of information). The processing of their own performance evaluations may occur briefly at the end of the lesson and, most certainly, at the team's next planning meeting.

Teaching cooperative lessons on a regular, frequent basis has many benefits. Team members have the opportunity to observe colleagues' demonstrations of new or exemplary instructional approaches and to learn from their colleagues' models. The members also have the opportunity to be observed by trusted colleagues who jointly are acquiring knowledge and competence in using cooperative learning in the classroom. Peer coaching models, such as that offered by Carol Cummings (1985), provide a structure for teammates to refine their instructional skills by receiving specific constructive feedback. Finally, regular and frequent implementation of cooperative lessons builds a teaching team's cumulative history of successes—examples of strategies that have worked to address various challenges—as well as examples of less effective interventions, all of which inform the team of how to invent more successful future lessons. The cumulative history of successes also builds team confidence and cohesion, which, in turn, influences future success.

Multilevel Evaluation

If conducting a cooperative lesson is an opportunity for data collection, then evaluation is an opportunity to use data to improve student and teacher success with cooperative learning structures. Evaluation of student performance occurs during the lesson and continues following the lesson, with the "grading" of student outputs and processing of student social and academic behavior at subsequent planning meetings of the cooperative education team.

One of the first items on the agenda of any planning meeting that follows a cooperative lesson should be an evaluation of the team's performance; that is, an evaluation of the integrity of the lesson's delivery, the effectiveness of the team's instruction, the team members' ability to coordinate their actions and work together, and the team's acquisition or refinement of skills through the teaming process. Evaluation results inform the team of how future lessons may be better designed and conducted.

Table 20.2 offers a series of evaluation questions that cooperative education teams may wish to address in meetings. Of course, all the questions rely on observational data collected when the lesson was delivered. Questions that deal with the behavior of team members also require a high level of trust among teammates and skills in giving and receiving negative and positive feedback (Johnson & Johnson, 1998).

The Power of Reward Interdependence in Evaluation Self-reflection, self-evaluation, processing of successes and failures with others, and the evaluation of others' (student and adult) performances are all evaluative actions that promote professional growth among members of the cooperative education team, as well as improve cooperative learning experiences for students. When members of cooperative education teams are

Table 20.2. Sample evaluation questions for cooperative learning teaching teams to consider

Integrity of cooperative group learning lesson delivery

To what extent was the lesson delivered as designed? Did team members perform their designated roles? What could be done to improve members' role performance?

Did adjustments need to be made? Why? What was learned from making the adjustments?

To what extent were the critical elements of face-to-face interaction, positive interdependence, individual accountability, and social skill development and processing structured into the lesson?

To what extent was attention to academic and social skill objectives balanced?

To what extent did team members successfully anticipate problem areas and employ effective interventions? What are likely future problems and appropriate interventions?

Use of effective instructional methods

Were the academic and social skill objectives appropriate for the learners? What are appropriate objectives for the next lesson? How did or will team members provide additional guided practice or enrichment for those who need it?

Do certain individuals or groups of students require individualized objectives, materials, or performance criteria in the future? If so, what will be done to individualize and measure student success?

Did team members respond to students in a consistent manner?

Was the explanation of the objectives, process, and expected outcomes clear? How might it be improved in subsequent lessons?

How did the team check for students' understanding of the content and the cooperative group task? What are alternative ways of checking for understanding in future lessons.

Modeling of collaboration

How did the team members provide a model of effective collaboration for their students? How might the team provide an even more effective model of collaboration in future lessons?

Did team members fulfill their agreed-upon roles and responsibilities in the design, implementation, and evaluation of the lesson? What is each team member most proud of in designing, implementing, and evaluating the lesson?

Do team members feel that they equitably distributed responsibility for instructing, monitoring, and evaluating the performance of all of the students in the class?

Skill acquisition

What did each team member learn from watching his or her colleague teach?

Do team members want to set individual professional growth objectives for the next lesson? How do team members want their colleagues to support them to monitor and attain the objectives?

Team membership

Does the team need additional expertise? What resources exist to provide training, modeling, coaching, and feedback?

Is it time for the team to expand or dissolve? If so, for what purpose?

---

evaluating and providing feedback to one another, it is especially important for them to remember to structure reward interdependence; that is, shared rewards and celebrations for the team's collective work. Reward interdependence means that the recognition of one member's contributions does not overshadow the equally important, but possibly less visible, contributions of another. A norm within effective collaborative education teams is that successes are celebrated collectively—no one person receives special recognition. As a result, when goals are achieved, all members share in the gratification of having contributed to the achievement. A responsibility of cooperative education teams and of the administrators that support their work is to jointly explore and identify what it is that team members view as a reward or incentive for continued collaboration. At a minimum, teams should structure celebration time into every meeting's agenda (see Figure 20.2). During this time, each member shares at least one positive statement about cooperative lesson-related activities, the students, or other professional accomplishments.

It must be remembered that responsibility comes with joint rewards. There will be times when a lesson goes poorly, a student presents an unexpected exceptional challenge, and things, in general, do not work out as hoped. Teams that swim together also must sink together. When a team faces disappointments or failures, it is the collective "we" and not a single person who accepts responsibility.

CASE STUDIES: EXEMPLIFYING TEACHER ROLES AND DECISIONS

The following are three examples of cooperative education teams in action. Each is a composite of the actual experiences of a number of cooperative education teams functioning in Vermont schools. The descriptions are intended to illustrate the diversity among teams in terms of composition, size, and the way in which they handle the critical elements of cooperative learning structures.

An Elementary Language Arts Team

In a school committed to providing children with heterogeneous learning opportunities, a 15-year veteran teacher of the fourth grade and a novice special educator collaborated to meet the needs of all of the students placed in the fourth-grade classroom. Fourth graders who were eligible for special education or other special services received their support within this general education classroom.

The two teachers differed tremendously in training background and experiences. In the past, the fourth-grade teacher relied primarily on a basal series to teach her students to read; the special educator was trained to deliver instruction in phonics to individuals or small groups of learners. One commonality was mutual interest in cooperative learning. The fourth-grade teacher had recently completed a course in cooperative learning and the special educator had had experience with cooperative groups in his graduate training program. This team decided to use cooperative learning groups in two areas of reading: drill and practice in sound–symbol relations and answering comprehension questions about passages in the basal reading text. They met at least twice a week to plan and every day they co-instructed during the 45-minute reading block.

From the start, the two teachers shared responsibility for selecting objectives and materials. Every lesson included a review of phonetic skills and a set of comprehension questions for student groups to answer. During the first marking period, the fourth-grade teacher assumed primary responsibility for the lesson design. She presented the task to the students while the special educator assisted in monitoring student progress in social skill acquisition. The classroom teacher collected anecdotal data for four student groups; the special educator collected data for three groups. Both teachers provided students with feedback regarding their use of collaborative skills. The classroom teacher graded all the papers and provided feedback regarding academic performance to the students and their parents.

During the second marking period, the special educator took on a more active role and co-designed lessons with the classroom teacher. On occasion, he also explained the task and social skill objectives to the students. By the third marking period, the classroom teacher and the special educator were rotating roles and responsibilities on a daily basis. One explained the objectives, the task, and the expected outcomes, while the other assumed primary responsibility for monitoring and processing individual and group performance of the desired social skills. They also took equal responsibility for grading student products, meeting with parents during parent–teacher conferences, and providing one another with feedback regarding their instruction.

Both teachers found this partnership professionally valuable and stimulating. In an effort to further refine their skills and meet student needs, they decided to expand the membership of their cooperative education team. They invited a Title I teacher, who had expertise in alternative strategies for teaching reading and the development of thematic units, to team teach with them and to attend their Tuesday and Thursday planning meetings. The original two-member team believed the Title I teacher could help them to develop interdisciplinary units, motivate the students, and breathe new life into the team. The Title I teacher accepted because she wanted to learn cooperative group instructional methodology so she could meet the needs of her students through a classroom rather than a pull-out service delivery model. She also welcomed the opportunity to develop a closer professional relationship with her colleagues. Two years later, all three instructors continue to meet twice weekly for planning and to team up to deliver language arts instruction a minimum of 4 days per week.

A Middle School Social Studies Team

A sixth-grade social studies teacher and a special educator have worked as a cooperative education team for 4 years. They team teach a minimum of 3 days a week. This team does not have a set meeting time for planning; instead, they mutually decide, from week to week, when and where they will conduct the next planning meeting. Neither team member has had "formal" training in cooperative group learning, but both have had the opportunity to team teach extensively with other school personnel who are considered outstanding in the design and delivery of cooperative group learning experiences. In addition, both team members have had training in effective instruction and collaborative teaming (Thousand & Villa, 2000). They try to employ the principles of cooperative teaming when they meet to plan cooperative learning lessons.

This team chose to split academic and social instructional responsibilities. Because of his knowledge of social studies content and his enthusiasm for the subject matter, the classroom teacher determined and explained the academic objectives. The special educator, who is familiar with various social skills curricula and is experienced in facilitating social skills groups for middle-level students, determined and explained the social skill objectives. Both teachers monitored student progress and intervened to teach academic and social skills. The classroom teacher made sure that students summarized their learning daily, whereas the special educator guided the processing related to the cooperative skill objectives.

The members of this team recently decided to take a cooperative learning summer graduate course together and to invite colleagues with more experience and expertise in cooperative group learning to observe and provide them with feedback at least once each marking period.

A Secondary School Science Team

A high school science teacher, who relied primarily on whole-group instruction and lab activities to teach homogeneous groups of high-ability students, decided to try cooperative learning structures. She stated two reasons for taking this new instructional approach. First, she had received strong written negative feedback from her department chair about her continued failure to use a variety of instructional approaches. Second, the school board had adopted a policy that virtually eliminated homogeneous grouping and tracking from the high school. The teacher recognized that soon the composition of her classes would be more diverse and that new instructional strategies, such as cooperative group learning, might enable her to better meet her students' needs and to please her supervisors.

During the previous year, the science teacher had overheard several teachers in the lounge commenting on how a special educator (referred to as a collaborating teacher in this school system) with expertise in speech and language had assisted them to acquire or refine their cooperative learning instructional skills. The science teacher thought that this collaborating teacher had a great sense of humor and might be an enjoyable work partner. The science teacher approached the collaborating teacher with an invitation to form a cooperative education team for the class period prior to lunch. The invitation was quickly accepted. The collaborating teacher saw it as an opportunity to acquire content knowledge that would assist him in working with students who are eligible for speech-language services and who struggled with the vocabulary and content of the science classes.

The science teacher (with her expertise in science) and the collaborating teacher (with his expertise in cooperative learning, verbal and nonverbal communication, effective instruction, and individualizing and adapting instruction) formed a cooperative education team. During the first year, they had numerous differences in educational philosophy and approaches to teaching and classroom management. Initially, the collaborating teacher reported feeling more like a teaching assistant than a teacher during the actual instructional period. In retrospect, he identified the primary source of those feelings as his lack of content mastery during the first year of the team relationship. The science teacher noted that she felt very dependent on the collaborating teacher for the design and presentation of the cooperative learning segments of lessons. She also stated that without the skill and patience of the collaborating teacher, she would have given up using cooperative learning structures.

The science teacher readily acknowledges the many skills she has acquired to design more active student-learning experiences and to accommodate student differences. The collaborating teacher points to the science content he has acquired and the skills in conflict resolution that were refined as he and his teammate developed a classroom management system that was mutually acceptable. Interestingly, both acknowledged that discipline problems diminished when the students were trained in how to work as a member of a cooperative learning group and given more responsibility for their own and one another's acquisition of academic and social skills.

During the second year of the team relationship, a student with Down syndrome enrolled in the team's "college-level" biology course. She provided the team with the opportunity to refine skills in designing group-learning experiences in which student objectives are individualized. The team wanted this learner both to contribute meaningfully to group activities and to achieve her individualized education program (IEP) objectives. They decided on several strategies. First, they decided to use a peer tutor to preteach some of the science content to the young woman during her study hall. The science teacher recruited a former student who had demonstrated mastery in the science content of this class as the peer tutor. The collaborating teacher provided initial and ongoing training, support, and evaluative feedback to the peer tutor. Second, they frequently assigned to the student with Down syndrome the role of timekeeper in her group, thus addressing the time-telling and time-keeping needs identified in her IEP. Third, they reduced the amount of content for which this student was held accountable. Fourth, with the permission of the young woman and her parents, the members of her cooperative groups assisted her and her teachers to determine appropriate instructional and social skill objectives, accommodations, and modifications.

The members of this cooperative education team expressed confidence in their ability to design exciting and appropriate group-learning experiences. Both are involved in planning the transition of a young man with multiple disabilities to their school. The science teacher has requested that this young man be placed in one of her classes and, with her collaborating teacher teammate, has begun designing cooperative group science lessons to address his IEP goals for increased vocalization, communication board use, and age-appropriate social interactions, along with the academic and social skills objectives of the other students in the science class.

DISCUSSION AND ADVICE

We have described how classroom teachers and support personnel can effectively share expertise and responsibility for designing, conducting, and evaluating cooperative learning experiences and, in this way, personalizing curriculum and instruction for students who, by nature, are unique and have variable needs. As the case studies illustrate, teaching need not be a "lonely profession" (Sarason, Levine, Godenberg, Cherlin, & Bennet, 1966, p. 74), and the traditional pull-out and special class arrangements of compensatory and special education need not be the solution to the challenges of increasing adult-to-student ratios, individualizing instruction, and accommodating student differences. When members of the school community work together to foster the academic and collaborative skill development of students, they offer the students a valuable model of collaboration in action as well as provide opportunities for their own professional and interpersonal growth.

It is important to remember that it may take a cooperative education team some time to become as effective and efficient as it would like. Teams evolve through the forming, functioning, formulating, and fermenting stages of group development, particularly if their members regularly examine the role clarification questions in Table 20.1 and the evaluation questions in Table 20.2 and if they process how well they perform small-group social skills. Numerous teams also report that the agenda format presented in Figure 20.2 is most helpful in alerting them to the critical elements of an effective team (i.e., frequent face-to-face interaction, positive interdependence, individual accountability, social skill performance, periodic assessment, processing instructional and interpersonal effectiveness).

The task of educating an increasingly diverse student population can be overwhelming. No one teacher is capable of successfully meeting this challenge alone. We propose that collaboration among students (through cooperative learning structures) and adults (through cooperative education teams) is a key to meeting the challenge of educating a heterogeneous student population. We are pleased to report that students now have joined adults as partners in cooperative education teams and have proven to be creative resources in formulating objectives, instructional methods, and accommodations for individual students. When the work of the traditional teacher is divided between two or more people, both teachers and students should more fully experience the power of being able to meet increasingly diverse educational and psychological student needs, to free themselves from isolation and the sole responsibility for student learning, and to experience the fun and feeling of belonging that result when people reinvent education together.

REFERENCES

Cummings, C. (1985). *Peering in on peers.* Edmonds, WA: Snohomish.

Glasser, W. (1998). *Control theory in the classroom* (Rev. ed.). New York: Perennial.

Glickman, C.D., Gordon, S., & Ross-Gordon, J. (1997). *Supervision of instruction: A developmental approach* (4th ed.). Needham Heights, MA: Allyn & Bacon.

Johnson, D.W., & Johnson, R.T. (1989). *Cooperation and competition: Theory and research.* Edina, MN: Interaction Book Company.

Johnson, D.W., & Johnson, R.T. (1998). *Learning together and alone: Cooperation, competition, and individualization* (5th ed.). Upper Saddle River, NJ: Prentice-Hall.

Johnson, D.W., Johnson, R.T., & Holubec, E. (1998). *Circles of learning* (2nd ed.). Arlington, VA: Association for Supervision and Curriculum Development.

Parnes, S.J. (1988). *Visionizing: State-of-the-art process for encouraging innovative excellence.* East Aurora, NY: D.O.K. Publishers.

Parnes, S.J. (1997). *Optimize the magic of your mind.* Buffalo, NY: Creative Education Foundation Press.

Sarason, S., Levine, M., Godenberg, I., Cherlin, D., & Bennet, E. (1966). *Psychology in community settings: Clinical, educational, vocational, and social aspects.* New York: John Wiley & Sons.

Showers, B., Joyce, B., & Bennett, B. (1987). Synthesis of research on staff development: A framework for future study and a state-of-the-art analysis. *Educational Leadership, 45*(3), 77–87.

Skrtic, T. (1991). *Behind special education: A critical analysis of professional culture and school organization.* Denver: Love Publishing.

Slavin, R.E. (1989). Research on cooperative learning: Consensus and controversy. *Educational Leadership, 47*(4), 52–54.

Thousand, J.S., & Villa, R.A. (1990). Sharing expertise and responsibilities through teaching teams. In W. Stainback & S. Stainback (Eds.), *Support networks for inclusive schooling: Interdependent integrated education* (pp. 151–166). Baltimore: Paul H. Brookes Publishing Co.

Thousand, J.S., & Villa, R.A. (2000). Collaborative teams: A powerful tool in school restructuring. In R.P. Villa, & J.S. Thousand (Eds.), *Restructuring for caring and effective education: Piecing the puzzle together* (2nd ed., pp. 254–291). Baltimore: Paul H. Brookes Publishing Co.

Cooperative Group Lesson Plans

Ann I. Nevin
Jacqueline S. Thousand
Richard A. Villa

Creative cooperative group lesson plans can be used to teach students at the preschool, primary, upper elementary, middle, junior, or senior high school levels as well as within in-service education workshops. Cooperative group learning models are the most researched educational approach to promote heterogeneous student grouping (see Chapters 11 through 14). They are gaining popularity and acceptance as school personnel simultaneously recognize the need to 1) address students' social and interpersonal skill development and 2) create heterogeneous school communities that reflect and prepare students for the "real world" of the 21st century where diversity (e.g., cultural, racial, ability, ethnic, sexual preference, language, economic) is the norm.

Administrators, classroom teachers, and support personnel (e.g., special educators, guidance personnel, speech-language pathologists, compensatory education personnel) are becoming more and more knowledgeable in cooperative learning methods. Parents of students with disabilities are becoming better equipped to advocate for cooperative group learning methods when their children are included in the general education classroom.

Many school personnel who have a history of working in isolation (e.g., in self-contained general or special environments) are mystified by the idea of collaborating to educate a more diverse group of learners through interactive processes. Cooperative group learning provides a viable, step-by-step option for teachers, parents, and students to explore and expand their academic and social-emotional growth.

Cooperative group learning lesson plans appeal to teachers, parents, advocates, and administrators who want to meet the needs of their multicultural and ethnically and linguistically diverse learners without mislabeling them as students with disabilities. Many researchers and practitioners in the area of bilingual education and teaching English as a second language (ESL) have identified cooperative group learning as "best practice" that results in increased English language proficiency. For example, Walter (1998) suggested that cooperative group learning provides a way for teachers to use specific ESL strategies such as focusing on academic content, scaffolding of English language objectives with academic standards, and enabling peer support strategies to strengthen both expressive language and comprehension.

In this chapter, cooperative group lesson plans representing preschool, primary, upper elementary, middle, high school, and adult levels are featured. The lesson plans follow the format described in Chapter 20 of this book. A variety of grade levels and curriculum areas (e.g., science, mathematics, language arts, oral expression) are featured. The lesson plans emphasize how general and special education teachers have adapted their instruction to meet the unique needs of students with varying abilities (e.g., learning disabilities, gifts and talents, emotional challenges, mild–moderate special education needs, learning ESL).

In addition, there are two lesson plans that introduce cooperative learning methods to middle school teachers and other adult learners (e.g., teachers and parents participating in in-service education programs). The story behind the creation of each lesson plan is provided, followed by an anecdote describing the results of implementing the lesson. The essential elements of cooperative learning lessons are marked with an asterisk (*). At the end of each lesson, the teacher checks that these essential elements were included in the lesson. Readers have permission to photocopy the lesson plans in this chapter for educational purposes. The range and variety of the lessons are illustrated by their titles:

1. Elementary Science for a Student with Visual Impairments, by M.K. Monley

2. Upper Elementary Mathematics for a Student Who Is Gifted and Talented (and Has Challenging Interpersonal Behaviors), by C. Conn-Powers

3. "The Universe Holds Many Mysteries" Lesson for Students with Language Learning Disabilities and Learning English as a Second Language, by A.M.L. Quiocho

4. Introducing Middle School Students to Cooperative Learning Groups: The Fishbowl Technique, by R.A. Villa and J.S. Thousand

5. Junior High School Language Arts for a Student with Behavior Disorders, by C. Conn-Powers

6. Non-violence: Another Response to War for a Student with Emotional and Learning Disabilities and for Classmates Learning English as a Second Language, by D. Barton and N. Cardosa

7. Introducing Adults to Cooperative Learning as a Strategy for Integrating Students with Disabilities, by J.S. Thousand

REFERENCE

Walter, T. (1998). *Amazing English!* New York: Addison-Wesley.

Elementary Science for a Student with Visual Impairments

Lesson name: Fruit seeds
Grade level: Preschool to second grade
Time: 40 minutes

Author: M.K. Monley
Content area: Science

Monley (1989), an educational specialist intern, worked with a primary school teacher to adapt a regularly scheduled science lesson for a learner with visual impairments who had no oral language and no formal means of communication.

ACADEMIC OBJECTIVES ••••••••••••••••••••••••••••••••••••

What are the prerequisite skills?	Object identification (naming fruits); concepts of "same," "different," and "seed"
What are the academic objectives?	Students learn that different fruits have different kinds of seeds. Students describe and/or compare the seeds by color, size, shape, and number.
How do students demonstrate the academic objectives?	Students demonstrate these objectives by saying and doing the following: When handling a specific fruit, the students say, "This (fruit name) has (number) seeds that look like (shape) and are (color name) and that is similar to/different from this (fruit name), which has (number) seeds that look like (shape) and are (color name)."
What are the criteria for success?	Students are successful if they include at least three fruits and draw shapes that accurately portray the number, size, and shape of the relevant seed(s).
What are the modifications for learner(s) with special education needs?	J. has a visual impairment, is nonverbal, and has no formal means of communication yet. J. explores the different fruits tactually. J. listens to a description of each fruit so as to increase his receptive understanding of these objects. Say, "J., you're holding a banana. It is long and has a peel." Peel it together, feel the peel, and talk about it (e.g., "On the inside, it is squishy").
How does a learner with special education needs demonstrate the academic objectives?	J. demonstrates these objectives by saying and doing the following: When touching a fruit, J. moves it from hand to hand. When explanations are given, J. is "ear-oriented" to the speaker and demonstrates receptive language by following directions (e.g., when asked to touch the peel, J. touches the peel).
What are the criteria for success for the learner with special needs?	J. is successful if he explores each fruit both independently and with guidance and sits with the group during the entire lesson.

FACE-TO-FACE INTERACTION DECISIONS* ••••••••••••••••••

What is the group size?	There are 18 students in the class—six groups of three children.
How are students assigned to groups?	To ensure heterogeneity, students are assigned to groups randomly by counting backward from 6 ("6–5–4–3–2–1") with all the "6s" working as a group, all the "5s" working as a group, and so forth.
What is the room arrangement?	The room is arranged so that cut-outs of numbers 1–6 hang from the ceiling. Students move their desks to the area that matches their numbers and then arrange themselves so that they are facing each other.

STRUCTURING POSITIVE INTERDEPENDENCE* ••••••••••••

	Members get the messages: "We sink or swim together," "Do your work—we're counting on you," and, "How can I help you to do better?"
What is the structure—a single product, one group goal, or a shared outcome?	There is one collage per group (six for the class). The teacher explains to the group, "Your poster will have at least three fruit and seed drawings (one for each group member). You decide and agree among yourselves who will draw which fruit and seeds. There will be only one poster and one set of crayons so you will have to decide and agree on how you want to manage the drawing. Your group will have only one fruit at a time and will have to pass the fruit to another group, who will give you theirs, and so forth so that everyone gets a chance to look at all the fruits. So, what should your poster look like?" (Check for understanding by having a student paraphrase.)
Is a group reward structured?	Groups that create posters that meet criteria and whose group members can tell about the color, shape, size, and number of seeds receive a colorful sticker for each member of the group.
Are student roles assigned?	No.
What are the other divisions of labor besides roles?	This emerges as the group decides how they will draw their fruits and seeds.
How are materials arranged?	To promote positive interdependence among all groups, various fruits (apples, pears, bananas, oranges, melons, cherries, grapes) are rotated among the groups. Poster-size paper (six pieces, one per group) and crayons (six containers, one per group) are distributed.
Optional: *What other ways are used to promote positive interdependence—intergroup cooperation, intergroup competition, positive fantasy mission, or identity interdependence (e.g., group name)?*	In this lesson, intergroup cooperation is structured by rotating the fruits among the groups, and at the end, everyone makes a fruit salad by cutting up all the fruit.

ESTABLISHING SOCIAL SKILL PERFORMANCE* •••••••••••

What are the social skills objectives?	Using "smiley faces" and "smiley face words," students demonstrate the social skill of giving encouragement by smiling when group members contribute and by saying encouraging statements, such as "Good job!" "Good idea!" or, "The tiny oval seed you drew for an apple looks like it's real!" The social skill for J. is to sit with his group during the lesson.
How is the need for each social skill communicated?	Ask students what happens when they hear words such as "Good job," "Good idea," or "You're right on!" (Acknowledge students' responses—they might say they feel happy inside, they want to work more—or elicit ideas from them; for example, "Do you think you'll feel like talking more if you hear "Good idea!" than if you hear "Your idea is wrong"?) Say, "That's why we'll be practicing smiley faces and smiley face words while you make your posters."
How are social skills explained, demonstrated, role-played, or practiced?	Ask students to volunteer how they sound and what their faces look like when they make smiley faces and say smiley face words. Praise appropriate demonstrations and give corrective feedback until the students get the idea.
How are social skills assigned to group members?	All group members are responsible for demonstrating the smiley faces and smiley face words.

SOCIAL SKILL PERFORMANCE ••••••••••••••••••••••••••••
Teacher Monitoring and Intervention*

What is the process (how and who) for monitoring groups?	The teacher visits each group to observe and monitor group interactions—approximately 1 minute per group at least three times during the lesson.
What is the process for feedback (how and who) to groups if social skills are being used?	The teacher shares "on the spot" that the group is doing a great job with smiley faces and smiley face words.
What is the process for feedback (how and who) to groups if social skills are not being used?	The teacher asks the group, "What does it look like and sound like to practice smiley faces and smiley face words? I'll come back in a few minutes, and I expect to hear and see you, okay?"
What collaboration problems are anticipated?	Arguments about who will draw; one person doing all the drawing
What are interventions to avoid or remedy the anticipated problems?	*Rules:* When you feel like intervening, don't. If you must intervene, then do it with questions, not answers. Move away as soon as you can, even if it is only 3 feet. Remind the group that arguing is okay as long as smiley faces and smiley face words are being used. Ask how the others feel if one person does all the work (e.g., "Does it feel fair?" "What can you do to share the work?").

SOCIAL SKILL PERFORMANCE ······························
Student Monitoring

What is the student observer selection and training process (what and who)?	Students are asked to monitor their own use of smiley faces and smiley face words.
How are social skills monitored?	The frequency of smiley faces and smiley face words is monitored by the teacher via tally marks by the names of children in each group.
Do students observe more than one group?	No.
Do students observe for an entire lesson?	Yes.
How and when do students share their observations?	As the teacher listens to each group, he or she can "catch the students" engaging in smiley faces and smiley face words and ask them to share. Also, at the end, during the processing, the teacher can randomly select a student from one or two groups to share their examples of smiley faces and smiley face words.

STRUCTURING INDIVIDUAL ACCOUNTABILITY* ············

Are individual quizzes assigned?	No.
Is there a random selection of group members to answer questions?	For social skills practice, students are randomly selected to share their examples of smiley faces and smiley face words.

SETTING THE TASK ································

What is the process for explanation of the academic task and criteria for success (when and who)?	"Today you'll work in groups to learn more about these fruits. As a class, please name each of these fruits as I hold them up. Your job is to find out all you can about the seeds inside the fruits. You'll want to look at how they are the same and how they are different. You'll need to look carefully at the size of the different seeds. What size are they—big, little, or tiny? What color are they—red, brown, or green? What shape are they—round or oval? How many are there—only one, a few, or a lot? Each of you should draw a different fruit and its seeds on the poster paper. Then share with the class what part of the poster your buddy drew. You'll tell the class what you found out about the seeds—color, size, shape, and number. If each of you can do this, your poster will receive a sticker!"

How are social skills and criteria for success explained (when and who)?

Just before the students begin their poster preparation, the teacher explains smiley faces and smiley face words: "I'll expect each person in the group to practice smiley faces and smiley face words, and I'll come around to your groups to hear and see you, okay? I expect to hear quiet voices while you discuss your discoveries and decide which fruit and seed you will draw before you start. Make sure each person has a fruit and seed to draw." The teacher checks for understanding: "What will I be checking for?" (Acknowledge students who paraphrase the above directions and give corrective feedback until students understand.)

CLOSURE AND PROCESSING* •••••••••••••••••••••••••••••••••

What is the process for closure (students summarize what they learned)?

Each group comes to the front of the room to show their poster and to share what they found out about the seeds—color, shape, size, and number. If criteria were met, then the poster gets a prize sticker and each student receives a sticker.

What is the process for feedback on academic performance (how, who, and when)?

If a poster does not meet criteria, then ask the group what they can do to fix it. Have the group fix it after all the other groups present their posters. If a group member does not accurately share or know the information about the seeds, then ask the group to help provide the answer. They may choose to return as a group and present again after the other presentations are complete.

How are the teacher's observations shared?

Rule: Share negative comments in private and positive comments in public and private. The teacher shares summary data on frequency and impact of using smiley faces and smiley face words.

What is the process for assessment of individual and group success in using social skills (how and when)?

After the presentations, the teacher asks each group to take a few minutes to compare how well they did on the poster and how well they used smiley faces and smiley face words. Notice any impact. Ask the class as a whole, "What have you liked about working with this group? What didn't you like? What will you do differently when you work together later today?"

AFTER THE LESSON ••••••••••••••••••••••••••••••••••••••

How does the teacher evaluate the success of the lesson?

The teacher checks to see that the essential elements (noted with asterisks) of cooperative learning lessons were included. The next lesson is planned so that the students can practice student monitoring by tallying the frequency of their smiley face words. This integrates the graphing skills they are learning in math class. In addition, the teacher plans to schedule a written quiz to check individual understanding of the seeds of fruits.

ANECDOTE ••

This lesson was a great success. J. participated for the entire lesson, and his group members guided him appropriately to tactually explore each fruit. They came up with the idea of having J. paste on parts of the fruits and seeds instead of drawing them. The entire class helped cut up the fruit and enjoyed a tasty, healthy fruit salad as a class bonus.

REFERENCE

Monley, M.K. (1989). *Cooperative group lesson plan.* Unpublished manuscript submitted in partial fulfillment of requirements for the Educational Specialist graduate program, Professor J. Thousand, University of Vermont, Department of Special Education, College of Education and Social Services, Burlington.

Upper Elementary Mathematics for a Student Who Is Gifted and Talented (and Has Challenging Interpersonal Behaviors)

Lesson name: Math disagreements
Grade level: Fifth to sixth grade
  (intermediate)
Time: 40 minutes

Author: C. Conn-Powers
Content area: Mathematics

Conn-Powers (1988), a special education graduate intern, worked with a sixth-grade teacher to implement this lesson. The special features of the lesson included attention to students' reasoning skills and their interpersonal skills when confronted with different opinions. Math story problems were used to stimulate disagreement, or at least discussion, about different ways of solving the same problem and to dispel the myth that mathematics is "cut and dry."

ACADEMIC OBJECTIVES ••••••••••••••••••••••••••••••••••••••

What are the prerequisite skills?	Computational skills through fractions and reading skills
What are the academic objectives?	Students solve math story problems requiring reasoning and basic computational skills.
How do students demonstrate the academic objectives?	Students demonstrate these objectives by saying and doing the following: "I think we should go about solving the problem this way because. . . ."
What are the criteria for success?	If four problems are assigned, then students must show alternative solutions for at least three to receive an *A*, two for a *B*, and one for a *C*.
What are the modifications for learner(s) with special education needs?	D. is a student with gifts and talents and challenging interpersonal behaviors. He tends to advocate only for his ideas as the "right" ones and ridicules his classmates' contributions. His GATE (gifted and talented education) teacher is assisting him to become responsible for the effects of his behaviors on his classmates during two sessions he attends each week. In this lesson, D. will practice one of his new skills by serving as the "encourager" who asks others, in a friendly way, to share their ideas for solutions.
How does a learner with special education needs demonstrate the academic objectives?	D. demonstrates the same academic objectives as his classmates. To incorporate what he has been learning from his GATE teacher, D. demonstrates the skill of encouragement by saying and doing: "Why do you think that's a way to solve it?" or, "How about we try it this way?"
What are the criteria for success for the learner with special needs?	D. is successful if he asks at least two encouraging questions of each team member during the 20-minute lesson.

FACE-TO-FACE INTERACTION DECISIONS* •••••••••••••••••

What is the group size?	There are 24 students in the class—four students to each group, six groups total.
How are students assigned to groups?	To ensure heterogeneity, students are assigned to groups by the teacher so that there is equal distribution of boys and girls, high and low achievers, and students who speak Spanish. The teacher prepares name cards for each student using index cards that are marked with Spanish numbers in words—*uno, dos, tres, quatro, cinco,* and *seis.*
What is the room arrangement?	The room is arranged so that numbers 1–6 hang from the ceiling. Students move their desks to the area that matches their number and arrange their desks so that they are facing each other.

STRUCTURING POSITIVE INTERDEPENDENCE* •••••••••••••

	Members get the messages: "We sink or swim together," "Do your work—we're counting on you," and, "How can I help you to do better?"
What is the structure—a single product, one group goal, or a shared outcome?	There is one answer sheet per group (six for the class). The teacher explains, "Your group has a large newsprint to make a poster showing two or three ways to solve each problem. You have different color markers to make it easy for us to see your different solutions. You can be as creative as you like—make pictures, diagrams, flow charts, or use words and songs. So, what should your poster look like?" (Acknowledge students' responses or give corrective feedback until they show they understand the directions.)
Is a group reward structured?	Yes. The teacher might say, "Groups that create posters that meet criteria and whose group members can each tell about the reasons why the different solutions work or do not work will have the chance to work at the math games table for 10 minutes before the next math class. The music teacher told me that you are learning a special way of using math to harmonize. Any group that can creatively incorporate this skill in one or more of their solutions will earn an extra 5 minutes at the math games table."
Are student roles assigned?	Yes. The recorder role will be assigned so that each student practices recording the group's agreed-upon solutions on a rotating basis. The decision as to who serves as recorder first is based on whose first name has the most letters.
What are the other divisions of labor besides roles?	This emerges as the group decides how to draw its solutions.
How are materials arranged?	To promote positive interdependence among all groups, special colored markers (e.g., purple, fluorescent pink) can be rotated among groups; poster-size paper (six pieces, one per group), water-based magic markers (six containers), and any four math story problems can be used.

Optional: *What other ways to promote positive interdependence are used—intergroup cooperation, intergroup competition, positive fantasy mission, or identity interdependence (e.g., group name)?*

Whole-class cooperation is structured by having the special markers rotated among the groups. At the end, the class can invite another sixth-grade class to come in for a 10-minute gallery of solutions demonstration. The music teacher can be invited to comment on the creative applications of her lesson on harmony.

ESTABLISHING SOCIAL SKILL PERFORMANCE* • • • • • • • • • • • •

What are the social skills objectives?

The controversy skills of friendly disagreement (Brewster, 1990) are practiced. The teacher writes five ways to disagree in a friendly way on the board, on an overhead transparency, or on a poster to place in a prominent area for students to see while they work on their lesson. (These skills have been introduced and practiced by the class during a previous social studies lesson.)

1. Ask for different opinions: "Why do you think that's best? What is your opinion? What is your answer?"

2. Ask others to explain why: "Explain how you got your answer, please. Explain that last part. Show me how that works. How will that solve the problem?"

3. Add on or modify: "Could we expand on that answer? How about if we added this? Could we change . . . ?"

4. Offer alternatives: "What do you think about . . . ? Wouldn't this work also? Here is a different way of looking at things."

5. State disagreement: "I have a different idea. My answer is different. Here is why I think this way."

How is the need for each social skill communicated?

Ask students how they feel when they hear words such as "I don't agree with you" said in a friendly tone with a smile or an unfriendly tone with a frown. (Demonstrate. Acknowledge students' responses—they might say how they feel, they might want to work more—or elicit from them those ideas [e.g., "Do you think you'll feel like talking more if you hear a friendly or an unfriendly tone?"]. Acknowledge contributions and give corrective feedback until students get the idea.) "That's why we'll be practicing friendly disagreement while you work your math problems today."

How are social skills explained, demonstrated, role-played, or practiced?

Ask students to volunteer to demonstrate how they would sound and what their faces would look like when disagreeing in a friendly manner.

How are social skills assigned to group members?

All group members are responsible for demonstrating at least two of the five ways to disagree in a friendly way.

SOCIAL SKILL PERFORMANCE ••••••••••••••••••••••••••••
Teacher Monitoring and Intervention*

What is the process (how and who) for monitoring groups?	The teacher visits each group to observe and monitor group interactions—approximately 1 minute per group, at least three rotations during the lesson.
What is the process for feedback (how and who) to groups if social skills are being used?	The teacher shares "on the spot" those things that the group is doing well.
What is the process for feedback (how and who) to groups if social skills are not being used?	Ask the group, "What does it look like and sound like to practice friendly disagreement?" (Acknowledge student responses.) "That's right! I'll come back in a few minutes, and I expect to hear and see you, okay?"
What collaboration problems are anticipated?	Argument over who will write on the poster; one person doing all the writing
What are interventions to avoid or remedy the anticipated problems?	*Rules:* When you feel like intervening, don't. If you must intervene, then do it with questions, not answers. Move away as soon as you can, even if it is only 3 feet. Remind students that arguing is okay as long as they are disagreeing in a friendly way. Ask how the others feel if one person does all the work. "Does it feel fair? Remember that the recorder role is to be shared by each person."

SOCIAL SKILL PERFORMANCE ••••••••••••••••••••••••••••
Student Monitoring

What is the student observer(s) selection and training process (what and who)?	Students use an observation form that they created during social studies class on which each of the five ways to disagree in a friendly manner is listed. Students monitor their own friendly disagreeing.
How are social skills monitored?	Friendly disagreement is tallied on the student-generated observation form.
Do students observe more than one group?	No.
Do students observe for an entire lesson?	Yes.
How and when do students share their observations?	As the teacher listens to each group, he or she can "catch the students" engaging in friendly disagreement and ask them to share. Also, during the process, the teacher can randomly select a student from one or two groups to share his or her examples of friendly disagreement.

STRUCTURING INDIVIDUAL ACCOUNTABILITY* ・・・・・・・・・・・・

Are individual quizzes assigned?

No.

Is there a random selection of group members to answer questions?

Yes. At the end of the lesson when the teacher processes the social skills interactions, students are randomly selected to share their examples of friendly disagreeing.

SETTING THE TASK ・・・・・・・・・・・・・・・・・・・・・・・・・・・・・・

What is the process for explanation of the academic task and criteria for success (when and who)?

The teacher begins the lesson by talking about math story problems and the math (computational) and thinking skills that are needed to solve them. "How many of you think that mathematicians always agree?" (Acknowledge responses.) "What do you think they do when they don't agree?" (Acknowledge responses.) "Today we're going to find out what you do when you don't agree!"

"I want you to use your reasoning skills to determine which math operation (addition, subtraction, multiplication, or division) to use to solve the problem. I'll be looking for how you use different ways to solve the same problem. You'll need to find at least two different ways for each problem. Your group will make a poster to show the different ways you discover. If three of the four problems have two solutions, then each person in your group earns an *A;* if two have alternative solutions, then your group earns a *B;* if one has alternative solutions, your group earns a *C;* and if your group provides no alternative solutions, then you will have a chance to solve them after recess."

How are social skills and criteria for success explained (when and who)?

"I expect each person in the group to practice friendly disagreement, and I will come around to your groups to hear and see you, okay? I expect to hear quiet voices while you discuss your solutions and decide how you will make your poster before you start. Make sure each person can explain the different solutions. What will I be checking for?" (Acknowledge students who paraphrase the above directions.)

CLOSURE AND PROCESSING* ・・・・・・・・・・・・・・・・・・・・・・・・

What is the process for closure (students summarize what they learned)?

Each group comes to the front of the room to show its poster. Each buddy shares what his or her buddy contributed and what he or she found out about the solutions.

What is the process for feedback on academic performance (how, who, and when)?

If criteria are met, then each student in the group receives a ticket to work at the math games table for 10 minutes. For groups that incorporate harmony, each student receives a ticket to work at the math games table for 5 extra minutes. If a group's poster does not meet criteria, then ask the group what they can do to fix it. Have them fix it after all groups share. If a group member does not accurately share or know the information about the solutions, then ask the others in the group to help him or her. They may choose to return as a group and present again after the other presentations are complete.

How are the teacher's observations shared?

Rule: Share negative comments in private and positive comments in public and private.

The teacher shares summary data on the frequency and impact of using friendly disagreement. If there is time, the teacher shares a story about how a famous mathematician disagreed with an accepted solution and came up with another way. What is the process for assessment of individual and group success in using social skills (how and when)?

After the presentations, the teacher asks each group to take a few minutes to compare how well they did on the poster and how well they used friendly disagreement skills. Pass out index cards for groups to record what skills they practiced very well and what skills they plan to practice the next time. Students sign the cards and hand them in for the teacher to review.

Ask the class as a whole, "What did you like about working with this group? What didn't you like? What will you do differently when you work together later today?"

AFTER THE LESSON ••••••••••••••••••••••••••••••••

How does the teacher evaluate the success of the lesson?

The teacher checks to see that the essential elements (noted with asterisks) of cooperative learning lessons were included. Both the academic and social skills objectives were met, especially for D. The teacher decided to expand the friendly disagreeing skills to playground activities to ensure maximum generalization.

ANECDOTE ••••••••••••••••••••••••••••••••••••••

This lesson was quite successful. All six groups met criteria and earned tickets for the math games table. Two of the groups (including the one of which D. was a member) incorporated the harmony skills and earned an extra 5 minutes at the math games table. D. participated for the entire lesson and his group members told him that they appreciated how he encouraged them to disagree! Later, at recess, the teacher overheard D. practicing one of the friendly disagreement skills while playing tether ball with another group from his class. In addition, during a science class the next day, the students spontaneously began to use the friendly disagreement skills to address a challenging series of questions.

REFERENCE

Conn-Powers, C. (1988). *Cooperative group lesson plan.* Unpublished manuscript submitted in partial fulfillment of requirements for the Educational Specialist graduate program, Professor J. Thousand, University of Vermont, Department of Special Education, College of Education and Social Services, Burlington.

"The Universe Holds Many Mysteries" Lesson for Students with Language Learning Disabilities and Learning English as a Second Language

Lesson name: The universe holds many mysteries

Grade level: Fourth to sixth grade

Time: 1 hour 30 minutes

Author: A.M.L. Quiocho

Content area: Science, language arts (listening, speaking, reading, writing), English language syntax, grammar, and vocabulary

ACADEMIC OBJECTIVES[1] ....

The objectives are derived from the Reading/Language Arts Framework for Public Schools fifth grade (O'Malley & Brynelson, 1999, pp. 129–132):

Reading 1.0: Word Analysis, Fluency, and Systematic Vocabulary Development

Students use their knowledge of word origins and word relationships, as well as historical and literary context clues, to determine the meaning of specialized vocabulary and to understand the precise meaning of grade-level appropriate words.

Writing 1.0: Strategies

Students write clear, coherent, and focused essays and establish a topic, important ideas, or events in sequence or chronological order.

Listening and Speaking 1.0: Strategies

Students deliver focused, coherent presentations that convey ideas clearly (using standard American English); ask questions that seek information not already discussed; clarify and support spoken ideas with evidence and examples.

What are the prerequisite skills?

Be a member of the class. Students can read text at the 1.5 grade equivalent and above. Students have had previous experiences with the collaborative process. Students have practiced evaluating their participation as well as how the group worked or did not work collaboratively and how to improve the process.

---

[1]These objectives provide complex challenging material to stimulate the cognitive academic language proficiency of students learning English as a second language.

How do students demonstrate the academic objectives?	Students orally predict explanations people might give about the origin of the stars. Students create a model showing how the planets rotate around the sun and describe the characteristics of the planets in the solar system either orally or in writing. After reading and responding to poems about the sun and moon as a model, students write poems or stories about planets and stars.
What are the criteria for success?	Criteria for success include 1) 90%–100% accuracy of factual information based on text, 2) model of the planet with 90%–100% accurate information, and 3) or oral presentation in English of at least 30 words in correct syntax and accurate vocabulary related to the model of the planet.
What are the modifications for learners with special education needs?	Scaffolding of information is provided for students learning ESL; specifically the Think-Pair-Share (Kagan, 1995) technique encourages oral expression of ideas before writing ideas and the K-W-L (What We Already *K*now/What We *W*ant to Learn/What We *L*earned) chart (Ogle, 1986) encourages students to make predictions and ask questions (thus expressing ideas in English). The written information on the K-W-L chart gives students models of written English syntax, grammar, and vocabulary. For students with learning disabilities, the hands-on demonstration and creation of a model solar system provide concrete tactile experiences.

FACE-TO-FACE INTERACTION DECISIONS* • • • • • • • • • • • • • • • • •

How are students assigned to groups?	The students will be assigned to the partnerships by the teacher before the class session. The teacher sets up the partnerships so that monolingual Spanish-speaking students are paired with bilingual English/Spanish–speaking students; and the two students with learning disabilities are each paired up with students who have been taught how to use the writer's process to tutor the development of written expression. As the students enter the room, the teacher hands them an index card with one half of a photograph of one of the planets or moons of the solar system. The students must find the other half and thus their planetary system partnership for today's lesson. Thus, if there are 24 students in the class, there will be 12 partners–nine partners can be assigned one of the nine planets–Mercury, Venus, Earth, Mars, Jupiter, Saturn, Uranus, Neptune, and Pluto; three partners can be assigned the Earth's moon, the sun, and the manned space station.
What is the room arrangement?	For this lesson, the desks are arranged in pairs.
How are materials arranged?	Materials for the assignment have been collected in a planetary basket for each partnership. Each basket includes scissors, crayons, magic markers, large poster paper for drawings, and construction

paper for creating the models of the planets. The teacher posts NASA photographs of the planets around the room for realistic models for the children to emulate.

Instructional materials include at least three different types of readings related to the solar system.

1. Bryan, A. (1992). *Sing to the sun.* New York: HarperCollins.

2. Gutierrez, D., & Oliver, M.F. (1998). *The night of the stars.* La Jolla, CA: Kane/Miller Book Publishers.

3. Krulik, N. (1991). *My picture book of the planets.* New York: Scholastic.

STRUCTURING POSITIVE INTERDEPENDENCE* ••••••••••••••

Members get the messages: "We sink or swim together," "Do your work—we're counting on you," and, "How can I help you to do better?"

What is the structure—a single product, one group goal, a shared outcome, or a group reward?

There will be a shared outcome—one item from the planetary system from each of the partners—and a class product—a model of all the planets circling the sun.

Are student roles assigned?

Yes. Partners will take turns being reader and listener or writer and drawer as the lesson progresses.

What are the other divisions of labor besides roles?

Other divisions of labor may emerge as the partners work together. For example, one student may volunteer to look up more information about his or her planet in the encyclopedia or on the Internet and report back to the partnership. Another student may volunteer to find a different myth about the origin of the planets and report back to the partnership.

How are materials arranged?

Materials are arranged so that students must share in order to accomplish the task. For each partnership, there will be at least one book of poems about the sun and moon, at least one storybook showing a legend about the stars, and at least one science-related book showing what scientists know about the solar system. At least one of the books will describe the solar system in Spanish. The reading levels of the books should range from a grade-equivalent of 1.5 to 7.5 to ensure a wide readability range.

Optional: *What other ways to promote positive interdependence are used— intergroup cooperation, intergroup competition, positive fantasy mission, or identity interdependence (e.g., group name)?*

The entire class will decorate the classroom as an interplanetary voyager might see it.

ESTABLISHING SOCIAL SKILL PERFORMANCE* • • • • • • • • • • • •

What are the social skills objectives?

There are two major social skills that are emphasized in this lesson. The first social skill is listening with respect. Students will show they are listening by facing the speaker or reader and asking questions that indicate they heard what was being said or read.

The second social skill is summarizing. Students will show they can summarize by asking questions and by writing or drawing.

How is the need for each social skill communicated?

The teacher says, "The more we learn about our universe, the better we understand it. How do we learn?" (Pause for ideas from the students. Acknowledge all answers. Paraphrase so that some of the answers include "reading what other people say about it," "listening," "watching videos," and "talking to other people about their ideas.") "Yes, that's good thinking, class! We learn by asking questions, listening to ideas, watching the world itself, and summarizing what we have discovered! Today we'll be emphasizing two of these skills: listening and summarizing."

How are social skills explained, demonstrated, role-played, or practiced?

As the group work begins, the teacher reminds students of previous lessons in which explanations of the social skills have been presented. Children's charts showing what the social skills "sound like" (words or phrases they can use to summarize, such as "I think what José just read means that the planet revolves around the sun, and the moon revolves around the planet. Is that right?") and "look like" (head nods, smiles, quizzical faces if more information is needed) are posted on the wall.

How are social skills assigned to group members?

Students, working as partners, will take turns being listener and summarizer as the lesson progresses.

SOCIAL SKILL PERFORMANCE* •
Teacher Monitoring and Intervention

What is the process (how and who) for monitoring groups?

The teacher will visit each partnership as the students are working. The teacher will monitor how the students are listening, writing, speaking, and summarizing as they create their model of the planet assigned to them.

What is the process for feedback (how and who) to groups if social skills are being used?

As the groups are working, the teacher will decide whether to interrupt the group process to 1) provide feedback on the frequency of the social skills being used and 2) make any comments about the accuracy of the summaries of information.

What is the process for feedback (how and who) to groups if social skills are not being used?

The teacher will use "on the spot" immediate correction.

What collaboration problems are anticipated?	Monolingual Spanish-speaking students and/or monolingual English-speaking students speaking only with each other rather than with their assigned partners.
What are interventions to avoid or remedy anticipated problems?	*Rules:* When you feel like intervening, don't. If you must intervene, do it with a question, not an answer. Move away as soon as you can, even if it is only 3 feet. Ask the students to use Think-Pair-Share with the entire group rather than with just one person, starting with the bilingual person. This will give the monolingual students a chance to hear and cognitively rehearse what they want to say.

SOCIAL SKILL PERFORMANCE ••••••••••••••••••••••••••••
Student Monitoring

What is the student observer(s) selection and training process (what and who)?	Specifically trained student observers are not used in this lesson.
How are social skills monitored?	Summarizing is tallied by the teacher.
Do students observe more than one group?	No.
Do students observe for an entire lesson?	No.
How and when do the teacher or students share their observations?	At the end of the lesson, the teacher debriefs with students. This can be done with the whole group as well as with groups of partners while the others might still be working on completing their planets. The teacher asks, "What was easy about today's learning/collaboration?" "What was hard?" "How did you collaborate with your partner?" "If someone was having trouble being a good collaborator, what would you say to that person?"

STRUCTURING INDIVIDUAL ACCOUNTABILITY* ••••••••••••

	First, model for students how to self-evaluate in terms of being a good collaborative member of a group. Then ask students to self-evaluate their performance as a member of and as a contributor to their group and the group product.
Are individual quizzes assigned?	No.
Is there random selection of group members to answer questions?	Yes. Random selection of group members' poems and sentences can occur.

SETTING THE TASK ••••••••••••••••••••••••••••••••••••••

What is the process for explanation of the academic task and criteria for success (when and who)?

The teacher says, "Today you will work as partners in your two-person planet partnerships to learn about the different explanations for why the universe is as it is. First, you will be a listener to what is being read by your partner, then you will be a thinker, then you will pair up with your partner to share your summary of what you learned. In the summary, you can write a sentence together or draw a picture to show your understanding. After you have taken turns being reader and listener, you will then compare your ideas with each other. Are you with me? This means you will have how many summary sentences or pictures?" (Accept all answers.) "Yes, you are good listeners. This means there will be two summary sentences or pictures. Then, your two-person planet partnership will make a model of your assigned planet. By the end of the class, you will place your planet into the class model of the solar system, turning our classroom into a solar system! Are you ready for the journey?"

(On a large piece of newsprint sectioned into thirds, the teacher has prepared a three-column K-W-L chart with the headings What We Already **K**now/What We **W**ant to Learn/What We **L**earned.) "Good! Let's start first by making a very big K-W-L chart to find out what we already know and what we'd like to learn about, and then at the end of the class we will fill out the what we learned today section."

"We will use our Think-Pair-Share system to begin. So, everyone think about what you already know about the sun, the moon, and the stars." (Pause for 1 minute.) "Okay, raise your hand if you have an idea already." (Glance around the room. Typically only a few students will raise their hands.) "Thank you. Now let's think a different way. Pair up with your partner. The partner with the longest hair starts by asking, 'What's your idea?'" (Pause for 1 minute to let the partners share.) "Thank you, class. That's good! I'm hearing lots of good ideas. Now it's the other partner's turn. Partner with the shorter hair, you ask your partner, 'What's YOUR idea?'" (Pause for 1 minute as more oral language expression continues.) "Good thinking aloud, class! Now let's get at least four or five of these ideas on the newsprint. Who would like to share what your partner said?" (Call on two people, write down their ideas in the What We Know column?) "Good! You've done a great job of showing that you listened to your partner. Do you agree, partners?" (Wait for head nods or smiles.) "This is what I'll be looking for when you do your group work."

"Let's continue. Now think about what you WANT to learn about." (Pause for 1 minute.) "It's time to ask your partner again. This time, the partner with the shorter hair begins by asking, 'What do you want to learn about?'" (Pause for 1 minute while they share ideas.) "Good! I'm hearing lots of great things that you are curious about learning! It's time to take turns. Partner with the longer hair, it's your turn to ask." (Pause for 1 minute for oral expression.) "Thank you! Let's write down four or five things in the What We Want to Learn column. Raise your hand if your partner has a great idea of what she or he wants to learn." (Pause. Notice how many hands are raised. By now, with the safe environment for oral expression having been established, nearly 100%

of the class should be raising their hands!) "Great! I see that you are eager to share what your partner wants to learn. Let's write down four or five ideas quickly." (Call on four or five students and quickly write down their ideas.)

"Now you are really ready to begin your journey. The first thing we'll be doing is listening to a folktale about why there are stars in the sky. I'm going to read the story, and you will listen. I will ask you to draw a picture in your mind's eye as the folktale is being read. Then, you will share your mental picture with your planet partnership. Let's go. The story is. . . ." (Show the book you've selected, read the title, and begin reading.) Twice during the story, pause to ask, "Ask your partner, what do you think will happen next?" This reinforces listening, and allows for a brief moment for oral expression and checking for understanding. Pause for about 1 minute. Solicit one or two predictions. "Let's find out." (Continue reading until the story is complete.) "Now it's your turn. Tell your partner the mental picture you had as you listened. For example, you might say, 'I saw bright colors in my mind's eye' or 'I heard a song in my mental picture.'" (Pause for about 1 minute as each person shares.)

"Now it's your turn to read and listen. Using the books at your desk, you and your partner will choose one book to share reading and listening for the next 8–10 minutes. At the end of the reading and listening time, you will write a sentence or draw a picture to summarize what you learned. You may begin." (Circulate to eavesdrop as students take turns reading and listening or writing and drawing summary sentences. Make sure they are reading brief passages—about 1 or 2 minutes for each segment of oral reading. Keep the pace moving. The writing/drawing may take a little longer.)

"Good working and thinking! I'm hearing some very good summarizing, too. Now it's time to share. Show your sentences and pictures to each other and be ready to post them on the bulletin board." (Pause for 2 minutes while the sentences/pictures are shared. Collect them and begin posting.)

"Now you are ready to construct your planets. You have 10–15 minutes to make the model of your planet. Use as much information that you learned about your planet as you can."

Circulate to each of the planet partnerships to check progress. At the end of 10 minutes, give the class a time check, saying, "You have 3 minutes to complete your model and bring it up here to place in the class model of the solar system."

"What do you notice about our solar system? Does it match some of the pictures that are on our classroom walls taken by scientists who have sent probes to some of our planets?" (Pause to check for head nods or smiles.) "Yes! Good job, class! Now let's double check to find out if we learned what we said we wanted to learn." (Refer to the K-W-L chart, reading and checking off the items that the class mentioned that they wanted to learn.) "What else have you learned today? Raise your hand if you learned something else." (Pause. There should be many hands raised. Just in case some students are still shy to orally express, allow for one more Think-Pair-Share opportunity.) "Thank you! Before you share what else you've learned, ask your partner! Take turns!" (Pause while partners exchange.) "Now, raise your hand to share what your partner said!" (If some of the students formerly reluctant to volunteer are raising their hands, call on them!) "Thank you. Let's write four or five of these ideas down. You've done a lot of good thinking today!"

"Now, are you ready for some fun? It's time to write a poem with the information you've learned about your planet today. Remember what your mental pictures were when you were listening to the folktale? Now it's your turn to create a word picture–a poem. Make sure your poem includes at least two of the pieces of information your team summarized from your readings. You have 10 minutes! Go for it!" (Circulate to each partner, make sure the large poster paper is being used so that the poems can be posted.) "Good job! I notice that some of you have used more than the information you summarized. This tells me that you have been listening to the class discussion from the K-W-L chart where we summarized what else we learned! Now let's post all the poems near the class solar system model for everyone to enjoy. As you go to recess, be sure to read some of these poems! We'll use them tomorrow to help us review and remember what we learned today! Have fun at recess. Good-bye." (Dismiss the class to the next activity, or recess.)

How are social skills and criteria for success explained (when and who)?

The teacher says, "I expect you to take turns at least three times today as you think and then share your ideas. I expect you to write at least one summary statement either in a sentence or as a picture. And I expect you to share your ideas as your team makes the model of the planet."

CLOSURE AND PROCESSING* ●

What is the process for closure (students summarize what they learned)?

In addition to posting the model of the planet, sentences, pictures, and poems, the students will orally complete the class K-W-L chart (as described previously), showing what they have learned about the details of the solar system.

What is the process for feedback on academic performance (how, who, and when)?

The teacher asks the students to compare the class model of the solar system with NASA photographs. Similarities and differences are acknowledged.

How are the teacher's observations shared?

Rule: Share negative comments in private and positive comments in public and private.

The teacher shares summary data on frequency and impact of using listening and summarizing skills. The teacher connects the model created by the whole class to the ability of each person in each partnership to listen carefully and then summarize what they learned.

What is the process for assessment of individual and group success in using social skills (how and when)?

The teacher provides a summary of the listening and summarizes what was accomplished, especially connecting the social skills to the achievement of the partners' summary sentences, pictures, and poems that have been posted along with the class solar system model.

AFTER THE LESSON ••••••••••••••••••••••••••••••••••

How does the teacher evaluate the success of the lesson?

The teacher checks to see that the essential elements (noted with asterisks) of cooperative learning lessons were included. Both the academic content objectives (science content and literature/folklore) and social skills objectives (listening and summarizing) were met, especially for the students with learning disabilities and those learning English as their second language. In this particular cooperative group lesson, the teacher also evaluated how well the scaffolding techniques of Think-Pair-Share and the K-W-L chart worked to ensure that children orally rehearsed the concepts using standard English grammar, syntax, and vocabulary.

ANECDOTE ••

The teacher used the cognitive academic language learning approach (CALLA; Quiocho, Croghan, & Diaz-Greenberg, 1999) in this cooperative group learning lesson with her fifth-grade class. She had been trying to teach them about planets in the traditional way—read the science book, look at the illustrations, try to make sense of the text, and then answer the questions. It wasn't working.

With the use of multiple resources, the lesson was brought to life. The myths helped the students understand that everyone has a way to explain the unexplainable. The teacher felt that because she used multiple sources to get students to where she wanted to get them—to understand the system of planets—they were able to use creative thinking strategies to develop their schema about the planets.

Because students were paired together, they were able to share their knowledge with each other. Students who were developing English language skills obtained information from their own partner as well as from other pairs of students. They cognitively rehearsed what they were going to say when giving their oral presentations. This extra practice allowed students who were usually reluctant to speak in class to gain more confidence. Two students with learning disabilities in written expression were excited that their sentences and drawings were posted along with their classmates' products. By the time the sharing was completed, the shy students became less inhibited and participated actively in the learning process.

REFERENCES

Kagan, S. (1995). *Cooperative learning* (Rev. ed.). San Clemente, CA: Kagan Publishing.

Ogle, J. (1986). K-W-L: A teaching model that develops active reading of expository text. *The Reading Teacher, 3,* 564–570.

O'Malley, E., & Brynelson, N. (1999). *Reading/language arts framework for California public schools, K-12 grade.* Sacramento: California Department of Education.

Quiocho, A., Croghan, M., & Diaz-Greenberg, R. (1999, Nov.) *CALLA (Cognitive Academic Language Learning Approach) and SDAIE (Specifically Designed Academic Instruction in English) strategies: Teach . . . Light up the future.* Paper presented at the meeting of the National Association for Multicultural Education, San Diego, CA.

Introducing Middle School Students to Cooperative Learning Groups: The Fishbowl Technique

Lesson name: Introduction to cooperative learning
Grade level: Middle school students
Time: 50 minutes

Authors: R.A. Villa and J.S. Thousand
Content area: Group dynamics

Many teachers wonder how to teach the social skills necessary for cooperative groups to be effective. Villa and Thousand (1987) developed this lesson as a demonstration for middle school teachers to observe. Villa was the teacher for a group of 21 middle school students who volunteered to show their teachers how they would behave in classrooms where cooperative learning was being practiced. The 21 students filed into a classroom that was set up with desks in traditionally aligned rows. Their teachers were arranged in the back of the room to observe the instruction. The lesson began with a whole-class discussion that was followed by students working in pairs to answer four questions. Volunteers then formed a cooperative group to accomplish a language arts assignment that was observed by their classmates and teachers. The lesson concluded with the entire class working as members of cooperative groups.

ACADEMIC OBJECTIVE ••••••••••••••••••••••••••••••••••

What are the prerequisite skills?

Be a member of the student body of the middle school.

What are the academic objectives?

1. Identify what has worked well and what has not worked well when students worked in groups in the past.

2. Identify advantages of working in a group for students and teachers.

3. Identify skills needed to work in a cooperative group, explain why the skills are needed, and give examples of each skill.

4. Identify examples of encouraging and sharing social skills demonstrated by a volunteer group of students.

How do students demonstrate the academic objectives?

After interviewing a classmate, each student contributes the classmate's ideas to the discussion. During the fishbowl demonstration of a cooperative learning lesson, students work with a partner to complete a checklist, noting frequencies of cooperative skills.

What are the criteria for success?

For the whole class, at least six publicly shared statements related to each of the four objectives are expected.

What are the modifications for learners with special education needs?

Several middle school students have attention-deficit/hyperactivity disorders that interfere with their ability to focus. To increase their listening skills, they are assigned to a study buddy. Their role with the study buddy is to "check for understanding"—to ask specific questions related to the task, to assess understanding, and to answer questions their buddy might have. In this way, they are given added cognitive rehearsal of the material and they have a legitimate way of asking for clarification. During this lesson, each member of the class is paired with a study buddy.

How do learners with special education needs demonstrate the academic objectives?

The students with special needs demonstrate the academic objectives in the same way as other students—by participating in the class discussion first by checking answers with his or her study buddy and then by sharing answers with the whole class.

What are the criteria for success for learners with special needs?

Each student with special needs offers at least one idea during the discussion of advantages, skills needed for cooperative group work, and things that have and have not worked well in the past.

FACE-TO-FACE INTERACTION DECISIONS* ･････････････････

What is the group size?

There are 21 students in the class. Five students volunteer to practice in "fishbowl" fashion while the other 16 students observe.

How are students assigned to groups?

Random selection of student volunteers

What is the room arrangement?

Desks are arranged in a circle of five desks with the other 16 students arranged in a semicircle for ease in listening to the volunteer group.

STRUCTURING POSITIVE INTERDEPENDENCE* ･････････････

Members get the messages: "We sink or swim together," "Do your work—we're counting on you," and, "How can I help you to do better?"

What is the structure—a single product, one group goal, or a shared outcome?

1. Study buddies generate a single set of brainstormed lists of advantages, skills needed for cooperative group work, and things that have and have not worked well in the past.

2. Study buddies share these ideas during the whole-class discussion so that the class lists a set of brainstormed advantages, skills, and things that have and have not worked well in the past.

3. Study buddies complete an observation sheet during the fishbowl demonstration.

Are student roles assigned?

Students watching the demonstration group are assigned study buddies to observe the cooperative skills being practiced in the demonstration group. Students in the demonstration group are assigned cooperative behavior roles (encourager, sharer) as well as leadership roles (observer, timekeeper, recorder).

What are the other divisions of labor besides roles?

None.

How are materials arranged?

One paper containing the story is distributed to the demonstration group. Each study buddy pair receives an observer sheet to record their observations of cooperative behaviors shown by the demonstration group.

Optional: *What other ways to promote positive interdependence will be used—intergroup cooperation, intergroup competition, positive fantasy mission, or identity interdependence (e.g., group name)?*

None.

ESTABLISHING SOCIAL SKILL PERFORMANCE* • • • • • • • • • • •

What are the social skills objectives?

Students increase their knowledge and/or practice of the social skills needed for cooperative groups to work effectively.

How is the need for each social skill communicated?

During a class discussion, the teacher elicits from the students their experiences of working in groups in the past with a focus on what worked well and what did not work well and why the skills are needed, giving an example of each skill.

How are social skills explained, demonstrated, role-played, or practiced?

The volunteers are asked to model the behaviors of encouraging and sharing. During the fishbowl demonstration, the demonstration group shows how encouraging and sharing ideas leads to a creative ending to a story.

How are social skills assigned to group members?

The teacher assigns the social skills at random.

SOCIAL SKILL PERFORMANCE •
Teacher Monitoring and Intervention*

What is the process (how and who) for monitoring groups?

Monitoring occurs at three levels. The demonstration group has a student observer, classmates observe, and the teacher observes to monitor how well the group members share, encourage, and practice their leadership roles.

What is the process for feedback (how and who) to groups if social skills are being used?

The teacher stops the work at least once to offer specific feedback.

What is the process for feedback (how and who) to groups if social skills are not being used?

The teacher may ask the student observer to report to the group his or her results and ask the group to remember to practice the social skills of encouraging and sharing.

What collaboration problems are anticipated?

Lack of volunteers

What are interventions to avoid or remedy the anticipated problems?	*Rules:* When you feel like intervening, don't. If you must intervene, do it with questions, not answers. Move away as soon as you can, even if it is only 3 feet. Have all students count off 1–4. Those with the number 4 become the demonstration group.

SOCIAL SKILL PERFORMANCE ....
Student Monitoring

What is the student observer(s) selection and training process (what and who)?	1. The teacher models for all students how to use the observation form when giving instructions to the volunteer group. 2. Study buddy pairs are assigned by the teacher. 3. The teacher selects randomly from the student volunteers one student to be a silent observer.
How are social skills monitored?	One student in the demonstration group monitors by completing the observation form. Students observing the demonstration group complete the form with a partner.
Do students observe more than one group?	No.
Do students observe for an entire lesson?	Yes.
How and when do students share their observations?	At the completion of the demonstration, the teacher solicits comments randomly from study buddy pairs, and the observer in the demonstration group reports his or her results.

STRUCTURING INDIVIDUAL ACCOUNTABILITY* ....

Are individual quizzes assigned?	No.
Is there a random selection of group members to answer questions?	Study buddies are randomly called on to volunteer their observations.

SETTING THE TASK ....

What is the process for explanation of the academic task and criteria for success (when and who)?	The teacher leads a class discussion focusing on cooperation and group work. "How many of you have worked in groups that have been successful?" (Acknowledge those who raise their hands or orally indicate they have.) "And how many of you have worked in groups that have not worked so well?" (Acknowledge those who participate.) "Today we will focus on two key characteristics of what makes groups

successful—from Olympic champion teams to business teams to winning football teams—and we will start by making sure you are a winner! First, you will find your study buddy—the person who has a championship badge that matches yours. Your job is to be a 'checker for understanding' with your buddy. Throughout this class session, I will stop every once in a while to ask you to ask your buddy if he or she has any questions or ideas to contribute. Your job is to make sure that the question gets answered before we move on and to make sure that your buddy's idea is heard by the class. Raise your buddy's hand now to show that you are partners."

"Good! Now, please check with your buddy to find out three things that have worked well and three things that have not worked well in the groups in which you have been members. You have 3 minutes to do this, so work efficiently." (Pause, circulate to listen to the buddies.) "Thank you. Now, let's get your great ideas on the board. I'll scribe while you tell me what you have come up with. First, let's hear from the buddy with the shortest hair." (List as many ideas as you can in about 3 minutes. Print on newsprint with two columns: Things that Work Well and Things that Don't Work Well.) "Thank you! This shows that you all have some great experiences to build on. Now let's find out from your buddy the advantages to working in groups for yourselves and for your teachers. I'll give you 3 minutes to listen to each other's ideas." (Pause, listen to buddies, and return in about 3 minutes.) "Good work! Now let's hear from the buddy with the longest hair and I'll scribe as you tell me the results of your interviews." (List advantages in two columns: Advantages to Learners and Advantages to Teachers.) "You have certainly identified some key ideas that even executives in businesses have agreed are important for workers and their bosses as advantages for good group members. Now, let's see if we can practice what we are preaching."

"Now, please ask your buddy to tell you what he or she thinks are the important skills he or she needs to work in a cooperative group. Be specific and tell why the skill is needed. Think of at least two skills." (Pause, listen to buddies, and return in about 3 minutes.) "You folks are really thinking up some great skills. Let's get them on newsprint real fast. This time let's hear from the person who has on the wildest footwear." (List as many skills as you can and spot check for reasons why they named the skill.) "We'll need five volunteers to show the class how to practice two key roles—encouraging and sharing ideas—as they finish the ending to a short story."

Select five students randomly and arrange them in a circle in the center of the room with the remaining students in a semicircle around them in "fishbowl" fashion. Listen as they complete a short story. Follow the directions below.

INSTRUCTIONS FOR THE
FISHBOWL DEMONSTRATION GROUP •••••••••••••••••••

"Thank you for agreeing to work as a group today. You will complete one paper that you will sign, indicating you agree with the ending to the story that your group has created. Signatures indicate that you agree with the content of the sentences, the sequence of the sentences, and the grammatical accuracy. You will each receive the grade that this story earns. You will receive an *A* for stories with at least three complete sentences in a logical sequence and with no grammatical errors; a *B* for stories with at least two complete sentences in a logical sequence with three to five grammatical errors; a *C* for stories with one sentence and five to seven errors; and a *D* for less than one sentence. The group will be evaluated for completing the academic task in the assigned time and for practicing 1) the cooperative behaviors of encouraging and sharing ideas and 2) the leadership behaviors of timekeeper, recorder, and observer. If your classmates judge that you have met these criteria, then they will give you a round of applause!"

ROLE ASSIGNMENTS •

Students count off 1–5: 1 serves as the recorder who writes down the group's sentences, 2 is the timekeeper who makes sure the task is completed in the time allotted, 3 is the encourager who lets teammates know their ideas are appreciated and invites contributions from everyone, 4 is the observer who completes the cooperative skills observation form and provides feedback to the group, and 5 is the checker who checks to make sure everyone agrees and understands. Each student receives a job card that details each of the roles. The teacher asks each student to read his or her job card out loud. Students are encouraged to remember that they have two jobs to do: One is to practice the social skill of the role and the other job is to thank their teammates when they also practice the role.

DIRECTIONS FOR THE ACADEMIC TASK •

Read the following story. Brainstorm and record possible ending sentences. Select at least three sentences to finish the story. Agree on grammar, punctuation, and sequence of the sentences. Record the selected sentences on the back of the page. Proofread the three sentences. Make sure all group members sign, indicating agreement with the decisions.

STORY •

The most unusual things happened to me during the last couple of weeks of school. At the time I was a little nervous about what was going on. Now, when I look back, a lot of it seems funny to me.

Directions to observer: Write the names of your group members in the boxes numbered 1–5. Place a tally mark each time you observe the cooperative skills. If you have time, jot down specific examples of the skills so you can share them later during group processing.

How are social skills and criteria for success explained (when and who)?	Encouraging and sharing are indications of groups that work well. The brainstormed list of what works well in successful groups is sure to yield both behaviors and the list of what does not work well is sure to yield their opposites (e.g., put-downs, not sharing). The teacher makes a point of connecting these skills to the students' shared experiences.

CLOSURE AND PROCESSING* •

What is the process for closure (students summarize what they learned)?	At the end of the demonstration lesson, the teacher solicits comments from the study buddies' observations of the strengths and weaknesses of the demonstration group members' performance of the cooperative behaviors (encouraging, sharing) and leadership behaviors (observer, timekeeper, recorder).
What is the process for feedback on academic performance (how, who, and when)?	The teacher comments on the grammatical accuracy of the story ending and the creativity of the ending itself.
How are the teacher's observations shared?	*Rule:* Share negative comments in private and positive comments in public and private. After the students have shared, the teacher shares his or her observations.
What is the process for assessment of individual and group success in using social skills (how and when)?	The student observer shares results of the observation and makes comments about various team members' participation. The study buddies interview each other to find out what behaviors they observed. The teacher randomly calls on a student to report what his or her buddy observed. The teacher tries to show how the behaviors of encouraging and sharing are correlated with the creative process.

AFTER THE LESSON •

How does the teacher evaluate the success of the lesson?	The teacher checks to make sure the essential elements (marked by asterisks) of cooperative learning groups were completed. The teacher schedules a series of classes in which students continue to practice working in cooperative groups.

ANECDOTE •

The students in the fishbowl accomplished their task and received feedback from their classmates and the teacher. Immediately following the lesson, the rest of the class was divided into cooperative groups, and the groups were assigned the same academic task, roles, and social behaviors as the fishbowl group. Each member of the fishbowl was an observer in the newly formed groups.

The teachers who observed and the students who participated in the lesson reported that they enjoyed the lesson. The charts that were generated during the class discussion were used for lessons that were subsequently developed by the middle school teachers. It was clear that the students enjoyed being consulted about their experiences with group work and that they were committed to improving the way they worked together.

REFERENCE

Villa, R., & Thousand, J. (1987). *Cooperative group lesson plan.* Unpublished manuscript developed as part of an in-service staff development activity for A.A. Kingston Middle School faculty (New York), Center for Developmental Disabilities, University of Vermont, Burlington.

Junior High School Language Arts for a Student with Behavior Disorders

Lesson name: Newspaper ads
Grade level: Seventh to ninth grade
Time: 40 minutes

Author: C. Conn-Powers
Content area: Language arts

Conn-Powers (1988), a special education intern, collaborated with a junior high school language arts teacher who wanted to infuse creative writing skills into a reading lesson in a practical way. This was quite a challenge, especially considering the large size of the class, the range of students' reading abilities, and the inclusion of a student with behavior disorders. The two teachers consciously selected cooperative learning groups as a way to individualize instruction and ensure a high level of accountability for student participation. The social skills and role assignments enabled the language arts teacher to "multiply" himself; he knew many of the students needed to be "coached" in reading and comprehension. The teachers found it easy to adapt the cooperative group lesson for the student with behavior disorders. The guidance counselor met with them in advance to explain the anger management strategy the student used and to update them on the student's progress in using it.

ACADEMIC OBJECTIVES ....

What are the prerequisite skills?	Reading skills at least at the fourth- to fifth-grade level
What are the academic objectives?	Students define classified ads, state the benefits to the community of having classified ads, locate ads according to type of service wanted, and accurately match examples of ads to appropriate categories. Students write a creative story that illustrates the benefits and accurately matches the type of classified ad.
How do students demonstrate the academic objectives?	Students demonstrate these objectives by saying and doing the following: "I need this service or these goods and can find people to help me by looking in this section of the classified ads. The benefits include . . . because. . . ."
What are the criteria for success?	Students who can locate an appropriate classified ad and write and tell a story consisting of at least one paragraph of four or more sentences explaining two benefits of the ad earn an *A* on this assignment; stories with one or two sentences or only one benefit earn a *B*; stories with one or two sentences and no benefits earn a *C*.
What are the modifications for learners with special education needs?	No modifications were needed for the academic objectives. L. is an adolescent female with behavior disorders whose IEP includes objectives related to increasing self-control, especially when confronted with difficult or time-consuming academic tasks. Instead of throwing a tantrum (e.g., throwing her books and materials on the floor, stomping her feet) or withdrawing (e.g., leaving the room), L. is practicing "counting to 10 while taking deep inhalations and long slow exhalations" while staying at her seat. This technique has been taught to her by the guidance counselor.

How do learners with special education needs demonstrate the academic objectives?	The teacher asks L. privately to show how she practices calming down by breathing deeply and counting to 10 and lets her know that today's lesson may be a good time for her to show this skill. The teacher asks L. what kind of support she would like to receive from her group. (Possible requests: "Don't stop talking while I practice breathing because I can still listen." "Is it okay if I ask for help in reading the small print?")
What are the criteria for success for the learners with special needs?	L. stays with her group to complete the lesson. She practices "counting to 10 and deep breathing" any and every time she needs to.

FACE-TO-FACE INTERACTION DECISIONS* • • • • • • • • • • • • • • •

What is the group size?	There are 32 students in the class—four students to each group, eight groups total.
How are students assigned to groups?	To ensure heterogeneity, students are assigned to groups by the teacher by classified ads categories: Apartments for Rent, Miscellaneous for Sale, Home Furnishings for Sale, Dogs, Help Wanted (General), Houses for Sale, Personals, and Automobiles (Foreign) for Sale. The teacher makes sure that each group has at least one student who can read the material, boys and girls are distributed equally, and so forth.
What is the room arrangement?	Students move their desks into eight clusters so that they are facing each other.
How are materials arranged?	Each group receives one newspaper that includes a classified ads section, one blank piece of paper, and one set of colored pens.

STRUCTURING POSITIVE INTERDEPENDENCE* • • • • • • • • • • • •

	Members get the messages: "We sink or swim together," "Do your work—we're counting on you," and, "How can I help you to do better?"
What is the structure—a single product, one group goal, a shared outcome, or a group reward?	Each group selects one ad that accurately reflects its assigned category. Each person reads the ad and explains what it means. The group then writes a story about the person who placed the ad and what beneficial things happen to him or her when the ad is answered.
Are student roles assigned?	To promote positive interdependence, students are assigned roles by the teacher. The teacher hands out prepared "role cards" on index cards: Recorder: A person who writes the story the group creates Checker: A person who makes sure that everyone in the group agrees Ad reader: A person who reads the ad in the assigned category Encourager: A person who energizes the group by asking for or praising ideas

What are the other divisions of labor besides roles?	This emerges as the group decides the content of its story.
How are materials arranged?	To promote positive interdependence, only one newspaper is given to each group so that team members must share the paper.
Optional: *What other ways to promote positive interdependence are used— intergroup cooperation, intergroup competition, positive fantasy mission, or identity interdependence (e.g., group name)?*	Intergroup cooperation is encouraged by having groups listen in on each others' story lines.

ESTABLISHING SOCIAL SKILL PEFORMANCE* •••••••••••••

What are the social skills objectives?	Based on student performance during other group work, the teacher decides that the social skill of paraphrasing will be emphasized in this lesson.
How is the need for each social skill communicated?	Ask students what happens when they share an idea and nobody says anything. (Acknowledge student responses along the lines of, "I don't think my idea is good," or, "I don't feel like saying anything anymore.") "What are some better ways than silence to handle this?" (Acknowledge student contributions [e.g., Say, "Thanks for the idea," "Okay," or, "I didn't know that"]. "Another way we can handle it is to restate or paraphrase what that person said. Paraphrasing is saying what someone else said in another way."
How are social skills explained, demonstrated, role-played, or practiced?	Ask students to volunteer to demonstrate how they would sound and what their faces would look like when paraphrasing a statement. Praise appropriate demonstrations and correct until students get the idea. Write on the board or on poster paper some of their examples under two columns: "Paraphrasing sounds like. . . ." and "Paraphrasing looks like. . . ."
How are social skills assigned to group members?	All group members are responsible for practicing paraphrasing at least two times during the lesson.

SOCIAL SKILL PERFORMANCE •••••••••••••••••••••••••••
Teacher Monitoring and Intervention

What is the process (how and who) for monitoring groups?	During the lesson, the teacher observes and monitors group interactions for about 1–2 minutes per group for at least three rotations.
What is the process for feedback (how and who) to groups if social skills are being used?	The teacher shares "on the spot" when the group is doing a great job at paraphrasing.

What is the process for feedback (how and who) to groups if social skills are not being used?	Ask the group, "What does it look like and sound like to paraphrase?" (Acknowledge student responses.) "That's right! I'll come back in a few minutes and I expect to hear and see you, okay?"
What collaboration problems are anticipated?	One person not contributing to the story; one person taking over the story
What are interventions to avoid or remedy anticipated problems?	*Rules:* When you feel like intervening, don't. If you must intervene, then do it with a question, not an answer. Move away as soon as you can, even if it is only 3 feet. Ask the group, "How can you rearrange the way you're working to make sure that everyone's ideas are in the story?" (Acknowledge student responses.) "You have some really good ideas. I expect if you use one or two of them, you'll write a more creative story. I'll be back in a few minutes to see how you're doing."

SOCIAL SKILL PERFORMANCE ....

Student Monitoring

What is the student observer(s) selection and training process (what and who)?	Specifically trained student observers are not used.
How are social skills monitored?	Paraphrasing is tallied by the teacher.
Do students observe more than one group?	No.
Do students observe for an entire lesson?	No.
How and when do the teacher or students share their observations?	Students share during the closure part of the lesson when the teacher randomly calls on students to do so. As the teacher listens in on each group, he or she can "catch the students" engaging in the skill of paraphrasing.

STRUCTURING INDIVIDUAL ACCOUNTABILITY ....

Are individual quizzes assigned?	No.
Is there random selection of group members to answer questions?	Students are randomly selected to read their group's story about the ads. For social skills processing, students are randomly selected to share their examples of paraphrasing.

SETTING THE TASK ••••••••••••••••••••••••••••••••••

What is the process for explanation of the academic task and criteria for success (when and who)?

The teacher says, "Today you'll be working as a group to learn more about classified ads. What are classified ads?" (Acknowledge student responses and correct misconceptions.) "Where are they located in the newspaper?" (Acknowledge accurate responses.) "What kind of information are you able to get from the classified ads?" (Acknowledge accurate responses.) "People place ads and others read ads to learn about people in our town. The ads help people get jobs, find housing, and transact business. What are some ads that you or your family might place in the paper?" (Write all responses on the board.) "In what sections of the classified ads would you find these ads?" (Acknowledge or coach accurate responses.) "Ad readers, open your group's paper to the 'For Free' section. Group members, help your ad reader find the section and praise him or her for finding it quickly. Now, read the first ad. Who in the room would like that free item?" (Acknowledge responses.)

"Today you will be reading a specific section of the classified ads. Help your ad reader select one ad that accurately reflects your assigned category. Be sure each person can explain what it means. Your group should then write a story about the person who placed the ad and what beneficial things happen to him or her when the ad is answered. You have 20 minutes to do this. I'll be looking for at least four complete sentences in your story explaining at least two benefits. Groups that meet criteria will have their stories posted on the Young Authors' Award board."

How are social skills and criteria for success explained (when and who)?

"I expect each person in the group to practice paraphrasing at least twice during this 20-minute lesson. I will place a checkmark every time I hear your group paraphrase." Teacher checks for understanding by asking, "What will I be checking for?" (Acknowledge students who paraphrase the previous directions and give corrective feedback until they get the idea.)

CLOSURE AND PROCESSING* ••••••••••••••••••••••••••••

What is the process for closure (students summarize what they learned)?

One or two randomly selected groups comes to the front of the room to read their stories.

What is the process for feedback on academic performance (how, who, and when)?

If criteria are met, the teacher prominently displays story and authors' names on the Young Authors' Award board.

How are the teacher's observations shared?

Rule: Share negative comments in private and positive comments in public and private.

The teacher notes exemplary displays of paraphrasing, commenting on how the ideas flowed and explaining the relationship between sharing lots of ideas and "process gain"—how no one person could have come up with what the group did.

What is the process for assessment of individual and group success in using social skills (how and when)?

Pass out one index card per group for group members to record what went well and what skills they plan to practice the next time. Students sign the card and hand it in. The next time the groups work together, the teacher distributes their commitment cards.

Ask the class as a whole, "What did you like about working with this group? What didn't you like? What will you do differently when you work together next time?"

AFTER THE LESSON •

How does the teacher evaluate the success of the lesson?

The teacher checks to see that the five elements (marked by asterisks) of cooperative learning lessons were included. The next social skill the teacher introduces is "piggy-backing on ideas," which extends the concept of paraphrasing to include building on the positive aspects of ideas that are contributed.

ANECDOTE •

Each group decided on an interesting ad and wrote a one-page story, which represented many more than four sentences in a 20-minute period—an unexpected outcome. They cooperated and worked well together. Two groups had trouble getting started and after sending a team member to listen to other groups, they managed to get inspired. L. became frustrated twice and used her intervention technique to great advantage. Her group was happy that she shared her ideas and used them to create a different twist to their story. In their story, the person who placed the ad needed to know how to deep-breathe in order to use scuba diving gear that was for sale. The scuba gear did not sell, but it was used to save another person's life. According to Conn-Powers and her partner teacher, the most impressive aspect of the lesson was that the students were so eager to hear each other's stories. The class decided to create a composite story using ideas from all eight stories and send it to the school newspaper. It was published the next month, creating an unexpected whole-class reward.

REFERENCE

Conn-Powers, C. (1988). *Cooperative group lesson plan.* Unpublished manuscript submitted in partial fulfillment of requirements for the Educational Specialist graduate program, Professor J. Thousand, University of Vermont, Department of Special Education, College of Education and Social Services, Burlington.

Non-violence: Another Response to War for a Student with Emotional and Learning Disabilities and for Classmates Learning English as a Second Language

Lesson name: Non-violence:
  There is another way
Grade level: High school students
Time: 50 minutes
  (introductory lesson)

Authors: D. Barton and N. Cardosa
Content area: History, multicultural
  studies, conflict resolution, collaboration, language arts

Diane Barton and Nancy Cardosa (1999) developed this lesson plan to include Cassie in the general education high school social studies class. The social studies teacher had developed a multimedia unit on the concept of *power* to help the freshmen students understand the post–World War II era. Cassie was reading at a preprimer level, but the activity required at least a sixth-grade reading and writing skills level. Cassie often walked out of the classroom when frustrated and had violent outbursts when stressed (although she was learning more appropriate ways to manage her anger during a support group process once a week). She was artistic but had a short attention span. Sometimes she liked being with a group, and other times she needed to work alone. She liked to do nonacademic jobs in the classroom.

ACADEMIC OBJECTIVES •••••••••••••••••••••••••••••••••••••

Students will learn different philosophies of non-violence and relate them to their own lives.

Given the words to a popular song about war, the student will contribute at least two opinions or speculations regarding three questions about attitudes toward war; come to consensus as to the answers to each question, and accurately describe at least one response from each of the answers orally or in writing.

What are the prerequisite skills?

Students must know how to complete a "free write" exercise (writing on an assigned topic without interruption or editing for 3–5 minutes). Students have completed a thematic integrated instructional unit on World War II and Vietnam. Students follow directions and ask clarifying questions. Students have had previous experiences with working in cooperative learning groups.

How do students demonstrate the academic objectives?

There are three major ways that students demonstrate the academic objectives.

1. Orally expressing and writing quotations and examples from videotapes and written material about Mohandas K. Gandhi

2. Visually and orally representing the philosophy of non-violence expressed in the short stories about Martin Luther King, Jr., or Chico Mendes

3. Writing an essay that shows how their own life experiences reflect the non-violent philosophies of Mohandas K. Gandhi, Martin Luther King, Jr., or Chico Mendes

What are the criteria for success?

The criteria for success were that the citations, posters, and essays accurately included at least one element of non-violent philosophies.

What are the modifications for learners with special education needs?

The group roles were assigned to specifically capitalize on each student's strengths. In Cassie's case, she could orally express ideas, watch the video, or listen to the song. She was paired with a peer tutor who had been coached in the process of co-reading the short stories assigned to her group. Cassie's artistic ability helped the group produce a poster that was colorful and appropriate to the topic. Cassie's desire to do nonacademic jobs made it logical for her to be assigned the role of "materials procurer"—as the group needed a specific item, Cassie went to the teacher or the storage area to get it. Cassie dictated her essay to the peer tutor (or, if she preferred to work alone, Cassie was allowed to tape record her essay).

Other accommodations: Because this class has a large number of students who are learning ESL, the teacher scaffolded the concepts and information by using peer tutors who were bilingual and who had successfully completed U.S. history with a grade of *C* or better. The peer tutors were available twice a week to work in this classroom.

FACE-TO-FACE INTERACTION DECISIONS* • • • • • • • • • • • • • • • • •

How are students assigned to groups?

Students are assigned randomly to groups. As each student enters the classroom, hand him or her one red, orange, green, yellow, purple, or blue lollipop. (Be careful to count four lollipops of each color).

What is the room arrangement?

Ask students to move the furniture to the sides of the classrooms and arrange chairs in circle groups of four so that they sit face-to-face. Students with the red lollipops sit in a circle together, those with blue sit together, and so forth.

How are materials arranged?

The tape recorder/music system is set up so that all students can easily hear the music to the 1970 tune, *War.* In addition, each student has a copy of the lyrics so they are able to read as the song is played.

Each student has an individual packet of materials. All students receive a summary of the Gandhi information (as a model for the scope of their poster). This summary includes a list of the people, the political leaders, a map of India, and a timeline showing approximately 10 important dates, places, and events.

All students receive short readings related to Martin Luther King, Jr., and Chico Mendes along with examples of quotes (e.g., "Let freedom ring from every hill and molehill of Mississippi, from every mountainside, let freedom ring."; "Our fight is the fight of all the peoples of the forest").

All students complete a study guide of six items:

1. Of what empire was India a part?

2. What are the two main religions in India?

3. Describe the relationship of reincarnation, the caste system, and the untouchable caste.

4. Describe the philosophy of non-violence. Be sure to include its purpose regarding the oppressor.

5. Write a paragraph about the background of Chico Mendes. Include information about the rain forest and the rubber-tapping industry.

6. Write a paragraph about the background of Martin Luther King, Jr. Include information about the Jim Crow laws and segregation.

STRUCTURING POSITIVE INTERDEPENDENCE* • • • • • • • • • • • • •

Members get the messages: "We sink or swim together," "Do your work—we're counting on you," and, "How can I help you to do better?"

What is the structure—a single product, one group goal, a shared outcome, or a group reward?

As a group of four, students will come to a consensus on the 10 strongest images of war as they are presented in the song.

Over the course of the week of study, the group goal is to create an attractive poster to visually display the non-violent philosophies of Martin Luther King, Jr., or Chico Mendes, including a timeline with seven events, three significant quotes from either person, and two background comments.

Are student roles assigned?

There are four roles assigned by the teacher (to specifically capitalize on each student's strengths).

1. Recorder: On the sheet provided, the recorder writes the name of who contributed what idea.

2. Layout artist: The layout artist drafts the poster on the layout paper, showing the location of the quotes selected, background statements, map, and timeline, including the colors and what other items there will be.

3. Liaison: The liaison checks the recorder's information and the layout design with the teacher and will obtain any materials from the teacher that are needed to complete the poster.

4. Presenter: The presenter orally expresses the key points of the poster to the class.

What are the other divisions of labor besides roles?

Other divisions of labor may emerge as the poster is created. For example, the role of "consensus builder" may need to be added in the case of groups in which consensus seems to be absent.

How are materials arranged?

To promote positive interdependence among the members of the groups, one handout, one extra piece of paper for the recorder, one sheet of poster board, and one pencil are assigned to each group.

Optional: *What other ways to promote positive interdependence are used—intergroup cooperation, intergroup competition, positive fantasy mission, or identity interdependence (e.g., group name)?*

Each of the groups will report their 10 strongest images, thus creating a "class consensus" of the "top 10" strongest images all together. All the groups will share their posters, thus creating a "class gallery" that could be opened for other classes to view.

HIGH SCHOOL

ESTABLISHING SOCIAL SKILL PERFORMANCE* • • • • • • • • • • •

What are the social skills objectives?	The teacher selects two skills based on performance in previous group work: active listening and contributing ideas.
How is the need for each social skill communicated?	The need for the social skills of active listening and contributing ideas will be communicated through a 3-minute scripted role play of inappropriate group behavior; a group brainstorm of what could be done better, along with expressing the feelings tied to the inappropriate behavior; and the consequences, followed by a second 3-minute scripted role play of appropriate group behavior. Students will then be asked to volunteer to demonstrate how they would sound and what their faces would look like during active listening and when they contribute ideas.
How are social skills explained, demonstrated, role-played, or practiced?	The teacher shares "on the spot" when the group is doing a great job of contributing and active listening.
How are social skills assigned to group members?	All group members are responsible for practicing active listening at least twice during each class session. All must contribute at least two ideas to the group poster.

SOCIAL SKILL PERFORMANCE •
Teacher Monitoring and Intervention

What is the process (how and who) for monitoring groups?	The teacher circulates to visit each group at least twice during each class period.
What is the process for feedback (how and who) to groups if social skills are being used?	The teacher acknowledges instances of active listening and/or positive contributions "on the spot," or the teacher asks the recorder to report to the group and asks the group to comment.
What is the process for feedback (how and who) to groups if social skills are not being used?	The teacher briefly sits with the group to listen to their evaluation of their group process (after the recorder has shared what has been written, specifically showing nonparticipation of some members or overparticipation from others). The teacher re-creates the scenario presented at the beginning of class showing inappropriate and appropriate active listening and/or expressing contributions.
	Group members may be asked to observe/eavesdrop on another group and report back to the group what they observed with respect to appropriate active listening and/or expressing contributions.
	The teacher may also say, "I'm going to leave you right now for a few minutes while you come up with a plan to show active listening (or make sure that all contributions are being heard). I'll check back with you in a 5 minutes." (Then return to hear their resolution.)
What collaboration problems are anticipated?	Students may work independently without gaining contributions from other group members.
	Students may not want to participate in the activity because of some previous altercation with a member of the group.

Students may fear that their ideas about non-violence will be denigrated or disrespected (especially if there is a gang culture in the school).

What are interventions to avoid or remedy anticipated problems?

Rules: When you feel like intervening, don't. If you must intervene, do it with a question, not an answer. Move away as soon as you can, even if it is only 3 feet.

The teacher can redistribute the tasks and roles to rotate the responsibilities so as to create a more balanced division of labor and thus gain positive interdependence through shared resources.

The teacher may say, "Do you think Martin Luther King, Jr., faced people who disagreed with him? How about Chico Mendes or Mohandas K. Gandhi? What advice do you think they might give you for handling this disagreement you are having?"

Later, the teacher can add, "Remember it's okay to have disagreements. Use your friendly disagreeing voice. In fact, people who disagree and really listen to the other person's reasons for disagreeing often learn a better way to understand the concepts and one another."

SOCIAL SKILL PERFORMANCE •
Student Monitoring

What is the student observer(s) selection and training process (what and who)?

Specifically trained student observers are not used. However, students will record the contributions of each group member for the group poster.

How are social skills monitored?

The recorder for each group will write the names of each group member and their contributions.

Do students observe more than one group?

No.

Do students observe for an entire lesson?

No.

How and when do the teacher or students share their observations?

During and at the end of the lesson

STRUCTURING INDIVIDUAL ACCOUNTABILITY • • • • • • • • • • • • •

Each group member contributes two or more items for the poster. The recorder records who and what each member contributes. The liaison reports this information to the teacher. Each person receives a grade from the teacher calculated as follows:

• Cooperative efforts for the group poster: 5 points

• Detail and accuracy of the poster: 5 points

HIGH SCHOOL

- Individual "free writes" with group comment page: 5 points

- Individual score for essay about non-violence/significance to the student: 5 points

- Individual accuracy and completion of unit packet: 5 points

- Teacher–student private evaluation of student's group and individual work: 1–5 points

Are individual quizzes assigned?	No.
Is there random selection of group members to answer questions?	Yes.

SETTING THE TASK •••••••••••••••••••••••••••••••••••••

What is the process for explanation of the academic task and criteria for success (when and who)?

The teacher says, "Today we'll be summarizing what we've learned about World War II and Vietnam by listening to a song titled *War* that shows how our society has changed its attitude about war. This will launch our study of three leaders who have helped to change society's attitudes–Mohandas K. Gandhi, Martin Luther King, Jr., and Chico Mendes." (Point to a newsprint with the questions posted.) "Here are the questions that will guide our study today."

1. What attitudes and emotions about war are expressed in this song?

2. Why might the public have had those attitudes during that year (1970)?

3. Think of a time in your life when you or a member of your family felt threatened by someone else. What was your reaction? How could you change the way you reacted?

(Show movie clips of *Gandhi*.) "What are your ideas about what Mohandas K. Gandhi said and did that show his philosophy of non-violence?" (Acknowledge responses, write on the overhead key phrases and ideas.) "Good! This is what you will be doing to summarize the key ideas of your selected leader–Martin Luther King, Jr., or Chico Mendes."

CLOSURE AND PROCESSING* •••••••••••••••••••••••••••••••

What is the process for closure (students summarize what they learned)?

Each group creates a "we believe" statement about non-violent movements and chorally states the response as the teacher conducts sharing by calling on each group in random order.

What is the process for feedback on academic performance (how, who, and when)?

After listening to the song, partners orally report their images. The teacher writes the images on an overhead, showing how images overlap or are distinct.

Each group orally reports the content of their posters on Martin Luther King, Jr., or Chico Mendes. The posters are displayed on a section of the classroom wall titled *Non-violent Methods for Change.* Individual students' sentences and paragraphs are attractively displayed around the posters.

How are the teacher's observations shared?

Rule: Share negative comments in private and positive comments in public and private.

The teacher evaluates each group by discussing the effective qualities they demonstrated while working on the poster. Positive comments are publicly shared throughout the process, becoming an important component of positive interdependence between the students and the teacher and the students and the group. Comments are specifically selected to help the students increase their awareness of their actions and how those actions helped the group achieve the desired outcome.

What is the process for assessment of individual and group success in using social skills (how and when)?

The teacher visits each group to monitor the quality and accuracy of the statements by listening during 3- to 5-minute time samples for each group. While circulating to visit each group, the teacher notices and acknowledges acceptable active listening and expression of contributions as they occur.

At the completion of the lesson, the teacher asks each person to write appreciation statements. (Show on an overhead transparency with the sentence structure, "I appreciate [write your group member's name here] contribution [write what the person did or said].") The teacher says, "Review what you and your group accomplished in this lesson. Think of three or four things that happened that made your group successful. Was it something one person said or did? Did one person do an especially good job at something? These might be what you appreciate."

AFTER THE LESSON •

How does the teacher evaluate the success of the lesson?

During the whole-class presentation of the posters, the teacher checks for accuracy of their statements and provides explicit feedback. Individually meeting with each student later in the week, the teacher elicits from each person self-evaluation of their oral and written expression and together set up a plan for future performance.

ANECDOTE •

Cassie was pleased that her group's poster was included. In addition, Cassie expressed her disagreements without walking out of the room or having a violent outburst. When she read that Martin Luther King, Jr., was known as a boy who would rather talk his way out of arguments than fight, she decided she would learn to do that, too!

REFERENCE

Barton, D., & Cardosa, N. (1999). *Non-violence: An alternative response to war: Cooperative group lesson plan.* Unpublished manuscript submitted in partial fulfillment of requirements for Fall 1999 EDMX 627, Professor J. Thousand, California State University San Marcos, Department of Special Education, College of Education, San Marcos.

Introducing Adults to Cooperative Learning as a Strategy for Integrating Students with Disabilities

Lesson name: Cooperative learning
for adults
Grade level: Adult
Time: 55 minutes

Author: J.S. Thousand
Content area: Language arts
and appreciating diversity

Jacqueline S. Thousand developed this lesson plan for teachers and other adults who want to make sure that students with disabilities are meaningfully included in cooperative learning groups. The role play embedded in the lesson enables the adults to empathize with students who might have the sensory, intellectual, psychological, or learning challenges that they simulate. Teachers have enthusiastically embraced both the simulation and the task of reading and sharing their reactions to one of the poems from Silverstein's (1981) classic book, *A Light in the Attic*. The excerpt is likely to evoke strong feelings and empathy for the alienation that comes when people feel incompetent.

ACADEMIC OBJECTIVES ••••••••••••••••••••••••••••••••••

What are the prerequisite skills?

Membership in the class (i.e., selecting this session to attend during the in-service); in each group, someone must be able to read the poem and write, and there must be comprehension of the language used in the poem.

What are the academic objectives?

Group members interpret the poem about diversity and feelings.

How do students demonstrate the academic objectives?

Group members are observed to be giving at least one answer per question and individually answering one of the three questions with the answer that matches the group's answer. They are observed producing at least five answers per question, selecting and circling the agreed-upon answer, and initialing to indicate agreement with answers.

What are the criteria for success?

Contributing at least one answer per question and initialing to indicate agreement

What are the modifications for learners with special education needs?

Participants are assigned role cards that instruct them to simulate students with various challenges. Modifications for the challenges are also described on the cards. A student with visual impairments needs a fellow student to serve as a reader; a student who does not read needs a fellow student to serve as a reader; a student with cerebral palsy who uses a computer to write is assigned the role of recorder for the group; a student who likes to get the group "off task" needs an engaging role such as "checker for understanding"; and a student who is academically gifted, likes to work alone, and sees little value in others' contributions needs to play a supportive role, such as "encourager."

FACE-TO-FACE INTERACTION DECISIONS* ••••••••••••••••

What is the group size?	Participants work in groups of five.
How are students assigned to groups?	There must be at least one person who can read the poem and one who can write. Otherwise, the group is heterogeneously mixed according to gender, culture, and ethnic background or according to race, gifts, challenges, and achievement (e.g., one high-achieving, three average-achieving, and one low-achieving student in each group). The teacher, not the students, decides who is in each group.
What is the room arrangement?	Participants arrange their seats in a circle with or without a table so they may be seated face to face and close enough to have eye contact, hear one another, and do their work jointly. There should be enough space for the teacher to move from group to group.

STRUCTURING POSITIVE INTERDEPENDENCE* ••••••••••••

	Members get the messages: "We sink or swim together," "Do your work—we're counting on you," and, "How can I help you to do better?"
What is the structure—a single product, a group goal, a shared outcome, or a group reward?	The teacher says, "I want one set of answers from each group that all members agree to, as indicated by the signature of your initials on the group product. Initialing indicates that you have participated and that you understand and agree to the answers. Each group can earn up to 100 points for the group answer sheet. There are 20 points for each of your four answers and an additional 20 points if all members sign their initials on the answer sheet within 20 minutes."
Are student roles assigned?	Role cards with definitions for each role are prepared and distributed as follows: The encourager role is assigned to the "gifted" learner, the timekeeper role to a nonreader who knows how to tell time, the checker role to the student with visual impairment, the reader role to the student who gets the group off task, and the recorder role to the student who uses a computer to write.

Role Definitions
Encourager/Equalizer

Watch to make certain all group members are contributing. Invite silent members by asking them for their opinions and help.

Timekeeper

Notify the group of approaching time limits (e.g., 5 or 10 minutes). Move the group along to the next step in the assignment. Allot no more than 5 minutes for each question. Make sure signatures (initials) are secured within the time limit.

Checker

Check to make certain each member can state each answer. Check to make sure members agree on reasons for the answers. Check at any time during the discussion. Try a "quiz" for each of the group members.

Recorder

Summarize answers until the group is satisfied. Record all answers. Secure signatures (initials) within the time limit.

Reader

Read aloud to the group as often as requested.

What are the other divisions of labor besides roles?

This may emerge as the students participate in the lesson. The role of "jargon buster" may be needed if the adults begin discussing the interventions for students with various disabilities. The jargon buster signals when a specialized term that might not be understood by everyone is used; the jargon user is then asked to define the term.

How is material arranged to promote positive interdependence?

Each group shares two copies of the Silverstein poem, "The Little Boy and the Old Man", that includes a set of four questions for the group to answer. One copy is for the reader; the other is for the recorder to record the group's answers on the computer.

The Little Boy and the Old Man

Said the little boy, "Sometimes I drop my spoon."
Said the old man, "I do that too."
The little boy whispered, "I wet my pants."
"I do that too," laughed the little old man.
Said the little boy, "I often cry."
The old man nodded, "So do I."
"But worst of all," said the boy, "it seems
Grown-ups don't pay attention to me."
And he felt the warmth of a wrinkled old hand.
"I know what you mean," said the old man.
(Silverstein, 1981, p. 95)

Instructions: Please share your answers to each question. Recorders list all answers given.
   As a group, circle the favorite answer for each question.

1.   What is the poet saying?

2.   What emotion(s) does the poem evoke in you? (How does this poem make you feel?)

3.   What are two key words in the poem? Why did you select these words?

4. How does the content of this poem relate to your feelings about people with disabilities?

Sign your initials indicating you have participated and you understand and agree to the answers.

ESTABLISHING SOCIAL SKILL PERFORMANCE* • • • • • • • • • • •

What are the social skills objectives?

Group members contribute at least one idea for each question. Group members praise each other's contributions at least once.

How is the need for each social skill communicated?

The instructor asks the group, "What do you think is the least used social skill in adult groups?" (List all answers on newsprint.) "Thank you! Yes, it's true. Adults rarely praise each other's contributions, especially adults in the helping professions. Today, we'll be focusing on the use of praise or encouragement, particularly because the poem is likely to evoke strong feelings that may result in reluctance to share."

How are social skills explained, demonstrated, role-played, or practiced?

The instructor says, "Please check with the two people next to you to find out their favorite, most authentic praise statements. I'll check back with you in 2 minutes to list them on the newsprint." (Wait for 2 minutes and then list the responses on newsprint so that the participants can easily see them.) "Thank you! Now these are visible to all encouragers and remember that the encourager's role is twofold: Modeling how to praise by actually praising your team members' contributions and monitoring your team members to ensure that they are praising also! I'll be coming around to each of your groups to listen for these important social skills."

SOCIAL SKILL PERFORMANCE •
Monitoring and Intervention*

What is the process (how and when) for monitoring groups?

The instructor systematically visits each group to listen in for 3–5 minutes to 1) ensure that group members understand and are following the directions, 2) ensure that the social skills of contributing and praising are being practiced, 3) check that group members are performing assigned roles, and 4) intervene if necessary. Use the observation form (see Figure 21.1) to take note of significant examples of cooperative behaviors to share during the closure part of the lesson. Place a tally mark (/) each time the skill is observed. Write brief descriptive comments to illustrate the content of the collaborative skill.

What is the process for feedback (how and when) to groups if social skills are being used?

During a debriefing discussion at the end of the lesson, provide examples to each group on their use of the social skills. Be specific by giving verbatim phrases and describing the situation and, if possible, the result (e.g., the impact on the group's creativity, attitude, or cohesiveness).

Collaborative skills	Team A Group members	Team B Group members	Team C Group members
Contributing			
Comments			
Praising			
Comments			
Checking for understanding			
Comments			
Asking questions			
Comments			
Encouraging others			
Comments			

Figure 21.1.　Sample observation form.

What is the process for feedback (how and when) to groups if social skills are not being used?

If an interaction problem is observed, encourage the group to stop and solve it before continuing. Ensure that the encourager is facing the board where the list of praise statements can be seen. Ask the group to brainstorm other statements that might be more authentic or believable to the group.

What collaboration problems are anticipated?

Due to the emotional sensitivity of the poem, some adults may be reluctant to share. In some cases, loss of a child or older family member may be remembered. Another likely problem is superficial answers.

What are the interventions to avoid or remedy the anticipated problems?

Rule: When you feel like intervening, don't. If you must intervene, do it with questions, not answers. Move away as soon as you can, even if it is only 3 feet.

Encourage the group to allow psychological space for deep emotions by letting each person experience whatever emotions may surface. Do not try to stop the flow of emotions or soothe or mask them. Instead, let them be. It may be helpful for each person to write about his or her feelings. Invite each person to share and allow an individual to "pass" if he or she prefers.

If superficial answers are surfacing, then interrupt the group and gently challenge the participants to explore interesting answers or elaborate on the superficial ones.

ADULT

SOCIAL SKILL PERFORMANCE ·······················
Student Monitoring

What is the student observer(s) selection and training process? (what and who)?	In this lesson, there are no student observers.
How are social skills monitored?	The teacher monitors with an observation form as shown in Figure 21.1.
Do students observe more than one group?	No.
Do students observe for the entire lesson?	No.
How do students share their observations?	Participants are asked to share their reactions to the process.

STRUCTURING INDIVIDUAL ACCOUNTABILITY* ············

Are individual quizzes assigned?	No.
Is there random selection of group members to answer questions?	The instructor tells the class, "After the lesson, I will collect your group papers and ask each group member to answer in writing one of the four major questions. You won't know ahead of time which of the questions I will ask you, so be prepared to answer them all. Remember that you will need to generate some creative alternatives to writing for the student who is visually impaired and for the nonwriter so that they, too, can give their individual answers. Remember that when you sign your initials on the group product, it means that you have participated and that you understand and agree to the answers."

SETTING THE TASK ······························

What is the process for explanation of the academic task and criteria for success (when and who)?	"Remember what the objectives for this lesson are—I've printed them on newsprint for you. For the last 3 weeks we've been reading the poems of various American poets. Each of you has composed a number of poems with themes you have selected yourselves. You may find yourself wanting to compose a poem today! Poetry is a way for each of us to express our feelings and ideas in a creative way. Poetry is a form of literature that some people enjoy reading; similar to music, poetry is rhythm, and rhyme can be quite beautiful. The poem for today deals with emotions. Your task, as a group, is to read or listen to the poem, "The Little Boy and the Old Man," and answer some questions.

I want your group to generate at least five possible answers for each question and then circle your group's favorite answer."

"Each group can earn up to 100 points. Your group can earn a total of 100 points for the group answer sheet–20 points for each of your four answers and an additional 20 points if all members initial the answer sheet within 20 minutes. Signing your initials indicates that you have participated and that you understand and agree to the answers."

How are social skills and criteria for success explained (when and who)?

The instructor continues, "I expect each of you to contribute at least one idea for each of the questions. I expect to see and hear you as you listen and praise other team members' ideas. I'll be looking for at least one praise statement to someone else. Finally, I want to see you pushing for many possible answers (at least five) before deciding on one answer. Also, each group member has a role. I'll be counting on the checkers to share how well you performed your roles and the social skills of contributing, praising, and pushing for more answers."

CLOSURE AND PROCESSING* •

What is the process for closure (students summarize what they learned)?

The instructor randomly "beams" questions to individuals in each group and asks them to share the group's answer.

What is the process for feedback on academic performance (when and who)?

The instructor scores group and individual responses and returns the work at the start of the next day's class period.

How are the instructor's observations shared?

Rule: Share negative comments in private and positive comments both in public and private.

The instructor shares examples of observations of group members performing their assigned roles and examples of contributing, listening, and praising.

What is the process for assessment of individual and group success in using social skills (how and when)?

The instructor asks each group to huddle for 3 minutes to write their answers as a group to these questions:

1. What social skills did we do well?

2. What do we need to improve?

3. How well did we perform our roles?

4. What do we need to perform them better?

The checker facilitates the discussion, and the encourager records the group's answers and hands them in to the instructor. The instructor solicits one answer from each group as a class closure.

ADULT

AFTER THE LESSON ••••••••••••••••••••••••••••••••••••

How does the instructor evaluate the success of the lesson?

The instructor checks to see that the essential elements (marked with asterisks) of effective cooperative learning lessons were included.

ANECDOTE ••••••••••••••••••••••••••••••••••••••

Those who participated in this lesson realized that their group's performance depended on each individual member's contribution and the group's ability to accommodate for the individual differences among the group members. They experienced the importance of achieving the academic task (i.e., understanding the poem) and maintaining positive interactions with group members (i.e., engaging in specific interpersonal skills such as encourager). This combination yielded an appreciation for the feelings their own students may experience when working in cooperative learning groups.

REFERENCE

Silverstein, S. (1981). *A light in the attic.* New York: Harper & Row.

Creating and Supporting Peer Tutor Partnerships in Secondary Schools

Pamela J. Villalobos
Deborah Tweit-Hull
Amie Wong

Ensuring that all students have the support they need to be successful in school may seem a lofty goal. But, as LaPlant and Zane show (see Chapter 18), schoolwide systems of peer supports are in place in many schools and have contributed greatly toward achieving this goal. One smaller, yet critical, piece of this puzzle involves the development of supportive peer tutor programs. The process discussed and described in this chapter focuses on the creation of peer tutor supports for secondary students with disabilities, although these strategies have been applied toward the development of more schoolwide partner learning systems as well (LaPlant & Zane, 1994).

Peer tutor programs can have many different "looks." Often, tutor programs, as with any other program, need to be tailored to the resources and culture of a particular school. In some instances, however, the development of an effective and respectful peer tutor program can also have a positive influence on the culture of the school and may serve to help create a more positive and supportive school climate. To facilitate this kind of positive energy or direction, it is critical that the peer tutor program emphasize the values of respect, mutual benefit, and advocacy. As articulated by Van der Klift and Kunc (see Chapter 3), relationships between individuals with and without disabilities (such as that developed between a tutor and "tutee") must emphasize a sharing of power, reciprocity, appreciation for differences, and recognition of each other's talents and limitations. It is important that the peer tutor relationship not result in an unequal balance of power and status such that one individual is always in the role of "helper" and the other in the role of "helpee." Instead, the focus should be on developing capacity within oneself and others. These core values are infused within the lesson plans presented in the next chapter.

Students are an extremely valuable resource on which secondary schools in particular need to capitalize. Utilizing students as peer tutors is one of many ways that students can contribute to and actively participate in the larger school community. However, effective peer tutor programs do not occur spontaneously or in isolation. As with any effective strategy or program, active planning, support, and facilitation are required to maximize this resource.

This chapter presents practical strategies and resources to create and support a peer tutor program and student partnerships in secondary schools. Actual hands-on lesson plans to train peer tutors for their instructional support role, while embracing the core values of respect, mutual benefit, and advocacy, are provided in the next chapter. Finally, this chapter is organized to address the components of effective partner learning systems (modified from LaPlant and Zane, Chapter 18), including 1) organizing and administering a peer tutor program, 2) identifying tutees, 3) recruiting and selecting peer tutors, 4) training peer tutors, 5) supervising and supporting peer tutors, 6) evaluating peer tutors, and 7) celebrating participation in a peer tutor program.

ORGANIZING AND ADMINISTERING A PEER TUTOR PROGRAM

To establish an effective peer tutor program at a secondary school, at least one person must commit to setting up and coordinating the program. This role entails overseeing the planning and implementation of a peer tutor class, as well as assuming the ongoing and daily responsibilities involved in selecting, training, supporting, and evaluating peer tutors. At most schools, a special education teacher often assumes this role because he or she is typically responsible for coordinating and providing supports to students with disabilities who are included in general education classes. Peer tutors can play a critical role in this milieu of supports provided to such a student. In addition, the special education teacher is usually the most knowledgeable about the needs of students who receive support and is familiar with the general education classrooms and teachers. This is not to say that other teachers and support staff are not involved in supporting or working with peer tutors. In fact, the general education teacher who has a peer tutor working with a student in his or her class will assume some responsibilities, as may other special education teachers, counselors, and paraeducators. Ideally, the special education teacher will receive support from other key players at the school, such as a counselor, a service learning coordinator, a Future Educators of America (FEA) club advisor, and/or office support staff, to coordinate, oversee, and maintain the program. Together, the special educator and other involved personnel develop the program components that best meet the needs of their students and school.

Setting Up a Peer Tutor Program

How a peer tutor program "looks" at a particular school will vary depending on the school structure, student needs, and other unique features of the school, staff, and student body. Several examples follow that depict a typical high school, a secondary school with a nontraditional structure, and a secondary school that offers no elective courses.

Parker High School

At Parker High School, the peer tutor class is set up as an elective course. Students may select peer tutoring as one of many electives such as drama, art, photography, and so forth. At Parker, one of the special education teachers, Ms. Philippe, has assumed primary coordination responsibilities for their peer tutor program and is listed as the course instructor for the peer tutor class elective. Ms. Philippe is responsible for all aspects of the course including daily attendance, course curriculum, peer tutor training, ongoing support and supervision, and grading. Ms. Philippe is also one of the inclusion support teachers at Parker and is responsible for meeting the needs of students with disabilities who are included in the general education core curriculum. In this capacity, the teacher is available to meet the peer tutors at the beginning of each class period or block, maintain attendance records, and deal with student absences to ensure adequate support is provided to students who receive support in their general education classes. The peer tutors are enrolled in a peer tutor elective course, and during this period they are responsible for providing instructional support to a designated student. The support is provided in the tutees' general education classes, which may be a core academic or an elective class. When tutored students are absent, the peer tutors may be requested to support different students (with whom they are familiar) for that day or may assist Ms. Philippe and the general education teachers to develop adapted materials for the tutored students. At the beginning of the school year, and periodically throughout the year, peer tutors will also be "pulled" from the general education classrooms to receive training. Peer tutor training is discussed in more depth later in this chapter. This type of peer tutor program model basically requires the establishment of a peer tutor course that is recognized, for a grade, in the school and the advanced scheduling of peer tutors (usually over the summer) to ensure the availability of peer tutors across the school day and when particularly needed.

Caesar Chavez Middle School

At Caesar Chavez Middle School, the establishment of a peer tutor program required some creativity and planning. Chavez Middle School is organized into six educational "families" that function as six separate schools within a school. Consequently, one educational family may follow a typical seven-period schedule each day, whereas another family may organize their instructional time around extended block periods. Another educational family may operate a "hybrid" version of both and engage in a 3-day rotational modified block schedule, sometimes referred to as an "ABC" schedule (i.e., day one is block schedule A, day two is block schedule B, day three may be all periods or may represent a third block schedule C). However, this school offers an extensive service learning program that seventh and eighth graders may select in lieu of their one elective course. Peer tutoring has been established as an option within the service learning program, and students receive a grade, as with any elective and service learning class. Teachers at Chavez determined that peer tutors should work with students outside of their own educational family, primarily for the purpose of confidentiality. Consequently, this posed somewhat of a scheduling challenge given the difference in schedules across educational families. Students serve as peer tutors during their own elective period and are supervised by the special education support teacher of the student and educational family they are tutoring. It is the responsibility of that special educator to plan, support, and supervise that peer tutor's experience. Depending on the peer tutor's elective schedule, he or she may tutor 5 days a week at the same time, 5 days a week at different times, or two or three times a week for a longer period of time. The supervising special education teacher may schedule the peer tutor's time to work specifically with one student in the same class (e.g., humanities) or across several classes (e.g., humanities, math, computers). The peer tutor may also be involved in working with two different students during the week within one subject area (e.g., science) or may spend part of his or her time supporting a student in class and the other part assisting the special education and general education teachers to develop modified/adapted materials for the student and other "special assignments." In this model, a large number of teachers share responsibility for the overall and day-to-day coordination and operation of the peer tutor program. Two special education support teachers engage in the overall coordinating activities and meet with the peer tutors for general training and support meetings once a week during the homebase period (25 minutes). Each special education support teacher is responsible for student-specific training, scheduling, ongoing support/supervision, and grading of each peer tutor providing support to students within their educational family. And, during the period that each special education support teacher is monitoring the learning center, he or she is responsible for assisting peer tutors to sign in/out, record absences, and pass on alternative assignments when tutees are absent. During their elective period/block, peer tutors follow the schedule provided by the special education support teacher (largely involving working with students in their general education classes) and once a week attend a special peer tutor homebase for 25 minutes at the beginning of the school day.

Nathaniel Junior High School

Nathaniel Junior High School was faced with a particularly challenging situation as they were involved in developing their peer tutor program: Students at the school had no elective courses. All students took Spanish and physical education in addition to their core academic classes and attended a shortened advisory period once a day (which was a common time across the school). The only exceptions to "no electives" were band and chorus, which were offered to a limited number of students during the advisory period. The solution was that students could sign up for the peer tutor course during their physical education period and then have their physical education class during the advisory period. The special education teacher who coordinated the peer tutor program co-taught the advisory period/physical education class along with a volunteer teacher from the physical education department. The special education teacher found that using the advisory period to teach physical education to the peer tutors provided an additional opportunity to create a relationship and a sense of "family" and teamwork with peer tutors that positively impacted the peer tutor program and experience. Furthermore, she was able to positively influence the physical education department who had been previously reluctant to actively include students with special needs in the physical education program at Nathaniel. This was accomplished by her collaborative, co-teaching relationship with a key physical education teacher and by including students with disabilities in the advisory period/physical education class, thus modeling effective strategies and supports.

Securing Administrative Support

Obviously, establishing a peer tutor program requires administrative support and approval. Before this can occur, a model and plan for implementation needs to be well developed. If possible, a small committee can be organized for the purpose of developing the model and plan based on the unique characteristics of their school. An initial step of the committee is to examine and, if possible, visit other programs/models in place. Next, the committee must craft out a model that will fit their school and resources. As shown in the previous examples, this may require some creative and collaborative brainstorming to develop a viable model. Once the model and plan of implementation have been developed, the next step involves securing administrative support and approval. Having a well-developed and thought out plan may be enough. However, depending on the culture and politics of a particular school, some "selling" of the idea to key stakeholders may be required as well. Other stakeholders that may be particularly affected include counselors and the person or people responsible for scheduling students in classes. Therefore, it may also be critical to provide a solid rationale for the development of a peer tutor program that describes the benefits and anticipated outcomes of peer tutoring.

Once approved, the implementation plan will most likely need to be revisited and perhaps modified to accommodate the needs of other stakeholders. This may include the process for scheduling peer tutors for the fall semester and, possibly, for determining the schedules of the tutees as well. It may also be possible, or necessary, to secure the involvement of other teachers or counselors to assist with coordination of activities and to facilitate the recruitment and selection process. Furthermore, a detailed implementation plan (or the steps to setting up a peer tutor class) must consider the following:

- Logistics concerning course enrollment

- Determining tutor eligibility

- Informing the faculty of the new peer tutor course

- Informing the student body and their families of the new peer tutor course

- Procedures for coordinating and scheduling peer tutors

- Training procedures and content for peer tutors

Table 22.1 outlines the actions and resources necessary to address the considerations.

Identifying Tutees

Once administrative support has been secured and the peer tutor course is set up, the next major issue that must be addressed concerns the actual *size* of the peer tutor program. In other words, how many students need or desire peer tutor support, and how many peer tutors can the program (at this stage) realistically train and support? The peer tutor program may initially be set up to meet the needs of a small number of students. Eventually, as the program gains popularity and/or recognition and increased capacity to manage a larger number of students, the program can gradually expand. Ideally, the program might eventually evolve into a schoolwide resource in which any student can request and benefit from peer assistance.

Initially, the number of peer tutors the program can support must be identified. In turn, this will most likely represent the number of students who will be using peer tutor support. Subsequently, these students will need to be identified and prioritized. Again, how this is done will largely be determined by the needs, interests, and characteristics of the school and students. When making this determination, a number of student characteristics need to be considered, including the following:

- Students who are over-reliant on adult support

- Students who require personal support to initiate, maintain, or complete an assignment

- Students who are more resistant to adult support (i.e., don't want the stigma but may be open to support from a peer)

- Students who could benefit from additional one-to-one support or attention (but who may not receive much adult support)

- Students who are identified as "creating disruptions" in the class

- Students who have individualized education program (IEP) goals related to working with peers (Using an IEP may be one way to address this goal for students who have difficulty interacting with peers due to communication and/or behavioral considerations.)

In addition to these considerations, a number of questions require attention on the part of the peer tutor committee and the peer tutor coordinator:

Table 22.1. Setting up a peer tutor class

Goals	Actions	Resources
Obtain administrative approval and support.	Provide proposal that identifies program benefits for students with and without disabilities; plan for program implementation, coordination, and evaluation; and identify timeline and personnel needs. Determine course status (e.g., elective/5-unit course).	Research summary for benefits of peer tutoring and examples of successful programs at other schools (see Chapter 16) Prepared course description, requirements, and course materials
Determine logistics for course enrollment.	Meet with personnel responsible for student schedules. Describe rationale for peer tutor class, benefits to all students, course status, and requirements. Identify teacher for class, and assign course number.	Approved proposal for peer tutor course Prepared course description, requirements, and course materials
Determine tutor eligibility.	Determine number of peer tutors needed. Decide on course eligibility requirements based on needs of students who will be tutored and anticipated level of support available to peer tutors.	Examples of course eligibility requirements at other schools
Inform faculty of new course.	Determine how faculty will be informed with administrator. Provide faculty with rationale and program benefits summary. Define faculty's role and list strategies to assist peer tutors and tutees.	Rationale and program benefits List of strategies to work with students
Inform students and their families of new class.	Publish a description of the peer tutor course in the school's catalog of course offerings. Publish articles in the school's newspaper and parent newsletter. Ask faculty members to share information about the class with all of their students.	Description of peer tutor class Articles published at other schools Summary of peer tutor class and benefits to students
Determine logistics for peer tutors.	Set up system for attendance, communication, training, and evaluation. Determine requirements and logistics for peer tutor sign-in, daily communication, and completion of assignments.	Evaluation forms Sign-in sheet Peer tutor folders Journal forms
Train peer tutors.	Determine time and duration of training. Prepare training checklist and lessons. Provide initial general training. Provide ongoing individualized training (relevant to student-supported and general education class in which student is included). Provide ongoing support and supervision to peer tutors.	Training schedule Training topics and lessons Peer tutor assignments

- With the proper peer tutor (i.e., a good match), will the student benefit from peer tutor support?

- What kind of support will the peer tutor need to successfully support the tutee?

- Will this support come from the general education teacher, the special education teacher, a paraprofessional, or another more experienced peer tutor?

- How much support will be provided and how will it be faded and monitored?

Often, students with the most intensive needs are identified to receive peer tutor support, but this should not preclude looking at other students who may also benefit. With some students, adult versus peer support may need to be balanced over the course of a typical school day. For one student, the goal may be to fade direct adult support over the course of the school year. The committee should also consider the students who are quiet, but perhaps struggling—who will not call attention to themselves but could benefit from additional attention, instruction, or modeling.

Recruiting and Selecting Peer Tutors

At middle and high schools where peer tutor programs thrive, people have discovered that the best way to recruit peer tutors is to empower peer tutors and students who have received peer support to do the recruiting themselves. In fact, the best form of public relations for a peer tutor program occurs naturally through informal word-of-mouth communication between students as the program evolves and expands with increasingly more students positively affected by the experience. The peer tutor coordinator and supporting committee can be instrumental in setting the stage for recruitment at their school site by making sure that all students potentially have the opportunity to become peer tutors by setting up the logistics for peer tutor recruitment activities on campus and, finally, supporting interested students to prepare for and lead recruitment efforts. The most personal and effective way of promoting a peer tutor program is for peers to present their experiences at club meetings or during class presentations to enable students to learn firsthand about the benefits of providing and receiving support from peers. Table 22.2 shows benefits and additional strategies that can be discussed with students or initiated by the peer tutor coordinator and other key players at the school when a program is introduced at a campus. An example of a flier that can be used as a recruitment tool is depicted in Figure 22.1.

Whenever possible, students should be recruited, selected, and enrolled in a peer tutor program prior to the beginning of the next school year. With adequate time, the person or people in charge of student schedules can ensure that an adequate number of peer tutors are assigned throughout the school day to meet the needs of students who need support. When peer tutors are ready to start on the first day of school, the focus is appropriately placed on training them rather than trying to scramble to find more peer tutors.

The selection of peer tutors may be limited by when potential peer tutors are available to support their peers. Schools that offer a peer tutor class for elective credit, such as Parker High School (previously described in this chapter), offer the most flexibility and access for students to enroll in the class throughout the day. At other schools, such as Chavez Middle School and Nathaniel Junior High, specific course requirements and schedules could limit the opportunities for students to become peer tutors. With commitment to the peer tutor program from the school administration and faculty, creative solutions can and have been discovered to work around these barriers.

Table 22.2.   Peer tutor recruitment strategies

Recruitment strategies	Examples of methods
Create a flier to introduce and create awareness for the peer tutor class.	Distribute flier to students through counseling office, advisory period, and administrative office.
	Post flier in library, office, and throughout school campus.
Publicize information about peer tutoring.	Publish an article about peer tutoring in the school's newsletter that is mailed to students and their families.
	Publish an article about peer tutoring in the school newspaper.
	Feature peer tutors and the peer tutor class in the school's yearbook.
	Announce information about peer tutoring in the daily school bulletins and/or newscast.
Teachers discuss opportunities to peer tutor with their students.	Discuss during their advisory period.
	Discuss during their classes.
Meet with school's student leadership (e.g., student council, ASB).	Inform them about the peer tutor class.
	Ask for their support and suggestions for recruitment of tutors.
Visit classes, club meetings, and school assemblies to make presentations about the peer tutor class.	Have current peer tutors and students who receive tutoring lead presentations and share the benefits of peer tutoring.
Meet with counseling staff (or other staff who complete student schedules).	Provide information about the peer tutor class and benefits of peer tutoring to both students who receive and provide support.
	Discuss eligibility requirements and preferences for peer tutor characteristics.
	Update them on student success stories resulting from peer tutoring.
	Request preferred number of peer tutors.
Peer tutors complete projects to create awareness and recruit new peer tutors.	Create a mural on campus.
	Create bulletin board displays throughout campus to provide information about and benefits of peer tutoring.

Beyond the scheduling considerations, deciding who to select as peer tutors is also individually determined at schools. Some programs without formal selection criteria rely on the guidance counselor or another school staff member to recommend students. Peer tutors are selected on an individualized basis by considering their unique strengths and desire to learn and grow through the experience. In fact, many students who have had either academic and/or social concerns at school appreciate the opportunity to make a positive contribution and personal connection with a peer, often becoming more empowered in their own lives and compelling as a peer tutor.

Other programs choose to establish a formal selection criteria and require that interested students complete an application and interview and provide references, thus supporting the school-to-career goals prevalent at secondary schools today. Common examples of established selection criteria include the following:

- Upper-class status

- Teacher recommendation

- Above-average grades (citizenship and academic)

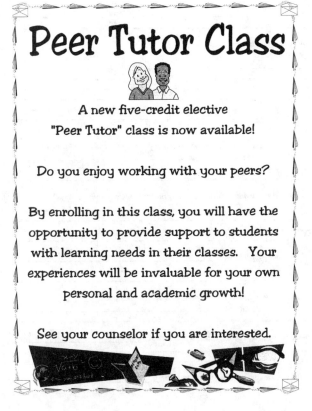

Figure 22.1. Peer tutor flier.

- Leadership and responsibility

- Strong interest and desire to contribute to the school community and to support peers

- Appreciation of human diversity

Whether an informal or formal process of selection is employed, it is always preferable to include students with disabilities who have received or will receive peer support to participate in interviews with the peer tutor candidates and assist with selection decisions. Once peer tutors are selected, letters of acceptance can be provided and a pool of alternates identified. It is critical to select a realistic number of peer tutors to ensure that appropriate training and ongoing support can be provided. At the onset of a new program, it is best to focus on the integrity of the program by limiting the number of peer tutors to ensure that the students and general education teachers receive the initial and ongoing support necessary. Again, the best public relations for the program rest with the students who want to share their positive experiences when part of a well-supported peer tutoring partnership.

Assigning Peer Tutors

Once peer tutors are selected, the job of carefully placing students into tutorial partnerships begins. Many peer tutor program coordinators take the time to talk with newly selected peer tutors to gain a sense of their strengths, interests, confidence level, school involvement, and relationships with specific teachers and/or preferences for specific subject areas. A peer tutor survey, as illustrated in Figure 22.2, provides the coordinator with a written record for each peer tutor.

Name	Date
Block/Period	Grade level

1-Please list your current schedule:

Block/Period	Class	Teacher

2-Please list any extra-curricular activities you are involved in, including clubs, sports teams, government, other:_____

3-Please list your favorite classes. Why did/do you enjoy these classes?

4-What are your interests?_____

5-Do you have any hobbies and/or special skills? Please list._____

6-Why did you sign up to become a peer tutor? _____

7-Have you ever been a peer tutor before?_____

*If you need more space, please write on the back of this page.

Figure 22.2. Peer tutor survey.

By examining the needs and interests of students who need support, their general education classes and teachers, and the qualities that each peer tutor brings (much like carefully considering all of the pieces in a puzzle), the peer tutor coordinator attempts to arrive at the best fit to establish student partnerships. Some strategies to consider for peer tutor assignment include

- Matching the peer tutor's academic or interpersonal strengths with the tutee's needs and/or classroom teacher's preferences

- Pairing students together who already share a positive relationship or have a strong desire to work together

- Pairing students together who share similar interests

- Pairing a peer tutor who is well-connected at the school with a student who has a limited social network

- Pairing a confident and competent peer tutor with a student with more intensive needs

Although the relationship between peer tutors and the students they support is paramount, it is also critical to focus on the needs of the general education classroom teachers in the context of supporting their curricular content and the teaching strategies they employ. Peer tutors should not be limited, nor limit the students they support, by providing one-to-one tutoring that is perceived as separate from the rest of the class. Instead, peer tutors must be viewed as a resource to all students in the classroom and strategically placed with teachers who best utilize their unique strengths. Figure 22.3 is a sample peer tutor information sheet that can be provided to the general education teachers to better inform them of the assigned peer tutor's strengths and interests as well as suggested ways the peer tutor can support the tutee and the class as a whole.

TRAINING PEER TUTORS

The success of a peer tutor program is largely determined by the quality of training provided to the peer tutors. Effective training strategies and ongoing support provide peer tutors with the necessary tools to ensure a rewarding experience for all.

Training Logistics

Ideally, a peer tutor training plan includes at least two phases: an initial orientation and ongoing follow-ups or supplemental trainings that occur throughout the school year. The initial orientation should occur at the start of the school year and provide more intensive training on the basics of peer tutoring. The basic training topics may include getting started, getting to know your student, working in the classroom, assigning roles and responsibilities, and teaching basic instructional strategies—both general as well as those tailored to the individual student being tutored and others (e.g., curriculum adaptations, positive behavior support strategies, communication, social relationships). Other training sessions should be scheduled throughout the school year that reinforce the initial training topics as well as provide new information and strategies, such as effective problem solving, advo-

Peer Tutor Information Sheet
Date_____

Peer Tutor_____ Grade_____	Period/Block_____
Peer Tutor Coordinator_____	Telephone _____
Classroom Teacher(s)/Classes Assigned To_____	
Student(s) Peer Tutor Will Support_____	

Peer tutor interests & extracurricular activities_____

Peer tutor academic & learning strengths_____

Peer tutor's experience providing peer support_____

Suggested ways the peer tutor may support the student(s) in your classroom_____

Suggested activities for peer tutor to support the classroom teacher(s)_____

Procedural Information
· Peer tutors are required to check in/out in with the Peer Tutor Coordinator at the beginning and end of their assigned tutorial time period each day
· In the event that the tutee (student who receives peer tutoring) is absent, please contact the Peer Tutor Coordinator. The peer tutor working in your classroom may receive an alternate assignment for that day
· Teachers will be provided with an evaluation form to assess the performance of the peer tutor working in their classrooms and to give input into their grade

Figure 22.3. Peer tutor information sheet.

cacy, leadership, instructional strategies, and ongoing support for each tutoring relationship. A list of suggested training topics with indexes to the lessons presented in Chapter 23 are in Table 22.3. A variety of the actual hands-on and interactive lessons identified in the index are included in Chapters 23 and 24.

Training Considerations

Ultimately, a master "training plan" must be developed prior to the initiation of the peer tutor program. One of the first key steps in developing this plan involves identifying the goals and objectives of the training. What are the *real* lessons that you want the peer tutors to walk away with at the end of the orientation and at the end of the school year? Obviously, one goal is for the peer tutors to learn and apply effective tutoring/instructional

Table 22.3. Topical areas and lesson index

Training topics	Chapter 23: Peer tutor lesson index	Chapter 24: Leadership lesson index
Peer tutor roles and responsibilities	Do's and Don'ts/Lesson 1 Get Moving with RESPECT/Lesson 3	
Inclusion		Visualizing Inclusion/Lesson 1 INCLUDE Values/Lesson 2 Posting Our Values/Lesson 3 Inclusion Jeopardy!/Lesson 4 Who Am I?/Lesson 5 A Walk with Courage/Lesson 6 Speak to Us/Lesson 7 Speak Up Through Song/Lesson 9 Wake Up Now!/Lesson 13
Celebrating human diversity	We're People First/Lesson 2 We're Smart!/Lesson 6	A Walk with Courage/Lesson 6 Speak to Us/Lesson 7 Label Me, Negate Me?/Lesson 8 How Big Is Your Circle?/Lesson 14
Disability rights and social justice	We're People First/Lesson 2	A Walk with Courage/Lesson 6 Speak to Us/Lesson 7 Speak Up Through Song/Lesson 9 It's the Law!/Lesson 10 A Rainbow of Justice/Lesson 11 Wake Up Now!/Lesson 12 How Big Is Your Circle?/Lesson 13
Providing support to peers	Do's and Don'ts/Lesson 1 Get Moving with RESPECT/Lesson 3 Ain't Misbehavin'!/Lesson 4	Speak Up Through Song/Lesson 9
Learning and teaching	Can I Pick Your Brain?/Lesson 5 We're Smart!/Lesson 6 Right on Cue!/Lesson 7	
Relationships	Get Moving with RESPECT/Lesson 3	Who Am I?/Lesson 5 Speak Up Through Song/Lesson 9
Communication	Something To Talk About/Lesson 8	
Curriculum adaptation	Ins and Outs of Curriculum Adaptation/Lesson 9 Just Adapt!/Lesson 10	
Reflection and action planning		3-2-1 Reflect!/Lesson 14 School MAPs/Lesson 15

strategies. However, another important goal may also be for the peer tutors to understand and value diversity with respect to abilities, talents, strengths, and interests. Traditional peer tutor programs, often unintentionally, can create a "helping" mindset and send conscious/unconscious messages such as, "I am assisting this poor, helpless person"; "The tutor is a wonderful person for helping this deserving person with a disability"; and, "I, the tutor, have much to offer, and need a pat on the back in return." These sentiments create unequal relationships in which one individual (the tutor) is perceived as the giver and the other individual (the tutee) is perceived as the taker/receiver. One goal, then, may be to examine ways in which the relationship can become more "two-directional"—that is, in some instances, the tutee is the giver and the tutor is the receiver. One way to achieve this is to begin by addressing issues of respect, relationships, advocacy, leadership, and social justice within the context of the overall peer tutor training plan and activities. In turn, as Van der Klift and Kunc point out (see Chapter 3), opportunities for reciprocity must be created and tutors helped to understand and actively merge the concepts of respect and help. These concepts must be reinforced and modeled throughout the peer tutor experience, via training, support, and evaluation activities and requirements. Several of the sample lesson plans contained in Chapter 23 address the issues of respect and relationships. In addition, a number of lessons dealing with advocacy and leadership, which are pertinent to a peer tutor training program, are included in Chapter 24.

Once the goals and objectives of the training activities have been identified, the next step is to develop the actual training content and sequence that supports the goals and objectives. As mentioned previously, develop an initial orientation training plan and then a subsequent, follow-up plan that can be implemented over the course of the school year or semester. Again, Table 22.3 can be used to guide this process.

It is important to also become aware of the ways in which we approach training peer tutors, as this will have a powerful influence on their understanding and application of learning and teaching. In essence, we need to "walk the talk" by ensuring that training sessions make use of and model active and cooperative teaching strategies that engage the peer tutors in learning. It is also preferable to involve experienced peer tutors and students with disabilities in teaching roles throughout the actual training sessions to offer their invaluable insights, expertise, and leadership to the newly selected peer tutors. Finally, it is important to provide peer tutors with time to reflect on the information and experiences encountered during the lesson activities and to complete a brief evaluation of the training session. Figure 22.4 illustrates this kind of evaluation in the form of a "3–2–1 reflection," which allows the students to focus on what they learned as well as express their own learning and support needs as a peer tutor.

Examples of School Training Models

Time for training, as with time for collaboration and anything else in schools, must be identified and planned. Many have identified ways to create time for training based on their own school's structure and schedules. The following three scenarios provide several unique "solutions" to the time for training dilemma.

Parker High School

When the faculty at Parker High School decided to restructure to 90-minute block periods within a quarter system, a tutorial block was created. The tutorial is a separate block of time that does not interfere with students' other classes. Students use the tutorial to gain access to their teachers for additional assistance with course assignments, to make up tests or assign-

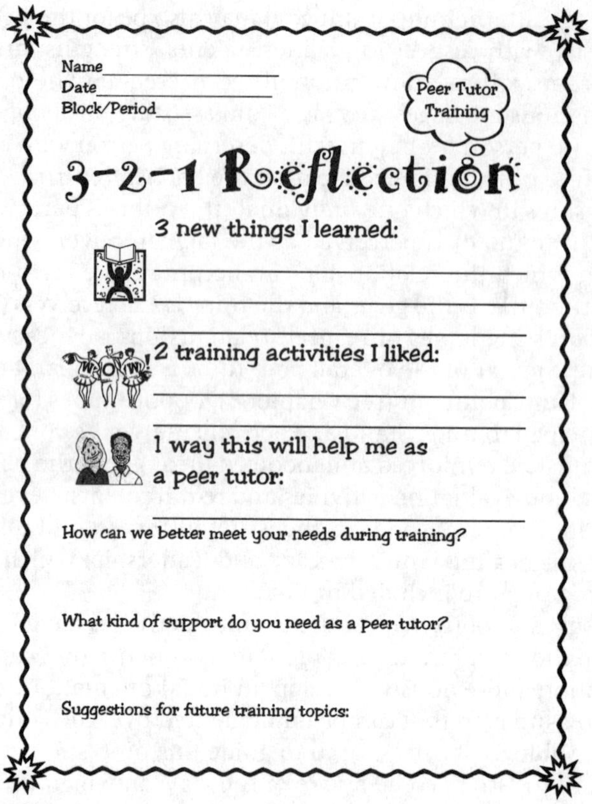

Name_____
Date_____
Block/Period_____

Peer Tutor
Training

3-2-1 Reflection

3 new things I learned:

_____
_____
_____

2 training activities I liked:

_____
_____

1 way this will help me as a peer tutor:

_____

How can we better meet your needs during training?

What kind of support do you need as a peer tutor?

Suggestions for future training topics:

Figure 22.4. Peer tutor training evaluation.

ments, or to meet with group members to work on projects and/or complete homework. This block of time provides an ideal opportunity for the peer tutor teacher to bring all peer tutors together for training without the need to remove them from the general education classes and students they are supporting. Initially, peer tutors are required to attend three training sessions during tutorial for the first 2 weeks of the quarter in order to benefit from more intensive initial training. Subsequently, peer tutors attend the tutorial once per week to receive ongoing training and to have the opportunity to reflect on their role and the need to empower the students they are supporting. The peer tutor teacher is also available during tutorial on a daily basis to meet with individual peer tutors or together with the students who are supported to address their specific needs and to assist with final project completion. The staff at Parker High found this school schedule to be ideal for providing the personalized training needed for peer tutors to be effective in the classroom and to allow them to grow in their capacity to examine and act on the challenges of their role and relationship to the students they support.

Caesar Chavez Middle School

Caesar Chavez Middle School, which serves 1,500 students, is organized into six educational "families" (or "houses") that each serve as their own school within a school. As a result, each educational family has their own schedule (e.g., traditional seven periods, mixed block) that includes a discovery period (e.g., elective courses) and a homebase. During the discovery period (which is at different times for each educational family), students may also opt for a service learning course/credit. Peer tutoring is one of the options that students may choose from within the service learning program. The school determined that because homebase was the one common time/period at the beginning of the day across educational families, it could be utilized to pull peer tutors from across educational families for some common training time. For the first 2 weeks, the peer tutors attend a specially designed peer tutor class twice a week for initial training and once a week thereafter for ongoing training and support sessions. At the same time, over the first 2 weeks of school, the peer tutors receive individualized/small-group training during their discovery/service learning period (when they will be peer tutoring) that is specific to the student they are assigned to support. This requires a significant time commitment from the supporting special education teachers at the beginning, but they have found this initial training time to be time well spent.

Nathaniel Junior High School

At Nathaniel Junior High School it was determined that the only training time available was during the actual periods that the peer tutors tutored. Given the importance that the staff placed on initial peer tutor training, the training was designed to occur during the first 2 weeks of school. For the first 2 weeks of school, instead of reporting to their assigned tutee and class, the peer tutors reported to the special education teacher who coordinated the peer tutor program. Every day for 2 weeks, the peer tutors (for that class period) engaged in hands-on training and introductory activities. This meant that the special education teacher who coordinated the peer tutor program committed every period of every day for 2 weeks to training the peer tutors. The paraeducators who worked with the special educator and who had been engaged in training activities before the start of the school year provided in-class support to students. This strategy also required the support and active involvement of the general education teachers who had students with disabilities included in their classes. They recognized that for the first 2 weeks of school they would not receive much support but felt that having quality, trained peer tutors for the remainder of the semester/school year was a beneficial trade-off. In addition, the general education teachers found that the start of the school year was a time for themselves and the students to get to know each other and to establish their routines and expectations. Not having much support was advantageous because they took the initiative to get to know *all* of the students and were better able to establish a relationship with their student(s) with special needs as a result of this experience. Knowing and establishing a relationship with their student(s) with disabilities thus enabled the general education teachers to better support the peer tutors to assist students in their classes.

Training Components

The 10 lessons in Chapter 23 cover a range of activities to use when training peer tutors who will provide support in inclusive secondary classrooms. In this context, the peer tutor's primary role involves supporting the student to participate along with classmates in all class activities and assignments. The peer tutor is not responsible for replacing the direct instruction provided by the teacher but instead for providing the accommodations for the student and/or adapting the activities and the core curriculum used by the classroom teacher. The selected lessons are intended to prepare peer tutors for this kind of support role. Again, Table 22.3 offers a listing of topical areas and lessons indexed from Chapters 23 and 24. Peer tutor training should also cover additional topics (not covered in the indexed lessons) as exemplified by the *Peer Tutor Training Manual* developed for the Exceptional Programs Department in the San Diego Unified School District (Mauri, Radetski, & Wong, 1995). The other examples of training information and/or lessons this manual provides include overall course information, safety procedures, getting to know your partner, suggestions for assisting students in class, understanding disability, communication, and appropriate interactions. In addition to the lessons described in Chapter 23, these additional topics and the lessons indexed from Chapter 24 should also be considered as part of a school's overall peer tutor training plan.

SUPERVISING AND SUPPORTING PEER TUTORS

With the peer tutors selected and trained and the program up and running, one might expect that the program can now basically "run" on its own. However, once trained, peer tutors require ongoing support and supervision to ensure that the students receiving support are satisfied and that their needs are being addressed appropriately. Peer tutors need and value the guidance, feedback, and collaborative teamwork provided by a support teacher to learn how to respectfully and skillfully provide academic and social support to their peers. Consequently, supervision and ongoing support are just as critical to the success of the program as are the recruitment and training components. Supervision and support are needed to

- Ensure that students are being supported in a positive and sensitive way

- Provide strategies and tips on how to motivate students to learn

- Utilize appropriate instructional strategies

- Support the tutor/tutee relationship

- Guide the development of materials and adapted classwork

- Ensure that the rules and procedures of the program are being followed

- Ensure that any relevant IEP goals are being met

One method of supervising peer tutors is through the use of daily journal logs. The journals are an excellent tool for enhancing and facilitating communication and keeping track of tutor/tutee activities, accomplishments, and concerns on a daily basis. In the journal, the peer tutor is responsible for documenting:

- Class assignments and activities

- How the tutor supported the tutee

- What the tutee was able to accomplish or how he or she participated in activities

- Overall reflection on the class period

- Any questions or concerns that may need to be addressed

An example of a weekly journal format used in several high schools is depicted in Figure 22.5. Journal logs can be very helpful; however, if they are to be used, it is important that peer tutors receive training and models of what is expected in the writings.

Another method of supervision is "spot-checking" the peer tutors. This requires the peer tutor program coordinator(s) to designate some time to spend with the peer tutor and

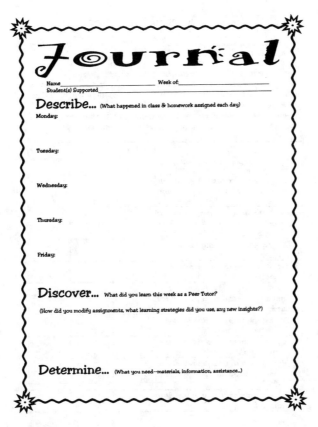

Figure 22.5. Journal log.

tutee each week while they are in class. Spot-checking allows the teacher to follow the progress of the tutors and tutees by witnessing first-hand how the situation is playing out. While spot-checking, the teacher can provide guidance and feedback to the tutor, spend time with the tutee, and also touch base with the general education teacher to get his or her feedback on the situation. In addition, this also provides the opportunity for the peer tutor coordinator to model effective strategies for the tutor and general education teacher, if needed.

Many peer tutor programs require that the peer tutors go to a designated place (e.g., learning center, resource room/office) to check in prior to reporting to their tutoring class assignment. Being available and monitoring this time at the start of each period allows the coordinator/support teacher to touch base and talk for a few moments with peer tutors. These brief conversations can be used to 1) share specific support or motivational strategies; 2) get a feel for how things are going from the peer tutor's perspective; 3) follow up on curriculum adaptations/modifications; and 4) discuss upcoming activities, assignments, or projects. Finally, having the ability to conduct ongoing training and meetings throughout the school year provides another opportunity for support and monitoring of the tutor's and tutee's progress and their relationship.

EVALUATING PEER TUTORS

With the number of people involved in one student's experience as a peer tutor in middle and high school inclusive classrooms, an evaluation process, rather than a single tool or

Self-Evaluation for Peer Tutors

Name_____

Date_____

Please answer the following questions to evaluate yourself as a peer tutor. This process may help you to become more aware of your own skills and to identify areas you would like to improve in. Your responses will also help us to be more aware of your strengths, as well as enable us to provide you with the training or information you may need. Mark an "X" in the box which best answers each question.

	Great	Okay	Want to improve
1. How has your attendance been?			
2. Do you feel comfortable with your role in the general education classroom?			
3. Do you use your time wisely to assist students with their assignments?			
4. Do you really listen and respond to students?			
5. Do you treat all students with respect?			
6. Do you show independence and initiative to adapt class assignments for students?			
7. Do you ask for help from teachers whenever you need it?			
8. Do you share your ideas and communicate well with others?			
9. How well do you know about students' learning strengths and skills?			
10. How prepared are you to deal with safety issues?			

Figure 22.6. Peer tutor self-evaluation.

criteria, is essential. Such a process should honor the voice of the student who receives the peer tutor's support, incorporate feedback from the general education classroom teachers, be aligned with the peer tutor course requirements as monitored by the peer tutor coordinator, and, perhaps most important, promote self-reflection and growth by the peer tutors themselves. Although an individual's interpersonal and academic skills may determine, in part, their ultimate success as a peer tutor, it is hoped that the evaluation process will look beyond the student's initial skills. Ultimately, one must question whether the training activities and assignments, ongoing support and feedback from the teachers involved, and the actual in-class experiences contribute to the peer tutor's understanding of peer support in relation to respect, reciprocity, and empowerment. For each peer tutor, this understanding should develop and deepen when an evaluation process occurs and includes the opportunity for self-reflection.

The journals previously discussed as a communication and supervision tool (see Figure 22.5) provide a daily opportunity for peer tutors to informally reflect on their role. For a more formal assessment of their skills and growth, completion of a self-evaluation form can be an empowering process in itself as a way for peer tutors to periodically celebrate their strengths and identify areas that they need to focus on for improvement. A sample self-evaluation form is depicted in Figure 22.6.

Peer tutors at a Kentucky high school are required to develop their own self-evaluation matrix as a culminating final activity (Longwill & Kleinert, 1998). The peer tutors individually determine the five characteristics that they believe are essential to peer tutoring. They evaluate themselves using their own rubric delineating four performance levels. Finally, they provide a written explanation of the self-evaluation of their performance as a peer tutor.

Tutee Evaluation of Peer Tutor

Evaluation Completed By: Date:

Peer Tutor's Name:

General Education Class/Teacher:

1) Does the peer tutor arrive to your class when expected?

    Yes   Most of the time   Sometimes   No

2) Does the peer tutor support you to participate in class activities?

    Yes   Most of the time   Sometimes   No

3) Does the peer tutor provide support that allows you to complete your own class assignments?

    Yes   Most of the time   Sometimes   No

4) Does the peer tutor really listen to you and respond to your needs?

    Yes   Most of the time   Sometimes   No

5) Does the peer tutor understand your learning strengths and needs?

    Yes   No   I'm not sure

6) Does the peer tutor get along well with you, the teacher, and the other students?

    Yes   Most of the time   Sometimes   No

7) Does the peer tutor support you to talk and work with other students in the class?

    Yes   Most of the time   Sometimes   No

8) Overall, are you satisfied with the peer tutor who supports you in this class?

    Yes   No

    a) What do you like most about <u>how</u> this peer tutor supports you?

    _____

    b) How can this peer tutor <u>do a better job</u> supporting you?

    _____

9) Would you like to meet (with the Peer Tutor teacher) to discuss this peer tutor?

                         _____Yes   _____Not at this time

Other Comments:_____

_____

Figure 22.7. Tutee evaluation of peer tutor.

Evaluation of Peer Tutor

To:

From:

Date:

Please answer the following questions to evaluate _____ as a peer tutor in your classroom. Your responses will inform us about the student's strengths and areas in which s/he needs more support, training, and information.

Please return the evaluation to my mailbox by _____. Thank you for your feedback!

1) Is the peer tutor in class regularly? Does s/he arrive on time and stay for the entire class?

    Always   Most of the time   There are problems

2) How well do you think the peer tutor works with the student being supported in your class?

    Very well   Okay   Needs more training

3) Does the peer tutor adapt assignments (if needed) for the student being supported?

    Yes   Most of the time   Needs more training

4) Does the peer tutor maintain focus on the student being supported?

    Yes   Most of the time   There are problems

5) Is the peer tutor an effective communicator with staff and students?

    Yes   Most of the time   There are problems

6) Is the peer tutor respectful toward all students in your class?

    Yes   Most of the time   There are problems

7) Would you like to meet to discuss this peer tutor and/or the student being supported in your class?   _____Yes   _____Not at this time

Recommended grade based on the peer tutor's performance in your class:_____.

Comments:_____

_____

Figure 22.8. Teacher evaluation of peer tutor.

PEER TUTOR COURSE REQUIREMENTS

Teacher's Name
Room #:
Telephone:

Course Description:
The Peer Tutor course (5 credits) provides you with the opportunity to support students with learning needs in their classes. As a peer tutor, you will assist students to succeed in class by helping them to complete class assignments and participate in class. You will receive direction and assistance from the classroom teacher and support staff. It is very important to ask questions and give us feedback to ensure a successful experience for you and the student(s) you will support.

You are required to check-in daily and pick up your folder at Room # _____. We will provide you with necessary materials and information for the specific student(s) and class(es) at that time.

Every Friday, you are required to turn in your Journal assignment.

Grades:
Peer Tutor grades are based on:
1. Daily attendance (consistency is very important!)
2. Your assistance given to students with learning needs
3. Positive interaction skills with students and school staff
4. Positive "on-the-job" work habits including: Following directions, showing initiative, accepting responsibility, communicating your ideas, questions, and needs
5. Completion of Peer Tutor assignments and final project
6. Adapting assignments to meet individual student learning needs

ATTENDANCE IS CRITICAL!
· Consistent with our school policy, excessive absences will result in a lowered grade (if no make-ups completed)
· All excused absences can be made-up
· Please inform the Peer Tutor class teacher if you know you will be absent on specific days (to enable us to plan for student support in your absence)

Figure 22.9. Peer tutor course requirements.

The tutee's evaluation of the peer tutor depicted in Figure 22.7 can be used to obtain ongoing feedback from the student who receives support from the peer tutor. A trusted adult can support the student to complete this evaluation. The student's feedback should be shared with and carefully considered by the peer tutor coordinator. The students who receive peer tutor support must know that their needs and opinions are vitally important. The student may choose to share his or her responses with the peer tutor informally or with support from the peer tutor coordinator to give both positive feedback to the peer tutor and/or discuss any areas of concern.

Evaluations completed by the general education teachers are also indispensable as the teachers observe and work with the peer tutors in their classrooms on a daily basis. The form illustrated in Figure 22.8 can be useful for ongoing feedback and also as a means to collaborate with the general education teacher to determine the peer tutor's grade.

The syllabus used for a peer tutor course should clearly communicate how grades are determined. Figure 22.9 provides an example of a peer tutor course description and grading considerations.

In this example, a final project represents a portion of the peer tutor's grade. This assignment provides the peer tutor with a final opportunity to reflect on his or her experiences and share his or her message with a wider audience through an individual and unique project design. A description of this project and final project proposal form are depicted in Figures 22.10 and 22.11.

In several high schools where final projects are required, peer tutors have overwhelmingly expressed a sentiment of personal growth and mutual reciprocity gained from the experience in creative and personalized projects. Figure 22.12 illustrates a profound

Peer Tutor
Final Project

Your final assignment for the Peer Tutor class will be due at the end of the semester. Please choose from the following projects in order to best express what you have learned from your experiences as a peer tutor this semester. Additional project ideas are welcome! If you feel more comfortable with an activity which is not listed, let's discuss your plan. You may also elect to complete a traditional written final instead. You must complete the attached Project Proposal by _____.

The goal for this project is for you to either:
1) Reflect on your experiences as a peer tutor; or
2) To provide information about peer tutoring, inclusion, and/or issues of diversity.
Guiding questions and several examples of possible projects are listed as either "Reflection" or "Informative." Please do not hesitate to ask for help with your Project Proposal and with your project. Remember, the goal is for you to best express what you have learned. Good luck!

1) Reflection
You may want to use one or more of the following guiding questions to get you started. How did your participation and experiences as a peer tutor affect you as a student and a person? Have you changed in any way? How does this class compare to other experiences in school? What have you learned about inclusion? (or respecting differences, or yourself, or teaching and learning)

Examples: -Video interview
-Photo essay
-Collage
-Letter to principal, counseling staff, District administration
-Presentation to counseling staff
-Journal format
-Artwork

2) Informative
You may want to use one or more of the following guiding questions to get you started. What would you want new peer tutors to know about your experiences to help them get started? In what ways can other students be informed about the Peer Tutor class and/or inclusion?

Examples: -Create a flyer
-Write & submit an article/letter to editor for school paper
-School broadcast
-Plan additional 9th grade presentation activities
-Create a mural, poster, or T-shirt design

In what ways can teachers learn more about the positive aspects of inclusion and peer tutoring?

Examples: -Prepare presentation to faculty meeting or department meetings
-Based on your observations & insights as a peer tutor, describe the teaching strategies and activities which seem to work well for all students
-Describe the positive experiences for the student you support (video interview, in writing, or other visual arts project)

Figure 22.10. Final project.

Peer Tutor
Final Project Proposal

Name_____   Date_____
Period/Block____

This proposal is due on_____

I plan to complete: (select one of the following)

_____ **Reflection Project**
(Reflect on your experiences as a peer tutor)

_____ **Informative Project**
(Provide information about peer tutoring, inclusion, and/or issues of human diversity)

_____ **Written Final**

Project Description:

I will create the following project:_____
_____
_____

Questions to consider:
How will your project express what you have learned from your experiences as a peer tutor? How are you planning to reflect on or inform others about peer tutoring, inclusion, and/or embracing human diversity?

Comments/Questions?
_____
_____

Figure 22.11. Final project proposal.

Final Project
Amanda Bohy, Peer Tutor

I have chosen to reflect on my experiences as a peer tutor for my final project. Please share this letter with anyone you would like to. I hope it will show them how beneficial being a peer tutor can be in your life.

I began working with Ricky about a month into the school year.
I did it because I didn't have a sixth period and my counselor suggested that
I should become a peer tutor. He said it would be good community service
and would look good on college applications. So I decided to give it a shot.
I was a little nervous at first. I wasn't sure if I would be able to relate with
Ricky in a way that we could work together, alone, for an hour.
I soon discovered we could. Right away, Ricky and I become friends.
He was always smiling and seemed like a really happy person.
Before I met Rick, I was very unhappy.
Quite frankly, I believed that life was not enjoyable at all.
I was depressed and I didn't smile very much. I had a lot of problems with
my friends and family. I hated coming to school.
Ricky changed all that. First off, his smile was contagious.
I found myself smiling all through sixth period. I started looking forward to
that class everyday. Just thinking about Rick made me smile.
He made me realize that no matter how bad your life is, you can always make
it better. So, I began smiling all the time.
I started looking on the bright side of everything.
Even my dad noticed a change in me.
He said I seemed much happier and he also credited Ricky for that.
I felt better about myself because
just as Ricky was helping me, I was helping him.
He depended on me everyday for his sixth period. Together, we work on his
homework, class work, or anything else he needs to get done.
However at the same time we laugh together,
share stories and past experiences.
We talk about the future and who we want to be. We talk about life.
Ricky and I have become good friends.
I am on the road recovering from my depression
and I give Rick partial credit for that.
He taught me how to smile.

Figure 22.12. Project example/letter.

1

self-reflection in the form of a letter addressed to the peer tutor course teacher. Figure 22.13 is an example of a creative endeavor that sums up the peer tutoring experience using a mind map.

The peer tutor evaluation process ends with some form of final feedback, perhaps in the form of a grade and/or course credit. Many peer tutor coordinators choose to provide peer tutors with a written letter of support and recommendation that is affirming to the peer tutor and espouses a more personalized form of evaluation. The evaluation process can finally begin anew with the peer tutor's evaluation of the course, including his or her assessment of the quality of training and support he or she received throughout his or her experiences. Figure 22.14 is a sample of a peer tutor evaluation. The voices of the peer tutors bring the evaluation process full circle when we share the vision of empowering all students to contribute to each other's social experiences, education, and personal growth.

CELEBRATING PARTICIPATION IN A PEER TUTOR PROGRAM

LaPlant and Zane discuss both formal and informal reinforcement systems for participation in partner learning in Chapter 18. At secondary schools, providing opportunities for student partnerships to celebrate their shared contributions together can be an empowering and renewing experience. The "RESPECT" lesson described in Chapter 23 specifically addresses the need to celebrate in reciprocal and mutually respectful relationships. It is important not to communicate an attitude of benevolence by providing the peer tutors with rewards for the assistance they provide to their "less fortunate" peers.

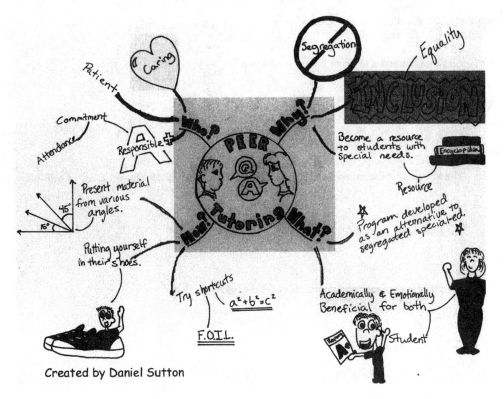

Created by Daniel Sutton

Figure 22.13. Project example/mind map.

**PEER TUTOR COURSE/EXPERIENCE
EVALUATION**

Name_____ Period/Block____ Date_____

	Stronly Agree	Agree	Not Sure	Disagree	Strongly Disagree
1. My instructor(s)/supervisor appeared to be knowledgeable about the subject matter.	5	4	3	2	1
2. My instructor(s)/supervisor were able to clearly communicate the subject content.	5	4	3	2	1
3. My instructor(s)/supervisor was approachable and responsive to my needs	5	4	3	2	1
4. My instructor(s)/supervisor was available to discuss issues, concerns and ideas.	5	4	3	2	1
5. The course content was relevant to my tutoring experience and useful.	5	4	3	2	1
6. I feel that I have gained new knowledge and skills as a result of this course and experience.	5	4	3	2	1
7. The general education teacher(s) was/were supportive and approachable.	5	4	3	2	1
8. I was able to apply much of the information gained in this course to my tutoring experience.	5	4	3	2	1
9. I enjoyed working with and getting know the person(s) I tutored.	5	4	3	2	1
10. I feel that I learned a lot from the person(s) that I tutored.	5	4	3	2	1
11. I would recommend this course and experience to others.	5	4	3	2	1

12.   The lesson(s)/information that I felt were most useful and helpful to my situation was/were:

13.   The best thing about this course/experience were:

14.   What I would change about this course/experience:

15.   Other comments:

Figure 22.14.   Peer tutor evaluation of course.

Table 22.4. Peer tutor celebration ideas

Recognize the importance of peer support.

Honor and celebrate all students involved in the peer tutor program during school assemblies and awards events.

Invite student partners to parties at lunch–treat them to pizza or ice cream sundaes, and express your appreciation for all they do and are learning together.

Hold an end-of-the-year celebration banquet for students who have been involved as peer tutors or tutees throughout the school year.

Give peer tutors and tutees notes of appreciation throughout the semester for their commitment, teamwork, and individual attributes.

Announce appreciation for peer support in the daily school bulletins and/or newscast.

Create bulletin board displays throughout campus honoring peer support.

Encourage students to invite peer tutors to participate in their individualized education program (IEP) meetings as friends and advocates.

Feature "peers supporting peers" and the peer tutor program in the school's yearbook.

Encourage students to write thank-you notes to express what they've learned from each other and for the unique gifts their partner brings to their relationship.

Provide opportunities for students to learn more about human diversity, team building, and peer support.

Publish an article about peer tutoring in the school newspaper, written by peer tutor partners.

Provide opportunities for peer tutors and tutees to plan and participate in field trips (e.g., Museum of Tolerance, ROPES, conferences).

Invite peer tutors and tutees to participate in districtwide and/or interdistrict student conferences.

During training sessions, class and club presentations, and other recruitment activities, invite peer tutors and tutees to express what they have learned from their shared experiences.

Ensuring that all students are honored, recognized, and appreciated for the growth that occurs individually and within a partnership demonstrates utmost respect from the teachers and staff involved with peer tutoring and is definitely worth celebrating. Several ideas to begin the celebration are listed in Table 22.4.

REFERENCES

LaPlant, L., & Zane, N. (1994). Partner learning systems. In J.S. Thousand, R.A. Villa, & A.I. Nevin (Eds.), *Creativity and collaborative learning: A practical guide to empowering students and teachers* (pp. 261–273). Baltimore: Paul H. Brookes Publishing Co.

Longwill, A.W., & Kleinert, H.L. (1998). The unexpected benefits of high school peer tutoring. *Teaching Exceptional Children, 30*(4), 60–65.

Mauri, C., Radetski, K., & Wong, A. (1995). *Peer tutor training manual.* San Diego: San Diego City Schools, Exceptional Programs Department.

23

Creating and Supporting Peer Tutor Partnerships

Lesson Plans

Pamela J. Villalobos
Deborah Tweit-Hull
Amie Wong

Lesson 1—
Do's and Don'ts

Purpose

Students will identify positive peer tutoring practices, reflect on their own strengths and needs, and set one goal for personal improvement in response to reading the "Do/Don't List" for peer tutors. This lesson can be used

- To describe specific strategies for peer tutors to provide positive and respectful support to their peers, to communicate and collaborate with others, and to demonstrate responsibility and initiative

- To assist peer tutors to identify their own strengths and areas of improvement

- To assist peer tutors to set goals and improve their skills as a peer tutor

- As an introductory lesson for a unit on support strategies

Materials

- "Reflections" graphic organizer for each student

- "Do/Don't List" for each student

- Highlighter pens (two different colors)

Activity

- Students receive a copy of the "Reflections" graphic organizer (see Figure 23.1).

- Students are directed to respond to the first prompt, "The great thing about being a peer tutor is . . . ," by writing their answer on the graphic organizer. Students are invited to share their responses with each other in pairs or to the whole group.

- The teacher distributes the "Do/Don't List" (see Figure 23.2), and students volunteer to read each suggestion aloud. Students may share their experience with specific issues.

- Students are instructed to use highlighter pens to focus on at least three areas of strength and improvement, using one color to highlight the "Do's" areas of strength and a different color to highlight the "Don'ts" areas for improvement.

- Students are directed to select the area they feel is their strongest peer tutoring skill under the "Do" column. Next, they write down a word or picture on the "Reflections" graphic organizer (next to the "+" sign) to describe their most important strength. They are then directed to select one peer tutoring skill that they need and want to improve. Again, they record their response on the graphic organizer, next to the delta symbol/triangle (signifying change).

- Students may volunteer to share their responses with the group or in pairs.

- To end the activity, peer tutors are instructed to write down their thoughts about "How I make a difference . . ." on the graphic organizer. This prompt should not be limited to their roles as peer tutors and may include family life, community life, or extracurricular activities.

Acknowledgments

Pamela J. Villalobos and her colleagues at Santana High School created the "Do/Don't List." Pamela later developed this activity for peer tutor training completed in schools across the Grossmont Union High School District in La Mesa, California.

Figure 23.1. Reflections graphic organizer.

Successful Peer Tutoring:
Considerations for Providing Support

As a peer tutor, you are now expected to provide support to students in their classes. You may have many questions regarding your responsibilities. If this is your first experience as a peer tutor, you have an opportunity to learn from the positive suggestions and to avoid some of the mistakes listed in the "Do & Don't" list. If you have been a peer tutor in the past, you can use this list to improve your skills as well as celebrate yourself for all the "Do's" you already "do"! Please refer to this list often in order to challenge yourself to be the best you can be. All of your hard work, creativity, and commitment are important to others and very much appreciated!

Do...	Don't...
Focus on each student's unique gifts, skills and interests.	Don't focus on what someone cannot do.
Share conversation, interests, & ideas with the student--get to know each other.	Don't ignore the student by talking to other friends without including the student in your conversation.
Treat all people with respect.	Don't be disrespectful to the teacher or any student in the class. You are now in a leadership role.
Use *People First Language* when speaking about a person with a disability (see article by Snow, K.).	Don't refer to students by disability labels.
Assist students to talk to & make friends with others in their class.	Don't forget how important it is to us all to feel included and to have friends.
Ask the student questions & explain how you want to help before you provide support.	Don't just tell a student what to do.
Ask for help from a teacher whenever you need it. All of your questions are important! We want you to share your ideas & concerns.	Don't be afraid to ask for help. Sometimes teachers seem too busy to ask, however, your needs are very important.
Be cooperative & flexible! Have a positive attitude.	Don't be unwilling to respond to students' changing needs.
When necessary, modify class assignments to increase the student's participation in class activities & opportunities to learn.	Don't take a student out of a class because the class activity or assignment seems too difficult to participate in.

Figure 23.2. Do/Don't List.

Figure 23.2. *(continued)*

Do...	Don't...
Practice common sense & safety. Pay attention to student needs.	Don't misuse student equipment, ignore student needs, etc.
Be reliable & accountable to your teachers, & more importantly, to the student you are supporting.	Don't ever leave the class without telling the student & receiving permission from the teacher.
The best way to help/support students is to make sure they learn to do things for themselves.	Don't do work for a student. Even if a student is able to do only part of an assignment, it is better than you doing all of the work instead.
Facilitate opportunities for the student to work with all students and be sure he or she is included in all aspects of the class.	Don't just provide one-to-one tutoring separate from the other students in the class.
Support the student to stay organized (e.g., assignments are turned into the teacher, put into the correct notebook section, & written down with due dates).	Don't assume the student will receive help from someone else to organize his/her notebook. If necessary, use some of your time together to work on organizational skills.
If the teacher is lecturing, focus on the student's specific learning needs (e.g., take notes, write key words from the lecture, use pictures. mind mapping, graphic organizers).	Don't stop providing support when the teacher is lecturing. You can always help the student to learn more and/or prepare learning materials based on the information being presented by the teacher.
When the class is working in cooperative groups, be sure the student is included in a group & is assigned specific duties.	Don't provide individualized tutoring during group work. Work with the student & group members to come up with roles & responsibilities for everyone.
Inform the teacher if you think a student needs support with his/her behavior.	Do not discuss a student's behavior with other students...respect the student's right to confidentiality.
Be honest regarding your own needs. If you are uncomfortable with your role or any aspect of your responsibilities, talk to a teacher.	Don't ignore your needs! It is not uncommon to feel uncomfortable about your skills for a specific class or to need help to better support a student. We all need to support each other.
Celebrate your shared successes with your partner! You are making a difference in one another's lives.	Don't focus on the problems you encounter. Instead, focus on your solutions & positive experiences together.

Lesson 2—
We're People First

Purpose

Students will identify and make personal connections to the effects of labeling. As a result of reading the article dealing with people-first language, students will expand their understanding of the disability community, disability rights, attitudinal barriers, and the powerful impact of language and labeling and look at positive examples of people-first language. This lesson can be used with peer tutors

- As an introductory activity for training dealing with issues of providing support to others

- To make connections between the personal experience of being labeled and the effects of labeling on people with disabilities

- To share the detrimental effects of labeling any group of people with others and to model the importance of using people-first language in everyday conversations and in writing

Materials

- Picket sign or T-shirt with the message, "Label jars, not people!"

- Student copies of the article (Snow, 1998) or selected reading that addresses labeling or people-first language

- Overhead projector and overhead transparency of the cartoon (Giangreco, 1998)

- Literature circles worksheets delineating each role and responsibilities

- 3–2–1 Reflection sheets for each student

Activity

- The teacher will begin this activity by walking in with a picket sign (or wearing a shirt) that reads, "Label jars, not people!" Students are asked what they think about the message of the sign. As a group, the students are directed to call out examples of labels that are used to describe groups of people at their school, and the teacher writes these labels on the board.

- Students are asked to share their personal experiences with labels and/or discuss whether labels are useful, harmful, informative, and so forth.

- The teacher introduces the connection between labeling and people with disabilities by sharing a cartoon on the overhead projector depicting the concept, "The most appropriate label is usually the one people's parents have given them" (see Giangreco, 1998).

- Students are then placed into "literature circles" to read the article, *To Achieve Inclusion, Community, and Freedom for People with Disabilities, We Must Use People First Language,* written by Kathie Snow (1998). The teacher assigns and explains the literature circle roles for students to assume as they read the article. Possible roles include artful artist, passage picker, word finder, discussion director, and connector. With six students or more, students can be grouped with role-alike members to read the article and prepare for their role in the upcoming discussion. For example, student pairs could be assigned to three of the five possible roles. The discussion director role needs to be assigned to ensure that students, rather than the teacher, lead the discussion. The student groups and role assignments are easily modified to meet the needs of students participating in the lesson.

- Students are provided with teacher-prepared worksheets (or they can use the worksheets prepared in Daniels [1998]) to fill in, either individually or as a group if there are enough students to form role-alike groups, as they read through the article to prepare for the subsequent discussion with their group members. The worksheets need to include the name and description of each student's assigned role with corresponding directions and questions to help prepare the students to participate in the subsequent literature circle discussion. For example, the discussion director is responsible for preparing a list of questions to help the group discuss the big ideas in the reading and to elicit the

Acknowledgments

This lesson was developed by Pamela J. Villalobos.

410 · · ·

Lesson 2—continued

Resources

Daniels, H. (1998). *Literature circles: Voice and choice in the student-centered classroom.* York, ME: Stenhouse.

Giangreco, M. (1998). *Flying by the seat of your pants* (p. 18). Minnetonka, MN: Peytral Publications.

Snow, K. (1998). To achieve inclusion, community, and freedom for people with disabilities, we must use people first language. *TASH Newsletter,* 14–16.

Activity

students' thoughts and feelings about the topic. Sample questions to prepare could include, "What were the three most important ideas in this article?" or, "How did you feel about what the author said about . . . ?"

- Next, students meet together in groups with different roles to discuss the article and share their contributions based on their assigned role (using their completed worksheets). The teacher may wrap up the discussion by asking students to comment on the use of slang, such as *retard* and *lame,* in everyday language after reading and discussing the article. As the discussion finishes, the teacher will challenge students to notice when friends, family, and the media (including printed materials in newspapers, magazines, etc.) do not use people-first language and ask them to share what they think they can and will do.

- Students individually complete a 3–2–1 Reflection form (see Figure 24.14) to express three things they learned about labeling and people with disabilities, two things they will share about labeling with others, and one change they will make to put people first.

Lesson 3—
Get Moving with RESPECT

Purpose

Students will identify and relate to how people feel respected and give respect as presented in the acronym RESPECT. This lesson can be used

- As an introductory activity for peer tutor training dealing with issues of providing support to others

- To make connections between the personal need to feel respected and the need to show respect to others

- To understand the importance of respect for people with disabilities

- To apply the meaning of respect to the peer tutor role and the peer tutor's everyday interactions with the students he or she supports

Materials

- *Respect* by Aretha Franklin

- Tape or CD player or VCR

- "Respect" passage copied for each student (Shapiro-Barnard et al., 1996)

- Overhead projector and overhead transparency of the "Respect" passage

- Poster boards, markers, magazines, scissors, computer graphics, and glue sticks

Activity

- The song *Respect* by Aretha Franklin will be played. As the song starts, students will stand up and follow along with the teacher's hand motions, each followed by two claps to the rhythm of the music. The teacher will use motions to express the meaning of each word that represents how we can give respect and feel respected through the acronym RESPECT.

  - *R*ecognize (salute)

  - *E*mbrace our differences (one hand is placed over the chest, then the other hand crosses it on the chest)

  - *S*ynergize (hands clasp together then raise upward)

  - *P*repare (point to head and then down to watch on wrist)

  - *E*mpower (hold up one fist and raise it upward)

  - *C*elebrate (wave one hand then the other hand above the head)

  - *T*rust (one hand is raised with palm facing out and then placed over the heart)

- For example, "recognize" can be expressed by a salute with two separate motions—touching the forehead and pushing out the hand, followed by two claps. All motions representing the acronym should have two parts in order to follow the beat of the song. Each motion and double clap are repeated to enable the students to follow along. The motions are repeated as the song plays until the students begin to remember the sequence.

- Students are provided with the RESPECT acronym written vertically on the page. The students are asked to guess each word in the acronym based on the hand motions. As each word in the acronym is identified, the teacher elaborates on the meaning of the word and its relevance to the peer tutors' relationships with the students they support and to their role as peer tutors. The following examples can be used:

  - *R*ecognize: Ensure that the student is a contributing member of the class and is able to provide, as well as receive, support from others.

  - *E*mbrace: Respect individual learning styles, use people-first language, and model acceptance of diversity to others.

Acknowledgments

Lori Eshilian and Pamela J. Villalobos created the RESPECT acronym and content motions and have facilitated this activity during conference presentations and with student groups.

Lesson 3—continued

Resources

Franklin, A. (1995). Respect. *I never loved a man the way I love you* [CD]. Atlantic Recording Corporation.

Shapiro-Barnard, S., Tashie, C., Martin, J., Malloy, J., Schuh, M., Piet, J., Lichtenstein, S., & Nisbet, J. (1996). *Petroglyphs: The writing on the wall* (pp. 26–27). Concord: University of New Hampshire Institute on Disability.

For further information on using content motions, iconic posters, and other strategies to engage students in learning, see Abernathy, R., & Reardon, M. (1998). *Hot tips: Increasing student engagement.* Oceanside, CA: Firstborn Publications.

Activity

• **S**ynergize: Communicate with the student and teachers to figure out ways the student can benefit from your support (e.g., participate fully in class activities, develop relationships with others, improve academic performance). *Note:* The word *synergize* is used to describe the exponential power of two or more people working together as opposed to working separately. In other words, by sharing ideas and brainstorming with others, the creative effect is enhanced substantially.

• **P**repare: Partners involved in peer tutoring can show their respect by being prepared, as expressed by the motions meant to indicate planning ahead and using time effectively. Other ways peer tutors can prepare include keeping up with their weekly journals and learning new strategies to support the student.

• **E**mpower: Peer tutors must avoid communicating for or doing the work for the student but instead must enable the student to advocate for him- or herself.

• **C**elebrate: Student partners need to focus on and enjoy their shared accomplishments and positive experiences.

• **T**rust: Without trust, there is no respect. Student partners can demonstrate respect by trusting that each is learning from their shared experiences.

• Students receive a copy of the "Respect" passage (Figure 23.3) taken from *Petroglyphs: The Writing on the Wall* (Shapiro-Barnard et al., 1996). The passage is projected on the wall with an overhead projector. All students read the passage aloud together in a choral reading. Students are asked to make connections between this passage and the words previously discussed in the RESPECT acronym.

• Students work in small groups to create iconic posters to visually express the meaning of respect by drawing pictures and/or symbols, selecting magazine pictures, or using computer graphics using the acronym RESPECT.

• Students share their posters with each other and hang them in the classroom.

• *Respect* is played again. The students will stand and try to remember the hand motions together.

RESPECT

We used to think
disabilities were bigger than
people.
That students' days were best
filled with what someone said
they couldn't - wouldn't -
shouldn't do.
So we pulled them out of English
class to do physical therapy.
Out of math to work on speech.
Out of lunch to learn social skills
in a restaurant.
And although it's difficult to
admit, we often believed that a
student with disabilities was in
need of repair.
So if we could remediate the
disability, we could help the
student learn more.
Live more.
Become a better person.

We now know
students with disabilities are not
broken.
That unlike automobiles,
people don't need to be fixed.
We now see past a student's label
and learn the student's name.
Past the IQ score
to find the student's talent.
We now know people are people.
(Scary to think that this is
something new.)
And so we talk with students,
not about them.
We plan with students,
not for them.
We follow, not lead.
Ask, not tell.
Respect, not change.

Figure 23.3. Respect passage. (From Shapiro-Barnard, S., Tashie, C., Martin, J., Malloy, J., Schuh, M., Piet, J., Lichtenstein, S., & Nisbet, J. [1996]. *Petroglyphs: The writing on the wall* (pp. 26–27). Concord: University of New Hampshire Institute on Disability; reprinted by permission).

Lesson 4—
Ain't Misbehavin'!

Purpose

Occasionally, a tutor (or other support person) may encounter a situation in which the student he or she is supporting engages in a behavior that proves "challenging." The intent of this activity is to discuss and share with a small group of individuals 1) how they would handle/respond to the situation and 2) what the underlying reason for the behavior might be. The resulting brainstormed ideas will be shared with the larger group, with additional discussion and sharing of strategies provided by the facilitator/trainer.

Materials

• Index cards with a single, written behavior (examples are provided in the lesson—feel free to modify, add, or delete)

Resources

Carr, E.G., Levin, L., McConnachie, G., Carlson, J.I., Kemp, D.C., & Smith, C.E. (1994). *Communication-based intervention for problem behavior: A user's guide for producing positive change.* Baltimore: Paul H. Brookes Publishing Co.

Janney, R., & Snell, M.E. (2000). *Behavioral support: Teachers' guides to inclusive practices.* Baltimore: Paul H. Brookes Publishing Co.

Lovett, H. (1996). *Learning to listen: Positive approaches and people with difficult behavior.* Baltimore: Paul H. Brookes Publishing Co.

Activity

Ask participants to pick a partner (or divide into 18 groups—equivalent to the number of examples provided). Each pair (or group) will receive an index card with a "challenging" behavior printed on it. Each person will be asked to share his or her behavior with the group. The group will then brainstorm the following: 1) possible ways to respond to or resolve the situation and 2) reasons why the student may be engaging in the behavior.

Stubborn
Repeats what you say
Hits/kicks/pinches/pulls hair of
   another student
Talks (out of turn; when teacher
   is talking)
Falls asleep
Unmotivated (will not complete
   work)
Says bad words
Acts silly
Talks nonsense (intentionally)
Picks his or her nose

Does not pay attention
Passes gas
Restless/does not stay in his or
   her seat
Runs away from people
Uncooperative (refuses to do
   work, engages in disruptive
   behaviors)
Screams
Keeps asking for lunch or to go
   home
Touches his or her "private
   parts"

Acknowledgments

This lesson was created by Deborah Tweit-Hull.

Lesson 5—
Can I Pick Your Brain?

Purpose

Students will identify six key factors that facilitate learning based on brain research. Then, students will apply this information to determine a variety of strategies (e.g., using mind mapping, graphic organizers, and pictorial vocabulary cards) they can use when providing instructional support to students in the classroom.

This lesson can be used

- As an introductory lesson for a unit on learning and teaching

- To prepare peer tutors with specific information and strategies to improve their skills when providing academic support to students

Materials

- K-W-L format

- "Can I Pick Your Brain?" graphic organizer (Figure 23.4)

- Examples of graphic organizers, mind maps, and other visual tools

Resources

Bromley, K., Irwin-Devitis, L., & Modlo, M. (1995). *Graphic organizers: Visual strategies for active learning.* New York: Scholastic Professional Books.

Flynn, K. (1995). *Graphic organizers: Helping children think visually.* Cypress, CA: Creative Teaching Press.

Jensen, E. (1998). *Teaching with the brain in mind.* Alexandria, VA: Association

Activity

- Students will use the K-W-L format (refer to Figure 24.9 in Chapter 24 of this book) to discuss, as a group, what they *know*, *want* to know, and subsequently, what they *learn* about "brain-compatible" learning or what helps them pay attention and remember the content that is presented in their classes. The teacher should encourage the students to think of a teacher who they remember to be very effective and brainstorm the strategies used by the teacher.

- In the *K* column, the teacher or student volunteer will record the students' responses to identify what they already know about how they learn best.

- In the *W* column, the students will share what they want to know about what helps the human brain learn and remember new information.

- The teacher will then ask the students, "Can I pick your brain?," and write the acronym PCKENS on the board. Students will pair up to propose the six key factors that help us learn based on brain research using the acronym (each letter in the acronym stands for the first letter of the factors involved).

- The teacher will use an overhead projection of a graphic organizer that depicts the six key factors as illustrated in Figure 23.4 and may elaborate on brain-compatible learning using one of the resources listed in the left-hand column.

- For each factor, the students will brainstorm strategies they can use to support students in class incorporating that factor. For example, the letter *C* stands for color. Peer tutors may support students to use color when taking notes, to draw pictures to illustrate important concepts, to outline the information being presented, to use different colored highlighter pens to review key information, or to color code different sections of their notebooks. The teacher may share examples of a variety of graphic organizers, mind maps (refer to the mind map depicted in Figure 22.13 of Chapter 22 as one example), and other visual tools, as well as provide peer tutors with blank graphic organizers to use while peer tutoring and/or prepare supplemental learning materials.

- Students will complete the last column of the K-W-L by recording what they learned as a result of using the acronym PCKENS.

Acknowledgments

Pamela J. Villalobos developed this activity for peer tutor training completed in schools within the Grossmont Union High School District in La Mesa, California.

Lesson 5—continued

Resources

for Supervision and Curriculum Development.

Kagan, M. (1997). *Graphic organizers smartcard.* San Clemente, CA: Kagan Publishing.

Kagan, M. (1997). *Mind mapping smartcard.* San Clemente, CA: Kagan Publishing.

Margulies, N. (1991). *Mapping inner space: Learning and teaching mind mapping.* Tucson, AZ: Zephyr Press.

Margulies, N. (1995). *MAP IT! Tools for charting the vast territories of your mind.* Tucson, AZ: Zephyr Press.

Margulies, N. (1999). *Inside Brian's brain.* Tucson, AZ: Zephyr Press.

Activity

• The teacher may elect to assign homework activities or continue to explore this topic in future lessons with the following activities:

• Students will read the interactive comic book, *Inside Brian's Brain* (see Resources), to discuss and use for a lesson during the next training session.

• Students will read and complete the interactive comic book, *MAP IT! Tools for Charting the Vast Territories of Your Mind* (Margulies, 1995). The students will learn the skills necessary to use mind mapping to enhance their note-taking ability and academic support to students.

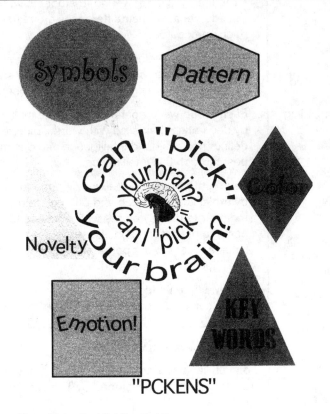

Figure 23.4. Can I Pick Your Brain?

Lesson 6—
We're Smart!

Purpose

Students will participate in a variety of active learning experiences to discover, identify, and describe the eight multiple intelligences (as defined by Gardner [1983] in his theory of multiple intelligences). With this knowledge, students will understand that all students are smart (in eight different ways) and will learn more. They express this knowledge when provided with the opportunity to participate in learning activities that incorporate ways they can use their strongest intelligences. This lesson can be used

- As an introductory lesson for a unit on learning and teaching

- To assist peer tutors to become aware of their own learning strengths and needs

- To provide information and strategies to assist peer tutors to address the individualized learning needs of each student when providing instructional support

Materials

- Human Intelligence Hunt/ Bingo card for each student

- Resource materials for each group to learn about each of the eight intelligences

- Large butcher paper cut into eight slices that form a large circle (pizza) to display on classroom wall

- Markers, watercolor paints and brushes, magazines, scissors, glue sticks, and computer graphics

Activity

- Students will participate in a scavenger hunt, obtaining signatures from their peers who have the characteristics or talents described in the Human Intelligence Hunt/Bingo card, as shown in Figure 23.5. The first student to fill one horizontal, vertical, or diagonal line of their card with names shouts out, "We're smart!"

- The teacher will give a brief introduction to the theory of multiple intelligences by sharing the following big ideas, as visually displayed in a mind map or graphic organizer:

- Howard Gardner (1983) developed the theory that changes the way we think about what it means to be smart and how we think about culture and identified the criteria (connected to brain research, culture, development, and exceptional individuals) for the eight different intelligences (as opposed to a single entity that can be measured by an IQ test).

- Every person has all eight of the intelligences, and there are many ways to express and strengthen each intelligence.

- Schools typically favor the verbal/linguistic and logical/mathematical intelligences and do not capitalize on student strengths in the other intelligences.

- The theory is empowering to students with diverse learning needs because their differences are respected and accommodated.

- Students are divided into eight groups to study each of the intelligences. Resources are listed to provide students with materials to use when learning about the intelligences.

- Each group will prepare a slice of the multiple intelligence pizza by decorating their slice with words, pictures, and symbols to define their assigned intelligence and describe how people learn best through this intelligence.

- Each group presents their intelligence to the rest of the students by explaining their slice and putting the multiple intelligence pizza together to display on the wall. The teacher also challenges students to brainstorm specific strategies to use each multiple intelligence theory to support students after each multiple intelligence slice is shared.

- Finally, students form pairs to share their strongest and weakest multiple intelligences in a Pair-Share.

Acknowledgments

Lori Eshilian and Pamela J. Villalobos created this lesson by adapting activities developed by Thomas Armstrong (1994).

Lesson 6—continued

Resources

Armstrong, T. (1994). *Multiple intelligences in the classroom.* Alexandria, VA: Association for Supervision and Curriculum Development.

DePorter, B., Reardon, M., & Singer-Nourie, S. (1999). Orchestrating dynamic design. In B. DePorter, M. Reardon, & S. Singer-Nourie (Eds.), *Quantum teaching: Orchestrating student success.* (pp. 96–100). Needham Heights, MA: Allyn & Bacon.

Gardner, H. (1983). *Frames of mind. The theory of multiple intelligences.* New York: Basic Books.

Gardner, H. (1993). *Multiple intelligences. The theory in practice.* New York: Basic Books.

Kagan, M. (1997). *Multiple intelligences smartcard.* San Clemente, CA: Kagan Publishing.

Kagan, S., & Kagan, M. (1998). *Multiple intelligences: The complete MI book.* San Clemente, CA: Kagan Publishing.

Lazear, D., & Margulies, N. (1999). *Tap your multiple intelligences posters.* Tucson, AZ: Zephyr Press.

Margulies, N. (1999). *The magic 7: Tools for building your multiple intelligences.* Tucson, AZ: Zephyr Press.

For additional resources to teach students about multiple intelligences:

Kagan Publishing
(800) WEE CO-OP
http://www.KaganCoopLearn.com

Zephyr Press
(800) 232-2187
http://www.zephyrpress.com

Figure 23.5. Multiple intelligences (MI) Bingo.

Lesson 7—
Right on Cue!

Purpose

Students will define natural cues, the levels of instructional prompts/cues, and fading. Students will also be able to use this information to improve their support to students by avoiding "hovering" and fostering dependence on their support and by fading their support to students when appropriate. This lesson can be used

• To prepare peer tutors with specific information and strategies to improve their skills when providing academic support to students

Materials

• Cartoons (see Giangreco, 1998)

• An overhead transparency and copies for each student of the "Instructional Prompts" list (Figure 23.6)

• Index cards with a variety of instructional tasks and prompt levels (at least one per student pair)

• 3–2–1 Reflection sheets

Resources

Cartoons to use for student pair discussions:
Giangreco, M.F. (1998). *Ants in his pants: Absurdities and realities of special education.* Port Chester, NY: National Professional Resource.
  • Helping or Hovering? (p. 74)
  • Island in the Mainstream (p. 27)

Activity

• The students will pair up or meet in small groups to receive a copy of one of five cartoons that demonstrate inappropriate support provided to a student (see Giangreco [1998] for cartoons dealing with providing instructional support to students in the classroom). The students will discuss what's going on in the cartoon, how it relates to their role as a peer tutor and relationship to the student they support, and how the situation could be improved.

• Student pairs/groups will share their reactions to their cartoon with the rest of the students. A copy of each cartoon may be projected on the overhead projector during the presentations.

• The teacher will introduce the concepts of natural cues and instructional prompts and define each prompt level while using an overhead transparency list of the levels of prompts as shown in Figure 23.6.

• The teacher should include the following information when discussing these concepts (and relate back to the cartoons where appropriate):

  • Natural cues refer to the information that ordinarily exists to let us know when or how to do certain things.

  • *Prompts* are defined as different levels of assistance you can give to a student to facilitate his or her learning.

  • When providing prompts to a student, you can teach the student to become more independent by attending to the natural cues that exist in the classroom environment (and providing examples).

  • The goal is to strike a balance between providing enough support for the student to participate and learn from the activity and providing too much support ("overprompting").

  • The choice of prompts used depends on the student and his or her individualized needs for each instructional activity.

  • By fading your support (gradually reducing the levels of prompting or actively assisting other students, leaving the classroom to run an errand for the teacher, etc.), you assist the student to become as independent as possible.

Acknowledgments

Pamela J. Villalobos developed this activity using resources developed by Deborah Tweit-Hull, Pamela J. Villalobos, and Carina York for the video, *The Paraprofessional's Role in Inclusive Classrooms: Parts 1 and 2.*

Lesson 7—continued

Resources

- Learning to Not Make a Move (p. 104)
- Speaking Loudly (p. 101)
- Unintended Distractions (p. 82)

For resources to teach about providing instruction and prompt levels:

Falvey, M.A., & Grenot-Scheyer, M. (1995). Instructional strategies. In M.A. Falvey (Ed.), *Inclusive and heterogeneous schooling: Assessment, curriculum, and instruction* (pp. 148–150). Baltimore: Paul H. Brookes Publishing Co.

Tweit-Hull, D., Villalobos, P., & York, C. (1999). *The paraprofessional's role in inclusive classrooms: Parts 1 and 2* [Video]. Sacramento, CA: The Department of Education, Special Education Division; and San Diego: Interwork Institute/San Diego State University.

Tweit-Hull, D., Villalobos, P., & York, C. (1999). Instructional strategies. In D. Tweit-Hull, P. Villalobos, & C. York (Eds.), *The paraprofessional's role in inclusive classrooms: Support manual* (pp. 23–25). Sacramento, CA: The Department of Education, Special Education Division; and San Diego: Interwork Institute/San Diego State University.

Activity

- Strategies to avoid overprompting include the following:

  - Allow the student time to respond before "jumping in."

  - Show other students how to prompt the student.

  - Don't "hover"; only provide as much help as the student actually needs.

- Students should take notes on their own copies of the "Instructional Prompts" handout (Figure 23.6).

- Next, student pairs will receive an index card with a sample classroom task and specific instructional prompt level(s). Examples of tasks could include saying "Hi" to a classmate, turning on and using the computer, getting a pen out of his or her backpack, or recording his or her response for a test question. Each student pair will complete a role play for the rest of the students by having one student play the part of the peer tutor and the other student act as the student receiving support to complete the task. For example, if the task is turning on and using the computer and the corresponding prompt level is physical, then the peer tutor would physically prompt the student to complete the steps necessary to use the computer.

- The rest of the students guess what task the student pairs are doing and what prompt levels are being used.

- After all pairs have completed their role plays, all students individually complete a 3–2–1 Reflection form (see Figure 24.14) by writing down three new vocabulary words they learned related to instructional prompts, two ways to avoid overprompting, and one way they can fade support for the student they support.

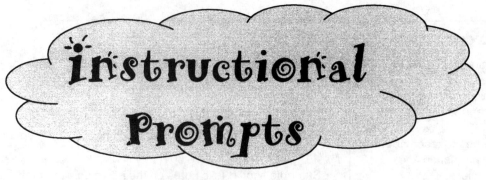

- Natural cues
- Gestures
- Verbal
  - -Indirect
  - -Direct
- Modeling
- Physical
  - -Partial
  - -Full

Figure 23.6.　Prompt Levels Handout.

Lesson 8—
Something To Talk About

Purpose

Define, discuss, and provide examples of the various forms of communication, including verbal and augmentative and alternative communication. Be sure to include gestures, sign language, communication boards/books, and some high- and low-tech examples.

Materials

- Index cards with a single, written expression (14 sample expressions are listed)

- Examples of augmentative and alternative communication systems

Resources

Fried-Oken, M., & Bersani, H.A. (2000). *Speaking up and spelling it out: Personal essays on augmentative and alternative communication.* Baltimore: Paul H. Brookes Publishing Co.

Johnson, J.M., Baumgart, D., Helmstetter, E., & Curry, C.A. (1996). *Augmenting basic communication in natural contexts.* Baltimore: Paul H. Brookes Publishing Co.

Activity

Ask participants to pick a partner (or divide the class into 14 groups—equivalent to the number of examples provided). Each pair (or group) will receive an index card with an expression printed on it. Tell them they must try to convey what is on the expression card to their partners/group without talking. Have the pairs/groups switch cards with another group. Have them repeat the process so that each person gets a turn. The index cards are printed with the following expressions (feel free to add your own):

What are we doing today?	I don't have a pencil.
What is for lunch?	I forgot my binder.
Why can't I do that?	Can I go outside?
I am sick.	I am tired.
I am bored.	I am hot.
I am hungry.	I need to use the bathroom.
I don't understand.	Be my friend.

At the end of the activity, discuss the following questions with the large group:

- What was easily communicated? What was more difficult?

- If your partner began to get the wrong idea, how did you respond?

- How did it feel not to be understood?

- What happened when the "listener" became frustrated?

Acknowledgments

Deborah Tweit-Hull modified this lesson on communication from one presented in the San Diego City Schools Peer Tutor Manual.

Lesson 9—
The Ins and Outs of Curriculum Adaptation

Purpose

Students will define curriculum adaptations and describe the process of learning in terms of "input" and "output." Students will determine a variety of ways to use curriculum adaptations to provide individualized instructional support to students in the classroom. This lesson can be used

• To prepare peer tutors with specific information and strategies to improve their skills when providing academic support to students

Materials

• Overhead transparency of "Bringing It All Together" iconic poster (Figure 23.7)

• Guided note-taking worksheets for each student (Figure 23.8)

• "The Many Paths of Curriculum Adaptation" handout for each student (Figure 23.9)

• Venn diagram iconic poster (large enough to post on the board with room to paste on examples of curriculum adaptation strategies)

Resources

Tweit-Hull, D., Villalobos, P., & York, C. (1999). *The paraprofessional's role in inclusive classrooms* [Video]. (Available from the California Department of Education, Special Education Division, 515 L Street, Room 270, Sacramento, CA 95814, [916] 445-4613)

For a copy of the complete paraprofessional support manual, including additional resources on examples of adaptation ideas across all subject areas:

Activity

• The teacher will introduce and define curriculum adaptations, input, and output by projecting an overhead summarizing these concepts using the "Bringing It All Together" iconic poster (see Figure 23.7). The teacher should describe the following components of the iconic poster:

• The student is pictured in the middle of the page, hanging onto the curriculum content (as depicted by the flying books) presented in class.

• In order to learn the content, the student must input or get the information and have the opportunity to output or "show what he or she knows" as a result of participating in learning experiences.

• The supports that the student will need to learn the curriculum content are depicted by the building blocks (acronym IAMMPT) under the student.

• IAMMPT is easily recalled by the phrase, "I am a marvelous peer tutor."

• These supports must be *i*ndividualized to meet the student's unique needs, may include student *a*ccommodations and curriculum *m*odifications that are created by providing adapted or additional *m*aterials having *p*ersonalized support (e.g., peer support, adult assistance) and *t*echnology.

• Next, the students will each receive a copy of "The Ins and Outs of Curriculum Adaptation Guided Note-Taking" worksheet as illustrated in Figure 23.8. As the teacher reviews the information, students fill in the appropriate terms in the underlined sections of the worksheet (the answers as recorded in Figure 23.8 need to be deleted prior to providing the worksheet to the students). The teacher may also use the video, *The Paraprofessional's Role in the Inclusive Classroom* (Tweit-Hull, Villalobos, & York, 1999), which covers the same material in the "Materials and Adaptation Development" section in Part 2 of the video (a support manual developed to accompany this video contains the fill-in format as modified in the worksheet depicted in Figure 23.8). If using the video, the teacher will need to pause at various points to allow time for students to complete the worksheet and to further elaborate on the specific examples presented.

• The teacher will distribute "The Many Paths of Curriculum Adaptation" handout (see Figure 23.9) to each student to read and

Acknowledgments

This lesson was created by Pamela J. Villalobos. The "Bringing It All Together" iconic poster was adapted from the visual created by Lori Eshilian and Mary Jane Hibbard at Whittier High School.

Lesson 9—continued

Resources

Tweit-Hull, D., Villalobos, P., & York, C. (1999). *The paraprofessional's role in inclusive classrooms: Support manual.* Sacramento: California Department of Education.

For resources to develop iconic posters:

Abernathy, R., & Reardon, M. (1998). *Hot tips: Increasing student engagement.* Oceanside, CA: Firstborn Publications.

For resources on the Venn graphic organizer:

Bromley, K., Irwin-Devitis, L., & Modlo, M. (1995). *Graphic organizers: Visual strategies for active learning.* New York: Scholastic Professional Books.

Activity

save with their peer tutor training materials. The examples of the "paths of curriculum adaptation" will be written on colorful sticky notes. Students will take turns placing each sticky note example on the large Venn diagram posted on the board. Students will determine whether their "path" can be classified as an example of input (far left circle of the Venn), both input and output (shared middle portion between two circles of the Venn), or output (far right circle of the Venn). After reading the example aloud and posting it on the Venn, the rest of the students determine whether this response is correct.

• As a final review of the concepts learned, students will pair up to review the "Bringing It All Together" overhead (Figure 23.7), working together to recall the definitions of curriculum adaptations, input, and output as well as the components needed to support student learning (listed in the IAMMPT acronym).

Bringing it all together...

Input
1-*Get* information
2-Have access to learning the same content

Output
1-*Give* information
2-"Show what they know"

Curricular Content

i
A M
M P T

Figure 23.7. Input and Output.

LESSON 9

The Ins & Outs of Curriculum Adaptation: Guided Note-Taking

CURRICULUM ADAPTATIONS are defined as <u>changes</u> made to the classroom environment, assignments, or activities with the purpose of enhancing a student's <u>participation</u> and <u>performance</u>. One of your responsibilities will most likely involve assisting in the construction or <u>creation</u> of <u>adaptations</u> under teacher supervision.

INPUT AND OUTPUT

"Input" refers to how students <u>get</u> and <u>learn about</u>_____ new information and how information is <u>presented</u> to the student. Some of the ways you can assist the student to understand or learn new information being presented in class include:

1. Using <u>additional</u> materials such as:
   - books on tape
   - <u>enlarged text</u>
   - pictures
2. Focusing on <u>less</u> information by:
   - learning ___<u>"big ideas"</u> rather than detailed information
   - using <u>simplified</u> versions of core literature
3. With <u>individualized</u>____ support by:
   - allowing the student to <u>listen</u> as peers read aloud
   - giving <u>extra help</u> to further explain concepts
   - assisting the student to search a <u>computer program</u>
4. At a <u>different</u> pace by:
   - having <u>extra time</u> in the classroom for new information to really "stick"

"Output" refers to how students <u>show</u> what they have learned. Some ways that you can assist the student to more effectively demonstrate what they have learned may involve:

1. <u>Changing</u> the assignment to:
   - giving an ___<u>oral report</u> with or without peer assistance
   - drawing a picture or diagram relating to the subject
2. Using <u>additional</u> or <u>different</u> materials such as:
   - a computer or <u>calculator</u>
   - using self-stick labels
3. <u>Reducing</u> the workload by:
   - assuming a specific and less involved <u>role</u> for a group activity
   - being assigned fewer or <u>easier</u> vocabulary words or math problems
   - reading chapter <u>summaries</u>
   - taking a simplified test, being responsible for only a few big ideas
4. Having more support or <u>time</u> by:
   - <u>dictating</u>___ answers to an adult or peer
   - allowing <u>more time</u> to complete assignments

Four important considerations should guide all decisions about how to adapt curriculum. Curriculum adaptations should:

1. Be age <u>appropriate</u>
2. Look as <u>similar</u> to the other students' class work as possible
3. Increase the student's <u>independence</u> and self-reliance
4. Address and teach relevant IEP _____<u>goals and objectives</u>

Figure 23.8. Curriculum Fill-in.

The Many Paths of Curriculum Adaptation

Curriculum adaptations can be <u>any change to the learning process</u> including:

1. How students are grouped (or not) during the learning activity

2. Learning materials used

3. Environmental conditions (e.g., inside/outside, listening to music, seating arrangements, lighting)

4. How information is provided to students (e.g., teacher talking, visual aids used, watching a movie)

5. How students demonstrate what they learned (e.g., written essay, picture collage, answers on a multiple choice test, oral presentation)

6. <u>Amount</u> of work the students complete for an assignment or test (e.g., number of math problems, number of themes discussed from a book, number of steps in a project)

7. Level of <u>difficulty</u> of the assignment

8. Amount of <u>time</u> allowed to complete assignment

9. What is learned (content may need to be personalized)

10. Level of support needed to fully participate (e.g., technology, peer assistance, group work)

When students and teachers work together to adapt curriculum, creative and effective ways to support students to learn and participate as members of the general education classroom are discovered!

Figure 23.9. Paths of Adaptation.

Lesson 10—

Just Adapt!

Purpose

Providing support to a student in a general education class requires the understanding of how to use and create adaptations to classroom assignments and activities. Although the teachers have the overall responsibility of designing and developing appropriate adaptations, peer tutors may assist in this process; and for those unplanned or spontaneous classroom activities, may be called on to "just adapt!" This activity provides an opportunity to practice the development of curriculum adaptations under the guidance of a teacher/facilitator.

Materials

- Five stations set up around the room

- Five adaptation scenarios that each highlight a different subject area (e.g., math, English, history, Spanish, science); feel free to use the examples provided or create your own scenarios that more closely reflect your school's curriculum

- A typical general education math assignment/worksheet (from your school's curriculum) to use with Station 1

Resources

Barry, C., Bjorgan, H., Blanchard, J., Christ, C., Gold, R., Hamilton, M., Kearny, A., Kessler, T., Lee, L., Nusbaum, E., Oliver, K. (2000). *Adapting curriculum and modifying instruction for all*

Activity

- Five stations will be set up around the room. The participants will be divided into five groups with each group assigned to one of the five stations. Each station highlights a different subject area (e.g., math, English, history, Spanish, science—or pick your own!) and provides a scenario of an activity that involves one or more students.

- Instruct the groups to read their scenario and to adapt the proposed assignment for the student(s) presented. Each group can rotate through each of the five stations.

- After each group has had a chance to work through each of the stations, bring the groups back together to share what they have developed for each station/scenario. Possible scenarios follow. (Or create your own!)

Station 1: Math

- Turn to page 19 in the math packet.

- Adapt the assignment on this page for Abel.

- Abel is learning to count on his own. He can count to 5 before he starts to make mistakes. He is learning how to use the calculator with a lot of hand-over-hand help, to match pictures, to copy numbers and words, and to count objects to help him recognize numbers. Math will look different for Abel, but he can still work on the same things as his peers. He just needs to have his work modified.

- How can you help Abel with this assignment?

Station 2: English

- The class assignment is journal writing. The topic the students have to write about is, "Should the drinking age be lowered to 18?"

- Please adapt this assignment for Belinda and Suri.

- Belinda needs hand-over-hand help with writing. She likes to use the computer but is still learning how. If you ask her questions, she will answer you with some prompting. She primarily speaks Spanish, but she speaks some English, too. She is shy and needs to learn to work cooperatively with others. Belinda is easily distracted and needs reminders to wipe her mouth periodically. She tends to rush through her work and is learning to focus on the quality of her work (not finishing it as fast as she can!).

- Suri can trace words. She loves to color and get involved with all the activities the students in her classes are doing. Suri needs to learn to copy (i.e., print) words. She needs her words written large enough for her to see, otherwise the letters look too confusing. Suri needs to talk louder and learn to be as independent in class as possible.

- How can you help Belinda and Suri with this assignment?

Lesson 10—continued

Resources

students: A guide for all educators. San Francisco: San Francisco Unified School District.

How to differentiate instruction. (September, 2000). *Educational Leadership, 58*(1).

Janney, R., & Snell, M.E. (2000). *Modifying schoolwork: Teachers' guides to inclusive practices* (4 vols.). Baltimore: Paul H. Brookes Publishing Co.

Villa, R.A., & Thousand, J.S. (2000). *Restructuring for caring and effective education: Piecing the puzzle together* (2nd ed.). Baltimore: Paul H. Brookes Publishing Co.

Activity

Station 3: History

- The students are studying the Renaissance era. The assignment is to choose from one of the following projects: 1) a book report and a collage, 2) a book report and creating an artifact from the Renaissance era, or 3) a videotaped report that shows a visual of this era of time.

- Please adapt this assignment for Richard.

- Richard can copy words, type—with help—on the computer (but be watchful when he's at the computer—Richard is very curious!), and answer questions with little prompting. Richard likes to color, but he also likes to color on himself. Richard needs to use his spoken language more and learn to ask for help. Remember that Richard likes to keep busy at all times.

- Which assignment would you do with Richard, and how would you adapt it?

Station 4: Spanish

- There is a class lecture on the Day of the Dead, a Mexican celebration.

- What would you do for Francisco during the class lecture?

- Francisco can speak Spanish and English. He likes to work with his classmates and others but is very shy. He will eventually warm up to you. Francisco can copy off the board and from notes taken for him. He does not write very fast, and too much writing will overwhelm him. He colors and draws well. He can use the computer with help.

Station 5: Science

- The class is dissecting a frog and needs to label the parts on a diagram. The students also need to write a summary of the experience. During this type of activity, there is usually a lot of commotion going on in the class due to the excitement.

- Please adapt this assignment for Michael.

- Michael is learning to use a switch to activate various assistive technology and other devices. He uses a Bigmack switch (which is programmed by his peer partners) to answer questions and help out in presentations. His switches have also been hooked up to a tape recorder, class overhead/slide projectors, and to a SpeakEasy (voice-output device). Michael is also learning to respond to yes/no questions by nodding and shaking his head. He is just beginning to use the computer and his IntelliKeys. Michael enjoys working in groups with his classmates and helping out his science teacher.

- How would you involve Michael in this activity?

24

Empowering Secondary Students to Take the Lead

Training Activities to Promote Advocacy, Inclusion, and Social Justice

Pamela J. Villalobos
Lori Eshilian
Jeff Moyer

High school campuses are dynamic places of learning, social change, and increasing demands on both youth and adults to meet a growing list of expectations and standards for excellence. As we write this chapter, another tragic event has both horrified and saddened us. At a high school that is internationally known for providing inclusive education for students with disabilities, a young man has taken the lives of two students and injured 13 others during a shooting rampage. It is imperative that we not only explore the potential causes to such horrific incidents and ways to make our schools safe places for our youth but that we also act now to ensure that all schools are pro-actively addressing the need for all students to belong. The 15 student leadership lessons described in this chapter can represent one small step toward this end.

Student leadership training builds on the principles of critical pedagogy and liberatory education that are described in Chapter 6 of this text. Particularly, such training is intended to promote the experience of *praxis*, the cycle of action–reflection–new action (i.e., self-determination) that can transform an individual's experience of the world, as well as the world itself. Although many of the lessons included in this chapter focus specifically on inclusion and the rights of people with disabilities, the intent of student leadership training is to empower all students to advocate for themselves, to accept and appreciate human diversity, and to effect social change.

STUDENT PARTICIPANTS

Students "recruited" to participate in the lessons should represent a diverse and heterogeneous group and not be limited to students who, in the established view, might be considered the leaders at the school. In other words, the leadership activities are not intended to be a "project" in which student leaders are "doing for" or helping students with disabilities. This is not a "special" program or a helping model but a forum for all students to learn leadership skills together for the purpose of changing their school.

Table 24.1.   Secondary school models: Student leadership training

School models for training	Participants/organizations
Classroom presentations (student "teach-ins")	Students within one school plan who participate in training activities
Club activities	
Extracurricular activities (e.g., friendship clubs)	Associated Student Body (i.e., student body governance)
Assemblies (e.g., speaker, performance troupes that address human diversity)	Clubs (e.g., Human Relations, Key Club, Future Educators of America)
Field trips (e.g., Museum of Tolerance, Self-Advocacy Conference, Youth Resiliency)	Peer counselors and tutors
Service-learning[a] (e.g., Habitat for Humanity)	
Team-building programs	ROPES/Outward Bound
	Inclusion retreats
Regional student conferences	Inter-district: Students representing schools from different districts attend a conference together (see sample agenda, Figure 24.7)
	Districtwide: Students from schools in one district attend a conference together

[a]Project SUCCESS is an example of an inclusive service-learning experience project supported by the United Cerebral Palsy Association, the Corporation for National Service, and Serve America (Brannon, 1998).

COORDINATING LEADERSHIP TRAINING

To implement student leadership training at a school, at least one staff member must take on the responsibility of administering and coordinating the activities involved. At one author's school, the student leadership efforts were facilitated by a special educator with close coordination with a guidance counselor and an advisor for two important student leadership organizations on campus: the Human Relations Club and the Associated Student Body (student governance body). By working closely with key players, the special educator received the support to identify and follow through on the logistics required for introducing student activities on campus. Being affiliated with the Associated Student Body, the special educator could easily gain access to student leaders for guidance during the planning stage and support for participation in the training activities throughout the school year.

Whoever takes on the coordination responsibilities for student leadership training needs to be sure to customize the training model, with the students involved, so that it best matches the culture of the school and district. Table 24.1 examines certain training dimensions that need to be considered when customizing a model.

What follows are 15 specific lessons for activities that can be used with any training model. The brief introduction that precedes the lessons may be used with students, teachers, administrators, and parents to orient them to the intent and scope of the student leadership training activities.

INTRODUCTION TO STUDENT LEADERSHIP LESSONS

Purpose and Goals of Training

The purpose of student leadership training is to empower students to

- Explore their personal experiences and values in relation to human diversity

- Expand their knowledge base about historical and current social practices of excluding and including people with disabilities

- Use that knowledge to advocate for a school where everyone belongs and each student's contribution is valued

An ultimate goal, then, of empowerment training is to motivate students to take action when they become aware of any form of injustice that occurs at their school and in their community. Actions can range from daily and personal acts of acceptance and inclusion of others to participation in more formal planning and problem-solving processes. The outcome is to change the culture of a school from one that devalues students based on their membership or lack of membership in perceived cliques, ethnic groups, or any other labeled group to one of acceptance and celebration of human differences.

Lesson Activities

The 15 lessons included here are a sampling of activities that have been used in secondary schools to promote student advocacy and leadership regarding issues of human diversity, social justice, and inclusion. The lesson activities are active learning experiences that respect students' diversity in learning styles and allow them to express their multiple intelligences. Students with disabilities assume a teaching and leadership role when the lessons are presented because their perspective and participation is crucial when students are

Table 24.2. Index to student leadership lessons by topical areas

Lesson titles	Authors
Belonging/inclusion	
1. Visualizing Inclusion	Eshilian, L. & Villalobos, P.J.
2. INCLUDE Values	Holloway, M.A. & Villalobos, P.J.
3. Posting Our Values	Holloway, M.A. & Villalobos, P.J.
4. Inclusion Jeopardy!	Holloway, M.A. & Villalobos, P.J.
5. Who Am I?	Eshilian, L.
Celebrating diversity/social justice	
6. A Walk with Courage	Eshilian, L. & Villalobos, P.J.
7. Speak to Us	Eshilian, L. & Villalobos, P.J.
8. Label Me, Negate Me?	Eshilian, L.
9. Speak Up Through Song	Eshilian, L. & Villalobos, P.J.
10. It's the Law!	Eshilian, L. & Villalobos, P.J.
11. A Rainbow of Justice	Eshilian, L. & Villalobos, P.J.
12. Wake Up Now!	Moyer, J.
13. How Big Is Your Circle?	Moyer, J.
Reflection/action planning	
14. 3–2–1 Reflect!	Eshilian, L., & Villalobos, P.J.
15. School MAPs	Eshilian, L.

learning about the rights and inclusion of people with disabilities. Table 24.2 provides an "at-a-glance" preview of the 15 lessons by topical area. As you examine the lessons you will notice that many lessons address issues across all three topical areas.

REFERENCES

Abernathy, R., & Reardon, M. (1998). *Hot tips: Increasing student engagement.* Oceanside, CA: Firstborn Publications.

Armstrong, T. (2000). *Multiple intelligences in the classroom* (2nd ed.). Alexandria, VA: Association for Supervision and Curriculum Development.

Blue, B. (1990). Courage. *Starting small* [Cassette].

Brannon, M. (1998). *Project SUCCESS: An inclusive service-learning curriculum for youth.* Washington, DC: United Cerebral Palsy, Corporation for National Service and Learn, and Serve America.

Bromley, K., Irwin-Devitis, L., & Modlo, M. (1995). *Graphic organizers: Visual strategies for active learning.* New York: Scholastic Professional Books.

Falvey, M., Grenot-Scheyer, M., Coots, J., & Bishop, K. (1995). Services for students with disabilities: Past and present. In M. Falvey (Ed.), *Inclusive and heterogeneous schooling: Assessment, curriculum, and instruction* (pp. 23–39). Baltimore: Paul H. Brookes Publishing Co.

Kagan, M. (1997). *Multiple intelligences smartcard.* San Clemente, CA: Kagan Publishing.

Kagan, S., & Kagan, M. (1998). *Multiple intelligences: The complete MI book.* San Clemente, CA: Kagan Publishing.

Krutein, W., & Pomeranz, D. (1987). *In every one of us* [Video]. San Francisco: New Era Media.

Kunc, N., & Van der Klift, E. (1995). *A credo for support* [Video]. (Available from Axis Consultation & Training Ltd., 340 Machleary Street, Nanaimo, British Columbia, Canada V9R 2G9; telephone: [250] 754-9939).

Lazear, D., & Margulies, N. *Tap your multiple intelligences posters.* Tucson, AZ: Zephyr Press.

Margulies, N. (1991). *Mapping inner space: Learning and teaching mind mapping.* Tucson, AZ: Zephyr Press.

Minnesota Governors Planning Council for Developmental Disabilities. (1999). *Parallels in time* [CD-ROM]. Minneapolis, MN: Author.

Moyer, J. (1995). Wake up now! On *We're people first: A celebration of diversity* [CD and activity guide]. Cleveland, OH: Jeff Moyer Music.

Moyer, J. (2000). How big is your circle? On *A musical promoting healing of exclusion, ridicule, and violence* [CD, script, and activity guide]. Cleveland, OH: Jeff Moyer Music.

National Information Center for Children and Youth with Disabilities. (1999). *Disability fact sheets.* Washington, DC: Author.

Perske, R. (1989). *Circle of friends.* Nashville, TN: Abingdon Press.

Pierpoint, J. (1992). *Exclusion/inclusion mind map* [Poster]. Toronto: Inclusion Press International.

Sabia (1989). Never turning back. On *Live! En vivo!* [CD]. Chicago: Flying Fish Records.

Sapon-Shevin, M. (1999). *Because we can change the world.* Needham Heights, MA: Allyn & Bacon.

Lesson 1—
Visualizing Inclusion

Purpose

Students will develop a visual image of their school, class, or club to examine the inclusive or exclusive practices that currently exist. This lesson can be used

- As an introductory activity to engage students in thinking about inclusion

- To provide the opportunity for students to make a personal connection with inclusive and exclusive experiences

Activity

- Group or individual students identify what inclusion and exclusion mean.

- Students can use dictionaries or a group discussion or reflect on a time they felt included or excluded.

- Teacher can elaborate with use of visual mind map of society's inclusive and exclusive practices (see Resource section).

- In small groups, students can complete the Needs Assessment for an Inclusive School (see Figure 24.1) to evaluate the inclusive practices at their school.

- In these same groups, students design and create a visual that represents what inclusion and exclusion looks like at their school.

- Students explain their visual product.

Materials

- Colorful marking pens and/or pencils

- Butcher or poster paper

- Dictionaries

- Visual of society's inclusive and exclusive practices (see Resource section)

- Needs Assessment for an Inclusive School

Resource

Pierpoint, J. (1992). *Exclusion/inclusion mind map.* [Poster]. Toronto: Inclusion Press International.

Acknowledgments

This lesson was created by Lori Eshilian and Pamela J. Villalobos. The Needs Assessment for an Inclusive School was adapted from *Full Inclusion Student Council Needs Assessment,* a tool utilized by the University Affiliated Project for Self Advocacy (University of Southern California.).

Needs Assessment for an Inclusive School

School:_____ Date:_____

Names of persons filling out this form: _____

_____

_____

Resources used: (Administrators, Special Education Teachers, Resource Specialists, Program Specialists)

_____

_____

General Information about your school:
1. How many students are enrolled? _____
2. How many students have IEPs (Individual Educational Plans)?_____
   a. How many students are in the *Resource Program*? _____
   b. How many students are in *special day* classes all day? _____
   c. How many students are *mainstreamed* part of the day (RSP & SDC)? ____
   d. How many students are *fully included*? _____
   e. How many students with or without IEPs use wheelchairs or have physical needs that require modifications or adaptations? _____
3. Of the students mainstreamed and fully included...
   a. How many are in academic classes? _____
      List examples _____

      _____

      _____

      _____

      _____
   b. How many are in PE or elective classes? _____
      List examples _____

      _____

      _____

      _____

      _____

Architectural Design: (suggestion: have someone on the committee who uses a wheelchair to assess this area)
1. How many entrances are there to your school? _____
   a. Do all students use the same entrance? _____YES____NO Why or Why not? _____
   b. Where do the buses drop off students? _____

   _____
2. Does the school have steps entering the buildings? _____YES____NO Where? _____
   Does your school have ramps as well? _____YES____NO Where? _____

   _____
3. Can students who use wheelchairs get to all places on campus?____YES____NO
4. Are all bathrooms wheelchair accessible? (i.e. wider doors, hand rails, lowered sinks, soap or towel dispenser) _____

   _____
5. Are your buildings two or more stories? _____YES____NO Are there elevators for any building that is two or more stories? __YES____NO
6. Classrooms:
   a. Are the doors wide enough for wheelchairs? _____YES____NO
   b. Is there enough space inside for wheelchairs?____YES ____NO
   c. Are there tables high enough for wheelchairs?____YES____NO

Figure 24.1. Needs Assessment for an Inclusive School.

Figure 24.1. *(continued)*

7. Are there any other architectural barriers in your school facilities:
   a. Gym and locker rooms? _____

   _____

   b. Cafeteria?_____

   _____

   c. Science Labs?_____

   _____

   d. Art or Woodshop Classes?_____

   _____

   e. Library?_____

   _____

   f. Other _____

   _____

Extracurricular/ Social Opportunities & Participation:
1. Do all students with IEPs have the same nutrition, lunch and passing periods?
   _____YES____NO If No, why not? _____

   _____

2. Do all students with IEPs sit and blend together at lunch and nutrition?
   _____YES____NO Explain: _____

   _____

3. How many clubs are there on campus? _____
   a. Are students with IEPs involved in clubs?_____YES____NO
   b. What are some activities that clubs organize? _____

   _____

   c. Could students with IEPs participate in all activities?____YES___NO
4. How many students are involved in student government (ASB & Grade Level)?_____
   a. Are there any students with IEPs in student government?____YES____NO
5. Are students with IEPs involved with sports? ____YES___NO
   a. In what sports? _____

   _____

   _____

6. How many performances were there (band, drama, comedy, lip-sync etc.)?_____
   a. How many students with IEPs were in the performances?_____Which ones?_

   _____

   b. How many students with IEPs attended the performances? _____
7. How many school dances were there? _____
   a. Did students with IEPs attend?____YES___NO
8. Other activities in your school that most students participate in? _____

   _____

   _____

   _____

Rate your school - Our school does an excellent job including students with disabilities:

```
   |    |    |    |    |    |    |    |    |    |
   1    2    3    4    5    6    7    8    9    10
Strongly Disagree                        Strongly Agree
```

Lesson 2—
INCLUDE Values

Purpose

Students will relate to the values of inclusion presented in the acronym INCLUDE. This lesson can be used

- As an introductory activity for student leadership groups, classroom presentations, and team-building activities

- As a review or ongoing activity for students who participate in interactive groups and explore the specific values of inclusion

Activity

- Teacher and/or student volunteers/leaders will utilize the Review-Preview cards to introduce the values of inclusion by holding up posters with the letters and corresponding values contained in the acronym INCLUDE (see Figure 24.2). When each card is held up, all students call out the name of the value written on the poster. As the poster is flipped over, revealing a short phrase that expresses the value, all students chorally read the phrase.

- After a couple experiences with calling out the values on the posters in order, students can learn "content motions" along with the values. These are hand, arm, or body motions that are paired with the content of each poster and that help students remember the concepts being taught.

- Posters can be held up randomly to further challenge the students to remember the values of inclusion. As the posters are held up, students can chorally respond to the values represented in each poster.

- All students complete the 3–2–1 Reflection sheet (see Lesson 14) at the end of the activity.

Materials

- INCLUDE poster Review-Preview cards

- 3–2–1 Reflection sheet handouts

Resources

For further information about using the Review-Preview cards and content motions activities, as well as 28 other strategies to increase student engagement in learning, see

Abernathy, R., & Reardon, M. (1998). *Hot tips: Increasing student engagement.* Oceanside, CA: Firstborn Publications.

Acknowledgments

Mary Ann Holloway (teacher at West Hills High School, Santee, California) and Pamela J. Villalobos created the acronym INCLUDE and the related activities with peer tutors from West Hills High School to focus on inclusive education values during presentations to freshmen classes at West Hills.

The values of inclusion are expressed by the acronym

"INCLUDE"

"I" for Inclusion: All students learn together!

"N" for Need: All students need to belong!

"C" for Classmates: Classmates support each other!

"L" for Learn: All students have the right to learn!

"U" for Unity: Together we're better!

"D" for Diversity: Respect and celebrate our differences!

"E" for Everyone: Everyone can make a difference!

Figure 24.2. INCLUDE values.

Lesson 3—
Posting Our Values

Purpose

Students will explore and relate to the values of inclusion by working collaboratively with peers in a jigsaw cooperative group activity to create posters reflecting the values of inclusion. This lesson can be used

- As an introduction to the concept of inclusive education

- To provide an opportunity to make a personal connection and to teach others

Materials

- Seven folders with directions and materials for the interactive activities needed for each expert group (one folder for each letter from INCLUDE)

- Blank letters cut out (large enough to decorate) for each INCLUDE expert group folder

- Markers, crayons, colored pencils, glue sticks, glitter, and stickers

- Strips of paper to glue the decorated letters to for the home group posters

- INCLUDE poster Review-Preview cards

- 3–2–1 Reflection sheets for each student

Resources

Krutein, W., & Pomeranz, D. (1987). *In every one of us.* [Video]. San Francisco: New Era Media. (Available through New Era Media, 425 Alabama Street, Post Office Box 410685-W, San

Activity

- Students within "home groups" will be divided into expert groups according to each letter in the acronym INCLUDE. (There should be seven students in each home group).

- Once students join their expert group, they will become involved in interactive activities to deepen their understanding of the value that each letter represents (see the values that each letter represents in Lesson 2: Review-Preview INCLUDE).

- Each group will have an activity folder containing directions and materials to guide students through activities to further explore their INCLUDE value. One example of an activity is watching the video *In Every One of Us* (see Resources section) and completing a 3–2–1 Reflection sheet (see Lesson 15) to bring home the value of respecting and celebrating our *differences* as represented by *D* in the INCLUDE acronym. Several of the lessons presented in this chapter could be used for these small-group activities. Lesson 6: A Walk with Courage could be used for the letter *E* in INCLUDE because the message of the song exemplifies that "everyone can make a difference." Lesson 5: Who Am I? provides an activity for students to recognize the group(s) they belong to and where they have developed their friendships. Students ultimately connect with the notion that "everyone *needs* to belong" (as expressed in the *N* of INCLUDE). The *L* in INCLUDE (all students have the right to *learn*) could be further explored by completing portions of Lesson 10 that deal with current state and federal laws and court rulings that support this value. These and other activities can be incorporated into the seven expert group activity folders for each of the INCLUDE values. The book *Circle of Friends* is listed in the Resources section to further assist with the development of group activities.

- Teachers should assist each group by ensuring that students understand the directions and activities involved. If student leaders are assisting with this lesson, then at least one student leader should join each expert group to facilitate the discussion around the specific value of inclusion.
  Together, expert group members should discuss issues reflecting their designated INCLUDE value and individually decorate cut-out letters to visually express this value.

- Students then return to their original home group to present their expert knowledge regarding each value. Each student will review

Acknowledgments

Mary Ann Holloway, Pamela J. Villalobos, peer tutors, and student leaders presented this lesson to freshmen classes at West Hills High School in Santee, California.

Lesson 3—continued

Resources

Francisco, CA 94141-0685; telephone: [415] 863-3555)

For resources to develop activity folders, the following book provides wonderful short stories for students to read together and respond to questions that can be developed for specific INCLUDE values:

Perske, R. (1989). *Circle of friends.* Nashville: Abingdon Press.

Activity

his or her value, describe how his or her decorated letter represents the value, and paste his or her letter on a strip of paper to ultimately spell and create their group INCLUDE poster.

• Each group then hangs their completed poster in the classroom or school hallway and selects one member of their group to stand in front of the room to facilitate the final activity.

• The final activity can include the whole class in a final (loud!) call-out of the inclusion values by holding up the Review-Preview cards (see Lesson 2).

• All students complete the 3–2–1 Reflection sheet (see Lesson 14).

Lesson 4—
Inclusion Jeopardy!

Purpose

Students will demonstrate the knowledge they have gained about inclusive educational values, practices, legislation, and historical influences. This lesson can be used

- As a final and celebratory activity after participating in a variety of student leadership activities

Activity

- Students are divided into teams (the same home teams as established in Lesson 3 can be used).

- Students can "warm up" using Preview-Review cards (see Lesson 2).

- Jeopardy! question categories are posted on the board in the front of the classroom with point values listed below each category. Sample categories, point values, and corresponding questions are provided in Figure 24.3.

- Teacher and/or student leaders can explain the game rules and review categories of questions as listed on the board.

- One team is chosen at random to begin by selecting a category and point value question. The teacher or student leader will ask the corresponding question. The entire team will have the opportunity to share ideas and refer to their note-taking pages before deciding on their final answer.

- The teams continue taking turns until time runs out. If there is a tie, the teacher or student leader will ask Double Jeopardy! questions to determine the final winning team.

- The winning team leads the whole class in the INCLUDE values call-out with the Review-Preview cards as a final celebration!

Materials

- Jeopardy! questions (Figure 24.3)

- Question categories and point levels displayed on the board

- Review-Preview cards from Lesson 2

Resources

Other lessons included in this chapter and in Chapter 23 of this text.

Acknowledgments

Peer tutors at West Hills High School in Santee, California, recommended that Jeopardy! be used to keep the presentation interesting. Mary Ann Holloway (West Hills High School teacher) and Pamela J. Villalobos created the questions for use as a final evaluation/celebration during the freshmen class presentations.

Jeopardy! Questions

Values of Inclusion	More Values	Support for Inclusion	Inclusion Facts	Inclusion at our school
50 What does the "U" stand for in "INCLUDE" & show the motions	50 What does the "I" stand for in "INCLUDE" & show the motions	50 How can you show respect to someone with disabilities when providing support? *refer to Credo	50 Name the federal law which gives students with disabilities the right to attend general ed. classes with support?	50 Identify 3 examples of how students are labeled at your school (& related stereotypes)
50 What does the "L" stand for in "INCLUDE" & show the motions	50 What does the "D" stand for in "INCLUDE" & show the motions	50 What are accommodations?	50 What was the name of the Supreme Court case which found that "Separate is not equal?"	50 Name 3 kinds of accommodations students with learning needs might use when learning in classes?
40 What does the "E" in "INCLUDE" stand for (use E-word & entire phrase)	40 What does the "N" in "INCLUDE" stand for (use N-word & entire phrase)	40 Who can support the student in class (e.g., to take notes, complete assignments)	40 Give a definition of inclusion	40 Describe at least two clubs at your school which promote the values of "INCLUDE" & explain how
30 What does the "C" in "INCLUDE" stand for?	30 What's the opposite of inclusion?	30 Give an example of how you could support a student with learning needs in one of your classes	30 Why not educate students with disabilities in separate schools? *Separate is not equal	30 Give an example of how your school tries to promote unity among all students
Double Jeopardy Questions				
When was the federal law IDEA first enacted? *1975	What year was the Brown v. Board of Education case decided? *1954	What is the full name for the federal law which goes by the acronym A.D.A.? *Americans With Disabilities Act	What is the name of the video (powerful messages about respect & support) by Norman Kunc & Emma Van der Klift?	Name at least five of the eight multiple intelligences

Figure 24.3. Jeopardy! questions.

Lesson 5—
Who Am I?

Purpose

Students will identify some of their personal characteristics as defined by the groups they belong to, the things they like to do, who their friends are, and where they develop friendships. This lesson can be used

- As a self-awareness activity to explore the idea and importance of "belonging"

- As one of the interactive activities described in Lesson 3.

Materials

Graphic organizer "Who Am I?" (see Figure 24.4)

Activity

- Have students use the graphic organizer (see Figure 24.4) to brainstorm answers to the question boxes: "Where do I belong?" "What do I like to do?" "Who are my friends?" and, "Where did I meet my friends?"

- Have students share their answers in pair-share or a small group.

- Group discussion questions include

  - Is your circle of friends diverse?

  - Is your circle of friends inclusive?

  - Can all kids participate in the group(s) or club(s) you belong to?

  - What makes it inclusive or exclusive? Why?

  - How can we make all extracurricular activities inclusive?

  - How can we make sure all students feel welcome?

- The teacher should facilitate the discussion, touching on the main points:

  - It is important to recognize that most of us make friends through the extracurricular activities we *choose* to participate in (e.g., band, sports teams, drama, clubs, church, skateboarding). If students are excluded from extracurricular activities of their choice, then they are denied access to friendships with people who share similar interests.

  - It is important to examine whether our extracurricular activities as well as our classrooms and school environments are inclusive.

  - It is important to recognize the systemic limitations (e.g., lack of transportation, lack of support services, narrow view of how people can participate) that cause limited access for people in our schools to make friends and fully belong.

Acknowledgments

Lori Eshilian created the courage open head graphic organizer and facilitated this activity during an interdistrict student leadership conference and used it with numerous classroom lessons.

WHO AM I?

Who are my friends?

Where did I meet my friends?

What "groups" do I belong to?

What do I like to do?

Figure 24.4. Who Am I?

Lesson 6—
A Walk with Courage

Purpose

Students will reflect on their own experiences in response to hearing the song *Courage*. This lesson can be used

- To make connections between injustices committed throughout history and everyday discrimination of individuals

- To understand the power of one person acting to stop injustice and make a difference in the lives of others

- To make connections between the universal need to belong and the values of inclusion

- As one of the interactive activities as described in Lesson 3.

Materials

- *Courage* music or video (Blue, 1990)

- Tape or CD player or VCR

- *Courage* lyrics copied for each student or pair (Figure 24.5)

- Courage open head graphic organizer for each student (Figure 24.6)

- List of discussion questions

- 3–2–1 Reflection sheet for each student (see Figure 24.14)

Activity

- Students listen to the song *Courage* or watch the video as sung by a middle school student (Blue, 1990). A copy of the lyrics (see Figure 24.5) can be distributed to all students or student pairs to read along with as the song plays.

- Students are provided with the courage open head graphic organizer with directions to write a personal reflection and to answer the questions listed (see Figure 24.6).

- The whole class or small groups discuss their reaction to the song. The teacher facilitates the discussion by asking questions or may provide small groups with a list of questions to keep their discussion going. Examples of questions may include

  - Why is this song called *Courage?*

  - Why did the singer refer to " . . . gas chamber, bomber, and gun in Auschwitz, Japan, and My Lai"?

  - Who is bullied at our school?

  - What keeps us from acting when we witness someone being treated unfairly?

- Students complete individual 3–2–1 Reflections (see Lesson 14).

- The last question should deal with how students can take a stand about an issue that is important to them.

Resources

Blue, B. (1990). Courage. On *Starting small* [Cassette]. (Available at 54 Walnut Street, Apartment 2B, Waltham, MA 02154)

Acknowledgments

Lori Eshilian created the courage open head graphic organizer and facilitated this activity during an interdistrict student leadership conference and during numerous classroom presentations.

Courage
By Bob Blue

A small thing once happened at school
That brought up a question for me.
And somehow, it forced me to see
The price that I pay to be cool.
Diane is a girl that I know.
She's strange, like she doesn't belong.
I don't mean to say that it's wrong.
We don't like to be with her, though.
And so when we all made a plan
To have this big party at Sue's,
Most kids in our school got the news,
But no one invited Diane.

The thing about Taft Junior High,
Is secrets don't last very long.
I acted like nothing was wrong
When I saw Diane start to cry.
I know you may think that I'm cruel.
It doesn't make me very proud.
I just went along with the crowd.
It's sad but you have to in school.
You can't pick the friends you prefer.
You fit in as well as you can.
I couldn't be friends with Diane,
'Cause then they would treat me like
her.

In one class at Taft Junior High,
We study what people have done.
With gas chamber, bomber and gun
In Auschwitz, Japan, and My Lai.
I don't understand all I learn
Sometimes I just sit there and cry.
The whole world stood idly by
To watch as the innocent burned.
Like robots obeying some rule,
Atrocities done by the mob.
All innocent, doing their job.
And what was it for? Was it cool?

The world was aware of this hell
But nobody cried out in shame.
No heroes and no one to blame,
A story that no one dared tell.
I promise to do what I can
To not let it happen again.
To care for all women and men.
I'll start by inviting Diane.

Figure 24.5. *Courage* lyrics.

A Walk With Courage

Practice "walking in someone else's shoes." After listening to the song "Courage," what are your thoughts and feelings? Do you relate more to the girl singing or to Diane? Write a personal reflection inside this head...

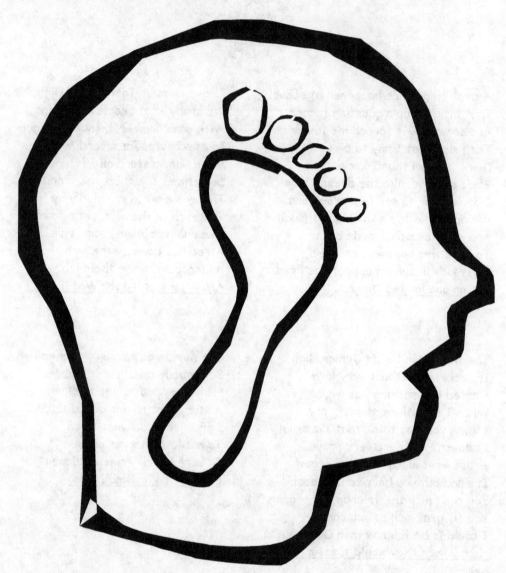

Figure 24.6. Courage open head.

Lesson 7—
Speak to Us

Purpose

Students will relate to and reflect on a speaker's personal experience with disability and inclusion. This lesson can be used

- As an introductory or celebratory activity during a student leadership group meeting, classroom presentations, schoolwide assemblies, and/or team-building activities

- During interdistrict or districtwide student leadership conferences to inspire and motivate students around the issues of human diversity, social justice, and inclusion (Figure 24.7 is an example of an agenda used for an interdistrict student leadership conference)

- As a presentation for groups of general education administrators and teachers who are unfamiliar and/or resistant to the inclusion of special education students in their schools and classes

Materials

- List of discussion questions

- 3–2–1 Reflection sheet for each student

Resources

Norman Kunc and Emma Van der Klift
Axis Consultation & Training Ltd.
340 Machleary Street
Nanaimo, British Columbia
Canada   V9R 2G9
Telephone: (250) 754-9939
http://www.normemma.com

Activity

- A speaker with disabilities presents to students in a formal presentation and/or an informal discussion. Suggested topics may include

  - Their personal experiences with disability, schooling, work, support needs, and so forth

  - The universal need to belong

  - Self-advocacy and disability rights activism

  - The importance of having dreams

- Formal presentations are effective for student conferences or school assemblies. Ideally, students would have the opportunity to listen to the speaker first and then break into small groups to discuss follow-up questions that address the speaker's presentation and help the students make connections to their own lives, values, and actions. Some examples of discussion questions used by a speaker include

  - What did you learn about people with disabilities that you didn't know before this presentation?

  - Explain why the speaker does not want to be cured of his or her disability. What do you think about not wanting to be cured?

- Informal presentations may be appropriate for meeting with school leadership groups and/or clubs as a follow-up meeting to a formal presentation or as a planning session. The speaker could briefly present and then support the students to work together to develop an action plan for their school (see Lesson 15). Goals for the planning activities would be to make sure all students are included in classes and activities and to ensure that all students at school feel accepted and valued, as well as to celebrate diversity.

- Students complete individual 3–2–1 Reflection sheets specific to this activity (see Lesson 14). The final question prompt should deal with how they will make a difference at their school.

Full Inclusion Student Council Youth Leadership Training
March 10, 1998
USC University Affiliated Program

AGENDA

TIME	ACTIVITY/PRESENTATION	SPEAKER
8:30-9:00	The Shadow of Hate	Videotape by Teaching Tolerance Southern Poverty Law Center
9:00-9:10	Welcome to Training	Barbara Wheeler, Ph.D. Director, Self-Advocacy Project Robert Jacobs, M.D., MPH Director, USC UAP
9:10-10:10	Disability and Society: Past, Present, and Future	Colleen Wieck, Ph.D. Exec. Dir. Governor's Planning Council On Developmental Disabilities St. Paul, Minnesota
10:10-10:20	Break	
10:25- 11:15	Membership, Belonging & Friendships "Courage"	Lori Eshilian, M.A. Educational Consultant Song
11:15-12:00	Augmentative Communication and Understanding My Disability	Ryan Duncanwood
12:00-12:30	Lunch	
12:30-12:45	Icebreaker	Westside Leadership Magnet
12:45-12:50	"Credo for Support"	Videotape
12:50-1:00	Introduction to Inclusion/ Exclusion Visual	Lori Eshilian
1:00-1:45	Break Into Groups to Develop the Visuals	
1:45-2:15	Groups Report Back on their Visuals	
2:15-2:30	Closing Remarks`	Barbara Wheeler

Figure 24.7. Conference agenda.

Lesson 8—
Label Me, Negate Me?

Purpose

Students will explore the basic stereotypes and prejudices our society has, identify the labels that are often used for people or groups of people in our society, and understand how their own experiences can shape their behavior and prejudices. This lesson can be used

- As a follow up to "A Walk with Courage" (Lesson 6)

- As an introductory activity to begin to explore how our prejudiced beliefs can place limits on others as well as ourselves

Materials

- Overhead transparencies of stereotypical adolescents (it is easy to get pictures from a variety of cross-cultural magazines and have color overhead transparencies made of them)

- Overhead projector

- Handouts (Figure 24.8) copied for all students, or have students label the columns on their own paper

Activity

- Show students slides or overhead transparencies of "stereotypical" adolescents. (e.g., a "gang member," a "skater," a "jock," a "nerd," a "cheerleader," a "low-rider," a "Gothic," a "punker," a "druggie"). Include pictures of adolescents who have identifiable disabilities.

- Have students use the handout depicted in Figure 24.8 for recording their responses. In the first column, "Stereotypes," have students play an association game whereby they write down the first "label" that comes to their mind when they see the picture. Go through the pictures quickly so that the students do not think too hard about their answers. Students can be made to feel more comfortable if they are reminded that the labels we think of first are not always representative of our personal beliefs but of society's or the media's stereotypes.

- Show the pictures a second time and have students offer their labels. Offer some of your own or some that you've heard other people use, especially if students are feeling too self-conscious to share their "prejudiced" thoughts.

- Identify whether the stereotypical label is a positive or negative label in the second and third columns of the handout. This often leads to interesting discussions because some students don't think some labels are "bad" or negative.

- Move to the last column of the handout to discuss and write down if the prejudices we have for people, as reflected in our labels, lead to discriminatory treatment of them. Use an "if . . . then" format for discussion questions. For example, if we call this person "wheelchair bound," then how might we treat them? Or, if we label this person "retarded," then what are our expectations? Or, if a storeowner thinks a person belongs to a gang, then how does he or she treat the person?

- Have students share if they have been stereotyped based on the way they look or act. Examine how this makes them feel or how it may limit them.

Acknowledgments

Lori Eshilian developed this activity for an interdistrict student leadership conference and used it with numerous classroom lessons for students to identify their own stereotypes and prejudices.

LESSON 8

451

Stereotyping / Prejudices

	Association The Stereotypical Labels That comes to mind "If we call them ...	+ Positive Label	- Negative	Prejudices Discriminatory Actions Treatment Then ...
Slide #1				
#2				
#3				
#4				
#5				
#6				
#7				
#8				
#9				
#10				

Figure 24.8. Stereotype chart.

Lesson 9—
Speak Up Through Song

Purpose

Students will identify songs that communicate messages of social justice, unity, activism, and self-advocacy and/or celebrate human diversity. This lesson can be used for students to

- Demonstrate understanding of selected lyrics through movement or other creative forms of expression
- Make connections between the messages of selected songs and specific injustices or forms of discrimination that are occurring in their school or community
- Brainstorm ideas to help bring about social change

Materials

- CD or tape player
- Poster board, sticks
- Markers, paint
- Computer access with PowerPoint program
- Overhead projector
- Overheads with lyrics of songs
- Resources
- Lyrics communicating social justice messages, such as
  - John Lennon–*Imagine*
  - Sabia–*Never Turning Back*
  - Bob Marley–*Redemption Song*
  - Indigo Girls–*Let it Be Me* and *This Train*
  - Jewel–*Hands* and *Life Uncommon*
  - Tracy Chapman–*Talkin' 'Bout a Revolution*
  - Arrested Development–*Mr. Wendell*
  - *We Shall Overcome*

Activity

- Students will learn the movement and lyrics to a song concerning social justice. Initially, students learn the beat of the song (three stomps and two claps while standing). Each verse and chorus are projected on the overhead screen while students learn each part. (Simple and repetitive dance movements and sign language can be used to represent lyrics.)

- In small groups, students will select their own song that communicates a message of social justice, unity, activism, and self-advocacy and/or celebrates human diversity, either from their own music collections or from music provided by the teacher.

- Groups will give a classroom presentation in which they play the song, distribute the lyrics to class members, and express the message of the song through motions, a PowerPoint presentation, picket signs, or iconic posters.

Acknowledgments

Lori Eshilian and Pamela J. Villalobos used the song *Never Turning Back* by Sabia to teach conference participants dance and signing as a team-building activity with a social justice message.

Lesson 10—
It's the Law!

Purpose

To teach students about the current civil rights court cases and laws in the United States of America, which are intended to promote equity and social justice for people with disabilities. (Americans with Disabilities Act [ADA] of 1990, PL 101-336; Individuals with Disabilities Education Act [IDEA] of 1990, PL 101-476; Individuals with Disabilities Education Act [IDEA] Amendments of 1997, PL 105-17; Rehabilitation Act of 1973, PL 93-112). This lesson can be used

- To increase student knowledge regarding the civil rights and social justice movement for people with disabilities in the United States of America

- As one of the interactive activities as described in Lesson 3

Materials

- CD-ROM (see Resources)

- K-W-L form for all students (Figure 24.9)

- Note-taking page for all students (Figure 24.10)

- Poster paper or overhead transparency

- Overhead projector

Activity

- Introduce that disability rights is a movement that doesn't have to work to create new laws but fights for the fair enforcement of the current laws—IDEA 1997 and the ADA.

- Ask students to volunteer what they "know" about how people with disabilities have been treated throughout history, and ask them to record all responses using a K-W-L graphic organizer (see Figure 24.9). Students should also share and list "what they want to know" in the next column.

- Show the CD-ROM *Parallels in Time/Learning Center* to show the history of treatment of people with disabilities. Students should use the K-W-L graphic organizer to take notes.

- Divide the class into expert groups to study each court case or current law that protects the civil rights of people with disabilities (e.g., ADA, IDEA 1997).

  - Students will need a variety of resources to research the court cases and laws.

  - Students can use another K-W-L form for gathering information about each case or law.

- Students will create a "mind map" poster or overhead with words *and images* to describe the case or law to present to the rest of the students in the class. Their mind map will include the full name of the legislation or court case, defendants and plaintiffs (identify it), date of court case or legislation (date it), the court ruling or description of what is legislated by the law (describe it), and the resulting impact on our society (deal with it).

- Students use the note-taking page during each student group presentation (see Figure 24.10).

Acknowledgments

This lesson was created by Lori Eshilian and Pamela J. Villalobos. The *Parallels in Time* CD was presented by Colleen Wieck, Ph.D., Executive Director of the Governor's Planning Council on Developmental Disabilities, St. Paul, Minnesota, during an interdistrict student conference (Full Inclusion Student Council Youth Leadership Training, March 1998) involving school districts throughout the Los Angeles area (organized by University of Southern California University Affiliated Program) as an effective way to introduce student leaders to the historical treatment of people with disabilities.

454 • • •

Resources

Bromley, K., Irwin-Devitis, L., & Modlo, M. (1995). *Graphic organizers: Visual strategies for active learning.* New York: Scholastic Professional Books.

Falvey, M., Grenot-Scheyer, M., Coots, J., & Bishop, K. (1995). Services for students with disabilities: Past and present. In M. Falvey (Ed.), *Inclusive and heterogeneous schooling: Assessment, curriculum, and instruction* (pp. 23–39). Baltimore: Paul H. Brookes Publishing Co.

Margulies, N. (1991). *Mapping inner space: Learning and teaching mind mapping.* Tucson, AZ: Zephyr Press.

Minnesota Governors Planning Council on Developmental Disabilities. (1999). *Parallels in time* [CD-ROM]. Minneapolis, MN: Author.

For information on IDEA 1997 contact the National Information Center for Children and Youth with Disabilities at (800) 695-0285 or http://www.nichcy.org.

Activity

• The teacher can use the Jeopardy! format (see Lesson 3) and/or ask students to construct a timeline including all of the cases and legislation presented as a final assessment of the information learned through this process.

K-W-L Form

K- What do you KNOW?	W- What do you WANT to know?	L- What have you LEARNED?

Figure 24.9. K-W-L form.

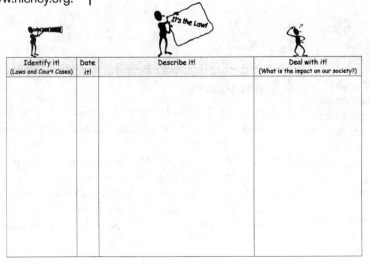

Identify it! (Laws and Court Cases)	Date it!	Describe it!	Deal with it! (What is the impact on our society?)

Figure 24.10. It's the Law! notes.

Lesson 11—
A Rainbow of Justice

Purpose

Students will explore the concept of social justice through a variety of learning strategies that address the eight human intelligences of verbal-linguistic, mathematical-logical, spatial, musical, body-kinesthetic, naturalist, interpersonal, and intrapersonal. Students will define *social justice* as a set of values that teaches fair practices, emphasizes a sense of equity and respect for all people, and promotes not only the welfare of individuals but also of our communities. This lesson can be used

- As an active learning lesson that address a variety of learning styles and serves to teach students about social justice through their own exploration and critical thinking

Materials

- Activity cards for each intelligence group (see Figure 24.11)

- A different colored arch (large enough to record all student group products and to display on wall) representing each color of the rainbow; eight different colors for each multiple intelligences group

- Marking pens; Polaroid camera and film or digital camera and computer access

- Masking tape

Activity

- Students will be introduced to the concept of social justice in a discussion facilitated by the teacher. Together, the students will brainstorm the definition of *social justice* and identify movements and/or events in history that exemplify social justice in our society. Students' ideas will be graphically organized on the board using a web (with the word *social justice* in the middle).

- Students will form pairs to complete a pair-share to review the eight human intelligences (see Lesson 6 in Chapter 23 of this text and/or the Resources section of Lesson 6 for ideas to teach and learn about multiple intelligences).

- Students will be divided up into eight cooperative learning groups.

- Students will rotate to each station and spend approximately 10 minutes actively involved in the activity stated on each activity card. Sample activity cards for each intelligence are depicted in Figure 24.11.

- Students will complete the activity with group members, placing their product, list, or outcome onto the large rainbow arch in each station.

- When each group has visited all eight stations and returned to the original station, then the groups will construct the rainbow by connecting each colored arch together.

- Students will discuss and comment on the similarities and differences in each group's product.

Acknowledgments

This lesson was created by Lori Eshilian and Pamela J. Villalobos.

Resources

Armstrong, T. (1994). *Multiple intelligences in the classroom.* Alexandria, VA: Association for Supervision and Curriculum Development.

Kagan, M. (1997). *Multiple intelligences smartcard.* San Clemente, CA: Kagan Publishing.

Kagan, S., & Kagan, M. (1998). *Multiple intelligences: The complete MI book.* San Clemente, CA: Kagan Publishing.

Lazear, D., & Margulies, N. *Tap your multiple intelligences posters.* Tucson, AZ: Zephyr Press.

A Rainbow of Justice Activity Cards

Intrapersonal -Think of a time when you spoke up for a social justice cause. How did it feel? What would you do differently? And, how has it affected your life? Write a label or phrase on the rainbow for your personal experience (each group member completes their own).

Body Kinesthetic - Create a formation (by positioning your bodies together) that would be symbolic of social justice. Have a Polaroid picture taken of your group members in this formation and tape it on the rainbow.

Naturalist – What are examples of "social justice" evident in nature (in the animal or plant communities). Draw a picture or diagram of your examples.

Interpersonal – Brainstorm with your group members different organizations that you know of that non-violently fight for social justice. Write down the groups, how they work together, and their cause on the rainbow.

Musical – Think of, or create a chant or song that is representative of social justice and/or inclusion. Write down the words on the rainbow and be ready to perform your chant or song.

Spatial – Draw symbols, pictures, or create a mind map that represent social justice on the rainbow.

Mathematical/Logical – Divide your group in half and debate the pros and cons to acts of civil disobedience that support a social justice cause. Write these in a chart on the rainbow.

Verbal/Linguistic – Discuss and list the connection of social justice and inclusion in our schools. List these on the rainbow.

Figure 24.11. Justice activity cards.

Lesson 12—
Wake Up Now!

Purpose

This section will review one of 12 classroom activities accompanied by the song *We're People First* by Jeff Moyer. This section will address song 10, *Wake Up Now!* The book provides a structured and easy-to-follow guide for a student leader or a teacher to follow. This summary condenses these elements for the purpose of brevity. Sections include Benefits for the Student, Background for the Teacher/Leader, Suggested Classroom Activities, Creative Variations, and Lyrics.

The purpose of the activities surrounding the content of *Wake Up Now!* is to stimulate thinking and action concerning the rights of students with disabilities to be included in all activities in school and in the community, including employment. The song was written with a group of young people with disabilities and presents their ideas. The song is based on the fundamental rights protected under the ADA and other disability rights legislation and urges proactive involvement to protect and ensure the full participation of students with disabilities.

Activity

- Review the background of *Wake Up Now!*, and ask students to think about specific situations faced by kids with disabilities their own age.

- Discuss the meaning of being proactive and how the students in your class can identify the need for and create social change.

- Obtain age-appropriate materials on the ADA, and introduce this historic piece of national legislation.

- Provide students with a copy of the lyrics as depicted in Figure 24.12, and teach the song using the full-performance track on the CD.

- Sing the song using the accompaniment track on the CD.

Materials

- *We're People First* Activity Guide includes
  - Background information and activity suggestions for each of 12 age-graded songs
  - Lyric sheets for copying
  - Lead sheets with melody and chords
- *We're People First* CD includes
  - Full performance tracks of 12 songs with varying styles, themes, and forms—six for younger students and six for older students.
  - One song performed by an inclusive group of teenagers that includes one student singing using his augmentative and alternative communication (AAC) device; other performers include people who are deaf, have visual impairments, and use a wheelchair. Lyrics address these differences and commonality of experience.
  - Accompaniment-only tracks for each song.
  - Program song files for each song in male and female pitch range that can be downloaded into certain AAC devices to enable inclusive singing.

Resources

We're people first: A celebration of diversity is available through Jeff Moyer Music at http://www.jeffmoyer.com; telephone: (888) 323-0626; fax: (440) 449-4652.

Acknowledgments

The song *Wake Up Now!* was written as an outgrowth of a songwriting and advocacy workshop conducted with Third Street Kids, an inclusive performing arts program in Tucson, Arizona. These materials have been used by student leaders from high schools with younger students and their application as disability-awareness activities facilitated by students with disabilities, parents, teacher advocates, and school counselors.

Wake Up Now!
Lyrics:

1. We want to ride the bus you ride,
We want to use the doors you use.
We want to read the signs you read,
We want to choose the path you choose.
The telephone can draw us close,
If it is there for all.
But if you can't hear, speak or reach the slot,
Then you can't make the call.

2. With access we can surely grow,
If schools had open doors.
For knowledge is much more than books
It's arts and sports and more.
We want to share in all of school,
To flourish and to thrive.
In attitude we find the key.
We grow. Awake. Alive.
(Chorus)
© 1995 Jeff Moyer

Chorus:
We've got to wake up now.
We've got to look and see.
Things aren't the way,
That they ought to be.

3. Now working is the human way.
It builds community.
Yet millions are excluded.
        Just by disability.
We have the skills and hearts and
    minds.
We're equal to the task.
And ADA has paved the way.
We've seen the light at last.
(Chorus)

Figure 24.12. *Wake Up Now!* lyrics.

Lesson 13—
How Big Is Your Circle?

Purpose

How Big Is Your Circle? is a musical for schools that promotes student initiatives and personal responsibility toward the healing of exclusion, ridicule, and violence against students who are devalued because of their differences. The play contains eight scenes and eight songs and can be performed as a classroom reading or as a full production that can include actors, a chorus, and a string orchestra. The materials also include a classroom discussion guide with questions that evoke the exploration of how the play's content relates to school culture and behaviors specific to the individual school and locale. School leaders are encouraged to facilitate group processes within the school community to adapt the play to local issues, slang, and situations.

The play frames the problem of exclusion, ridicule, and verbal and physical violence as problems faced by all children who are devalued because of their differences, including those with disabilities, obesity, racial differences, poverty, academic excellence, short or tall stature, and newness to the school community. During the course of the play, students come to recognize the similarity of their experiences and agree to take individual responsibility and courageous action to create a safe school community for all learners. The content of the play was written with the advice and counsel of many students with and with-

Activity

These are materials that are highly flexible in their application. Each of the eight scenes in the play include a song (lyrics are shown in Figure 24.13), background information, and questions for classroom discussion. The recording that accompanies the book contains both full performance and accompaniment tracks for each song. Students can learn the songs or simply listen to their performance.

Scene 1 summary: A group of students in an informal setting exchange an array of negative put-downs concerning other students. Offstage the sound arises of a student being bullied by a group. One student rushes to join the assault as the others look on passively. Slowly, the dialogue shifts to the growing awareness that it could be any of them being victimized by the pushing and shoving.

From the Activity Guide

This scene shows a school culture in which put-downs, ridicule, and violence are passively accepted as the norm. The seed of opposition to this cycle of negative treatment begins to grow, resulting in personal revelation and the community building toward positive change. However, such problems are typically not solved because they generally are not addressed at the subtle levels of passive acceptance, such as being a bystander and falling prey to the insidious undertow of peer pressure. Take heart, the play resolves what it addresses.

Questions for Discussion

• What problems occurred during this scene that negatively affected the safety and well-being of the school community?

• During this scene, who contributed to the problems? In what ways?

• During the pushing circle, who was responsible for what was happening to Michael? How?

• Why didn't any of the students watching the pushing circle take action to stop it?

• What is empathy? During this scene, who expresses empathetic ideas? What is the impact of that expression?

Acknowledgments

Among the applications of these materials has been the performance of the play by an inclusive group of actors from Clearfork High School and Middle School in Mansfield, Ohio, as a disability-awareness and community-building activity. In addition, the Fort Lauderdale Children's Theatre performed the musical with an inclusive cast at the 2000 TASH conference

Lesson 13—continued

Purpose

out disabilities and reflects what those students considered to be honest portrayals of student behavior and accurate expressions of contemporary slang.

Materials

- *How Big Is Your Circle?* script and activity guide includes
  - Script to be copied
  - Director's score for chorus and string orchestra
  - Individual string and choral parts to be copied
  - Activity guide for each scene
- *How Big Is Your Circle?* CD includes:
  - Full performance tracks of eight songs, including performances by youth chorus and string orchestra.
  - Professional accompaniment tracks for use during performance or classroom singing

Resources

How big is your circle?: A musical promoting healing of exclusion, ridicule, and violence is available through Jeff Moyer Music at http://www.jeffmoyer.com; telephone: (888) 323-0626; fax: (440) 449-4652.

Acknowledgments

in Miami, Florida, and will continue to produce the show as a character education piece for schools local to Fort Lauderdale. The production of the materials and the performance on the CD were developed in collaboration with The School of Fine Arts, an inclusive community school of the arts in Willoughby, Ohio.

Lyrics:
We're Different

1. We're tall and short, we're thin and round, we're big and small from farm and town.
We come from Calgary, Cleveland, Lagos, and Japan.
We're young and old and shy and bold, we're sometimes hot and sometimes cold.
We're olive, amber, black, brown, white, and tan.
Oh yes we speak with many accents, yes we speak in many tongues.
We speak with sounds and gestures, words and eyes and hands.
We play in snow and on the beach, we study, learn, we share and teach.
We come from many cultures, many different lands.
Chorus:
Oh yes we're different, different, different, very different, different, different,
Just as different, different, different as can be.
Oh yes we're different, different, different, very different, different, different, different,
That's the beauty of humanity.

2. We come from different kinds of families, some kids live in foster homes.
Some live with mom or dad or grandma 'til they're grown.
Some live in tiny, tiny families and some great big families sprawl.
But stop and think they're families one and all.
We live in huts and high-rise towers and in houses in a row.
We live in towns and burghs and cities on the map.
We're good at sports, we're good at art, each in our way we play our part.
We all have many talents that we learn to tap.
(Chorus)

3. We walk and run, we wheel around, use canes and crutches on the ground.
We're average students and we're gifted and we're slow.
We learn to learn, we learn to share, each in our way we learn to care.
As on through different lives we each do go.
We read with eyes and ears and fingers, we use hearing aids and sign.
We use technology now that helps us speak our minds.
We find the way around our problems and in our diversity
We are unique examples of humanity.

4. Now do you think it really matters that we're not all just the same?
The rainbow would be boring with no different hues.
A team needs different kinds of players, games need different kinds of teams.
We're stronger for our differences its true.
We share one Earth one sky one atmosphere, one tiny planet home,
And deep inside we all want love and dignity.
If you think hard about the matter of our great diversity,
You'll celebrate our varied world community.
© 2000 Jeff Moyer

Figure 24.13. *We're Different* lyrics.

Lesson 14—

3-2-1 Reflect!

Purpose

Students will reflect on what they have learned and then practice personal empowerment goal setting to "make a difference." This lesson can be used

- As a culminating activity for a group Making Action Plans (MAPs) lesson, in-service training on values of inclusion, or listening to a speaker

- A routine activity to close each lesson or group meeting

Materials

- 3-2-1 Reflection sheet (Figure 24.14)

Activity

- Teachers can use the 3-2-1 Reflection sheet format as depicted in Figure 24.14, modifying the questions in relation to the specific lesson.

- Students, individually or in small groups, will respond to the three questions by completing the graphically organized boxes.

- Through pair-share or as a whole group, students will share their responses to one or more of the prompts.

Acknowledgments

The 3-2-1 format was originally developed by Janice Vitullo and Mary K. Kastanis (as presented at the 1998 Association for Supervision and Curriculum Development Annual Conference) and modified for a variety of purposes by Lori Eshilian and Pamela J. Villalobos to engage students to reflect and set goals.

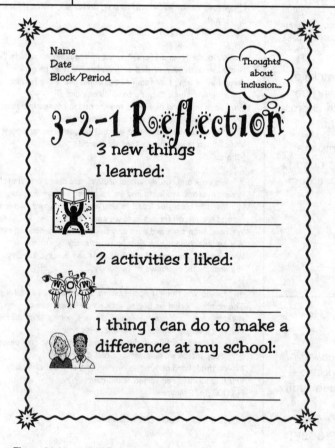

Figure 24.14. 3-2-1 Reflection sheet.

Lesson 15—

School MAPs

Purpose

To empower students to be self-advocates and to advocate for positive changes at their school. This lesson can be used

- As a culminating activity to close a conference or student leadership meeting

- As a culminating activity after completing the "Needs Assessment for an Inclusive School"

- As a quarterly activity completed by student leadership groups to assess and plan for ongoing change and development

Materials

- Butcher paper or overhead transparency

- Marking pens

Resources

Falvey, M., Forest, M., Rosenberg, R., & Pierpoint, J., in Chapter 4 of this text.

Activity

- Use an overhead transparency or large butcher paper and draw a circular graphic, identifying the "topic" for change, such as inclusion, tolerance, respect, belonging, or friendship, at the top, as shown in Figure 24.15.

- If the "Needs Assessment for an Inclusive School" (Figure 24.1) was completed during Lesson 1, then the group may want to refer to the findings when answering the following questions.

- Brainstorm each step with students either in small groups or in the larger group.

  - Step 1: What does our school look like now? What is our history when it comes to _____ (e.g., inclusion, respect, tolerance)? Include both positive and negative aspects of the campus.

  - Step 2: What would the group like their school to be like (the group's dreams)?

  - Step 3: If nothing changes, what is the worst that can happen (the group's nightmares)?

  - Step 4: Identify what the group can really do given their realm of influence, their resources, and their passion (the group's goal).

  - Step 5: Outline a sequential plan of up to five activities the group could do immediately. Identify who is responsible for each activity and prepare a timeline for completion so that an ongoing plan can be followed.

Acknowledgments

This lesson was created by Lori Eshilian and used during an interdistrict student conference and with a high school student's peers with whom he would be included in classes.

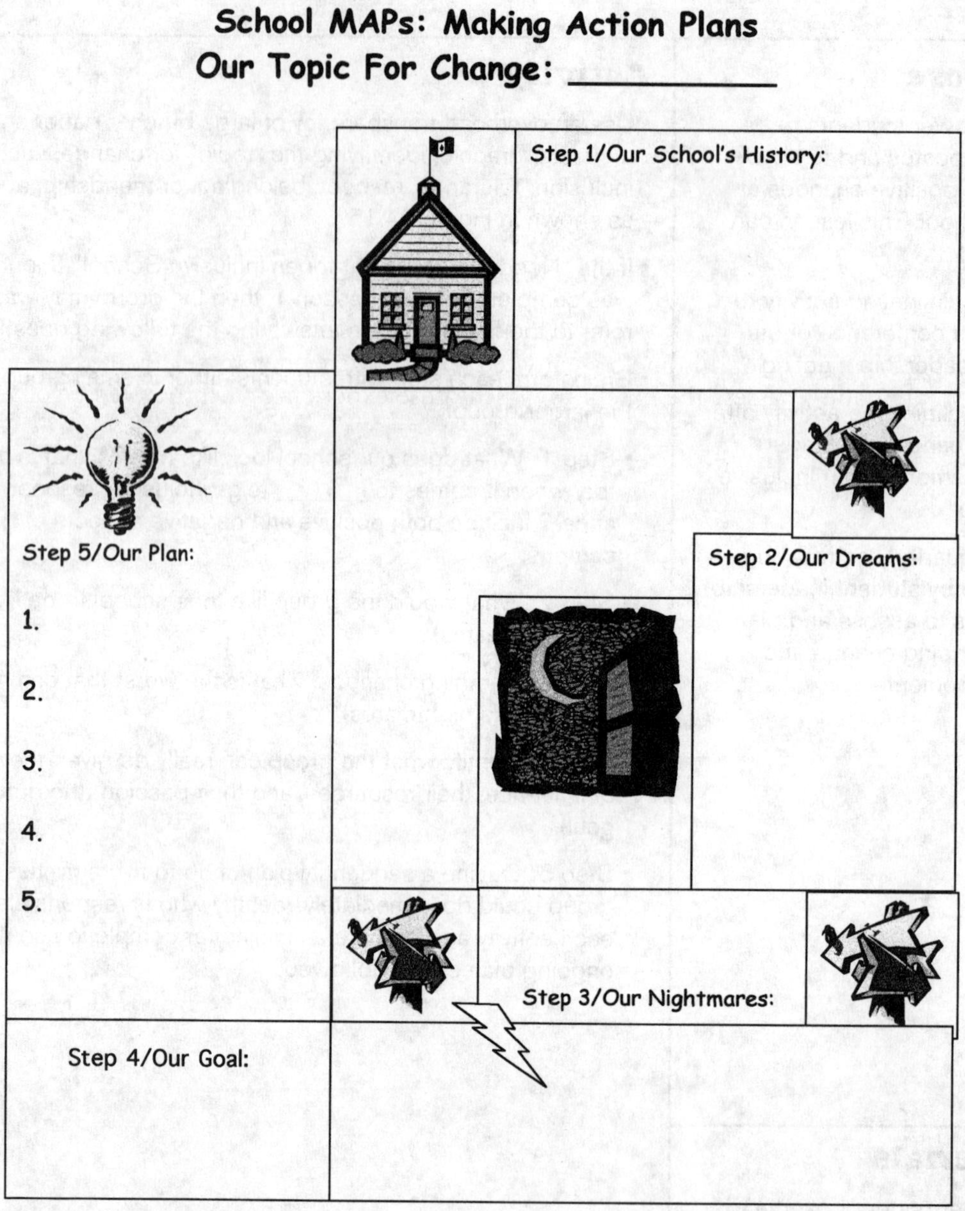

School MAPs: Making Action Plans
Our Topic For Change: _____

Step 1/Our School's History:

Step 5/Our Plan:

1.

2.

3.

4.

5.

Step 2/Our Dreams:

Step 3/Our Nightmares:

Step 4/Our Goal:

Figure 24.15. School MAPs.

Afterword

At the beginning of this book, we invited you to reflect on your personal experiences as a student and to assess the extent to which those experiences incorporated a collaborative and creative approach. Unless your educational experiences were different from most adults who have taken the Student Collaboration Quiz, the majority of your responses probably were "never" and "rarely."

Now that you have completed the book, we invite you to envision yourself as a student in a school that uses the recommended peer empowerment strategies, collaborative planning and teaching skills, and creative solution-finding techniques described in the book and retake the Student Collaboration Quiz. We are confident that you will be able to circle more ratings of "often" and "very often" compared with your initial ratings. We hope that the dramatic positive change in the scores will motivate you to expand your implementation of the collaborative and creative strategies explored throughout this book.

It is imperative for us to demonstrate wisdom and courage by acting to change schools now so that students may be more actively engaged in their own and others' acquisition of humanistic ethics; communication, information-seeking, and problem-solving skills; and core curriculum deemed essential by their community. Starting points for change include the implementation of the strategies presented in this book. After implementing the strategies described in this book, we encourage you to administer the Student Collaboration Quiz to your students and to process with them the role that these strategies play in preparing learners to live in an increasingly complex, global, diverse, interdependent, democratic, technological, and inclusive society.

Jacqueline S. Thousand, Richard A. Villa, and Ann I. Nevin

Index